WHITE SALT-GLAZED STONEWARE
of the British Isles

WHITE SALT-GLAZED STONEWARE
of the British Isles

Diana Edwards and Rodney Hampson

ANTIQUE COLLECTORS' CLUB

©2005 Diana Edwards and Rodney Hampson
World copyright reserved

The right of Diana Edwards and Rodney Hampson to be identified as authors of this work
has been asserted by them in accordance with the Copyright, Designs and Patents Act 1988

ISBN 1 85149 480 4

All rights reserved. No part of this publication may be reproduced, stored in a retrieval
system, or transmitted in any form or by any means electronic, mechanical, photocopying,
recording or otherwise, without the prior permission of the publisher

British Library Cataloguing-in-Publication Data
A catalogue record for this book is available from the British Library

---

FRONTISPIECE: **Stand or grand plat ménage,** *Staffordshire, c.1760-70 (see Colour Plate 99).*
TITLE-PAGE: **Loving cup,** *Staffordshire, 1748 (see Colour Plate 17).*
PAGE 7: **Teapot,** *Staffordshire, c.1755-60 (see Colour Plate 30).*

Printed in England
for the Antique Collectors' Club Ltd., Sandy Lane, Old Martlesham,
Woodbridge, Suffolk, IP12 4SD

Antique Collectors' Club

Formed in 1966, the Antique Collectors' Club is now a world-renowned publisher of top quality books for the collector. It also publishes the only independently-run monthly antiques magazine, *Antique Collecting*, which rose quickly from humble beginnings to a network of worldwide subscribers.

The magazine, whose motto is *For Collectors-By Collectors-About Collecting*, is aimed at collectors interested in widening their knowledge of antiques both by increasing their awareness of quality and by discussion of the factors influencing prices.

Subscription to Antique Collecting is open to anyone interested in antiques and subscribers receive ten issues a year. Well-illustrated articles deal with practical aspects of collecting and provide numerous tips on prices, features of value, investment potential, fakes and forgeries. Offers of related books at special reduced prices are also available only to subscribers.

In response to the enormous demand for information on 'what to pay', ACC introduced in 1968 the famous price guide series. The first title, *The Price Guide to Antique Furniture* (since renamed *British Antique Furniture: Price Guide and Reasons for Values*), is still in constant demand. Since those pioneering days, ACC has gone from strength to strength, publishing many of today's standard works of reference on all things antique and collectable, from *Tiaras* to *20th Century Ceramic Designers in Britain*.

Not only has ACC continued to cater strongly for its original audience, it has also branched out to produce excellent titles on many subjects including art reference, architecture, garden design, gardens, and textiles. All ACC's publications are available through bookshops worldwide and a catalogue is available free of charge from the addresses below.

For further information please contact:

ANTIQUE COLLECTORS' CLUB

www.antique-acc.com

Sandy Lane, Old Martlesham
Woodbridge, Suffolk IP12 4SD, UK
Tel: 01394 389950 Fax: 01394 389999
Email: info@antique-acc.com
or
Eastworks, 116 Pleasant Street – Suite #60B
Easthampton, MA01027, USA
Tel: (413) 529-0861 Fax: (413) 529-0862
Email: info@antiquecc.com

Dedicated to the memory of
Arnold R. Mountford, CBE, MA, FRSA, FMA
former Director of the
City Museums and Art Gallery,
Stoke-on-Trent

Other Books by the Authors

Diana Edwards
Tea and Sympathy: Post-Revolutionary Ceramics in the Stamford Historical Society
The Castleford Pottery 1790-1821
Neale Pottery and Porcelain
Black Basalt

Diana Edwards with Catherine Rogers Arthur
Taste and Table: A Century of Ceramics in Early Maryland

Rodney Hampson
Longton Potters 1700-1865
Churchill China: Great British Potters since 1795
Pottery References in the Staffordshire Advertiser 1795-1865

Diana Edwards and Rodney Hampson
English Dry-Bodied Stoneware

Contents

Acknowledgements		8
Introduction		9
CHAPTER I	Early Development of White Salt-Glazed Stoneware	11
CHAPTER II	Early Industrial Stonewares	20
CHAPTER III	The Demand for Salt-Glazed Stoneware	48
CHAPTER IV	Raw Materials	64
CHAPTER V	Making the Pots	71
CHAPTER VI	Marketing in Britain and Europe	142
CHAPTER VII	English White Salt-Glazed Stoneware for the American Market	159
CHAPTER VIII	The Collectors	177
CHAPTER IX	Thirteen Potters and the Pots they made	183
Appendix 1	Thomas Wedgwoods of the Overhouse	241
Appendix 2	Salt-Glaze Potters	246
Appendix 3	Price Lists	283
Appendix 4	Patterns, Shapes and Tiles	286
Appendix 5	Customers for White Salt-Glazed Stoneware	288
Bibliography		295
References		300
Index		329

Acknowledgements

We are grateful to Brian Adams, Garry Atkins, Katie Banks, David Barker, Robert Barth, Richard Beech, Mavis Bimson, Harold Blakey, Tracey Booth, Noel Boothroyd, Gilbert Bradley, Bernard Bumpus, Sandra Burgess, Helen Burton, Philip Bye, Bernice Cardy, B. Carpenter, Mr. and Mrs. Dudley Catzen, John and Joyce Cockerill, Jacques Coplo, Allison Cowling, Alwyn and Angela Cox, Aileen Dawson, Lu Ann De Cunzo, Kerry Dickins, Stephen Dixon, Michael Donnelly, Julie Edwards, Robin Emmerson, Oliver Fairclough, Andrew Fletcher, Kevin Freyer, Henry Ginsburg, Geoffrey Godden, Harriet Goldweitz, Miranda Goodby, Jonathan Gray, Chris Green, Joy Green, Shauna Gregg, John Griffin, Pat Halfpenny, Helen Hallesy, Peter Hammond, Alan Hibbs, Robin Hildyard, Lyn and Maurice Hillis, Christopher Hilton, Jonathan Horne, Mollie Hosking, Ray Howard, Jack Howarth, Lisa Hudgins, Rod Jellicoe, Mr. and Mrs. Harwood A. Johnson, Matthew Jones, Henry Kelly, Roger Kemp, J. Lamond, Thelma Lancaster, Amanda Lange, Mike Lewis, Al Luckenbach, K. McGoverin, J.V.G. Mallet, Errol Manners, Martha Mayberry, the late Leoni Mero, Michel Montefroy, John Oxford, Clare Parsons, Barbara Perry, Martin Phillips, John Pike, Martha Pinello, Bill Pitman, Roger Pomfret, the late Kenneth Quinn, Ben Read, Dinah Reynolds, L. Richardson, Louise Richardson, Peter Roden, Michael Signy, Janine Skerry, Patricia Hughes Smithson, Susan Stein, Deborah Stevenson, James Stevenson, Rosalind Sword, Olive Talbot, Sue Taylor, Neville Thompson, Alan Townsend, Jill Turnbull, George Twigg, Jessica Tyree, Tom Walford, Noel Walley, M. Ward, Andrew Watts, Gregory Weidman, Mrs. Henry Weldon and the late Henry H. Weldon, Peter White, Timothy Wilson, Tamsin Wragg, Hilary Young and John Yule, and those inadvertently overlooked.

We thank John Mountford for permission to quote from the late Arnold Mountford's thesis and Gaye Blake Roberts and fellow Trustees of the Wedgwood Museum for permission to quote from the Wedgwood papers, on deposit at Keele University. For their translations, we owe a special debt of gratitude to Peter and the late Tursten Berg, Francis Celoria, Bernard Dragesco and Helen Smith.

Finally, we gratefully acknowledge our spouses, Eileen Hampson and the late Francis D. Murnaghan, Jr., for their unstinting support and wise advice during the writing of this book.

The authors are grateful to the Winterthur Museum, Delaware, for offering the first Dwight Lanmon scholarship to work on this subject to Diana Edwards. Ceramica Stiftung helped to make the publication of this book possible with their generous grant, for which we are most appreciative.

Introduction

There comes a time when it seems appropriate, given the accumulation of new information, to add to and re-evaluate the previous work on a subject. In this book we have brought together archaeological and documentary research in white salt-glazed stoneware since the last major publication over thirty years ago. In-depth study on both sides of the Atlantic was already developing then and has flourished since. We have had the benefit of all this work and taken part in it. We hope that our present conspectus will encourage further research as more sites, more documentary sources and more pots come to light.

In all, we have looked at around 150 possible salt-glaze potters and given our reasons for confirming 125 as producers, about one hundred of them in Staffordshire. Salt-glaze potters did not mark their wares and of these 125 we have been able to relate only thirteen of them to the pots they made. Nine of these thirteen makers were found or confirmed by archaeological investigation. Six of the thirteen are outside Staffordshire and that disproportion demonstrates the relative ease of locating and excavating single sites compared with the multiplicity of sites in Staffordshire. Likewise, our detailed research is distorted by the random survival of documents.

Post-medieval archaeology has developed apace in the past fifty years in Britain and America and contributed greatly to information about the makers and consumers of salt-glazed ware. We have been able to utilise published and unpublished work and shards to complement documentary evidence.

The dealer, the collector and the curator have an important role in the subject. Dry documents and broken pots have their place, but interest would be greatly diminished without a demand for whole examples, from Horace Walpole in the eighteenth century to today's collectors, great and small. An archaeologist by another name, it is the dealer who finds the pieces and facilitates their acquisition by collector or curator. Only because of the generosity of dealers and collectors and the cooperation of curators are we able to illustrate our subject so profusely.

Charles Luxmoore was already quoting the Wedgwood papers for salt-glaze references by 1914 and we have used them extensively to identify Staffordshire salt-glaze potters and customers countrywide. Josiah Wedgwood's administration of the estate of his eldest brother, Thomas Wedgwood, has provided a detailed case study of an individual salt-glaze potter. Arnold Mountford secured the surviving records and products of Thomas and John Wedgwood and studied them in depth, and we are privileged to make use of his M.A. thesis.

We have been fortunate in having available the recently published work on German stoneware by David Gaimster and on John Dwight by Chris Green (preceded by that of Dennis Haselgrove and John Murray) and on other London potters by Rhoda Edwards. The 'out-potteries' in Britain and America have also had attention in the last thirty years and we have drawn upon both published and unpublished studies of them.

In 1971 Arnold Mountford's fine book *The Illustrated Guide to Staffordshire Salt-Glazed Stoneware* appeared. As an overview to his Master of Arts thesis on *Thomas Wedgwood, John Wedgwood and Jonah Malkin Potters of Burslem* (University of Keele, 1972), Mountford, more than any other ceramic historian, chronicled the development of a pottery fabric which was a staple in British and Colonial households for many years and was undoubtedly widely exported to the Continent. Mountford's was the most recent book on the subject which began with Charles Luxmoore's monograph *English Saltglazed Earthenware*, written by 1914, published in 1924, and reprinted c.1970. Luxmoore's work is still the most comprehensive in illustrating the models and moulds used for producing the intricate moulded bodies in salt-glazed stoneware after about 1740. We also look back to William Burton in 1904, Edwin Atlee Barber in 1906 and J.F. Blacker in 1922, but Luxmoore and Mountford are the two seminal works which have been most generally associated with the manufacture of salt-glaze.

We believe that our work reveals a great deal that is new about the industry as a whole, both the making and the marketing, and also about those who collected these timelessly appealing wares.

Tea Canister. The incised decoration reads 'Henry Muskit 1760 L' and on the other side, 'Elizabeth Cannon 1760 Liverp.' See page 263. (Courtesy of the National Museums, Liverpool (The Walker)')

CHAPTER I

Early Development of White Salt-Glazed Stoneware

It would not be an exaggeration to say that salt-glazed stoneware revolutionised the ceramic world. From its first introduction, in the early sixteenth century in the Westerwald, and its subsequent introduction by German and Dutch potters into England in the mid-seventeenth century, salt-glazed stoneware vessels, impermeable to liquids and made hygienic by their clear, lustrous silica glaze, vastly changed food storage and consumption habits.[1] Initially used for storage containers and drinking vessels in medieval German homes, the introduction of Chinese porcelains for drinking tea and later coffee in seventeenth century England spurred on local potters, such as John Dwight, into attempting a domestic industry in white salt-glazed stonewares emulating the coveted Chinese porcelains. Eventually tea and table wares joined the repertoire of jugs, mugs and food storage vessels. The impact of white salt-glazed stoneware in England, in the colonies and abroad was, from the early years of the eighteenth century, the most revolutionary ceramic development until Chinese export porcelain devoured the market after the first quarter of the eighteenth century and creamware exploded in the 1770s.[2] Stoneware competed, of course, with other ceramics, including a comprehensive and concomitant delftware industry as well as pewter and glass, all of which were slightly cheaper and more pervasive in the market place.

Properties and Technology of Stonewares
Earthenware clays, composed primarily of silica and aluminium oxide mixed with water and fired at temperatures generally below 1000 degrees centigrade, are typified by containing impurities; therefore they flux and vitrify at different levels. Stoneware clay must be highly refractory and be able to withstand temperatures of between 1200 and 1300 degrees centigrade. Impurities such as iron, and other minerals which also make colours, act as fluxes and so clays located above coal seams containing less than three per cent iron are usually more refractory and used for producing stoneware.[3] Owing to the high firing which fuses the body, making it non-porous, stoneware can remain unglazed and can be utilised for containing liquids. However, stoneware is the only body to be glazed by salt. The salt provides sheen and allows additional colour to be added to the surface of the pot. The sodium mixture for salt-glaze ($NaSi_2Cl$), consisting of sodium chloride and water, is introduced into the kiln late in the firing when the temperature reaches at least 1150 degrees centigrade.[4] Salt is added for up to six hours, the sodium volatilising on to the pots followed by a clear fire when the chlorine gas is emitted as a noxious by-product and spewed out of the kiln vents. A more comprehensive account of the properties of clay, flint and salt is considered in Chapter IV.

That salt-glazed stoneware was an immense *tour de force* in the ceramic world is no surprise. The sturdy, vitrified salt-glazed stonewares revolutionised food storage and consumption patterns. Potteries located in and around Siegburg, Raeren, Frechen, Cologne, Höhr and Grenzhausen produced salt-glazed stoneware which by the sixteenth century included sophisticated moulded relief and coloured embellishment. Both the Westerwald mountains on the east bank of the Rhine and the Eiffel mountains in the west,

Colour Plate 1. **Mug,** *salt-glazed stoneware gorge-shaped mug, one of four to be attributed to Francis Place, Dinsdale, Yorkshire who was making stoneware in the late 17th century. The mug is attributed to Place by family descent and by the inclusion of a similar mug in a self-portrait of Place in the Patrick Allan-Fraser of Hospitalfield Trust, Arbroath, Scotland. Francis Place, c.1690. 3½in. (8.89cm) high. (Mint Museum of Art, Charlotte, North Carolina, gift of the Delhom Service League, 1998.40)*

between the Moselle and the Rhine, had abundant deposits of clay. Kilns were initially fired with wood from the local forests.[5] The grey-bodied stonewares, often with manganese or cobalt decoration, produced principally in the Westerwald but also in Raeren were traded locally and exported across Europe, to North America, Africa and the Far East.[6]

John Dwight and the Development of an English Stoneware Industry

From the early seventeenth century archaeological sites in England and throughout North America indicate a lively trade in brown and grey-bodied stoneware jugs from the Rhineland. In 1673 *John Dwight* (1630s-1703) gave evidence to a House of Lords committee declaring he could 'make as good as much Cologne ware as would supply England'.[7] The previous year he had taken out a patent to produce 'Cologne ware' along with 'transparent earthy ware',[8] the latter clearly intended to compete with the Chinese imports entering the country in vast quantities. Indeed, wasters of transparent white porcelain and of cobalt painted jugs and mugs with medallion relief decoration in the Museum of London indicate Dwight was producing wares in imitation of both Westerwald and Chinese imports at Fulham around 1675.

Brown-bodied stoneware from the Raeren and Frechen areas were equally popular exports concomitant with those wares being sent from the Westerwald. In England an indigenous industry following the German tradition emerged and brown stoneware bellarmine bottles were produced. In 1676 the London Glass Sellers Company, unable to fill all their orders, requisitioned John Dwight of Fulham to manufacture '...the Cullen or brown stone wares...' 'fine Browne Bottles Juggs and and all other sorts of fine Browne stone wares'.[9] The initial agreement, on 25 March 1676, was between Windsor Sandys of Saint Martin-in-the-Fields and John Dwight of Fulham and the second agreement, on 1 May 1677, was between the Company and John Dwight alone, suggesting that by that date Dwight was working alone.[10] It was, until fairly recently, thought that Dwight was the only domestic manufacturer of salt-glazed stoneware in the seventeenth century. However, there were two prior attempts at manufacture of the brown stoneware bellarmines thought to have been exclusively made at Frechen and Cologne, one at *Woolwich*, a Thames bank site in south-east London, around 1640 to 1650 where excavations include a kiln and wasters in the Frechen style[11] and another by Captain William Killegrew in Southampton around the same time as the patent taken out by Dwight, c.1672.[12]

The only other identified potter to make salt-glazed stoneware in the seventeenth century was *Francis Place* (1647-1728) who was making white and brown salt-glazed stoneware mugs and cups in north-east England in the 1680s. Place was a landscape artist working in various mediums and a mezzotint engraver as well as a potter working in the Dwight style. He produced gorges in marbled stoneware, the bulbous bases and turned elongated necks following silver and other metal shapes popular at the time (Colour Plate 1).[13] Only four mugs can be authenticated to Place, the attribution being based on family history, Place's activities as a potter, and a self-portrait including a mug of similar form and decoration.[14]

White stoneware was manufactured at Siegburg from at least the fifteenth century with an early tradition of producing tall, white-bodied, cylindrical jugs and mugs.[15] The industry was destroyed in the Civil War of the Truchsess Apostasy (1583-8) and Siegburg potters relocated in the Westerwald, augmenting the established pottery industry and increasing the quality and output.[16] Immigrant potters from Siegburg brought their moulds with them, often bearing the dates from the previous century and consequently adding confusion to the dating and manufacturing site of these vessels. The foreign monopoly on white stoneware production was not challenged until the third quarter of the seventeenth century when John Dwight took out a patent in 1672 for 'the mistery of transparent Earthen ware commonly knowne by the names of Porcelane or China and Persian ware as also the misterie of the stone ware vulgarly called Cologne ware'.[17] John Dwight was producing it all in the third quarter of the seventeenth century: brown and grey-bodied Westerwald type salt-glazed wares, white salt-glazed stoneware and experimental porcelain. It is to Dwight that any account of the subsequent development of the industry must look.[18]

John Dwight, of course, was the watershed potter in English ceramics. He separated the previous centuries of potting in England from what was to become its future. He realised the possibilities of firing pottery to temperatures producing wares combining strength and beauty which could compete with Oriental imports. In essence Dwight laid the ceramic foundations for the upcoming century thirty years before its arrival and some seventy-five years before the development of an actual English porcelain industry.

There is no indication that John Dwight had any previous association with the pottery industry before he applied for his famous patent in 1672. Prior to that Dwight, who was educated at Christ Church Oxford where he studied civil law and 'Physick a little, but most Chemistry',[19] undoubtedly worked with Robert Hooke and others in the famous laboratory of Robert Boyle in a salient period in the late 1650s, just when a brilliant group was at work there on many branches of science.[20] In 1661, after the Restoration, Dwight was secretary to successive bishops of Chester, including one John Wilkins. Wilkins, a fellow of the Royal Society, brought a suit against Dwight for mishandling diocesan funds. If indeed Dwight did embezzle funds it seems poor timing as a friend like Wilkins in high circles could have been a much needed patron.[21] After the debacle with Wilkins Dwight moved to Fulham some time between December 1671 and May 1673.[22] He arrived in London with the patronage of Hooke and Boyle[23] which undoubtedly brought with it financial advantages. As a gentleman settling his pottery in Fulham, close to the river Thames, Dwight probably selected the site for its proximity to the City of London as well as the advantages offered by the river of transport of raw materials and finished products.

A body of historical documentation initiated by Mavis Bimson (1961) and Rhoda Edwards (1974), followed by

Fig. 1. ***A Deed of Lease to John Dwight of Fulham*** whereby William Penn, as Proprietor of Pennsylvania, deeded Dwight five hundred acres of land in the Province of Pennsylvania. The deed is dated 22 March 1685/6 and was the first step in a two-part transfer of the land. The next day a signed deed of release completed the transaction for £22. The right to buy the land was sold out of the family following Dwight's death in 1703 and, when it eventually was surveyed in 1709 (perhaps after Lydia Dwight's death), the actual land was located in Warminster Township, Bucks County, north of Philadelphia. (Former collection Tracy and Harwood Johnson, Wallingford, Pennsylvania. See Harwood A. Johnson 'John Dwight of Fulham's Purchase of Land in Pennsylvania', Ars Ceramica No. 10, 1993, 21-25)

Fig. 1a. ***The name of John Dwight*** and the signature of William Penn as it appears on the document.

Dennis Haselgrove and John Murray's comprehensive publication of all the documentary information in 1979 and 1992, with the detailed report on the extensive excavations of the Fulham site by Chris Green (1999) and a previous exhibition and catalogue provided by Jonathan Horne (1992), combine to make John Dwight the best-documented potter after Josiah Wedgwood.

A look at the contemporary ceramic scenario might be in order to place Dwight's venture in perspective. As has been suggested earlier, two types of ceramics were cheaply imported into England in the seventeenth century, Rhenish stoneware and Chinese porcelain; the latter, however, was substantially curtailed in 1635 when Jingdezhen was in turmoil from the civil war which eventually led to the fall of the Ming dynasty to the Manchus who set up the Qing dynasty after 1644.[24] Trade was further hampered by various Anglo-Dutch conflicts in ensuing years. The difficulty of obtaining the highly coveted Chinese porcelains just when the fashion had been established sparked the wide production of tin-glazed earthenwares. Archaeological and documentary evidence seems to indicate that the market for Chinese porcelains was not fully satisfied until the first quarter of the eighteenth century.[25] Dependency on imports, particularly where political conflicts abound, presented a challenge to a man such as Dwight with his scientific inclinations. And, although there can be little doubt that

Colour Plate 3. **Bust of Lydia Dwight,** white salt-glazed stoneware. John Dwight, Fulham, c.1680. 6⅞in. (17.53cm) high. (Willett collection, 1887, British Museum)

Colour Plate 2. **Figure of a sportsman** in contemporary dress with a hare slung over his shoulder and a dog at his side, white salt-glazed stoneware. John Dwight, Fulham, c.1680. 9⅕in. (23.37cm) high. (Reynolds collection, Franks collection 1887, British Museum)

Colour Plate 4. **Figure of Athena** adapted from a marble in the Parthenon, white salt-glazed stoneware. John Dwight, c.1680. 6⅛in. (15.56) high. (Reynolds collection, Willett collection, 1887, British Museum)

Chapter I – Early Development of White Salt-Glazed Stoneware

*Colour Plate 6. **Figure of Meleager** with long hair in the 17th century style; quiver slung over his shoulder. His dog is nosing the boar's head on the ground. White salt-glazed stoneware, John Dwight, Fulham, c.1680. 11in. (27.94cm) high. (Reynolds collection, Franks collection, 1887, British Museum)*

*Colour Plate 7. **Figure of a girl** standing between two lambs, white salt-glazed stoneware of fine texture and colour, translucent in places. John Dwight, Fulham, c.1680. 8¾in. (22.23cm) high. (Reynolds collection, Franks collection, 1887, British Museum)*

*Colour Plate 5. **Figure of Flora**, white salt-glazed stoneware. John Dwight, Fulham, c.1680. 11¾in. (29.85cm) high. (Reynolds collection, Franks collection, 1889, British Museum)*

Chapter I – Early Development of White Salt-Glazed Stoneware

*Fig. 2. **Two mugs**, gorge-shaped. Above, white-slipped salt-glazed stoneware with a silver rim. 4in. (10.16cm) high, made by John Dwight, Fulham, c.1685. Below, blanc de chine Chinese porcelain, 3¾in. (9.53cm) high. c.1690. (Harriet Carlton Goldweitz collection)*

Fulham was intended to be a porcelain manufactory, it is for the important contribution to the development of the stoneware industry in England that Dwight's factory will be principally remembered.

A chronology of Dwight's accomplishments combining the documentary and archaeological data would suggest that prior to 1675 he was preoccupied with the production of porcelain which, although probably not commercially viable, did establish him as the first manufacturer of porcelain in the country. However, the figures in the British Museum and the Victoria and Albert Museum (Colour Plates 2-7) in the greyish-white stoneware are the finest legacy to the skills of John Dwight. Indeed, they stand at the pinnacle of figure production by any English manufacturer in earthenware or in porcelain. The bread and butter trade was by 1674 the so-called Cologne stonewares or bellarmine bottles with which he intended to supply England.[26] It would be interesting to know just how commercially competitive Dwight's prices were. He continued to produce good quality stoneware into the 1690s, including white stoneware produced both during his lifetime and by his widow and son after his death well into the eighteenth century, precursors to the fine Staffordshire industry.

In the main white salt-glazed stoneware from the seventeenth century pottery at Fulham was left undecorated, but some was gilded, enamel painted, or marbled. The painting was perhaps done by independent decorators working for the glass industry. It will be remembered that Dwight agreed to supply the London Glass Sellers Company brown bottles made to regulation sizes overseen by the Company itself for a period of three years in 1676 and so decorators may have been enamelling and gilding on both glass and ceramics. In 1677 Dwight suggested that his 'transparent *Earth*'… '*Statues* or *Figures*' could be decorated with '*colours of Iron, Copper, Brass,* and *party-colour'd,* as some *Achat – Stones*'.[27] Certainly the Glass Sellers Company patronage, which extended to buying only Dwight's products to the exclusion of foreign imports, was a serious boost to Dwight's business as well as his reputation.

In the 1680s Dwight expanded his range of wares and took out a second patent for another fourteen years in 1684. The patent was taken out two years before the expiry of the 1672 patent, presumably to remind threatening competition of his hegemony in the field. The 1684 patent specifies that Dwight was making white and marbled wares, red stoneware tewares and figures and statues.[28]

Dwight's patent was allegedly infringed by thirteen other potters, initiated by in-house espionage resulting in the defection of John Chandler, a Dwight labourer, who went over to the *Elers brothers-James Morley* of Nottingham camp in the 1690s. Other potters of note accused of infringement included three members of the *Wedgwood* family, *Aaron, Thomas I and Richard* and *Matthew Garner. Luke Talbot, Richard White* and *Moses Johnson* of Southwark were accused in 1695 and in 1697 three more Staffordshire potters were also cited, *Moses Middleton, Cornelius Hammersley* and *Joshua Astbury*.[29]

The temptation to other potters to cash in on the manufacture and market for salt-glazed ware brought about the series of lawsuits from 1693 to 1698. An argument put forward by Cornelius Hammersley against the accusation of

*Fig. 3. **Coffee/chocolate pot,** lighthouse shaped white-slipped salt-glazed stoneware with an iron-dipped rim, knop, spout and handle tip. This is the only example of a Dwight coffee pot of this shape known. John Dwight or successor Lydia Dwight or Dr. Samuel Dwight, Fulham c.1695-1710. 4in. (10.16cm) high. (British Museum, Franks collection No.35)*

patent infringement was that the Fulham venture did not involve a new invention but was merely an extension of existing potters' knowledge.[30] Apparently Dwight did negotiate with some potters to allow their productions. The Elers brothers were allowed by licence to continue producing red stoneware in both Vauxhall and in Staffordshire.

An interesting addendum to the chronology of Dwight achievements was his purchase in 1685 of property in Pennsylvania from William Penn, a parcel of land consisting of five hundred acres located in Bucks county just north of Philadelphia (Figs. 1, 1a). Dwight paid £22 for the land but his intentions for its use were never divulged. Harwood Johnson, who owns the deed of lease and has written about the transaction,[31] speculates that it may have been simply a business venture or possibly a potential resettlement for either himself or for his family. The possibility that he might have intended the property to be a source of clay for his pottery seems unlikely, although, of course, Josiah Wedgwood was bringing back clay from North Carolina and from Australia in the late eighteenth century for that very purpose.

White salt-glazed pottery produced by John Dwight is typified by mugs which were white dipped stoneware in gorge forms (Figs. 2, 199). One mug (Fig. 199) in the Victoria and Albert Museum is dated 1682 on the silver rim, a good benchmark for the production of this popular shape

CHAPTER I – EARLY DEVELOPMENT OF WHITE SALT-GLAZED STONEWARE

*Colour Plate 8. **Two mugs**, white-slipped salt-glazed stoneware with iron-dipped rim and handle tips. Staffordshire, c.1700-25. Left, 5in. (12.7cm) high (ex Helas collection); right, 3½in. (8.89cm) high. (Private collection)*

produced by Dwight. Jugs and cylindrical mugs are also known as well as one apparently unique lighthouse shaped coffee pot (Fig. 3) in the British Museum. Pottery from the Fulham manufactory of John Dwight was excavated in a pit at 16 Tunsgate, Guildford, Surrey in 1991 where a jug and a teapot in salt-glazed stoneware were uncovered (Figs. 4, 200, 201).[32] In America, Dwight salt-glazed mugs and a coffee pot (Figs. 5, 6) were found in Maryland in an early eighteenth century context at London Town (see Chapter VII); other Dwight salt-glaze was excavated at

*Fig. 4. **Jug**, white-slipped pear-shaped jug with iron-dipped rim and top of handle. The partially reconstructed jug, excavated at 16 Tunsgate, Guildford, Surrey in 1991, is a unique example of this type to have come to light made by one of the Dwight family, Fulham between 1700 and 1710. 5¾in. (14.61cm) high. (Guildford Museum)*

*Fig. 5. **Mug**, partially reconstructed white-slipped salt-glazed stoneware with iron-dipped rim and upper handle. The mug was excavated at Rumney's Tavern, London Town, Maryland's western shore. The knife-cut terminal and fine articulation of the turned base link the mug to Dwight's manufactory at Fulham, c.1700-1720. 6½in. (16.51cm) high. (Anne Arundel County, Lost Towns Project)*

Colour Plate 9. **Shoe,** *salt-glazed stoneware with a white-slip covering a darker body with applied motifs and brown slip. The shoe is very rare in stoneware, more often seen in delftware. Staffordshire, c.1710-20. 5⅛in. (13.02cm) long. (Photograph courtesy of Jonathan Horne)*

Jamestown, Virginia.

White salt-glazed wares produced by John Dwight (d.1703) and his wife Lydia, who took over the manufactory until around 1708, and subsequently his son Dr. Samuel Dwight (1709-37) were grey stoneware bodies dipped in a white engobe slip which when fired tended to pull away from the body. To camouflage the greyish rims which were exposed after firing the Dwights either had silver rims produced for the necks of mugs or dipped the rims in an iron oxide producing a brown line.

By 1698 Dwight is described as being ill[33] and nothing more is heard of him until his death in 1703. It seems that the last decade of his life was spent trying to vanquish his rivals and the expense and preoccupation involved in litigation undoubtedly undermined his own industry. Nevertheless, John Dwight initiated a tradition in producing white high-fired wares which turned the tide in the English pottery industry from earthenware production to a stoneware for every man's taste and table.

Fig. 6. **Fragments of a coffee pot,** *white salt-glazed stoneware with upper half dipped in an iron wash. These were excavated at Rumney's Tavern, London Town, Maryland in a trash pit with the latest material dating to 1723/4. The potting and ferruginous wash relate to the teapot in fig. 201 excavated at 16 Tunsgate in Guildford. Probably John Dwight or successor family potters at Fulham, c.1700-10. (Anne Arundel County, Lost Towns Project)*

CHAPTER II

Early Industrial Stonewares

Frustratingly little is known about the production of white stoneware after *John Dwight's* salient decade from 1685 to 1695 until one finds primary source documentation, such as newspaper advertisements and business letters, in the mid-eighteenth century. That there were legions of manufacturers attests to the success of the industry in a ware which could be as beguiling and serviceable as Chinese porcelain and as cheap as delftware. The documentation of salt-glazed stoneware is difficult, and made more so by the fact that the manufacturers were not bound by ego or entrepreneurship to mark their wares. Few acknowledgements of manufacture exist prior to the *Josiah Wedgwood I* years and the opening of the factory at Etruria in 1769, which seems to herald the beginning of marking of wares in Staffordshire pottery. There are more questions to be asked than answers available about the pottery industry: its wages, terms of hiring, supply and demand, transport domestically and abroad. For example, undecorated salt-glaze is being excavated in the Netherlands in considerable quantities but there is precious little supporting evidence to corroborate its existence there. No rate books or company documents exist in Staffordshire for the early years of the eighteenth century as they do in London.

In order to look into these years one has to examine the excavated archaeological material. In London *Dr. Samuel Dwight*, John Dwight's son, continued producing pottery on the Fulham site. He inherited the pottery from his mother in 1709 and his obituary in the *Gentleman's Magazine*, November 1737, claimed: 'He was the first that found out the Secret to colour Earthen-Ware like China'.[1] Many examples of white-slipped, iron-dipped vessels have been identified from the period following John Dwight, that is from as early as 1695 to 1710 (Figs. 3-6, 200, 201; Colour Plates 10, 11). These wares are often refined white or pale grey stoneware, thrown, and lathe-turned at the base. Some of the examples are grooved for a rim mount. Chris Green suggests that they were possibly sent immediately to the silversmith for mounting before being offered for sale. There is a teapot excavated at 16 Tunsgate, Guildford (Fig. 201) with an iron wash on the upper half of the vessel, a form not yet found elsewhere. The teapot is decorated in a manner similar to excavated shards of a coffee pot (Fig. 6) with a pear-shaped body and iron-washed decoration on the upper half of the body at Rumney's Tavern at London Town on Maryland's western shore around 1723/4. Handle terminals on Fulham mugs and jugs are finished with a knife-cut kick (Colour Plate 10).[2] Mugs with lathe-turned bodies and similar knife-cut kicks among the vessels recovered at Rumney's Tavern, London Town (Fig. 5). An unusual light-house shaped coffee pot in the British Museum (Fig.3) with white engobe slip and iron rim, handle tip and knop is hard to date, but it could have been made by John Dwight at the end of his career or by his wife Lydia or son Dr. Samuel Dwight a few years later. The Fulham vessels are distinguished from

*Fig. 6a. **Tea jar**, white salt-glazed stoneware with moulded panels very closely allied to a red stoneware tea jar of Elers manufacture in the Hampshire County Museum (illustrated by Gordon Elliott,* John and David Elers *(London: Jonathan Horne Publications, 1998, Plate 3B). Tantalising in its rarity and for the implied suggestion that the Elers may have also been making salt-glazed stoneware. Staffordshire or London, c.1695-1700. 4½in. (11.43cm). (Photograph courtesy of Jonathan Horne)*

their Staffordshire counterparts (Colour Plate 8; Fig. 5) of a similar period by the better quality of workmanship. The lathe-turned foot is more defined and the engobe thinner, allowing for finer articulation of the details such as lathe turning and handle grooving. The use of white engobe slip covering a coarser grey body was not unique to Dwight and later English potters. The technique was used by Chinese potters toward the end of the T'ang dynasty in the ninth and tenth centuries to achieve the effect of the recently produced first porcelains.[3] It becomes an exercise in futility to speculate whether Dwight was aware of these pots or if he reinvented the technique. Certainly he was very conversant with a wide range of Chinese forms and techniques as discussed in his patents and the signature gorge mug was, of course, a classic Chinese form in *blanc de chine* (Fig. 2).

The Staffordshire debt to Fulham has long been accepted. The lawsuits of plagiarism were not apocryphal and had their genesis in reality with obvious benefits to the industry. The debt to Fulham, and its one pottery, for both shapes and technology, must be acknowledged in Staffordshire; however, assessing and dating Staffordshire artefacts with its multiplicity of sites is another game indeed.

The potteries in Staffordshire offer vast quantities of material associated with the sites but uncertainties incumbent with urban salvage archaeology make dating, and sometimes attribution, difficult. In the absence of general written information one has to rely on the occasional excerpt from a will, or an entry in a parish register, or possibly a name on an indenture, hard scrabble for the researcher who desires the kind of primary documentation more easily obtainable after 1760. An ameliorating dating tool can be New World archaeological sites, some of which have not been overridden by subsequent development. The so-called Lost Towns in Anne Arundel County, Maryland are

*Fig. 7. **Teabowl fragment,** white salt-glazed stoneware with ribbed body and annular turning at the base and a small flared foot. Excavated at the Richard Shortridge House site, Deer Street, Portsmouth, New Hampshire in the fill between two house lots. Staffordshire, probably Shelton Farm, c.1720-22. 2⅛in. (5.4cm) diameter. (Strawbery Banke Museum, A 780)*

a case in point. Underneath the plough zone is material dating to the first half of the eighteenth century. Other North American sites yield similar information which are frustrated again by lack of identification by marks of manufacture. Occasionally, however, one can link up an excavated shard from an archaeological site with another from the urban salvage of a particular pottery (Figs. 7, 8). This is eureka: not always an attribution, but a likely one and, perhaps more importantly, a dating device for the social and art historian. Potteries have the finite life to which social and ceramic historians cling.

Previous written records often reiterate myths within the

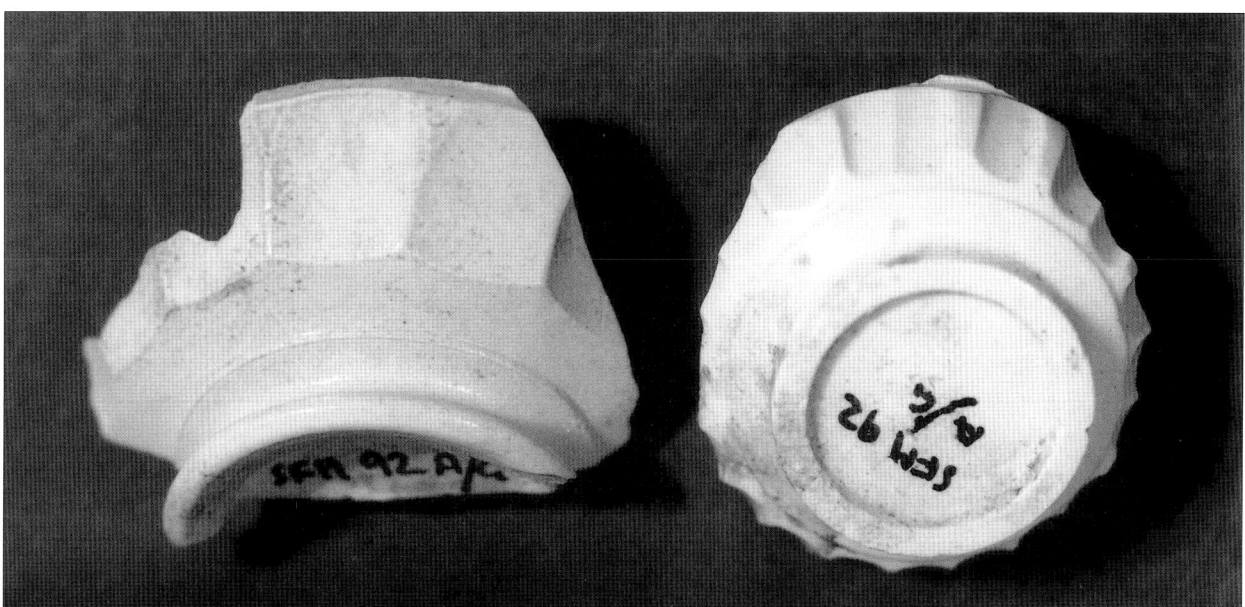

*Fig. 8. **Two teabowl fragments,** white salt-glazed stoneware with ribbed bodies and annular turning at the base with flared foot rims. Staffordshire, excavated at Shelton Farm, Hanley, c.1720-22. (Potteries Museum and Art Gallery, Stoke-on-Trent, SFM 92)*

*Colour Plate 10. **Mugs,** brown and white salt-glazed stoneware with iron-dipped surface colouring. Left and centre, Staffordshire c.1720-40; right, London, Dwight's factory c.1700-25. (Photograph courtesy of Jonathan Horne)*

industry and perpetuate downright mistakes. However, fine historians such as Dr. Robert Plot[4] have clarified pottery nomenclature such as the potter's count:

> they reckon them by the piece, i.e. Quart, in hollow ware, so that 6 pottle, or 3 gallon bottles make a dozen, and so more or less to a dozen, as they are of greater or lesser content; the flat wares are also reckoned by pieces and dozens, but not (as the hollow) according to their content but their different bredths…[5]

By 1750 Burslem had been the centre of the salt-glaze stoneware industry for two or three decades. Slip-casting, the pouring of liquid clay into moulds, had by that time been a function of the pottery industry for about ten years. The moulding process, either by slip-casting or pressing, forecast the industrialisation which would take place in the 1760s.

The challenge to the historian writing about salt-glaze is in elucidating the development in the first half of the eighteenth century when pottery production was effectively functioning as a cottage industry. Here, as suggested, archaeology comes into play. A deposit in a cellar c.1723/4 of ceramics and glass from Rumney's Tavern, operating on the South River of Maryland's western seaboard from around the last decade of the seventeenth century and through the first half of the eighteenth, included dipped white salt-glazed stoneware mugs, jugs and teabowls. (Figs. 5, 6; Colour Plates 11, 12, 138-141). Given the date of deposit, the salt-glaze must have been coming to North America straight from the London kilns. Furthermore, an export business was clearly in place in the first two decades of the eighteenth century. Chapter VII discusses trade to America and the salt-glaze markets. Newspapers and probated estate inventories in the American colonies and early federated republic tell us a great deal about the ceramics available in given periods. Combined with archaeological data the three sources provide a general overview of a period prior to surviving written records, most of which exist only after the mid-eighteenth century in Britain.

A list of the 'Pot Works in Burslem about the year 1710 to 15' was written by Josiah Wedgwood in his own hand in 1776 (Fig. 26). The list includes forty potters, the ware they made, the 'Suppos'd amo' (amount of sales?) and their residence. A second list includes names of seven potters working in Hanley. He adds that there were only two houses in Stoke, 'Wards & Poulsons'.[6] Although the salt-glazed potters are included in the general gazetteer of potters working in salt-glaze in Chapter IX and in Appendix 2, it is interesting to see the names as mentioned by Josiah Wedgwood some sixty years later:

Moses Marsh Stone Ware.   6 - -   Middle of the Town
Aaron Shaw Stone or Dipp'd w[t]
                          6 - -   Next on the East side
Tho[s] Taylor Stone Ware & Freckld
                          6 - -   Next to the North
Moses Shaw D[o]   6 - -   Middle of the Town
Sam[l] Edge Stone Ware   6 - -   Next to the West
R[d] Wedgwood Stone Ware 6 - -   Middle of Town[7]

No stoneware potters were specifically noted in Hanley.

Another page breaks down the workmen, their wages and the raw materials necessary to make an oven of black and mottled ware, and the expected profit for the Master. Although this is not a salt-glaze kiln one would expect similar data would apply toward the production of a salt-glaze firing. The list is transcribed in full for 'an Oven of Black & Motled per Week & other expenses':

6 Men 3@ 4/per week & 3@ 6/	1-10-
4 Boys @ 1/3	-5-
1-2 Lead ore _____ @8/	-12-
Manganese	-3-
Clay 2 Cart Load[s] @2/	-4-
Coals 4 Horse Loads @ 2ᵈ	-8-
Carrᵈ of Dº @ 1/	-6-
Rent of Works @ 5 per Annᵐ	-2-
Wear & Tear of ovens, Utensils &c 10p annᵐ	-4-
Straw for Packing 3 Thraves of 24 Sheaves to the Thrave @ 4	-1-
The Masters Profit besides 6/ for his Labor	-10-
	£4.05-

If we are to believe Josiah Wedgwood there were forty-seven potters firing ovens in Burslem and Hanley in the second decade of the eighteenth century. The reality is that most of these potbanks were operating only one oven, employing as few labourers as necessary to work the pottery and existing on a small margin of profitability. Only one firing could take place in a week. And yet these pots, many of which were salt-glazed, were being transported down to London and up to Liverpool, even sent abroad, as we shall see in Chapters VI and VII. Similar conditions existed for the production of

*Colour Plate 12. **Partially reconstructed teabowl and saucer**, white-slipped salt-glazed stoneware excavated at Rumney's Tavern, London Town, Maryland in context with many other Dwight salt-glazed wares. This teabowl and saucer is very finely potted with thin walls, a waisted high foot and flaring rim. Although no teabowls and saucers have been yet identified as from the Dwight manufacture at Fulham, the early 1723/4 context also suggests that these too may be his family's product. London or Staffordshire c.1710-20. Teabowl 1½in. (3.81cm) high, saucer 4⅛in. (10.5cm) diameter. (Anne Arundel Country, Lost Towns Project)*

pottery until *Thomas and John Wedgwood* began adding ovens or amalgamating potteries in an effort to turn the individual potbank into a pottery industry in 1743. At that time Shaw tells us that Thomas and John Wedgwood erected a pottery with three ovens which they soon expanded to five, causing censure for extravagance amongst the inhabitants of the town.[8] With their vision and later subsequent expansion Thomas and John Wedgwood were essentially the first to industrialise the pottery industry in North Staffordshire. By 1762 Burslem Potters submitted a case in Parliament for a road to be turnpiked between Burslem and the Red Bull in Cheshire and at the time it was claimed there were 150 potteries. The claim was that the industry was burgeoning at such a rate that it had increased by two-thirds in the previous fourteen years.[9] In 1769 Arthur Young maintained that there were three hundred potteries in the six towns employing an estimated twenty hands each or 6,000 plus ancillary workers which would be an estimated 10,000 people employed in all.[10] If Young is correct, the number of potteries had doubled in seven years.

Of course, any pot works which made salt-glazed stoneware and earthenware on the same premises would have to have more than one oven, so that as early as 1714 Aaron Shaw was working two ovens in the middle of Burslem.[11] According to Wedgwood Aaron Shaw was making 'dippᵗ Wᵉ'

*Colour Plate 11. **Partially reconstructed jug**, white-slipped salt-glazed stoneware with iron-dipped rim. Excavated at Rumney's Tavern, London Town, Maryland in a 1723/4 context, the jug appears from the fine general articulation to be of London manufacture but the handle has not been identified as being of Dwight manufacture. Found among other salt-glazed wares of Dwight/Fulham manufacture, the jug has to be considered to be of London manufacture also. London or Staffordshire, c.1700-20. 6⅞in. (17.46cm) high. (Anne Arundel Country, Lost Towns Project)*

CHAPTER II – EARLY INDUSTRIAL STONEWARES

stoneware, the body of which consisted of grey or buff colour local marl covered with an engobe of pipe clay and calcined flint. This was due to the paucity of local white-firing clays. These pots often have an iron wash on the rim and, in the case of mugs and handled cups, another touch of iron at the top of the handle. Not for decoration alone, the iron wash served to disguise the engobe slip which had a tendency to pull away from the body at the rim, handle and spout during firing, exposing the fabric underneath. After about 1720, plastic white-firing ball clay began being imported from Devon and Dorset into the Potteries.[12] White engobe slip was initially used on all salt-glazed white stonewares. After 1720 teawares and higher-end white stoneware were produced with an all white-firing or ball clay. Engobe white slips continued to be used on some less important salt-glazed stoneware, such as chamber pots and wash basins, throughout the life of the manufacture of white stoneware. Indeed, a white-dipped mug was retrieved from one of the British vessels sunk at Yorktown in 1781.[13]

Another document confirms the early expansion of the one-kiln potbank into a larger complex of buildings designed to accommodate the production of a wider range of pottery. In 1731 *Dr. Thomas Wedgwood II* (not to be confused with potters *Thomas and John Wedgwood* of the Big House), whose father was described as producing 'Brown Stone' in 1710-15,[14] bought a pottery from a John Taylor of Silkstone, Yorkshire for £50. The transaction included a 'House wherein Samuel Malkin, Burslem, mold-man doth now resp'fully inhabit & dwell…Pott' Houses, Workhouses, Ware-houses, beating-houses, molding-houses, throwing-houses, smoke houses, Pott-ovens, kilns, hovels, ground…in Burslem'.[15]

Fig. 9. **Mug,** *white-slipped salt-glaze stoneware with iron-dipped rim and handle tip and scratch-brown decoration E:W 17:23. Staffordshire, c.1723. 5¼in. (13.34cm) high. (Potteries Museum and Art Gallery, Stoke-on-Trent)*

Fig. 10. **Two-handled cup,** *white salt-glazed stoneware incised* Mrs Mary Sandbach her cup anno dom 1720. *Staffordshire, c.1720. 6in. (15.24cm) high. (The Nelson Atkins Museum of Art, Kansas City, Missouri (Gift of Mr. and Mrs. F.P. Burnap) 41-23/675, ex Revelstoke collection)*

CHAPTER II – EARLY INDUSTRIAL STONEWARES

Fig. 11. ***Two-handled cup,*** *white-slipped salt-glazed stoneware commemorating the marriage of Martha Barlar and Cornelius Toft incised* c martha Barlar T/1727:8 *and on the other side* WB martha Barlar Ct/ Cornelius Toft 1727/8 *hand (Cornelius Toft was christened in Stoke-on-Trent 17 December 1703, the son of Mathei and Dorothy Toft). Staffordshire, c.1727/8. 6in. (15.24cm) high. (Central Museum and Art Gallery, Northampton, Manfield bequest, 1920.1d1.86)*

This is one of the earliest surviving records documenting the purchase of a pottery. Note the site contained more than one kiln. It also tells us that *Samuel Malkin* was a 'mold-man' in 1731. What kind of a mould maker was he? Could he have been a hump-mould maker for the production of plates? 1731 is an early date for the industrial press moulded wares so often associated with salt-glaze production, a decade or so before the usually accepted date of the introduction of press-moulded and even slip-cast wares. Dr. Thomas Wedgwood's indenture of Aaron Wood, shortly after he bought the Burslem pottery, in August 1731,[16] is of particular interest in that the then fourteen year old boy, who was to become the master mould maker, may have been apprenticed to Samuel Malkin to learn the trade. There is a master mould of a spittoon signed by Aaron Wood in the British Museum (Fig. 77, Chapter V). Aaron Wood went on to augment his legacy by fathering the great modeller Ralph Wood. At least fifteen moulds marked by Ralph Wood have survived, some of which are dated.[17]

Early Dated Salt-Glaze

The earliest surviving dated white salt-glaze stoneware is a two-handled cup in the Burnap collection in the Nelson-Atkins Gallery, Kansas City, incised *Mrs. Mary Sandbach her cup anno dom 1720*. The cup is a thrown white body, lathe-turned with rolled handles (Fig. 10). The earliest white-engobe slipped dated piece is a mug in the Potteries Museum with brown sgraffito-type decoration *E:W 17:23* (Fig. 9). Two vessels dated 1724 exist, a scent bottle marked *T.W.1724* on the base, in the Glaisher collection,[18] and a flask, slip-decorated in scratch-brown, marked *IM 1724*.[19] Another two-handled cup in the Central Museum and Art Gallery, Northampton (Figs. 11, 11a), is incised into the white body *c martha Barlar T/1727:8 and on the other side WB martha Barlar Ct/ Cornelius Toft 1727/8 hand*. In the Potteries Museum, Stoke-on-Trent, there is a crucifix (Fig. 12), moulded and hand-modelled, dated 1732. This would appear to be a unique piece and was made by *Aaron Wedgwood* or his sons John and Thomas of the Big House, Burslem.[20] The

Fig. 11a. ***Inscription on cup*** *(fig. 11).*

Chapter II – Early Industrial Stonewares

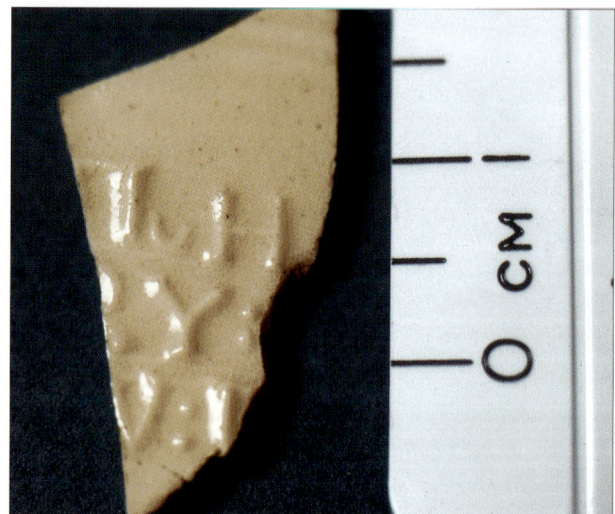

*Fig. 12. **Crucifix**, white salt-glazed stoneware moulded and hand modelled dated 1732. This would appear to be a unique piece and was made by Aaron Wedgwood or his sons John and Thomas of the Big House, Burslem. 4¼in. (10.8cm) high. (Potteries Museum and Art Gallery, Stoke-on-Trent)*

*Fig. 13. **Master mould for a teapot** commemorating the victory of Admiral Vernon at Portobello in 1739. Staffordshire, c.1739. 5⅛in. (13.02cm) high. (Potteries Museum and Art Gallery, Stoke-on-Trent, 713)*

*Fig. 14. **Mug depicting the victory at Portobello** by Admiral Vernon. White salt-glazed stoneware with rouletted neck and base with sprig relief moulding of Admiral Vernon, a cannon and six ships which reads: The British Glory Revived by Admiral Vernon He took Portobello with six ships only. Staffordshire, c.1739. 7in. (17.78cm) high. (Victoria and Albert Museum, Schreiber collection, 71)*

*Fig. 15. **Shard from a Portobello mug**, white salt-glazed stoneware excavated at the Dr. Hall Jackson site in Portsmouth, New Hampshire. Staffordshire, c.1739. (Private collection)*

*Colour Plate 13. **Teapot depicting the victory at Puerto Bello (Portobello)** (white salt-glazed stoneware) on the Spanish main when Admiral Lord Vernon captured the town to secure another stronghold for transportation of South American treasure to Europe in 1739. The teapot has PORTO/BELLO/TAKEN on one side and on the reverse BY AD/VERNON and FORT/CHAGRE. At the time of the victory many medals were struck in London, probably taken from contemporary maps of the area and further mementos, such as this teapot, would probably have been moulded from similar sources. Staffordshire, c.1740-45. 5½in. (13.97cm) high. (The Henry H. Weldon Collection, Colonial Williamsburg Foundation, photography by Gavin Ashworth)*

moulded parts of this unusual crucifix indicate the early ability to mould hollow wares in fire-clay moulds before the introduction of plaster of Paris which appears to have been a few years later. Further discussion of moulds and mould-makers is included in Chapter V.

At least two examples dated 1735 are recorded: a puzzle jug with *1735* in scratch-brown and applied iron-brown reliefs on the neck in the Potteries Museum, and a two-handled cup marked *W.A. 1735* with ear-shaped handles pinched at the terminals and turned and rouletted bands around the body from the Earle collection.[21]

1739 was an important date for commemoratives and one cannot be sure that all of the mugs and teapots commemorating the Battle of Portobello, when Admiral Edward Vernon (1684-1757) defeated the Spanish 'with six ships only', were actually produced in that year. It is likely many were not. Portobello was, of course, the anglicised *Puerto Bello*. A master mould for a Portobello teapot is in the Potteries Museum (Fig. 13). One shard from a mug was found in Portsmouth, New Hampshire, on the Dr. Hall Jackson (1739-1797) site where a well on the property was excavated (Fig. 15). The context, which included material up to the end of the famous physician's life, gives no clue to the date of purchase, which was probably part of a legacy. A further battle of Admiral Vernon's in 1740 at the fort of San Lorenzo protected the town of Chagre. This victory allowed Vernon to secure another Spanish stronghold for transport of South American treasure to Europe. In 1741 another battle at Cartagena, the key port of the Spanish Main, on the Caribbean coast of what is currently Columbia, was a defeat to the British fleet whose troops were decimated by yellow fever and thus the battle was lost. Captain Lawrence Washington, the brother of the future first President, was decorated for bravery in the battle. Staffordshire potters were less inclined to celebrate the lost battle in pottery but a few Cartagena teapots exist, also commemorating both Portobello and Chagre.

Most of the 1739 dated salt-glaze pieces are historical commemoratives of these battles. but another jug with cross-hatched decoration and a strap handle in the Earle collection is inscribed:

I
T A
1739.[22]

There are a few pieces dated 1740 and 1741. An inkpot, marked *I.B., 1742* in perforated dots, was lost in the 1873 fire at Alexandra Palace.[23] 1742 is the year when one finds

Chapter II – Early Industrial Stonewares

*Fig. 16. **Two-handled cup**, white salt-glazed stoneware with finely ribbed rouletted neck and scratch-brown incised decoration which reads* Sarah Jones 1744. *Staffordshire, 1744. 7⅜in. (18.73cm) high. (British Museum, 1919,053.61)*

the first dated examples of scratch-blue decoration on salt-glazed stoneware. Scratch-brown (Figs. 9, 16; Colour Plates 16, 18) had been used to decorate English stoneware from the early 1720s, but in 1742 one finds the first of a long list of dated scratch-blue (or 'blue and white stone' as the newspaper advertisements described it). Two examples survive, a mug decorated with birds and flowers and inscribed *17 Enoch Booth 42* in the Glaisher collection (Colour Plate 14). There is also a bowl (Colour Plate 15) incised *EG 1742* in the Greg collection.

Scratch-blue dated examples are found frequently from 1742 until 1778, the last of the dated salt-glazed stoneware in general. Scratch-blue decoration appears to be predominant in the decorated salt-glaze market until the mid-1750s when enamel decoration became popular. There are two earlier dated examples of enamel-decorated salt-glaze, a mug in the Victoria and Albert Museum dated 1739 and another at Colonial Williamsburg dated 1746 (Colour Plate 93 a-e). The suggestion that they may have been decorated in London workshops (and not in Dutch workshops) seems likely when the decoration is compared with the enamelling done at the time on Chinese porcelains and in the 1740s on English porcelains. These mugs will be discussed in Chapter V.

Eighteenth century Pottery Economics

Wages for skilled pottery labour had essentially remained the same from the 1710 to 1715 period according to Josiah Wedgwood's document listing the forty-seven potters extant in Burslem and Hanley (Fig. 26) until mid-century. In 1710 a man was paid 4s. or 6s. a week and a child 1s.3d. per week.[24] In 1748 *Jonah Malkin* hired Daniel Heath and Joseph Burn for

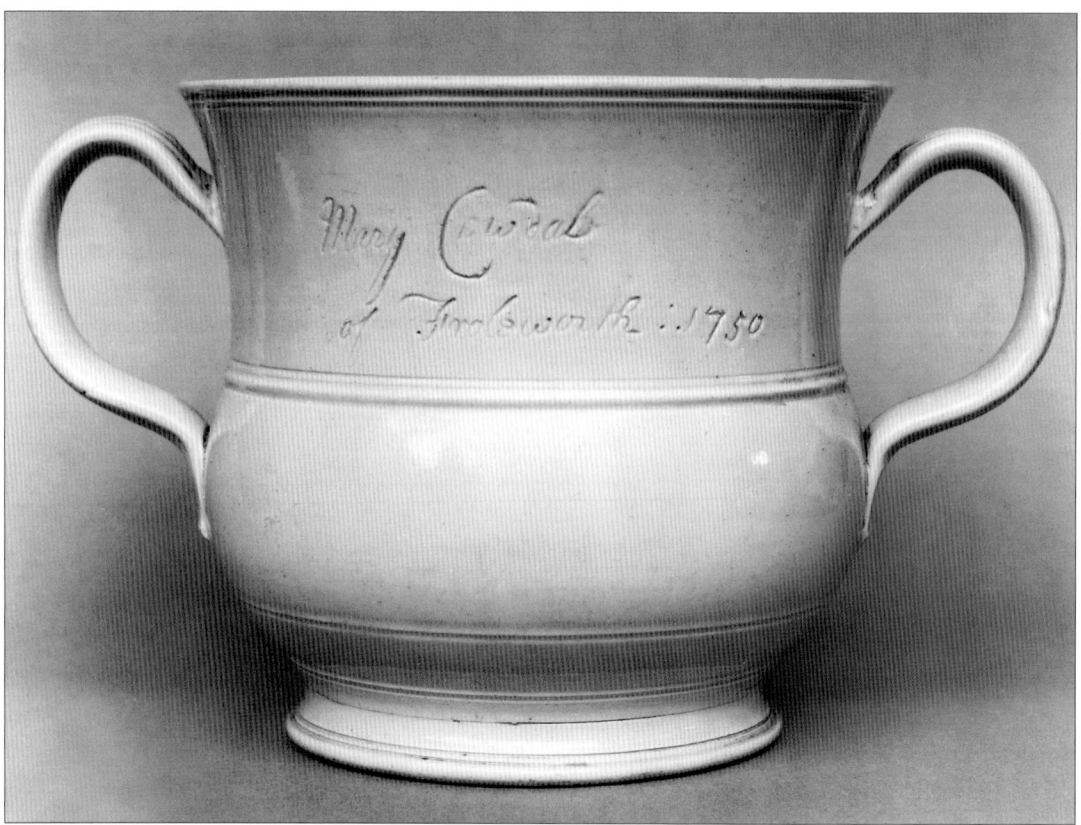

*Fig. 17. **Two-handled cup**, white salt-glazed stoneware incised* Mary Cowdal of Frolsworth:1750 *(Frolsworth is near Lutterworth in Leicestershire). Staffordshire, 1750. 4⅜in. (11.11cm) high. (British Museum, Willett collection, 1887,0210.160)*

CHAPTER II – EARLY INDUSTRIAL STONEWARES

Fig. 18. **Mug,** *white salt-glazed stoneware with scratch-blue incised motto:* Drink your drink and Stand your Ground for this is Cal d the ploughmans Round....Edwa'd Plant 1750/1. *Staffordshire, 1750. 5⅛in. (13.14cm) high. (Harriet Carlton Goldweitz collection)*

Fig 18a. **Mug** *(fig. 18) viewed from obverse.*

Fig. 19. **Two plates,** *white salt-glazed stoneware press-moulded, the left plate with the motto* THE KING OF PRUSSIA, *enamel decorated. In a letter to Horace Mann, Horace Walpole wrote:*

Mr. Pitt is in bed with the gout and the King of Prussia writing sonnets to Voltaire; but his Majesty's lyre is not half so charming as his sword; If he does not take care Alexander will ride home upon his verses. All England kept his birthday: it has taken its place in our calendar next to Admiral Vernon's & my Lord Blakeney's, & the people, I believe, think that Prussia is part of *Old England*. (1758)

Staffordshire, c.1758. 9¼in. (23.5cm) diameter. (British Museum, Franks collection, 1887)

Chapter II – Early Industrial Stonewares

*Colour Plate 14. **Mug**, white salt-glazed stoneware with scratch-blue decoration of birds and flowers. The base is incised 17 Enoch Booth 42. Although it is tempting to think this mug was made by Enoch Booth it was probably made for him. Staffordshire, 1742. 4½in. (11.43cm) high. (Fitzwilliam Museum, Glaisher collection, 507-1928)*

*Colour Plate 15. **Bowl**, white salt-glazed stoneware with scratch-blue decoration incised with EG 1742. This bowl and the Enoch Booth mug (Colour Plate 14) are the two earliest dated scratch-blue examples known. Staffordshire, 1742. 7½in. (19.05cm) high. (City Art Gallery, Manchester, Greg collection, 1923-540)*

*Colour Plate 16. **Inkwell** (with screw top), white salt-glazed stoneware with scratch-brown decoration incised: Alex Ready, Esq.r: 1745. Staffordshire, 1745. 2½in. (6.35cm) high. (Photograph courtesy of Jonathan Horne)*

6s. a week and their sons for 1s.7d. and 1s.8d. respectively.[25] An account book of *Thomas Whieldon* of 1749 indicated that a turner or a saggar maker could make up to 8s. per week whereas some unspecified jobs only paid only 5s.[26] According to the Bank of England (in 1999) the equivalent buying power of £1 in 1720 would require £74.59.[27] A wage of 6s. a week in 1710 to 1748 would be the equivalent of about £21 per week in contemporary wages.

Some prices of goods in London in 1745/6 included gold (coin) @ £3.17s. per ounce, silver @ 5s.3d. an ounce, a beaver skin 3s. to 3s.6d., Jamaican rum 3s.9d. per gallon and Jamaican coffee £4.10s.-£5.10s. (measurement unspecified); Virginia tobacco was available at the astonishing price of 2½-5d. per pound, Bohea Tea at 5s.3d., Green 6s.6d. and Hyson 15s., black pepper was 12½d., all per pound; refined sugar was expensive at £4.6s. the pound; gunpowder, sold in 100 pound increments, was £3.5s. Insurance was available on goods from London to Carolina and vice versa at nearly twice the cost. There were provisions for the mode of transport, on a convoy or in a man-of-war, the latter being half the price.[28]

The buying power of the pound remained the same from 1670 to 1720. By 1770, probably owing to increased demand for labour and competition due to the Industrial Revolution, £1 was equivalent to £56.59 in purchasing power.

Salt-Glaze Ascendancy

It is difficult to pinpoint *the* heyday of salt-glazed stoneware by date or even decade. If one considers the earliest dated piece, 1720 (Fig. 10), and contrasts it to the latest one, 1778 (Colour Plates 190, 190a; Fig. 25), one has a documentable period of almost six decades when salt-glaze made history. However, it would appear to be more complex than that. With a hundred year manufacturing history, from 1685 to

CHAPTER II – EARLY INDUSTRIAL STONEWARES

Colour Plate 17. **Loving cup,** *white salt-glazed stoneware with overall scratch-blue decoration inscribed M B 1748. Staffordshire, 1748. 6⅜in. (16.19cm) high. (Potteries Museum and Art Gallery, Stoke-on-Trent, 3662)*

Colour Plate 18. **Large mug,** *white salt-glazed stoneware with scratch-brown incised initials IK and 1749. Staffordshire, 1749. 6¾in. (17.15cm) high. (The Henry H. Weldon Collection, Colonial Williamsburg Foundation, photography by Gavin Ashworth)*

Colour Plate 19. **Jug and mug,** *white salt-glazed stoneware with scratch-blue floral decoration, mug incised: M:B 1751. 5in. (12.7cm) high. Staffordshire, 1751; jug, 3in. (7.62cm) high. Staffordshire, c.1750. (Central Museum and Art Gallery, Northampton, Manfield collection, 1920-1 d1.89; 11.77)*

Chapter II – Early Industrial Stonewares

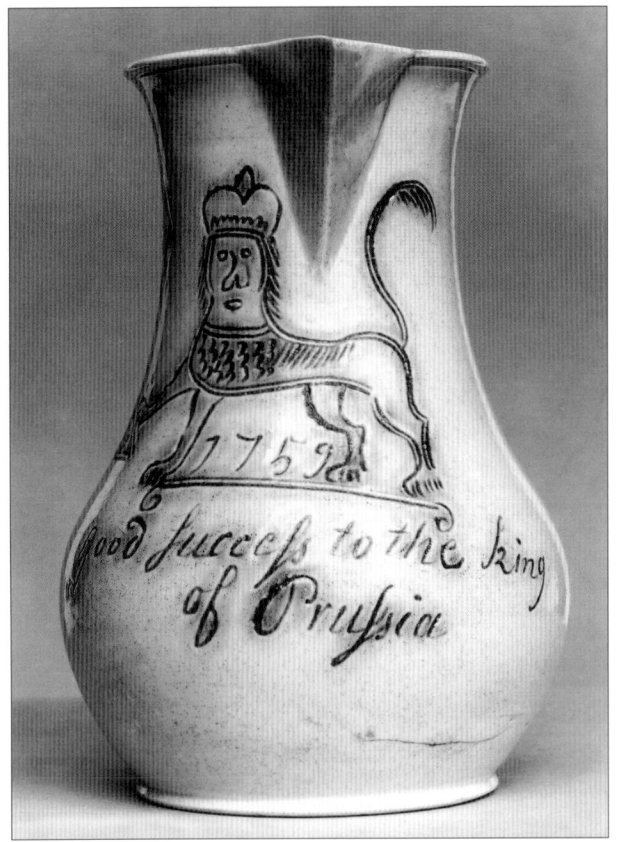

Fig. 20. **Jug,** *white salt-glazed stoneware with scratch-blue decoration commemorating the Seven Years War inscribed* 1759 Good Success to the King of Prussia *surmounted by a crowned lion. Probably Staffordshire, 1759. 7in. (17.78cm) high. (British Museum, 1938,0314.26)*

Fig. 21. **Plate,** *white salt-glazed stoneware with scratch-blue incised decoration including a lion surmounted by a cross representing the British alliance with Frederick, King of Prussia during the Seven Years War. Probably Staffordshire, c.1756-63. 8½in. (21.59cm) diameter.* **Tea canister,** *scratch-blue white salt-glazed stoneware incised* Grace Nichols 1770. *Bovey Tracey, Devon, 1770. 5¼in. (13.34cm) high. (Photograph courtesy of Jonathan Horne)*

CHAPTER II – EARLY INDUSTRIAL STONEWARES

*Fig. 22. **Mug**, white salt-glazed stoneware scratch-blue decorated with incised flowers inscribed: B.T 1759. Staffordshire, c.1759. 5¾in. (14.61cm) high. (Catzen collection)*

*Fig. 22a. **Handle** on mug in fig. 22.*

*Fig. 23. **Punch bowl**, white salt-glazed stoneware with scratch-blue floral decoration incised* Edward ★ Saddler 1759 *on the exterior and on the interior*
    Fill up the Bowl
        Let not our Wife us Control
Probably Staffordshire, 1759. 5½in. (13.97cm). (Photograph courtesy of Jonathan Horne)

Colour Plate 20. **Mug,** *white salt-glazed stoneware with scratch-blue decoration commemorating Bonnie Prince Charlie incised 1753 I F. Probably Staffordshire, 1753. 5in. (12.7cm) high. (Photograph courtesy of Hall Auctioneers, Shrewsbury)*

Colour Plate 21. **Inkwell,** *white salt-glazed stoneware personalised in scratch-blue with the initials WM 1761. 2¼in. (5.72cm) high. Right, a unique salt-glazed stoneware* **leech jar** *with a pierced lid incised in scratch-blue Dr. Alexdr Smollet and on the base P.E./1753. Perhaps Staffordshire, 1753. 9¼in. (23.4cm) high. (Photograph courtesy of Jonathan Horne)*

approximately 1785, the salient period would probably have to include the period of highest visibility and creativity, the period when the moulding, casting and decoration were aimed initially at competing with Chinese and English porcelains, and targeting the market in 'curious'[29] teapots intended to charm the gentry by

Fig. 24. **Shard of tea canister?,** *white salt-glazed stoneware with scratch-blue decoration incised 1769. The shard was found in a field near Totnes, Devon. Bovey Tracey, 1769. 1⅝ x 1⅜in. (4.13 x 3.49cm). (Photograph courtesy of Brian Adams)*

whimsy rather than expense. On occasion the whimsical salt-glaze forms reverberated back to the Chinese and one sees the West to East phenomenon such as in the shell-shaped jug (Fig. 27) whose handle, feet and moulding are pure salt-glaze. Those squirrel (Colour Plate 24), camel (Colour Plate 25), house (Figs. 29, 72; Colour Plate 56), shell (Figs. 30-32), heart-shaped (Fig. 33) and commemorative pots must have revolutionised the tea table with their own special grace.

Alongside these decorative and whimsical wares was always an underlying production of plain and moulded tea and table wares of a utilitarian nature which undoubtedly provided the financial underpinnings of the salt-glaze industry. What we know about their use and that of other salt-glazed stoneware is woefully sparse; we can only piece together strands and hope to come out with a small cord which gives us some understanding about the popularity of certain well-known patterns in certain time frames. There are a few manufacturers with identifiable pots, who are discussed in Chapter IX. Salt-glaze in the social context will be discussed more thoroughly in Chapter III. Chronologically, the emerging interest in salt-glaze in the most prominent five decades of its importance will be looked into through the documents as we proceed.

Certainly one of the most prominent, documentable manufacturers of salt-glazed stoneware was Thomas

CHAPTER II – EARLY INDUSTRIAL STONEWARES

Fig. 25. **Bowl,** *white salt-glazed stoneware with scratch-blue incised motto:*
   Long May we Live hapy May we be
   Blest with Content and from all dangers free
   Willm Fillipes His Bowl– March 12th Swansea 1778
Swansea, 1778. 9in. (22.86cm) high. (Photograph courtesy of Jonathan Horne)

Colour Plate 22. **Tea canister,** *white salt-glazed stoneware with scratch-blue rococo swirl and floral cartouche, the centre of which is inscribed* Joan Dunley 1767. *Probably Staffordshire, 1767. 5½in. (13.97cm) high. (Central Museum and Art Gallery, Northampton, Manfield collection, 1920-1d1-87)*

Colour Plate 23. **Flask,** *white salt-glazed stoneware with scratch-blue floral decoration inscribed* Bengamin Mellor 1775. *Probably Staffordshire, 1775. 6⅜in. (16.19cm)high. (Potteries Museum and Art Gallery, Stoke-on-Trent)*

35

Chapter II – Early Industrial Stonewares

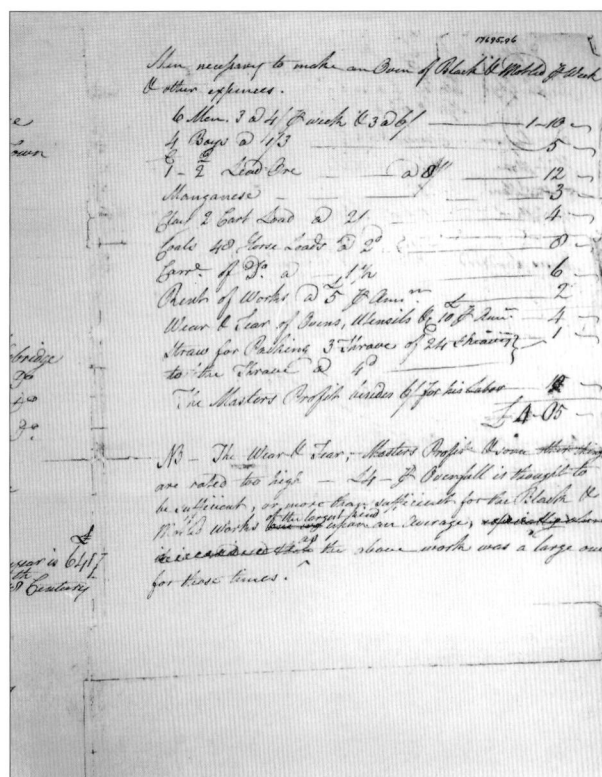

Fig. 26. **List of potters in Burslem 1710–15,** Wedgwood MS 96/17695.

Fig. 27. **Jug,** Chinese porcelain with enamel decoration moulded in a pecten shell form with feet and handle in the English stoneware and earthenware tradition. China, mid-18th century. 4in. (10.16cm) high. (Photograph courtesy of E.H. Manners)

Fig. 28. **Teapot,** white salt-glazed stoneware slip-cast in the shape of a camel with exotic figures and a faceted handle. The nearly flat lid is surmounted with a kylin knop. Staffordshire, c.1750. 6½in. (16.51cm) high. (British Museum, 1919.0503.39)

Whieldon, who is discussed in detail in Chapter IX. He began potting at Fenton Vivian in 1747, making both salt-glaze, cream-coloured and tortoise wares in 1749, as illustrated in the following invoice:

    Mr. Thos. Fletcher, Dr.
To 1 doz. Plates, Tor. [toiseshell]	0.8.0
2½ do. plate	0.2.6
To 2 2 dishes	0.2.0
" 1 do. painted	0.2.0
" 1 do. Cream Colr.	0.2.6
" 5 pails	0.2.6[30]

The 'painted' must be salt-glaze.

In 1755 the Duke of Bedford purchased a set of dinner ware from Thomas Whieldon and Robert Garner, his apprentice. A bill for £6.13s.6d. was attached to the following list:

    For the Duchess of Bedford
4 large oblong Dishes	@ 4/6	£0.18. 0
4 less dº	@ 3/6	14. 0
4 less dº	@ 2/6	10. 0
4 less dº	@ 2/	8. 0
4 less dº	@ 18^d	6. 0
4 less dº	@ 12^d	4. 0
4 less dº	@ 10^d	3. 4
4 Doz Tables Plates	@ 5/-	1. 0. 0
2 Doz small Bread & Butter plates 3/-		6. 0
1 Tureen & Stand		10. 6
12 fruit Dishes		18. 0
6 Sauce boats		3. 0
1 Doz of Small Basons (?Brown) plates (or plats)		3. 0
		£6.13.10
1 Doz of Plates with Colers		6. 0
		£6.19. 0
& Box 4^d		4
		£6.13.10[31]

The descriptions of the service make it highly likely that it was salt-glazed stoneware and not earthenware. The invoice gives a complete picture of the graduated sizes of a dinner service for twenty-four people and attendant serving dishes and their retail prices.

The duchess placed a smaller order from Thomas Whieldon on 23 October 1755:

10 fruit plates @ 10^d each ?	1.7.0
1 Doz small mosaick plates	3.0
1 Tureen & stand	5.0
6 milk pots	1.6
Boy	1.6
	£1.18.0

The bill was paid by His Grace the Duke of Bedford on 16 January 1756.[32] 'Mosaick' as a description was an early reference to what we currently call dot, diaper and scroll moulded relief.[33] In this case it was a border pattern for plates, but was also commonly seen on sauceboats and other hollow wares. In November 1757 the *Daily Advertiser* advertised 'fine Mosaick Stone Ware',[34] a term which by then apparently was part of the current lexicon for basketweave moulding (for example Fig. 41). From 1755 one begins to see mention of the ubiquitous mosaic pattern in invoices and advertisements with great frequency. In 1760 William Greatbatch was making salt-glazed teapots in various patterns, mosaic, foxglove and fluted. He was also making 'Cornu Copias', or salt-glazed wall pockets.[35] In 1761 and 1762 both gadrooned-edge and mosaic pattern plates and dishes appear with nearly equal frequency on invoices and sales receipts.[36]

An earlier invoice of 1752[37] documents the buying-in of salt-glazed plates and dishes by *Thomas Wedgwood IV* from *John Baddeley*.

4 Doz of ed'g flow d plates @	0.16.0
4 Doz of Scollpt Dº	0.16.0 @5
6 Small Sq flow d Dishes @ 9	0. 4.6 @12

The flow'd [flowered] plates probably referred to the rim moulding of flowers which could have possibly been like Fig. 136 or Fig. 151.

In 1762/3 *Aaron Wedgwood* was producing, along with his 'flummery cups' and 'buttercups', many toy ceramics, all possibly salt-glaze, including toy porringers, cups and saucers.[38] Blue teapots and cups and saucers of the Littler-Wedgwood variety were being sold by Aaron Wedgwood in existing accounts from 1762 to 1764[39] (Colour Plates 91, 92). In 1764 he also was selling Josiah Wedgwood '1 doz. best Fine blue saucers 0.10.6 2 doz Cups Dº Dº 0.5.3.[40] These were, of course, the brilliant mazarine blue salt-glazed wares for which Aaron Wedgwood was so famed. Aaron Wedgwood was not the only manufacturer of the Littler-Wedgwood blue wares. In the 1766 to 1768 period *Anthony Keeling* was providing Josiah Wedgwood with a variety of coffee and tea wares in the mazarine blue, including tea canisters.[41] Thomas Whieldon was also producing blue teawares at the pottery at Fenton Vivian (Colour Plate 194). Blue wares were still on inventories as late as 1775.[42]

Moulded borders and ground patterns, which began to appear on German porcelains of the 1735-40 period, may have been the inspiration for their counterparts on English white salt-glazed stoneware. German porcelain had been considered a threat to the newly established English porcelain industry prior to 1751 when advertisements and auction notices for German porcelains became more familiar in England.[43] However, the Seven Years War following shortly thereafter cut off the supply of German porcelains when the British allied themselves with the Prussians. Nevertheless, it seems possible that the German porcelain borders influenced the English salt-glazed ones; although not necessarily the same the trend was indisputable. Some borders also became

Chapter II – Early Industrial Stonewares

Colour Plate 24. **Teapot** in white salt-glazed stoneware slip-cast in the form of a squirrel. Staffordshire, c.1745-50. 6in. (15.24cm) high. (The Henry H. Weldon Collection, Colonial Williamsburg Foundation, Photography by Gavin Ashworth)

Colour Plate 25b. **Bourdalou** (coach pot), white salt-glazed stoneware. Probably Staffordshire, c.1745-65. 3⅝ x 10in. (9.21 x 25.4cm). (Tom Walford collection)

Colour Plate 25a. **Teapot handle** (fig. 25).

CHAPTER II – EARLY INDUSTRIAL STONEWARES

Colour Plate 25.
Teapot, *white salt-glazed stoneware slip-cast in the form of a camel. Staffordshire, c.1745-55. 5¾in. (14.61cm) high. (Central Museum and Art Gallery, Northampton, Manfield collection, 1920-1d1-81)*

Colour Plate 27. **Shards from mazarine blue teawares,** *white salt-glazed stoneware with blue dip, excavated from Thomas Whieldon's Fenton Vivian pottery site. Staffordshire, Thomas Whieldon, c.1750-1770. Bowl foot 1½in. (3.81cm) diameter, rim shard maximum 1¼in. (3.18cm). (Potteries Museum and Art Gallery, Stoke-on-Trent)*

Colour Plate 26. **Teapot,** *white salt-glazed stoneware with mazarine blue dip, known as Littler-Wedgwood blue. Staffordshire, c.1750-55. 4⅝in. (11.75cm) high. (Private collection)*

39

CHAPTER II – EARLY INDUSTRIAL STONEWARES

*Fig. 29. **Group of teapots,** white salt-glazed stoneware slip-cast, two in the shape of houses. Staffordshire, c.1745-55. Right, 7¾in. (19.69cm) high. (British Museum, Willett collection, 1887)*

*Fig. 30. **Teapot (minus lid),** white salt-glazed stoneware slip-cast in the form of a shell with three lion mask feet and faceted, notched handle. Staffordshire, possibly Humphrey Palmer, c.1745-55. 4in. (10.16cm) high. (Olive Talbot collection)*

CHAPTER II – EARLY INDUSTRIAL STONEWARES

*Fig. 31. **Two shards and a waster** of shell-shaped teapots or cream jugs of white salt-glazed stoneware excavated from the Town Road site of Humphrey Palmer. Waster 3in. (7.62cm) long. (Potteries Museum and Art Gallery, Stoke-on-Trent, K3 274 1985)*

*Fig. 32. **Cream jug**, white salt-glazed stoneware slip-cast with crisp pecten shell moulding. Staffordshire, c.1745-55. 3in. (7.62cm) high. (Harriet Carlton Goldweitz collection)*

ground patterns, such as a seed-type border of around 1760, which is also identified as the barleycorn pattern, a term immediately followed in English salt-glazed stoneware.[44] 'Dresden or Barley Corn Tureens' are mentioned in a list of 1763/4 suggesting that 'Dresden' may be another terminology for barleycorn.[45] By 1762 English invoices and inventories of stock all included wares with the popular barleycorn pattern, and frequent mention of gadrooned plates and dishes. Barleycorn plates and dishes were sometimes described as with or without 'work', which may mean piercing.[46] Barleycorn was also produced in most hollow wares (for example in Fig. 60) including, although rarely, teapots. Barleycorn continued to appear on invoices and sales records until at least 1780.[47] Gadroon borders continued to be seen on lists of salt-glazed wares until at least 1777.[48] Mosaic moulded salt-glazed stoneware had been popular since at least 1755 (Fig. 42). Mosaic as a pattern seems to be in decline as few invoices include wares described as mosaic by 1763. However, the terminology changed from mosaic to 'basket work' in 1763 to describe the popular pattern.[49] Nevertheless, there are fewer entries in invoices for basketwork after 1764 than for barleycorn or gadrooned wares.[50] Agate ware appears on many invoices in 1763, heralding the ascendancy of the lead-glazed earthenwares and what would eventually be the death-knell to the salt-glazed stonewares.

41

CHAPTER II – EARLY INDUSTRIAL STONEWARES

*Fig. 33. **Teapot,** fancifully modelled in the shape of a heart, white salt-glazed stoneware with grape and vine leaf relief decoration. Staffordshire, c.1750-60. 6½in. (16.51cm) long. (Potteries Museum and Art Gallery, Stoke-on-Trent, 947)*

*Fig. 34. **Teapot,** white salt-glazed stoneware slip-cast in a square form with fanciful moulded relief including male faces, a frond base (similar to jester pantaloons), a salamander finial, serpent handle and spout. Staffordshire, c.1745-55. 4½in. (11.43cm) high. (Catzen collection)*

*Fig. 35. **Partially reconstructed food storage container,** ovoid-shaped white salt-glazed stoneware with pale iron colouring to shoulder and rim excavated at Deer Street, Portsmouth, New Hampshire in an extension (referred to as the 'linty') of the Fernald house erected in 1702. The deposit appears to have been mid-18th century. Possibly Staffordshire, 1700-50. 8⅜in. (21.27cm) high. (Strawbery Banke Museum, A633)*

*Fig. 36. **Partially reconstructed chamber pot,** white salt-glazed stoneware with a rolled rim and strap handle excavated at Deer Street, Portsmouth, New Hampshire on the site of a home of a licensed vintner. Probably Staffordshire, c.1730-60. 6⅛in. (15.56cm) high, 8in. (20.32cm) diameter. (Strawbery Banke Museum, A621)*

CHAPTER II – EARLY INDUSTRIAL STONEWARES

*Fig. 37. **Group of utilitarian wares and teawares,** plain white salt-glazed stoneware including a stoolpan, punch pot, two jugs and two teapots. Staffordshire, c.1740-70. Punch pot 9½in. (24.13cm) high; toy teapot 1⅞in. (4.76cm) high. (Potteries Museum and Art Gallery, Stoke-on-Trent, left to right (rear), 230P 1965, 1930.7, 76P 1975 (front) 229P 1990, c.341.1&2 2000, 185P 1988)*

*Fig. 38. **Group of moulds,** white salt-glazed stoneware moulds and pettys in various forms: star, double star, Turk's cap, melon, fluted and triangular-shaped. Staffordshire, c.1750-70. Melon 4½in. (11.43cm) long. (Potteries Museum and Art Gallery, Stoke-on-Trent)*

*Fig. 39. **Group of utilitarian wares** consisting of a teabowl, plate, and a patty pan in white salt-glazed stoneware. These were excavated from the James Geddy House site, second occupation James Geddy, Jr. (1760-1777) in Williamsburg, Virginia. Probably Staffordshire, c.1750-70, Plate 9in. (22.86cm) diameter; patty pan 5⅛in. (13.02cm) diameter; teabowl 3in. (7.62cm) diameter, 2in. (5.08cm) high. (Colonial Williamsburg Foundation)*

*Fig. 40. **Two partially reconstructed plates,** white salt-glazed stoneware with moulded relief. Staffordshire, c.1755-70. Left, gadrooned-edged 9in. (22.86cm) plate; right, twiffler, 7in. (17.78cm), of royal shape with barleycorn pattern. (Colonial Williamsburg Foundation)*

CHAPTER II – EARLY INDUSTRIAL STONEWARES

*Fig. 41. **Sauceboat,** white salt-glazed stoneware press-moulded in the mosaic pattern. The term 'mosaick' is mentioned in 1755 in the Duke of Bedford's inventory of wares purchased from Thomas Whieldon. By 1763 'mosaic' wares were generally called 'basketweave' or what has later been termed 'dot, diaper and scroll'. One of the most popular of all salt-glazed moulded relief patterns, it was made by nearly all the identified manufacturers. Staffordshire, c.1750-60. 4½in. (11.43cm) high. (Private collection)*

*Fig. 42. **Caster, plate and candlestick,** white salt-glazed stoneware in the barleycorn pattern which popularly appeared in invoices and sales from around 1760 until 1780. Sometimes referred to as the 'seed' or 'Dresden' pattern, barleycorn was produced in nearly all shapes, but rarely on teawares. Staffordshire, c.1760-80. Caster, 5in. (12.7cm) high; plate 9¾in. (24.77cm) diameter; candlestick, 10in. (25.4cm) high. (Ex Cecil Baring collection. Potteries Museum and Art Gallery, Stoke-on-Trent, 4256, 4081, 291)*

CHAPTER II – EARLY INDUSTRIAL STONEWARES

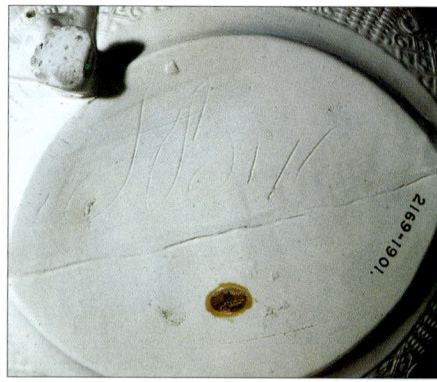

Colour Plate 28. **Tureen and cover,** *white salt-glazed stoneware press-moulded in the mosaic or basketweave pattern with three lion mask paw feet. Incised on base JB 1769?. Staffordshire, possibly John Baddeley, c.1769. 8⅞in. (22.54cm) high. (Victoria and Albert Museum, 2169B-1901)*

Colour Plate 28a. **Tureen base** *incised with JB 1769[?] illustrated in Colour Plate 28.*

Fig. 43. **Two sauceboats,** *white salt-glazed stoneware press-moulded in a variation of the barleycorn pattern. On 14 December 1763 John Smith sold 'Barley corn Sauce boats with covers' to Josiah Wedgwood (Wedgwood MS 30/22978). Staffordshire, c.1760-80. 2in. (5.08cm) high. (Catzen collection)*

But salt-glaze production continued to function successfully throughout the 1760s alongside creamware in its many manifestations. Small moulds in various salt-glaze forms, such as shells, melon, heart and flower triangular moulds, star pettys and cups, salt and table spoons (sometimes with holes) were being purveyed in quantity (Figs. 38, 46, Colour Plate 29).[51]

Apart from his partnerships with John Harrison I and Thomas Whieldon, there is no certain evidence that Josiah Wedgwood made salt-glazed stoneware in the eighteenth century. The Wedgwood factory did make a limited amount of salt-glaze in the nineteenth century. Wedgwood had wares fired by certain other potters in their salt-glaze kilns. It may be that Wedgwood was moulding the pots in the creamware body and having John Smith of Burslem, later Hanley Green, and others fire the green ware in their salt-glaze kilns, sometimes indicating they should be sent directly up to London for sale.[52]

Josiah Wedgwood bought in some of the salt-glaze he was selling from *Thomas and Isaiah Taylor* in 1763, items which, although the body is not specified, were principally produced in salt-glaze: strainers, pettys, gadrooned (dishes), and barleycorn plates, twifflers, dishes and teapots.[53] In 1768 second cousins *Thomas and John Wedgwood* provided him with '42 doz plain hearts' and 'Starr cups'.[54] Josiah also bought in 'barley corn plates and baskets' and other salt-glaze from *Thomas Daniel II*,[55] as well as *Warburton & Stone*.[56] Other potters also supplied white salt-glazed stoneware to Josiah Wedgwood, their invoices providing much of our evidence for salt-glaze potters in Appendix 2.

The Decline of White Salt-Glaze

By 1770 salt-glaze had been nearly replaced by the beautiful creamwares which had taken the market by storm over the previous decade.

Twenty-seven white salt-glaze potters met in 1770 and

*Fig. 44. **Partially reconstructed sauceboat,** a white salt-glazed stoneware press-moulded waster in the barleycorn pattern excavated at the Foley site, Fenton. Staffordshire, Foley, Fenton, c.1760-80. 3in. (7.62cm) high. (Potteries Museum and Art Gallery, Stoke-on-Trent)*

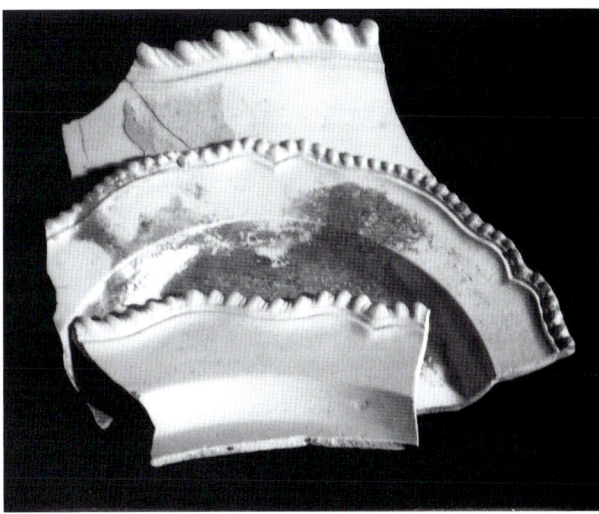

*Fig. 45. **Three gadrooned-edged plate rims,** white salt-glazed stoneware moulded with beaded or gadrooned edges excavated at the Foley site, Staffordshire, Foley, Fenton, c.1760-80. Middle 6½in. (16.51cm) long. (Potteries Museum and Art Gallery, Stoke-on-Trent)*

*Colour Plate 29. **Spoon,** white salt-glazed stoneware press-moulded with a modified 'fiddle-back'. Probably Staffordshire, c.1750-70. 5⅜in. (13.65cm) long. (Photograph courtesy of Winterthur Museum, 1958-0897)*

*Fig. 46. **Three spoons,** white salt-glazed stoneware press-moulded with shell tipped handles. Staffordshire, c.1760-70. Left and middle 7¼in. (18.42cm) long; right 5⅝in. (14.29cm) long. (Potteries Museum and Art Gallery, Stoke-on-Trent, 214P 1965, 216P, 1965, 217P, 1965)*

agreed 'To sell to the Manufactures [sic] of Earthen ware at the Above Prices' (see Appendix 3), confirming that by that period much of their business was coming from the makers of creamware. The pricing was specified for the form, that is, tureens, nappies, etc., as well as for the quality: 'Best, Best Seconds, Worser [Seconds]'.[57]

The decade of the 1770s witnessed the ascendancy of creamware and a rapid decline in interest in and sales of salt-glazed stoneware. Although the popular barleycorn, basket and gadroon-moulded ware continued to be produced, the major manufacturers were making cream-ware exclusively with some of the smaller ones producing salt-glaze in the old patterns.

Littler-Wedgwood blue also continued to be seen on lists until at least 1775. Salt-glaze appeared on a few inventories and sales receipts in the 1780s.[58] *Ralph Bucknall and Son of* Cobridge produced both white salt-glaze patterns and royal pattern in the 1780s. Utilitarian wares, such as chamber pots, ewers and hand wash basins, and wares for the dairy continued to be produced in white salt-glaze for some considerable time, although the body is rarely specified in these items and one can only speculate about the quantities.

CHAPTER III

The Demand for Salt-Glazed Stoneware

By the mid-eighteenth century the high demand for British white stoneware would have been fuelled by a variety of internal and external economic and social forces which began more than a century before. The forces which were responsible for the creation of white salt-glazed stoneware were not indigenous. The salt-glazed stoneware tradition was, as we mentioned in the first chapter, the direct result of wares imported into Britain from the various German areas of production around Raeren, Frechen and Siegburg. The influences of the porcellaneous white colour, the shape and frequently the decoration of the white salt-glazed stoneware emanated from the porcelains which came into the country in vast shiploads in the seventeenth century and continued to be popularly imported throughout the eighteenth century.

These two extraneous threads were the major influences in the creation of the white stoneware which, by the first decade of the eighteenth century, had centres of manufacture in both London and in Staffordshire and ultimately would penetrate into most of the Midlands, to Chester, Derby, Oxford, Swansea, Devon, Lancashire, Yorkshire, and up to Scotland. In spite of the two foreign infusions white salt-glazed stoneware was purely English, invented in London, appreciated throughout the country, exported abroad in vast quantities; in short, a successful ceramic staple for three-quarters of a century. The demand for the ware can also be laid at the feet of the social, political and economic forces at play in the seventeenth and eighteenth centuries: population increase in urban areas, the emergence of a middle class, and changing demographics, as the city became the social epicentre. These forces and others combined to change the drinking and dining customs which so dramatically influenced the ceramic industry.

Population shifts beginning in the seventeenth century played no small role in creating a ready market for attractive tea and table ware which aped porcelain (Colour Plates 30, 31). At the close of the seventeenth century London was, within the walls, the largest city in the country, with approximately 70,000 inhabitants in its ninety-seven parishes and over half a million in the suburbs. Not only the largest city in Britain, London was the most populous city in Europe in the eighteenth century. The next largest city in the country was Norwich with 30,000 inhabitants. In the 1730s Bristol overtook Norwich as the second largest city. At the beginning of the eighteenth century Birmingham had only about 12,000 inhabitants, Newcastle-upon-Tyne perhaps 15,000 and Leeds and Manchester about 10,000 each. The eighteenth century saw continued population shifts from rural to urban areas as people moved into the rapidly growing industrial towns.[1] In 1700, however, Britain was overwhelmingly rural. Of the approximately seven million inhabitants only eleven per cent lived in towns of 5,000 or more.[2] By 1801, the time of the first census, the country had grown to nine and a quarter million inhabitants, of which 17½ per cent lived in towns of over 20,000 people.[3]

Life in seventeenth century Britain was punctuated by social and political upheaval, civil war and judicial murder. That such a background, fuelled by the Catholicism and authoritarian tendencies of James I of the House of Stuart, which put the Hanoverian George, elector of Brunswick-Lüneburg, on the English throne in 1714,[4] could presage a subsequent long period of peace and prosperity seems unlikely in the extreme. Nevertheless, that was exactly what happened. But the foundations were laid in the previous century in spite of the chaotic politics of the last three quarters of that century.

Fig. 47. **Mug,** white salt-glazed stoneware with a wide band of decoration turned on the lathe. The raised band has then been cross-hatched with an incising tool while still on the lathe. The mug has a flared foot and sprig florets at the neck. The handle is typical of Staffordshire handles excavated at both the Greatbatch and Humphrey Palmer sites. Staffordshire, c.1740-50, possibly Humphrey Palmer. 6⅝in. (16.83cm) high. (Potteries Museum and Art Gallery, Stoke-on-Trent, 281)

*Fig. 48. **Teapot,** white salt-glazed stoneware with three feet and foliate handle and spout. The body and lid have rouletted decoration and the shoulder has applied sprig foliage. Staffordshire, c.1740. 4in. (10.16cm) high. (Photograph courtesy of Garry Atkins)*

*Fig. 49. **Teapot,** drab-coloured salt-glaze stoneware with white pipe clay crabstock spout, handle, finial and shell-moulded feet. The body is decorated with trailed grape and vine leaf tendrils in white with additional blue grape clusters and foliage. Staffordshire, c.1750. 4in. (10.16cm) high. (Harriet Carlton Goldweitz collection)*

The rapid expansion of towns and urban centres in the seventeenth century required a commensurate provision for catering and the result was increased specialisation of drinking and dining establishments as inns, taverns and ale houses, coffee houses and cookshops proliferated.

From the first decades of the seventeenth century ale houses began to provide fixed-price meals and a wider range of foods. The advent of the London 'season' in the first years of the century moved the gentry into town for several months each year as they entertained and socialised to marry off their daughters and sons. Not only were many more elegant eating establishments required, but London townhouses required furnishing with sufficiently high quality accoutrements to impress one's peers and betters in

Chapter III – The Demand for Salt-Glazed Stoneware

*Colour Plate 30. **Teapot**, white salt-glazed stoneware with applied sprig decoration picked out in translucent colours, the body painted in enamel colours with additional flowers and foliage. Staffordshire, c.1755-60. 3½in. (8.89cm) high. (Photograph courtesy of Garry Atkins)*

the social whirl. London taverns were located along all the principal roads with particular concentration near the political centre at Whitehall and in the mercantile areas of the City. Inns were mostly located around the outskirts of the City where travellers might wish overnight accommodation. For the most part taverns were the centre of London social life.[5] Taverns provided food and drink and often began to acquire a flavour of their own, garnering clientele of a homogeneous nature. Thus the tavern became the predecessor to the social, political and literary clubs which followed. Clubs such as the Beefsteak of Addison and Steele, the Rumpsteak or Liberty Club, set up in opposition to Walpole's Tory Government in 1734, and others which have survived to this day such as White's, Brooks's and Boodle's, were all established in the eighteenth century.[6]

The rise of coffee, tea and chocolate

Taverns sold wine almost exclusively and surprisingly admitted women.[7] In the middle of the seventeenth century coffee houses began to spring up. The first was in Oxford in 1650[8] followed by London in 1652 in St. Michael's Alley, Cornhill. Coffee was lauded for its qualities which promoted alertness 'making one fit for business.' By 1663 there were eighty-three coffee houses in the metropolis.[9] Coffee houses seldom served anything but beverages, coffee, tea and chocolate. One proprietor offered in addition 'lemon-, rose- and violet-perfumed sherbets'.[10] The coffee house became the conduit for the news of the day. English 'newsbooks' had been available at intervals from 1620 but throughout the Commonwealth and the Restoration printed news was strictly regulated. It was Milton who argued in his famous *Areopagitica* of 1644 against treating news as a monopoly and in 1665 the *Oxford Gazette* (*London Gazette* 1666) was established as the official vehicle for news. By 1705 a number of newspapers and news-sheets with single page layouts existed including the thrice weekly *British Mercury*,

*Colour Plate 31. **Mug**, white salt-glazed stoneware with chinoiserie decoration in opaque enamel colours. Staffordshire, c.1755-65. 5in. (12.7cm) high. (Photograph courtesy of Jonathan Horne)*

CHAPTER III – THE DEMAND FOR SALT-GLAZED STONEWARE

Colour Plate 32. **Table with a chocolate set,** *white salt-glazed stoneware, mixed and matched as might have been seen on a tea table of the mid-18th century, Shipley Room, Winterthur Museum. (Photograph courtesy of Winterthur Museum)*

Colour Plate 33. **Teapot,** *white salt-glazed stoneware with undecorated globular body, wish-bone handle and faceted spout. The handle, spout and lid are similar to examples excavated at Shelton Farm. Staffordshire, c.1720-25, possibly Shelton Farm, Stoke-on-Trent. 3¼in. (8.26cm) high. (Private collection)*

Colour Plate 34. **Capuchin or chocolate cup,** *white salt-glazed stoneware with high foot and band around lower shaft. The shape of the cup and the handle, ratcheted at the base, have been excavated at Shelton Farm. Staffordshire, c.1720-25, probably Shelton Farm, Stoke-on-Trent. 2¾in. (6.99cm) high. (Private collection)*

51

*Fig. 50. **Teapot**, white salt-glazed stoneware decorated with a band of incised lozenges between two bands of clay chips. The spout is a face mask and the handle a dragon moulded form. The kylin knop on the lid is surrounded by another band of clay chips, Staffordshire, c.1740. 4¾in. (12.07cm) high. (Harriet Carlton Goldweitz collection)*

published by the Sun Fire Insurance Company.[11] Literacy can only be estimated, but it has been suggested that as many as half of the population were literate[12] and newspapers were distributed and read in coffee houses.

Chocolate was a greater luxury than coffee (Colour Plate 32) and more exotic and difficult to prepare. Originally from Mexico, it arrived in England in the 1650s via Spain. The cost, initially 10s. to 15s. per pound, set it, aside with tea, as a drink for the elite.[13]

Coffee, tea and chocolate were the latest in drinking fashion from the mid-seventeenth century and profoundly influenced social life and equipage. Some of the rituals surrounding the serving and drinking of these hot beverages have remained more or less intact to the present day. Tea, popular in Britain, less so in France and rarely drunk in Germany, Scandinavia, Spain or Italy, where coffee reigned supreme, continues to be served in the English speaking world as an afternoon repast with much the same ado as in the seventeenth century. High taxes on tea, not reduced until 1784, guaranteed it remained the drink most associated with the life of the gentry. Ale was the drink of the poor. After 1784 tea became the drink of the masses.[14]

Tea, its cultivation, preparation and history has been the subject of volumes. It continues to fascinate. The association with the upper classes which kept it artificially costly through taxes, the identity with smuggling to avoid the taxes and other intrigues founded on myths of its medicinal qualities, both positive and negative, have kept the fascination alive. The taxation insured a lively smuggling trade which passed through Cornwall, Dorset and Kent. It is estimated that smugglers provided about half the tea drunk in England (along with other contraband such as tobacco, silk and brandy). Scruples about smuggling of tea did not seem to disturb many of the wealthy and upright. Charles Lamb and many others applauded the practice. Lamb said 'I like a smuggler. He is the only honest thief. He robs nothing but the revenue – an abstraction I never really cared about'. In 1777 Mrs. Elizabeth Montagu wrote to her sister requesting a 'couple of pounds of good smuggled tea at Margate…' She goes on to say that after she has paid for it she will drink it in good conscience. Socially tea was schizophrenic, being contrived by some as a metaphor for irrational self-indulgence and, conversely, as a symbol of domestic order.[15] Introduced from China through Portugal and the Dutch East India Company initially, tea was served after dinner, a late afternoon meal, prepared in the drawing room by women while the men stayed on in the dining room drinking wine. As dining moved on later in the day tea became a late afternoon custom to stave off hunger where it was accompanied by cakes and sweet breads and to entertain friends of both sexes. Afternoon tea was one of the most civilising of all ceremonies in bringing men and women into conversation when theretofore dialogue between the sexes was stilted and artificial. However, tea, coffee and chocolate increasingly became synonymous with social gatherings at any time as seen in eighteenth and nineteenth century portraits where all the beverages were served in various parts of the house, the bedroom, drawing room and dining room, or *en plein air* whenever a group was gathered.

Ceramics for the Tea Table

The popularity of the drinking of chocolate, coffee and tea, particularly tea, cannot be overestimated in the development of the ceramic industry in Britain. All three of these drinks could be taken with milk, although initially green or unfermented tea was not traditionally taken with milk. After the introduction of black tea, which soon became popular, milk was regularly used. Additional vessels became a part of the tea service, where one frequently

*Fig. 51. **Teapot,** white salt-glazed stoneware with wide band of cross-hatched decoration on the body and sprig relief flowers and foliage on the shoulder, Staffordshire, c.1725-40. 4¾in. (12.07cm) high. (Photograph courtesy of Winterthur Museum, 1998.0022,AB)*

found two tea canisters marked with **G** and **B** for Green and for Bohea, the most common black tea (Fig. 53).

Green tea which sold for 10s.6d. per pound was almost twice as expensive as Bohea tea at 5s.6d.[16] A typical advertisement of 1764 from London merchant Charles Vere, located at the corner of Salisbury Court and Fleet Street, offered:

Setts all sorts of Fine China Ware, the finest Hyson, Congon Teas, Coffee & Chocolate, fine Snuffs, India Tea Tables... N.B. Setts of Chinaware for Exportation.[17]

Teasets commonly included, in addition to the teapot, a milk jug, tea canister(s), slop basin, and sometimes a sugar pot and tea tray. Containers for sugar were not always a part of the service, although they were brought in from Paris in 1659,[18] and one does see references to them in inventories from as early as 1729.[19] As a regular part of the tea service sugar pots or 'dishes', as they were generally referred to, became common after around 1760. After about 1760 it was also common to supply an additional hot water jug (or urn) to dilute the tea after serving. Cup shapes varied for coffee, tea and chocolate with services containing two or three shapes of cup, but only one set of saucers. Chocolate pots were often distinguished from coffee pots by a spout at a ninety degree angle to the handle (Figs. 3, 93).

During the seventeenth century porcelains became the primary vessels from which to enjoy hot beverages, which couldn't be drunk out of silver or pewter comfortably. In effect the ascendancy of tea drinking made it necessary to have porcelain or another substitute from which to imbibe these liquids. Initially delftware was the humble man's porcelain, but the friable nature of the fabric made it an unsatisfactory substitute.

John Dwight was attempting porcelain manufacture in the fashion when he took out his patent in 1672 (see Chapter I; Chapter IX, *John Dwight*). The salt-glazed stoneware, white, brown and variegated, which resulted was largely composed of vessels to hold or dispense tea, coffee or chocolate and ale. The earliest known ceramic chocolate pot (Fig. 3) was a product of the Dwight factory at Fulham as were the many *gorges* (Colour Plate 1) and other drinking and serving vessels.

The Middle Class and Dining

With the urbanisation of Britain came the emergence of a middle class which was estimated to be as many as one million of the seven or so million total population in the early eighteenth century. On the one hand this middle group was beginning to distinguish itself socially and politically from the patrician elite and the working classes.[20] On the other, the tendency to adopt the so-called social graces and mores of the upper echelons was to be part and parcel of the burgeoning of a middle class which in turn imitated the tastes of their social superiors and promoted the market for the accoutrements necessary to civilise their lives.

Books on cookery proliferated and were fuelled by interest in dining and entertaining at home. From 1500-1700 cookery books were mostly concerned with hints on how to improve domestic life and could include anything from how to correct the colour of dyes or remedy various ailments. The Restoration period saw a marked change in audience aimed at a shift from the large estate to the private home of the emerging middle class with books such as Hannah Wolley's *The Cook's Guide* and *The Gentlewoman's Companion* (c.1670). The first thirty years or so of the eighteenth century saw cookery books emerge with an emphasis on high style court cooking which either emanated from the French *haute cuisine* such as Patricia Lamb's *Royal Cookery* (1710) and Charles Carter's *The Complete Practical Cook* (1730) or reacted

CHAPTER III – THE DEMAND FOR SALT-GLAZED STONEWARE

Colour Plate 35. **Teapot,** *white salt-glazed stoneware with three high rising mask-head feet, faceted handle, faceted spout and applied floral decoration stained blue. The mask head and paw feet and the spout are associated with Humphrey Palmer's factory, Hanley through excavated waster shards (see figs. 215, 223). Palmer also incorporated blue sprigging into the decoration of some of his teapots (Colour Plate 187). Staffordshire, c.1750, possibly Humphrey Palmer. 3⅛in. (7.94cm) high. (Private collection)*

Colour Plate 36. **Group of scratch-blue wares,** *white salt-glazed stoneware with cobalt scratch-blue decoration. Probably Staffordshire, c.1750-70. Pail 3¼in. (8.26cm) high, double tea canister 5⅞in. (14.92cm) high, cup 2⅝in. (6.67cm) high. (Potteries Museum and Art Gallery, Stoke-on-Trent, 1925.17, 239, 923)*

Colour Plate 38. **Barber's basin or bleeding bowl,** *white salt-glazed stoneware with slight scratch-blue decoration. Probably Staffordshire, c.1750-70. 10in. (25.4cm) diameter. (Historic Deerfield, Inc, Deerfield, Massachusetts, 59.144)*

Colour Plate 37. **Tea canister,** *white salt-glazed stoneware with scratch-blue decoration inscribed Mary Pugsle/1768 and on the reverse Mary Winsor, both names which occur in Bovey Tracey parish registers. Devonshire, Bovey Tracey Pottery, c.1768. 4¼in. (10.8cm) high. (Photograph courtesy of Winterthur Museum, 1971.0193)*

hostilely to French taste while plagiarising their recipes with Hannah Glasse's *The Art of Cookery Made Plain and Easy* (1747).[21]

It is certain that, in large part, the success of white salt-glazed stoneware was due to the gentrification of society through the creation of a middle-income group which could not afford porcelains for its tea and dining tables, yet wished to be perceived as having such. So successful did the pottery industry become at imitating the designs that only a refined eye could tell the difference from a distance between the white stoneware and its prototypes. It is interesting to note that on occasion the Chinese imitated western forms; in the case of the jug in Fig. 27 the pecten shell Chinese porcelain jug was taken from a salt-glaze prototype.

When setting the scene for the economic prosperity of the eighteenth century one cannot overlook the importance of waves of foreign settlers – Flemings in the fourteenth century, Dutch and Walloons in the sixteenth and Huguenots in the seventeenth century. These various immigrant peoples introduced the 'new draperies' into the woollen industry, revived the decaying silk industry, introduced the making of fine linen, established the copper and brass industries, practically created glass-making, promoted the growth of steel and the cutlery trades, and developed the china, paper and cordage industries. In addition they drained the Fens, made harbours and improved the art of dyeing. The Huguenots, in particular, stimulated every branch of the economy with their infiltration into society bringing with them skills in all the arts as well as technological gifts.[22]

With the new disposable money pleasures outside the home became *de rigeur*. Innkeepers and victuallers, realising the potential as consumers of the socially aspirant, were quick to advertise both the quality and variety of their fare, from turtle to whitebait, the extent of the cellar and the novel and fashionable fittings of the house. Such were the foundations of the modern day restaurant, literally a *restauratif (ive)* which came into being around 1760. Eating became fashionable. Establishments serving food produced recipe books in the eighteenth century and a wide range of offerings tempted the customer who became the butt of the satirists' pen for his gustatorial interest.

Dining in the eighteenth century is difficult to picture from the exterior of a showcase in a museum where objects are lined up on shelves. But how these vessels were used is well understood from historical and current writings on the subject. In Britain and in the Americas the order of ceramic succession from Chinese porcelains, which in fact were never totally supplanted by any of the newcomers, was thus: Chinese porcelain to delftware, both English and to a lesser extent to Dutch, to salt-glazed stoneware and then to creamware.[23]

As early as 1635 mustard pots, salt cellars, jugs and mugs and chamber pots for European markets were being commissioned from Chinese kilns. Mustard pots and salt cellars were taken from silver and pewter prototypes. The barber's bowl or letting/ bleeding bowl (Colour Plate 38), which again is taken from metal models, was also produced in

Colour Plate 39. **Candlestick,** *white salt-glazed stoneware with press-moulded rococo base in silver form. Staffordshire, c.1750. 6½in. (16.51cm). (Photograph courtesy of Jonathan Horne)*

porcelain at the time.[24] Although the seventeenth century did not see the manufacture of any of these forms except for mugs and jugs in white salt-glazed stoneware, they became familiar objects in the eighteenth century production line. Mustard pots were frequently mentioned in inventories and in advertisements in Colonial America (see Chapter VII). Fashions in dining dictated the vessels which were needed. In 1643 and 1644 orders for vegetable dishes appear in Dutch East India Company manifests[25] corresponding to more frequent service of vegetables with the main meal.

Dining hours followed both the available light and the dictates of fashion. In the seventeenth century the main meal of the day was usually mid-afternoon, becoming later as the century progressed. Four o'clock was the appointed hour for a long period, when available light could provide illumination and the cost of tallow or beeswax candles could be avoided. All candles were artificially expensive due to a tax instituted in 1709 which not only influenced the dining customs, but caused the candle ends to be saved and remelted. Neither dinner nor tea services included candlesticks, but candlesticks were made in all materials, including many in salt-glazed stoneware (Figs. 54-58; Colour Plate 39). Because of the cost of candles, and also probably for fire precautionary reasons, it was customary to carry them around from room to room as required. The invention of the Argand lamp in 1782 made it possible to dine later, after which it became polite to entertain in the evening.

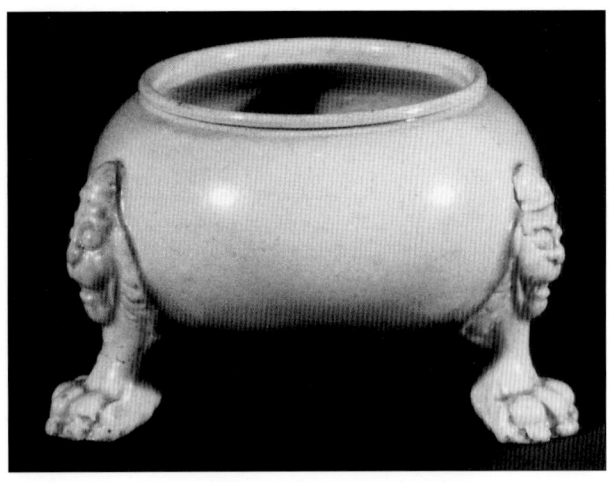

Fig. 52. ***Salt,*** *white salt-glazed stoneware with three lion mask feet. Staffordshire, probably Humphrey Palmer, c.1750-60. 1¾in. (4.45cm) high. (Catzen collection)*

Fig. 53. ***Invoice*** *from John Fleetwood, China-man and Glass-Seller, Leaden Hall Street, London, 10 October 1757. Fleetwood also sold Green leaf and teas in canisters. (Photograph courtesy of Winterthur Library: Joseph Downs Collection of Manuscripts and Ephemera, 60 x 8.12)*

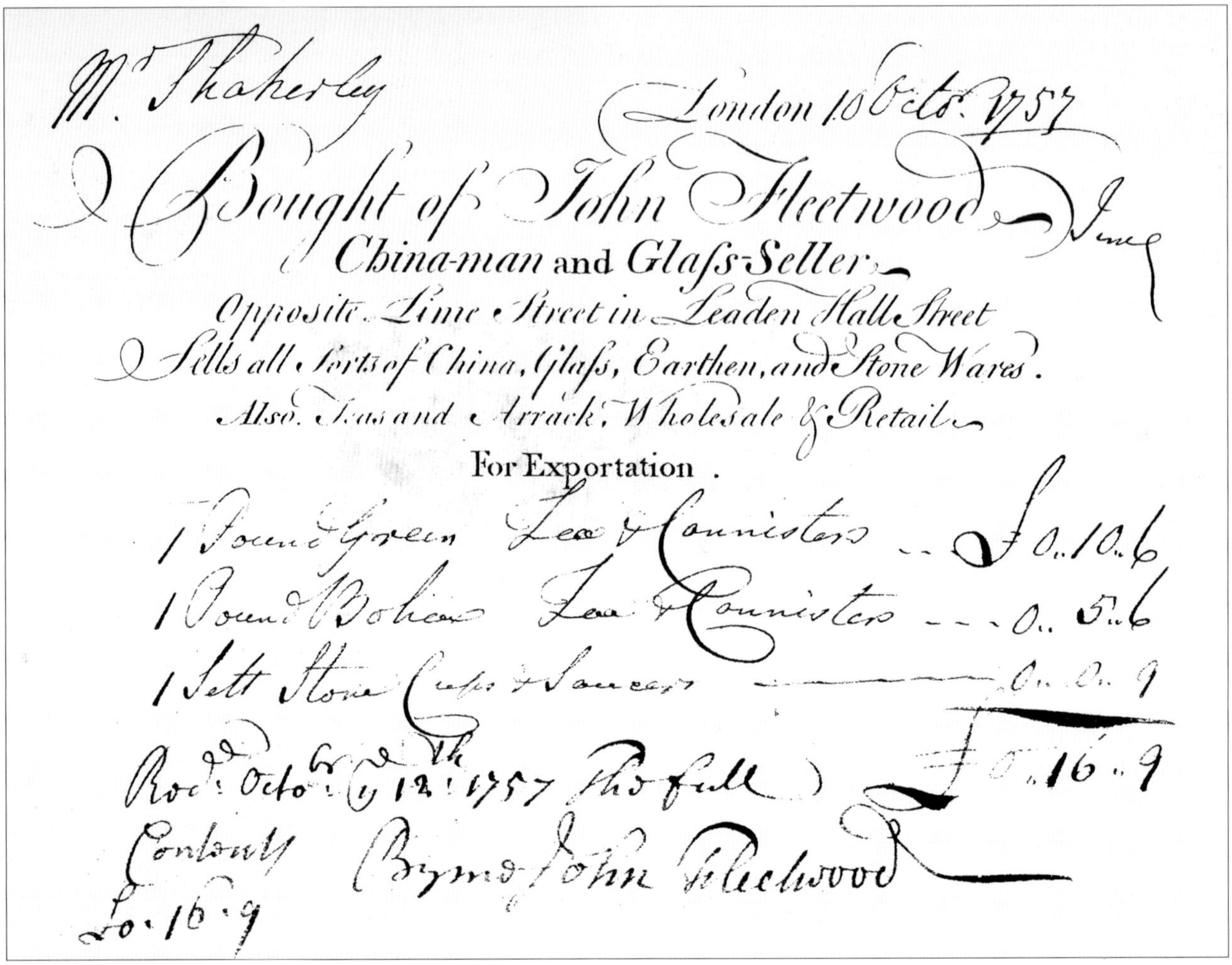

Mr Shakerley London 10 Octr 1757

Bought of John Fleetwood

China-man and Glass-Seller

Opposite Lime Street in Leaden Hall Street

Sells all Sorts of China, Glass, Earthen, and Stone Wares.

Also Teas and Arrack, Wholesale & Retail

For Exportation .

1 Pound Green Tea & Cannisters .. £0..10..6

1 Pound Bohea Tea & Cannisters ... 0.. 5..6

1 Sett Stone Cups & Saucers ——— 0.. 0.. 9

£0..16..9

Recd Octor ye 12: 1757 the full Contents By me John Fleetwood

£0.16.9

For the English aristocracy and the nobility in the seventeenth century dining customs were primarily influenced by the French taste of Louis XIV, whose court became the model for refinement and innovation. Charles II, whose mother was French, initiated many of the French refinements in dining which were adopted by upper society.[26] One of these was dining *à la française,* a more informal service at the table where the host and hostess served certain courses such as soup and fish, or carved roasts, and guests helped themselves to the accompanying dishes which were laid out in front of them. Dining *à la française* required new centrepieces, tureens, dish-covers, sauceboats and condiment dishes, extending the earlier requirements of simple platters and serving dishes in a variety of sizes. Both the porcelain and white salt-glaze manufactories expanded their production of shapes to meet the demand of the new entertaining. Dining *à la française* left servants free to provide clean plates and cutlery, remove courses and add others. After

CHAPTER III – THE DEMAND FOR SALT-GLAZED STONEWARE

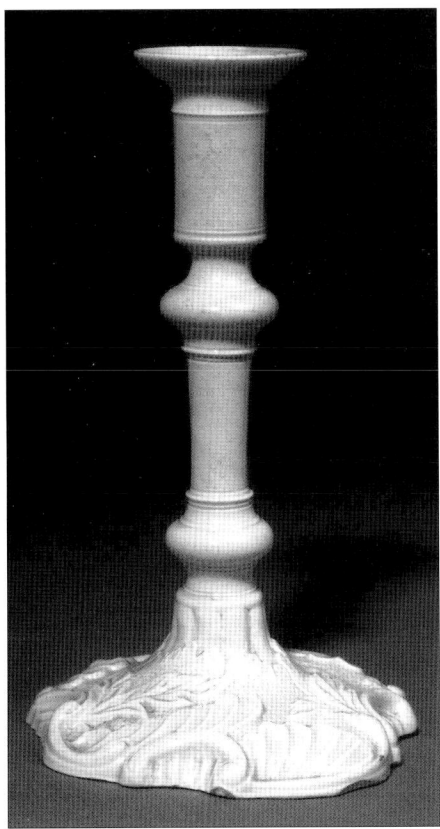 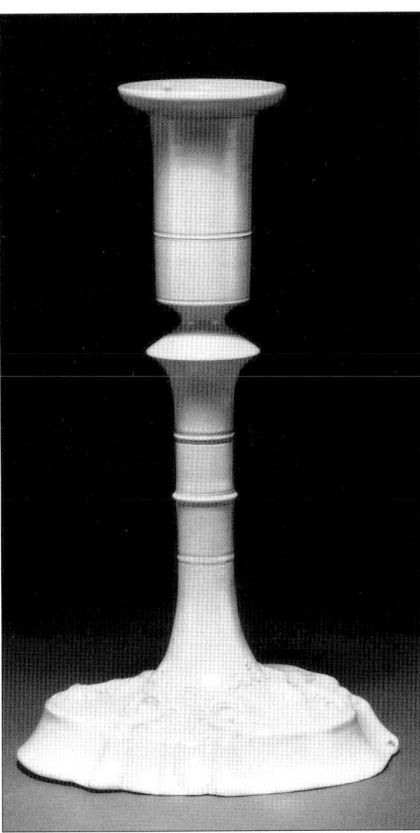 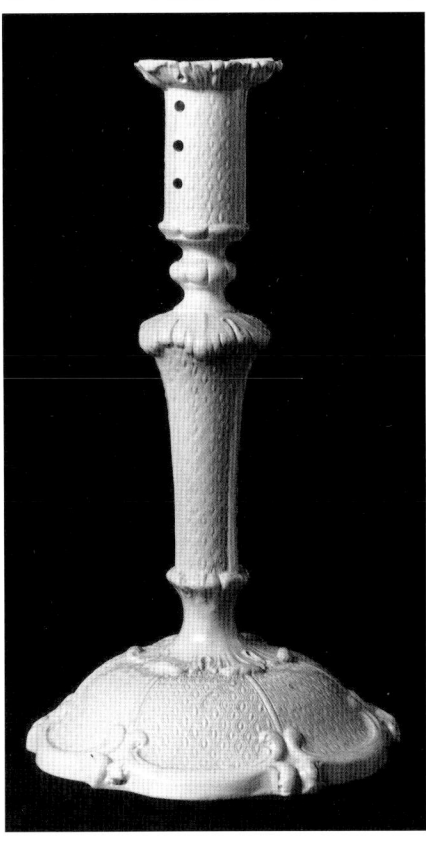

*Fig. 54. **Candlestick,** white salt-glazed stoneware with moulded rococo base adapted from a silver shape. Staffordshire, c.1750. 9in. (22.86cm). (Photograph courtesy of Christie's, London)*

*Fig. 55. **Candlestick,** white salt-glazed stoneware with rococo moulded base. Staffordshire, c.1755. 8½in. (21.59cm) high. (British Museum, Willett collection 1887)*

*Fig. 56. **Candlestick,** white salt-glazed stoneware press-moulded in the rococo style with a barleycorn or seed pattern. Probably Staffordshire, c.1760-70. 9¾in. (24.77cm) high. (Photograph courtesy of Winterthur Museum, gift of Mr. and Mrs. John Mayer, 1982.0130)*

the serving of the dessert, servants generally left guests to themselves. Dining *à la française* continued in practice until the nineteenth century when service *à la russe*, or individually plated courses provided from the sideboard were offered to guests by the servants.[27]

Dinner sets[28] of porcelain were always Chinese until the middle of the eighteenth century when French porcelain and English porcelain from the Chelsea factory became available to the aristocracy. German porcelain dinner sets were also available but seem to have been less in demand in England. It was late in the century before many English factories were able to provide sets of similar size and variety to meet the requirements of the nation. However, two other fabrics did offer the widest possible range of wares: from around 1740 white salt-glazed stoneware and, after 1760, locally produced creamware.

The dinner set, if one permits the use of the term, is loosely designated as such in this context. A wide variety of vessel forms was available by around 1740 when both the documentary and archaeological evidence seems to indicate that plates were first being produced in white salt-glazed stoneware (see Chapter VII). Sets *per se* were not being made in 1740; however, mass production from hump moulds with a limited variety of border patterns could produce plates in large quantities inexpensively. Soon other vessels were in demand, such as serving dishes, tureens, sauceboats, etc. These were also produced in the same rather restricted patterns by press-moulding methods consisting principally of mosaic and barleycorn motifs which could be combined by the retailers with matching plates, twifflers and muffins. The plates and serving-dish amalgams became the so-called dinner sets in white stoneware, equivalent to the intentionally executed dinner sets made in a grander fashion by the major porcelain factories.

Salt-glaze, like creamware, seemed to cut a swathe right across social strata, being found in homes of all classes. In 1755 the Duchess of Bedford placed a large order with *Thomas Whieldon* for a service for forty-eight which was presumably white salt-glazed stoneware or, less likely, earthenware, including seven different sizes of oblong 'Dishes', the largest @ 4s.6d. per dozen, the smallest at 10d. per dozen. In addition she ordered four dozen 'Table plates' @ 5s. a dozen, two dozen small 'Bread & Butter' plates at 3s., one tureen and stand at 10s.6d. and twelve fruit dishes for 18s. (These must have been fruit baskets, judging from the cost; Fig. 59.) She also ordered six sauceboats, a dozen

Chapter III – The Demand for Salt-Glazed Stoneware

Colour Plate 40. **Teapot and bowl,** *white salt-glazed stoneware painted in enamels in Oriental motifs, the teapot in kakiemon style, the bowl in opaque enamels in the famille rose style with flowers on the outside and fish on the interior. Staffordshire, c.1760. Bowl 9⅝in. (24.45cm) diameter. (Photograph courtesy of Jonathan Horne)*

Colour Plate 41. **Plate,** *white salt-glazed stoneware painted in enamel colours with kakiemon decoration. Staffordshire, possibly decorated in London, c.1760. 4½in. (11.43cm) diameter. (Historic Deerfield, Inc, 58.060.2)*

*Colour Plate 42. **Toy teapot; large jug** in white salt-glazed stoneware with enamel chinoiserie floral decoration. Staffordshire, c.1760-70. Teapot, 2in. (5.08cm) high, jug, 9¾in. (24.77cm) high. (Photograph courtesy of Jonathan Horne)*

small 'Basons', one dozen plates with 'colers' (coolers? or colours?) The total order came to £6.13s.6d.[29] The following year the Duchess was purchasing more fruit plates and one dozen 'mosaick' plates, which were the so-called diaper, basket and scroll border pattern, one tureen and stand, and six milk pots.[30] White salt-glazed stoneware is found in nearly all domestic sites in Colonial America which date to the period of its manufacture, regardless of the wealth of the household.

No manufacturer could ignore the vagaries that taste and fashion played in society. Ceramics were just as susceptible to the fickleness of fashionable scrutiny as dress or household furnishings. White salt-glazed stoneware was no exception in following the taste of the times.

Initially ceramics were left undecorated, or sparsely decorated with a dipped iron rim (to obscure the way in which the white slip pulled away from the grey stoneware body during firing). Early decoration included simply etched names or motifs in brown (iron oxide); after about 1740 the etched or scratched decoration was produced mainly in blue. In the 1750s one began to see enamel decoration following the Chinese and Japanese taste, often in opaque enamels of the *famille rose* or *famille verte* palette (Colour Plates 40, 44, 97, 104, 113). European decoration on salt-glazed stoneware (Fig. 61; Colour Plates 113-115) was largely a factor of the taste of the times as well and was

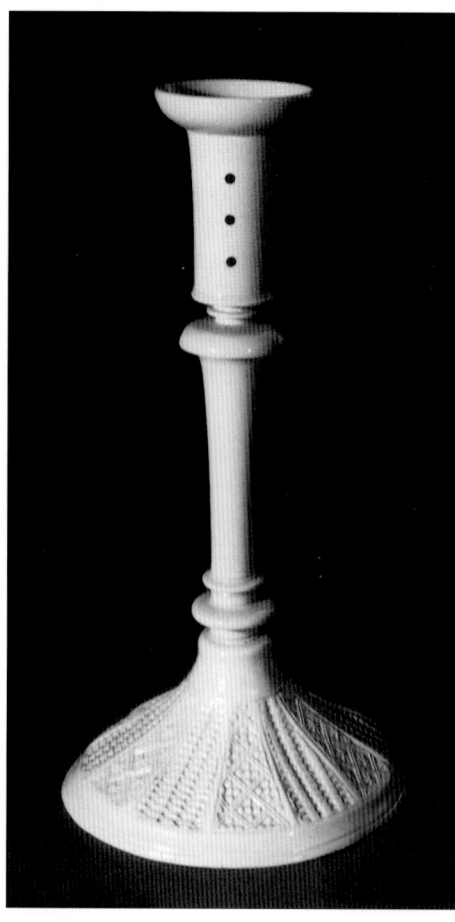

*Fig. 57. **Candlestick,** white salt-glazed stoneware press-moulded with a mosaic or basketweave base. Probably Staffordshire, c.1755-70. 9¾in. (24.77cm) high. (Victoria and Albert Museum, 414-1885)*

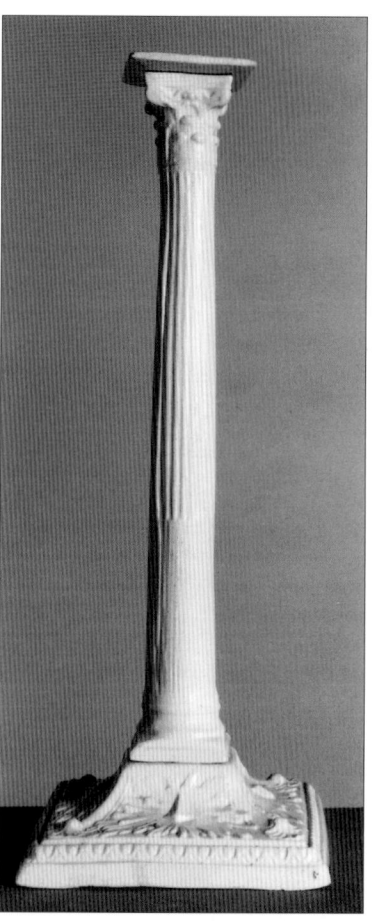

*Fig. 58. **Candlestick,** white salt-glazed stoneware in neo-classical style with square base and reeded column. Staffordshire, c.1760-70. 5in. (12.7cm) high. (Photograph courtesy of Winterthur Museum, 1958.0904)*

*Fig. 59. **Fruit basket,** white salt-glazed stoneware with pierced lattice and foliate designs on the outside and moulded tree relief on the interior. Staffordshire, c.1760-70. 13¾in. (34.9cm) long. (Potteries Museum and Art Gallery, 2917, ex Boynton collection sale 24 March 1920, 388)*

CHAPTER III – THE DEMAND FOR SALT-GLAZED STONEWARE

*Fig. 60. **Caster, plate and candlestick,** white salt-glazed stoneware in the barleycorn pattern which popularly appeared in invoices and sales from around 1760 until 1780. Sometimes referred to as the 'seed' or 'Dresden' pattern, barleycorn was produced in nearly all shapes, but rarely on teawares. Staffordshire, c.1760-80. Caster, 5in. (12.7cm) high, Plate 9¾in. (24.77cm) diameter, Candlestick, 10in. (25.4cm) high. (Ex Cecil Baring collection. Potteries Museum and Art Gallery, Stoke-on-Trent, 4256, 4081, 291.)*

particularly prevalent in the 1760s. Some commemorative wares, such as the King of Prussia wares (Figs. 19-21; Colour Plates 130, 132), or the Bonnie Prince Charlie scratch-blue mugs and cups (Colour Plates 20, 112, 113) were exceptionally decorated to assert political alliances. These trends are further discussed in Chapter V. Nevertheless, one cannot underestimate the role of fashion in influencing the responses of manufacturers and decorators in the production of ceramics, whether a humble ware or a grand one.

Expansion of Markets

It has been suggested that two factors contributed to the expansion of commerce and opened up wider fields of opportunity to the entrepreneur: the discovery of America and of a sea route to India, and a sense of nationalism which wanted to protect foreign markets, both import and export, from one's political enemies. The 'new money' of the eighteenth century was both stimulated by and a stimulus to the export market.[31] Between 1700 and 1760 English foreign trade nearly doubled and shipping doubled commensurately. Although Europe continued to command the largest market for England's export trade,[32] the American and the West Indian colonies were growing rapidly. In 1760 the American population was six times larger than in 1700[33] and the material cultural ties to the motherland were formidable. Long before the Industrial Revolution England had the reputation for manufacturing textiles, watches, cutlery, leather, ceramics and glass of high quality. Indeed England had been described as 'the workshop of the world'.[34]

London was, of course, the major market for the North Staffordshire potters. London shopkeepers not only supplied the needs of the city, but also acted as wholesalers for the exportation of ceramics all over the globe. Pottery was

*Fig 61. **Mug,** white salt-glazed stoneware with chinoiserie enamel decoration, probably decorated in London. Staffordshire or London, c. 1740-45, 3⅞in. (9.9cm). (Courtesy Bonhams, Tom Walford photograph)*

61

CHAPTER III – THE DEMAND FOR SALT-GLAZED STONEWARE

Colour Plate 43. **Sauceboat,** *white salt-glazed stoneware press-moulded with opaque enamel flowers and lion mask paw feet. Staffordshire, c.1755-60. 6½in. (16.51cm) long. (Photograph courtesy of Jonathan Horne)*

Colour Plate 44. **Bottle,** *white salt-glazed stoneware with sophisticated enamel decoration in the* famille rose *palette. Staffordshire, possibly London decorated, c.1760. 8½in. (21.59cm) high. (Photograph courtesy of Winterthur Museum, 1977.0093)*

also sent to the ports of Bristol and Liverpool from Staffordshire for local sale and export by merchants. Lorna Weatherill suggested in her excellent book on the pottery trade in North Staffordshire that wares were exported to America as early as the 1740s.[35] More recent information gleaned from further excavations on North American sites suggests that the wares were being exported nearly as soon as they were produced. Certainly wares of Dwight manufacture, either *John Dwight* or more probably *Lydia* or *Dr. Stephen Dwight*, have been found in pre-1725 contexts in both Jamestown, Virginia and London Town, Maryland (see Chapter VII). Archaeologists have found wares which correspond to some of the earliest datable white stoneware manufacturers, such as *John Fenton and Thomas Hill* at Shelton Farm, who were producing white salt-glazed stoneware in the 1720s. The context in which a probable Shelton Farm teabowl shard (Fig. 7) was found in Portsmouth, New Hampshire was commensurate with the decade of its manufacture.

Throughout the eighteenth century manufacturers found it possible to pursue the quest for wealth as profitably inside England as outside it. Ceramics manufacturers never lost sight of the home market for their wares and bowing to the taste (and to the purse) of the consumer kept their eyes peeled to the fashion of the day, assuming in the end that what was good for an Englishman was good for the rest of the world.

CHAPTER III – THE DEMAND FOR SALT-GLAZED STONEWARE

Colour Plate 45. **Punch pot,** *white salt-glazed stoneware with enamel chinoiserie decoration. Staffordshire, c.1760. 12¼in. (31.16cm). (Historic Deerfield, Inc., 65-231)*

Colour Plate 46. **Punch pot,** *white salt-glazed stoneware with an enamelled scene of Bacchus astride a wine barrel. This punch pot was made in more than one version (see Colour Plate 47). A punch pot of this description was sold in 1920 from the Boynton collection, ex Solon collection. Staffordshire, c.1760. 11in. (27.94cm) high (***cup,*** 2⅜in. (6.03cm) high). (Potteries Museum and Art Gallery, Stoke-on-Trent, 2287, 1164)*

Colour Plate 47. **Punch pot,** *white salt-glazed stoneware with enamel painting similar to that in Colour Plate 46. Staffordshire, c.1760. 10⅞in. (27.62cm). (Photograph courtesy of Jonathan Horne)*

CHAPTER IV

Raw Materials

CLAY
Clay is the defining raw material for pottery: flint, bone or other materials may be added, but clay is the essential ingredient. *John Dwight* of Fulham may have been influenced to make white stoneware by the grey-white salt-glazed ware imported from Germany, along with the brown 'Cologne ware', which he also patented. Made earlier at Siegburg, these grey-white wares came from the Westerwald in the later seventeenth century, formed from the white-firing highly plastic clays found there.[1]

White-burning clays occur in various parts of Britain and were used for pottery and tile decoration from the thirteenth century.[2] The consumption of tobacco, so widespread by 1604 that King James I published a *Counterblaste to Tobacco*,[3] led to increased demand for clay pipes and the white-burning clay to make them. To make white salt-glazed stoneware, potters needed such a white-burning, vitrifiable clay. Earlier references are to 'tobacco-pipe clay' and 'pipe clay' but it gradually became known as 'ball clay' for ceramic purposes. It is generally thought that this name derived from the 'balls' of clay, around 35lb., into which the clay was cut, although in Dorset it is held that the name comes from the *tubal*, an adze-like tool used for digging the clay.[4]

White-burning 'pipe' clay was available in various parts of the country, sufficient for local tobacco-pipemakers, but the large deposits are in Dorset, North Devon and South Devon. The traditional explanation of the formation of these large beds has been that the products of weathering of the granite mass in Devon were carried away by streams, settling as sediment in the Bovey Basin in South Devon, around Petrockstow in North Devon and carried further afield by a river to its estuary in Dorset.[5] More recently it has been held that at least the Petrockstow clay was derived from shales and sandstones, supported by the fact that there are overseas deposits of ball clay which are not associated with granite.[6] Tables of analyses of twenty-six ball clays, published in 1963, include clays from Dorset, Devon, Meissen, the Westerwald and other sources in Germany, Canada, and Tennessee and Kentucky in the USA.[7]

Simply defined, ball clay is a very plastic secondary clay which, compared with most other secondary clays, is relatively free of iron oxide and therefore white or cream burning.[8] For those who wish to know more on the subject, probably the most extensive study of ball clays was made by the British Ceramic Research Association between 1949 and 1956.[9]

Dorset Clay for London Potters
John Dwight of Fulham had been at Wigan between 1666 and 1671 and was said to have made his first ceramic discoveries on 'a whitish yellowish Earth, in a field near the *Kennel-pits* at *Haigh*' nearby.[10] Dwight was said by Robert Hooke to use 'tobacco pipe clay' to make his 'English china' in 1673/74,[11] though Robert Plot wrote by 1677 that Dwight made 'stone *Bottles* of a *Clay* in appearance like to *Tobacco-pipe clay*, which will not make *Tobacco-pipes*'.[12]

We are on surer ground in 1697/98, when Sir John Lowther, having interviewed Dwight, wrote that John Dwight's 'clay comes from about Pool, in Dorsetshire' and 'His [Dwight's] is Tobacco Pipe clay'. Dwight himself told Lowther's agent at the same time that 'stone Pots (not Holland [delft] but cologne Ware) are made of Tobacco Pipe Cley [*sic*] with some fine sand intermixd'.[13] Whilst it was only suggested that Dwight used pipe clay in 1674, his 1684 patent for white gorges shows that he did use it by 1684, confirmed by him to Lowther in 1698. The other pre-1700 London potters who may have used pipe clay to make salt-glazed stoneware were *Matthew Garner and Luke Talbot,* and *Moses Johnson*.

Tobacco pipe clay from Dorset was readily available in London in the seventeenth century. An agreement was made in 1618 for tobacco pipe clay to be dug in Dorset,[14] and in 1633 459 tons of pipe clay was shipped coastwise from Poole. Not all stayed in England. Pipe clay was being brought from Poole to London and then exported in 1627; and in 1629 200 tons went from Poole and Southampton to Rotterdam in Holland.[15] Export of pipe clay was forbidden in 1662, an Act repealed only in 1780.[16] In 1691 Poole shipped 3,114 tons of clay, 2,215 tons of it for London alone.[17] John Dwight would have had no difficulty in obtaining pipe clay in London by the time that he obtained his first patent in 1672 and it would continue to be available.

The only other pre-1700 maker of white salt-glazed stoneware, *Francis Place* of York, seems to have only worked on a small scale on salt-glazed ware and would have been able to obtain modest quantities of pipe clay locally.[18]

Dutch Clay for Derby Potters
Reinhold Angerstein described white salt-glazed stoneware manufacture at *Derby* in 1754,[19] and stated that the body

consists of half 'dutch pipe-clay' and half calcined and ground black flint, a material which is not found in this place and has to come by water from other provinces in England. The clay also has to be calcined and ground before mixing with the flint.

The phrase 'dutch pipe-clay' was placed in inverted commas by the translators, as a trade term for which no clarification was available. Derby was accessible by water from the North Sea via the Rivers Humber, Trent and Derwent,[20] so that clay could have been brought from Holland – or did Angerstein or his Swedish transcribers mean Dorset? Calcining clay seems unlikely: warnings about burning slip in slip kilns in 1860 and china clay in Cornish 'dries' c.1970 have been found,[21] confirming that burnt clay was to be avoided. Perhaps Angerstein confused clay and flint here.

Staffordshire Clay for Staffordshire Potters
Apart from accusations of potters digging clay in the highways, our first clear information about clay used by potters in North Staffordshire comes from Robert Plot. Having published his *Natural History of Oxfordshire*[22] in 1677, Plot published a similar history of Staffordshire in 1686, which included his famous description of pot-making at Burslem.[23]

Plot also described the available clays. A pipemaker at Newcastle-under-Lyme, only three miles from Burslem, used three sorts of white-burning clay, found between Shelton and Hanley, and also north-west of Newcastle.[24] The Burslem potters had four throwing clays, including '*White-clay*, so called because it seems though of a blewish colour, and used for making yellow-colour'd *ware*, because yellow is the *lightest* colour they make any *Ware* of'.

They also had slips to paint their wares, including 'the *white Slip*' which made the ware yellow. These clays may have been the locally obtainable white-burning pipe clay also used by the Newcastle pipemaker. Decorated slipware of this period appears distinctly yellow, but a broken piece shows a much whiter slip under the yellow-tinged lead glaze, confirming that Staffordshire potters used a whitish clay in Plot's time.

Dwight's well-known 1693, 1695 and 1697 lawsuits,[25] which might be expected to show what clays were being used by the Staffordshire potters, are ambiguous: all are accused of breaching his 1684 patent for making white and marbled ware, fine stoneware never previously made, porcelain and fine redware, though not for making 'Cologne ware', which was also in his patent. Because Dwight's accusations were about copying any of his wares, it is not certain whether the Staffordshire potters named (*Aaron Wedgwood, Thomas Wedgwood and Richard Wedgwood* of Burslem in 1693 and *Moses Middleton* of Shelton, *Cornelius Hammersley* of Fowle Ley and *Joshua Astbury* of Shelton in 1697) were making white or any other kind of salt-glazed ware, or making fine redware. A group of them, led by the Wedgwoods, protested to the Privy Council on 11 June 1696[26] that Dwight was obstructing them in their trade by his 1684 patent, without revealing what they were making.

Only Hammersley replied to Dwight's accusations.[27] He maintained that he had particularly good clay on his own land (which contained red-burning clay), so that Hammersley may well have been making fine redware, like his neighbours, *John and David Elers*. It must be borne in mind that Dwight had reached agreement with the Elers brothers for them to continue making fine redware in late 1693 and that the Elers may have prompted Dwight to sue Hammersley, Middleton and Astbury in 1697, for copying his and their product.

Although not a contemporary reporter, William Pitt, writing in 1817, gives an acceptable account of Staffordshire salt-glaze potters, from making brown (Crouch) salt-glazed ware from 'can marl' found in local coalpits, through to a white salt-glazed ware, again from local clay but with a covering of Devonshire clay. After describing lead-glazed 'specimens' with 'medals of King William and Queen Mary' attached to the sides of the ware (so not made before 1689), and with the dust of lead ore inside and out, he continued:

> together with a variety frequently found, *glazed with salt*, and bearing the initials WM. WR. AR. surmounted by a crown, and others ornamented with medals of Queen Anne, tolerably executed in basso-relievo. These pieces appear to be composed of the clay found in the coal-pits in and near Burslem, and then called can-marl; whilst others have been found, formed of this clay and a mixture of white sand or pounded gritstone, procured at Mole Cop [Mow Cop, local to Burslem], and well covered with a salt glaze. This last is known by the name of CROUCH WARE, and proves that the salt glaze had at that time been introduced.[28]

After mentioning ornamental slipware, Pitt went on:

> From these facts it would appear, that the salt glaze was used long previous to the introduction either of flint, or white clay, particularly in making Crouch-ware; the body of it being at first formed of a reddish clay, and afterwards of a dark greyish clay, dug from the coal-pits, which, when exposed to an intense heat, became of a light greyish colour. This clay, mixed with pounded sand from Mole Cop, produced a whitish body, then called STONE WARE, which was for some time generally used, and further improved by several manufacturers, who dipped it into a slip produced from the whitest clay from Devonshire.[29]

Pitt was describing a transition from using only locally found clay to the first use of imported ball clay.

'Crouch' ware continued to be made in Staffordshire, presumably from the local clay described by Pitt. *Thomas Cartlich* of Burslem supplied both Josiah Wedgwood and his brother *Thomas Wedgwood IV of the Overhouse* with Crouch ware in 1764-65; and Josiah Wedgwood's head clerk, Peter Swift, went into partnership with *John Cobb* to make Crouch ware in 1777.

North Devon Clay for Staffordshire Potters

The earliest reliable information about the use of ball clay in North Staffordshire comes in 1721, in documents relating to the partnership of *John Fenton and Thomas Hill*, potters at Shelton. In 1720, they agreed to buy clay, salt and flint, implying at least a white-burning clay, suitable for making white salt-glazed stoneware. When they dissolved partnership in 1721, the inventory taken included specifically 'Clodds of Clay brought from Bridgnorth or Liverpool'. A 1722 partnership agreement between *John Mare* of Longton and Richard Taylor included a similar agreement to buy 'Coles, Clay, Salt, fflint and other materials', again implying the availability of pipe clay.

The 1721 reference to 'Clodds of Clay brought from Bridgnorth or Liverpool' tell us that ball clay was being brought to North Staffordshire as a matter of routine by then. Liverpool is of course well known as a port, but Bridgnorth was also a minor port, on the River Severn. The nearest source of pipe clay to both these ports is from North Devon, shipped from Bideford.

The North Devon pipe clay comes from the Petrockstow Basin, nine miles south of Bideford. It was used by local potters for decorative slip and glaze, but was also shipped up the Bristol Channel. John Greening made two or three voyages a year between 1654 and 1688 with pipe clay, from Bideford to Gloucester.[30] Gloucester is the inland limit for sea-going vessels up the River Severn, and freight was transferred there to river boats, plying to Bridgnorth and Shrewsbury.[31] There was thus a transport route from North Devon already available for the 1721 'Clodds of Clay brought [forty miles] from Bridgnorth' to Shelton.

Some of Fenton and Hill's 1721 clay was brought from Liverpool, also served by coastal boats from Bideford. Daniel Defoe commented by 1724 that at Bideford he had seen several ships employed to go to Liverpool and up to Warrington to fetch rock salt,[32] ships which could easily have carried pipe clay on their outward journey. In his 1829 history, Shaw referred several times to Bideford clay,[33] showing that the term was in common use in the Potteries.

Shaw also referred to '*Chester Clay*',[34] named for another west coast port served by Bideford ships. Chester was a centre for tobacco pipe making, using North Devon clay,[35] but shipments of clay from Bideford to Chester trebled between 1691 and 1730,[36] a massive increase, surely caused by demand from North Staffordshire potters.

At forty miles, Chester and Bridgnorth were equidistant from North Staffordshire, but haulage from those two ports had to be by land, initially by pack-horses. Liverpool was considerably further at over fifty miles, but one can assume it was also initially reached by pack-horses.[37] The increasing production of Cheshire salt led to agitation for the River Weaver to be made navigable, from 1699 onward,[38] but it was 1732 before the river was made navigable from the River Mersey up to Winsford,[39] only twenty miles from the Potteries. Shallow-draught boats could then carry merchandise from Liverpool up the Mersey and Weaver. The seminal study by Lorna Weatherill[40] shows that pipe clay began to be taken up the River Weaver in 1734, starting from something over a hundred tons in that year and rising to almost 2,000 tons in 1760, supplying the clay needed for North Staffordshire's mature white salt-glazed stoneware production and emerging cream-coloured earthenware business.

Clay from South Devon

As has been shown, pipe clay was shipped from Dorset in 1633 and from North Devon from 1654, the earliest sources of pipe clay in quantity. South Devon pipe clay began to be exploited later. Up to 1852, Exeter port records included Teignmouth, which was and still is the actual port for pipe clay.[41] Six and a half tons were shipped from 'Exeter' to Plymouth in 1691, twenty-eight tons to London in 1721, and six cargoes totalling 129 tons were exported to London in 1730. Cargoes to Liverpool started in 1741, rising to ten a year in 1758.[42] By 1765, exports to Liverpool were over 2,000 tons,[43] matching the tonnage taken up the Weaver Navigation in 1760. A Dorset man, William Crawford of Poole, was the first successful clay merchant in South Devon, leasing clay-bearing land and exporting 490 tons of clay to London between 1726 and 1729.[44] His Dorset origin suggests that Crawford was already in the pipe clay business there and saw the opportunity to exploit the large deposits of pipe clay in South Devon. Writing of 1754, Angerstein stated that pipe clay cost 35s. a ton.[45]

The sources of ball clay and the methods of transport were now well established to supply the increasing demands of salt-glaze potters, both in Staffordshire and elsewhere in Britain.

FLINT
Use of flint in potting

The general subject of flint in pottery and flint milling is admirably described in Robert Copeland's *A short history of pottery raw materials and the Cheddleton Flint Mill*.[46] Some form of silica is an essential ingredient in white salt-glazed stoneware, in part to provide the basis for reaction with salt vapour to form the salt-glaze.[47] Ground sand or calcined and ground flint can provide the silica needed.[48] In the seventeenth century John Dwight of London used sand from Woolwich and the Isle of Wight in preference to calcined flint. Dwight knew about calcined flint; his acquaintance, Robert Hooke, noted that he 'Saw calcin'd flints as white as flower [*sic*, flour]' at a London glasshouse in 1673, and that 'Dwights secret consist only in flint powdered' in 1674.[49]

John Dwight left two notebooks, dated between 1689 and 1698. He mentioned flint only twice: his first entry, dated April 1689, is for a 'fine flint glasse [glaze]', using powdered flints or white sand. Dwight's second mention of flint is probably in 1698. Describing how to make white earth, he wrote 'Note yᵗ [that] calcin'd beaten & sifted flints will doe instead of white sand, & rather whiter, but ye charge & trouble is more'. Dwight frequently mentioned fine white sand and told how to calcine it.[50]

Dwight told Gilpen in 1697/98 that Cologne ware was

made with clay and 'fine sand' and Gilpen enlarged this to 'a fine smale [small] sort of sand which is brought from the Isle of Wight'.[51] The inference is that, although Dwight knew all about calcined flint, he preferred white sand.

Staffordshire potters first used local grit from the gritstone ridges north and east of the Potteries to provide the silica for their stoneware, but later turned to using calcined flint. In 1686 Plot described millstones quarried at Mole Cop (Mow Cop), north of the Potteries, but made no mention of the use of millstone grit by potters then. After the end of salt-glazed ware production, William Pitt wrote in 1817 of the early use of pounded sand from Mole Cop to make a whitish body, and another body which included pounded gritstone from (local) Baddeley Edge and Mole Cop.[52]

Recipes for stoneware bodies quoted in the eighteenth century are four, five or six of clay to one of flint. After earlier and obviously erroneous attempts, Reinhold Angerstein finally settled for five and a half of pipe clay to one of flint, at Hanley in 1754.[53] Gabriel Jars, who visited North Staffordshire about 1765, gave the proportions of clay to flint as six to one or five to one for white salt-glazed stoneware.[54] Between 1768 and 1771 a French artist, François Joseph Bélanger, drew elevations and plans of two kilns, probably at *Derby*.[55] A note on the plans gives a stoneware body: four parts of clay to one part of flint.

The legend of Astbury learning about calcined flint when his horse needed treatment at Dunstable is on record thirty years earlier than previously thought.[56] Dr. Richard Wilkes was told the story in Hanley in 1743, only a generation after the supposed occurrence of the incident. Dr. Richard Wilkes (1691-1760) researched a never-completed history of Staffordshire,[57] and amongst other papers left a diary, compiled from 1739 to 1754, which includes information about a visit to Hanley in 1739.[58] Wilkes wrote:

[1739 Feb 16] At Hanley Green I was told by M^r. Jo^h Burslem & M^r. Joshua Heat [*sic*, query Heath] two head Potters yt. [that] Some years ago a Parcel of Dutch Men came & made Pots at Bradwel [*sic*] near Newcastle [-under-Lyme]: yt. one M^r. George Astbury a joyner [*sic*] being employ'd by them in making Lathes & other machines at length got a notion of the Pottery Trade: yt. he about 30 years ago [so c.1709] began to make a sort of white Ware of calcin'd Pebbles: yt one M^r. Dwight of Fulham had a Patent for making such Kind of Muggs: yt. one Time w[he]ⁿ he was at y^e [the] Cock in Redburn [*sic*, Redbourn] his Horse having a sore Back ye Horseler [ostler] undertook to cure it in a few Hours by strewing ye powder of calcin'd Flint upon it: y^t when he saw it whither yn [*sic*, whiter than] the calcin'd Pebbles he resolv'd to try to make Cups of it, in w[hi]^{ch} he succeeded & was the first who made y^t kind of Ware in these Parts. This M^r. Astbury got a considerable Estate by this Business, & so have many more since.

This appears to be by far the earliest account yet found of two 'legends' of the Staffordshire Potteries: the theft of Elers' secrets and recognition of the value of calcined flint.

Wilkes' account is still over forty years after the presence of the Elers brothers in Staffordshire (1693-98), and some thirty years after the 'horse-flint-ostler' event. The Cock Inn at Redbourn, Herts., on the main road south to London, did exist between 1636 and 1781.[59] *George* Astbury has not been traced, and *Joshua Astbury* (1676-1721/22) seems the most likely candidate (with very similar names) who was a salt-glaze potter and died wealthy. It is interesting that there was this Staffordshire 'folk-tale' in 1743, when calcining flint was well known in London seventy years earlier, in 1673. There were certainly less romantic ways of learning about the procedure in the early eighteenth century. However the Staffordshire potters learnt about the use of flint, there are records of large mortars in potters' inventories in the 1710s and reference to pounded flint by 1720.

When Reinhold Angerstein visited Derby in 1754, he found the white salt-glazed stoneware makers using calcined black flint, brought by water from other parts of England.[60] The Derby potters followed Staffordshire practices, and were well placed for flint supplies, already passing up the River Trent *en route* for North Staffordshire. For Staffordshire he quoted raw flint from Liverpool, Chester and other ports as costing 20s. a ton.

Sources of flint

A modern textbook tells us that 'The Chalk of southern and eastern England contains many nodular and shapeless masses of black or grey chalcedonic silica, called *flint*.'[61] Because of the continual erosion of chalk cliffs, flint pebbles are found in abundance on the adjoining seashores. Long before its value for pottery was realised, flint was used by primitive man for edged tools and weapons, and in historic times for building and road-making, for ignition in general and particularly for gun-flints when the flintlock was invented. Thus there was already an elementary supply system from quarry or seashore.

Chalk, containing flint, occurs in the south-east of England and in north-west France. The south bank of the River Thames, near Gravesend was a source of flint-bearing chalk. Because of its nearness to London it was perhaps the earliest to be exploited for glass and pottery purposes and was easily available to John Dwight and the other London stoneware potters. The Sussex coast was another source for potters' flints: The manor court of Meeching, which covered Newhaven, was told in 1748 that persons were digging chalk boulders and selling them without leave.[62] 'Blue boulders', flints for the Potteries, continued to be collected from the seashore at Rye Harbour, Sussex until c.1960.[63]

Gabriel Jars, French industrial spy, recorded c.1765 that 'the flint, which is used in quantity [in North Staffordshire] is obtained from Gravesend or, rather, the banks of the Thames.'[64] Josiah Wedgwood noted in his experiment book in 1759 or later 'The best and purest flint is got in the Chalk Pits at and near Gravesend. That which is picked from the shores, or has been exposed to the air or common soil out of its natural bed of chalk, has acquired a metallic tinge, and is generally or <u>always</u> bad'.[65] Surviving correspondence shows that he received flint from 'London' via Liverpool in 1777.[66]

Josiah Wedgwood agreed to take flints in payment for ware from a Norwich merchant, Ralph Lewis, in 1763-64, presumably flint of Norfolk origin. Lewis told him in 1764 that he had a good stock of lump flint at Willington and at the mill.[67] *John Baddeley* paid freight for flint from Gravesend and Norfolk in 1766, and from Gravesend and 'french' in 1767.[68] Edward West, dealer in flints, 3 Darkhouse Lane, London, insured his property in 1767 and Edmund Elsden of King's Lynn, Norfolk, flint and general merchant, did so in 1766.[69] Amongst a variety of payments for sand and freight of sand, *John Baddeley* paid Edmund Elsden £7.12s.4d. in 1758.[70]

Transport of flint
The most direct route from the south-east coast to the Staffordshire potteries was by sea to the Humber estuary and up the navigable River Trent to Willington. From there, flint was carted some thirty miles to the Potteries mills. An alternative and less obvious route was by sea to Liverpool, initially with a longer overland haul to Staffordshire. The River Weaver was made navigable in 1733, making a shorter land journey to the water mills east and south of the Potteries, shortened still further with the completion of the Trent and Mersey Canal in 1777.

In 1769 Arthur Young noted that 'flints from the Thames are all brought rough by sea, either to *Liverpool* or *Hull*, and so by *Burton* [Willington].'[71] In 1772, the *London Magazine* confirmed the westerly route: 'Flints come from the Thames, round the land's end [*sic*] to Liverpool, and up the River Weaver, into the heart of Cheshire, and carried by land to Burslem and its neighbourhood.'[72] L. Weatherill has shown that flintstones began to be brought up the River Weaver from 1733, from 230 tons in the first full year of 1734 to a maximum of 720 tons in 1753, but with wildly fluctuating tonnages from year to year.[73]

Calcining and grinding flint
Potters prepared clay themselves. Initially the potters, moving on from using local grit, also prepared flint, calcining the pebbles and then pounding the calcined pebbles by hand in mortars. Calcining was done industrially by burning alternate layers of coal and flints in a vertical kiln, but no information has been found about the earliest practices, though obviously potters had the kiln expertise for calcining small quantities.[74]

Pounding was both laborious and dangerous, and only feasible for small quantities. Benson, patentee of wet grinding, spelt out the hazard of dry grinding in 1726: 'any person ever so healthful or strong working in that business cannot probably survive above two yeares [*sic*] occasioned by the dust sucked into his body by the air he breaths [*sic*], which being of a ponderous nature, fixes there so closely that nothing can remove it'.[75] Wet grinding was safer and, perhaps more importantly, allowed much greater production.

There is documentary confirmation that flint was pounded by hand before 1721. When *Samuel Edge* died in that year,[76] the inventory of his possessions included '3 Mortars & pestills [pestles]' worth £2.5s.0d.[77] These could have been used for pounding lead for lead-glazed ware, but because of their value are more likely to have been large and therefore for pounding calcined flint, used for the body of stoneware.[78] *Joshua Astbury* also died in 1721 and his inventory shows that he had 'sifting boxes and mortars worth £9'. Like Edge's mortars, these could have been used for pounding lead, but there is no doubt about a third 1721 reference. When *John Fenton and Thomas Hill* started their partnership in 1720, they agreed to buy 'fflint'. At the end of the partnership in 1721, the raw materials divided included 'all unpounded fflint', and Fenton took 'punned [pounded] fflint',[79] clear confirmation that flint was being powdered by hand in that year.

Thomas Benson took out two patents for the wet grinding of flint. The first, 5 November 1726, provided for flint stones to be first wetted and crushed by iron wheels, then pulverised by iron balls in circular iron pans. His second patent, six years later, used the same method, but this time the the iron pans and balls were replaced by stone pans and balls, obviating the possibility of contaminating the flint by iron.[80] When *John Meir* of Fenton Vivian died in 1729,[81] the inventory of his effects included 'fflint burn'd & pounded … & fflint unburn'd', showing that he at least still pounded his flint.

Wet grinding in pans called for wind, water, horse and later steam power to turn the mill. Windmills did exist, but water power was available on the hilly Pennine slopes, and existing corn water-mills were adapted to grind flint, with the addition of calcining kilns. Nearly two hundred water mills of all periods and for all purposes have been identified within a twenty miles radius of Newcastle-under-Lyme, the market town of the Potteries.[82]

Existing mills were converted and new ones built, some by master potters, venturing into vertical organisation by milling their own raw materials. *John Peat*, a farmer and potter, bought Gom's Mill, a corn mill and smithy at Longton in 1732.[83] When he sold it in 1745[84] it had acquired a kiln, suggesting that Peat had adapted the former corn mill to be a flint mill. After 1742 Peat also built a flint mill on the River Trent, near Fenton Hall, which was bought by *Thomas Whieldon*, another potter, in 1749.[85]

Angerstein, in Staffordshire in 1754, described crushing calcined flint by an edge-runner mill (by his sketch apparently horse-driven), next sieved and then ground in conventional pans, water-powered. He noted there that raw flint cost 20s. a ton, with another 5d. a hundred-weight (8s.4d. a ton if of 20 hundred-weight) for coal for calcining. The resultant 'flint flour' was sold for 1s. per 16 pints.[86]

James Brindley, famous as a canal engineer, built flint mills: water-, wind- and steam-powered.[87] His notebook records that he and John Baddeley visited 'Matherso [Moddershall, near Stone, Staffs.]' on 15 March 1757, where at least a new mill-wheel was required. Brindley drew plans and set out the wheel-race, and the wheel turned by August. On 22 February 1758, Brindley 'began to work the Engen [sic, engine] for Mr John Baddles [Baddeley's] flint mill' and in the same year incorporated a 'niew [sic] invention' at Mr. Griffith's New Inn flint mill at Hanford, south-west of the Potteries. In the same year, Brindley installed a fire-engine (steam engine) at Fenton Colliery, so it is conceivable that he also installed a fire-engine for Baddeley, but not necessarily at Moddershall. Brindley himself patented a 'Fire Engine' in 1758, for pumping water and other purposes.[88] (At that period, fire engines were used for pumping back water to re-use over water wheels.)

Brindley also built a windmill to grind flint and pump water in 1758, at the Jenkins, north-east of Burslem.[89] An undated plan in Staffordshire Record Office shows a horse-powered flint mill, 'Mr. Shaw's flint mill in Burslem', circular in form, with provision for 'the Pole that the Horse draws by' and six grinding pans.[90]

Flint Miller and Potter: John Baddeley
The activities of *John Baddeley* as a flint miller illustrate well the sophistication of the supply of flint at the height of production of salt-glazed ware in North Staffordshire. His surviving records show that the supply of flint to individual potters was well-organised in the 1750s and '60s, with suppliers, shippers, many mills, specialist carters and frequent deliveries.[91] Of course, a flint and ball-clay body was also being used for cream-coloured ware by this period.

Simeon Shaw wrote that 'Mr. John Baddeley was the son of the flint grinder at Mothersall [sic]',[92] a good example of the germ of truth in Shaw's reporting of oral history. The Baddeley family is highly concentrated north of the Potteries and the name does not occur in parish records covering Moddershall.[93] John Baddeley was in fact baptised on 26 February 1725/26 at Wolstanton Church,[94] the 'mother-church' for the north of the Potteries, and it was he himself who became 'the flint grinder at Mothersall' as part of his potting activities.

John Baddeley had partners in his milling business: James Kent (a potter at Lane Delph)[95] and a Moses Keeling were his partners in 1756-57,[96] and Thomas Fletcher in the 1760s.[97] Baddeley's sources for flint were Norfolk,[98] Gravesend,[99] and 'Cressey',[100] possibly the unidentified source of the 'french' flints bought in 1767.[101] He bought through merchants: Maddison in 1763 and 1766,[102] and Blaydes of Hull in 1765.[103] Flints came to Baddeley's mills by both east coast (Hull, Gainsborough[104] and Willington[105]) and west coast (Liverpool[106] and Winsford[107]) routes. His principal carrier was Ward and Smith,[108] but he also used the Nottingham Boat Company,[109] and Lowe.[110]

Baddeley had several mills in the Moddershall valley near Stone, Staffs: New Mill, Old Mill and Upper or Shorts Mill between 1758 and 1763,[111] and Lower Mill from 1764 to 1766.[112] Other mills in which he was concerned include Botteslow Mill in 1758-63,[113] Meir and Goatshead Mills in 1762-66,[114] Furnace Mill from 1762 to 1763[115] and Lower Old Field Mill at Hanley in 1761.[116] When he died in1772, Baddeley owned but apparently did not operate Ivy House Mill, near Hanley.[117]

His accounts include many details of repairing, staffing and running these mills, and of the local carters who delivered 'pecks'[118] of flint to many North Staffordshire potters, in this period of course makers of salt-glazed ware and makers of cream-coloured ware. Supplies of flint by Baddeley to salt-glaze potters are noted under their names.

SALT
Clay defines pottery in general; ball clay and flint define white pottery, but salt for glazing is the defining raw material for this study in ceramic history. The origin of the use of salt to glaze pottery is not known, but salt-glazing was established in Germany by the sixteenth century.[119] This method of glazing came fully fledged to Britain from Germany or Belgium. The practice came first to Woolwich around 1650,[120] then to coastal Southampton about 1666,[121] and to London c.1672, before spreading to Staffordshire, possibly in the 1690s but more certainly after 1700.

Sources of salt
For London, John Dwight's 1698 'Memoriall [sic]' to Parliament gives some evidence of his source of salt, where he complained that he had to bear and pay a considerable tax for *foreign* salt.[122] The source of salt for the North Staffordshire potters is much more likely to have been nearby Staffordshire or Cheshire. Although Cheshire is the obvious local source of salt for North Staffordshire potters, salt was also produced at Shirleywich near Stafford, only twenty miles south of Burslem. Made by evaporating brine, salt was made there from c.1680 until c.1900.[123] It would therefore have been available to Staffordshire potters, but there is no contemporary evidence of its supply.

Cheshire had produced salt from Roman times, again by evaporating brine, until rock salt was discovered at Marbury in 1670 during a search for coal, the fuel needed by then for heating the brine tanks. Wood had been the first fuel used, but its increasing use in industry far outstripped its availability, and the more expensive coal took its place. (Salt pans have some affinity to potters' slip kilns, both used to evaporate water by under-floor heat.) Cheshire salt was taken far and wide, both by land and by sea from the River Mersey. Defoe reported in 1724 that 'several [Bideford, North Devon] ships were employ'd to go to Leverpool [sic], and up the river Mersey to Warrington, to fetch the rock salt'.[124]

The main centres of salt production in Cheshire were Nantwich and Middlewich, equidistant from Burslem at sixteen miles, and Northwich, considerably further. In 1750, Dr. Pococke mentioned a salt works at Lawton, only seven miles from Burslem.[125]

Transport of salt
Coal was used for evaporating the brine by 1636,[126] and a 1656 account states that 'Pit-coals' were used, 'whereof there is great abundance not far off in the Confines

between the two Counties of *Chester* and *Stafford*',[127] i.e., in North Staffordshire. Figures given in 1682 mention the weekly consumption of over 400 tons of coal by Cheshire salt works, brought from North Staffordshire and North East Cheshire mines by horse-drawn waggons.[128] In proposals to canalise the Cheshire River Weaver in 1699, it was argued that it would enable coal for the salt works to be brought upstream from Lancashire cheaper than land-hauled Staffordshire coal, confirming that Staffordshire coal was used. In opposition, it was said that Cheshire farmers' leases took account of 'the advantage of carrying salt and coal',[129] showing that they carried both commodities. A study of 'saltways' in Cheshire has not traced 'any eastward from Nantwich …. It is reasonable to postulate a saltway to Newcastle-under-Lyme but evidence of it is lacking'.[130] The lack of evidence may be because the coal carters took salt on their outward journeys to the North Staffordshire coal mines.

Consumption of salt

Thomas Wedgwood IV of Overhouse bought eight or nine bushels of salt each week in 1772[131] at 3s.10d. per bushel. *John Baddeley* of Shelton bought similar values of salt at frequent intervals in 1762.[132] The only mention of salt in a potter's inventory so far found was '8 bushells of Bay salt' left by Nathaniel Oade, a London tin-glaze and brown stoneware potter, in 1726.[133] Eight or nine bushels seems to represent the quantity of salt needed for a single firing, about four hundredweight of salt.[134] It is apparent that salt was bought for each oven firing and salting, and no stock kept.

Baddeley's supplier was Robert Gardner of whom nothing more is known, whilst *Thomas Wedgwood IV of Overhouse* bought his salt from a Mr. Graham. He seems to have been a Burslem ironmonger, who also supplied nails, oil, rope, hinges, paint, smalts and zaffre.[135] His son, *John Graham junior,* was a salt-glaze potter in 1784. References to potters in association with salt are rare. Apart from John Baddeley's and Thomas Wedgwood's purchases and Oade's inventory, *John Fenton and Thomas Hill* agreed to buy it in 1720, as did *Richard Taylor and John Mare* in 1722. *Thomas Stevenson* left a 'salt bag' in 1758.[136]

No evidence has been found of where Gardner or Graham obtained their salt supplies, which were of course also needed locally for cooking and preserving food.

Gabriel Jars, a contemporary reporter, writing of c.1765 practice, said that Staffordshire potters used sea salt,[137] but he went on to state that 'The salt used … is very white and large-grained, to some extent similar to that produced at Lons-le-Saunier for consumption by the Swiss'. Lons-le-Saunier is an inland town, famous for its salt mines, so Jars' comparison was with mined rock salt rather than evaporated sea salt.

The 1762 petition of the potters for a turnpike road stated: 'In Burslem and its neighbourhood are near one hundred and fifty separate potteries for making various kinds of stone and earthen ware … as much salt is consumed in glazing one species of it [Burslem ware] as pays annually near £5,000 duty to government' and goes on to describe the ancillary trades supported by the pottery industry, including 'men employed in the salt works' and 'not one foreigner is employed in, or any material imported from abroad for, any branch of it'.[138] The potters wanted a road *inter alia* to bring in salt made within Britain, by Britons, paying duty to the British government. With inland sources such as Cheshire and Staffordshire on their own doorstep, it seems unlikely that Staffordshire potters would use 'sea salt'.

The 'near £5,000 duty' paid can be quantified into consumption of salt by potters. Salt Duty was 3s.4d. per bushel,[139] meaning that almost 30,000 bushels of salt were used for firing salt-glaze ovens annually in about 1761. At eight bushels per firing, 3,750 ovens were fired in a year, or about seventy-five a week. Our research has identified about sixty potters in the 1761-70 decade, reasonably close to the notional seventy-five ovens fired per week then. The quantity of salt used by the North Staffordshire potters was not large in comparison with clay, flint and coal: in total about fifteen tons a week in 1761.[140]

Thomas Wedgwood IV of Overhouse (1717-1773) (see Appendix 1) was a representative salt-glaze potter near the end of our period, when the supply chain was thoroughly organised. He bought clay via Winsford in Cheshire and his son bought clay first from Liverpool and then from Longport, the local canal wharf, after the Trent and Mersey Canal was opened throughout in 1777. They bought flint regularly in small quantities, from local millers, and salt week by week. By this time, the supplies were so reliable that there was no need to hold stocks.

CHAPTER V

Making the Pots

The manufacture of white salt-glazed stoneware in Britain was one more stage in the development of pottery making. Tin-glaze techniques spread from Holland first to Norwich and then to London, whilst salt-glazing methods came from Germany to Woolwich, London and Southampton. Salt-glazing spread to Staffordshire, an area where redware potting was indigenous.

White salt-glazed stoneware manufacture was described by several eighteenth century foreign visitors: Reinhold Angerstein, a Swedish industrial spy who visited England and Wales between 1753 and 1755,[1] noted his visits to white salt-glazed stoneware makers at Derby, Burslem and Hanley in 1754; a French arcanist, Jacques Louis Brolliet, reported on English white salt-glazed stoneware manufacture c.1755;[2] a French industrial spy, Gabriel Jars, described Staffordshire white salt-glazed stoneware processes in 1765;[3] and a French artist, François Joseph Bélanger, drew elevations and plans of two kilns at Derby between 1768 and 1771.[4] An English chemist, Dr. R. Watson, writing as late as 1784, also gave a brief description.[5]

Robert Plot's description of pot-making in Burslem c.1680,[6] often quoted, is a remarkably detailed account of coarse redware manufacture. He mentions as equipment a wheel, a slip-trailer, a square pit for steeping the clay, a beating board and spatula, a wageing (wedging) board and wire; an outside drying place, a wire brush and a pencil (paintbrush), a means of crushing and calcining lead ore, an oven, saggars and kiln furniture.

A 1709 document survives of the lease of a 'Workhouse and Pott Oven adjoyning thereto' at Lane Delph, from Thomas Basset of Barlaston, clerk, to Thomas Dakin and William Chatterley of Hanley Green, potters.[7] It confirms Plot's account, and exemplifies the simplicity of equipment needed then for a *coarse* redware potter, typical of Staffordshire potters, some of whom went on to make fine redware, whilst others progressed to increasingly sophisticated white salt-glaze stoneware manufacture. Redware manufacture by Dakin and Chatterley is confirmed by permission to get clay in Basset's land 'for their said oven only' (i.e., not to sell) between November and March.

The equipment amounted in all to a single pot wheel, forty six-foot (1.83m) boards, one mortar and pestle, a set of oven bricks, materials for a kiln, a poker and a drawing iron, a girdle for the oven, and planks to make slip pots.

Body preparation
The first stage in the making of pots is the preparation of the 'body'. Redware required the removal of impurities from the clay, done by liquefying it and sieving it, and allowing impurities to settle. For a body to make cooking pots, sand or grit would be added to 'open' the body so that the pot would be suitable for use with fire. A similar sequence was needed to make white stoneware. The standard body included pipe clay and silica in the form of sand or calcined flints. Pipe clay was received from Dorset or Devon in solid foot-square 'balls' (hence its later name of ball-clay). It had to be mixed with the sand or calcined flint, liquefied and stirred, to ensure a homogeneous body.

John Dwight's pottery at Fulham has been the subject of intensive archaeological investigation[8] and clay preparation features found there might be considered representative of 'London' potters' practice, both tin-glaze and salt-glaze. The only physical evidence found is two small double-compartment brick tanks,[9] provisionally regarded as being for clay settlement. The smallness of these tanks is suggestive of preparing small amounts of 'fine' body.

William Gilpen noted in 1698 that pipe clay was used at Fulham, brought in foot-square balls from Dorset, ground between millstones, sieved and mixed with sand, then mixed with water, and 'wrought to a plyable temper'. Next the mixture was put in a pit and 'there Mixed and wrought well together by treading'.[10] Gilpen does not mention any 'purifying' of the clay, by sieving out pebbles etc.

There is no convenient contemporary 'Gilpen'-type record for Staffordshire, but Plot, writing in 1686 of coarse redware, was conscious of the need for purifying local clays, when he stated that 'Neither of which *clays* or *Slips* must have any *gravel* or *Sand* in them; upon this account, before it be brought to the *wheel* they prepare the *clay* by steeping it in water in a square pit, till it be of a due consistence'.[11]

Neither Plot nor his successors, Angerstein and Jars, mentioned 'weathering' clay, exposing clay to the elements for months or years before use, though Shaw recommended weathering marl for making saggars in 1829.[12] Exposure of clay to the weather

> helps to oxidise any pyrite present, rendering it soluble, so that this and other soluble impurities are to some extent leached out; the water content also becomes more uniform and agglomerates of clay are broken down with a consequent increase in plasticity.[13]

Clay could be weathered at the pottery, if space permitted, or at canal or river wharfs. When *Thomas Stevenson*, a salt-glaze potter, died in 1757, he had 'Clay in Burslem about 50 load £2.10s.' and 'Clay in the ffield fifty load £1.5s.', besides 'Flint & Chester Clay' in his works. A related process, 'ageing' or 'souring' of prepared body by storing, usually in cellars, enables the water to become more uniformly dispersed.[14]

71

Chapter V – Making the Pots

A French chemist, Jean Hellot, noted a process for making something like English white salt-glazed stoneware in 1751, using only calcined and ground flint, dipped in a salt and water solution before firing.[15] He was doubtful of its practicality and the best that can be said is that it is a garbled and incomplete description of the real method. There are descriptions of clay preparation in Staffordshire in 1754 and 1765. In his 1754 peregrination, Reinhold Angerstein noted (surely in error for the proportions) at *Derby* that the white ware body was 'half "dutch pipe-clay" and half calcined and ground black flint' and at *Liverpool* that Staffordshire white ware was 'half pipe clay and half flint'.[16] When he reached Burslem he recorded that 'The composition of white ware is one part clay and 5½ parts of flint' and only when he reached Hanley did he learn 'that the proportions of 'pipe clay to flint flour were 5½ to 1', proportions confirmed by Jars in 1765.[17] Angerstein went on to describe mixing clay and flint at Derby:

> The clay also has to be calcined and ground before mixing with the flint, which takes place in two boxes, one above the other, through which the slurry of water and ground materials flow and is blended. Subsequently it is placed in a tank made of brick heated by a fire underneath, where it is dried to consistency convenient for throwing or modelling.

Calcining clay seems unusual, and there is no mention of sieving the materials or mixed body. His accompanying sketch shows two raised boxes with drains, over a shallow pit, and a separate sketch of a brick tank with a floor raised above three 'fireholes' on a long side, a slip-kiln. Boxes, pit and tank are all oblong in plan.[18]

Angerstein later described body preparation at Burslem.[19] Pipe clay was 'dispersed in water and sieved through haircloth', with no mention of calcining or grinding as was done at Derby. The flint was calcined and next crushed by an edge-runner mill, his sketch suggesting that the mill was worked by a horse. The crushed flint was then ground in circular pans, Angerstein's sketch showing the grinding stones pushed round by a geared drive from a water wheel. In the text, mixing was as at *Derby*, slip descending through two tanks into a third 'which is built of thick bricks and provided with a fire grate underneath, where coal is burnt'. The drawing shows a cistern emptying into an oblong tank and a separate oblong slip kiln with a single firebox at one end and a tall chimney at the other, unlike the Derby one described above.

Gabriel Jars' 1765 account of potting in Staffordshire seems to be solely about the making of white salt-glazed stoneware, although the manufacture of cream-coloured lead-glazed ware was well established by then. Jars gave the proportion of clay to flint. After fine sieving of both clay and flint, they were mixed in the proportion of one of flint to either five or six of clay, depending on the type of ball clay used, care being taken to see that the two liquids were of the same consistency. After mixing well, the resultant body was sieved twice more, and then dried out on a slip kiln.[20] He wrote:[21]

> Clay is put into a tank with water to make it sloppy. Water is well mixed with it by stirring it with a piece of board. The water holding this clay is put through a large sieve to separate what has not been dissolved in the water and is caught in the sieve, being returned to the original tank. As to the clay which passes through, one waits until there is a sufficient quantity of it and then it is agitated vigorously in the water it is in, being passed through a finer sieve.

Dr. R. Watson, writing as late as 1784, also gave a brief description:[22]

> The *flint* or *white-stone* ware, is made in Staffordshire, and other places, in the following manner:- Tobacco-pipe clay, which they have from Dorsetshire, is beat much in water; by this process the finer parts of the clay remain suspended in the water, whilst the coarser sand, and other impurities, fall to the bottom. The thick liquid, consisting of water and the finer parts of the clay, is further purified, by being passed through hair and lawn [silk] sieves of different degrees of fineness: the clay is then sufficiently prepared to be mixed with powdered flint, the other ingredient in the stone-ware.

Between 1768 and 1771, a French artist, François Joseph Bélanger, drew elevations and plans of two kilns (see *Derby: Nottingham Road*).[23] One kiln elevation and plan is endorsed with two notes. Translated, the second note gives a stoneware body recipe: four parts of clay to one part of flint, a variation on Jars' proportions.

Mention is made here of the use of a fine white dip to improve the appearance of a coarse stoneware body. *John Dwight* of Fulham made *inter alia* both brown and white salt-glazed ware, and is thought to have used a white engobe or dip to improve coarse-bodied ware in the 1690s.[24] Use of a fine white dip over a coarse body gives the same outward appearance, with much less expense for fine materials, reducing the price and thus expanding the market. It has been suggested that this dipping was one of the secrets learned from Dwight by Staffordshire potters.

Staffordshire potters certainly did use the same technique, to which they were no strangers, Plot describing them 'makeing the ground' with '*Orange Slip*' in 1680,[25] and Pitt wrote in 1817:

> This [coal-pit] clay, mixed with pounded sand from Mole Cop, produced a whitish body, then called STONE WARE, which was for some time generally used, and further improved by several manufacturers, who dipped it into a slip produced from the whitest clay from Devonshire.[26]

Pitt was describing a transition from using only locally found clay to the first economical use of imported ball clay. Josiah Wedgwood's list of 1710-15 Staffordshire potters[27] (Figure 26) named *Aaron Shaw* who made 'Stone & dippt wit [dipped white]', though there is no other evidence of him making salt-glazed ware. Shaw suggested that *Thomas Heath (I)* of Lane Delph used 'the Wash of Pipe Clay',[28] possibly no more than folk-memory, but with the usual kernel of fact.

Dipped ware continued to be produced, meeting a demand for a cheaper product: *Jonah Malkin* sold his 'first oven full of Dipt white' in 1747, and went on selling dipped ware until 1750/51. *John Peat* of Fenton Vivian leased out his whiteware warehouse and dipware warehouse in 1752. Dipped shards were found on the 1750s Fenton Vivian site of *Thomas Whieldon* (Colour Plates 192-193). Nor was the technique confined to Fulham and Staffordshire; dipped shards have been found at white salt-glazed stoneware production sites in Devon at *Bovey Tracey* (Colour Plate 166), at *Isleworth* in Middlesex (though this could have been from sales stock, rather than production), and in *Shropshire* at Benthall. Arnold Mountford had this dipped ware analysed, showing that the covering engobe contained flint, whilst the underlying body did not. He pointed out that this dipped ware is never as white as solid white stoneware, it is usually thicker (for obvious reasons) and that there is a tendency for the white dip covering to craze.[29]

Staffordshire coarseware potters had used 'sun kilns' for drying out their purified clay. Shaw described them in detail – an outdoor shallow pit, where the liquefied clay dried out by the heat of the sun – and indicated where at least four were still in use in the Staffordshire Potteries in 1829.[30] Angerstein illustrated them in use at *Prescot* in 1754[31] and an example survives at Weatheriggs Pottery in Cumbria.[32] Whilst adequate for potters like Dakin and Chatterley (above), who got their clay between November and March, dependence on the fugitive sun in North Staffordshire was not reliable enough for 'mass production'.

The concept of a heated kiln for drying out liquefied materials was well known before 1700. In Europe, Agricola described brine pans somewhat similar to slip kilns in 1550.[33] In Cheshire, the next county to Staffordshire, rules for gathering wood for 'lead pans' used for evaporating brine to make salt were promulgated at Nantwich in 1538, and there is a detailed description of iron salt-pans with coal-fired furnace holes beneath at the same place in 1675.[34] This knowledge of evaporation by heat would be easily accessible to Staffordshire potters. Dwight's 1689-1698 'recipe books' refer to putting the both fine white and fine dark body into stone pans to be dried on a furnace in the hot arch.[35] This sounds like a small scale operation, perhaps reflecting the small scale of his 'fine white' production.

The method was known in Staffordshire for redware clay by 1709. As mentioned above, Basset's 1709 lease included 'materials for a kiln' distinguished from a set of oven bricks and a girdle for the oven. In 1718-19 an arbitration award against John Middleton of Shelton, earth potter, revealed that he had a 'kiln or boyler' and a stove in one of his buildings, and an oven which annoyed his neighbours by 'smoak'. Middleton had to remove his kiln and not re-build in the same place 'to be used in or about the boyling of clay and preparing it for making of potts'; build his stove pipe larger, and 'raise the case [hovel] of his pott oven to be nine yards high'.[36] His neighbours, *John Fenton and Thomas Hill,* took over a kiln, assumed to be a 'slip kiln', in 1720. Although filter presses for de-watering slip were patented in 1853,[37] slip kilns continued to be used into the twentieth century.[38]

Angerstein saw a slip kiln at Derby in 1754, described above. Jars described Staffordshire slip kilns, by reference to those at Newcastle-upon-Tyne: 'a long tank or kind of pan made of bricks, supported underneath by iron bars. There is an iron grate for a coal fire and a chimney at the end of the tank to take up the smoke. The mixture suspended in water is put in these tanks to evaporate off moisture to reach a consistency adequate for wedging. Then the clay is taken out to place it on a level surface made of slabs, or on boards',[39] to 'beat' or 'wedge' any air-pockets out of the body before using it. *Aaron Shaw III* left 'beaten clay' in 1737 and *'Doctor' Thomas Wedgwood II* left a 'wedging Board' in the same year; *John Baddeley* had beating flag(stone)s in 1761, and *Thomas Wedgwood IV of the Overhouse* had a 'beating stone'.

There are occasional mentions of clay preparation equipment in contemporary documents. The inventories of salt-glaze potters include paddles, sieves and lawns – see *Samuel Edge* in 1721, *Aaron Shaw III* in 1737, *Thomas Stevenson* in 1757, *Peter Bagnall* in 1761 and *Thomas Wedgwood IV of Overhouse* in 1773. To quote Jars, paddles were used for stirring ('blunging') the clay when it was 'put into a tank with water to make it sloppy… stirring it with a piece of board'; and also for mixing the 'sloppy' clay with calcined flint.

The end result of all this preparatory activity was what was later called the 'body', the mixture of clay and flint, ready for making pots. *Thomas and John Wedgwood* termed it 'Clay prepared for the Wheele' in the 1770s, and *Thomas Wedgwood IV of the Overhouse* left 'Made up clay' in 1773.

Continental and English potters made brown salt-glazed stoneware at the same time that white salt-glazed stoneware was made: London potters and Staffordshire potters, not to mention Nottingham, Derbyshire and other potters who only made brown salt-glazed ware. The Staffordshire term for brown salt-glazed ware was 'Crouch Ware', though it was Lancashire which provided an early definition of the term, in a *Prescot* auction advertisement of 1770 for a 'Mug or Earthenware Works, with two ovens, the one for burning the Crouch or Nottingham ware'.[40] Angerstein's 1754 description of the 'coffee-brown' salt-glazed ware made at Crich in Derbyshire confirms its production there,[41] leaving no doubt that 'Crouch' meant 'Crich'. It seems to have been usual to describe ware by its original place of manufacture: 'Nottingham ware' and 'Burslem ware' are examples, and 'Crouch' was used in the same way. John Wyke of Liverpool ordered white stone 'Boslam [*sic,* Burslem]' ware in 1763.[42] There are many instances of brown salt-glazed ware being unearthed in the Potteries and one report of brown salt-glazed wasters being found in Burslem.[43] *Thomas Cartlich* of Burslem was supplying crouch ware in the 1760s.

*Colour Plate 48. **Teapot,** drab-coloured salt-glazed stoneware with white crabstock handle and spout and sprig-relief decoration. This teapot was thrown and appears to pre-date the two manufacturers known through excavations to have made drab wares, Thomas Whieldon and Humphrey Palmer. Staffordshire, c.1745-50. 3in. (7.62cm) high. (Private collection)*

*Colour Plate 49. **Teapot,** drab-coloured salt-glazed stoneware with white crabstock handle, spout and shell-paw feet. The sprig relief is white with occasional blue-stained flowers. Staffordshire, c.1750. 4in. (10.16cm) high. (Harriet Carlton Goldweitz collection)*

Chapter V – Making the Pots

Colour Plate 50. **Milk jug,** *drab-coloured salt-glazed stoneware with white pipe clay handle, spout, feet and sprigging, some of which is stained blue. Staffordshire, c.1750. 4⅞in. (12.38cm) high. (Tom Walford collection, Luxmoore, Plate 25)*

Colour Plate 51. **Partially reconstructed milk jug and teapot,** *drab-coloured salt-glazed stoneware with jewel-like white sprigging characteristic of Humphrey Palmer. These were both excavated at the Town Road site of Palmer's factory in Hanley. Staffordshire, Humphrey Palmer, c.1750-55. Milk jug 3½in. (8.89cm) high. (Potteries Museum and Art Gallery, Stoke-on-Trent, K3.552.1985)*

Colour Plate 52. **Group of four drab wares,** *salt-glazed stoneware with drab-coloured bodies and white sprig relief and white handles and spouts and finials. The planter and stand and two teapots have the jewel-like sprig relief characteristic of Humphrey Palmer's factory at Hanley. Similar grape and vine leaf sprigging was also excavated at the Palmer site. Staffordshire, all possibly Humphrey Palmer, c.1750-55. Planter 4⅛in. (10.48cm) high. (Potteries Museum and Art Gallery, Stoke-on-Trent, left to right, 3581, 243P 1965, 912, 3544)*

Brown salt-glaze is not our concern, but shapes have survived in what is now called 'drab ware', probably 'ash' in the eighteenth century. In 1750, Dr. Pococke commented that 'they [Staffordshire potters] make Dove-colour and Brown',[44] 'Dove' possibly a reference to drab or 'ash' (Fig. 49, Colour Plates 48-52). Angerstein referred to grey crockery being made in Staffordshire in 1754, but it is not clear whether he is referring to salt-glazed or to lead-glazed ware. He noted

In order to make the grey or so-called embossed crockery, a grey flour is mixed in. In this way it is also possible to make marbled crockery by mixing grey clay with white. That which is grey or decorated with other colours must be fired twice, namely once for the ordinary glazing with salt, and a second time for the blue colour or enamel, which, as I was told, is mixed with clay.[45]

By 'embossed' or 'Bost' ware, Angerstein seems to mean pressed plates and dishes, and he does not mention pressed hollow-ware.[46] He wrote under 'Hanley' that 'plates and dishes that are embossed are first formed roughly to shape, then allowed to dry somewhat in front of a fire before pressing, illustrating both round and octagonal dishes on a rack before a blazing open fire. Earlier, Angerstein had written that 'Bost [embossed]' ware or 'fine pots of light yellow colour' were made by Wilson at Newcastle-under-Lyme, and at Burslem he had distinguished between white ware, tortoise-shell, 'bost', black and red ware. His Burslem price list is headed '*Sales Prices of embossed* [authors' emphasis] *and tortoise-shell ware*' but includes (salt-glazed) white ware, cream colour ware with lead glazing, 'Bush'[47] grey colour with lead glazing, red china not glazed, agate ware, lead glazed and finally and most expensive, white ware, enamelled.[48]

Either a different colour of clay, or some kind of metallic stain (Angerstein's 'grey flour') seems required, for the body colour to be darkened. *Thomas Wedgwood IV of Overhouse* supplied 'Ash coloured' to London dealers in 1753. *Thomas and John Wedgwood* sold various shapes in 'Ash' between 1770 and 1772: teapots, saffron pots, flower pots and stands, jugs and beakers, including flower pots and stands and pint and quart jugs 'Sent to Mr. Brindley for his son to take to America in Mar 1772'. Their crate book also mentions teapots, white ground with ash sprigs in various sizes in 1770.[49] The dates given depend on surviving documents, and there are surviving examples of 'drab ware' which appear of earlier manufacture than 1750-1770.[50] Salt-glazed 'agate' cats are known, made of mingled white and grey clay.

A drabware teapot with white sprigging was recovered from the Town Road, Hanley site. Described as a 'waster', it was probably made by *Humphrey Palmer*, on the site from 1750. Enoch Wood used the term 'Ash colour' in 1835 and 1836,[51] but specimens from his own collection were catalogued as 'Drab-coloured ware' from 1855.[52]

Shaping
Throwing and moulding are the methods of shaping the prepared clay into vessels. For Staffordshire, Plot referred only to the wheel for making either hollow or flat redware c.1680,[53] which could have been shaped solely by hand, though scrapers or elementary profiles[54] were probably used to finish the ware. *John Dwight* in Fulham was making much more sophisticated brown and white salt-glazed ware. If his accusations of plagiarism against other London, Nottingham and Staffordshire potters from 1693 onward have any substance, those potters were also using his techniques. Staffordshire potters *Joshua Astbury* and *Samuel Edge* had lathes as well as wheels by 1721, whilst *Fenton and Hill* named not only lathes but also moulds when they parted in 1722.

Wheels may have been kick-wheels at this early date, the turntable rotated by a flywheel below, kicked round by the thrower himself, either directly or by kicking a bar attached to a cranked spindle. In 1747, Campbell in *The London Tradesman* described the activity:

The Potter uses a Wheel, which he turns round with his Foot. The Clay he makes up into Lumps, according to the Largeness of the Cup, Plate or other Vessel he intends to form; he places one of these lumps upon the Head of the Wheel before him; which he turns round while he forms the Vessel with his Finger and Thumb.[55]

Campbell was probably writing of London tin-glaze and stoneware potters.

The crank wheel, where a boy pushed a rod attached to a crank, was an advance on the cranked kick-wheel, as it relieved the thrower from actually turning the wheel, probably enabling him to make finer vessels. Angerstein described and illustrated another type of crank wheel in use at *Prescot*, where the boy worked a remote crank, connected to the throwing-wheel by pulleys and cord, and a string or great wheel also used there.[56] At Hanley in 1754 he noted that 'a potter's wheel is used for throwing, but it is always turned by a boy to increase the speed', and illustrated a great wheel.[57]

Jars described throwing with the great wheel in Staffordshire in 1765: 'All the vessels which are not to be shaped are made on a wheel with a vertical shaft kept in motion by a little boy turning a wheel'.[58] Arthur Young had visited the Potteries by 1770, and he noted the great wheel in use: 'A boy turns a perpendicular wheel, which, by means of thongs, turns a small horizontal one, just before the thrower'.[59] These detailed descriptions suggest that the string wheel was of recent introduction. Famously, Thomas Bentley *turned the wheel* for Josiah Wedgwood to throw their 'First Day's Vases' on 13 June 1769.[60] Using information given to him by the Wedgwood family c.1795, John Aikin attributed an improvement which greatly accelerated the potter's wheel to 'an ingenious mechanic in the neighbourhood [of the Staffordshire potteries], Mr. Alsager'.[61] Whoever applied the improvement to the potter's wheel, it could well have been suggested by the familiar spinning wheel. Potter *William Taylor I* of Hanley had both a long and a little (spinning) wheel in his kitchen in 1738.

Thrown ware could be improved by shaping with a

Fig. 62. ***Two partially reconstructed pudding moulds***, *white salt-glazed stoneware in the form of a bundt mould used for puddings or jellies. These were sometimes referred to as 'Turk's cap' moulds. Moulds of this type were slip-cast and have been excavated at both the Greatbatch and Palmer sites and were probably made by other potters as well. Staffordshire, perhaps Palmer or Greatbatch c.1750-70. Right mould 3½ x 7¾in. (8.89 x 19.69cm). (Potteries Museum and Art Gallery, Stoke-on-Trent, 79P 1960, 432)*

profile or paring whilst rotating vertically on the wheel, but the introduction of the lathe enabled the surface and fineness to be adjusted more accurately by rotating horizontally when the pot had dried to 'leather-hardness'. ('Carved' ware is recorded in the 1760s, but it is not known whether the 1760s carved ware was hand-carved or made with a particular moulding.) Lathes were already in general use by metalworkers and woodworkers,[62] so that they were available for adaptation to the use of the potter. London potters seem to have lacked lathes in the early eighteenth century,[63] although it has been convincingly argued that *John and David Elers*, who moved from Fulham to Staffordshire c.1691, used lathes in Staffordshire.[64] In 1743 Wilkes was told that the Elers employed a local joiner to make lathes,[65] so that the 'know-how' was available locally before 1700.

Native Staffordshire potters certainly had simple lathes by 1721. *Joshua Astbury* left three lathes and two wheels then, and *Samuel Edge* left two of each, whilst Fenton of *Fenton and Hill* kept the lathes when he and Hill parted in the same year. Later potters followed Astbury in having more lathes than wheels: *'Doctor' Thomas Wedgwood II* left two lathes and one wheel in 1737 and *Thomas Wedgwood IV of Overhouse* had one wheel but three lathes and a hand lathe when he died in 1773. This proportion reflects Simeon Shaw's assessment of '[one] thrower, two turners' amongst the employees of a pottery up to 1740.[66] Like the child to turn the wheel, the separation of turning from throwing was a further division of labour. One thrower could keep two or three turners working, making a more uniform product.

Only circular forms could be made on wheels and lathes. Hollow-ware (mugs, jugs, jars, bowls) are obvious examples of the thrower's craft, but plates and dishes could also be made on the wheel. It was stated in 1970 that 'there is as yet no unequivocal evidence that white salt-glaze plates were made before the early 1740's',[67] and no evidence has been found since. However, absence of evidence is not evidence of absence, and the question remains open. Tin-glaze plates and dishes were made in plenty before 1740 and it seems surprising that the salt-glaze potters did not challenge the pewterers and tin-glaze potters for this important market. Unfortunately, Shelton Farm (see *Fenton and Hill*) where white salt-glazed ware was only made between 1720 and 1722 yielded 'no plates in stratified levels'.[68]

The nineteenth century 'jigger' for plate-making is only an adaptation of a potter's wheel, requiring a hump mould to give the internal shape and a hand-held profile[69] to form the under-side of the plate or dish, so it seems perfectly possible for salt-glazed plates and dishes to have been made at an earlier date than 1740.

Moulding

'Moulding', shaping the pot, ranges from the potter's wheel to the making of the finest of Wedgwood's jasper ornaments. The wheel itself gives circularity as a first step beyond irregular hand-made pottery, and the simple gauge stick, stuck in a lump of clay beside the wheel, is the next aid, enabling the thrower to make pots of uniform height and diameter of rim. Even the humble redware butter pot had to have uniform capacity and be marked. An Act of 1662 required butter pots to contain fourteen pounds of butter and to be marked with the empty weight and the maker's name. An example, stamped 'W DANIEL' round a figure 4, was excavated in Burslem in 1955, the stamp an early use of a mould.[70] A hand-held profile gives regularity of shape, and callipers help the lathe turner to maintain regularity of diameter. 'Turning', whether done on the wheel or on the lathe, gave the opportunity for simple decorative effects, such as incised lines or 'pedestal' footrims. In our field of salt-glazed ware, ornamental moulds had been used to apply decoration in Europe from the Middle Ages,[71] taken up by Dwight and his fellow London potters in the late seventeenth century. 'Uniformity' and 'regularity' are the key words: the gauge stick, the profile, callipers and the mould are prepared in

*Fig. 63. **Jug**, a simple thrown white salt-glazed jug with side pouring spout. This jug has a date of 1743 on the bottom, but could have been made any time from the beginning of the 18th century on as the form and handle were not particularly subject to the trends of fashion. Inscribed on the bottom 'the Groyal [sic, or troyal] of ye first oven, Nov. 24 1743'. Staffordshire, possibly Thomas and John Wedgwood, Burslem, 1743. 2in. (5.08cm) high. (Potteries Museum and Art Gallery, Stoke-on-Trent, 233P 1965)*

advance and used repeatedly to achieve identical results.

Moulds can be used to make shapes other than circular, or to give surface decoration to pottery, the decorative element either integral to the shape mould or applied later. Generally speaking, applied ornamental moulds seem to have been used earlier than shape moulds, and the transition may have been from ornamental moulds through handle, spout and feet moulds to complete body shapes. Many other trades used moulds before the British potter. In the vessel trade, goldsmiths, silversmiths, brass workers and pewterers all did so. Whatever the trade, moulds enable the reliable repetition of the modeller's skill by less skilled workers, a step towards mass production.

Distinctions need to be emphasised about the terminology surrounding moulds. The elementary one is between the moulds used by the potter to shape his ware, and the moulds which he produced for kitchen use: salt moulds, jelly moulds and fruit moulds (Figs. 38, 62).[72] The more difficult distinction is in the names used for the successive stages of mould making. Ceramic historians and curators frequently refer to *block* moulds when they are really describing *models* or *case* moulds. The modeller makes a positive model, from which a negative master block is made. A positive master case is next made, followed by a negative working block. Actual pottery shapes could be made from this, but for mass production a further two stages are made, a working case and a working mould.[73] A positive mould which shows seams, indicative of itself being moulded, is likely to be a case mould, rather than an original model.[74]

Twenty brass stamps and one copper mould are in the British Museum, carefully catalogued in 1903 as 'stated to have been found in a pot on the site of *Dwight's* works at Fulham about 1865'.[75] Recent detailed study confirms the seventeenth century manufacture of the twenty stamps, themselves cast from positives, and made with metal tangs to attach to wooden handles 'like a bookbinder's stamp'.[76] These stamps are of busts, human and animal figures, natural forms and a single landscape, and the same study identifies three salt-glazed bottles on which the stamps have been used. *John and David Elers* have been shown to have used similar metal moulds for decoration of redware in Staffordshire in the 1690s.[77] The earliest documentary evidence of Staffordshire salt-glaze potters having moulds is when *John Fenton and Thomas Hill* of Shelton Farm dissolved partnership in 1721 and Fenton took 'Modells, Moulds'. From the evidence of recovered shards, these are likely to have been for ornamental sprigs, rather than shapes.

The technique was to fill the negative stamp with soft clay and apply the stamp and clay to the soft clay pot. The clay positive adhered to the pot, the brass stamp accidentally leaving some outline as evidence of the manner of application. One 'Dwight' stamp has been identified as the work of a well-known die-sinker or medallist, an indication of the source of such stamps. In 1763, David Rhodes, then a Leeds enameller, apologised to Josiah Wedgwood because a Leeds engraver was unable to copy a brass mould and he had been obliged to send it to 'Saml. Ellis a very good Dye [sic] sinker at Sheffield',[78] confirming die-sinkers as a source for brass moulds.

Salt-glazed shards found at Shelton Farm show that *Fenton and Hill* used 'roulettes' or 'runners'[79] as well as models and moulds. Runners are like pastry wheels, with a pattern engraved round the rim of a brass wheel, used by the thrower or turner to impress decorative bands around their ware.

Moulds and runners all have to be originated by an artist and it is likely that the early salt-glaze potters bought in ready-made designs from engravers, type-founders, bookbinders or jewellers for their ornamental moulds. The working moulds were made as required in clay, to be fired, or in plaster. Fired clay models and moulds were much more durable than plaster, and some clay models or cases survive, because of their value and essential durability.[80] Brass models were presumably melted down for scrap value. The plaster working moulds were consumables, discarded when too worn for further use. William Pitt, in 1817, suggested that *Ralph Daniel*, a Cobridge potter, brought the idea of using plaster for moulds from France.[81] Born in 1722, Daniel would not have travelled to France before the 1740s, and it is now believed that Elers used plaster moulds in the 1690s.[82]

Joseph Banks epitomised the use of plaster moulds when he noted of his visit to Burslem in 1767 'Plates & dishes are made on a mould of Alabaster burnt or what we call Plaster'.[83] Alabaster itself, available in Staffordshire and easily carved, has been used for models. John Ward recorded in 1843 that 'Mr. Wood has in his Museum many moulds of brass and iron, used by the earlier potters, and several of *chiselled Alabaster*'.[84] Four such alabaster models are in the Potteries Museum and Art Gallery,[85] a positive model in alabaster for a triangular pickle tray, upper and lower moulds for a sweetmeat tray in alabaster, bound in iron, and a single negative heart-shaped alabaster sweetmeat mould, also bound in iron (Fig. 65). These four alabaster

*Fig. 64. **Three master moulds** for white salt-glazed stoneware. Left to right: a floral bordered plate and two leaf dish moulds. Staffordshire, c.1755-65. Plate 10½in. (26.67cm) diameter. (Potteries Museum and Art Gallery, Stoke-on-Trent, 436, 434, 1735)*

moulds must be the original work of a modeller, from which plaster moulds would be taken, and it is notable that they are for simple rather than ornate shapes, suitable for 'chiselling'. Wax is also a material used for modelling. Eighteenth century waxes survived in Wedgwood's Etruria Works, included in the Wedgwood Museum by 1909.[86]

Small ornamental moulds were used to commemorate the capture of Portobello by Admiral Vernon in November 1739. A white salt-glazed mug with sprigs of ships, cannon, a fortified seaport and figures of Vernon is in the Victoria and Albert Museum (Fig. 14).[87] Similar sprigs were used with white clay on a redware bowl in the British Museum.[88] These survivals suggest the existence then of an independent modeller, seizing the opportunity to sell sets of commemorative moulds c.1740. He or a fellow modeller also made solid teapot models with differing relief decoration commemorating the same 1739 incident, showing that casting or press-moulding techniques were also in use c.1740.[89] When *William Taylor I* of Hanley died in 1738, he left thirty-two sprigs worth 21s. As late as 1762, *John Baddeley* bought sprigs from Jos Giles, a Birmingham engraver, presumably metal master moulds. Birmingham, with its toy, jewellery and button trades, was a convenient source for such thing as sprigs.

The British Museum Portobello bowl shows the attractive contrast of white sprigs on redware, and salt-glaze potters also used this technique: in their case, white sprigs on ash (drab) bodies,[90] ash sprigs on white bodies ('1 peice Teapot w[hi]te ground Ash sprigs'[91]), and brown sprigs and blue sprigs on white.[92] White clay was presumably stained to make the blue sprigs. 'Vining' was used to simulate stems: thin rolls of white clay between, typically, blue 'bunch of grapes' sprigs on an ash body. Staffordshire vined teapots, whether salt-glazed or redware, were well known enough in 1740 to be celebrated in a poem: 'See how the charming vine twines all about! Lord! what a handle! Jesus! what a spout!'.[93] The handle and spout may have been of crabstock form, themselves press-moulded, imitating imported ware from China.[94] Angerstein noted at Hanley in 1754 that 'Flowers and leaves that were placed on teapots were also pressed, but in moulds, and generally of whiter material than the grey base.[95]

The vines and simple handles may have been either hand made or extruded from a box, described by Angerstein at both *Derby* and Hanley in 1754, and illustrated: 'For making handles and small vines to place on the outside of teapots, etc, they had a machine that pressed the clay out through a hole, giving it the same shape as the hole'.[96] Joseph Banks wrote much the same in 1767: 'in the Bottom of which is a hole properly shap'd to answer the pattern intended the top of this is moveable & by the power of a strong screw presses the Clay that is in the Box through the hole which consequently takes the impression its shape & size has given to it'.[97]

Chapter V – Making the Pots

*Fig. 65. **Two alabaster master moulds** for a white salt-glazed stoneware sauceboat and a leaf dish. Staffordshire, 1748 and 1744. Sauceboat 2⅞ x 6½in. (7.3cm x 16.64cm) incised RW 1748 on base; heart (iron bound) 6¾in. (17.14cm) long incised 1744 on rim. (Potteries Museum and Art Gallery, Stoke-on-Trent, 1752, 4351)*

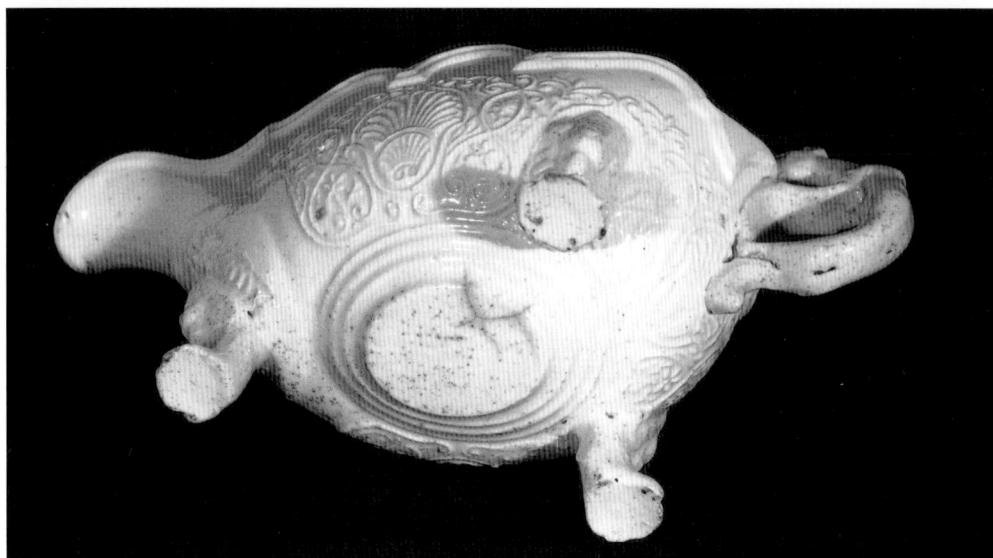

*Fig. 65a. **Sauceboat,** base of white salt-glazed stoneware sauceboat with mould rings and form illustrated in Fig. 65. The sauceboat is shown upright in Fig. 65b.*

*Fig. 65b. **Sauceboat,** white slip-cast salt-glazed stoneware moulded with shell and floral relief. The prominent paws on the lion's head feet contrast with the delicate handle in the form of a salamander. Staffordshire, c.1748-55. 2½in. (6.48cm) high. (Catzen collection, ex Joseph Downs collection)*

'Measure' marks were a specialised form of sprig. From 1700, ale and beer had to be sold in vessels of the correct standard measures, 'stampt or marked' with WR and a crown.[98] The 1700 Act made no provision for altering the sovereign's initials, but AR or GR and crown marks are found. Generally, it is brown salt-glaze mugs which are found with such sprig marks, but later in the eighteenth century, white salt-glazed mugs and jugs were made with crown over GR sprigs. *Thomas Cartlich* of Burslem made crouch (brown salt-glaze) mugs etc. in 1764 for John Douglas of Whitehaven, who urged him to make them 'Right Misers [correct measures] according to orders'. *Samuel Kirk and Co.*, also of Burslem, probably made *white* salt-glazed measure ware, being asked by Douglas for 'small miserd[*sic*] Quart Mugs' in 1763, suggesting that these were to be short measure. To counterbalance, Charles Kinkead of Strabane asked *Thomas Wedgwood IV of Overhouse* in 1764 for goods 'large in the mes [measure]'.

Plain circular objects were made by wheel and lathe (Fig. 63), but other shapes and those with integral decoration required moulds, made from an original model. Imported Chinese redware was an early source, along with silver.[99] One indirect Chinese source was Johan Nieuhoff's 1665 travel book *An Embassy from the East-India Company…*, shown to be the source for many low-relief scenes on teaware and a few three-dimensional figures, in salt-glazed stoneware (Colour Plate 54a).[100] Within the Potteries copying of designs was and is rife. In 1914 a Potteries designer wrote 'we have been infringing one another's moral copyright ever since potteries of any importance existed in the district, and probably will do to the end'.[101] In the eighteenth century buyers could order the same or very similar designs from many potters.

It was a natural progression from throwing pots from soft body to pressing the same body into moulds for both ornaments and shapes. For hollow-ware, moulds could be a single mould, or in two or more parts. The single mould is typified by a fluted cup mould found at *Dwight's* Fulham site.[102] It has, and any one-piece mould must have, at least a slight flare outward to release the slightly shrunken pressed (or cast) cup or bowl. A single mould or the parts had to be lined with a layer of body, the parts assembled and the seams made up with strips of body, then left to dry and shrink away from the mould. Moulds so used were quite durable, needing only superficial drying before re-use. 'Pressers' who performed this operation, were considered less skilled than throwers, being paid 8s. to 9s. a week in 1769, compared with the thrower's 9s. to 12s.[103] ('Handlers, who fix hands, and other kinds of finishers, for adding sprigs, horns &c.' were paid as throwers.)

Although liquid body (slip) had been used traditionally for decoration, drying out on the surface of the decorated pot, casting seems likely to have come into use later than pressing. When used for casting shapes in plaster moulds, the mould parts had to be held tightly together, filled with slip and left for a crust to form inside as the plaster took up moisture from the slip. Surplus slip was poured off, and the cast left in the mould to harden by drying.[104] Moulds so used had to be thoroughly dried after each use, deteriorating more quickly than press-moulds, so that more moulds were needed. This expense was somewhat counterbalanced by the lower cost of casting: casting was quicker than pressing and 'Moulders in plaister of *Paris*' were paid only 8s. per week in 1769, slightly less than the pressers mentioned above.[105]

Casting produced lighter, finer shapes than did pressing. Angerstein wrote of slip-casting of *Derby* porcelain in 1754 and, although he hardly mentioned moulding in Staffordshire, he quoted the cost of 'Plaster of Paris from Derbyshire for the moulds' at 18 pence a hundred-weight.[106] Brolliet described slip-casting in England in 1759[107] and in 1765 Jars described press-moulding of handles and slip-casting of spouts in *cream-coloured ware* at Newcastle-upon-Tyne, but only press-moulding of salt-glazed ware in Staffordshire.[108] Of course, this is not to say that slip-casting was unknown in Staffordshire, merely that Angerstein and Jars failed to mention it. (It has been shown that the Elers brothers practised slip-casting in Staffordshire before 1700.[109])

John Baddeley bought 'Blocks' from a *John* Greatbatch in 1761-62.[110] Assuming that our understanding of the nomenclature is correct, Baddeley was buying negative master moulds, the modeller retaining his master models, from which they were made. Baddeley also sold block moulds to *Samuel Chatterley* in the same period,[111] showing, unsurprisingly, that moulds were traded between potters. *Thomas Wedgwood IV of Overhouse* fired '3 Sagers ful of modles [*sic*]' and 'one Sager with Fruit modles' for *(Aaron), Thomas and John Wedgwood* in 1770.[112] *Thomas Wedgwood IV of Overhouse* had moulds in his 'stove house' when he died in 1773.

As has already been remarked, fired clay models and moulds were much more durable than plaster, and some clay models or cases survive, because of their value and durability. Examples are to be found in various collections, surveyed by Charles Luxmoore in 1914 (*sic*), Arnold Mountford in 1971, and most recently by Miranda Goodby in 1998.[113] Luxmoore gave a painstaking listing with illustrations of moulds then in the British Museum, Victoria and Albert Museum, the then Hanley, Stoke-on-Trent and Burslem Museums, the Liverpool Museum, and the Wedgwood Works Museum, then at Etruria, together with moulds in private collections at that time: his own and those of Dr. Sidebotham, the late L. Jahn and the late M. Solon. Almost all were positive models or case moulds, a few of them alabaster, wood or metal. Mr. Mountford drew upon the moulds in the Potteries Museum, almost all positive models or cases in pitcher clay or plaster. Exceptions are the alabaster models referred to above (Fig. 65).

Models require modellers to make them, persons with artistic ability. In Britain there had been modellers in stone, plaster, gold, silver, brass, pewter and similar trades for centuries before refined pottery was attempted. These modellers were available to teach apprentices and also to provide the originals from which similar pottery shapes could be created. In Birmingham, only forty miles from the

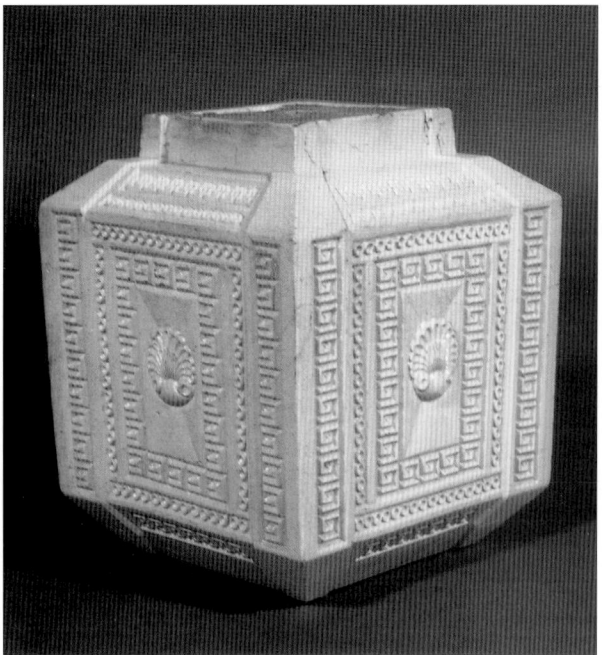 

*Fig. 66. **Master mould for a teapot** body in white salt-glazed stoneware. The four-sided body is decorated with Greek key and shell motifs and would have been a teapot which was not square but as viewed in a diamond shape. Staffordshire, c.1745-55. 4⅝in. (11.75cm) high. (Potteries Museum and Art Gallery, Stoke-on-Trent, 1745)*

*Fig. 67. **Master mould for a teapot** body in white salt-glazed stoneware. The four-sided body is decorated with Greek key and shell motifs similar to the one illustrated in Fig. 66. Staffordshire, c.1745-55. 4¾in. (12.07cm) high. (Potteries Museum and Art Gallery, Stoke-on-Trent, 1744)*

*Fig. 68. **Master mould for a teapot and the teapot** in white salt-glazed stoneware in the form of a shell. Staffordshire, c.1745-55. Teapot 4⅛in. (10.48cm) high. (Potteries Museum and Art Gallery, Stoke-on-Trent, 1714, 68P56)*

nascent Potteries, there were 'Two or Three Drawing Schools established in Birmingham for the Instruction of Youth in the Arts of Designing and Drawing'[114] in 1759. Chester, some thirty miles away and whence came to the Potteries the earliest supplies of ball-clay, had gold- and silversmiths from the sixteenth century.[115] Liverpool, fifty miles distant from the Potteries, had artists in the 1730s.[116] Indeed, the sister of the famous Potteries modellers, Ralph and Aaron Wood, married a Liverpool artist, William Caddick (1719-1795). Aaron Wood's son, Enoch Wood, was sent to Caddick's sons in Liverpool at the age of eleven in 1770 to learn drawing[117] and became a modeller and later a master potter. Newcastle-under-Lyme, market town for the Potteries, had its humble pewterer from as early as 1607.[118] 'Art education' was undoubtedly available in the provinces in the eighteenth century.

Some almost contemporary information about the principal eighteenth century Staffordshire modellers is given in a letter of 31 March 1805 from Thomas Byerley at Etruria to Josiah Wedgwood II in Dorset.[119] Their long-

*Fig. 69. **Master mould for a hexagonal teapot** in white salt-glazed stoneware. This is a favourite form with panels of Chinese figures in various activities and is seen more commonly in teapots in red stoneware and in multi-coloured oxide decoration in earthenware. Although shards of the same moulded relief have been found in both the Whieldon site at Fenton Vivian and at the Greatbatch site, the attribution remains indefinite because it appears this was a popular pattern and it is found on many other Staffordshire sites. (See Barker and Halfpenny,* Unearthing Staffordshire *(Stoke-on-Trent: City of Stoke-on-Trent Museum and Art Gallery, 1990, 56). Staffordshire, c.1760. 4in. (10.16cm) high. (Victoria and Albert Museum, 326-1889)*

*Fig. 69a. **Master mould for a hexagonal teapot,** another view.*

*Fig. 69b. **Master mould for a hexagonal teapot,** another view.*

time modeller, William Wood, had asked for an increase of salary and told Byerley that when he (William Wood) was almost out of his apprenticeship to Josiah Wedgwood I (c.1770[120]), he told Josiah I that 'at that time there were only 3 modellers in all the country. – W.G., Bullock and W.W.'s father'. 'All the country' means North Staffordshire. 'W.G.' was *William Greatbatch*, still working at Etruria when Byerley wrote in 1805 and well known enough to Byerley and his addressee for his initials to be understood. 'W.W.'s father' was Aaron Wood. 'Bullock' is much less known.

John Mallet noted that *John Baddeley* bought models from 'Bullock' in 1758, and from 'W. Bullock' in 1761, and that William Bullock was an 'earth potter' in Shelton in 1758.[121] A William Bullock was baptised at Stoke-on-Trent on 26 December 1716, son of John and Lydia, and a man of the same name married Elizabeth Barker at Stoke on 26 January 1741. They had a son named William, baptised at Stoke 1 November 1750.[122] It is possible that 'Bullock' was William Bullock baptised in 1716 and that it was his son, also William, baptised in 1750, who went on to be a jeweller, silversmith and chinaman in Liverpool c.1805.[123]

The brothers Ralph Wood (1715-1772) and Aaron Wood (1717-1785) are traditionally credited as the major modellers of salt-glazed pottery shapes. Ralph Wood was born in 1715, son of Ralph Wood, miller, and died in 1772. He had four daughters, and three sons, *Josiah, John and Ralph Wood (II)*, who all became master potters. Ralph Wood's reputation as a modeller rests on the numerous surviving models bearing his name or initials. It has been suggested that the Ralph Wood inscriptions denote prospective ownership rather than origin,[124] but no evidence has been found of this Ralph Wood being a master potter, and the obvious conclusion is that he was the maker of these models.

Chapter V – Making the Pots

Fig. 70. **Tea canister** *in white salt-glazed stoneware press-moulded with the same Chinese man holding a bird on a pole as in the master mould in Fig. 69b. The decoration was inspired by George Edwards and Matthew Darly's* New Book of Chinese Designs, *London 1754 – see Williams and Halfpenny,* A Passion for Pottery: further selections from the Henry H. Weldon Collection, Colonial Williamsburg Foundation *(New York: Sotheby's Publications, 2000, Pl. 12). Staffordshire, c.1760. 4⅛in. (10.48cm) high. (The Henry H. Weldon Collection, Colonial Williamsburg Foundation, photography by Gavin Ashworth)*

Colour Plate 53. **Tea canister,** *white salt-glazed stoneware press moulded in a square form with a Chinese woman and child. A shard of red stoneware with the same moulded relief was excavated on the Fenton Vivian site of Thomas Whieldon as illustrated in H.C. Goldweitz, 'An American Collection of English Pottery: A Chronology 1635-1778',* ECC Transactions, *Vol. XII, Part 1, 1984, Pl. 26. However, as has been pointed out by Barker and Halfpenny (Fig. 69), these were popular and have subsequently been found in several Staffordshire sites. Staffordshire, c.1760. 4½in. (11.43cm) high. (Harriet Carlton Goldweitz collection)*

Fig. 71. **Master mould for a teapot** *of octagonal form moulded with birds and game, some with heraldic coats of arms. Staffordshire, c.1745-5. 4⅛in. (10.48cm) high. (Potteries Museum and Art Gallery, Stoke-on-Trent, 236P65)*

*Colour Plate 54. **Master mould for a teapot** of octagonal form with panels of figures, birds and animals and heraldic motifs. Staffordshire, c.1745-50. 4⅞in. (12.38cm) high. (Victoria and Albert Museum, 2158-1901)*

*Colour Plate 54a. **Teapot,** white salt-glazed slip-cast stoneware moulded with panels from Johan Nieuhof's AN EMBASSY sent by the EAST-INDIA Company...to the GRAND TARTAR CHAM or EMPEROR OF CHINA, published in English in 1669. The photograph shows the 'Young Vice-Roy of Kanton' seated astride his horse. For further elucidation of the iconography of the teapot see L. Grigsby, The Henry H. Weldon Collection of English Pottery 1650-1800 (London: Sotheby's Publications, 1990), 66-7. Staffordshire, c.1745. 4½in. (11.43cm) high. (The Henry H. Weldon Collection, Colonial Williamsburg Foundation, photography by Gavin Ashworth)*

*Colour Plate 55. **Master mould for a teapot** of round form with a king and queen on one side and angels on the reverse. Staffordshire, c.1750. 4⅜in. (11.11cm) high. (Victoria and Albert Museum, C.87-1918)*

*Colour Plate 56. **Master mould for a house teapot** of Georgian style with three floors and a prominent slate roof and chimney. Staffordshire, c.1750. 6⅛in. (15.56cm) high. (Private collection)*

Chapter V – Making the Pots

*Fig. 72. **Teapot and master mould for the teapot body** in the form of a Georgian three storey house with figures in the doorway and a lion rampant above. Staffordshire, c.1750. 5⅛ and 4¾in. (13.02 and 12.07cm) high respectively. (Potteries Museum and Art Gallery, Stoke-on-Trent, 238P 1965, 3648)*

*Fig. 73. **Cream jug and master mould for the body.** The jug is moulded with reserve panels of a chinoiserie figure holding a parasol and large birds, one in flight. Mould impressed LONDON. Staffordshire, c.1750. 2¼ and 3⅜in. (5.72 and 8.58cm) high respectively. (Potteries Museum and Art Gallery, Stoke-on-Trent, 3656, 437)*

*Fig. 74. **Cream jug and master mould for the body.** The jug is moulded with variations of shell motifs. An identical mould is in the collection of the Victoria and Albert Museum marked RW 1749. Staffordshire, c.1749. 3½in. and 4¼in. (8.89 and 10.8cm) high respectively. (Potteries Museum and Art Gallery, Stoke-on-Trent, 922, 1724)*

CHAPTER V – MAKING THE POTS

*Fig. 75. **Master mould for a sauceboat and the sauceboat** moulded in the mosaic pattern. Mosaic pattern was popular from at least 1755, frequently being mentioned as such in invoices and advertisements. By 1763 the description of the same still popular pattern was generally 'basketwork'. The original model for this moulded sauceboat was done by Aaron Wood c.1755-57. 4¾in. and 7¾in. (12.07 and 19.69cm) long respectively. (Potteries Museum and Art Gallery, Stoke-on-Trent, 1729, 2832)*

Almost all our information about Ralph Wood comes from the records of *Thomas and John Wedgwood*, Burslem salt-glaze potters, held in the Potteries Museum and Art Gallery,[125] and from surviving signed models. Ralph Wood rented a house from Thomas and John Wedgwood in 1757, moved to their house 'at the Red Workhouse' in 1764, and was paying rent to them in 1770. The records show that Ralph Wood was employed by Thomas and John Wedgwood in 1757, 1758, 1763, 1767, 1768, 1770 and 1772, and his death on 11 December that year was noted by John Wedgwood. They paid him 9s. a week in 1763, a very similar wage to that of 'Useful' Thomas Wedgwood's £22 a year, when he agreed to serve his cousin Josiah Wedgwood I for six years in 1759,[126] both undoubtedly senior employees.

To quote the most recent writer on the subject,[127] 'At least fifteen moulds survive inscribed 'R.W' or 'Ralph Wood', and several of these are dated, ranging from 1748-1770'. As far as can be ascertained, all these are positive models from which the negative blocks, positive cases and negative working moulds were to be made. Most are salt-glazed and therefore high-fired, desirable both for durability and the sharpness of detail preserved.

Unlike his brother Aaron, Ralph Wood had no antiquarian son to promote his status as a modeller and thus he was not known to Pitt or Shaw, but, taking rent, wages and models together, the impression received is that Ralph Wood was a modeller, working continuously for Thomas and John Wedgwood from at least 1757 to 1772. It is likely that an eighteenth century modeller would also have been occupied in producing working moulds for his employer or customers.

Aaron Wood (1717-1785) has only one signed model to commemorate him. The only contemporary evidence of his work as a modeller is a single model for a spittoon, signed Aaron Wood, in the British Museum since 1891 (Fig. 77). It is described as 'Chinese shape, with globular body and spreading mouth; made of thick salt-glazed ware; ornamented with scallop-shells and vines in two compartments; fluted rim, with incised signature *Aaron Wood*', height 5¾in. (14.61cm).[128] As Aaron Wood is not known to have been a master potter, it can be accepted that his signature on the spittoon model is as modeller, not owner. The British Museum 1903 catalogue states that 'the best known basket-work pattern has been traced to Aaron Wood by means of a mould of his dated 1759',[129] also referred to by Professor Church in 1894,[130] but to which no present-day reference has been found by the authors.[131]

Two indentures have been published, neither of which makes any reference to Aaron Wood as a modeller. The earlier one states that Aaron Wood was apprenticed to *Dr. Thomas Wedgwood* from 11 November 1731 for seven years, to learn turning in the lathe, handling and trimming (but not throwing). The second, starting five years after the expiry of the first, shows that *John Mitchell*, earth potter, hired Aaron Wood, earth potter, for seven years from 11 November 1743, to 'perform all such service and business whatsoever relating to the trade of an earth-potter', for which Wood was to be paid 7s. a week during the seven years, and also 10s.6d. each 11 November. Wood was required to keep Mitchell's secrets, pay all money received to Mitchell and make account of all his activities to

Mitchell. Finally, and perhaps most significantly, Wood 'shall not have person or persons to work with him in the business that the said John Mitchell is to employ him but himself only'.[132] This was no ordinary hiring: Aaron Wood was to know Mitchell's secrets, handle money for him *and to work alone*, implying that Wood was to do original work, not to supervise staff.

Aaron Wood was born in 1717, married by 1740, had eight children and died in 1785.[133] His youngest son, Enoch Wood (1759-1840), himself a modeller, master potter and antiquarian, seems to have provided all other information about his father's activities. William Pitt, writing in 1817, transcribed the indentures and commented '7s. per week was considered sufficient for a man who was a modeller, and had the full management of the largest manufactory in the Pottery'. As the indenture does not include this information, it seems likely that Pitt is repeating Enoch Wood's remarks about his father. Pitt also wrote that Aaron Wood 'whose business it was to make models for the potters' imitated a plaster mould brought by Ralph Daniel from France.[134] In his own copy of Pitt's *History*, Enoch Wood noted that he helped his father to scrape off the seeds from the Barleycorn Pattern which Aaron Wood had previously modelled, to make a shape which became known as 'Queen's Pattern' in creamware.[135]

Twelve years later Simeon Shaw had the full cooperation of Enoch Wood whilst writing his *History* and we learn that Aaron Wood continued to work for Dr. Thomas Wedgwood after the end of his apprenticeship, that after leaving Mitchell he worked for different masters including *Thomas Whieldon*, and that he always worked alone. For Whieldon he made models and moulds of many different articles.[136] Some confirmation of Wood working for Whieldon is provided by an entry in Thomas Whieldon's notebook for 1 May 1753: 'Sett [*sic*, set, i.e. leased, rented] Mr Wood the house at the Mill Garden & find him fire & candle light p[er] year [£]3.3.0 paid 25 May 1754'.[137] As Aaron Wood was said always to work alone, the house may have been a workshop, rather than a residence. Enoch Wood himself wrote that his father was 'foreman to Whieldon at Stoke',[138] and told Shaw that his father pointed out to him 'a room, at Fenton, in which he produced the best models used by Mr. Whieldon'.[139]

Thomas Wedgwood IV of Overhouse was another of the 'different masters' for whom Aaron Wood worked. There was a

*Fig. 76. **Master mould for a teapot** commemorating the victory of Admiral Vernon at Portobello in 1739. Staffordshire, c.1739. 5⅛in. (13.02cm) high. (Potteries Museum and Art Gallery, Stoke-on-Trent, 713)*

*Colour Plate 57. **Teapot,** white salt-glazed stoneware, commemorating the Portobello victory in 1739, but not taken from the master mould in Fig. 76. Staffordshire, c.1740. 5½in. (14cm) high. (The Henry H. Weldon collection, Colonial Williamsburg Foundation, photography by Gavin Ashworth)*

CHAPTER V – MAKING THE POTS

Fig. 77. ***Master moulds (for making negative moulds).*** *Left a master mould for making a bottle or vase in the mosaic pattern, 9⅞in. (25.08cm) high. Right a master mould for making a spitting pot in a rococo and shell pattern incised* Aaron Wood *on the base, 5¾n. (14.61cm) high. Staffordshire, c.1750s. (British Museum, G 57, G56, gift of Capt. J.R. Lumley, 1891)*

Fig. 78. ***Spitting pot and bottle (vase),*** *white salt-glazed stoneware slip-cast from plaster moulds. The spitting pot is taken from a form commonly seen in tin-glazed earthenware. Left 3½in. (8.89cm) high. Right 4¼in. (10.8cm) high, c.1750-70. (Potteries Museum and Art Gallery, Stoke-on-Trent, 1930.8, 1679)*

89

settlement with him after Thomas Wedgwood's death:

> November 15th 1773 due five shillings to Aaron Wood from a recconing [sic, reckoning] on ye 13th February betwixt him and ye Late Mr. Wedgwood Uper [sic] house Deceas'd [received by] Thos Wedgwood [II][140]

The reckoning may have been for models or moulds supplied by Aaron Wood to Thomas Wedgwood I.

Enoch Wood inscribed several seed and basketwork oval dishes that they were 'Modelled by Aaron Wood about the Year 1760'[141] and left a note on the back of a portrait of Aaron Wood that 'He was modeller to all the potters in Staffordshire at the latter end of the time that white ware or white stoneware was made'.[142] A salt-glazed model for a sauceboat in the Victoria and Albert Museum has been attributed to Aaron Wood, on the evidence of Enoch Wood's inscribed dish.[143]

*Fig. 79. **Sauceboat**, white salt-glazed stoneware double-handled, footed sauceboat, slip-cast with radiating fronds along the lower body and a double row of Greek key relief. Staffordshire, c.1750. 3½in. (8.89cm) high. (Private collection)*

*Fig. 80. **Sauceboat**, white salt-glazed stoneware slip-cast with shell moulded relief, double handles and a flared foot. Staffordshire, c.1750. 2⅜in. (6.03cm) high. (Catzen collection)*

*Fig. 81. **Three sauceboats**, white salt-glazed stoneware with double handles slip-cast with frond and mask head relief (left) and shell relief (middle, right). Staffordshire, c.1750-60. Left to right 5⅞, 7½, 6in. (14.92, 19.05, 15.24cm) long respectively. (Potteries Museum and Art Gallery, Stoke-on-Trent, 1705, 934, 958)*

CHAPTER V – MAKING THE POTS

*Fig. 82. **Sauceboat,** white salt-glazed stoneware with double handles and three mask head and paw feet. The slip-cast relief includes a lion passant, birds and flowers. Staffordshire, c.1750. 3in. (7.62cm) high. (Olive Talbot collection)*

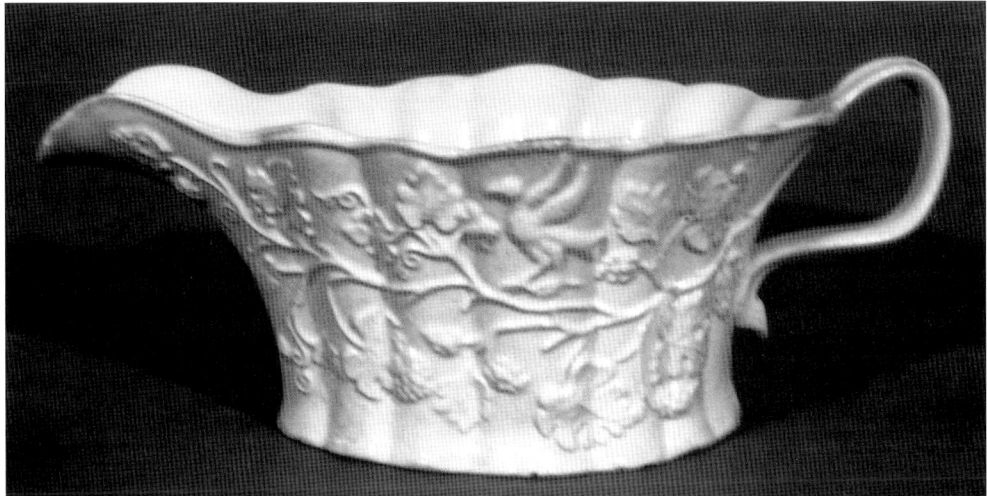

*Fig. 83. **Sauceboat,** white salt-glazed stoneware slip-cast and moulded in scalloped panels of vine and grape leaf relief with an exotic bird. Staffordshire, c.1755-60. 3in. (7.62cm) high. (Olive Talbot collection)*

*Fig. 84. **Sauceboat,** white salt-glazed stoneware with scalloped rim slip-cast with the 'boy in a tree' relief and vines and tendrils, lion mask and paw feet and a crimped handle. Staffordshire, c.1750. 2⅞in. (7.3cm) high. (Olive Talbot collection)*

*Fig. 85. **Four sauceboats** in white salt-glazed stoneware with various slip-cast moulded reliefs. Staffordshire, c.1750-65. 9⅜in. (23.81cm) maximum length. Potteries Museum and Art Gallery, Stoke-on-Trent, left to right, 935, 1699, 3658, 915.*

*Fig. 86. **Sauceboat,** white salt-glazed stoneware press-moulded with enamel colours. The three paw feet and fox handle were all separately press-moulded. The fox handle was also used on tin-glazed earthenware sauceboats. Staffordshire, c.1755. 6½in. (16.51cm) long. (Photograph courtesy of Jonathan Horne)*

*Colour Plate 58. **Sauceboat,** white salt-glazed stoneware with splashes of cobalt oxide. The double-ended sauceboat pours from dolphin spouts and is flanked by double-reeded strap handles. Staffordshire, c.1750. 6¼in. (15.88cm) long. (Harriet Carlton Goldweitz collection)*

CHAPTER V – MAKING THE POTS

Colour Plate 59. **Jug,** *white salt-glazed stoneware slip-cast in shell form with overall enamel colouring. The tripod feet are press-moulded with mask heads terminated by paws. Staffordshire, c.1750. 3in. (7.62cm) high. (The Henry H. Weldon Collection, Colonial Williamsburg Foundation, photography by Gavin Ashworth)*

Colour Plate 60. **Jug,** *white salt-glazed stoneware slip-cast after the 'Goat and Bee' jugs made by the Chelsea porcelain factory in the early triangle period (1745-49). Staffordshire, c.1750. 3⅛in. (7.94cm) high. (The Henry H. Weldon Collection, Colonial Williamsburg Foundation, photography by Gavin Ashworth)*

Colour Plate 61. **Teapot,** *white salt-glazed stoneware press-moulded in panels forming a lozenge shape with applied decorative motifs of flowers and a squirrel. Staffordshire, c.1745-50. 7¼in. (18.42cm) high. (Photograph courtesy of Jonathan Horne)*

Fig. 87. **Teapot,** *white salt-glazed stoneware slip-cast into panel forming a lozenge shape. The panels include one with the Royal seal and another with a seated gentleman and the inscription 'AD VERNON'; on the reverse there are ships in a harbour and 'PORTOBELLO TAKEN'. Staffordshire, c.1745-50. 6in. (15.24cm). (Photograph courtesy of Jonathan Horne)*

Fig. 88. **Bowl,** *white salt-glazed stoneware slip-cast in panels with elaborate exotic birds and foliage. Staffordshire, c.1745-50. 6¾in. (17.15cm) diameter. (Potteries Museum and Art Gallery, Stoke-on-Trent, 1672)*

*Fig. 88a. **Bowl**. White salt-glazed stoneware slip-cast in ten panels: 1) a crowned double-headed eagle with flowers and birds below, and two masks and scrolls above; 2) three women at a table drinking tea with a tea kettle on a hearth between a teapot and a cup and saucer below; 3) naked figure who carries a globe on his shoulder beckoning to a small boy with two cupids holding a crown over an altar below; 4) cloaked man with sword and grapes and a woman with a fan in ?Tudor dress; 5) fox and goose surmounted by a foliated medallion of a bearded and capped head between two masks; 6) trumpeting cherub astride a lion with a swimming swan below; 7) robed man and woman in crown-like caps; 8) reclining nude woman by a vine with a unicorn below; 9) man with bow and staff walking with two dogs by a tree containing a bird; 10) a shield of three fleur-de-lis between a chevron above a running deer and a bird. Staffordshire, c.1745-50. 3⅝in. (9.21cm) high. (Copyright National Museums & Galleries of Wales, A32268, W.J. Grant-Davidson collection)*

*Fig. 89. **Cup**, white salt-glazed stoneware slip-cast in panels of medieval motifs of a virgin capturing the unicorn along with contemporary motifs of shooting scenes. The handle is press moulded utilising a metal prototype. Staffordshire, c.1745-50. 2½in. (6.35cm) high. (Olive Talbot collection)*

*Fig. 90. **Bucket and ladle and two cups**, white salt-glazed stoneware. Bucket, 3¼in. (8.26cm) high. Ladle, 3¾in. (9.53cm) long, Staffordshire, c.1750-60 (A.H. Church collection, bequeathed by Dame Jemima Church, 1929.102, 103). Cup (centre) slip-cast in eight panels of exotic birds, animals and vegetation; 2¾in. (6.99cm) high. Staffordshire, c.1745-50 (Gift of C.D.E. Fortnum, C228 EF). Cup (right), fluted body with flaring rim and reeded strap handle with pinched kick. A rare form in salt-glaze, this form is more commonly seen in creamware; 2½in. (6.35cm) high. (Ashmolean Museum, Oxford, Church collection, 1929.100)*

Fig. 91. **Two mugs,** *of slip-cast white salt-glazed stoneware. The small mug consists of six panels of grotesque figures, birds and animals in relief. The large mug shows on its front a bust of George II and is inscribed 'God Save the/King and My Master'. The sides are covered with roundels and coats of arms representing families of importance. The connection is uncertain except that they were all in office between 1755-56. It may be an anti-Jacobite mug showing loyalty to the King. Staffordshire, c.1755. 4¼in. (10.8cm) high. (Photograph courtesy of Jonathan Horne)*

Fig. 92. **Cup, bowl and coffee pot,** *white salt-glazed stoneware, slip-cast in panels with medieval motifs and heraldry. The bowl has a cobalt blue wash in the panels. Staffordshire, c.1750-55.* Coffee pot 6in. (15.24cm) high. Potteries Museum and Art Gallery, Stoke-on-Trent, 2860 (coffee pot)

*Fig. 93. **Two coffee/chocolate pots,** white salt-glazed stoneware slip-cast coffee pots in lighthouse form cast in panels of grotesque subjects. Staffordshire, c.1745. 8½in. (21.59cm) maximum. (British Museum, left, G60 ex Willett collection; right G61 ex Franks collection)*

*Colour Plate 62. **Teapot,** white salt-glazed stoneware slip-cast with medieval scenes, horses and hounds and tavern motifs. The teapot sits on a flared foot and has a faceted handle, panelled spout and Fo lion finial. Staffordshire, c.1745-50. 6in. (15.24cm) high. (Central Museum and Art Gallery, Northampton, Manfield collection, 1920-1)*

CHAPTER V – MAKING THE POTS

Colour Plate 63. **Pickle dish and bowl,** of white salt-glazed stoneware. Pickle dish, triangular, press-moulded and decorated in enamel colours, the back with a crowned head facing to the right. The mould for this tray is in the Potteries Museum and Art Gallery, Stoke-on-Trent and is attributed by Mountford to Thomas and John Wedgwood of the Big House, Burslem. Staffordshire, c.1745. 5in. (12.7cm) long. Bowl, slip-cast teabowl with scratch-blue decoration, the master mould for which is in the Victoria and Albert Museum. Staffordshire, c.1740-45. 1½in. (3.81cm) high. (Photograph courtesy of Jonathan Horne)

Fig. 94. **Teapot,** white salt-glazed stoneware slip-cast in two parts in upper and lower body moulds. The relief decoration is grape and vine leaves; the round body sits on tripod mask head and paw feet and the cover has a crabstock finial. 4½in. (11.43cm) high. (Catzen collection)

*Colour Plate 64. **Knife haft**, white salt-glazed stoneware moulded with chinoiserie flowers and a bird on a branch. Staffordshire, c.1750-60. 3¼in. (8.26cm) long. (Private collection)*

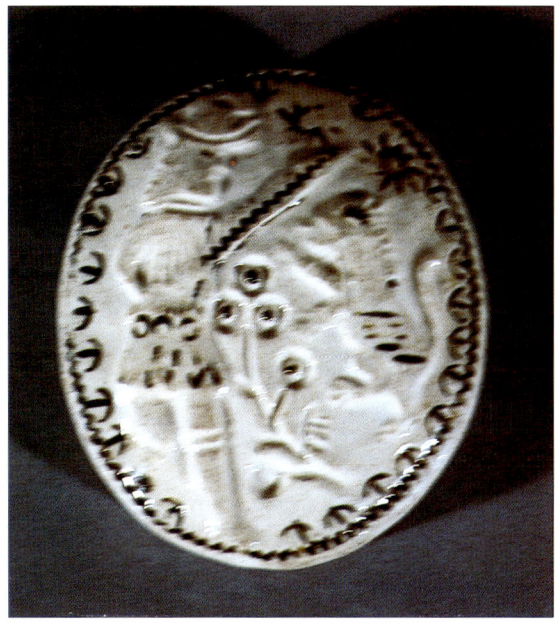

*Colour Plate 65. **Snuff box**, white salt-glazed stoneware moulded with a figure of a male holding a sword and lion rampant, brown slip decoration. Probably Staffordshire, c.1745-50. 2½ x 2¼in. (6.35 x 5.72cm). (Private collection)*

*Fig. 95. **Smelling flasks**, white salt-glazed stoneware press-moulded; left, in the form of a book with dark brown slip; (right) an octagonal flask with moulded relief of a unicorn and a sun face, the border zig-zag relief, Probably Staffordshire, c.1745-50. Both 2in. (5.08cm) high. (Photograph courtesy of Jonathan Horne; the book flask is now in The Henry H. Weldon Collection, Colonial Williamsburg Foundation)*

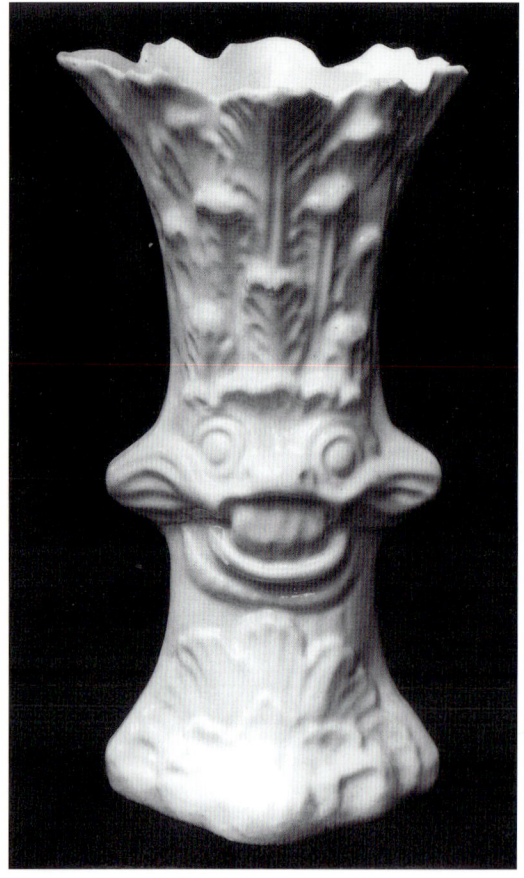

Fig. 96. **Vase,** *in beaker form with swelling middle and a grotesque mask. The press-moulded body is white, salt-glazed stoneware, the form probably inspired by the Limehouse porcelain example in Colour Plate 66. Possibly Staffordshire, c.1750. 4⅞in. (12.45cm) high. (British Museum, ex Willett collection, 1887, G52)*

Colour Plate 66. **Vase,** *soft-paste porcelain manufactured in London at Limehouse between 1745 and 1748 when the factory ceased operation. London, Limehouse, c.1745-48. 4¾in. (12.07cm). (Rod Jellicoe Antiques)*

Fig. 97. **Pew group,** *white salt-glazed stoneware picked out with brown clay. Staffordshire, c.1740. 6½in. (16.51cm) high. (Victoria and Albert Museum. Photograph courtesy of Jonathan Horne)*

CHAPTER V – MAKING THE POTS

*Colour Plate 67. **Pew group,** white salt-glazed stoneware with applied dark brown clay. The group is two trumpeters seated on a bench, the audience being three press-moulded faces appearing on the back of the bench presumably listening to the music with sceptical appreciation. Staffordshire, c.1740. 6½in. (16.51cm) high. (The Henry H. Weldon Collection, Colonial Williamsburg Foundation, photography by Gavin Ashworth)*

*Colour Plate 68. **Figure of a lady,** white salt-glazed stoneware with dark brown clay additions. The lady has her arms flanking her hoop skirt as if in readiness for a party. Staffordshire, c.1730-40. 7½in. (19.05cm) high. (Colonial Williamsburg Foundation, 1965-6)*

*Colour Plate 69. **Bell lady,** white salt-glazed stoneware with dark brown clay additions. The lady, in the form of a table bell, is one of the most sophisticated of its kind. Staffordshire, c.1740-50. 4½in. (11.43cm) high. (The Henry H. Weldon Collection, Colonial Williamsburg Foundation, photography by Gavin Ashworth)*

*Colour Plate 70. **Pair of lovers,** in white salt-glazed stoneware along with another somewhat similar pair in earthenware with underglaze brown clay and slip. Staffordshire, c.1745 and 1755 respectively. 5¼ and 4½in. (13.34 and 11.43cm) respectively. (Photograph courtesy of Jonathan Horne)*

Two models with unrecognised initials survived for Luxmoore to record: a salt-glazed dot-and-diaper sauceboat model with the initials KS incised, in the Victoria and Albert Museum; and another sauceboat model with relief roses and leaves, incised IS, in the Potteries Museum.[144] William Chaffers noted that John Stevenson, a Lowestoft modeller (for whom these initials would be appropriate), went from there to Worcester.[145] 'OB' has been suggested as a 'blockcutter [modeller]' for salt-glazed ware from initials on a jug (not a model) in the Colonial Williamsburg Collection.[146]

John Baddeley bought models from 'Harrop' and 'Bullock' in 1758, and from 'W. Bullock' in 1761.[147] Nothing more is known about Harrop. Baddeley paid a *John* Greatbatch for 'Blocks' on 21 November 1761, and 'Greatbatch' for further blocks around the same time.[148] Shaw credited a John Greatbatch with improving cream-coloured ware, also making the best china glaze, and making a body and a blue-printed glaze for the sons of John Baddeley.[149] At these dates, Baddeley may well have been buying models and blocks for cream-coloured ware, rather than salt-glaze.

Greatbatch is a common surname in the Potteries and *William Greatbatch*, potter and modeller, one of William Wood's '3 modellers', has been thoroughly researched by David Barker.[150] Shaw described William Greatbatch as an 'excellent modeller' making articles, of improved patterns and kinds'.[151] David Barker's research concludes that 'Greatbatch produced white salt-glazed stoneware in the traditional styles' and 'there is nothing to distinguish Greatbatch's [salt-glazed] wares from those of other manufacturers'. Starting business in the 1760s, Greatbatch was sensibly modelling shapes for fashionable creamware, not old-fashioned salt-glaze.

A third method of shaping, and the most primitive, was by hand. Besides human and animal figures press-moulded or cast in the usual way, individual figures and groups were assembled from hand-made parts, occasionally combined with moulded bases, and sometimes decorated with coloured clay[152] (for example, Fig. 97, Colour Plates 67-69).

Thrown or moulded ware, once made, had to be transported between workshops, traditionally done on ware boards five or six feet by one foot (1.5 or 1.8m to 0.3m), nonchalantly shouldered through narrow doorways and up and down rickety staircases. *Richard Daniel* had them as early as 1687, *Samuel Edge* had 108 boards in 1721, *Aaron Shaw III* had forty-nine in 1736, and *Thomas Wedgwood IV of Overhouse* left 500 foot [150m] of Work Boards' in 1773. Similar boards continue to be used.

In the proper order of processes, decoration under the glaze should be described here, but it seems logical to include it with 'on-glaze' decoration, as the interest of the final customer would be in its appearance, not in the technicalities of its application.

Ware, whether thrown, pressed or cast, was made from wet clay and had to be dried before firing, and plaster moulds had

CHAPTER V – MAKING THE POTS

*Colour Plate 71. **Figure of a woman**, white salt-glazed stoneware press-moulded and hand moulded. Staffordshire, c.1745. 7in. (17.78cm) high. (The Henry H. Weldon Collection, Colonial Williamsburg Foundation, photography by Gavin Ashworth)*

*Fig. 98. **Figure of a woman** (possibly Nancy Dawson) press-moulded in white salt-glazed stoneware. Staffordshire, c.1750-60. 4in. (10.16cm) high. (Catzen collection)*

*Fig. 99. **Figure of a bagpiper** press-moulded in white salt-glazed stoneware. Staffordshire, c.1740-50. 9in. (22.86cm) high. (The Henry H. Weldon Collection, Colonial Williamsburg Foundation. Photograph courtesy of Jonathan Horne)*

to be dried out after use. In Plot's 1680s the ware was 'set abroad to dry in fair weather, but by the fire in foule'.[153] Given England's moist climate, indoor and artificial drying was necessary for production on an industrial scale. 'Smokehouses' were the answer.[154] William Gilpen's description of Dwight's drying arrangements in 1698[155] may well be applicable to later 'Smoakhouses' (*sic*):

> the Roome in which it's dried being built to open on three sides for the more conveniency of wind and wether, and at the Close End there is a long Stoave, in which they put the Ashes and Embers that comes from their Furnaces, which keeps it allwayes warme Especially when its shut up close.

Samuel Edge of Burslem left 'smokehouses' when he died in 1721, '*Doctor*' *Thomas Wedgwood II* of Burslem bought 'smokehouses' amongst other pottery buildings in 1731, and in 1763 *William Banks* of Stoke had three 'smoak houses' to dry his ware and moulds.[156]

Of our contemporary reporters, Angerstein saw plates and dishes roughly formed then partially dried before pressing, and illustrated round and octagonal plates on a kind of easel before a roaring coal fire, in 1754.[157] Eleven years later, in 1765, Jars described pressing being 'done in a room with a fire' to keep the moulds dry and ensure the release of the moulded pieces, but both thrown and moulded wares were dried 'in the shade [outside, but not in the sun]',[158] so both Plot's methods were still in use.

Besides being dried, ware had to be 'fettled': thrown ware to be polished on the lathe, whilst moulded ware had the resulting seam ridges removed, sometimes by sponging. Aaron Wood, later famed as a modeller, but apprenticed in 1731 to learn 'turning in the lath[e], handling and *trimming*',[159] stands for all the men, women and children who tidied up the ware before it was fired.

Ovens

Salt-glaze ovens occurred in various designs. All have in common an entrance, firemouths, a firing area and flues. Oblong ovens have a long ancestry: a horizontal stoneware kiln of c.1400 has been excavated at Langerwehe in the Rhineland.[160] In England, Aubrey Toppin suggested that a

Fig. 100. **Group of five figures,** *four in white salt-glazed stoneware, the fifth in solid agate salt-glazed stoneware, all press-moulded. Pug, Staffordshire, c.1745-50, 2½in. (6.35cm) high (Gift of C.A. de Costa Andrade, 1968.380). Grotesque, Staffordshire, c.1745-50, 5¾in. (14.61cm) high (Gift of C.A. de Costa Andrade, 1968.380). Lady candle snuffer, Staffordshire, c.1740-45, 3in. (7.62cm) high (A.H. Church collection, gift of Dame Jemima Church, 1929.53). Ewe and lamb, Staffordshire, c.1755-65, 3½in. (8.89cm) high (Church collection, 1929.56). Lady (foreground), Staffordshire, c.1755 (Andrade collection, 1968.377. Ashmolean Museum, Oxford)*

Fig. 101. **Figure of a man and figure of a dog,** *in solid agate salt-glazed stoneware, the man's eyes picked out in brown slip, decorated with splashes of blue, the pug dog modelled in the same way. Staffordshire, both c.1750-60. Man 4¼in. (10.8cm) high; dog 2¾in. (6.99cm) high. The figure of the man is now in The Henry H. Weldon collection, Colonial Williamsburg Foundation. (Photograph courtesy of Jonathan Horne)*

*Colour Plate 72. **Two figures of 'Zhongliquan'** in white salt-glazed stoneware. One of the Eight Daoist Immortals, these figures are taken from examples originally produced in Chinese porcelain* blanc de chine, *then by Longton Hall. Staffordshire, c.1750. 7⅛in. (18.1cm) high. Another of these figures is in The Henry H. Weldon Collection, Colonial Williamsburg Foundation. (Victoria and Albert Museum, Schreiber collection, Sch. II 92)*

*Colour Plate 73. **Two figures of Louhans**, press-moulded white salt-glazed stoneware, the left figure with traces of gilding and red and green enamel. These Louhans or Buddhist monks are taken from* blanc de chine *porcelain originals from Fujian province. They are seated on lily pads in animated conversation. Staffordshire, c.1750. 4½in. (11.43cm) high. (Potteries Museum and Art Gallery, Stoke-on-Trent, 122 P49, 124 P49)*

square arched room in the cellar of a house in Lime Street, London EC3, was the kiln of Thomas Rous and Abraham Cullen, who obtained a monopoly for making (brown) stoneware in England etc. in 1626.¹⁶¹ Excavation of a c.1650 stoneware site at *Woolwich* revealed an oval horizontal oven base.

John Dwight of Fulham (c.1673-1703), whom we might expect to have experimented with various kiln designs, used a succession of rectangular kilns.¹⁶² C. Green provides a reconstruction on paper of a c.1685 kiln at Fulham, suggesting a rectangular brick structure with a single firing chamber at ground level, with flues in the ceiling to a first floor firing chamber, its arched roof having further flues to a tapering chimney above. It was noted that kiln remains had firing chamber corners blocked off, thought to be done to avoid 'cold spots'. This presaged the circular kiln which eliminated cold corners, although it had its own problem areas. Fragmentary quadrants of a perforated ceramic 'tube' found at Fulham may be the remains of a central vertical flue within a circular oven, another attempt by Dwight to avoid cold spots, this time in the centre of a circular oven.¹⁶³

A rectangular salt-glaze kiln survived in Fore Street, *Bovey Tracey* until the 1930s and was then removed to an industrial site at Heathfield,¹⁶⁴ where it remained in 1996. The potteries at Bovey Tracey in Devon had connections with both London and Staffordshire and this kiln may have been a 'London-type' salt-glazed kiln.

Reinhold Angerstein has left us a sketch of a Hanley pottery kiln which he saw in 1754, a simple domed oven within a hovel, with a doorway into the oven.¹⁶⁵ His sketch shows four semi-circular fireboxes and four salting holes on the shoulder of the dome, suggesting seven or eight fireboxes and holes in all, and a rudimentary scaffolding round the dome. He stated 'The kilns are everywhere in this district built as shown [in drawing no. 318]', unequivocal confirmation of the type of kiln in use in North Staffordshire in the 1750s.

*Fig. 102. **Three figures: Spinario, a Monk, Old Man,** in white salt-glazed stoneware. The figure of **Spinario,** perhaps taken from a Greek marble, inspired many bronze versions from as early as 1165 when the Spinario was recorded as being outside the Lateran Palace (Haskell and Penny, Taste and the Antique (New Haven and London: Yale University Press, 1981, 308). The Spinario is found in several other formats in salt-glazed stoneware (see Colour Plate 74). Staffordshire, c.1745-55. 4⅜in. (10.92cm) high. (Ex Soden-Smith, Franks Collection.) **Old Man,** is enamel decorated and stamped 'OLD AGE'. There is a marked figure by Walton in earthenware of the same form, perhaps taken from the salt-glazed figure. Staffordshire, c.1780. 6¾in. (17.15cm) high. (Ex Franks collection, British Museum, G 44, G45)*

*Colour Plate 74. **Figure of Spinario** in white salt-glazed stoneware press-moulded on a rectangular base. (See comments in Fig. 102.) Staffordshire, c.1755-65. 5¼in. (13.34cm) high. (Harriet Carlton Goldweitz collection, ex Rous Lench collection)*

*Colour Plate 75. **Box** with screw top in the form of a male head, white salt-glazed stoneware with enamel decoration. Staffordshire, c.1755-60. 2in. (5.08cm) high. (British Museum, 1919.5-3, 109)*

CHAPTER V – MAKING THE POTS

*Colour Plate 76. **Crane candlestick**, press-moulded white salt-glazed stoneware painted in enamels. The crane, next to the phoenix, was the most sacred bird in Chinese legend. Dehua figures of cranes came into Europe in the second quarter of the 18th century and may have inspired this English version of which the earliest may be the Longton Hall candlestick in the Victoria and Albert Museum c.1749 to 1753 (Grigsby, The Henry H. Weldon Collection of English Pottery 1650-1800 (London: Sotheby's Publications, 1990, 308). Staffordshire, c.1755-60. 11½in. (29.21cm) high. (The Henry H. Weldon Collection, Colonial Williamsburg Foundation, photography by Gavin Ashworth)*

His description of a circular white salt-glazed stoneware kiln at *Cockpit Hill, Derby* is of a similar oven. Angerstein wrote in 1754 that the whiteware factory had two large kilns. His sketch shows three semi-circular fireboxes with top openings, and three rectangular holes on the shoulder, for salting, suggesting that in the Derby ovens there were six fireboxes and six salting-holes in all. Angerstein stated that the flint or whiteware factory at Derby had originated from Newcastle in Staffordshire c.1751, so it is not surprising that this kiln resembled North Staffordshire salt-glaze kilns of that date.[166] Gabriel Jars observed Staffordshire salt-glaze ovens c.1765,[167] and noted eight firemouths with eight inner flues, brick boxes on the inside of the oven wall which directed the hot gases. The c.1755 salt-glaze oven at *Oxford* was circular.[168]

A French artist, François Joseph Bélanger, drew elevations and plans of two circular kilns,[169] made between 1768 and 1771, which *may* have been at *Derby*. Bélanger's 1768-71 sectional elevation of a salt-glaze kiln is much more sophisticated than Angerstein's 1754 sketches. All three are within protective hovels, but Bélanger's kiln has cylindrical sides and a domed roof whilst Angerstein's domes rise from floor level. Angerstein shows three round fireboxes at Derby

*Fig. 103. **Double crane candlestick**, white salt-glazed stoneware press-moulded. Staffordshire, c.1755. 11¾in. (29.85cm) high. (The Henry H. Weldon Collection, Colonial Williamsburg Foundation, photography by Gavin Ashworth)*

*Colour Plate 77. **Four swans** in press-moulded white salt-glazed stoneware, one pair with blue wash and solid brown clay tongues and the other enamel painted all over, also with blue tongues. Staffordshire, c.1755-60. 7⅝in. (19.38cm) high maximum. (The Henry H. Weldon Collection, Colonial Williamsburg Foundation, photography by Gavin Ashworth)*

*Fig. 104. **Figure of a hawk**, press-moulded white salt-glazed stoneware with brown washed base, enamel painted eyes and beak. Staffordshire, c.1755-60. 8⅞in. (22.54cm) high. (The Henry H. Weldon Collection, Colonial Williamsburg Foundation, photography by Gavin Ashworth)*

(indicating six in all) whilst Bélanger shows five rectangular ones (so ten in total). There is nothing contradictory about these variations: the same kiln may well have been completely rebuilt in the intervening fourteen years, or the drawings may be of different kilns at different works.

Other information about Staffordshire salt-glaze kilns is sparse. An excavation at *William Bourne's* works at 12 Westport Road, Burslem in 1974 revealed part of a floor of bricks laid in a curve, with glaze on the upper surface of some of the bricks.[170] It has been pointed out that salt-glaze ovens were unusable for other glazes.[171] When Staffordshire potters moved on to cream-coloured ware, they may have completely destroyed their salt-glaze ovens, including the bases, to make further use of the oven site.

CHAPTER V – MAKING THE POTS

*Fig. 105. **Figure of a hawk**, press-moulded white salt-glazed stoneware with washed-in enamel colours. Staffordshire, c.1755-60. 6½in. (16.51cm). (Photograph courtesy of Christie's)*

*Fig. 106. **Figure of a bird**, press-moulded in white salt-glazed stoneware. Staffordshire, c.1755-60. 5¾in. (14.61cm) (Photograph courtesy of Christie's)*

*Fig. 107. **Turtle mould, bird, ladle**, all of press-moulded white salt-glazed stoneware. All Staffordshire, c.1760-65. Mould 4⅞in. (12.38cm); bird 4¾in. (12.07cm) high; ladle 6⅛in. (15.56cm) long. (Photograph courtesy of Jonathan Horne)*

An 8ft.6in (2.5m) diameter oven base was noted at the Fenton Low site of *Edward Warburton,* but the reporter did not state that it was for salt-glazed ware. Shaw wrote that oven remains at Bradwell Hall, presumably left behind by *John and David Elers* in 1698 (see *London*) were measured by Enoch Wood and John Riley to be 5ft. (1.5m) inside diameter (so circular), compared by them with c.1700 Burslem ovens of 10ft. or 12ft. (3m or 3.7m).[172] The man who told Shaw that he had demolished this oven said that it was not like the salt-glaze ovens, and Shaw concluded

109

that only redware and black had been made by Elers at Bradwell. In 1817 Pitt noted that Staffordshire salt-glaze ovens were circular and 12ft. or 14ft. (3.7m or 4.3m) wide and 10ft. or 12ft. high (3m or 3.7m) inside, with seven or eight firemouths at equal distances.[173] The evidence available points to Staffordshire salt-glaze ovens being circular, as might be expected.

A hovel, the outer bottle-shaped building around and over the actual oven, was essential for control and enhancement of oven temperature, the lower part protecting the firemouths from the weather and its upper 'venturi' shape increasing the flow of hot gases through the kiln inside. Confirming Angerstein's 1754 sketch of a Staffordshire oven with a hovel, there are frequent documented mentions of hovels in Staffordshire: from *Fenton and Hill* in 1721 through *'Doctor' Thomas Wedgwood II* in 1731, *Humphrey Palmer* in 1750, *Thomas Alders* and *Thomas Taylor II*, both in 1751 and *Peter*

Fig. 108. **Owl jug,** *white salt-glazed stoneware thrown with applied decoration to form the feathers coloured in an iron slip. Staffordshire, c.1750. 8¼in. (20.96cm) high. (The Henry H. Weldon Collection, Colonial Williamsburg Foundation, photography by Gavin Ashworth)*

Colour Plate 78. **Candlestick** *of white salt-glazed stoneware in the form of a tree stump issuing from a rocky mound with shells, flowers, a snail and birds decorated in enamel colours. Staffordshire, c.1760. 10½in. (26.67) high. (Photograph courtesy of Jonathan Horne)*

Fig. 109. **Figure of an owl** *in white salt-glazed stoneware press-moulded. Staffordshire, c.1750. 8in. (20.32cm) high. (Photograph courtesy of Winterthur Museum, gift of Syd Levethan, ex Rous Lench collection)*

CHAPTER V – MAKING THE POTS

Fig. 110. **Figure of a lion,** *slip-cast white salt-glazed stoneware with brown slip eyes. Staffordshire, c.1760. 5⅜in. (13.65cm) high. (Catzen collection)*

Colour Plate 79. **Figure of a 'Dog of Fo',** *slip-cast white salt-glazed stoneware picked out in brown slip. This figure is copied from a Chinese* blanc de chine *original. Extra pieces of clay have been added to the slip-cast figure to enhance the ferocity of the dog. Staffordshire, c.1740. 8in. (20.32cm) high. (Photograph courtesy of Jonathan Horne)*

Colour Plate 80. **'Li tabio on lion'** *(Chinese boy resting on the back of a Fu lion), slip-cast white salt-glazed stoneware with cobalt blue additions. The Chinese exported versions of this figure in the 18th century and it was also produced in Longton Hall porcelain. (L. Grigsby,* The Henry H. Weldon Collection, Colonial Williamsburg Foundation, English Pottery 1650-1800 *(London: Sotheby's Publications, 1990, 292). Staffordshire, c.1750. 3¼in. (8.26cm) high. (The Henry H. Weldon Collection, Colonial Williamsburg Foundation, Colonial Williamsburg Foundation, photography by Gavin Ashworth)*

111

CHAPTER V – MAKING THE POTS

Colour Plate 81. **Rabbit figure** *press-moulded of solid agate salt-glazed stoneware. Staffordshire, c.1745. 3½in. (8.89cm) high. (Colonial Williamsburg Foundation, 1956-389)*

Colour Plate 82. **Cat figure,** *white salt-glazed stoneware with cobalt blue enamel eyes. The press-moulded figure is also seen in Limehouse porcelain c.1746-48. Probably Staffordshire, c.1750. 5⅞in. (14.92cm) high. (Harriet Carlton Goldweitz collection, ex Lowy and Chorley collections)*

Bagnall in 1761, *William Banks* in 1763 to *Thomas Wedgwood IV of Overhouse* in 1773. *William Littler* had 'ovens and ovenhouses' in 1745.

At *Rotherham* in Yorkshire *John Platt* laid the foundations for a new hovel for a 'white flint work' in 1766 and his hovels and kilns were damaged by heavy rain in 1767. All that is known of the *Chester* salt-glaze oven is a 1777 description of 'a large oven with Funnel or pipe… formerly made use of… for the burning or firing of Muggs'.

Bélanger's c.1770 Derby oven had a substantial building around it, with additional vents in the sloping roof, but still in essence a hovel.

Bélanger's c.1770 sketch of a *Derby* oven shows a combustion chamber surrounded by ten firemouths, beneath the actual firing space, somewhat like the paper reconstruction of *Dwight's* c.1685 Fulham kiln, the hot gases going up through holes in the firing chamber floor. Angerstein's 1754 sketches of salt-glaze kilns at Derby and Hanley show no

Colour Plate 83. **Pair of recumbent horses** *in white salt-glazed stoneware resting on grassy pads. Staffordshire, c.1750. Lengths 4⁵⁄₁₆in and 8⅝in. (10.95 and 21.91cm) respectively. (Colonial Williamsburg Foundation, 1961-218)*

*Colour Plate 84. **Bear jug**, thrown white salt-glazed stoneware with clay chips added to the body to simulate fur, and brown enamel collar, paws and eyes. Staffordshire, c.1740. 10⅛in. (25.72cm) high. (Harriet Carlton Goldweitz collection)*

*Colour Plate 85. **Boar figure**, press-moulded white salt-glazed stoneware probably taken from a Meissen figure by J.J. Kaendler. Staffordshire, c.1755-60. 2½in. (6.35cm) high. (The Henry H. Weldon Collection, Colonial Williamsburg Foundation, photography by Gavin Ashworth)*

combustion chamber and vertical half-cylinder fireboxes surrounding the actual firing chamber.

Although ironwork was often valued in inventories, no reference to firebars has been found, suggesting that the fires were laid on the firebox floor.[174] Gabriel Jars, who observed Staffordshire salt-glaze ovens c.1765,[175] made no mention of firebars, but noted eight firemouths with eight inner flues, brick boxes on the inside of the oven wall which directed the hot gases. Later Staffordshire ovens had also under-floor flues taking heat to the centre of the oven, serving the same purpose as Dwight's and Bélanger's under-floor combustion chambers, but Jars makes no mention of these.

Bands, or 'bonts', were oven ironwork which was often mentioned, the iron bars put round the cylindrical oven brickwork to hold it together in the intense heat of firing. *Joshua Astbury* of Shelton had 'ovenbands' which were valued at his death in 1721. Amongst other ironwork valued in inventories are *Samuel Edge's* crowbar, poker and tongs in

*Colour Plate 86. **Saggar with wasters**, white salt-glazed stoneware with holes for allowing the salt-vapour into the saggar for glazing the wares. Not infrequently wares would adhere to the sides, as in this illustration, fused by the salt or collapsed from overfiring. Provenance unknown, c.1740-70. 8 x 14½in. (20.32 x 36.83cm). (Jackfield Tile Museum, Ironbridge Museums Trust)*

Chapter V – Making the Pots

*Colour Plate 87. **Bowl**, white salt-glazed stoneware with scratch-blue decoration of waves and fronds. Staffordshire, c.1750-60. 3in. (7.62cm) high. (Private collection)*

1721 and the 'Pokers & Tongs Iron Rod Ladles & Shovels' of *Thomas Stevenson* of Burslem in 1757.

For heat to pass up and through an oven there must be a means of escape at the top and Angerstein shows the 'crown hole' in his Derby sketch (though not at Hanley).[176] He also shows the salting holes around the shoulder of the oven at both Derby and Hanley, a feature which may have been adopted for the 'quarter-holes' used to control draught on later ovens. Jars postulates eight shoulder holes, sixteen further up and six around the crown hole.

John Baddeley of Shelton paid for a hovel and an oven to be built in 1762, a time when he was making white salt-glazed stoneware, although this oven might not have been for salt-glaze. Obvious payments were for oven bricks, oven work, hovel work, lime (for mortar) for the hovel, and to the bricklayer. Less expected was *ale* in quantity: 14 August, ale at oven 4s.8d., 20 August, ale to hovel this week £1.2s., and finally on 21 August 'Ale at fin[i]s[hin]g Hovell 2s.6d.'.[177]

Saggars

To stack the prepared ware in the oven, it was 'placed' in 'saggars', open-topped drums. For the ware to be salt-glazed, holes were cut in the sides of the drum to allow the salt vapour to penetrate. Also, semi-circular notches were made in the rim so that the saggars could be prized apart when sealed together by the coating of glaze (Colour Plate 86).

Salt-glazed saggar shards are ideal evidence for salt-glaze production. Shards have been found at *Salem* in *America*, and in England at *Bovey Tracey* in Devon, *Chester*, Shropshire, and *Leeds* and *Swinton* in Yorkshire. Saggars were described contemporarily at Derby, at York and probably at Oxford. Whilst Staffordshire salt-glaze ovens are elusive, salt-glazed saggars and shards are frequently found in excavations in the area.

Saggars were made from mixed coarse fire-clay and ground up saggars, beaten out into slabs one or even two inches thick (2.5 or 5cm). Some were thrown,[178] but others were too heavy and were slab-built. The base was formed (knocked) within a metal ring, resting on a shoard (an iron plate). The side-wall was made by wrapping a slab round a wooden drum. The side-wall and base were placed on a saggar wheel, itself merely a turntable, fastened together and the holes cut out.

Thomas Stevenson of Burslem had a saggar wheel in 1757 and the 1773 inventory for *Thomas Wedgwood IV of Overhouse* showed that he had a saggar wheel, shoards and moulds (presumably saggar drums) in his saggar house. When made, saggars themselves had to be fired, probably as in later centuries at the top of the oven, filled with ware but bearing no weight.

Placing and Firing

'Placing' is almost self-explanatory, putting the dried ware into saggars before firing. *John Dwight* of Fulham used small saggars for single items of fine ware, but later potters used larger saggars. Large or small, the pieces of ware had to be separated in the saggar, so that the all-pervading salt-glaze vapour did not stick them together. 'Kiln furniture', not an eighteenth century term, was used for this purpose: small pieces of refractory clay with sharp edges or points. Like saggars, these items are good evidence of local salt-glaze production, noted for instance at *Bovey Tracey* and at *Derby Nottingham Road*, found in profusion at *John Dwight's* Fulham site,[179] and ubiquitously in Staffordshire. Salt-glazed 'stilt rings' form a major part of the evidence for manufacture of salt-glazed ware in *Liverpool*.

David Barker has written exhaustively on 'Bits and Bobs', using eighteenth century terminology for the title of his subject, eighteenth century Staffordshire kiln furniture.[180] Ingenuity born of experience devised many shapes: cones, cylinders, 'crowns', saw-toothed curves, stilts, inverted Ys and saddles are amongst the more sophisticated designs found. Saggar bases were covered with 'bits' (fragments of stone): and 'bobs' (lumps of clay) were primitive separators.

Gabriel Jars epitomised the making of 'supports' in Staffordshire in 1765: 'small children prepare supports which are small pieces of the same clay as that of the saggars, cut into rectangular prisms'.[181] He went on to describe the actual placing: 'While they [the wares] are still moist they are placed on roughly crushed grits which stick all over their surfaces. These grits are placed at the bottom of the saggars and one uses the prisms to support each piece. This is done so that there is no touching. The grits do not stick to the wares'. (See Colour Plate 86 and Figs. 147, 148, 156, 160, 164, 175, 202.)

The saggars were filled with ware, carefully separated by supports, and stacked in columns (*piles* in Jars' French, later called 'bungs') in the oven. Jars postulated that the top saggar in each column had a conical cover, to deflect the salt,[182] and Dr. Watson reported in 1784 'the top [of the saggars] being covered, to prevent the salt from falling upon the ware'.[183] Angerstein mentioned the insertion of 'pyrometers', in Burslem in 1754: 'the crockery should be thoroughly heated right through, which is ascertained by taking out small sample cups with an iron bar and breaking them';[184] and Brolliet wrote of 'small test pieces' at *Oxford* in the 1750s.[185] The finding of a salt-glaze pyrometer gauge at Fenton Low (see *Edward Warburton*) in 1924-25 was reported 'similar to those used later by Josiah Wedgwood' (which were small solid clay cylinders).[186] Angerstein noted that the kiln access entrance had to be bricked up before firing started.[187] An inventory of the contents of a salt-glaze oven, made when *Thomas Wedgwood IV of Overhouse* died in 1773, listed 360 dozen items, possibly 1½ tons in weight.

Firing required fuel. Wood was used for *Dwight's* late seventeenth century Fulham kilns,[188] possibly by the other London potters, and in America, but other salt-glaze potters had access to coal. Coal was the most bulky commodity used in the production of pottery and cheap and easy access was a prime factor in the location of pottery works. Estimates of the weight of coal used for a firing vary widely,[189] but a technical study of the firing of a large modern biscuit oven in 1942 gives 19 tons of coal for 16½ tons of ware.[190] (Angerstein intended to give the consumption of coal per kiln and firing in 1754, but unfortunately for us omitted to complete his text.[191]) Of course, coal was also used for firing the slip-kiln.

Coal was in stock when Walker took over the salt-glaze pottery at *Rotherham* in 1772, but otherwise coal never featured in inventories, probably because it was bought in every week. The accounts of *Thomas Wedgwood V of Overhouse* show that he bought coal weekly in 1782, admittedly when he was making creamware, but it seems likely that this was a long-standing practice. Other salt-glaze potters introduced a measure of vertical organisation by becoming partners in coal mines: see *Joshua Astbury* as early as 1721, *John Meir* in 1729, *John Brindley* in 1760 and *John Hales* in 1776.

Brolliet clearly identified wood as the fuel for a salt-glaze kiln at *Oxford* in the 1750s: 'remove all the wood and embers [from the fire-mouths]' although his correspondent, Hellot, noted that 'In the oven used to fire salt glaze or English ware you use coal'.[192] Angerstein knew about wood-firing at Chelsea porcelain works, but noted at Hanley in 1754 that 'the coal may be a little better in one place than another, which sometimes causes 2 to 3 hours difference in the time taken [for firing].[193] He estimated the firing took three days and two nights at *Derby* (say sixty hours); and forty-four to forty-six hours at Burslem.[194] Jars wrote of 1765 practice that firing in Staffordshire took forty-eight hours in total,[195] whilst Dr. Watson compromised in 1784 at forty-eight hours before salting.[196]

Pitt tells us that 'The *firing* generally commenced on the Thursday evening, and finished on the Saturday following about mid-day, something like 42 hours'.[197] The accounts from *Kirk* to Wedgwood for fired ware were all on Wednesdays: 29 August, 5 September, 19 September and 10 October 1764. The regularity of Wednesdays may signify the day of the week when the oven had been emptied after the traditional weekend firing, or merely the day on which *Kirk and Co.* made their deliveries or did their accounts.[198]

Colour Plate 88. ***Jug****, white salt-glazed stoneware with scratch-blue decoration, on three lion mask and paw feet. The paw feet and handle have been excavated at the Humphrey Palmer site in Hanley and Palmer also, along with nearly all the other Staffordshire potters, produced scratch-blue decorated wares. This jug also shows the translucency of some of Palmer's other wares (see Chapter IX; Fig. 229). Staffordshire, probably Humphrey Palmer, c.1750-55. 3¼in. (8.26cm) high. (Robert Barth collection)*

Salting

Salting to create a glaze is the key element of our subject, and fortunately there is enough contemporary information to provide a fair description of at least the 'Staffordshire' method. In Staffordshire and at Derby the kiln was built with holes around the top, the centre one to allow the hot gases to escape and the surrounding ones to control the air-flow through the kiln and for putting in the salt.[199] Scaffolding with planks was provided around the kiln and ladders for the men to reach it. Salt was bought in from local suppliers for each firing, typically eight or nine bushels a time, about four hundredweight, costing 3s.10d. a bushel.

Salting started after about forty hours' firing, when the heat was at its highest. Two men ascended the glazing ladder to the scaffold, taking a salt bag and iron ladle. Each hole was opened in turn, salt poured in and the hole closed again. This routine was carried out at half-hour intervals for up to six hours for each firing, using six to eight bushels of salt altogether. If more salt was used, at greater expense of course, a more even and smooth glaze developed.

As already mentioned, the top saggar of each bung was covered with a conical cap, so that the salt fell into the gaps between the circular bungs, meeting the hot gases rising from the firemouths below. The saggars had side openings, and the glassy vapour produced by salt and heat spread through the

Chapter V – Making the Pots

*Colour Plate 89. **Puzzle jug**, white salt-glazed stoneware with more flowing or debased scratch-blue decoration seen on tavern wares for some years after the more delicate table wares in scratch-blue had been out of fashion. Staffordshire, c.1760-80. 8in. (20.32cm) high. (Central Museum and Art Gallery, Northampton, Manfield collection, 1920-1 dl-95)*

saggars and reacted with the pots, coating them with a fine layer of glass – a *salt-glaze*.[200]

Jacques-Louis Brolliet described a different method of salt-glazing at *Oxford* in the 1750s. The six or eight wood-fired firemouths were cleared of wood and embers, a workman was placed at each firemouth with a basket (six and a half litres) of ordinary salt, and in a concerted movement, they threw the salt into the fire-mouths, creating a great noise, vaporising the salt which permeated the pierced saggars.[201] There is almost no evidence about *Dwight's* method at Fulham,[202] nor of what was done at *Bovey Tracey*.

The effect of throwing salt into a oven, heated to above 1100°C, is to produce sodium oxide which reacts with the silica in the stoneware body to form the glaze.[203] At the same time heavy white fumes are given off from the oven chimney, commented on frequently but first by Angerstein in Staffordshire in 1754:[204]

> When, as it sometimes happens, many kilns are glazed with salt at the same time, there is such a thick smoke of salt in these manufacturing towns, that people in the streets cannot see 6 feet [2m] ahead, which, however,

does not cause any difficulties. On the contrary, the smoke is considered so healthy that people who are ill come here from far away to breathe it.

Pitt made similar comments in 1817, adding that salting generally took place on Saturday mornings.[205]

After salting and the cessation of firing, the oven was allowed to cool over the weekend and 'drawn' (the saggars carried out and emptied). The ware was then looked over and sorted into best, second and third qualities, as shown in the 1773 inventory for *Thomas Wedgwood IV of the Overhouse*. Unsaleable ware (wasters to archaeologists) would be discarded and taken out of the factory for tipping, possibly by the carts which had brought in coal.

Decoration

Decoration in shape, relief or colour is not necessary for the pot to function. For the potter and the wholesale and retail sellers, it adds value and sales appeal to the product, with the consequent prospect of greater profit. To the final customer, decoration adds eye appeal to tempt purchase, with the anticipation of greater enjoyment in use. Additionally, there is no incentive to replace purely functional pots until they are worn out, whilst variety in decoration can inspire unnecessary purchases 'to keep in fashion'. We see this still reflected 250 years later, by the rarity of survival of plain, functional salt-glazed ware compared with relief moulded and decorated pieces.

Relief moulding is inseparable from making the pot, and so has been dealt with earlier in this chapter. Some coloured decoration was applied 'under-glaze', prior to firing, but it seems logical to include it here with 'on-glaze' decoration, as the interest of the final customer would be in its appearance, not in the technicalities of its application. Although sales of unfired ware from potter to potter are known,[206] 99.9% of under-glaze decoration would be applied by the actual maker. 'On-glaze' printed or enamelled decoration, however, could be applied equally well by the maker or by an independent decorator with a comparatively low temperature enamel kiln.

Under-glaze decoration

Coloured under-glaze decoration applied prior to firing had to be able to stand the heat of the salt-glaze oven and from surviving examples it seems that only blue and brown were used. *John Dwight* of London used both in the later seventeenth century, inspired by the German potters whose wares he imitated.

Cobalt blue and manganese were well known to British tin-glaze potters. Cobalt blue was used at *Woolwich* c.1650 and when John Robins, partner in the Pickleherring pothouse in Southwark, London, died in 1699, an inventory of the pothouse included both 'Saphir(e) [zaffre]' and 'Magnus [manganese]',[207] showing that London potters other than Dwight were familiar with these high temperature colours. Indeed, Pickleherring pothouse started out in 1604 as a facility for converting cobalt into smalt, blue pigment for painting earthenware. G. Smith published three recipes for blue colour for Delft ware in 1740, all including 'zaffer', and then stated 'Zaffer finely ground by itself, makes good blue, to paint on white glaz'd earthen ware'.[208]

Blue was obtained from cobalt, traditionally found in the Harz mountains of Saxony, and used in the form of smalts or zaffre for pottery decoration.[209] The demand for cobalt in Britain led to searches for it in Cornwall in the 1750s[210] and the mining of it in Scotland from 1759.[211] *John Baddeley* bought smalts for his china business in 1758.[212] In 1763 J.W. Pollmann, one of Josiah Wedgwood's London customers, sent him 'a sample of Zaffer received from Germany if you can dispose of a parcel I will order a Cask the price delivered there will be 2/6 p lb. [2s.6d. per pound weight]. It is very scarce abroad and cannot be afforded under'.[213]

By 1777 smalts and zaffre were available 'off the shelf' in Burslem. John Graham, ironmonger etc., invoiced *Thomas Wedgwood V of the Overhouse* for blue smalts on 1 July 1777 and six lots of 'Sapher 2 lb. at 3/6 [zaffre two pounds weight at 3s.6d.]' in 1778.[214]

Brown came from iron, or manganese which could also give a purple shade. Staffordshire potters had used '*Manganese*, by the *Workmen* call'd *Magnus*' on slipware by c.1680, as reported by Dr. Plot,[215] so that they were already familiar with it when they commenced making white salt-glazed stoneware. Half a ton of 'Magnus' was brought up the River Severn to Shrewsbury in 1699,[216] only thirty miles from the embryonic Potteries.

Dipping the upper part of a mug or jug rim in an iron or manganese solution is a very primitive form of decoration. It has been suggested that it was done to conceal the edge of the fine white dip used to improve coarse ware, but perhaps it was rather the continuation of a long tradition of parti-coloured drinking vessels, originally done to disguise discoloration of the drinking lip. 'Iron dip' shards were found on the 1750s site of *Thomas Whieldon* and at Benthall in *Shropshire*, showing that it continued to be done at the mid-century.[217]

One economical use of colour was for sprigged ornament. Every variation was used: ash on white and white on ash, and brown on white, which only involved coloured clay, and blue sprigs were also used, from clay stained with zaffre. Brown clay was also used as an inlay on white and for decorative touches on figures etc. (Colour Plates 5, 65, 67-69, 77, 79, Figs. 95, 97, 110).

Impressing or incising decoration into the pot began early. At its simplest, it takes the form of horizontal lines, made by a pointed implement whilst the pot rotates on the wheel or lathe. Use of a roller (a roulette, like a pastry wheel) with a relief pattern gives a more sophisticated appearance. A multi-pronged 'comb' was also used on the rotating pot or for simple freehand designs, as was the 'pointer'.

The use of blue to heighten scratched inscriptions or decoration seems to start in the early 1740s (see Colour Plates 14 and 15), then known as 'flowering' but termed 'scratch-blue' by collectors. Simeon Shaw described the technique: 'The *Flowerers* now *scratched* the jugs and tea ware, with a sharp pointed nail, and filled the interstices with ground zaffre, in rude imitation of the unmeaning scenery on foreign porcelain, and in this art women were instructed'.[218] Shaw was correct, confirmed by Angerstein's first-hand accounts.[219] He noted at *Derby* in 1754: 'When blue colour is required on the white-ware, they draw on the vessels and then strew smalt or cobalt into the hollows. The salt vapours which are used for the glaze then melt the smalt to a blue glass which adheres to the pattern, although not very uniformly.' He also saw the same process at Hanley: 'Crockery with a blue linear pattern, which can be finished in a single firing is also made but is seldom very even. This is carried out by sprinkling the blue pigment or smalt powder along lines drawn on the surface of the pottery or in score marks made with the point of a very sharp knife.'

Simple leaves and flowers were the most common incised decoration, and the process was known as flowering. The memorandum book of *Thomas Whieldon* yields the oft-quoted hiring on 24 August 1752 of 'little Bet Blour to learn to flower'.[220] *John Mitchell* of Burslem hired William Wood to learn flowering in 1760. *John Baddeley* was supplying 'flowd [flowered?]' dishes and plates in 1752 and *Peter Bagnall* left flowered saucers in 1761. 'Scratch-blue' shards have been found at pottery sites at *Bovey Tracey* in Devon and Jackfield in *Shropshire*. *Thomas Wedgwood IV of Overhouse* took orders for blue flowered ware in 1753 and 1763, and had forty-six dozen blue and white cups and saucers in stock when he died in 1773.

An obvious development of incising was the 'personalisation' of pots, scratching names, dates, places or messages to order, in the still-soft clay. Such inscribed pieces were treasured by their owners and families and therefore tend to survive. The earliest dated incised piece known to us is a two-handled bowl now in the Burnap Collection, inscribed 'Mrs. Mary Sandbach her Cup Anno Dom 1720' (Fig. 10).[221] No colour was used for the Sandbach bowl, nor for an inscribed 1727/8 marriage cup in the Northampton Museum (Fig. 11).[222]

It was a simple step forward to colour the inscriptions, either brown or blue. A mug in the Potteries Museum collection combines the attributes of being dipped white salt-glazed stoneware, with an iron dipped rim and also a brown incised inscription 'E:W/17:23' and freehand decoration of a bird, flowers etc. (Fig. 9).[223] Dated examples, often embellished with blue, continue through the century to the latest piece known to us, a bowl in the Glynn Vivian Art Gallery at *Swansea*, dated 1778 (Colour Plate 190).

Mugs and jugs with 'GR' measure mark sprigs are often found with solid areas of blue, crudely painted within the incised decoration, the so-called 'debased scratch-blue' (Colour Plates 162, 163). A.R. Mountford has shown that a mixture of clay and cobalt-oxide could have been used for 'flowering',[224] and it seems likely that a more liquid mixture was painted on this 'tavern ware', probably late in the eighteenth century when white salt-glaze was going downmarket fast and cobalt derivatives were cheaper (Fig. 126, Colour Plate 89).

Shaw's Patent

Salt-glazed wares covered entirely in brown or blue are known to collectors as 'Shaw's Patent' (brown) and 'Littler's

Colour Plate 90. **Bowl,** *brown stoneware with white slip incised with a combing tool to reveal the brown body, all of which is salt-glazed. This is an example of wares produced under Ralph Shaw's patent of 1733. Staffordshire, c.1733-40. 6¼ x 10in. (15.88 x 25.4cm). Potteries Museum and Art Gallery, Stoke-on-Trent, IIP38.*

Colour Plate 91. **Teapot,** *white salt-glazed stoneware with Littler-Wedgwood blue wash. Staffordshire, c.1750-55. 4⅝in. (11.75cm) high. (Private collection)*

attributes, fine white lines and also white sprig decoration,[227] and a tankard with similar bands and sprigging.[228] This tankard is compared with shards excavated on the 1750s Fenton Vivian site of *Thomas Whieldon*, which could have been made after the patent had expired. A similar teapot with the Royal Arms sprigged in white is in the Fitzwilliam Museum, Cambridge.[229]

Although he was the sole patentee, Shaw had two partners, both in potmaking and in his patent, a local farmer, Richard Bagnall, who left his share in the patent to his wife when he died in 1737, and named a Thomas Daniel as a third partner. Simeon Shaw was the first to describe Ralph Shaw's patent, and also a subsequent court case when *'J[ohn?]. Mitchell'* was unsuccessfully sued by Shaw in 1736 for infringement of his patent.[230] In 1750 Dr. Pococke commented that 'they [Staffordshire potters] make Dove-colour and Brown'.[231]

Ralph Shaw may have been the uncle of *William Littler* who became known for developing blue salt-glazed ware. William Littler's mother was Sarah Shaw, daughter of a Ralph Shaw.[232] She may have been the sister of Ralph Shaw, whose patented process has some similarity to the technique of 'Littler-Wedgwood Blue', an interesting connection, but not surprising in a close-knit community.

Littler-Wedgwood Blue

Salt-glazed stoneware survives, coloured all over in blue, in shades from pale blue to purple (Colour Plates 26, 27, 91-93, 137 and 194). It is found with decoration in white enamel, and also gilded. Littler-Wedgwood Blue has been compared with Sèvres *bleu de roi*,[233] more evenly applied than sponged-on *gros bleu* which was first used about 1749.[234]

The late Arnold Mountford had two sample shards analysed by the British Ceramic Research Association (BCRA, now Ceram Research), which reported that the blue layer was 0.026in. (0.66mm) thick and the salt-glaze layer was 0.004in. (0.1mm) thick. The BCRA stated that the most feasible method of making this ware would be to dip the unfired ware in a fusible mixture containing cobalt, followed by firing and salt-glazing.[235]

'Littler's Blue' is a collectors' term, taking its name from Simeon Shaw's 1829 account, itself only elaborated from what William Pitt wrote in 1817.[236] The essence of Pitt's description is that *William Littler* and his brother-in-law *Aaron Wedgwood* dipped unfired ware in a compound of zaffre, flint and clay before firing, producing a ware with a fine glassy surface.

Dating the introduction of Littler-Wedgwood Blue is problematical. *William Littler* was a salt-glaze potter at Burslem c.1745-1750, spent some time in Hanley and then went c.1751 to Longton Hall to make porcelain until 1760. Littler next appeared in Scotland in 1764. *Aaron Wedgwood* was also a salt-glaze potter in Burslem, producing from at least 1749 to 1770. No evidence has yet been found for a formal partnership, but they were brothers-in-law and could have co-operated in making 'Littler-Wedgwood Blue' before 1751 or between 1760 and 1764.

Blue'. To be accurate, 'Shaw's Patent' is brown salt-glazed stoneware, with white clay decoration, but its origin and quality justify its inclusion here.

Ralph Shaw of Burslem obtained a patent on 24 April 1733 for a ware 'of a true chocolate colour, striped with white… and glazed with salt'.[225] The Potteries Museum and Art Gallery has a brown salt-glazed bowl, the inside washed with white and with two stripes of white outside, these decorated by combing with a three-pronged tool (Colour Plate 90), and also a small unhandled cup made by the same technique.[226] A teapot is recorded with the same

*Colour Plate 92. **Teapot, basket, sauceboat,** white salt-glazed stoneware with Littler-Wedgwood blue dip, the teapot with traces of gilding. Staffordshire, c.1750-60. Teapot 3⅛in. (7.94cm) high, basket 8½in. (21.59cm) diameter. The Daily Advertiser 30 August 1753 offered 'Staffordshire White Ware at 1/6 per dozen … Blue at 12/- per dozen'. (Ashmolean Museum, Oxford, A.H. Church collection, 1929.77, 1929.138, 1929.65)*

There is documentary evidence that *Jonah Malkin* bought 'japand flowerd new collor [*sic*, japanned flowered new colour]' from *Aaron Wedgwood* on 10 September 1749, but this is ambiguous. 'Japanned' indicates lacquering or varnishing, and 'flowered' usually meant scratched decoration, leaving only 'new collor' as a possible reference to Littler-Wedgwood Blue.[237]

Ten years later, *Thomas and John Wedgwood* sold 'Gild d [*sic*] blue' to John Griffith of Backs, Bristol, on 12 May 1759.[238] Later references in their accounts associate 'blue' with *Aaron Wedgwood*, starting with 'Blue Ware Aarons' on 24 January 1760'.[239] The 1759 blue could of course also have been bought in from Aaron Wedgwood. There are invoices to Josiah Wedgwood for blue ware from salt-glaze potters from 1762 onward – see for examples *James Bold, Ralph Bucknall* and *Anthony Keeling*.

Contemporary literary references are also ambiguous. Dr. Richard Pococke visited the Potteries in 1750 and wrote 'At one place they make a dark blue glaze' but continued 'at another yellow, which when they are quite plain & well done look very much like China-tea-pots'.[240] Blue might have

*Colour Plate 93. **Sauceboat,** white salt-glazed stoneware slip-cast with vertical scallops and floral moulded relief decoration coloured overall with a Littler-Wedgwood blue wash. Staffordshire, c.1750. 4½in. (11.43cm) high. (Harriet Carlton Goldweitz collection, 182)*

been Littler-Wedgwood Blue and the yellow could have been early cream-coloured ware.[241]

Four years later, in 1754, Reinhold Angerstein noted 'That which is grey or decorated with other colours, must be fired twice, namely once for the ordinary glazing with salt, and a second time for the blue colour or enamel, which, as I was told, is mixed with clay.'[242] Out of this can be deduced that he was writing of salt-glazed ware and that the blue was mixed with clay. This agrees with the BCRA's 1970s definition of Littler-Wedgwood Blue, but a second firing was not needed for such an under-glaze dip.

A 1753 advertisement in the *Daily Advertiser*[243] seems to confirm that Littler-Wedgwood Blue was well known by that date:

…to be sold under prime cost. The stock of a person leaving off business next door to the Blue Ball and Stag, in King Street Bloomsbury, consisting of all sorts of Glass, Earthenware, Haberdashery and grocery. Staffordshire White Ware at 1/6 per dozen, ditto Black Ware at 2/- per doz., Red China at 5/- per doz., Tortoiseshell at 6/- per doz., *Blue* [authors' emphasis] at 12/- per dozen…

In the context and at such a high price, 'blue' would be Littler-Wedgwood salt-glazed ware.

With hindsight, the introduction of Littler-Wedgwood Blue seems scarcely revolutionary. Possibly cobalt became more plentiful and therefore cheaper and a new decorative feature would anyway command a higher price. From the information quoted above, it appears that Littler-Wedgwood Blue was developed by 1749.

Combinations of Glazes

There are several instances of combinations of salt-glaze and other glazes and it should be borne in mind that potters and decorators would use any practicable method to achieve a desired effect. The suggestion that red lead was added to salt can be traced back to Solon in 1883. He thought that the 'orange peel' appearance of salt-glazed ware was due to the glaze remaining as drops on the surface and that the addition of red lead made the drops 'hardly perceptible'.[244]

It has been proposed that two items made at *Swansea* were lead-glazed over salt-glaze, though there seems no logical explanation for covering 'scratch-blue', already protected by salt-glaze, with lead glaze.

Information about a salt-glazed stoneware crabstock teapot has recently been published, the body and cover a streaky brown and the handle, spout and knop coloured green, 'refired with a lead glaze',[245] the appearance (in a photograph) suggesting the use of coloured glazes.

Professor Alan Smith has put forward the theory that a group of twenty or more stoneware pots appear to have been biscuit-fired, dipped in tin-glaze and re-fired in a salt-glaze kiln, though allowing that the sequence might have been salt-glaze first followed by tin-glazing. Their *decorative* characteristics suggest a Liverpool origin,[246] but there are possible explanations of this process, which does not necessitate *manufacture* of these salt-glaze pieces in Liverpool.

Reinhold Angerstein visited Liverpool in 1754 and noted:[247]

one of the workers has recently found a way of glazing the so-called white ware, which one pottery intends putting into production. White ware is made in Staffordshire, the raw material consisting of half pipe clay and half flint, but there it is glazed with salt which is difficult and cannot be painted.

Angerstein seems to be referring to Staffordshire white ware, which was white salt-glazed stoneware at that date, and suggesting that a further glaze – tin-glaze? – was applied to it to facilitate painting.

John Sadler of Liverpool, printer and enameller, wrote to Josiah Wedgwood on 30 November 1764 about glazing. His letter was quoted in part by E.S. Price in 1948 and more briefly later[248] about a 'salt-glaze plate from Worcester, Printed blue and Glazed after', but the full letter reveals much more. On 27 March 1763 Sadler had written to Josiah Wedgwood in London that 'We are for trying a White Glaze, w[hi]ch may be of advantage'. There is nothing further which is relevant until the 30 November 1764 letter.

Sadler's 30 November 1764 letter[249] follows. (The authors have put certain words in italics for emphasis.)

Liverpool Novr 30 1764

Sir

Your's of the 22d should have been answer'd sooner (as you desired to know something about our Glazing *Flint*) but that I expected D Morris [the Burslem carrier] yesterday as you advis'd: However its as well as it is, for we could but make 2 Crates, besides the 4 left behind last Journey –

We are getting forward with your Ware as fast as we can; but the small Pieces are tedious, the days short &c. We shall fire next Week, and towards the End of the Week following shall have a good Quantity ready.

You know we have but little ware by us – no Coffee Pots – but very few T[ea]pots Mugs &c. –

We have all along had the putting a good White Glaze on *Flint* in view and we have made some Trials at Times – We have got together a p[ar]cel of different Ingredients for the Purpose Ground ready for mixing, and intend to have a Bout at it in earnest the first leisure we have; But we must first get into a stock of *Cream Col[ou]r* before we set about any Thing else; for our shipping will be going out in the spring, and we expect a good Demand.

Mr Luffingham[250] brought a salt Glaze Plate from Worcester, Printed Blue, and glaz'd after – He boasted much of it, and told us Mr Holdship [of the Worcester Porcelain Manufactory] said we could Print every Thing but Blue as well as himself, but That we could not manage – However we got the same Pattern engrav'd and Printed, glaz'd and burnt 2 Plates and 3 Mugs – Our Blue is much better than the Worcester (owing to its being firmer laid on) and our Glaze is whiter – Our Blue is as good as any I have seen on China. We shall send you some of the first pieces we do. You know the transparent Glaze for Blue and the Glaze for a fine White to print upon will be very different – As to the Glaze for Blue I would not desire a better than I think ours is. But as to the fine White Glaze to print Black Red &c. upon we have not made a thorough Trial yet, but shall acquaint you with our Progress (if we can make any) as we go on; for we would you partake with us of every Thing that is likely to afford either Honour or Profit

  I am Sir y[ou]r [ ] Serv[an]t

   John Sadler

I rec[eive]d the Zaffer, but have not tried it yet – We shall always be obliged to you for your Thoughts on the above affairs

Neither a response from Josiah Wedgwood nor any further reference in Sadler's surviving letters have been found.[251] When Sadler refers to 'Flint' he is writing of white salt-glazed stoneware, confirmed by his reference to 'Cream Colr' in the same paragraph. Our understanding of the above letter is (1) that Sadler had already succeeded in printing in blue on salt-glazed ware and over-glazing it, and (2) that he was ambitious to put a white glaze on to salt-glazed ware, suitable for printing on in black, red &c.

Given that tin-glazed ware was made in abundance in Liverpool at this period, is it not possible that Sadler actually applied a tin-glaze to salt-glazed pots, to provide a whiter basis for painted decoration?

Further puzzling combinations of glazes will no doubt come to light.

On-glaze decoration

Whilst under-glaze decoration by its nature must be applied by a manufacturer, on-glaze decoration, painted or printed, could be done by the manufacturer or by an independent decorator. The requisites were a potential demand for decorated ware, skill in painting or engraving, supplies of suitable colour, and a comparatively low temperature muffle kiln.

The Staffordshire historian, Pitt, writing in 1817,[252] ably summarised the likely inception of enamelling on white salt-glazed ware:

> This white [salt] glaze soon attracted the attention of enamellers from the china and Dutch-tile manufactories then established in different parts of the kingdom, who began to cover their carved work with fine enamel colours, and soon after made great progress in painting groups of figures, flowers, birds, &c. and in copying the paintings of the richest China from the East upon their tea, coffee, and dessert sets, as well as jars, cornucopiæ, figures, and other ornamental and useful articles.

Demand was already there: furniture, glass, and metal-ware had long been made more attractive and thus more saleable by surface decoration and, in our own discipline, tin-glazed earthenware and porcelain had been painted long before the advent of white salt-glazed stoneware. Thus the skills were already available in decorating workshops, and there must have been suppliers of the necessary colours, oils, spirits and brushes.

A 'muffle' or 'enamel' kiln was needed to fix the colours to the glazed surface of the ware, a fireproof cupboard to protect the enamelled or printed ware from the hot gases rising through surrounding flues from the fire-box below.[253] Unlike salt-glaze ovens, these muffles were small enough to be accommodated in a decorator's workshop, or in the rear premises of a pottery warehouse or showroom. Angerstein illustrated a 1754 muffle, but in connection with Derby porcelain works and for firing the ware, not for decorating.[254]

The London Tradesman of 1747 emphasised that 'Enamelling is properly of kin to the Potter; they use the same Colours, lay them on the same Way, and differ only in this, that the Ground work of one is earthen-ware, and that of the other Metal'.[255] Colours were also commercially available in the provinces. In 1748, there was a mill for grinding enamels at Bilston,[256] some thirty miles south of Burslem. A 30 September 1751 advertisement in *Aris's Birmingham Gazette* is explicit:

> Abraham Seeman, Enameller and Painter at Mrs. Weston's in Freeman Street, Birmingham, makes and sells all sort of enamelling colours, especially the Rose Colours, and likewise all sorts for china painters, at reasonable prices. N.B. Most of the eminent painters of Birmingham, Wednesbury and Bilston have made use of the above colours to their satisfaction.

His widow advertised in similar terms on 30 October 1752.[257] Mention of 'Birmingham, Wednesbury and Bilston' indicates use of colours for enamelled metalware, but the appeal of the 1751 advertisement is to china painters. J.E. Nightingale quoted a similar advertisement on 2 April 1753, and more cogently an advertisement in the same newspaper on 5 November 1753 by the China works at Bow, London, for 'Painters in the Blue and White Potting Way, and Enamellers on China-Ware'.[258] Clearly, Bow thought that such painters might be recruited within the area covered by the *Birmingham Gazette*, which then included the expanding Staffordshire Potteries, as well as the West Midlands enamellers.

Erroll Manners has been researching associated groups of enamel wares which appear to be similar, and may have been decorated in London. These consist of blank Chinese porcelains with English enamel decoration as well as similar salt-glazed examples. A mug dated 1739 in the Victoria and Albert Museum (Colour Plates 93a-c) and another one dated 1746 in the collection of Colonial Williamsburg (Colour Plates 93d, e) appear to fall into this category. So far the decorating workshops are not known.

Both Pococke and Angerstein mentioned difficulties in enamelling on salt-glazed ware in Staffordshire. Pococke wrote of Staffordshire potters in 1750[259] that 'they have… another kind they call enamelled; one sort of it is painted on white stone in colours & does not do well'. Angerstein was told at Liverpool in 1754 that 'White ware is made in Staffordshire … but there it is glazed with salt which is difficult and cannot be painted'. He went on from

Colour Plates 93a-c. **Mug**, white-dipped salt-glazed stoneware with double-rolled handle and enamel decoration in five panels depicting various exotic courting scenes involving Europeans and Orientals. The central panel is painted with a tower in the foreground attended by a turbaned black figure with a staff in hand. In the background one sees the masts of a square-rigged ship. The mug has many characteristics of those produced by the Dwight family in the early 18th century and the painting is similar to enamelling done in London workshops on Oriental porcelains. The date of 1739 at the base of the handle along with initials A M L is the earliest recorded on enamelled white salt-glazed stoneware. Probably Dr. Samuel Dwight's factory London 1739 (or earlier). 4½in. (11.43cm) high. (Victoria and Albert Museum)

Liverpool to Burslem and quoted the price of 'White ware, enamelled 8-12s[hillings]' a dozen, showing that any difficulties had been overcome. At Hanley, he priced 'Enamelled, white ware tea pots' at 10s. a dozen, and, obscurely, 'Ditto [tea pots?], blue and white 'Rond', salt glazed and enamelled' at 6s. a dozen.[260]

The difficulties were certainly overcome before 1759. Simeon Shaw had access to a drawing book, entitled 'Werner [*sic*] Edwards's Art of making Enamel Colours in a plain manner'. Warner Edwards of Shelton, Staffordshire, died in 1759[261] (see *Revd. John or Thomas Middleton*, potter). The book included details of suppliers of colour materials in London, Manchester and Liverpool, and detailed instructions on the preparations of colours, showing that the knowledge necessary for enamelling was available within the Staffordshire Potteries by 1759.

Gilding was an enhancement of enamelling, and Dr. Peter Bradshaw has written an exhaustive study which

*Colour Plates 93d, e. **Mug**, white salt-glazed stoneware with strap handle and flared turned base, enamel decorated and gilded lavishly with central cartouche of a drinking couple in a rococo enamel and gilded frame. The back of the mug is painted with opaque chinoiserie flowers. The mug is inscribed C ✱ Bacon; and dated 1746. Charles Bacon was a London decorator in the 1730s and 1740s. Staffordshire or London, probably decorated in London. 6½in. (16.51cm). (Colonial Williamsburg Foundation acc. no. 1963-67)*

describes the various methods used in the mid-eighteenth century, chiefly gold leaf or honey gilding.[262] Whatever the method known in the Staffordshire Potteries in the 1750s, *Thomas and John Wedgwood* of Burslem supplied 'Gild d blue' to John Griffith of Backs, Bristol, on 12 May 1759 (Colour Plate 92).[263]

Decoration of pottery and porcelain by transfer printing has also been studied in depth (Colour Plates 116-118, Fig. 112).[264] A design was incised into a copper plate, the incisions filled with metallic colour mixed with oil, the colour picked up on paper from the copper plate and the paper pressed down on the pot, effectively 'transferring' the design to the pot. A variation was to fill the incisions with oil, transfer the design to the pot by either paper or a flexible slab of glue, and dust the oil design with powdered colour. Both methods required firing in a muffle kiln to fix the colour on the pot. The technique of transfer printing was applied to enamels, porcelain, tin-glazed earthenware and white salt-glazed stoneware from the early 1750s, and in due course to cream-coloured earthenware.

In a petition for a patent on 25 January 1754, John Brooks of Battersea, engraver, claimed that his method of printing would enable him 'to supply foreign markets with the *stone* [our emphasis] and earthenware manufactories of this country beautifully printed and decorated', adding mention of stone and earthenware to his 1751 application for printing on enamel and china.[265] 'Stone' can be accepted as referring to white salt-glazed stoneware. Cyril Cook wrote specifically on the subject in 1958, listing twenty-seven different engraved designs on white salt-glazed ware, a few in three colours. He is convincing that this printing was done at York House, Battersea, with some engravings made by Robert Hancock. Cook quoted a 1756 advertisement for the auction of the York House stock, which included the phrase 'some hundred dozens of stone plates', a contemporary term for white salt-glazed stoneware plates.[266] Taken together, we have confirmation that 'outside decorators' bought in stocks of plain white salt-glazed ware and added value to it by embellishing it with prints of picturesque, commemorative, heraldic and many other saleable subjects.[267]

As with plaster moulds, the particular merit of transfer printing is that the design is prepared professionally in advance and can be repeated by unskilled workers, whereas free-hand painting depends on the personal skill of the individual artist. The skills could be combined, the same workshops adding enamel colour to printed designs, improving 'penny plain' to 'twopence coloured' to their further profit. Another variation was to apply separate transfers in different colours to the same pot.[268]

Colour Plate 94. **Teapot,** *white salt-glazed stoneware slip-cast in lobed pear-shaped form with shell moulded relief and 'Dog of Fo' knop. The ornate relief is enhanced by the addition of restrained enamel colouring. Staffordshire, c.1755. 6⅛in. (15.56cm) high. (Potteries Museum and Art Gallery, Stoke-on-Trent, 1694)*

Decorators

Who then were the decorators who embellished the plain ware with prints and enamels? Enamelling was not confined to pottery and porcelain: it was already applied to glass and copper and the same tradesmen were ready to use their skill on whatever new material came up. Decorators of glass, copper, tin-glazed earthenware and porcelain already existed in London and the largest provincial towns when white salt-glazed ware came on the scene. As demand for decorated salt-glazed ware increased, decoration would spread to the sources of production.

Decorators or enamellers are rare amongst the miscellany of customers (see Appendix 5), suggesting that they bought in small quantities from local wholesalers and not from manufacturers. Their work might have been 'to order' from china dealers or individual customers, or 'on spec.', keeping their employees busy when there were no specific orders to fill, to sell to wholesalers, retailers, or direct to the public.

A recent article has identified 'Giles' and 'Campman' as china painters in London in 1723, probably painting imported Chinese porcelain, and their surnames persisted as London decorators until late in the century, along with many others.[269] They would turn their hands to English porcelain, salt-glazed ware and cream-coloured ware in turn. One London decorator, William Duesbury, illustrated the spread of the technique by moving to Longton Hall in the Staffordshire Potteries in 1754, albeit to a porcelain works, before moving on to Derby in 1756. He had been decorating 'Staffd. Shepardsis [Staffordshire Shepherds]' and 'Staffordshir Birds' in London in 1751,[270] distinguished from items from 'Littler & Company', porcelain makers at Longton Hall, so surely white salt-glaze at that date.

In the Potteries, William Summerfield of Stoke-on-Trent, enameller and painter of earthenware, who insured his house, workhouses, warehouses, stable and carthouse, and stove room in 1755,[271] and James Wilson (enameller) Burslem, who was a trustee of the Derby to Newcastle-under-Lyme turnpike road in 1759,[272] would have bought and decorated white salt-glazed ware in that period. *William Banks*, a Stoke potter, insured a 'painting house' in 1763, although this might have been for ware other than salt-glaze. In 1764 Phillips and Greaves, also of Stoke-on-Trent, sold 'Enam'[elle]d 9s Teapots blue and w[hit[e]', spoon trays, sugar basins and covers to Josiah Wedgwood, so may have been decorators or potters.[273] Like Summerfield in 1755, Phillips and Greaves could also have enamelled salt-glazed ware. In 1767 William Locket of Burslem, potter, insured a house and adjoining shop tenanted by Thomas Anbury Enameller of Earthenware.[274] By then cream-coloured earthenware was available in quantity for decorating. On 9 May 1763 John Tidmarsh of London asked Josiah Wedgwood to 'Please to let your man pack ye En'[amelle]d Ware of Mr Thos Astbury'; and James Rigby of Liverpool wrote to Josiah Wedgwood 27 December 1763, complaining that a crate of enamelled cups and saucers from Mr. Ashbury of Burslem, ordered to come with Wedgwood's ware, had not been received.[275] It seems likely that all three surnames, underlined by us, refer to the same Burslem enameller, who would have been as ready to decorate salt-glazed ware as cream-coloured. This contemporary confusion over the name may excuse Simeon Shaw, who wrote that Josiah Wedgwood's 'tea ware required to be painted, was sent for that purpose to Mrs. Astbury, in Hot Lane'.[276]

No information has been found about the Dutchmen in Hot Lane,[277] or Mr. Daniel, of Cobridge, said by Shaw to have been the first enamellers in the Potteries,[278] nor of *Mrs. Ann Warburton* of Hot Lane as a decorator of salt-glazed ware,[279] who would have bought in undecorated ware. A payment of £1.8s.6d. to Mrs. Warburton on 30 July 1765 by Thomas and John Wedgwood was on behalf of their customer, William Baker of York, who had presumably bought ware from her.[280]

We have already quoted *Enoch and George Booth* as potters who were well known to John Dunbibin as enamellers by 1764 and indirectly supplied *Thomas and John Wedgwood* with 'Enamell Teapots' in 1767.[281] Enoch Booth senior is considered to have been a maker and decorator of cream-coloured ware from c.1743,[282] and this Booth partnership represents the combination of potter and

*Colour Plate 95. **Teapot**, white salt-glazed stoneware with chinoiserie enamel decoration which includes the 'blue rock' decoration, high mask head paw feet. Staffordshire, c.1755. 3⅛in. (7.94cm) high. (Private collection)*

*Colour Plate 96. **Teapot,** white salt-glazed stoneware with applied prunus decoration in the manner of Chelsea porcelain. The flowers are decorated in opaque enamel colours and the handle, spout and 'Dog of Fo' knop are all brown enamel. Staffordshire, c.1750-55. 4½in. (11.43cm) high. (Harriet Carlton Goldweitz collection)*

*Colour Plate 97. **Coffee or chocolate cup,** white salt-glazed stoneware with polychrome opaque enamel decoration in the* famille rose *palette. Staffordshire, c.1755. 2½in. (6.35cm) high. (Harriet Carlton Goldweitz collection)*

decorator which developed in Staffordshire from the mid-18th century.

As noted above, *Thomas and John Wedgwood* of Burslem supplied 'Gild d blue' to John Griffith of Backs, Bristol, on 12 May 1759,[283] suggesting either that there was a gilder in

*Colour Plate 98. **Pickle dish,** white salt-glazed stoneware, press-moulded in the form of a scallop shell with polychrome opaque chinoiserie enamels. Scallop shell pickle dishes were made at Limehouse and other English porcelain factories but are rare in salt-glaze. Probably Staffordshire, c.1755-60. 4¾in. (12.07cm). (Hollis Broderick Antiques, photograph by Robert Barth)*

the Potteries by then, or that they had the work done elsewhere to meet his order. Thomas and John Wedgwood sent 'goods in Cousin [Josiah or *Thomas IV*] Wedgwoods crate' to their customer 'Jasper Robison [*sic*] and Co. Briggate over against Geo[rge] in Leeds' on 1 April 1761.[284] This was a source for the 'enamel stoneware' which Robinson and Rhodes of the same address in Leeds boasted they could 'sell as cheap as in Staffordshire' in 1760.[285] In the letter of 21 November 1764,[286] in which David Rhodes told Josiah Wedgwood that 'my partner [Robinson] has turned over the business to me since last March and works for me at it', Rhodes requested, along with '6 quart mellon Coffee Pots – green & yellow' and other wares, '6 quart white d[itt]o. very good white' – white salt-glazed stoneware at that date.

There is also evidence of Yorkshire salt-glaze manufacturers who enamelled their wares. *John Platt and Samuel Walker* were salt-glaze potters at *Rotherham* in South Yorkshire from 1766 to 1770 and their (undated) trade card states that they 'Make & Sell *White Stone Ware*, Black, Tortoise Shell, Agate, Cream Colour, &c. also Gilt & Enamel Ware'.[287] Platt's diary survives and on 11 June 1767 he noted 'Building a muffle or kiln for ye painted or enamel ware pottery'.[288] This would be used for firing on the decoration of any of the types of ware produced, including an enamelled white salt-glazed stoneware jug, which survived in family possession until 1970, inscribed 'John Platt/1767',[289] possibly commemorating the new facility (Colour Plate 188).

An enamelled white salt-glazed punchbowl on pedestal, at Colonial Williamsburg, inscribed 'I,C,/1767',[290] has very similar numerals and might also be Platt and Walker's

*Colour Plate 99. **Stand or grand plat ménage,** white salt-glazed stoneware with each part press-moulded separately and washed with enamel colours. More commonly found in porcelain and in creamware, these are very rare in salt-glazed stoneware. Staffordshire, c.1760-70. 7in. (17.78cm). (Ashmolean Museum, Oxford, gift of F.V.C. de Costa Andrade, WA 1968.365)*

Chapter V – Making the Pots

Colour Plate 100. **Coffee pot** in white salt-glazed stoneware with polychrome opaque chinoiserie enamels of a woman in the foreground gesturing to a man behind and on the reverse a boy flying a kite. Staffordshire, c.1755-60. 7in. (17.78cm) high (minus lid). (Private collection)

*Colour Plate 101. **Coffee pot,** white salt-glazed stoneware with marbled enamels and a cartouche painted with a landscape. Spouts of similar type have been attributed to Derbyshire, Staffordshire and Yorkshire. Possibly Staffordshire, c.1755-60. 8in. (20.32cm) high. (Photograph courtesy of Jonathan Horne)*

*Colour Plate 102. **Coffee pot,** white salt-glazed stoneware in lighthouse form with chinoiserie enamel decoration. Staffordshire, c.1760-65. 5½in. (13.97). (Historic Deerfield, Inc., 66.032)*

*Colour Plate 103. **Large jug; figure of a shepherdess,** white salt-glazed stoneware, the jug enamel painted with English flowers. Both Staffordshire, c.1760-70. 9⅜ and 4⅞in. (23.81 and 12.38cm) respectively. (Central Museum and Art Gallery, Northampton, Manfield collection, 1920-1 D1.67, 1920-1 d1.172)*

*Fig. 111. **Plate,** white salt-glazed stoneware octagonal form press-moulded with diaper and scroll border and painted in enamel colours. Staffordshire, c.1760. 9in. (22.86cm) diameter. (Photograph courtesy of Jonathan Horne)*

*Colour Plate 104. **Plate,** white salt-glazed stoneware with press-moulded diaper and scroll border and chinoiserie opaque enamel decoration in the* famille rose *palette. Staffordshire, c.1760. 9¼in. (23.5cm) diameter. (Private collection)*

Colour Plate 105. **Two jugs**, *white salt-glazed stoneware enamel painted with coats of arms. Left, coat of arms of the Pratt family of Ryston Hall, Norfolk; right, a copy of the bookplate of George Thomas. Staffordshire, c.1760. 11⅝ and 8⅞in. (29.53 and 22.54cm) respectively. (Potteries Museum and Art Gallery, Stoke-on-Trent, 2888, 3659)*

Colour Plate 106. **Jug** *of white salt-glazed stoneware with replaced handle. The jug is enamel painted in the porcelain style with a courting couple with an elaborate border in diaper and rococo scroll enamel with gilding. Staffordshire, c.1760. 6⅝in. (16.83cm) high. (Private collection)*

Colour Plate 107. **Teapot,** *white salt-glazed stoneware enamel painted in puce and green with a central panel reserve painted with English flowers. Staffordshire, c.1755-60. 4in. (10.16cm) high. (Private collection)*

Colour Plate 108. **Punch pot and cup,** *white salt-glazed stoneware with elaborate enamel decoration of a drinking scene. Staffordshire, c.1760. 11 and 2⅜in. (27.94 and 6.03cm) respectively. (Potteries Museum and Art Gallery, Stoke-on-Trent, 2887, 1164)*

Colour Plate 109. **Teapot,** *pear-shaped white salt-glazed stoneware, landscape decorated in enamels. Staffordshire, c.1755. 4in. (10.16cm) high. (Photograph courtesy of Jonathan Horne)*

Colour Plate 110. **Two teapots and a milk jug,** *white salt-glazed stoneware enamel decorated with scenes of musicians. All Staffordshire, c.1755-65. Teapot right 5in. (12.7cm) high. (Ashmolean Museum, Oxford, left gift of C.A. de Costa Andrade, 1968.369, middle and right A.H. Church collection, gift of Dame Jemima Church, 1929.81, 1929.91)*

*Colour Plate 111. **Teapot**, white salt-glazed stoneware decorated in enamels simulating fossilised limestone. Staffordshire, c.1755-60. 4⅜in. (11.11cm) high. (Potteries Museum and Art Gallery, Stoke-on-Trent, 1162)*

*Colour Plate 112. **Bowl**, white salt-glazed stoneware with enamel decoration depicting 'Bonnie Prince Charlie'. Staffordshire, c.1755. 11in. (27.94cm) diameter. (Historic Deerfield, Inc., Massachusetts, photography by Amanda Merullo)*

*Colour Plate 113. **Teapot**, white salt-glazed stoneware in a form more commonly associated with Dutch tin-glazed earthenware and enamel decoration in a combination of famille rose palette and Dutch style enamel painting. The central figure is Bonnie Prince Charlie wielding a sword. Replacement lid. Staffordshire, c.1755. 3½in. (8.89cm) high (without lid). (Ashmolean Museum, Oxford, gift of C.A. de Costa Andrade, 1968.356)*

Colour Plate 114. **Teapot,** *pear-shaped white salt-glazed stoneware with Dutch enamel floral decoration and gilding. Staffordshire, c.1760. 5¼in. (13.34cm) high. (Harriet Carlton Goldweitz collection)*

Colour Plate 114a. **Teabowl** *from a child's tea service, white salt-glazed stoneware with Dutch enamel decoration. Staffordshire (Dutch decorated), c.1760. 1¼ x 2in. (3.18 x 5.08cm). (Private collection)*

Colour Plate 115. **Altar vase,** *white salt-glazed stoneware with enamel chinoiserie decoration, gilding. This unusual vase was intended for holy water. Staffordshire, c.1760. 7⅝in. (19.37cm) high. (The Henry H. Weldon Collection, Colonial Williamsburg Foundation, photography by Gavin Ashworth)*

manufacture (Colour Plates 189, 189a). An enamelled salt-glaze jug in a private collection, of similar size and shape to the Platt jug, inscribed 'John/Kirkham/1768', bears very similar lettering and numerals.[291]

White salt-glazed stoneware was also decorated in Holland. A Rotterdam merchant, Samuel Tabor, ordered 'white flint ware' and '10-12 complete Table Sets of best white stoneware' from Josiah Wedgwood in 1763 (see Chapter VI), items which could have been enamelled in nearby Delft. B. Rackham catalogued six items of white salt-glazed stoneware in the Schreiber Collection as being decorated in Holland, commenting 'designs unquestionably Dutch … show that the ware was sometimes enamelled at Delft'.[292] More recently there has been a suggestion that 'English stoneware' was decorated in Delft by 1740 (Figure 61, Colour Plates 114, 114a).[293] This decorating trade expanded and Dutch decoration survives much more frequently on cream-coloured earthenware.[294]

*Colour Plate 116. **Plate,** white press-moulded salt-glazed stoneware transfer-printed with a puce engraving of the 'Dog in the Manger', a print from Croxall's Fables of Aesop, cxxix. The border is enamel painted in turquoise. Staffordshire, c.1760. 8½in. (21.59cm) diameter. (Private collection)*

*Colour Plate 117. **Plate,** white press-moulded stoneware plate with diaper and scroll border. The red transfer print is from Croxall's Fables of Aesop, cxxix, 'The Dog in the Manger'. Staffordshire, perhaps printed in Liverpool, c.1760. 8⅞in. (22.54cm) diameter. (Potteries Museum and Art Gallery, Stoke-on-Trent, 3654, exhibited in Liverpool in 1907)*

W.B. Honey sounded a general alarm about 'the not uncommon old salt-glaze enamelled in modern times'[295] and the 1908 description by Thomas Greg, the Manchester collector, of twentieth century decoration on salt-glazed ware[296] serves well as a warning:

> Of late years it has been the habit of certain dealers to buy up common and uninteresting specimens of white salt glaze, and to send it over to Holland or France to be enamelled in colours… It cannot be too widely known that no piece of enamelled salt glaze should ever be treated as innocent until it has clearly proved itself by pedigree or expert opinion to be not guilty… About two years ago I sold a pair of salt-glaze flower vases to a dealer who is above and beyond suspicion. He sold them to another dealer soon after, and in about three months from their leaving my hands I saw this identical pair (one of which bore a mark by which I could infallibly recognise them) richly enamelled with modern colours, put up for sale at Sothebys, and bought by a friend of my own, for more than four times as much as I had sold them for and at least three times as much as they were worth.

Replicas
Replicas of white salt-glazed stoneware have been made over the two centuries since original production ceased.

Wedgwood of Etruria made replicas in the nineteenth century.[297] These should not be confused with smear-glazed stoneware, though a respected ceramic historian, G.W. Rhead, was deceived in 1910. He wrote then of 'tangible proof, if any were needed [that Josiah Wedgwood made salt-glaze] – a salt-glazed teapot marked Wedgwood'.[298] Rhead illustrated the piece, an 'artichoke' or 'cabbage' shape.[299] It was most probably white stoneware, smear-glazed, described by Robin Reilly as 'one of the artichoke teapots … available as late as 1845', made in Wedgwood's 'white stoneware', sometimes smear-glazed, and sometimes mistaken for salt-glaze.[300]

Minton of Stoke-on-Trent made small whitish salt-glazed stoneware fonts in 1866.[301] From the late 1920s to the late 1930s, Minton produced '18th century Staffordshire Saltglaze' wares, really made from an ivory body with a 'rather gritty matt finish in imitation of saltglaze', to appeal to the American market. Figures, animals, ornaments, tablewares and teapots were produced in this style, often thickly enamelled.[302]

In America, the Canonsburg Pottery Company of Canonsburg, Pennsylvania, produced Priscilla (later called Washington Colonial) designs based on salt-glazed shapes, from 1931. The firm closed in 1975.[303] All the foregoing reproductions are believed to be properly marked.

For a thoughtful study on 'Reproductions and Fakes of English Eighteenth-century Ceramics', see the paper with that title given by Wallace Elliot in 1937. Elliot described a 'spurious salt-glazed stoneware Cock', although in discussion this was suggested to be of Oriental origin; and a salt-glazed Adam and Eve 'Pew Group', copied from an original in the Glaisher Collection. He also drew attention

*Fig. 112. **Engraving** by Hayman from Simon François Ravenet engraving taken from T. Smollett's* Don Quixote *(1755), the print source for the plate in Colour Plate 116. (Harriet Carlton Goldweitz collection)*

*Colour Plate 118. **Plate,** white, press-moulded stoneware plate with diaper and scroll border transfer-printed in red over the salt-glaze. The print is Don Quixote and Sancho Panza designed by Hayman from a Ravenet print (see fig. 112). 9in. (22.86cm) diameter. (Harriet Carlton Goldweitz collection)*

to a spurious marbled cat in salt-glaze and a genuine salt-glazed mug, enamelled later with a portrait of the Young Pretender.[304]

G.W. Rhead alleged that the man who deceived L.M. Solon with slipware replicas also 'set up a salt-glaze oven and produced salt-glazed wares'.[305] For allegations of more recent reproductions, see reports of a well-publicised court case in 1994,[306] when it was sought to prove that salt-glazed and other eighteenth century English ceramics had been manufactured recently. The Black Museum, 30 Oxford Street, London W1, assembled by the late A.J. B. Kiddell of Sotheby's, contains examples of all kinds of 'innocent copies as well as out-and-out fakes and forgeries'.[307] *Caveat emptor* – let the buyer beware!

Masters, Works and Workers
Masters
Evidence surviving about master potters, their works and their employees is fragmentary. Restricted as we are to identifiable white salt-glazed stoneware production, statistics about eighteenth century population, even for an increasingly specialised district like the Staffordshire Potteries, are of limited value.[308] Figures for the Potteries villages published in 1843 do show the general upward trend of population in our period, from 4,000 in 1738 to 7,500 in 1762, and doubling again by 1785 to 15,000.[309] The twenty-four or so 'out-potteries' would make no impact on their local population numbers.

We have found some 125 white salt-glaze stoneware manufacturers,[310] ninety-seven of them in Staffordshire from, say, 1690 to 1790, and the rest scattered widely, as follows:

America (2) 1765-68 and 1782
Bovey Tracey, Devon 1766-75
Brentford, Middlesex 1759
Chester 1757-1777
Derby (2) 1751-1780 and 1770
Leeds, Yorkshire 1770
Liverpool, Lancashire (2) 1756
London (5) 1673-1737
Oxford 1755
Prescot, Lancashire 1751
Prestonpans, Scotland 1750-90
Rotherham, Yorkshire 1766-70
Rothwell, Yorkshire 1768
Shropshire (2) 1760s-70s
Swansea, Wales 1764-77
Swinton, Yorks 1769-75
Woolwich, Kent 1650
York 1683-93

The dates shown here and in the detailed description of potters are minimal, based on the firmest information found. In William Benson's first patent for grinding flint, granted in 1726, it was clearly stated 'that in Staffordshire *and some other parts of our kingdom* [our emphasis] there is a

*Fig.113. **Two plates,** press-moulded in white salt-glazed stoneware with unusual moulded relief decoration. Staffordshire, c.1755-70. Left, with a border moulded with melons/marrows and leaves. 9⅜in. (23.81cm diameter. Right, moulded overall with veining, leaves and acanthus leaves; 9½in. (24.13cm) diameter. (Ashmolean Museum, Oxford, A.H. Church collection, gift of Dame Jemima Church, 1929, 125, 126)*

manufacture carried on of making white pots, the chief ingredient of which is flint stone'.[311] Apart from Staffordshire, we have only found white salt-glaze stoneware manufacture in London at that date, but Benson's phrase allows manufacture elsewhere and we readily agree that there will be many other manufacturers still to be discovered, in different places and at different periods. Ireland is an obvious possibility.

Our earliest date is the possible production of white stoneware at Woolwich, in 1650, followed by *John Dwight* from 1673 and his London and Staffordshire competitors in the 1690s. Emphasising again that our information is fragmentary, we have found sixteen potters in the 1740s, thirty-one in the 1750s, a peak of sixty-one in the 1760s and a decline to twenty-three in the 1770s.

The latest, apart from revivals, are in the 1780s. In Staffordshire, there were *Thomas Barker, John Blackwell, Joseph Blackwell, Bourne, Wright and Co., Ralph Bucknall and Sons, John Graham junior, William Greatbatch,* and *Timothy and John Lockett.* Far afield, *Salem* in North Carolina in 1782 and *Prestonpans* in Scotland as late as the 1790s may have made our ware. Confirmation that production had almost ceased in Staffordshire in the 1780s comes from a letter of 5 May 1787 from Josiah Wedgwood to Madame Conradi, his customer in Dresden, when he told her that he had been very pressing upon the maker for the white stoneware, *'there being only one maker of it in this country* [our italics]'.[312] A last mention of white ware for H.C. Conradi, including Basket Work and Barley Corn, occurred in an Etruria memorandum dated 24 August 1790.[313]

*Fig. 114. **Figure of a woman,** white salt-glazed stoneware decorated in enamel colours, another example of which is in the Metropolitan Museum. Staffordshire c.1755. 5in. (12.7cm) high. **Tile,** press-moulded white salt-glazed stoneware. Examples of tiles are rare and some shards of similar tiles were excavated at the Fenton Vivian site of Thomas Whieldon. Staffordshire, possibly Whieldon, c.1750. 4⅞in. (12.38cm) square. (Photograph courtesy of Jonathan Horne, illustrated by Luxmoore Plate 88)*

Angerstein suggested thirty factories for white ware in Burslem and 430 'makers' (surely workers, not masters?) in

Colour Plate 119. **Sauceboat,** *white salt-glazed press-moulded sauceboat in the mosaic or basketweave pattern. Modelled by Aaron Wood, the same mould was used by Bow for making sauceboats. Staffordshire, c.1756-65. 3½in. (8.89cm) high. (Private collection)*

Hanley in 1754.[314] A figure of nearly 150 potters in Burslem and neighbourhood was given in a 1762 petition for a turnpike road, but this was immediately elaborated to be 'for making various kinds of stone and earthen ware'.[315] The same petition gave an annual amount of duty paid on salt consumed. Calculations given in our Chapter IV suggest seventy-five salt-glaze potters at that time, little more than the sixty-one we detail for the 1760s. Other mid-century estimates are also for all kinds of potters, Arthur Young suggesting some three hundred in 1768.[316] The 1770 Price Agreement (see Appendix 3) bears the signatures of twenty-seven salt-glaze potters, some measure of the number existing then, though it must be borne in mind that the signatories were only those salt-glaze potters who sold to earthenware potters, and that, for example, *Thomas and John Wedgwood* and *Thomas Wedgwood IV* of the Overhouse did not sign.

Inventories quoted show that early individual potters were also farmers, not solely dependent on pottery manufacture. *Joshua Astbury* of Shelton had ten cattle, six horses, two swine, corn, hay and farm implements when he died in 1721. *John Meir* left pottery, farming and coal-mining equipment in 1729. As late as 1773 *Thomas Wedgwood IV of Overhouse* had four horses, three carts, two cows, hay, oats and wheat, and a pair of harrows.

Partnerships show a development of this cross-financing. John Fenton, landowner, funded his young nephew Thomas Hill in a salt-glaze pottery (*Fenton and Hill*) at Shelton Farm in 1720. Richard Taylor, a Newcastle-under-Lyme iron-monger, became a partner to *John Mare*, a Longton salt-glaze potter in 1722, Taylor putting in £50 and not working, other than keeping accounts and selling ware.

Works

There are no contemporary statistics of the number of pot-works in the Staffordshire Potteries in the eighteenth century. Josiah Wedgwood estimated there to be seven making all types of stoneware in 1710-15 (Figure 26).[317] William Pitt wrote in 1817 of 'upwards of twenty ovens in the Parish of Burslem, all of which cast in their salt at the same time', but gave no date,[318] and Simeon Shaw estimated that 'fifty or sixty manufactories sent forth dense clouds of vapour',[319] again without date. All three estimates, seven, twenty, and fifty to sixty, may be correct according to their (unknown) dates, representing the gradual increase in businesses.

Fig. 115. **Tile,** *white salt-glazed stoneware press-moulded with a scene of the crucifixion. Incised Wm Simpkin on reverse. Staffordshire, c.1750. 5¼ x 5in. (13.34 x 12.7cm). (British Museum, 1919.0503.79; a larger identical tile was exhibited at the Burlington Fine Arts Club 1913-1914, Harland collection)*

Chapter V – Making the Pots

*Colour Plate 120. **Partially reconstructed plate** in white salt-glazed stoneware with press-moulded mosaic or basketweave border excavated at Deer Street in Portsmouth, New Hampshire. Mosaic plates were mentioned as early as 1757 in a London advertisement, and by John Bowcock of Bow in 1756. Staffordshire, c.1756-65. 10in. (25.4cm). (Strawbery Banke Museum, Portsmouth, New Hampshire, DS4 F. 48).*

There is very little *reliable* information about the size of the works. Lengthy lists of buildings in wills and title deeds are merely lawyers' attempts to include every conceivable type of premises and their only value is to confirm that the specialised workplaces named were known at that time. Inventories made after deaths and at bankruptcies are a dependable source, but even then there was no obligation on the assessors to name individual buildings or rooms. For larger estates it was convenient to list items room by room, and so the surviving information is skewed in favour of the bigger business. Insurance policies are another sound source, having to be specific to define the liability of the insurer.

Documents referring to *'Doctor' Thomas Wedgwood II* are a good example of lawyers' language which can be misunderstood. The lawyer drafting a title deed in 1731 stated that Wedgwood had bought 'Potthouses workhouses warehouses beating houses molding houses throwing houses smoakhouses, Pott-ovens killns hovells [sic]'in 1731.[320] When Thomas Wedgwood died in 1737, the assessors, Ralph Shawe and Moses Marsh, found only a solitary 'workhouse', very different from the impressive string of buildings allegedly bought by him six years previously. What the 1731 document does tell us is that all those buildings were known by then, even if Thomas Wedgwood really only possessed one workhouse.

The inventory made after the death of *Peter Bagnall* in 1761 shows that he had a large works: four warehouses, packing house, sliphouse, throwing house, turning house with a room over, an 'outshore' (lean-to building) adjoining the hovel, two or more ovens, and an 'Old Stove' (perhaps a drying room), in all ten or more locations, possibly most of them adjoining. The 1763 insurance record for *William Banks* detailed four hovels suggesting four ovens, a chamber to make dishes in, two Lathouses (lathe houses), a painting house and three 'Smoakhouses', about eleven workplaces altogether.

When *Thomas Wedgwood IV of Overhouse* died in 1773 an inventory of his works shows that he had a large workhouse, a throwing workhouse, a stove house, a hot house, a saggar house, a saggar house chamber and one oven, six workrooms and one oven in all. Thomas Wedgwood's single workplace in 1737, Bagnall's ten in 1761, Banks' 1763 eleven and Thomas Wedgwood's six in 1773 give some idea of the growth in the size of salt-glaze potworks in Staffordshire. For comparison, *John Baddeley*, a general potter making all kinds of ware, had about twenty workplaces in 1761.

Workers

As with potworks, we have widely differing estimates of the number of workers in Staffordshire, but of course not specific to salt-glaze manufacture. In 1754 Angerstein first wrote that 'In Hanley there are also nearly 430 makers of white ware and other pottery' and then 'The potteries are said to employ many thousands of people'.[321] Gabriel Jars said that it was claimed in 1765 that there were from 10,000 to 15,000 people employed in north Staffordshire, either in the coal mines or in the pottery factories, 'the latter form the greater number'.[322] Arthur Young, who visited the Staffordshire Potteries in late 1768, said that the '300 houses [potworks] … employ upon an average twenty hands each, or 6000 on the whole'.[323]

For individual potworks, we start with Josiah Wedgwood's estimate of ten workers (six men and four boys) in 1710-15 (Figure 26), for making 'Black and Mottled [ware]'.[324] A similar figure of ten employees applied when *Fenton and Hill* ended their partnership in 1721, this time nine men and one woman, specifically for salt-glaze manufacture. *Joshua Astbury*, another salt-glaze maker, was employing twelve to fourteen workers when he died in the same year.

In the mid-century, *Jonah Malkin*, briefly a salt-glaze potter at Burslem, hired three men and two boys in May 1748, whilst *Thomas Whieldon*, a general potter rather than salt-glaze specialist, employed between sixteen and twenty-five, including boys and girls, in the 1750s; and *John Baddeley*, another general potter, employed around forty workers in 1761-62.[325] The hiring book of *Thomas and John Wedgwood*, redware and salt-glaze potters, shows a maximum of thirteen employees in 1761: ten men, two women and one apprentice.[326]

Angerstein obliquely indicated the number of salt-glaze workers at *Derby* in 1754 as well over forty when he wrote that the china manufactory there employed forty people and the white-ware factory was much larger. If Angerstein is reliable, the Cockpit Hill salt-glaze works at Derby was larger than that of John Baddeley's general works at Shelton. There were over sixty workers at *Rotherham* in 1768, reduced to thirteen by 1772.

CHAPTER V – MAKING THE POTS

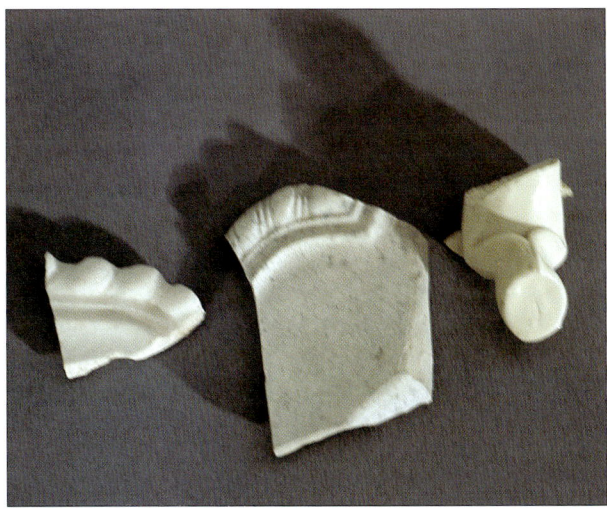

*Colour Plate 121. **Three shards** in white salt-glazed stoneware, a moulded edge of a plate with gadrooned pattern left, a bead and reel moulded edge, centre, a handle kick, all excavated from The Richard Shortridge house site, Deer Street, Portsmouth, New Hampshire. Staffordshire, c.1755-65. 1⅞in. (4.76cm) maximum. (Strawbery Banke Museum, Portsmouth, New Hampshire)*

Of the individual workers, few personal details survive. Master potters did employ more than one member of the same family, but the little information available is that they were paid individually, not as a family unit.[327] Separately from the fathers, *Jonah Malkin* hired Daniel Heath's son for 1s.7d. per week and Joseph Burn's son for 1s.8d. in 1748; and *Thomas and John Wedgwood* hired William Wedgwood for 7s. and his son for 16d. a week in 1766. Their hiring book includes employees' sons as apprentices: William Wedgwood's son for seven years from 1759 to throw and another son for seven years from 1762 to turn in the lathe.

*Colour Plate 122. **Plate rim shard**, white salt-glazed stoneware moulded with the seed or barleycorn pattern excavated from the Nims site, Deerfield, Massachusetts. Staffordshire, c.1755-65. (Photograph courtesy of Historic Deerfield, Inc.)*

The eighteenth century brought specialisation to workers. Simeon Shaw gave a general picture of the situation before 1740,[328] stating that a good workman could throw, turn and handle, and would work each week at two or three works, versatility indeed. He went on to say that the demand for white stoneware caused manufacturers to introduce formal hiring, binding each worker to one master and one craft. Specialisation brought increased health hazards. As early as 1726 Thomas Benson supported his application for a patent for wet grinding of potters' flint by stating that dry pounding and sifting had 'proved very destructive to mankind, insomuch that any person ever so healthfull or strong working in that business cannot probably survive above two yeares [*sic*], occasioned by the dust sucked into his body by the air he breath[e]s'.[329] Similar health risks attended fettlers who smoothed the dry but un-glazed ware all day.

We have referred earlier in this chapter to the well-known formal indentures of Aaron Wood, first as apprentice and then as 'journeyman'. Another surviving indenture is that of Josiah Wedgwood, bound to his brother for five years in 1744 to learn throwing and handling.[330] These are probably exceptional in being legally worded contracts. Much more usual would be *Thomas Whieldon's* casual notes, such as '1753 June 21. Hired Wm. Marsh for 3 years. He is to have 10s.6d. Earnest each year, and 7s. per week. I am to give an old Coat or something ab[ou]t 5s. value';[331] or *Thomas and John Wedgwood's* 'Hired Geo Greaves for 5/6 till Martinmas 1762 he never had nor askt [*sic*, asked for] any Earnest'.[332] ('Earnest' was an annual gift to the workman to bind the agreement, somewhat like a handshake to settle a deal.)

Because of inflation and improvement in standards of living, eighteenth century actual wage amounts have no relevance today, but can show the comparative standing of different skills. Arthur Young listed potters' wage rates in 1768, probably at Josiah Wedgwood's Burslem works:[333] pressers and moulders from 8s., throwers, handlers and other finishers from 9s., engine turners and painters from 10s., and gilders from 12s., though women gilders only received 7s.6d. Boys had 2s.9d. a week 'as they then learn nothing', but when apprenticed had initially 2s. per week, rising 3d. a year. The best-paid employee was one modeller who had £100 a year, possibly John Voyez. These variations in rates seem reasonable indications of the differing levels of skill required. Then, as now, London rates were better: Campbell suggested piece-work earnings of from 15s. per week for men pottery painters in 1747.[334]

Humble as the ordinary working potters were, they had the valuable 'know-how' of making salt-glazed ware, starting with the potters from Frechen in Germany, thought to have brought their skills to Woolwich c.1650, handed down to the Staffordshire men who took their in turn inherited abilities to Bovey Tracey in Devon and Cain Hoy in South Carolina in the 1760s. It is they and their countless colleagues who really made our much-admired white salt-glazed stoneware.

CHAPTER VI

Marketing in Britain and Europe

The purpose of producing pottery is to sell it. Whilst Hilary Young has written on marketing porcelain and Lorna Weatherill on the role of the pottery 'middleman' in the eighteenth century,[1] we limit ourselves to the sale of white salt-glazed stoneware. Information on the marketing of salt-glaze stoneware is lacking in the seventeenth century and first half of the eighteenth for the same reasons that thwart all conclusive evidence about potters and manufacture of the ware. Lack of information about the early salt-glaze industry is due to the utilitarian cottage industry nature of the business, a manufacture held in little regard by the consumer, just as later ceramics, like blue transfer-printed earthenware, were not regarded at the time of their manufacture as anything but common market products. Museums and collectors have subsequently given these wares an esteem not accorded them at the time.

Very little information is available for exports to the Continent or America. In America there is enough archaeological information, along with newspaper advertisements and estate inventories, to construct a broadly accurate picture of the use of salt-glaze stoneware in everyday life from 1720 to the late years of the eighteenth century. This is dealt with in Chapter VII. For Europe the picture is more obscure. English white stoneware is frequently uncovered in urban salvage excavations in the Netherlands and has been making its way back to dealers who are reselling these wares to museums and collectors. Amsterdam dealer Alexander Park was receiving large and frequent shipments of English pottery from *John Baddeley* of Shelton. According to Baddeley's account books, Park was receiving cargoes of ware sometimes totalling over a hundred crates at roughly two-monthly intervals between 1753 and 1767.[2] It seems likely that much of this was white salt-glazed stoneware and that there was widespread exportation to other parts of the Continent as well, although information is scanty.

John Dwight in London had a ready-made network of wholesalers and retailers in 1676 when he obtained a monopoly of selling stoneware, albeit brown stoneware, to the members of the London Company of Glass-Sellers.[3] The outlet for Staffordshire potters c.1680, making coarse red earthenware, was 'cheifly [sic] to the poor *Crate-men*, who carry them at their *backs* all over the *Countrey* [sic]'.[4] Thirteen years later the makers of stoneware were in active competition. Dwight, with his network of London outlets, was complaining that both London and Staffordshire potters had 'Made and sold very great quantityes [sic] of earthen wares' in imitation of his white and red wares 'for severall yeares [sic] last past'.[5]

Our information is drawn principally from the erratic survival of original documentation:

Jonah Malkin's sales ledger from 1747 consistently to 1750:   20 customers
Thomas Wedgwood IV of Overhouse's notebooks, at intervals from 1752 to 1773:   73 customers
Thomas and John Wedgwood's sales ledger and crate book, from 1755 consistently to 1776:   215 customers
Josiah Wedgwood's documents referring to the buying and selling of white salt-glazed stoneware surviving in the Wedgwood Accumulation, mostly 1763-64 with a few up to 1790:   35 customers

(These customers are listed in Appendix 5.) It can be seen that no detailed information is available from these sources

Fig. 116. **Vase,** *white salt-glazed stoneware with grape and vine sprig relief and slab moulded applied handles. Staffordshire, c.1740. 6in. (15.24cm) high. (Photograph courtesy of Winterthur Museum, gift of Mr and Mrs, John Mayer)*

before 1747, the year when Campbell wrote in *The London Tradesman*: 'The Earthen-Ware Shop is a Dependant on the Pot-House: They buy their Goods from several Houses in *England*, from *Holland,* and at the Sales of the *East-India Company*'. Campbell was probably referring to tin-glazed earthenware and Chinese porcelain, though he had a vague notion of stoneware 'only made near *Liverpool*' but 'much preferable to the Earthen-ware'.[6]

Dwight and his fellow London stoneware manufacturers lived in a commercial metropolis, with a long tradition of buying and selling. Although the Staffordshire potters lived in villages, they did have access to a nearby market town. Newcastle-under-Lyme was a chartered borough from 1173, had a market by 1203 and a guild merchant in 1235.[7] Amongst the trades represented there was a provider of tableware, James Shaw, a pewterer, who left £195 worth of 'brasse pewter moulds tooles & all other' when he died in 1607.[8] Commercial expertise was available from local lawyers and finance from embryonic bankers. Newcastle specialised in hat-making, and 'About 1730 Thomas Hall, head of a [hatmaking] firm [was] then considered the greatest export house in Europe',[9] showing that there was knowledge of national and overseas trading in the locality, for Staffordshire potters to draw upon. *John Mare* found finance from a Newcastle ironmonger for a salt-glaze pottery in 1722.

Customers came in many guises: wholesalers including exporters, overseas buyers, retailers and individuals, but also other potters and independent enamellers. Our admittedly unrepresentative list (see Appendix 5) includes all of these. Their locations were equally diverse: London and Liverpool, of course, but also scattered throughout England, from Newcastle-upon-Tyne and Whitehaven in the north to Plymouth in the south-west, to Dublin, Cork

Fig. 117. **Water bottle,** *white salt-glazed stoneware with applied sprig relief grapes, vines and birds. Staffordshire, c.1740-50. 8⅞in. (22.54cm) high. (Catzen collection)*

Fig. 118. **Stand for pickles or eggs?,** *white salt-glazed stoneware trefoil stand on an attached scalloped base with strap handle. Staffordshire, c.1755. 6⅛in. (15.56cm) long. (British Museum, Willett collection, 1887, G102)*

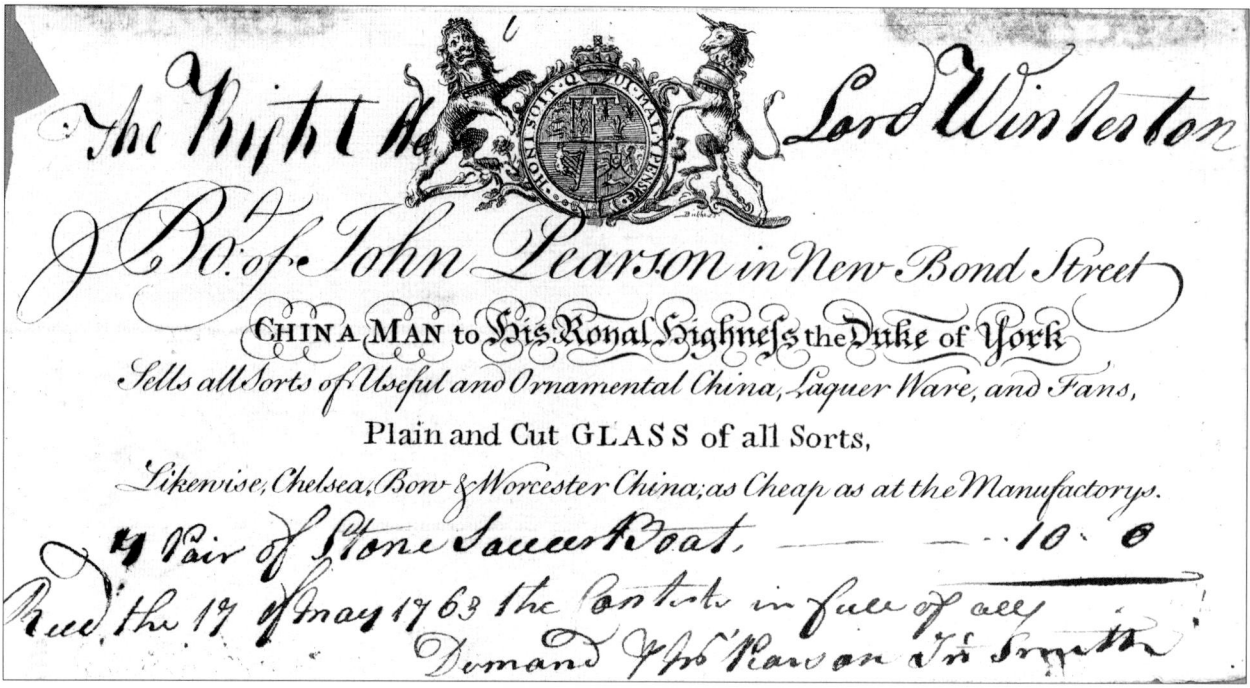

*Fig. 119. **Invoice** from John Pearson, New Bond Street, London to The Right Ho[nourable] Lord Winterton for the purchase of 'Pair of Stone Sauce Boat[s]' for 10s., 17 May 1763. (Courtesy the Winterthur Library: Joseph Downs Collection of Manuscripts and Printed Ephemera, 60 x 8.3. Photograph courtesy of Winterthur Museum)*

and Strabane in Ireland, and also to Hamburg, Rotterdam and far-off Dresden in Continental Europe.

No customers have been noted in Wales or Scotland, but it must be borne in mind that the four potters who provide most of our data were interrelated and likely to share business when necessary. We have no information about the customers of the many other salt-glaze potters who flourished in the same period. The surviving letters from wholesalers and retailers show their readiness to complain to the supplier, then as now.

London Dealers

The greatest mercantile activity was naturally in London. London was also where one would expect, and indeed did find, the widest variety and the latest in ceramic fashions. In 1746 the stock in trade of London china merchant Mrs. Revel, deceased, located at the corner of Little Queen Street, Holborn included a 'large Quantity of white Stone Ware of all Kinds, and brown ditto'.[10] One gets a glimpse of the character teapots which must have fascinated the tea drinking community with forms in the shape of camels (Colour Plate 25) monkeys, squirrels (Colour Plate 24) and houses (Figs. 29, 72) in an advertisement in the *Daily Advertiser* of 24 August 1747:

To be Sold

Facing the Door of the Old London Spaw, in the Spau Fields during Welch Fair.

All sorts of Welch Ware, Derby and Staffordshire fine Stone Ware, amongst which are great Variety of Curious Tea-Pots of all sizes, that far excel either Silver or China, both for Drawing or Pouring, and not inferior in beauty…

In the same year, Lady Findlater in Scotland bought from John Rickwood of Piccadilly a wide variety of stoneware shapes.[11] In 1757 John Fleetwood, 'China-man and Glass-Seller' located in Leadenhall Street opposite Lime Street, London, was selling for exportation along with Green and Bohea tea & 'Cannisters' 'Salt Stone Cups & Saucers'.[12] In 1763 John Guest, another London merchant, in addition to ordering black and red 'engraved [transfer-printed]' teapots, was ordering '1 doz Hawthorn Leaves, 1 doz Bird pattern, 1 doz Small Foxglove… 6 Lilley [sic] Candlesticks' which may have been salt-glazed stoneware.[13] John Pearson, the New Bond Street China Man (Fig. 119), sold Lord Winterton a pair of 'Stone Sauce Boats' which cost 10s. in 1763.[14] Pearson had bought from *Thomas and John Wedgwood* from 1756 until 1759, when he was insolvent,[15] but obviously continued to trade.

A 1727 London advertisement gives an early mention of white salt-glazed stoneware. William Watkinson, China-man, was bankrupt at his great China Shop between Catherine-Street and Exeter Exchange in the Strand, and his advertised stock included 'fine white Stone Ware'.[16] Eighteen years later, the 1745 billhead of Hannah Ashburner, corner of Fleet Bridge, London, included 'fine Stone Ware',[17] a business that probably became Lambden and Woods by 1769 (Fig. 120).

Messrs Addison & Abernathy, located on Hermitage Street, Wapping, purchased large quantities of wares from Josiah Wedgwood during 1763 and 1764. Thomas Abernathy placed an interesting order to Josiah Wedgwood in 1763 for:

25 White Worcester pattern Basket & Stands
24 Nutt pattern_____do
12 Largest White Bird Tureens & Stands

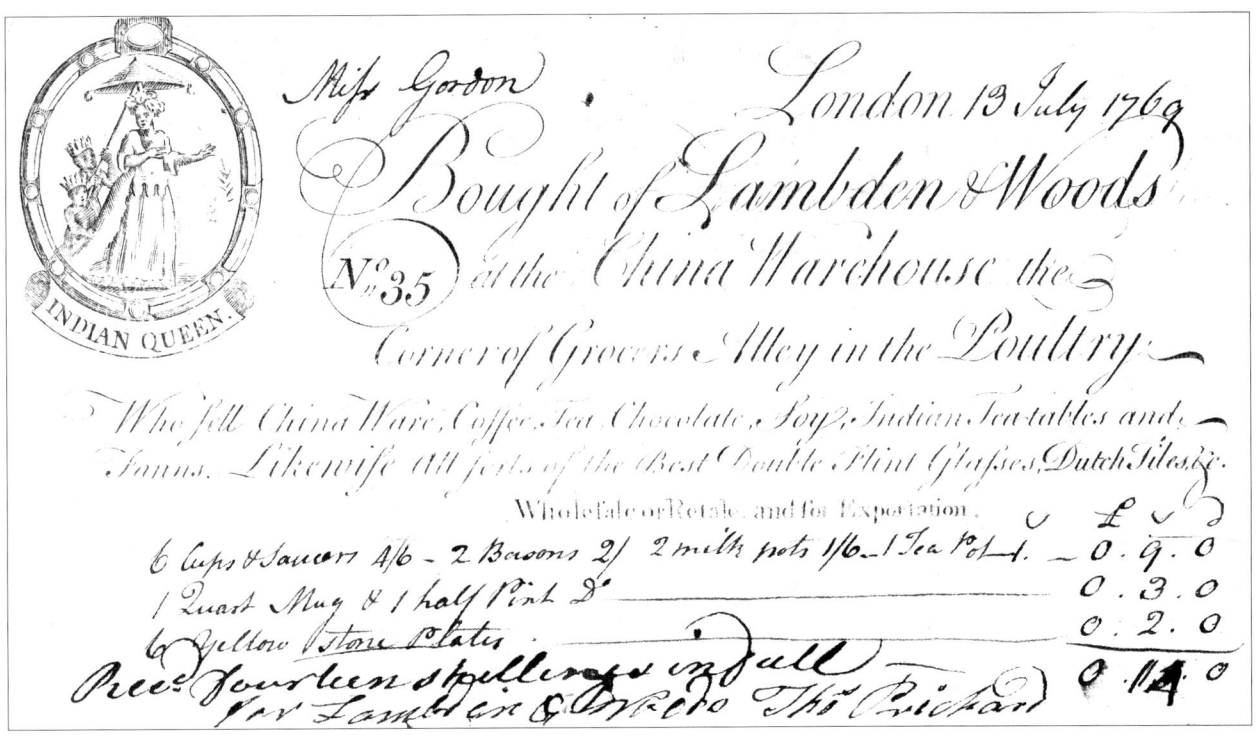

*Fig. 120. **Invoice** from Lambden & Woods, Corner of Grocers Alley, the Poultry, London to Miss Gordon for salt-glazed stoneware 13 July 1769. (Courtesy the Winterthur Library: Joseph Dowas Collection of Manuscripts and Printed Ephemera, 60 x 8.3. Photograph courtesy of Winterthur Museum)*

12 Smaller _____ do
12 Smallest _____ do
12 Sallad Bowles & Stands white
12 do ____Larger_____ do

NB. The above I mean to be White Stone the same shapes as those sent [in] Green … pray send us all the new patterns you can make … oval sallad [sic] Dishes Green & White would sell well of the French pattern – Mr. Booth is making some of them of 3 Sizes, 10, 12, & 14 Inches.[18]

A note appended to James Abernathy's order to Josiah Wedgwood in January 1764 said 'Mr. Abernathy has been in a Mistake when he mentioned barley corn and French pattern as different for we understand them as one'.[19] Another order from James Abernathy requested: '3 or 4 doz. Figures for Mantlepieces [sic] as Effigies of Turks, Dancers, Crooked Men & after the Chinese Taste & the Colours adapted accordingly, about 6 inches [15cm] in length'.[20] Along with the latest fashions in green and in tortoise-coloured wares the Abernathys were placing orders for considerable amounts of 'flint' in round, oblong [dishes] and fruit dishes, round butter tubs and stands, leaves, soop [sic] dishes, tureens and sauceboats.[21]

By February 1764 Abernathys were requesting that Wedgwood send no more white, an indication that the fashion for salt-glazed white stoneware was waning.[22] By August 1764 the Abernathys were trading as Abernathy & Livie, John Livie having been ordering from Wedgwood since at least March of that year from the Hermitage Street address.[23] Some orders continued to be placed for white stoneware, but they were vastly overshadowed by the interest in green and tortoise colour.

Chinaman Thomas Gilbert, located at Garlick Hill, London, was ordering from Wedgwood 'Square [teapots]' by the dozen with India figures in twelves, eighteens and twenty-fours.[24] In London Shoreditch dealer Robert Miller ordered among other typical wares of the day 'good white ware' in the form of chamber pots, teapots, 'pint porringers with round handles' from Josiah Wedgwood in 1763 and 1764 (Fig. 121).[25]

*Fig. 121. **Porringer,** white salt-glazed stoneware with shell-shaped and moulded handle pierced with one hole. Staffordshire, c.1730-50. 2½in. (6.35cm) high. (Private collection)*

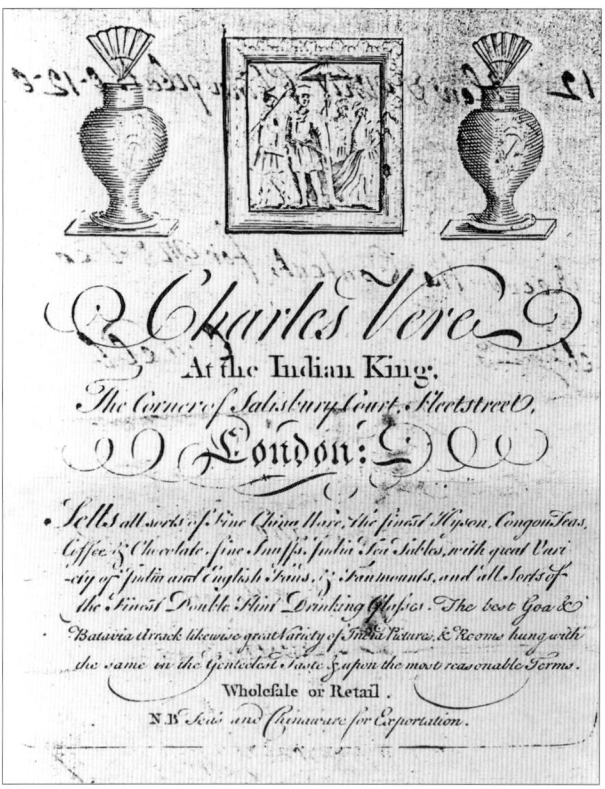

*Fig. 122. **Letterhead** for Charles Vere, the Corner of Salisbury Court, Fleet Street, London. Vere was operating in London in 1764. (Wedgwood MS 6/31180)*

Charles Vere, at the Indian King, corner of Salisbury Court and Fleet Street (Fig. 122), was a wholesale/retail merchant with colourful letterheads capitalising on the popularity of all things Oriental. He also exported and probably dealt in salt-glazed stoneware, although the one invoice to Wedgwood does not specify the fabric of the teacups and coffee cups and saucers purchased by Mr. Vere in 1764.[26]

Mr. William Philpot of London ordered two to three crates of gadrooned plates and oblong dishes in 1764, specifying they be 'all white'.[27] James Hayes opened up a new shop for 'China, Glass and Stoneware' in Fenchurch Street, London, in 1764. He placed an order to Josiah Wedgwood for barleycorn and gadrooned pattern stone sauceboats in several sizes as well as red stoneware teapots and melon and green earthenwares.[28] Other dealers such as John Buxton, 35 St. Paul's Churchyard, were still advertising the sale of white stoneware as late as 1769 when it was certainly beyond the height of fashion.[29] Lambden & Woods, No. 35 at the China Warehouse, corner of Grocer's Alley at the Poultry, advertised themselves as 'Wholesalers, Retailers and for Exportation' (Fig. 120). In 1769 they invoiced a sale which included '6 Yellow Stone Plates'[30] which were probably creamware, not stoneware, yellow being an early description for cream colour. If one was wealthy enough to have a servant, as was Charles Love, one could send him out to do one's shopping in 1769 with a note such as the following: 'To Mr. Hugh Gardner: Sir: Please to Send me by the Bearer Two of your Largest Stone Muggs and hope you will do me the favour to See there is [*sic*] no Cracks in Them....'[31] These might have been either brown or white salt-glazed ware, of course.

The usefulness of white stoneware continued to be expressed in the next two decades or so, with orders for utilitarian stonewares such as 'Gallipots, Spitting pots, Chamber pots, and nappies', particularly in the less fashionable parts of the city with dealers like Joseph Vanderkirk, whose address was simply 'Boro', an area south of the river Thames near Lambeth.[32]

The Staffordshire salt-glaze potters did not rise to the sophistication of later creamware makers. *Thomas Wedgwood IV of Overhouse* made occasional visits to London to obtain orders and collect debts and no doubt others did the same. *Joshua Astbury* rented a warehouse in London before 1721 and *William Banks* had a warehouse there by 1759. None is known to have had a *retail showroom* in London, as did Josiah Wedgwood, James Neale and John Turner for their later products. Nor is there any evidence of salt-glaze manufacturers 'hyping' their products by pretence of scarcity, as Wedgwood was to do.[33]

Provincial Dealers

Customers had to be found, and we have already mentioned Plot's poor cratemen of the 1680s, who went all over the country. A latter-day example was Sam Bryan of Lane End, who was probably of a late eighteenth century family of Bryans, potsellers, at Lane End (Longton).[34] He bought two crates from *Thomas and John Wedgwood* in 1765 (and never paid for them).[35] These hawkers came to the works and paid cash, mostly for seconds.

Travellers toured the country, gaining orders from shopkeepers and wholesalers. Simeon Shaw describes the travellers employed by *John Mitchell*, a major Burslem salt-glaze potter, in business from 1736 to 1763.[36] Mitchell employed four travellers, who all later settled in the West Country as glass and earthenware dealers: at Bridgwater in Somerset, Exeter and Plymouth in Devon and Falmouth in Cornwall. Their simple accounting method was to empty their pockets on return to Burslem, having already paid their travelling expenses!

William Hassells represents another method of distribution and sales. He advertised in an Ipswich newspaper in May and also October 1759 that he had just returned from his pot-house in Staffordshire with a variety of wares, including white and blue and white stoneware, to be sold wholesale in Bury St. Edmunds and at his own warehouse in Colchester.[37]

Richard Hargrave of Stamford, Lincolnshire, 'potter', who died c.1720, is an example of an early eighteenth century provincial shopkeeper. The 1720/21 inventory of his effects 'in the Shopp' show that he was purely a seller of pottery and glass, not a maker of pottery.[38] He had 'course [coarse] ware', 'Nottingham Muggs', 'Five fine Delph plates' at fivepence each, and 'Three dozen of Flatt Ware' at fourpence each, which might have been either pewter or pot. He also had 'White Muggs' and 'white Juggs' at a penny each, and 'white Tea Potts' at fourpence each. 'White' might be tin-glazed ware or salt-glazed stoneware.

The appraisers knew what Delph meant, and therefore it might be inferred that White meant salt-glazed ware.

In the provinces, dealers, literate or not, needed salt-glaze stoneware for their custom. From Chester Ann Parson wrote to Josiah Wedgwood for '8 paer of white corneycopes with the waer [eight pairs of white cornucopias with the ware]' (Fig. 123) along with green and white candlesticks (Colour Plates 39, 76, 78; Figs. 42, 54-58, 60, 103).[39] Chester dealers Alice and John Peers were also ordering white 'hand candlesticks, wash basons [sic]', wine measure quart mugs, barleycorn dishes and plates, toy teacups and teapots (Colour Plate 123).[40]

Dealer Elizabeth Cadman of Penkridge, Staffordshire, was ordering from Josiah Wedgwood in 1763 green and cream coloured ware but also baskets and stands in the 'old pattern' which was probably salt-glaze. She also wrote: 'I desire you will send me some Little Birds & Dogs____ about a dozen but send me no Cats for I think Mr. *Aaron Wedgwood* has stocked me very well with Cats & Kittens for a good while. Desire Mr. Aaron Wedgwood will send me

*Fig. 123. **Wall pocket cornucopia,** white salt-glazed stoneware press-moulded with a central cartouche with a female figure. Staffordshire, c.1750-55. 12in. (30.48cm) long. (Potteries Museum and Art Gallery, Stoke-on-Trent, 1676)*

*Colour Plate 123. **Teapot,** white salt-glazed stoneware in panels which may be the carved ware referred to occasionally in descriptions by merchants. Staffordshire, possibly Shelton Farm, c.1730-40. 5in. (12.7cm) high. (Victoria and Albert Museum, C464-1949)*

24 white half price floure [sic] horns to stand in the window'.⁴¹ Another modest request was for 'half a grose [sic, half a gross, 72] of white Galley pots if your Brother [*Thomas Wedgwood IV of Overhouse*] or any of your neighbours have any'.⁴²

Despite these simple orders, Elizabeth Cadman bought the latest in ceramic fashion, catering to the aristocracy with clients like Lord Gray, Lord Kildare and unspecified 'Ladies'. A request by her to 'send me a green gilt barley corn plat[e] a Large one' is significant in confirming that barleycorn moulds were used for green glazed ware.⁴³

In 1763 an invoice from Josiah Wedgwood to John Mitchell, location unspecified, gave an indication of the prices of white salt-glazed ware then. Inlet teapots size 24s were 2s.9d; common teapots 24s, 2s.6d; ewers and salts 36s, 2s.6d; both pint and half-pint mugs 2s.0d., and jugs 2s.0d., all per dozen.⁴⁴ More details of prices are given in Appendix 3. James Eaton, a Liverpool merchant, was buying enamelled white salt-glaze cups and saucers, teapots, sugar dishes and cream jugs by the dozen from Josiah Wedgwood in 1763.⁴⁵

In Nottingham retailer Ann Else principally placed orders for red stoneware coffee pots of silver shape and tortoise tea toys, and plain cream colour enamel teapots with natural flowers, but also asked for a blue coffee pot and two or three dozen small birds, these latter probably salt-glazed stoneware. She told the Nottingham carrier to obtain two dozen white mustard pot spoons from *Thomas and John Wedgwood*, who charged small amounts to her in 1762 and 1764.⁴⁶ Also in 1764 a Mr. Horner, location unknown, was placing orders exclusively for white stoneware in large quantities, seventy-two dozen white enamel teapots 18s and 24s, twenty-four white flummery shapes, diff(erent) figures, white toilet candlesticks and children's toys, as well as baking dishes, soup plates, twifflers, etc.⁴⁷

New money provided continual challenges to manufacturers in order to keep up with or, preferably, to anticipate changes in taste. A Mr. Arden of Macclesfield placed several orders for 'Tantalus Cups with Covers';⁴⁸ these were the Zeus or Bacchus cups with which he was perhaps supplying a tavern or inn. Some dealers, such as Emmanuel Boothroyd of Lindley near Huddersfield, complained that shell teapots didn't sell any more by 1764,⁴⁹ nor did white in general,⁵⁰ an indication that the stoneware was old fashioned and the more colourful naturalistic wares like the agates and fruit forms were more in demand. Red stoneware also continued to be widely appreciated during the mid-1760s.

Orders in the mid-1760s which do not specify the body could be salt-glazed stoneware, coloured ware, redware or creamware, although cream colour was still new enough to be more frequently specified in that period. So when one considers Whitehaven retailer John Douglas' order for forty dozen 'porrengers [sic]' 24s with the message appended 'you can't send too many', one must assume that these are more likely to be salt-glazed stoneware than any other fabric. Douglas was also ordering mustard pots (Colour Plate 124) and salts (Colour Plate 125), jugs and tankards, again probably in white stoneware.⁵¹

The letters from John Douglas to Josiah Wedgwood in 1763-64 illustrate the complexities of trade which were commonplace by then.⁵² Amongst many types of ware, he wanted (as)sorted blue and white ware, second flint sortable 'for I am sold out', barleycorn teapots, plain white flint and 'Crouch Misers'. These last were brown salt-glaze measure gill, pint and quart mugs and jugs, and he begged Wedgwood to 'charge them [the makers] to make them Right Misers according to orders or if they are not They are of very Littell [little] Service': Douglas wanted true measures.⁵³

Douglas also bought from Taylor Stevenson (see *Samuel Kirk and Co.*), Thomas Cartlich, William Parrott, Whieldon, Booth, *Thomas Wedgwood IV of Overhouse* and John Chatterley of Hanley Green. With such a range of suppliers it is not surprising to learn that Douglas visited the Potteries himself: in October 1763 he told Wedgwood that he would 'see you about Christmas'. He received his goods via 'Mr Wood', the wharfinger at Winsford and 'Mr. Brookes Horker [sic, hawker?] in Liverpool',⁵⁴ and had many complaints to make. Missing crates, crates left out of doors a long time, the straw and crate all rotten, white ware so slender that it will not stand carriage, get the next off someone who makes it stronger and puts more clay in it, are all paraphrases of Douglas' colourful criticisms. Douglas appeared to prosper: in 1772 he insured £600 worth of property occupied by others in Whitehaven Market Place.⁵⁵

In 1763 and 1764 dealer Charles Kinkead of Strabane in the north of Ireland sent two large orders to *Thomas Wedgwood IV of the Overhouse* for white salt-glazed stoneware, including blue and white and blue flow(ere)d cups and saucers.⁵⁶ He continued to place orders for similar wares in 1766 which included 'quart white jugs, canns, cup & saucers and chamber pots, Basons, Porengers [sic], Mustard Pots, Peper [sic] castors, silver edged Pleats [sic, plates]... Barley corne Pleats'.⁵⁷ Another Irish dealer, A. Coleman, located in Dundalk, wrote a letter of introduction to Josiah Wedgwood in 1764, requesting '1 crate of 1ˢᵗˢ, 1 of 2ⁿᵈˢ, 1 of 3ʳᵈˢ of white flint plates, Dishes, Chamber Pots, Jugs, from a quart to 3 quarts'.⁵⁸

Exporters

Statistics about English exports in the eighteenth century are too general to confirm what we expect to be the case; that 'To the Continent we send an amazing quantity of white stoneware', as Josiah Wedgwood wrote in 1765,⁵⁹ whichever continent he meant. Lorna Weatherill collated information about the export of pieces of glass and earthenware from England between 1697/8 and 1815, showing an increase from some 200 thousand items to 50 million in that period, noting that 'Trade statistics relating to pottery production are far from ideal and complete'.⁶⁰ To illustrate the exporting of salt-glazed ware, examples are quoted below from Liverpool, from London and one from Walsall, a town remote from any coast.

Liverpool was the obvious outlet for pottery exports from Staffordshire to cross-Atlantic destinations. Chapter VII gives some idea of the extent of exports of salt-glazed ware to America, though Bentley and Boardman of Liverpool, quoted there, is the only certain instance we have found of an exporter of white salt-glazed ware across the Atlantic. It is likely that John Dunbibin, Liverpool merchant and potter, mentioned below, was another, and there must have been many more, but sensible commercial secrecy dictated that buyers did not reveal the ultimate customers to their suppliers.

John Wyke of Liverpool, watch and clock maker,[61] received inquiries from Portugal in 1762 for various types of pottery and sent out patterns from Josiah Wedgwood and from *Aaron Wedgwood*, both of Burslem. Two orders followed in 1763, for white stone 'Boslam Ware [*sic*, Burslem Ware]', agate, tortoiseshell, pineapple etc. and red china, with stringent requirements for shapes, sizes, quality and packing.[62] The total order included 600 dozen half pint bowls, 400 dozen bowls, 350 dozen double coffee cups and also tewares, all of the same pattern, over 3,000 dozen pieces in all.[63] Another large order of a similar nature occurred the following month.[64]

Josiah Wedgwood recommended four Burslem salt-glaze pottery firms to provide the ware which he did not make himself and the reverse of Wyke's first order shows their initials and quantities. *Aaron Wedgwood*, already known to Wyke, apparently dealt direct. *Thomas and John Wedgwood* sent a hogshead (barrel) and a crate to Wyke on 23 July 1763,[65] whilst *Thomas Taylor III and Isaiah Taylor* despatched seven crates and *William Taylor II* supplied nineteen crates, paid for by Wyke on 23 August 1763.

Specifications of interest include French pattern stone plates, Globe teapots, Landscape stone painted teapots, and plates, dishes and small tureens with 'no frotted [*sic*, fretted, pierced?] work on the Brim only the scalloping & Moulding round the edge'. A single hand basin and beaker of 'Mazarine blew [blue]' ware was presumably to be supplied by *Aaron Wedgwood*. These transactions well illustrate the role of Josiah Wedgwood in receiving and passing on orders for white salt-glazed stoneware.

Thomas Bentley, well known as Josiah Wedgwood's partner for ornamental ware, was also in partnership with Samuel Boardman as general merchants in Liverpool. Wedgwood and Bentley were in correspondence in 1766 about a crate of white ware lost *en route* to Liverpool.[66] In 1769 Bentley and Boardman (mentioned in Chapter VII as exporting white salt-glazed ware to Boston in 1764) ordered from Wedgwood for Joseph Wright of Derby a number of items in creamware, but also some jugs, mugs, flagons, ewers and basins which may have been salt-glazed stoneware. They complained to Wedgwood of the breakage in the last shipment, particularly the spoons. Two months later Lady Derby placed an order for petty pans, again probably salt-glazed stoneware.[67] In 1769 Lord Ashburnham was also ordering a dozen soup plates in the barleycorn pattern and Sir Charles Smith wanted thirty or forty dozen plain white stoneware table plates in an order of an unspecified date, all examples showing that the use of salt-glazed stoneware cut across all social classes.[68]

Mary Forbes, near Old Dock, Liverpool, bought blue teaware, coffee cups and coffee pots and white salt-glazed ware in 1764, some for export, through Josiah Wedgwood. Her husband returned from the West Indies in September 1764, insolvent, and Mrs. Forbes was concerned that she would be involved. She owed money to many potters, including *Thomas Wedgwood IV of Overhouse*.[69] Continuing in business, Mrs. Forbes complained on 9 October 1764 that 'two crates of flint ware arrived yesterday & too late for the vessel', indicative of exporting, but not revealing the destination. Her complaint continued, that the goods were 'of an inferior quality' and 'whoever you had them from has not used you well'. *Thomas Wedgwood IV of Overhouse* still supplied her with 'best flint [ware, i.e. salt-glazed ware]' in 1765.[70]

Another exporter, Robert Perrin of Lancaster, shipped from Liverpool a wide variety of salt-glazed stoneware in 1763. He ordered gadrooned 'soops', flint coffee pots, 'Pint Pearl Enamel Coffee Potts', 'Enamel Sauce Boats' and cream jugs also in pearl enamel.[71] Mr. Blackburn, Salt House, Liverpool, was receiving the orders which continued into the autumn that year with 'flint enamel Mustard pots'.[72] 'Pearl enamel is a term which occurs in other orders around the same time and is not understood by the authors, but since it is distinguished from 'flint enamel' it is probably not salt-glazed stoneware.

Turning to London exporters, Jno. Will Pollmann ordered white salt-glazed stoneware through Josiah Wedgwood in 1763, to be sent to Pollmann's customers via Hull and Hamburg, and also via Newcastle-upon-Tyne.[73] On 19 April 1763 Pollmann asked for a 'neat assortment of Stone ware value about £26 or £27' to be sent to Hull for the first ship to Hamburg, 'chiefly Coffeepotts, Teapotts, & Milkpots of different patterns and Colours, a few Cups & Saucers, tureens and plates, and some other newfashioned articles'. This was 'a sample to a house abroad which deals largely – go near the wind to encourage them [keep the price down]'.[74]

Pollmann's dealings were not restricted to pottery. Wedgwood's Hull correspondent was to send six pieces of best pig lead with the order. Later, Pollmann sent Wedgwood a sample of zaffer (impure cobalt) received from Germany, to see if Wedgwood could sell it.[75] The surviving papers contain the usual complaints about prices, deliveries and quality, common from buyers to sellers, and detailed instructions such as sending before winter, presumably to avoid ice-bound rivers in Europe.

Wedgwood marked up Pollmann's 1 October 1763 order with the names of potters who were to supply salt-glazed ware: *William Taylor (II)* for 'Barley Corn' and Mr. *(John) Hales* for 'Basket Patt'n'.[76] *William Taylor II* duly invoiced Josiah Wedgwood on 24 October 1763 for one crate of barleycorn dishes, quart canisters, mustard pots, legged salts, candlesticks, carved boats, teapots and milks, and another crate of 100 dozen best cups, total £8.1s.2d.[77] The first crate bore the mark requested by Pollmann on 1 October 1763.[78] The second crate, with a different mark, agrees with an order to Wedgwood from Pollmann on 8 September 1763,[79] which Pollmann wanted sent before winter via Hull to Hamburg.

The part of Pollmann's 1 October 1763 order marked up by Wedgwood 'Basket Pattn Ordr for Mr. Hales' was for flat white table plates, soup plates, oval dishes in sizes, round dishes in sizes, breakfast plates, largest size tureens with feet and oval dishes, and two smaller sizes, sauceboats in sizes

*Colour Plate 124. **Mustard pot,** white salt-glazed stoneware. Staffordshire, c.1740-60. 3in. (7.62cm) high. (Robert Barth collection)*

*Colour Plate 125. **Salt (or wine cup),** white salt-glazed stoneware with dentil rouletting at the rim and applied sprig relief. The dentil rouletting was often seen on shards excavated from the Shelton Farm site. Staffordshire, c.1720-40. 2¼in. (5.72cm) high. (The Henry H. Weldon Collection, Colonial Williamsburg Foundation, photography by Gavin Ashworth)*

Colour Plate 126. Sauceboat, white salt-glazed sauceboat with slip-cast body and press-moulded foot in high rococo style. Staffordshire, c.1750-55. 5½in. (13.97cm) high. (Victoria and Albert Museum, C141-1993)

(Colour Plate 126), oval butter tubs with plates, mustard pots and covers, tea canisters, fruit baskets and plates, and candlesticks.[80] *John Hales* billed Wedgwood £14.2s.6d. for approximately these items on the 31st of the same month, in four crates.[81] Remarks in an earlier letter from Pollmann to Wedgwood[82] suggest that crates with the marks used by Hales were to be sent to Paul Jackson at Newcastle-upon-Tyne for shipment to Pollmann's directions.

Not all exporters were based in ports. In 1770 Cooper and Hodgskin were listed as merchants at Fountain Street, Walsall, in the West Midlands, far from any coast.[83] Walsall's main manufacture was saddlers' ironmongery, and it is likely that Cooper and Hodgskin were principally exporters of that commodity. They ordered all sorts of ware from Josiah Wedgwood between 1764 and 1769, including white salt-glazed stoneware, to be sent via Hull and Hamburg for a customer in Germany, probably J.D. Krause of Brunswick.[84]

Complaints arose as usual: for instance, Krause had called at Wedgwood's works in 1769 and been offered ware 10 or 15% cheaper.[85] Cooper and Hodgskin were persuaded to ship their pottery orders via Boardman and Bentley in Liverpool, and complained in 1768 that their customer was sent blue and white earthenware instead of blue and white stoneware, remarking 'those manufactured in Holland are

Fig. 124. Scent burner, white salt-glazed stoneware with petal-type perforations in the well of the dish. The top unscrews in the middle of the stem and the foot is hollow. Staffordshire or Yorkshire, c.1750. 4⅝in. (11.75cm) high. (Photograph courtesy of Winterthur Museum)

better in Quality and Price' and 'all of them [were] of the oldest fashion'.[86] A much more serious dispute arose when ware sent by Boardman and Bentley was lost at sea, and Bentley and Boardman had sent a bill of lading with the captain, contrary to custom.[87]

Krause's successor, Conrad Wilhelm Krause of Brunswick, wanted to deal direct with Josiah Wedgwood in 1771 for cream-coloured and stone wares, stating that he had previously received through friends.[88]

European Dealers

With one exception, all our information about direct sales of white salt-glazed stoneware to Europe comes from orders sent to Josiah Wedgwood. There is no evidence of *Jonah Malkin, John and Thomas Wedgwood* or *Thomas Wedgwood IV of Overhouse* dealing directly with overseas customers, other than in Ireland.

The exception is an order from a Potteries expatriate, Elijah Mayer, who sent a 'small order for white ware' to 'Mr. *William Taylor* [II]' at the Hill at Burslem' from Amsterdam on 9 January 1776, the ware to be sent via Mr. R. Coddington at Gainsborough to Mr. William Holmes at Hull. The order included common teapots, upright mugs, bowls, and London size and middle, 3rd, 4th and 5th size cups and saucers.[89] In an accompanying letter, Mayer referred to a previous delivery from Taylor, whose cups had been of good quality but the wrong shape, to be rounder and not so high in future. Mayer told Taylor that he might become a customer to him for cream ware. He could be sure of orders for white ware, as long as Taylor used him well.

In May 1763 Rotterdam merchant Samuel Tabor ordered three crates of 'white flint ware' along with red and black ware from Josiah Wedgwood. In June he added to the order '10-12 complete Table Sets of best white stoneware'. Tabor continued to place orders for sets of 'black printed ware', 'red printed bowls', and 'Basket pattern' which would be the only salt-glazed stoneware among that order.[90] Several dealers were purchasing salt-glaze from Wedgwood in Hamburg and other parts of Germany.

In Hamburg there were Will Coleman, Peter Mahler and William Seward. In April 1763 Coleman was ordering sophisticated wares in the form of '3 dozen 18s Teapots with feet and plates [stands], all white Sprig'd gilt'. He also ordered a large quantity of white stoneware 'flowered [which could mean raised flowers, scratch-blue or enamelled]' (Colour Plate 128), including two white stone 'Stands for Confectionary [sic]' and specified it be 'of the best sort'. Along with that order he requested '4 crates White Stone Plates & Dishes & half a dozen Tureens of the Newest Pattern flowered Borders & Soop plates'.[91]

Hamburg dealer Peter Mahler complained to Wedgwood in 1765 that his order for stoneware baskets, teapots, slop basins, sugar basins, coffee pots and sauce boats was left sitting on the docks in Hamburg and the high tides soaked the containers and breakage incurred. He listed the following breakage costs which in turn provides us with information about the cost of the white stoneware: teapots were 12s. to 18s. per dozen, slop basins and sugar basins 18s.

per dozen, sauceboats 24s. per dozen, coffee pots 6s. per dozen, the last figure seeming much too low.[92] William Seward, another Hamburg dealer, was recommended to Josiah Wedgwood through a Mr. Charles Metcalfe in 1764. Seward specifically wanted coffee pots 'without that long spout or pipe but with just a lip, like the Great Milk Pots'. With this request he also included a large order for other white stoneware, along with a similar order for red and black stoneware and coloured wares in cream colour.[93]

The sophisticated market for stoneware in central Europe is confirmed by an order from Christian Dethleffin (?) who was probably located near Flensburg on the German/Danish border. In 1763 his order to Wedgwood included 6 Blue gilded Coffee Pots with feet, 12 Teapots ditto, 6 Milk Pots without covers but curled on the edge with feet, and slop basins and sugar boxes with feet (not with raised flowers but gilded). He specified he wanted half these with birds upon the top and half with buttons. The order continues for blue flow(ered) coffee pots, teapots, slop basins, milkpots without covers but with curled edges, cream jugs long but small, sugar boxes and butter pots, followed by white gilded flint coffee and tea pots, butter pots with bird finials and common white flint chamber pots, and also black, agate and brown ware.[94]

The Germanic states were a prime destination for English white salt-glazed stoneware. Unsurprisingly, no information has been found about export of white salt-glazed stoneware to France, where the importation of many goods in the eighteenth century was only achieved by indirect means or outright smuggling.[95] There was a demand for English-type salt-glazed ware in France, and there were attempts to manufacture it at Montereau around 1750.[96]

A two-way correspondence of 1775 to 1793 between Madame Henrietta Charitas Conradi of Dresden in Saxony and Josiah Wedgwood shows the continued demand for white salt-glazed stoneware in Europe late in the eighteenth century and the problems of long-distance communication, winter weather and finally war.[97] Her first letter of 24 April 1775 was addressed 'Herrn Wichwood, London' and was twice endorsed 'not known in my part of Holborn', before reaching him. She told Wedgwood that she dealt in Foreign China and Stoneware, and already bought English stoneware in Hamburg, but wished to have a House in London 'as I can vend a very great deal of Stone ware when I import it from the manufacturer'. Gadroon, Basket and Dresden patterns would be wanted and both straw colour (creamware) and white (salt-glazed stoneware).

Early letters speak of a duty on 'English Stone Ware', which turned into a prohibition of import into Bohemia. By 1780 Mme. Conradi had obtained 'white earthenware articles, basket work and Barley Korn [sic]' from another place, but a few months later she wanted 'much in the future, as it is again much used here'. In February 1782 she complained that the barrels sent were very old and she had lost thirteen dozen white plates, barleycorn, which Wedgwood might replace with cream-coloured ones, via

Hamburg. Wedgwood apologised for the damage, but explained that he did not make the white stoneware plates 'and only bought them in for you, I can only apply to the maker… but fear it will be in vain'.

Orders for barleycorn and basket pattern tureens with stands, and sauceboats, followed in April 1782, with the injunction in July to send them speedily, as 'you know that they can not come up in the winter', presumably because of the ice-bound rivers. Dresden pattern salad dishes were included in a varied invoice of 13 May 1783, just in time to forestall a countermand from Madame Conradi on 14 May, 'as there is not the least call now for any White Earthen Ware'. In December 1786 Wedgwood promised to send Conradi 'black Satinet [fabric]' and all her other commands by the first ship in the spring, except 'the white stone ware Royal pattern' which was not made. In March 1787 Madame Conradi wanted both enamelled and white barleycorn and twisted basket ware, but later postponed despatch until September. Wedgwood replied in May that he had been very pressing upon the maker for the white stoneware, 'there being only one maker of it in this country', and added 'I have bought the white ware purposely for you, I must pay ready money for it'. In September 1788 came a note for stone goods for this winter 'to be sent off directly for Hamburg' and a last mention of white ware for H.C. Conradi, including 'Basket Work' and 'Barley Corn', occurs on an Etruria memorandum dated 24 August 1790.

Letters continued between Wedgwood, Sons and Byerley and Madame Conradi until 1793, when war with France intervened. Nine years later, on 3 January 1802, a single letter from Frederic William Conradi, postmarked 'Foreign Office Feb 2'. commenced 'As trade is secure after peace', and stated that he had hitherto obtained earthenware from Hamburg and other places and did considerable business. He asked Wedgwood for a price list and whether he could have certain items for spring, almost a repetition of Madame Conradi's first letter of 24 April 1775!

Potters as Customers
Considering *John Dwight's* attitude to other potters about infringement of his patent, it seems unlikely that he bought from them or sold to them. Staffordshire potters had no inhibitions about supplying their fellows. The fragmentary evidence surviving shows that salt-glaze potters sold both unfired and finished ware to both salt-glaze potters and creamware potters. The reasons would be varied: the salt-glaze potter-buyer might be out of stock of a particular shape for an urgent order, or he might have received an order for a shape which he did not make. Creamware potters would receive orders from their customers which included salt-glaze items. Even unfired ware was supplied, perhaps because the potter-buyer wanted shapes that he did not make and they were not available in a fired state.

Josiah Wedgwood is the prime example of a creamware potter receiving orders from customers for white salt-glazed stoneware and buying it in: prime because some of his records have survived. Much of our information about some thirty-three salt-glaze potters comes from their invoices to Wedgwood and, likewise, our knowledge of salt-glaze customers is greatly enhanced by their orders to Wedgwood. It is reasonable to infer that other creamware potters, such as *Palmer*, also received orders for white salt-glazed ware, but their records have not survived.

John Dunbibin was a delftware potter in Liverpool, and had warehouses there and in London for delftware, white stoneware and Nottingham ware.[98] He was buying from Josiah Wedgwood in 1763, placing orders specifically for a wide range of salt-glazed white stonewares, insisting that Wedgwood 'buy no ware for me unless worth the money'.[99] In addition to ordering 'moulded, cloudy' he ordered '1 doz inamel'd [sic] white Teapots'.[100] Dunbibin had a poor opinion of *Enoch Booth*, 'a very bad man', and his ware 'which turn out abominably for best'.[101] In 1763 he hoped that Booth's cousin, *George Booth*, who had offered him enamelled ware on moderate terms, would be a 'better man than his cousin'.[102] George Booth was enamelling salt-glazed stonewares and must have proved satisfactory, as one learns in a subsequent order by Dunbibin to Wedgwood.

On 17 January 1764 John Dunbibin asked Josiah Wedgwood[103] to 'get me from George Booth' the items listed below, the list significantly ending 'Enamel'd flint', i.e., white salt-glazed ware. On this occasion, an order from a customer to Wedgwood can be linked to an invoice from a salt-glaze potter. Ten days later, *Enoch & Geo. Booth* invoiced Josiah Wedgwood[104] for the items required.

Dunbibin's order	Booth's invoice		
	Enam'd ware		
6 Tea pots [size] 12s	6 teapots 12s	6/6	3.3
9 d[itt]o 18s	9 Do. 18	Do.	3.3
12 pint basons 12	12 Bowls 12	5/	5.0
Do. 24	12 Do 24	Do	2.6
18 double Coffees	[no coffees included]		
18 Ewers	18 Cream Jugs	3/-	1.6
6 doz[en] c[ups] & s[aucers]	6 Doz sprig Cups & Sau	2/	15.0
Enamel'd flint			

Apart from the absence of the 'double Coffees', Booths' invoice is an exact match for Dunbibin's request. In this example, Dunbibin already knew who would supply the enamelled items, but he was on bad terms with Enoch Booth and presumably preferred to deal through Wedgwood, who would charge commission on the order.

Humphrey Palmer, who progressed from salt-glaze potter to sophisticated maker of cream-colour, basalt and other wares, took salt-glazed ware from *Thomas and John Wedgwood*: 'fish', spoons, toys and mellons (*sic*) in 1759, in exchange for tureens, suns, moons, gadrooned and barley-corn ware; two salt-glaze potters each supplementing the other's production. Between 1766 and 1774 the Wedgwoods supplied Palmer with a great deal of unfired ware worth £731, mostly paid for by bills on James Neale of St. Pauls Churchyard, London, ending with a loss of £53

Colour Plate 127. **Scent burner,** *white salt-glazed stoneware with perforations in the well of the dish and a stem which screws to attach the top to the base. See fig. 124 for another example. Staffordshire or Yorkshire, c.1750. 4⅝in. (11.75cm). (The Henry H. Weldon Collection, Colonial Williamsburg Foundation, photography by Gavin Ashworth)*

on Palmer's failure in 1778.[105] Palmer could have salt-glazed the unfired ware, or biscuit fired, glazed and glost fired it as cream-coloured ware.

Thomas Shaw sold '4 Doz large Unburn'd Saucers' to Josiah Wedgwood in August 1764, unfired saucers which Wedgwood could fire and glaze as cream-coloured ware.[106] Likewise, *Thomas and John Wedgwood* sold unfired ware to Josiah Wedgwood between 1766 and 1775, to be biscuit fired, glazed and fired again to become cream-coloured ware. They also sold unfired ware to contemporary salt-glaze potters between 1768 and 1775: *Enoch Booth, John Bourne, John Hales, Thomas Heath II, Anthony Keeling, John and Thomas Lowe, Humphrey Palmer* (noted above), *Joseph Stephens* and *John and Ralph Wood*, presumably shapes urgently needed and not made by their customers. Phrases such as 'By allowance and Profitt [sic]', 'profet [sic] to be allow'd' and 'at half price' occur in *Thomas and John Wedgwood*'s ledger,[107] showing that they sold to their fellow potters at a reduced price. *Thomas and John Wedgwood* bought finished ware from fellow potters, and also sold it to them.[108]

Decorators or enamellers were also customers for white salt-glaze stoneware, though rarely found to be buying directly from manufacturers, presumably because they needed only small quantities of specific shapes (see Chapter V under Decoration).

Prices and Payment

As shown above, Bentley and Boardman of Liverpool obtained white salt-glazed stoneware through Josiah Wedgwood. On 16 February 1767, Josiah Wedgwood wrote in answer to a question from his future partner, Thomas Bentley:[109]

The proffit upon white stone is small, but your shareing it does not make the ware come a farthing higher. You sho[ul]d. not if you can help it allow disc[oun]t upon lowpriced white ware. Few of the Potters will allow it me.

*Colour Plate 128. **Teapot**, white salt-glazed stoneware with sprig applied leaves and veining, crabstock handle, spout and finial, traces of gilding. Staffordshire, c.1730-40. 4in. (10.16cm) high. (Harriet Carlton Goldweitz collection)*

Josiah Wedgwood's brother, *Thomas Wedgwood IV of Overhouse*, allowed Josiah 5% on salt-glazed ware in 1768.[110] At a time of bad trade, Wedgwood commented to Bentley, by then his London partner, on 21/22 April 1771 that 'Mr. Baddeley has reduced the prices of the [creamware] dishes to the prices of white stone Viz. 17 inches for 16d - 16 inches @ 14d &c.'[111] These prices were approximately those agreed by the salt-glaze potters a year earlier 'to sell to the Manufacturers of Earthen ware', 18d. and 15d. respectively, subject to 7½% discount. This discount is the small profit which Wedgwood wrote of in 1767.

The earliest price lists found are those given by Reinhold Angerstein He was a Swedish industrial spy who visited England and Wales between 1753 and 1755,[112] and noted his visits to white salt-glazed stoneware makers at Derby, Burslem and Hanley in 1754.

At *Derby* Angerstein noted a long list of 'Prices of whiteware' ranging from 1s. for a dozen of 24 sugar-cups to 2s.6d. per dozen (number not stated so presumably twelve) of the 'Ditto [Ordinary plates] with modelled roses'. Seconds were sold for 1s. for the dozens shown, and 5% was allowed for breakage.[113] His list of prices in the Staffordshire potteries includes unglazed redware, lead-glazed ware, and 'Tea pots, white ware 1s.6d.' and 'White ware, enamelled 8-12s.' both per dozen, which appear to be white salt-glazed items.[114]

The 1770 price list, which is transcribed and commented upon in detail in Appendix 3, is a remarkable survival. A handwritten copy is in Enoch Wood's Scrapbook, kept at the Potteries Museum and Art Gallery. On 14 February 1770 twenty-eight salt-glaze potters, starting with John Platt from distant Rotherham, agreed prices 'to sell to the Manufacturers of Earthen ware', with a penalty of £50 if they sold under the agreed prices. The need for such an agreement in 1770 underlines the extent to which salt-glaze producers were receiving orders through cream-colour manufacturers by then and their competition for the business. This list is for the 'staple' items such as dishes, plates, cups and saucers, sauceboats, butter dishes and toys, the common products of most manufacturers. An undated private price list for the less usual shapes made by *Thomas and John Wedgwood* is also reproduced in Appendix 3.

Unless there was another agreement which has not survived, the 1770 agreement left the salt-glaze potters free to sell direct to their own customers at whatever price they could obtain. It is notable that neither *Thomas Wedgwood IV of Overhouse* nor *Thomas and John Wedgwood*, leading salt-glaze potters, signed the agreement. In the same year, 1770, *Thomas and John Wedgwood* sold 15in. (38cm) plain round dishes at 15d. a dozen to their customer Rachel Jacob of Salisbury,[115] 3d. more than the 1770 price list. This shows that direct customers paid more, and that the prices quoted are for dozens, not single pieces.

As a comparison between creamware and salt-glazed ware prices in 1763, *William Greatbatch* sold creamware cups and saucers to Josiah Wedgwood at 24d. a dozen,[116] whilst *John Hales* sold salt-glaze cups and saucers to Wedgwood at 11d. a dozen in the same year.[117] In 1770 salt-glaze cups and saucers were 10d. a dozen, and in an inventory of *Thomas Wedgwood IV of Overhouse's* stock in 1773 best cups and saucers were still 10d. and 11d. a dozen.[118]

Reasons can be postulated for the 13d. difference between creamware and salt-glaze cups and saucers.

Basically, prices are what the buyer will pay. Salt-glazed ware, easily made by long practice and a common item in the market, had reached a standard price. Creamware was relatively new in 1763, it needed two firings, and it was desirable, so it could be expected to be expensive. Late in that year, in fact, *William Greatbatch* acknowledged a great fall in prices and reduced his creamware cups and saucers to 18d. a dozen.[119]

Whilst a London potter had a ready-made market close at hand, with a local population of around 600,000 in 1700,[120] potters in remote Staffordshire had to seek their markets far afield in order to expand a cottage craft to an industry. This could happen only if there was a reliable method of payment at a distance. The method used by Mrs. Ann Else of Nottingham as late as the 1760s was only an elementary improvement on Plot's 'poor crateman'. One of her notes was 'For Mr Thomas Jackson Staffordshire Carrier' to obtain ware from Josiah Wedgwood and *Thomas and John Wedgwood*, another promised 'I will remit cash by bearer' and a third ended 'for Mr. Jackson to pay'.[121]

A common method of payment in the eighteenth century was by bill of exchange, forerunner of the modern cheque. These promissory notes, forgotten now, were drawn by, say, the potter upon his customer for payment for pots supplied, in X months' time, and signed as accepted by the customer. The bill could then be immediately sold by the potter at a discount, to raise cash, or used by him to pay, for instance, his clay account, and re-used in the same way by the clay merchant. At the end of X months, the bill was presented by the last holder to the original customer for payment.[122] These bills formed an important addition to the public currency and are mentioned frequently in eighteenth century commercial correspondence.

John Douglas of Whitehaven, mentioned above, exemplified the varied methods of payment in use.[123] He sent a bill to Taylor Stevenson (see *Samuel Kirk and Co.*) and told him to pay Wedgwood £10, and on another occasion authorised Stevenson (through Wedgwood) to draw on him (Douglas) for £20. Again, he sent £32 to Stevenson with instructions to pay £20 to Parrott. Presumably, having been urged to pay Wedgwood's account, he worried about the untrustworthiness of merchants' bills and the problem of sending cash. A bill which Douglas had sent to *Thomas Wedgwood IV of Overhouse* had been returned, presumably dishonoured. He pleaded that his wife had died and he needed a good shopkeeper, so he hadn't been out collecting cash. Wedgwood was to pay cash to *Cartlidge* for crouchware as he made it, as they were poor and couldn't afford much credit.

Jo. Vanderkiste (also known as Vanderkirk), a prominent London dealer, obliquely apologised for failure to pay *Thomas Wedgwood IV of Overhouse* in January 1763, when he wrote 'I only wait for Frost to break that I may get into the Country for to collect a little money'.[124] He owed Thomas Wedgwood £63 in 1767, amongst some forty debtors who together owed £852.[125] *Thomas and John Wedgwood* had bad debts of £933 between 1757 and 1779, of which £222 was owed by bankrupts.[126]

Packing and Transport

Surviving invoices are necessarily full of references to crates, barrels and other containers for pottery. Crates were the most commonly named containers, but straw baskets and even a 'Twigen Hamper' are mentioned.[127] Crates were already being supplied in quantity in 1722, when John Fenton (of *Fenton and Hill*) noted purchases of thirty-nine, twenty-five and seventeen pairs of crates from William Lees.[128] The fact that these were *pairs* of crates indicates that they were for carriage by packhorses at that time. *John Baddeley* bought six baskets from John Henshaw and seventeen crates and covers from Wildblood in 1761. He also bought a load of straw, necessary for packing crates, and 'Cording', rope for securing the covers.[129] When *Peter Bagnall* died in 1761 he had baskets and cording.

With such a fragile cargo as pottery, packing inevitably gave rise to complaints. Wedgwood's salt-glaze customer Pollmann wrote in September 1763: 'the last goods were not well packed & terribly smashed'.[130] John Wyke of Liverpool, Josiah Wedgwood's customer for salt-glazed ware, sent patterns to Portugal in 1763 and complained in his idiosyncratic spelling 'And when the got them the Crate was Sadley Broak & plundered. Therefore for the fewture I must have them either packed up in large old Sugar Hogsheads [or] Strong stout and large Crates wickered all Round and a Grate [cover] well wickered, tied over the top in 6 or 8 places'. As noted above, Madame Conradi of Dresden complained in 1782 of losing thirteen dozen plates because the barrels were very old.

At retail level Mrs. Elizabeth Purefoy of Shalstone, Bucks., wrote to Mrs Ward at a China Shop near Surrey Street in the Strand, London in 1749 that 'The Box of China came safe all but the upper Plate w[hi]ch was put up under the cover of the Dish, & no straw being upon it, was broke'.[131] Mrs. Ward had warranted her packing and so she must replace the plate.

John Wyke wrote of crates, casks and hogsheads (large casks) in 1763.[132] A hogshead and crate with part of Wyke's order was sent by *Thomas and John Wedgwood* 'p[er] Daniel Morrice' on 23 July in that year.[133] Daniel Morris was the regular road carrier between Burslem and Liverpool, despite the alternative water transport on the Weaver Navigation, available from Winsford in Cheshire. As late as 1773, Morris billed Josiah Wedgwood for 'White Ware from Burslem to Liverpool by Land'.[134]

Earlier Burslem carriers included Robert Daniel in 1707, administering his father's estate,[135] and John Warburton, who had '7 old horses and all their materials for carrying' when he died in 1714. Moses Stevenson of Sneyd Green near Burslem, a carrier, had nine horses with pack saddles when he died in 1729.[136] When *John Mare and Richard Taylor* agreed to become partners in 1722, Mare was to buy one or more horses if necessary, which could have been for carting coal and clay or delivery of finished ware. At *Peter Bagnall's* death in 1761, he had three pack saddles and three pairs of panniers for his two mules. *Joseph Bucknall* of Cobridge, potter and carrier, wanted to sell his carrying business in 1760, waggon, cart and packhorses 'with the goodwill of the stage of carriage from Manchester Burslem and Coventry'.

The variety of carrying equipment and vehicles illustrate the state of roads in the eighteenth century. Packhorse routes and parish-maintained roads were being gradually supplemented by turnpike roads, the motorway toll roads of their day. North Staffordshire slowly became linked to the rest of the country by these purpose-made highways: London through Newcastle-under-Lyme to Carlisle in 1714, but not until 1759 for the next, from Newcastle through Stoke and Longton to Derby, followed by more local turnpikes in the 1760s.[137]

A major source for information about dealings in salt-glazed stoneware is *Thomas and John Wedgwood's* Crate Book,[138] containing detailed information about the contents of the packages which were sent to customers between 1770 and 1773. Unfortunately, because this book lists the contents, it rarely describes the container. In sixty-two pages, crate is only mentioned twice.

An entry for William Kell of Foot of the Side, Newcastle (-upon-Tyne) illustrates both packing and transport near the end of the 'salt-glaze' period. He was sent five crates on 12 May 1772. At the end of his entry he is charged for them: one at 9d., two at 15d. each and two at 18d. each, and five covers at 4d. each.[139]

The crate book and the relevant sales account book page show how crates were identified *en route* by being marked for sender and recipient: 'IW WK Newcastle I II III IV V ', IW for John Wedgwood and WK for William Kell, with a Roman numeral for each crate. The forwarding instructions noted illustrate the state of transport at that time: 'p[er] Heath [a carrier] to Stone [in Staffordshire, the then canal terminus] to go by Mr. Henshaw's Boats down the Canal and order'd ^{ym} [them] to Wm Fletcher W[h]arfinger Gainsb[o]rough and to his direction at Hull'.[140]

Heath, a carrier, was to take Kell's crates by horse-drawn waggon from Burslem to Stone, ten miles south. Stone at that date was the northern terminus of the Trent and Mersey canal, where Kell's crates could be loaded on to Henshaw's boat, to go by canal to the eastern end of the canal at Shardlow, and perhaps by the same boat down the Trent to Gainsborough, then to be sent by William Fletcher down the River Trent to Hull, thence up the east coast to Newcastle-upon-Tyne. By 1777 the Trent and Mersey canal was open throughout and Heath would have taken Kell's crates the two-mile (three-kilometre) journey to Burslem's nearest wharf at Longport. Heath's journeys were not only to Stone. Much earlier, in 1756, he took crates from *Thomas and John Wedgwood* to Wilden Ferry, thence to be sent via the River Trent and Gainsborough for shipment to London. In 1760 Heath took crates from *Thomas and John Wedgwood* to Chester for William Reid and in 1761 again to Chester *en route* for Dublin.[141]

Forty miles overland to Bridgnorth in Shropshire was one of the early routes for pottery traffic. Richard Whitworth, canal protagonist, said in 1760 that three pot waggons went every week from Newcastle and Burslem to Bridgnorth, carrying about eight tons of pot ware every week, loaded back with ten tons of white clay.[142] Chapter IV includes information about Devon clay coming to the Potteries via Bridgnorth, and Whitworth confirms the obvious corollary of the same carts taking pots from Staffordshire to Bridgnorth.

Shaw instanced a carter who was allowed four days to take crates to Bridgnorth, who had even gone to Exeter 'before there were regular carriers'.[143] From Bridgnorth, goods were taken down the River Severn to Gloucester or Bristol, for inland distribution or sea-going shipment. In 1749 *Jonah Malkin* sent salt-glazed ware to Joseph Jonson of Exeter, fourteen crates 'to bridgnorth [*sic*, in Shropshire, on the River Severn, presumably for shipment via Bristol] by Stockley' in September, and two crates 'from Bristol Decr. 20 1749 In the Elizabeth Capt. William Wood master'.[144]

Chester was another port, forty miles from North Staffordshire, and Chapter IV describes North Devon clay arriving there in increasing quantity from 1691 to 1730. It is reasonable to assume that pottery was sent to Chester by the same packhorses or waggons which brought the clay, but no evidence has been found. The isolated instance of Heath taking crates to Chester for Dublin in 1761 probably relates to the continuance of the Irish trade.[145]

The Dee estuary was increasingly impeded by silting. The River Weaver was made navigable from 1732, from the River Mersey up to Winsford, only twenty miles from the Potteries. This provided easier transport for both clay and pottery, upstream for clay and downstream for 'cratesware', to Liverpool, a thriving town and a port which combined coastal and ocean-going shipping facilities. Weaver Navigation 'Tonnage Books' from 1731 to 1772 and 'Day Books' from 1741 to 1755 survive.[146] Whilst incoming white clay and flint (see Chapter IV) could be considered to be for making white salt-glazed stoneware, the outgoing 'cratesware' could contain either salt-glazed ware or fine redware. Statistics show an increase from fifty tons of cratesware in 1734 to five hundred tons in 1751, but this can only be regarded as a general indication of increased production of pottery in North Staffordshire.[147]

'During a long time' Shaw's informant 'carried crates of Pottery to Winsford, and brought back Ball Clay; each of the five horses carried a crate on a pack-saddle and a small pannier on each side was used to hold two or three balls of clay'. 'Afterwards with a cart and four horses he went to Winsford and delivered his crates the same day'.[148]

To the east, the navigable River Trent gave access to Hull and the North Sea, for North-east England, Europe and London.[149] *William Taylor II* supplied white salt-glazed ware to Josiah Wedgwood for Pollmann in October 1763. Pollmann wanted ware sent via Hull to Hamburg, and Taylor's general account to Wedgwood for late 1763 included 'Carridge 13 Crates to the ferry',[150] the 'ferry' being Willington Ferry or Wilden Ferry, head of navigation on the River Trent.

London was reached either direct by land, or by sea, overland to Willington or Wilden, thence by the River Trent to Gainsborough or Hull, and onward by sea-going

Colour Plate 129. **Milk jug,** drab salt-glazed stoneware with white applied handle, spout and sprig moulded relief. Staffordshire, c.1750-55. 4¾in. (12.07cm) high. (The Henry H. Weldon Collection, Colonial Williamsburg Foundation, photography by Gavin Ashworth)

vessel. Appendix 5 lists over seventy London customers for Staffordshire salt-glazed ware.

The coming of the Trent and Mersey Canal to Staffordshire changed local transport arrangements. Actively promoted by Josiah Wedgwood and other potters, it was opened from Shardlow on the River Trent to the Potteries by late 1772 and throughout to Preston Brook in Cheshire, with access to the River Mersey, in 1777.[151] Used for the transport of flint, clay and all kinds of pottery, it would have no effect on the decline of salt-glaze production. Any reduction in transport cost would apply equally to salt-glazed ware and its supplanter, cream-coloured ware.

Overseas trade faced additional hazards, war, weather and shipwreck amongst them. In connection with his Portuguese customer's requirements of salt-glazed ware, John Wyke wrote to Josiah Wedgwood on 26 February 1763: 'No Vessels going from our Port [Liverpool] on Acc[oun]t of the Warr, it was Aug[us]t before I had an oportunity of sending the patterns I had from Mr. *Aaron Wedgwood* in April last'.[152] Wyke's 'Warr' was the Seven Years War, just ended.

As noted earlier, war interrupted Madame Conradi's business with Wedgwood, and winter weather was also a complication in their dealings, Wedgwood being reminded in July 1782 to send salt-glazed ware speedily to Dresden as 'you know that they can not come up in the winter', presumably because of the ice-bound rivers.[153] Again, in September 1788, in a note from Conradi, stone goods for this winter were to be sent off directly for Hamburg, to reach Dresden before the frost.[154] In September 1763 Pollmann, the London exporter, wanted his goods to be expedited before winter to Hull for Hamburg.[155]

Another hazard was shipwreck. Cooper and Hodgskin of Walsall bought salt-glazed ware through Josiah Wedgwood for their customer in Brunswick, Germany, and were persuaded to send a consignment via Bentley and Boardman of Liverpool instead of Hull.[156] In September 1768 they wrote: 'All the packages shipped from Liverpool were lost' and Wedgwood asked his friend Bentley 'what goods were lost in the ship cast away going to Altona?'[157] A prolonged dispute over insurance ensued.[158] Shipwreck was always a possibility, but a less anticipated problem was that of Peter Mahler, who complained that his consignment was left sitting on the docks in Hamburg and the high tide soaked the containers, causing breakage.[159] Further examples of packing and transport are given in Appendix 1.

CHAPTER VII

English White Salt-Glazed Stoneware for the American Market

Frustratingly little is known about the production of white stoneware from John Dwight's salient decade between 1685 and 1695 until one finds primary source documentation in the form of newspaper advertisements and business letters in the mid-eighteenth century. That there were legions of manufacturers attests to the achievement of an industry which in its most sophisticated manifestation could successfully rival the market demand for Chinese porcelains. At the lower end of the market, the wares were more durable than delftware and nearly as cheap. It is essential to keep in mind that the distinction between salt-glazed stonewares and the later creamware and pearlware was simply firing temperature and glaze. Lead-glazed earthenwares adhered to the same formula, often with similar spouts, handles and decoration. The markets, needless to say, were also shared.

Documentation for the early years of the eighteenth century is non-existent. The archaeological evidence is the principal key to distinguishing shapes from certain decades and to dating. Due to the fact that Staffordshire pottery sites are frequently part of urban salvage excavations, the most undisturbed archaeology is often North American domestic sites. Documentation regarding manufacturing and manufacturer is further thwarted by the cottage industry nature of the business, where potters were not bound by ego or entrepreneurship to identify their wares. After 1740 or so, when wares began to be mass-produced through moulds and casting, a few model and master mould makers such as Aaron Wood and Ralph Wood left signed examples of their moulds. At least fifteen moulds survive marked Ralph Wood, some of which are dated.[1] With the exception of a few other pots that are signed on the base by potters, such as the tureen in the V&A (Colour Plates 28, 28a) marked *JB 1769*, the historian might as well be a mystery writer in unravelling the manufacturers of the wares.

Salt-Glaze on Paper
In addressing the American market for white salt-glazed stoneware one needs to call into play newspaper advertisements and household probate inventories as well as the archaeological evidence.

Newspapers advertisements have a limited but very useful role in placing white salt-glazed stoneware in a social context. Through them one can construct a time line for supply and demand; that is, inception, peak and decline. Newspapers also frequently describe shapes available and occasionally decoration. Where they obviously fail is in delineating the manufacturer and usually even the port of shipment.

A number of published sources[2] and subsequent lecturers have cited the date of 17 January 1724 from a purported advertisement in the *Boston News-Letter* as the first mention of salt-glaze in an American advertisement.

> Just imported, and to be sold by William Randall, in the middle Of Cross-Street, at Capt. Philip Viscount's, Hogsheads of Earthenware, white stone Tea-cups and Saucers, Bowls, Plates, Salts, Milk Pots…
> Boston News-Letter, 17 Jan. 1724

Pat Halfpenny suggested in a lecture at Keele University[3] that the date was probably an error. The original advertisement is published in Dow's newspaper research in the *Arts & Crafts in New England*.[4] Complete microfilms of the January issues of the *Boston News-Letter* are difficult to find, but letters from two different curators at the Massachusetts Historical Society failed to confirm the existence of the advertisement for 17 January 1724. Another published advertisement from the same source for 17 January 1745 with identical wording suggests that Dow originally published it in error for the same date in 1724, an error which snowballed thereafter. Ivor Noël-Hume quoted this advertisement in an article in *Antiques* in February 1970 and, although he did not question the 1724 date, he did question the manufacture of plates at that date and rightly so. He conceded, publishing in bold type, 'there is as yet no unequivocal evidence that white salt-glaze plates were made before the early 1740s.'[5] With one possible exception, which will be cited later, there is nothing in probate inventories, newspaper advertisements or archaeological sites to substantially refute that, although delftware and other earthenware potters were manufacturing plates and it would seem inconsistent to think that salt-glazed stoneware potters couldn't also be producing plates.

The earliest advertisement referring to the availability of salt-glazed stoneware in America occurs again in the *Boston News-Letter* 23/30 April 1716 for 'Earthen and Stoneware in Parcels…' Given the date, one must be prepared to consider the possibility of Rhenish and not English stoneware. In 1728/9 other references occur for 'Stoneware in hampers …from Holland'.[6] An inventory for Chester County, Pennsylvania indicated that Edward Bennett of Thornbury had 'stone cups' in estate in 1715,[7] a surprisingly early date. One is hard pressed to think of any other stoneware which would be included in 1715 other than English white, or possibly Nottingham brown cups, although the survival of these is rare. In 1725 Joseph Prestbury of Baltimore County had '2 stone muggs & 1 chamber pot' valued 0/3/6 in his probated inventory.[8] In a Baltimore 1729 inventory Col. James Maxwell had white stone teacups and a stone teapot in a total estate valued at £1,192.[9] Again in 1729 in Talbot county, Maryland, Henry Troth's inventory listed '8 stone tea cups, slop basin, milk and sugar potts' among his other china, and delftware and ten slaves.[10] In May 1733, again in the *Boston News-Letter* one finds what may be the earliest reference to this ubiquitous white stoneware: 'White Earthen, Delph and Flint Ware … lately imported from Liverpool'. Flint, of course was an early synonym for white salt-glaze but was more commonly used for flint glassware. In the context of being 'lately imported from Liverpool', it seems likely that the advertisement refers to ceramics. As we shall see shortly, the archaeology record indicates much earlier use in America.

In 1739 the probated inventory of merchant Isaac Sumner of Portsmouth, New Hampshire listed among the stonewares '11 White Small Teapots'.[11] The following year merchant John Collins of Portsmouth left an inventory with many more shapes described, such as stone mugs, sauce dishes, seven brown teapots, three white ditto, sugar dishes, milk pots, a mustard pot and teacups and saucers.[12] In 1745 in Baltimore Major Acquilla Paca had '1 quart stone mug' in the probated inventory of his estate along with '2 elephant teapots' which were probably Chinese porcelain.[13] By 1746 inventories in the Portsmouth area were listing 'old Stone cups & Saucers about 1 Doz.[14] In 1749 the estate of Stephen Greenleaf listed among the stoneware the following shapes:

1 Old Stone Tea Pot	- 5-
5 ½pr. Stone Mugs	-15-
1 New England earthen Tea Pot	-1-
2 Stone Handle Cup	- 4-
1 Stone decanter	-12-
1 Salt	-6-
1 small Stone Jug	-12-
1 Stone Mustard Pot	- 3-[15]

Generally newspaper advertisement anticipated probate inventories. By 1737 the *Boston Gazette* was offering a 'choice sortment of Delph and Stone…'[16] In Philadelphia the *Pennsylvania Gazette* first offered 'earthen and stoneware in crates' on 15 August 1745. The *Boston Gazette* first advertised 'Blue and white sprigged Stone scollopped dishes' and 'blue & white Stone Mugs…' on 15 October 1751, five years before the scratch-blue was offered in Philadelphia, on 10 June 1756.[17] Blue and white, or scratch-blue as we now refer to it, was ubiquitous in Colonial America. The earliest dated examples found are a mug in the Glaisher collection inscribed *17 Enoch Booth 42* and a bowl in the Greg collection (Colour Plates 14, 15) also dated 1742. Scratch-blue continued in great demand as witnessed by frequent advertisements in Colonial America through the 1760s and included George Washington who purchased '1 doz blew & white stone Chamber Pots'[18] in 1761, possibly Westerwald or the so-called debased scratch-blue, which was a cruder version of the same decoration on beer mugs and chamber pots (Colour Plates 126, 145). He placed another order for six more in 1767.[19]

George Washington received via Thomas Knox of Bristol at Mount Vernon in December 1757 the following:

6 doz^n finest white stone plates	£ 1. 4.0
1 doz^n ditto Dishes 6 sizes	18.0
4 doz^n Patti pan 4 sizes	5.4
6 Quart Mugs	2.0
6 pint ditto	1.0
6 Tea Pots	1.0
12 Mustard pots	1.0[20]

By 1751 a full complement of vessel shapes was available in Boston shops, from tea Dishes to mugs and jugs in various sizes, as well as chamber pots. As an aside on the subject, the *Boston Gazette* advertised 'New fashion'd Turtle-shell Tureens' for sale in April, 1754.[21] It was reported in the *Boston Evening Post* that after 1 July 1754, an excise tax would be levied on certain luxury items: *An Act for granting unto his Majesty an excise upon Sundry Articles hereafter enumerated, for and towards the support of his Majesty's government of this Province.* The articles were tea and coffee and 'East-India wares called China-ware'.[22] Apparently that did not include English ceramics, which thereafter become more Chinese in decoration and form.

In 1752 the *Pennsylvania Gazette* advertised 'Lately imported from London and Liverpool … delph and flint ware…'.[23] Philadelphia was well supplied with luxury goods such as 'mourning rings engraved and enamelled after the neatest and newest fashions, as done in London' advertised by London jeweller Charles Duton in November of 1752.[24] In spite of Quaker admonitions against ostentation Philadelphia newspapers are rife with advertisements for Chinese porcelains 'enamelled and pencilled'[25] and there was much less interest in the common white stonewares preferred by Puritan New England. 1762 was the first advertisement in New York for enamelled stoneware when Keeling and Morris offered 'Enamelled Stone Tea-pots, Milkpots, Mugs, Bowls, and Cups and Saucers of all Sizes and of the newest Patterns…'.[26] The first reference found to enamelled stoneware in Philadelphia occurs in 1763.[27] Enamelled stoneware was not advertised in Boston until 1764.[28] 1763/64 is very late if one considers that the Whieldon notebook of 1749 includes an entry for 'painted [2-dish]'[29] which was probably salt-glazed stoneware because the next entry specifies 'Creamcol'r'.

In 1764 Thomas Bentley joined Samuel Boardman in Liverpool and began trading under the name Bentley and Boardman. In September of that year they placed with Josiah Wedgwood of Burslem 'a small order from a very careful man in Boston who has sent cash to pay [£27]'. He complained of the high price of ware which he had previously bought in Liverpool. The order began:

50 dozen white [missing words] half of them soop & half flat plates, some of them plain but the most carved 1/10

or 2/- per Dozen for which I expect firsts
4 Doz of flint white dishes from 14 Inches to 20 Inches some deep & some flat.
4 Doz Oval Do. 12 Inches to 16 some flat, some deep carved.
2 Doz small carved Dishes commonly called bread Baskets white.

He added: 6 Doz white flint muggs of several sizes.[30] Of course, Wedgwood was buying in his white ware from other suppliers, not actually producing it himself.

On 5 October 1764 Bentley and Boardman wrote to Josiah Wedgwood requesting a discount and the cost of carriage to Liverpool, urging the ware to be sent quickly or it would be there all winter. Another letter around the same time asks that the ware be well packed, strongest crates, with covers, not roped over, 'white ware in particular must be smooth and of a clean white'.[31] On 15 October the 'very careful and exact gentleman [from Boston]' ordered another £18 of flint or stoneware as follows:

10 Dozen of the flint white Stone plates plain & carved 22 pr Dozen, very white & well chosen not exceeding 2/- per Dozen
3 Dozen oval & round Dishes from 10 to 18 Inches, white, carved, very white smoothe [sic].[32]

On 8 November 1764 the firm wrote that 'A vessel & perhaps the only one that will sail for Boston this year, is now taking in her Loading and expects to sail <u>in the next week</u>. Please to forward your pots with all possible Dispatch for fear they should be too late'.[33]

In fact little stoneware is seen specifically noted in advertisements until 1766 in Philadelphia, after which time it is frequently noted, not entirely replacing Chinese porcelains but absorbing a great deal of the market.

The Seven Years War of 1756-63 presented an opportunity for potters to commemorate Frederick, King of Prussia, capitalising on the popularity of their valiant ally after his victory at Rossbach in 1757. Thus one begins to see advertisements such as this one in the *Boston Gazette* for 'White and black Stone Coffee Pots…' on 5 June 1758 (Colour Plates 132, 133) followed by 'White Stone, Prussian & Basket work'd Plates and Dishes' in November the same year (Colour Plate 130).[34] Fragments of two moulded plate rims which when whole read 'SUCCESS TO THE KING OF PRUSSIA AND HIS FORCES' were also found in the Wetherburn's Tavern excavations at Williamsburg.[35]

Hollow dining wares in salt-glaze were rarely mentioned in probate inventories, but a white stone fruit dish (valued at 2s.), specified as being used in the parlour where the 'china' was also displayed, and a tureen (5s.) (Colour Plate 131) were included in the estate inventory of Henry Woodward of Anne Arundel County, Maryland in 1762. Woodward was prosperous and owned twenty slaves.[36]

One of two of Maryland's most prominent and wealthy families were the Carrolls who emigrated to Maryland in 1688. Charles Carroll of Carrollton, a signer of the

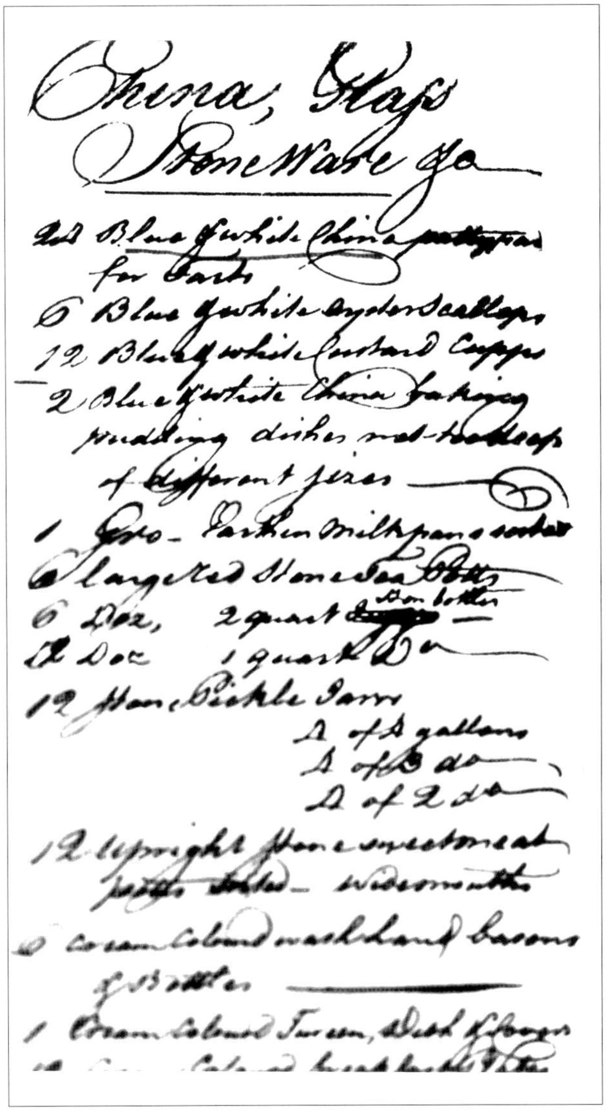

*Fig. 125. **Order from Charles Carroll of Carrollton** to his Annapolis and London agents, Wallace, Davidson and Johnson, for creamware and salt-glazed stoneware on 8 October 1771. Carroll continued to order salt-glazed stoneware through his agents until 1785, after which time stoneware was not mentioned. (Arents Letter Book, New York Public Library)*

Declaration of Independence, was responsible for feeding and clothing five hundred dependants in his principal home Doughoregan Manor and in the several homes of his children. Salt-glazed stoneware first appeared in the 1762 inventory of contents of Doughoregan Manor, one of the houses of his father, Charles Carroll of Annapolis, listing 'white stone patties' and 'Custard cups', 'Old ditto' as well as plates and 'soop plates' which were also probably salt-glazed stoneware.[37] From 1771 until the early nineteenth century 'the Signer,' as Charles Carroll of Carrollton was known, placed orders for most of the goods for his home and dependencies from his agents Wallace, Davidson and Johnson of Annapolis and London.[38] In 1771 (Fig. 125) Carroll ordered '6 largest Stone Teapots', '24 large white stone

Chapter VII – English White Salt-Glazed Stoneware for the American Market

Colour Plate 130. **Plate,** *white salt-glazed stoneware moulded with the basketweave or mosaic border impressed with* SUCCESS TO THE KING OF PRUSSIA AND HIS FORCES. *These plates were advertised for sale in America from 1758 and shards have been excavated at the site of Wetherburn's Tavern in Williamsburg, Virginia. Staffordshire, c.1756-1763 (or later). 9¼in. (23.5cm) diameter. (Robert Barth collection)*

Colour Plate 131. **Tureen,** *white salt-glazed stoneware press-moulded in the mosaic or basketweave pattern popular from 1756. This tureen has mask head and bold paw feet characteristic of those excavated at Humphrey Palmer's Town Road site, Hanley. Staffordshire, probably Humphrey Palmer, Hanley, c.1756-65. 7½in. (19.05cm). (Collection of the Colonial Dames, Moffatt Ladd House, Portsmouth, New Hampshire)*

Colour Plate 132. **Teapot,** *white salt-glazed stoneware with enamel overall decoration commemorating the alliance with England and Prussia in the Seven Years War. These may have been the 'black and cream-coloured stoneware' being advertised in Philadelphia in 1769, six years after the end of the war. Staffordshire, c.1756-69?. 3¾in. (9.53cm) high. (Private collection)*

Colour Plate 133. **Teapot,** *white salt-glazed stoneware with black fossilised limestone design and a central reserve panel painted with flowers. A rare decoration on salt-glazed stoneware, this would be less likely to be the design described in the advertisement in Philadelphia in 1769 for 'black and cream-coloured stoneware' (see comments in Colour Plate 132). Staffordshire, c.1760-65. 4⅝in. (11.75cm) high. (Winterthur Museum, 1954.0045.001A.B)*

CHAPTER VII – ENGLISH WHITE SALT-GLAZED STONEWARE FOR THE AMERICAN MARKET

*Fig. 126. **Two mugs,** white salt-glazed stoneware with the so-called debased scratch-blue decoration imitating Westerwald stoneware. These wares, which seem to have been popular in the late 1760s and 1770s for use in taverns and public houses, often bear GR (Georgus Rex) seals. In 1772 the* Pennsylvania Gazette *advertised 'blue and white GR [wares]…'. Staffordshire, c.1770-80. Left 4⅞in. (12.38cm) high. (Olive Talbot collection)*

chamber pots, '6 dozen stone bottles, 2 quart each, 6 gross quarts each'. At the same time he ordered '12 stone pickle jars, 12 upright stone sweetmeat pots from 1 quart to 2'.[39] The following year he continued to order utilitarian wares in salt-glazed stoneware: '24 white stone chamber pots, 24 strong coarse ditto for servants,' '12 white stone quart muggs 12 pint ditto', '12 stone juggs, 2 gallons each, 12 ditto 1 gallon'.[40] The orders continued in 1773 and 1775 for similar wares for chamber pots, food storage containers and plates and 'strong white stone bowls sorted', probably for servants.[41] Indeed, similar orders were placed in 1783 and 1785, after which stoneware is not mentioned.[42]

In Portsmouth, New Hampshire, the probated inventory of the estate of Elliott Vaughan in 1758 included among other stonewares '2 flowered beakers'. 'Enameld'd and every other kind of flint ware'… was still being advertised in the *New Hampshire Gazette* in 1772.[43] In Baltimore the 1765 inventory of the estate of James Phillips included '½ doz. Enameled stone plates' valued at 1.10s.0d. as well as a 'Chocolate pott' (1.1s.3d.) and a teapot in white stoneware.[44] Surprisingly, as late as 1769 'black and cream-coloured stoneware…' was still being purveyed in Philadelphia, six years after the end of the Seven Years War (Colour Plates 132, 133).[45]

In 1772 the *Pennsylvania Gazette* advertised 'blue and white G R (Georgus Rex) …and blue and white stoneware with China Glaze, consisting of table setts, &c…' (Fig. 126).[46] The so-called blue and white or scratch-blue was surprisingly long-lived, being frequently advertised from 1751 to 1774; the last mention in the *Pennsylvania Gazette* was in 1776.[47] The last dated scratch-blue pieces known are 1778.

In 1773 a Moravian store in Litiz, Pennsylvania was offering a variety of ceramics both fashionable and what would appear by then to be slightly *passé*: delft bowls, agate and black teapots and enamelled and white stoneware in tea and table wares. In a comparative list of prices plain creamware teapots were 6d. and 8d. each, enamelled creamware teapots much more expensive at 1s.4d. and 2s. each; agate 7d. and 11d. and black 7d.; enamelled stoneware sugar dishes at 16s. the dozen, and enamelled stoneware teapots at 14s. the dozen. Scratch-blue teapots were 7d. each. Of course all these prices are frustrated by lack of information regarding size.[48]

Just as creamware and enamelled salt-glaze co-existed in the 1760s and 1770s, delftware and salt-glazed stoneware co-habited for many years in merchants' inventories until about 1770. One invoice from Philadelphia merchants Mifflin & Massey (Colour Plate 134) dated 7 May 1763 gives the reader a good idea of the relative pricing of salt-glaze and delftware, delftware in some instances being more expensive than salt-glazed equivalents. For example, 'Table Plates' in stoneware were 3s. per dozen; 'fine Plates' in delftware were 3s.6d. per dozen.[49]

Inventories of estates and merchants' stock included a panoply of shapes: a Stone flagon (probably Rhenish) with a silver foot and top valued at 15s. in 1750,[50] chamber pots (1753),[51] stone porringers (1755) (Colour Plate 135),[52] stone tureens (1762, 1767),[53] 'Butter dishes or butter bowls', as they were sometimes described (1762, 1765),[54] 'punch strainer(s)' (1769),[55] pickle leaves (Colour Plate 136), salts and pepper boxes (1777)[56] and a variety of tea and tablewares which had been the stoneware staple since the early 1720s. A tantalising bill of sale from Philadelphia merchant James Gallagher to Mr. Samuel Rex which included '1 do[zen] delph Quart Mugs and 1 dº pint Tumblers' along with '1 dozen white Salts, 2 dº Soup Plates, 1 dº Sugar Dishes assorted' in 1791 leaves a great deal to the imagination regarding the wares purchased. The sale of so many delft mugs and tumblers and white stoneware is surprising for that late date (Fig. 127).[57]

Advertisements for stoneware have not been found in Philadelphia after 1783[58] but lingered in other regions. In 1789 the estate of Captain Ezra Allen, a mariner from Plymouth, Massachusetts, included plain white stoneware, '1 flow'd stone tea pot' valued at 6d. and '1 black tea pot' also valued at 6.[59] In 1800 the *New Hampshire Gazette* was still advertising stone mugs and jugs. In a shop inventory of 1808 (location unspecified) the stoneware was confined to jugs, mugs, pots and jars, in the main storage containers.[60]

In a survey of twenty-eight household inventories in Plymouth, Massachusetts plain white stone tableware first appears in 1767 and continues to be found frequently until 1789. Very little enamel stoneware is described. In two households 'yellow stone Plates' (1778, 1783) are described and '1 green stone Canister' and '1 green Cream Pot' are to be found in another inventory of 1781. These descriptions seems odd for stoneware. They are probably creamware and green-glazed earthenware. Only two 'flow'd' stonewares are listed, one plate (1784, 3d.) and a teapot (1789, 6d.).[61]

In 1770 Fredericksburg, Virginia, merchant Mann Page was ordering from John Norton & Sons, London exporters, '4 white quart stone Cans' and '4 pint–Do', in a long list of imported goods. For himself Page ordered white wash basins and chambers pots in stoneware and the more fashionable tea and coffee cups and of 'Queen China' and 'blue and white China bowls'.[62]

'Littler's Blue', or more correctly Littler-Wedgwood blue, makes an infrequent appearance on the American salt-glaze scene, unlike the ubiquitous scratch-blue, though a Chester County Pennsylvania inventory for Robert Wilson of Concord lists a 'blue stone Tea Pott' in 1766.[63]

Salt-Glaze below Ground

There is little evidence of Littler-Wedgwood blue found in North American archaeological sites. In three decades of excavations in Portsmouth, New Hampshire, only one shard was found.[64] Almost all of a teapot in blue with the typical crabstock handle and spout was excavated in New Market, Delaware[65] in a mid-eighteenth century context. Another teapot was excavated from a colonial farmstead area near Smyrna, Delaware, occupied by the William Strickland family from 1726 to 1764. Although the Stricklands were in the upper ten percent of the taxable income families in their district, nevertheless these were simply farmers who enjoyed the ritual of tea drinking.[66]

The most curious Littler-Wedgwood blue example was found at Cain Hoy, the John Bartlam's manufactory of creamware (1765-1773) near Charleston, South Carolina (Colour Plate 137). Although 129 pieces of white salt-glazed stoneware were found at the site, there was no indication that Bartlam ever produced salt-glazed stoneware in spite of the fact he was producing a wide range of English style creamware.[67] Two shards of Littler-Wedgwood blue were found which puzzle archaeologists, who continue to claim these as non-indigenous, while agreeing they are wasters.[68] White salt-glazed stoneware appears on Colonial American sites almost as early as it does on English sites – no surprise really when one considers the strong material attachment to the mother country.

London Town, in Anne Arundel county Maryland, was located on the South River which flows into Chesapeake Bay, where vessels often weighed anchor awaiting the harvesting of the tobacco crop. It was the site of public houses where sailors could while away the days, or weeks the crop maturation might entail. Rumney's Tavern, built around 1700 by Edward Rumney, who owned the tavern, operated a ferry and also worked as a boatbuilder, offered that maritime respite. Dr. Al Luckenbach and his archaeological team have done an analysis of the delftware deposit, which predominated ceramically. Working stylistically from decoration on dated examples, they have come up with a computer extract of a date of deposit of 1724. The salt-glazed ceramics in one cellar measuring 20ft. x 20ft. (6m x 6m) included eleven English white salt-glazed vessels: cups, bowls (Colour Plate 138), teabowls (Colour Plate 139), a coffee pot (Colour Plate 140) and mugs (Colour Plate 141). The mugs with their knife-cut handle terminals and fine lathe-turned bases are almost identical to ones excavated at Fulham (Colour Plate 142) in the 1695? to 1710 context when Dwight's widow Lydia and subsequently her son Dr. Samuel Dwight were working the pottery. According to Chris Green, the first white 'dipt' wares could have been made at Fulham as early as 1695, in Staffordshire possibly as early as 1697.[69] However, Green makes a strong argument that the London white salt-glaze ware was more refined in quality and craftsmanship than the wares coming out of Staffordshire at the same time.[70]

In Maryland the Calverts were side by side with the Carrolls in prominence, the descendants of the Lords Baltimore, the proprietors of Maryland. Salt-glazed stoneware gadrooned plates, enamelled tewares including a teapot (Colour Plate 143) and scratch-blue decorated tewares (Colour Plate 144) were unearthed at the site of the Calvert House on State House Circle in Annapolis. The house was occupied by Benedict Leonard Calvert, governor of the colony from 1728 to 1731. He attempted to return to England (dying on board ship) and the house was occupied by

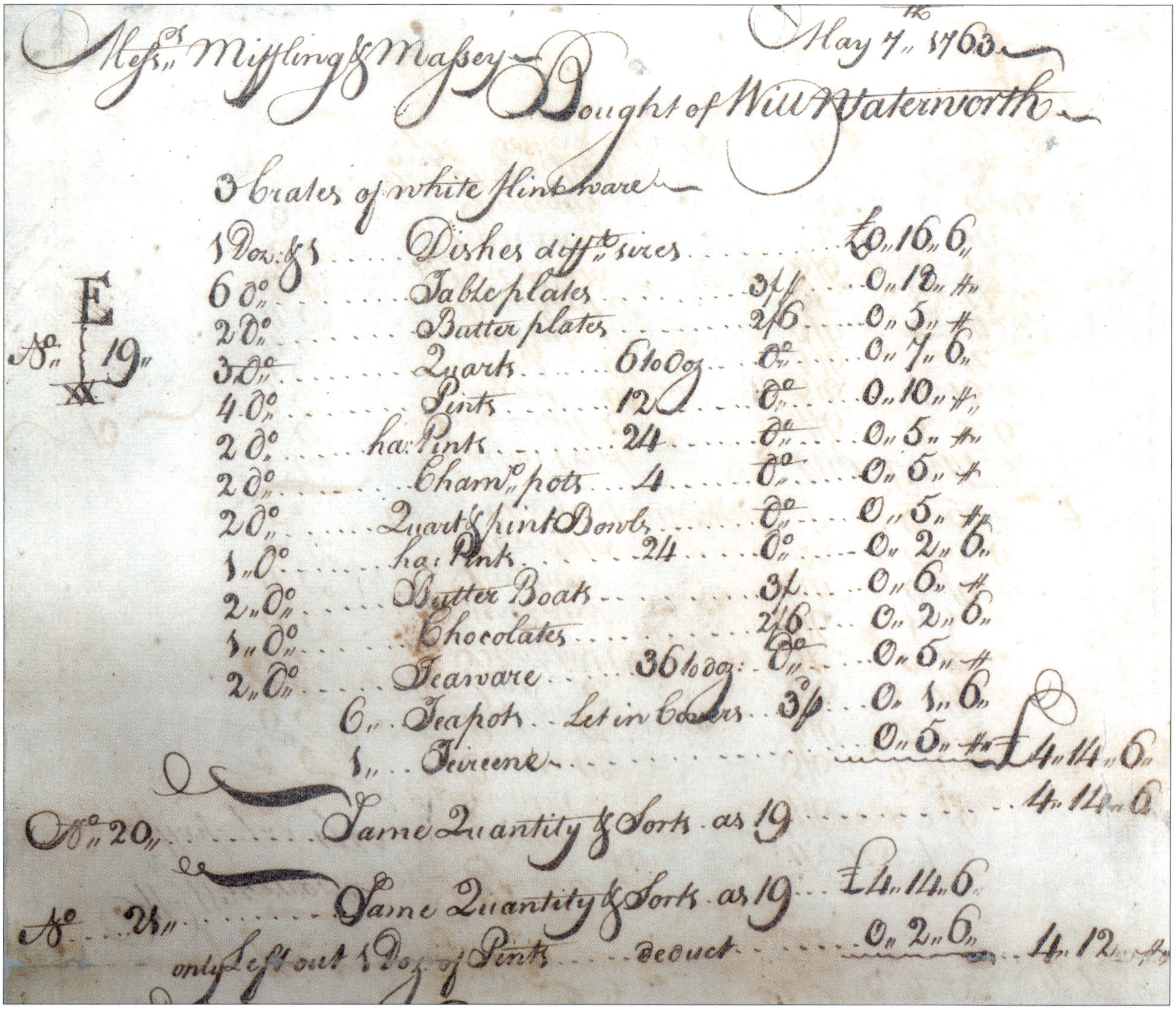
Messrs Miffling & Massey — May 7th 1763
Bought of Will Waterworth

3 Crates of white flint ware

No 19 E X	1 Doz: & 1	Dishes diffrt sizes		£0,,16,,6
	6 do	Tableplates	3/	0,,18,,–
	2 do	Butter plates	2/6	0,,5,,–
	3 do	Quarts 6 to doz	do	0,,7,,6
	4 do	Pints 12	do	0,,10,,–
	2 do	ha: Pints 24	do	0,,5,,–
	2 do	Chamr pots 4	do	0,,5,,–
	2 do	Quart & Pint Bowls	do	0,,5,,–
	1 do	ha: Pint 24	do	0,,2,,6
	2 do	Butter Boats	3/	0,,6,,–
	1 do	Chocolates	2/6	0,,2,,6
	2 do	Teaware 36 to doz	do	0,,5,,–
	6	Teapots Let in Covers	3/	0,,1,,6
	1	Tureene		0,,5,,– £4,,14,,6

No 20 ... Same Quantity & Sorts as 19 ... 4,,14,,6
No 21 ... Same Quantity & Sorts as 19 ... £4,,14,,6
only Left out 1 Doz of Pints ... deduct ... 0,,2,,6 ... 4,,12,,–

Colour Plate 134. **Invoice** *of purchases of white salt-glazed stoneware (flintware) from English agent Will Waterworth by Philadelphia retailers Messrs Miffling and Massey, 7 May 1763. (Courtesy the Winterthur Library: Joseph Downs Collection of Manuscripts and Printed Ephemera, 60 x 21.1)*

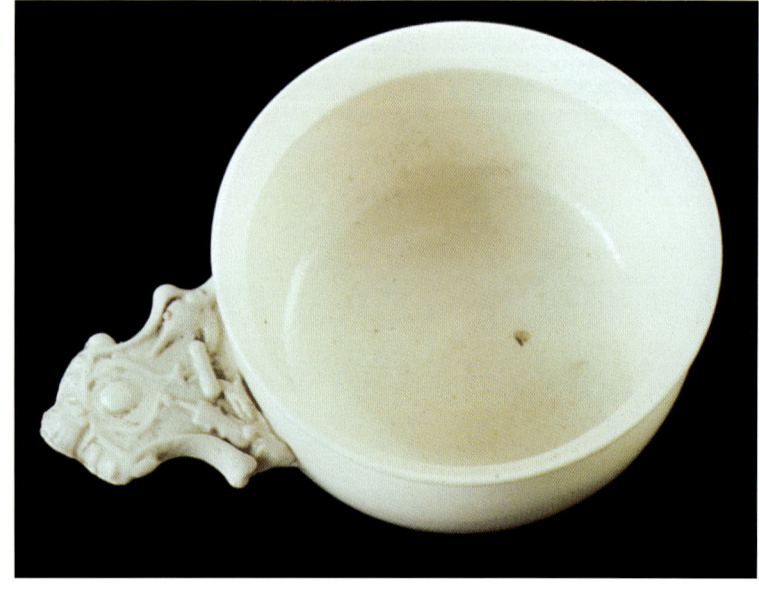

Colour Plate 135. **Porringer,** *white salt-glazed stoneware. Staffordshire, c.1740-55. 1½in. (3.81cm) high x 4in. (10.16cm) wide. (Winterthur Museum, 1976.0107)*

CHAPTER VII – ENGLISH WHITE SALT-GLAZED STONEWARE FOR THE AMERICAN MARKET

Colour Plate 136. **'Pickle leaf'**, white press-moulded salt-glazed stoneware with a bird on a branch in relief. Similar examples of leaves with birds facing to the left have been found among the excavated shards from Isleworth in biscuit creamware. Probably Staffordshire, c.1755. 4½in. (11.43cm) (John Paul Jones House, Portsmouth Historical Society, Portsmouth, New Hampshire)

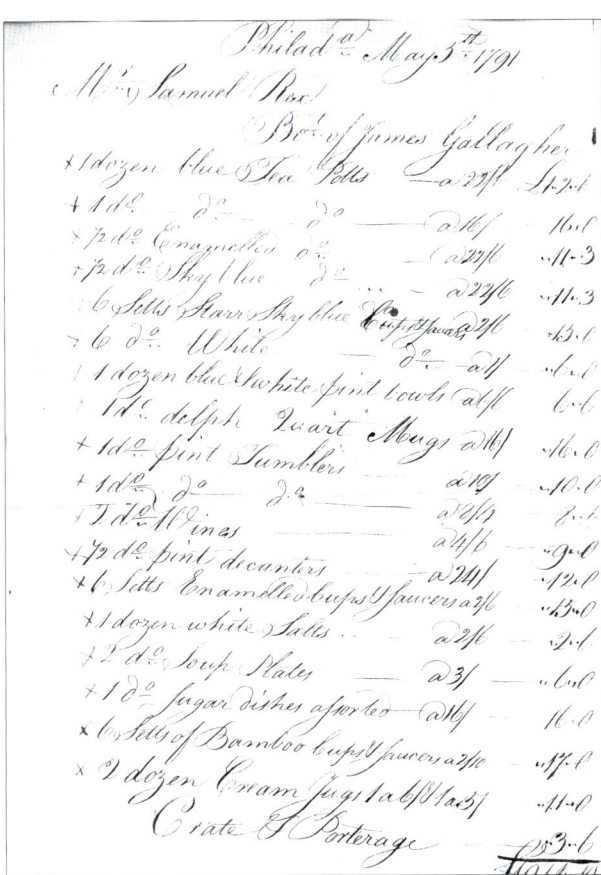

Fig. 127. **Invoice** of purchases by Samuel Rex, Philadelphia, from James Gallagher 5 May 1791. Note the mixture of delftware and 'white' salt-glazed stoneware (salts, soup plates and sugar dishes) with creamware, pearlware and caneware (bamboo). (Courtesy the Winterthur Library: Joseph Downs Collection of Manuscripts and Printed Ephemera, 73 x 113)

Colour Plate 137. **Waster shard,** white salt-glazed stoneware shard with Littler-Wedgwood blue dip found in the excavation of John Bartlam's creamware manufactory at Cain Hoy, South Carolina. Although salt-glazed shards were found on the site, along with this single waster decorated in Littler-Wedgwood blue, no other evidence of salt-glazed production was found in excavated material. Staffordshire or South Carolina, c.1765. (Photograph courtesy of University of South Carolina Department of Archaeology)

Colour Plate 138. **Bowl or cup,** partially reconstructed white salt-glazed engobe slip-decorated bowl with iron-dipped rim. Excavated in the cellar of Rumney's Tavern, London Town, Anne Arundel County, Maryland in a context c.1725. The thinly potted and finely executed bowl was found in a context with many other London delft and stonewares. Possibly London, Dwight's factory at Fulham c.1710-20. 2½in. (6.35cm) high. (Lost Towns Project, Anne Arundel County, Maryland)

his young niece, Elizabeth Calvert, who in 1748 married her cousin Benedict (Swingate) Calvert, moving him into the house where they lived until 1760 when they moved to Mount Airy plantation in Prince George's County. The ceramics illustrated probably reflect this occupancy.[71]

In St. Mary's, Maryland, in the south-eastern most corner of the state, a domestic site occupied by Captain John Hicks from 1723-43 yielded the following wares: four cups, twenty-four mugs, four vessels for dispensing liquid, three bowls, three teapots and three teacups and two saucers. Of a total vessel count of 277, salt-glazed stoneware numbered forty-eight, delftware fifty-five, porcelain twenty-one and earthenware 153.[72] One plate was found (the possible exception to the 1740 arbitrary date for production of plates by Noël Hume, but since the site was occupied from 1723-43 it is not reliable evidence for possible earlier production). Inventories from 1761-1763 in St. Mary's county indicate similar vessels and similar proportions of salt-glazed compared with the other ceramic bodies, but an increase in the number of plates and additional vessels, such as mustard pots.[73]

Naturally other North American sites boasted the same wares. In a trash pit between the house owned by the Read and Curtis families in Newcastle, Delaware and a house on the eastern lot owned by David French, a number of white salt-glazed vessels were excavated including this curious vessel with the pouring rim (Fig. 128) and a mug (Fig. 129). Related artefacts date the deposit to the 1720s-30s.

In Williamsburg, Virginia, excavations of eighteenth-century sites, Anthony Hay's cabinet shop (Anthony Hay died in 1770) yielded both press-moulded sauceboats and a slip-cast sauceboat with the 'boy in a tree' motif. A salt-glaze cup (c.1725) was found in the stream behind Hay's shop. A scratch-blue mug, and a scratch-brown fragment of a chamber pot, as well as a debased scratch-blue chamber pot, were also found associated with a later occupation of Anthony Hay's site (Colour Plate 145). A jug with a *terminus post quem* of 1728 was found nearby associated with John Brush's gunsmithing shop.[74] The James Geddy site[75] (1760-77; Colour Plates 146-148; Fig. 131) included typical salt-glaze of the period including plain salt-glaze which rarely survives outside archaeological sites making it unjustifiably interesting, as well as seed pattern and gadroon-edged moulded wares. A sauceboat moulded with farm animals was also excavated (Fig. 131).

Printed salt-glaze is rare above ground and almost non-existent below, but Williamsburg found portions of a salt-glaze plate printed in red with the *Dog in the Manger* (Colour Plates 117, 118) from Aesop's fables.[76]

In Charlottesville, Virginia, at Monticello, the home of Thomas Jefferson (built between 1767 and 1796), archaeologists found salt-glazed mugs (Fig. 132) among the Chinese porcelains and English creamware which predominated in the ceramic deposits.[77]

Fig. 128. Pouring vessel, white salt-glazed stoneware with wish-bone-shaped handle for pouring cream or other liquids. Excavated near the Read/Curtis House in Newcastle, Delaware, this vessel was found among artefacts dating from the 1720s-30s. Probably Staffordshire, c.1720-30. 2⅞in. (7.3cm) high. (University of Delaware Department of Archaeology)

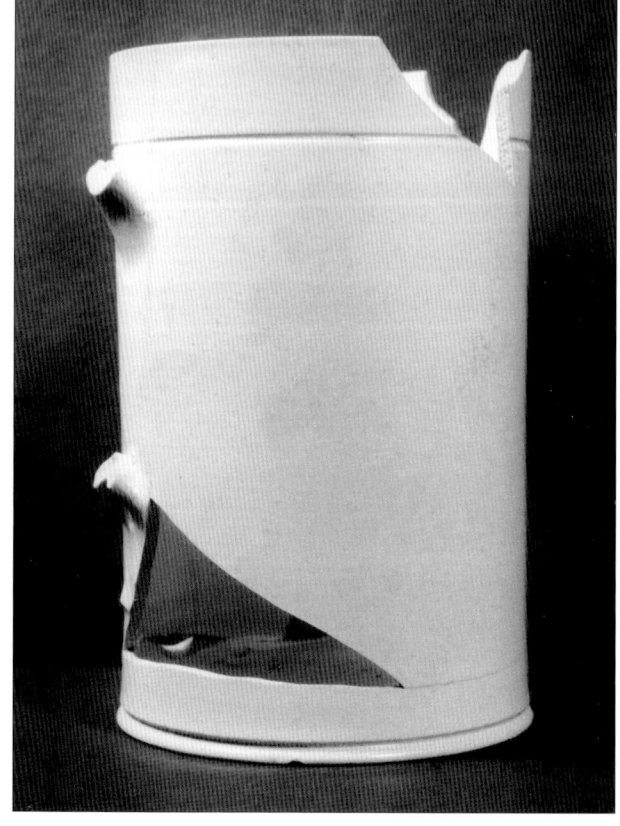

Fig. 129. Partially reconstructed mug, white salt-glazed stoneware. Probably Staffordshire, c.1720-30. 6⅜in. (16.19cm) high. (University of Delaware Department of Archaeology)

CHAPTER VII – ENGLISH WHITE SALT-GLAZED STONEWARE FOR THE AMERICAN MARKET

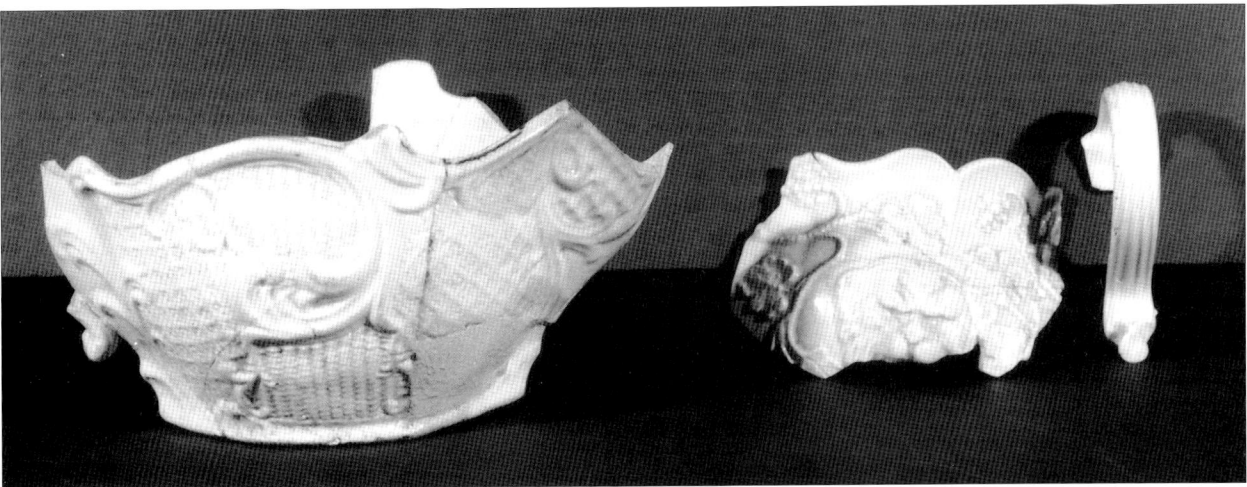

*Fig. 130. **Two partially reconstructed sauceboats,** white salt-glazed stoneware, the left pressmoulded with the mosaic or basketweave pattern: 2½in. (6.35cm) high; the right slip-cast with the 'Boy in the tree' pattern; 1⅞in. (4.76cm) high. These were excavated at Anthony Hay's house site (occupation 1760 to 1770). Staffordshire, c.1760-70. (Colonial Williamsburg Foundation Department of Archaeology)*

*Fig. 131. **Sauceboat,** partially reconstructed white salt-glazed stoneware slip-cast with farm animals in a bucolic setting. The sauceboat was excavated from the James Geddy house site, Colonial Williamsburg. Probably Staffordshire, c.1755-75. 3⅛in. (7.94cm) high. (Colonial Williamsburg Foundation, 01512-19B)*

*Fig. 132. **Two mugs,** of plain white salt-glazed stoneware with strap handles and waisted flared feet. These partially reconstructed mugs were excavated from a dry well deposit c.1770-71 at Monticello, the Virginia home of Thomas Jefferson. Staffordshire, c.1750-60. (Monticello, Thomas Jefferson Foundation, Inc., S.C.503, S.C.503)*

169

CHAPTER VII – ENGLISH WHITE SALT-GLAZED STONEWARE FOR THE AMERICAN MARKET

Colour Plate 139. **Teabowl and saucer,** *partially reconstructed white-slipped salt-glazed stoneware, thinly and finely potted. Excavated at Rumney's Tavern, London Town, Anne Arundel, County, Maryland. Probably London, Dwight's factory at Fulham, c.1715-20. Teabowl 1½in. (3.81cm) high; saucer 4⅛in. (10.48cm) diameter. (Lost Towns Project, Anne Arundel County, Maryland)*

Colour Plate 140. **Coffee pot fragments,** *white salt-glazed stoneware with iron-dipped upper half of body. Excavated at Rumney's Tavern, London Town, Anne Arundel County, Maryland. London, John Dwight's successor factory operated by Dr. Samuel Dwight, c.1715-20. (Lost Towns Project, Anne Arundel County, Maryland)*

Colour Plate 141. **Mug,** *partially reconstructed white-slipped salt-glazed stoneware with iron-dipped rim excavated at Rumney's Tavern, London Town, Anne Arundel, Maryland. London, Dwight's successor factory at Fulham operated by Lydia Dwight (1703-09) or her son Dr. Samuel Dwight (1709-37), c.1710-20, 6½in. (16.51cm) high. (Lost Towns Project, Anne Arundel County, Maryland)*

Colour Plate 142. **Two mugs,** *white slipped salt-glazed stoneware with iron-dipped rims. Left London, John Dwight's successor factory (note the handle with the notched terminal); right Staffordshire; both c.1710-20. 4¾in. (12.07cm). (Private collection)*

Colour Plate 143. **Partially reconstructed teapot,** *white salt-glazed stoneware enamel decorated with English flowers. Excavated at the Calvert House, State House Circle, Annapolis, Maryland, the ceramics were probably among the artefacts used by Elizabeth and Benedict Calvert who resided there from 1748 to 1760. Staffordshire, c.1755-60. 4⅛in. (10.48cm) high. (Historic Annapolis Foundation, V.562)*

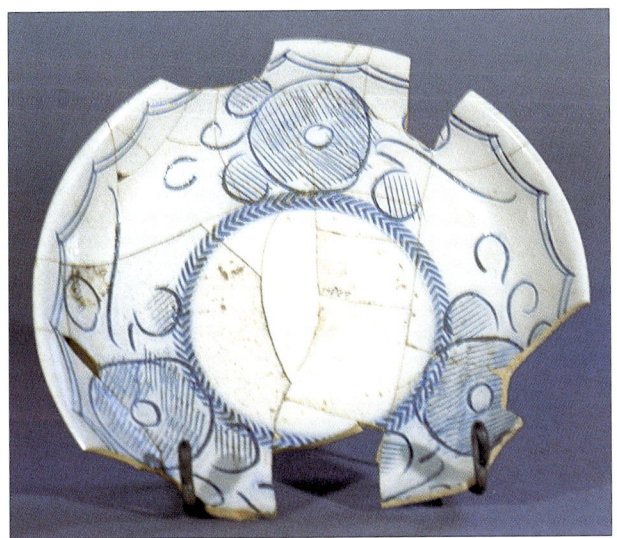

Colour Plate 144. **Partially reconstructed saucer,** *white salt-glazed stoneware with scratch-blue floral decoration excavated at the Calvert House, State House Circle, Annapolis, Maryland. Staffordshire, c.1750-60. 4¾in. (12.07cm) diameter. (Historic Annapolis Foundation)*

Colour Plate 145. **Partially reconstructed group of scratch-blue wares** *consisting of a mug, 3¾in. (9.53cm) high, lid, 3½in. (8.89cm) diameter, chamber pot, 5in. (12.7cm) high, all excavated at the Anthony Hay site, Colonial Williamsburg occupied from 1760 to 1770. (Colonial Williamsburg Foundation Department of Archaeology)*

Colour Plate 146. **Partially reconstructed plain vessels** *in white salt-glazed stoneware recovered from the James Geddy archaeological site, Williamsburg, Virginia. The salt-glaze is from the second occupation of the site by James Geddy, Jnr (1760-77). Plain stonewares were produced by all the factories including Bovey Tracey. Probably Staffordshire, c.1750-70; teabowl (01508-19BB), 2in. (5.08cm) high; plate (01517-19BB), 9in. (22.86cm) diameter; patty pan (01497-19BB), 5⅛in. (13.02cm) diameter (Colonial Williamsburg Foundation)*

Colour Plate 147. **Two plates** *partially reconstructed white salt-glazed stoneware with moulded edges in gadrooned and barleycorn (or seed) patterns. Excavated from the James Geddy house site, Colonial Williamsburg, the plates are probably Staffordshire, c.1755-75. Plate 9in. (22.86cm) diameter; twiffler 7in. (17.78cm) diameter. (Colonial Williamsburg Foundation, 01558-19BB, 01503-19BB)*

Colour Plate 148. **Partially reconstructed teabowl fragments and one saucer,** *white salt-glazed stoneware with enamel decoration excavated at the James Geddy house site Colonial Williamsburg. Staffordshire, c.1760-70. (Colonial Williamsburg Foundation Department of Archaeology)*

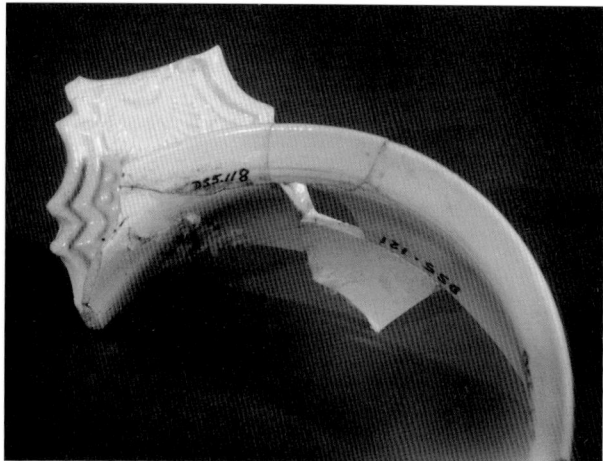

*Fig. 133. **Porringer,** partially reconstructed white salt-glazed stoneware. This vessel was excavated from a house site where the owner had a vintner's licence. Moulded porringer handles have been excavated at the Fenton Vivian site of Thomas Whieldon, at Humphrey Palmer's site, Hanley and at Bovey Tracey in Devon, but none actually matches these from Portsmouth. Porringers seem to fall out of fashion around the mid-18th century or around the beginning of these three factories. Probably Staffordshire, c.1740-55. 4½in. (11.43cm) long. (Strawbery Banke Museum, Portsmouth, New Hampshire, A0411)*

*Fig. 134. **Porringer handle** of white moulded salt-glazed stoneware excavated at Deer Street, Portsmouth, New Hampshire. Probably Staffordshire, c.1740-55, 2¼in. (5.72cm) high. (Strawbery Banke Museum, Portsmouth, New Hampshire, 02047)*

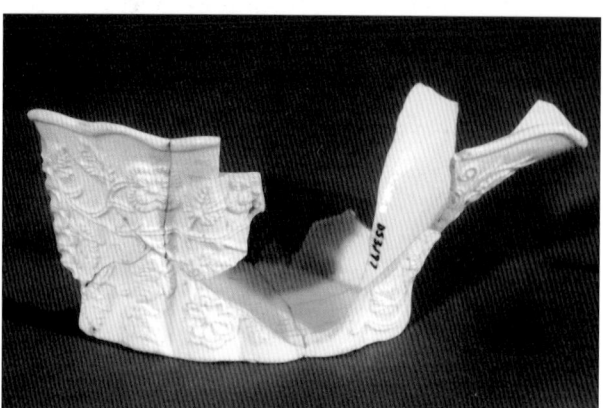

*Fig. 135. **Partially reconstructed sauceboat,** press-moulded white salt-glazed stoneware with scalloped body and relief floral decoration. Excavated on Deer Street, Portsmouth, New Hampshire. Staffordshire, c.1750-55. 2¼in. (5.72cm) base width. (Strawbery Banke Museum, Portsmouth, New Hampshire, A883)*

*Fig. 136. **Partially reconstructed plate rim** of white salt-glazed stoneware with a rim press-moulded with floral decoration excavated at the Warner House built by Captain Archibald Macpheadris (c.1716) in Portsmouth, New Hampshire. The artefacts found on the site date from the occupation of the house by his daughter Mary Warner and her husband c.1759-1814. Staffordshire, c.1759-70. 4¼in. (10.8cm) maximum. (Warner House Association)*

A great deal of domestic archaeology has been accomplished in the last thirty years in Portsmouth, New Hampshire, both in the Deer Street area where an entire neighbourhood was razed in 1969 for so-called urban renewal purposes, and at Strawbery Banke, a ten acre museum site with forty-two historic houses.

On Deer Street nothing was constructed on the site until 1988 when a Sheraton Hotel was erected. The early years of the 1980s, when the major digging occurred, were illuminating for archaeologists and social historians. The Hart-Shortridge House[78] yielded little salt-glaze because the deposit, c.1840, consisted mainly of later material. One sauceboat (Colour Plate 149) with the 'boy in the tree' as well as a large scratch-blue mug (Colour Plate 150) were included among the small number of salt-glazed vessels. The 1790 inventory of John Hart, the first occupant of the Hart-Shortridge House, indicated that some of the china in the closet was broken. Indeed the sauceboat had an old repair.

Other Deer Street area salt-glaze included porringers and handles (Figs. 133, 134), chamber pots (Colour Plate 151), another sauceboat with fluted panels (Fig. 135; Colour Plate 157), polychrome and scratch-blue decorated shards, a large food storage container (Colour Plate 152) and a fluted cup from the Richard Shortridge house site (Colour Plate 153) fluted in a manner similar to ones excavated at the Shelton Farm site in North Staffordshire

CHAPTER VII – ENGLISH WHITE SALT-GLAZED STONEWARE FOR THE AMERICAN MARKET

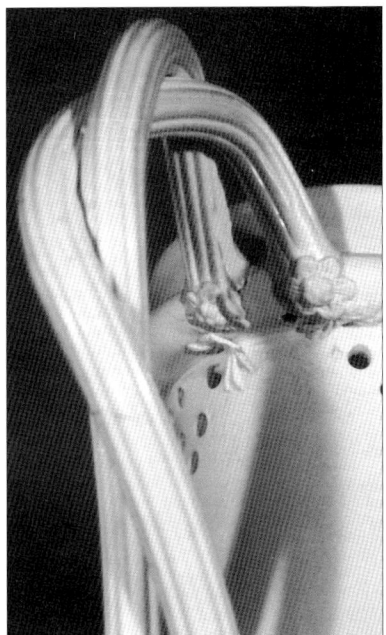

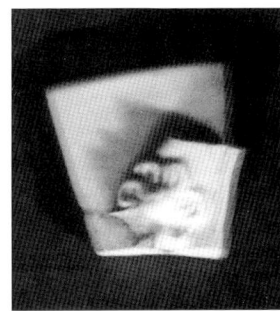

Figs. 137a and 137b. ***Close-up of puzzle jug and shard from puzzle jug*** *from the Dr. Hall Jackson site in Fig. 137. 1⅛in. (2.86cm) high. (Strawbery Banke Museum Collection, gift of Basil and Louise Richardson)*

Fig. 137. ***Puzzle jug,*** *white salt-glazed stoneware of rare form. The jug matches a shard found at the Dr. Hall Jackson excavation site in Portsmouth, New Hampshire. c.1780-90. 7¾in. (19.69cm) high. (Strawbery Banke Museum Collection, gift of Basil and Louise Richardson)*

(Colour Plate 154). Another handle excavated from the same house lot (Colour Plate 155) was similar to the unusual handle on a strainer (Colour Plate 156) with a long history in Deerfield, Massachusetts.

Excavations at nearby Warner House built for Captain Archibald Macpheadris, a wealthy merchant in 1716, yielded similar types of wares. All the salt-glaze dated to the later occupation of the house by his daughter Mary and her husband Jonathan Warner between 1759 and 1814 (Fig.136).

Dr. Hall Jackson (1739-1797), the revolutionary war physician who brought the smallpox vaccine to North America through his association with Dr. William Withering in Birmingham,[79] lived in Portsmouth. The well on his property was excavated in 1980 and included shards of a 'Battle of Portobello' mug (Colour Plate 158) and the terminal and rim shard from a jug similar to this puzzle jug (Figs. 137, 137a, b). Upcountry, on the shores of Lake Winnipesaukee, the last Royal Governor of New Hampshire, Governor John Wentworth, built a country estate in 1768 residing there part time until the revolution in 1775 when he was forced to flee the country. The house remained standing until 1820 when it burned, so most of the excavated ceramics are earthenware and porcelains of a later period. The salt-glaze uncovered included the expected moulded plates with diaper and

Chapter VII – English White Salt-Glazed Stoneware for the American Market

*Colour Plate 149. **Sauceboat,** partially reconstructed white salt-glazed stoneware slip-cast with the 'Boy in the tree' motif, excavated at the Hart-Shortridge House, Portsmouth, New Hampshire. Note the old repair to the lip. Staffordshire, c.1745-55. 8½in. (21.59cm) long. (Strawbery Banke Museum, Portsmouth, New Hampshire)*

*Colour Plate 150. **Large mug,** partially reconstructed white salt-glazed stoneware with scratch-blue floral decoration recovered from the Hart-Shortridge House excavation, Portsmouth, New Hampshire. Probably Staffordshire, c.1750-70. 3⅞in. (9.84cm) high. (Strawbery Banke Museum, Portsmouth, New Hampshire)*

*Colour Plate 151. **Chamber pot,** partially reconstructed white salt-glazed stoneware with rolled rim. The vessel was excavated on Deer Street, Portsmouth, New Hampshire on the site of a home of a licensed vintner. Probably Staffordshire, c.1730-60. 6⅛in. (15.56cm) high. (Strawbery Banke Museum, Portsmouth, New Hampshire, A621)*

*Colour Plate 152. **Food storage container** of white salt-glazed stoneware with pale iron colour to shoulder and rim, partially reconstructed ovoid storage jar excavated in an extension (referred to as the 'linty') of the Richard Shortridge house, Deer Street, Portsmouth, New Hampshire The jar's pale iron colour makes it difficult to place. First half of the 18th century. 8¾in. (22.23cm) high. (Strawbery Banke Museum, A633)*

CHAPTER VII – ENGLISH WHITE SALT-GLAZED STONEWARE FOR THE AMERICAN MARKET

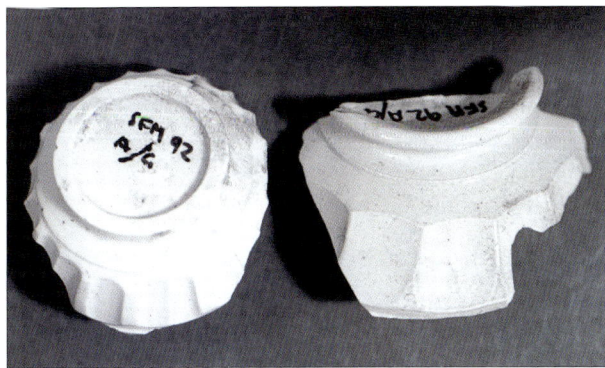

Colour Plate 153. **Teabowl fragment,** *white salt-glazed stoneware with fluted ribs, annular turned base and waisted foot. Excavated in the fill between two houses on Deer Street, Portsmouth, New Hampshire, the teabowl is similar to ones excavated at the Shelton Farm site, Staffordshire. Probably Shelton Farm, Staffordshire, c.1720-22. 2⅛in. (5.4cm) wide. (Strawbery Banke Museum, Portsmouth, New Hampshire, A780)*

Colour Plate 154. **Two teabowl fragments,** *white salt-glazed stoneware with fluted ribs and waisted feet excavated from the Shelton Farm site, Staffordshire. John Fenton and Thomas Hill, Shelton Farm, Stoke-on-Trent, c.1720-22. 1¾in. (4.45cm) diameter at base. (Strawbery Banke Museum, Portsmouth, New Hampshire, A780)*

Colour Plate 155. **Handle shard,** *white salt-glazed stoneware rolled handle for a porringer or a strainer excavated at the Richard Hart house, Portsmouth, New Hampshire. c.1730-40. 1½in. (3.81cm) long. (Strawbery Banke Museum, Portsmouth, New Hampshire, A2046)*

Colour Plate 157. **Sauceboat,** *press-moulded white salt-glazed sauceboat with scalloped form and floral relief decoration. Staffordshire, c.1750-55. 2¼in. (5.72cm) high. (Private collection)*

Colour Plate 156. **Strainer,** *white salt-glazed stoneware with rolled ram's horn handles. Descended in a Deerfield family, these handles are similar to the one in Colour Plate 155 excavated in Portsmouth, New Hampshire. Probably Staffordshire, c.1720-30. 1⅞ x 5 x 4in. (4.76 x 12.7 x 10.16cm). (Historic Deerfield, Inc, gift of Mr. John Mayer, 57.115)*

Colour Plate 158. **Shard from a Portobello mug,** *white salt-glazed stoneware excavated from the Dr. Hall Jackson site, Portsmouth, New Hampshire, c.1739. (Private collection)*

basket, gadrooned and seed borders as well as a scratch-blue teabowl.[80]

To recapitulate, white salt-glazed stoneware was available and in use in America by the early years of the 1720s, indeed probably by 1715, as the probated inventory of Edward Bennet of Chester County, Pennsylvania, indicated. The Fulham salt-glaze mugs and teawares excavated from London Town corroborate the use of salt-glaze in colonial America before 1720. Salt-glazed stoneware continued to be a part of household ceramic inventories through to the end of the century, playing a decreasing role in the last two decades with the ascendancy of creamware. Newspaper advertisements were occurring at least from 1733 in Boston. Both archaeology and newspaper advertisements for 'blue and white' confirm the popularity of scratch-blue decorated stoneware from 1751 to 1776 in colonial and early federated America. The imposition of an excise tax levied on Chinese porcelains and other luxury items in 1754 might have caused chinoiserie decorated stoneware to advance to fill that market; however, the paucity of advertisements for enamelled stoneware until 1763 does not confirm this was the case. Enamelled stoneware continued to be advertised frequently from 1763 until 1776. Initially tea and coffee wares, mugs and jugs and chamber pots were the predominant shapes. Around 1740 plates and other moulded wares were available. Delftware and white salt-glazed stoneware shared markets and were competitive in price, delftware being slightly cheaper. White salt-glazed stoneware graced both the graceful table of the wealthy Washingtons and Jeffersons as well as those in more humble establishments. The decline of stoneware, slightly grey, slightly gritty, was undoubtedly due to the introduction of creamware, the lead glazing providing a soft, sensuous texture easy on the palette, easy on the eye.

CHAPTER VIII

The Collectors

As my thoughts begin to disassemble, they touch down briefly on shelves of china. My Grandmother, too, collects china. She has lots of Staffordshire salt-glaze.
Barbara Trapido, *The Travelling Hornplayer*[1]

Whether white salt-glaze stoneware was the focus of an eighteenth century collector's interest is not something which will probably ever be known. That collectors such as Horace Walpole (1717-1797) had salt-glaze amongst their manifold other collections is known, but when Walpole made the inventory of the contents of Strawberry Hill in 1774 there were no actual listings of the salt-glaze in his collection amongst the wide range of Chinese, English and European ceramics.[2]

In the nineteenth century collectors such as Enoch Wood, L.M. Solon, Lady Charlotte Schreiber, Augustus Wollaston Franks, R. Soden-Smith and Professor A.H. Church included salt-glazed stoneware among their other ceramics. Salt-glaze in most instances was collected as part of a general pursuit of early English pottery and sometimes, as with Lady Charlotte and Franks, it included a highly developed interest in porcelain as well.

It was in the twentieth century, particularly the first half, that salt-glaze began to find a voice and make its way into museum collections in more than just a cursory way. Collectors like Sir Arthur Church, Wallace Elliot, Arthur Hurst, Louis Jahn, Charles F.C. Luxmoore, J. Henry Griffith, Micah Salt, Cyril Earle, Charles J. Lomax and Henry Willett were among those who populated the shelves in museum vitrines with salt-glaze, now regarded as not just pot amassing but a discriminating selection of wares, many of which are rare or even unique in the lexicon. Some of these collectors also wrote catalogues of their own collections, local museum collections or books on English ceramics. While most of the collectors of salt-glaze were interested in early English ceramics, at least one, Mr. Thomas B. Clarke of New York, collected salt-glaze because of its white glaze which he collected in conjunction with the lustrous Chinese white wares of the K'ang-hsi (1662-1722), Yung Chêng (1723-35) and Ch'ien-lung (1736-1795) periods. Clarke's collection sold at the American Art Galleries on Madison Square South, New York in January 1918.[3]

In recent years collectors such as Henry and Jimmy Weldon and Harriet Goldweitz have added to the repertoire with their discriminating selections, the Henry H. Weldon Collection of early English pottery having been recently given to Colonial Williamsburg. Both these collectors bought widely from other collections of English pottery including the Rous Lench sales (1986, 1990). The Weldons have salt-glaze from several important collections: Charles J. Lomax (1937), Mrs. F. Shand-Kydd, the Chorley, Price Glover and the Bertram K. and Nina Fletcher Little collection (1994). Harriet Goldweitz made purchases from many other well-known collections such as Lowy (1972), Gollancz (1975), Stretton (1984), and had pieces formerly in the Prescott, Tilley and Cyril Cook collections.

Dealers were not inconsequential in appealing to their clients, in some cases dictating their tastes. The *Connoisseur* showed that leading dealers in English ceramics included rare salt-glaze in their advertisements. The dealers who advertised with frequency in the first three to four decades of the twentieth century included Law, Foulsham & Cole at 7 South Moulton Street, Mortlocks Ltd at 31 & 32 Orchard Street (off Oxford Street), John Evelyn & Co. at 13 Exhibition Road, South Kensington, Stoner & Evans at 3 King Street, St. James's, and Cyril Andrade at the Dalmeny Galleries, 8 Duke Street, St. James's. In the case of Andrade he was a generous benefactor to the Ashmolean Museum adding not only pottery and porcelain to the museum's collections but many pieces of white salt-glazed stoneware until his death in 1973. At 47 Leicester Square auctioneers Puttick & Simpson advertised a limestone strata salt-glazed teapot (Colour Plates 111, 133) and a salt-glazed solid agate cat in November 1934. In 1935 Law, Foulsham & Cole advertised pieces of salt-glaze from the famous collection of Cecil Lord Revelstoke. Other dealers outside London who occasionally advertised salt-glazed stoneware were F.J. Morrall, 48 Liverpool Road, Stoke-on-Trent and F.W. Phillips, the Manor House, Hitchin, Hertfordshire, who advertised forty-eight pieces of enamel decorated white salt-glaze stoneware including the famous jug inscribed 'I T A 1739' in December 1907 which by 1915 was in the Earle collection.[4]

1914 was a landmark year for appreciation of early English pottery when the Burlington Fine Arts Club[5] launched a large exhibition (actually opening in December 1913), producing a catalogue which still stands as an important tome in ceramic libraries.[6] There were nearly two hundred pieces of white salt-glazed stoneware, including six by Dwight, agate and Littler-Wedgwood blue items. This exhibition, which put early English pottery and stoneware on the map, so to speak, boasted a list of contributors whose names populate accession cards in the major English museums. Lenders of salt-glazed stoneware included Mr. A.E. Clarke, Dr. Glaisher, Dr. E.J. Sidebotham,

Chapter VIII – The Collectors

Mr. Edward Sheldon, Mr. Thomas Greg, Capt. Charles Luxmoore, Mr. Brian T. Harland and Professor A.H. Church and others.

Perhaps the largest public collection of salt-glaze is in the Victoria and Albert Museum. Several collections were given to the museum which included large numbers of white salt-glazed stoneware. In 1901 the ceramics from the Museum of Practical Geology on Jermyn Street were incorporated into the collection at South Kensington. The Museum of Practical Geology had been set up in 1835 to illustrate geological and mineral resources in the British Isles. Gradually ceramics imitating natural substances were added to the collection which included a number of solid agate salt-glazed wares and other imitations of natural materials. In 1855 a *Catalogue of Specimens Illustrative of the Composition and Manufacture of British Pottery and Porcelain* was produced by the director of the museum, Sir Henry De La Beche, and curator Trenham Reeks. In 1901 the Science Museum was set up in South Kensington and the Museum of Practical Geology 'hived off the ceramics collections to the Victoria and Albert Museum under the rationalisation which had been recommended by Professor Church in 1881.'[7] Among the pieces going from the Jermyn Street collection to South Kensington was a master mould (Fig. 69) and a rare inscribed tureen and cover in the mosaic pattern (Colour Plate 28, 28a).

In a sense it is curious that the famous Lady Charlotte Schreiber (1812-1895) collection, a name synonymous with English ceramics, came to the South Kensington Museum. One would assume that Lady Charlotte's close association with Augustus Wollaston Franks would have made the British Museum the logical choice for its permanent home. Franks, who in addition to being a close friend, was the long-time curator and benefactor of the British Museum, helped in the preparation of the catalogue of her collection of over 2,000 pieces presented to South Kensington in 1884. Michael Archer in his chapter on 'The History of the Delftware Collection in the Victoria and Albert Museum' suggests that it may have been her friendship with Professor A.H. Church which encouraged her to donate her collection to the South Kensington Museum.[8] Of course, since the museum at South Kensington, later the Victoria and Albert Museum, was newly opened in 1868 it would have had the space to display the collection which the British Museum lacked. But it may simply have been Lady Charlotte's intention to see a more equable distribution of ceramics between the two museums, knowing that Franks' fine collection was going to the British Museum.

Lady Charlotte had been collecting early English ceramics since 1865. The catalogue of her collection was published in 1885 with ancillary help from Franks, A.H. Church and R.H. Soden-Smith. In the mid-nineteenth century, and for decades thereafter, very little was known about the rarity or values of early pottery and porcelain. Lady Charlotte was a bargain hunter with an amazing eye for fine early English ceramics. Her salt-glaze interests ranged in date from the earliest Dwight gorges (Fig. 199) to mid-eighteenth century Oriental figures (Colour Plate 72) and included many dated examples and commemoratives such as a mug of the Battle of Portobello (Fig. 14). As one of the leading dealers of the day, Mr. Mortlock of Oxford Street acknowledged that nearly everything he learned about English ceramics he gleaned from Lady Charlotte.[9]

Two other collectors made important contributions to the salt-glaze collection at the V & A: Wallace Elliot (1938) and Arthur Hurst (1940). Wallace Elliot (1867-1938) of Valley End House, Cobham, Surrey was a hugely important collector of a wide range of ceramics (and glass) of principally English manufacture. He was the second President of the English Porcelain Circle. In 1931 during his tenure the name was changed to the English Ceramic Circle and the scope enlarged. He gave some papers to the 'Circle' which were published in the *Transactions,* including an article on fakes in which he illustrated several examples of genuine and fake salt-glazed figures, animals and a pew group.[10] Elliot was apparently an exceptionally broadly versed man who combined his collecting interests with a talent for photography, was an accomplished watercolourist, could oversee the construction of a building, argue points of law with the best at the Bar and raise prize Jersey cattle.[11] He enjoyed a steady correspondence with Bernard Rackham, advising him on purchases for the Victoria and Albert Museum collection. In 1923 Elliot wrote to Rackham with a list of salt-glazed stoneware and other English pottery he thought would be of interest to the V & A including a square bowl he claimed was a unique one by Ralph Shaw.[12] Elliot had a plain white figure of Buddha in his collection (No. 27). In the A.E. Clarke sale of English pottery held at Sotheby's in June 1919 Elliot bought a solid agate cat (No. 48 WE Coll.) and a mug with the battle of Portobello relief decoration. Among other salt-glazed objects was a candlestick of two egrets facing in opposite directions (No. 97 WE Coll.) and an enormous enamel punch pot with a barbed crabstock handle, finial and spout illustrated in Rackham and Read's *English Pottery,* Plate 60.[13] Elliot purchased an important Dwight agate salt-glazed jug from the Brian T. Harland sale at Sotheby's on 11 February 1931. From another sale at Sotheby's on 4 June 1931 Elliot bought a pew group of two boys (one reading, the other holding two objects) which is marked 'Wedgwood' (No.687 WE Coll.), a reproduction which Elliot presumably purchased intentionally.[14] From the famous Lord Revelstoke collection, sold by Puttick and Simpson in November 1934, Elliot obtained six rare salt-glazed plaques, now in the Victoria and Albert Museum. Other salt-glaze in the Revelstoke collection included the Mary Sandbach cup dated 1720 (Fig. 10) which sold for £24.3s.[15]

When he died in 1938 the terms of his will indicated that Bernard Rackham of the Victoria and Albert and R.L. Hobson of the British Museum were to divide the collection between the two institutions up to the number of one hundred objects each. The remaining pieces of a still remarkably fine collection were sold in 435 lots at Sotheby's in May 1938.[16]

The Victoria and Albert Museum's collection of salt-glaze was enhanced by someone further afield, Arthur Hurst (1857-1940) of East Lodge, St. Peter's, York, whose bequest of 380 pieces of English pottery and stoneware came to the museum in 1940. Hurst was honorary curator of the Yorkshire Museum and wrote a catalogue of the Boynton bequest to the museum in 1922. Hurst's profile as a collector was not particularly distinguished. He did not participate in the important exhibition of early English ceramics sponsored by the Burlington Fine Arts Club in 1914. Hurst lived in York all his life and collected pottery, porcelain, enamels, glass, silver, prints, oils and watercolours. He left his Yorkshire pottery to the Yorkshire Museum and the remainder of his ceramics were divided between the V & A and the British Museum.[17] The quality of Hurst's ceramics, like Elliot's, was of such high standard that it vastly enriched the collection, often including rare examples which would have otherwise been unrepresented.

In addition to the Wallace Elliot and Arthur Hurst bequests to the British Museum collections, which included many salt-glazed stoneware pieces, two other donors greatly extended the museum collection, Augustus Wollaston Franks (1826-1897) and Henry Willett.

David Wilson described Franks as the 'second founder of the British Museum'. In doing so he suggested that when Franks came to the British Museum in 1851 it was dominated by its library collections and previous collecting policy had concentrated on those societies surrounding the Mediterranean.[18] After he died in 1897 the museum had virtually changed character with vast European, Oriental, pre-historical and English collections, all due to Franks' wide ranging cultivated eye. A major *Catalogue of the Collection of English Pottery* in the British Museum was published by the Trustees of the museum in 1903. Written by R.L. Hobson, the preface acknowledges Franks' role in the development of the collection. In 1904 *A Guide to the English Pottery and Porcelain in the Department of British and Medieval Antiquities* was published, also giving Franks the credit for the formation of the collection.

Specific to salt-glaze Franks added important objects to the virtually non-existent collection, accumulating fine pieces such as four Dwight figures (Colour Plates 2, 5-7), and in 1891 a figure of Spinario (Fig. 102) from R. Soden-Smith's collection.[19] Perhaps the earliest known example of a coffee/chocolate pot is the white-engobe dipped, iron-dipped one given by Franks (Fig. 3). He and Henry Willett also gave examples of lighthouse coffee pots in white salt-glaze in 1887 and 1888 (Fig. 93).

In what he entitled 'An Apology for my Life', Franks wrote: 'Collecting is an hereditary disease, and I fear incurable'.[20] He then went on to enumerate the various family members who had collected: a great-grandfather who collected Welsh and Irish printed books, a grandfather who collected hawks and fowls, a mother who was a mineral and plant collector, amongst others. But it was Franks himself who was the greatest collector, above and beyond all his other abilities. Franks collected ceramics from around 1850 until his death in 1897, not necessarily, as Aileen Dawson points out, the flashier European porcelains which were being avidly swept up by the Rothschilds who were filling vast houses, but with an eye to rarity and beauty within his means.[21] So highly regarded was he in his lifetime that he was offered the directorship of both the major South Kensington and British museums, both of which he turned down. It is as a museum visionary and connoisseur that he is commemorated.

Though most of Henry Willett's (1823-1905) collection at Arnold House, Brighton was given to the local museum in 1903, he supplied pottery to the British Museum from 1874 to 1896. Franks made a large purchase from Willett's collection for the museum in 1887. Some of these pieces include two Dwight figures (Colour Plates 3, 4), a candlestick (Fig. 55) and a dated cup (Fig. 17), the grotesque mask (Fig. 96) which is from the same model as a Limehouse porcelain example (Colour Plate 66), house teapots (Fig. 29) and an egg or pickle stand (Fig. 118). In 1899 most of the collection which went to the Brighton Museum in 1903 was shown at the Victoria and Albert's Bethnal Green Museum. A catalogue of the collection written by Willett was published.[22] The exhibition, which concentrated on historical British ceramics, did not include many salt-glazed wares but there were five pieces devoted to Admiral Edward Vernon's Battle at Portobello in 1739. After Willett's death Frank Freeth wrote an article on 'The Willett Collection at the Brighton Museum' in the *Connoisseur* (June 1905). Willett did not collect, as Franks did, as a connoisseur, but thematically, and in his own words because he felt the 'history of a country may be traced to its homely pottery'.[23]

Although many other museums have collections which include white salt-glazed stoneware, one other English museum boasts a vast collection, the Potteries Museum and Art Gallery, Stoke-on-Trent. Three local collections helped to furnish that collection: those of Louis Jahn, L.M. Solon and Micah Salt. Articles which came out in the *Connoisseur* in the first decade of the twentieth century began to draw attention to an already well-established collection of early pottery and porcelain. Frank Freeth wrote in November 1906 an article entitled 'A Glance Around the Hanley Museum'. The curator of the Public Museum, Stoke-on-Trent, was the little remembered Alfred J. Caddie who also contributed some articles on white salt-glazed stoneware to the *Connoisseur*. In his article 'Some Rare Specimens of Staffordshire Salt-Glazed Stoneware' (December 1906) Caddie illustrated the famous grotesque mask vase in the British Museum (Fig. 96) which has a twin in Limehouse porcelain (Colour Plate 66). He also illustrated an enamel painted jug in the Potteries museum inscribed 'James & Martha Jinkeuson 1764'.[24]

Louis Jahn (1839-1911), born in Oberweissbach, Thüringen, came to Mintons in 1862 and modelled vases for them for the London Exhibition. He worked for Brownfields as Art Director from 1872, when they began to make porcelain, until the early 1890s. From 1895 to 1901 he was back at Mintons as Art Director and from

CATALOGUE
OF THE
Pottery & Porcelain
IN THE COLLECTION OF
L. M. SOLON

TO BE SOLD BY AUCTION
WITHOUT RESERVE
ON
TUESDAY, WEDNESDAY AND THURSDAY
26th, 27th and 28th NOVEMBER, 1912
BY
MESSRS. CHARLES BUTTERS & SONS
AT THEIR PREMISES
TRINITY BUILDINGS, HANLEY
STOKE-ON-TRENT

The Collection will be on view at Trinity Buildings, Hanley, for Subscribers to the 10/6 Catalogues only, on Friday, 22nd November, and on Saturday and Monday, November 23rd and 25th, by Catalogue only, Price 1/-, to admit one person from 9 a.m. to 5 p.m.

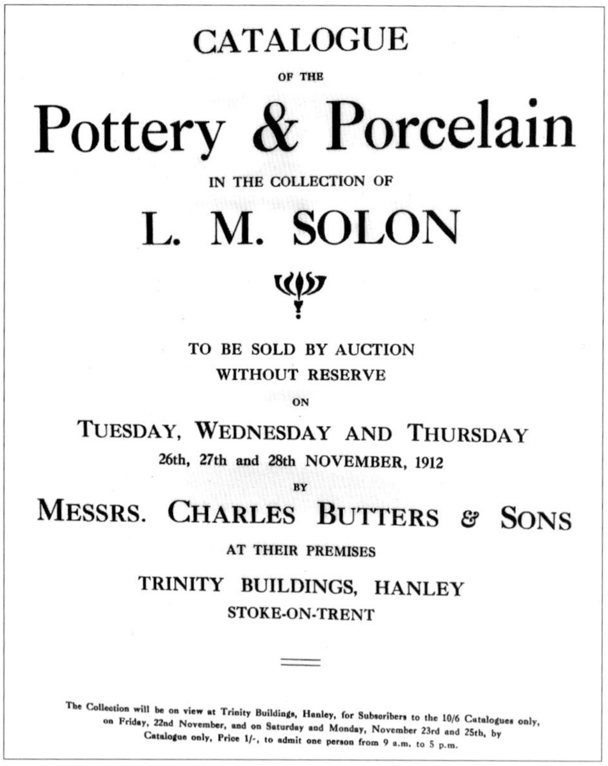

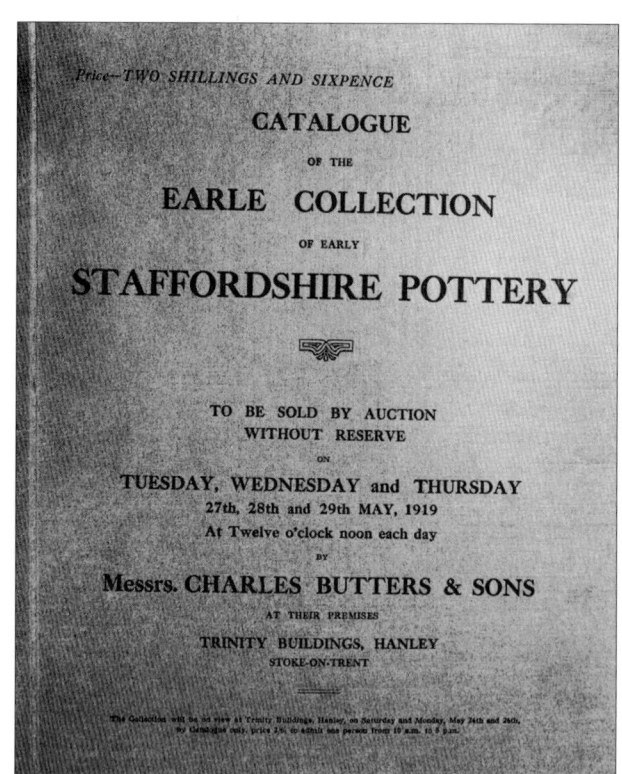

Fig. 138. ***Title page*** *of the catalogue of the Louis Marc Solon collection of pottery and porcelain sold at auction by Messrs. Charles Butters and Sons, Hanley, 26-28 November 1912. (Private collection)*

Price—TWO SHILLINGS AND SIXPENCE
CATALOGUE
OF THE
EARLE COLLECTION
OF EARLY
STAFFORDSHIRE POTTERY

TO BE SOLD BY AUCTION
WITHOUT RESERVE
ON
TUESDAY, WEDNESDAY and THURSDAY
27th, 28th and 29th MAY, 1919
At Twelve o'clock noon each day
BY
Messrs. CHARLES BUTTERS & SONS
AT THEIR PREMISES
TRINITY BUILDINGS, HANLEY
STOKE-ON-TRENT

The Collection will be on view at Trinity Buildings, Hanley, on Saturday and Monday, May 24th and 26th, by Catalogue only, price 2/6, to admit one person from 10 a.m. to 5 p.m.

Fig. 139. ***Title page*** *of the catalogue of the Earle collection of Staffordshire pottery sold at auction by Messrs. Charles Butters and Sons, Hanley, 27-29 May 1919. (Collection of Tracy and Harwood Johnson, Wallingford, Pennsylvania)*

1904 until his sudden death in 1911 he was Curator of the Hanley Museum.[25] His own pottery collection, and other personal effects realised nearly £2,000 when it was sold in 1911.[26] The auction was the first sale in the Potteries to realise high prices for the local pottery. Charles Butters & Son, Hanley conducted the auction from 24-27 October and the catalogue included thirty-seven lots of salt-glazed stoneware including several models for making teapot and coffee pot spouts, stamped with Ralph Wood's mark.[27] Several of these are illustrated by Luxmoore[28] and fetched high prices. Five models marked with either 'Edward Till, 1767'[29] or Ralph Wood 'R.W., 1748' brought £51 (lot 435). A previous lot of five models marked by Ralph Wood only brought £26 (lot 434). One 8in. (20.32cm) enamel jug decorated with a coat of arms brought £31 (lot 420).[30] In covering the auction on the following day the *Staffordshire Sentinel* paid tribute to Mr. Jahn's 'genius as a collector' and stated that the sale revealed the 'Potteries as an artistic centre which is able to hold its own'.

The name of Louis Marc Solon (1835-1913) was well known by the beginning of the twentieth century. Solon had published *The Art of the Old English Potter* originally in 1883 followed by a second edition in 1885. In 1890 he wrote the catalogue for an exhibition of his salt-glaze which was held in the 'Technical Museum at Hanley', the forerunner of the current Potteries Museum. The catalogue contained 112 items (twenty-four were brown, grey or German, the rest were white). In December 1901 and February 1902 he wrote two articles in the *Connoisseur* on the 'Solon Collection of Pre-Wedgwood English Pottery by the Collector'. The famous sale of his collection by Butters & Sons, Hanley took place from 26-28 November 1912 (Fig. 138). By the end of the third day 683 lots had been sold for a total of £5,849. Notable salt-glazed objects which fetched remarkably high prices included a Portobello mug with a lid with a male head for a knop (£110), an enamelled tea canister inscribed *Fine Bohea Tea* (£41), a King of Prussia teapot (£36) and the highest price paid to that date for a pew group which went to a New Zealand collector for £205.

Major Cyril Thornwicke Earle of Hull in Yorkshire (1871-1934) was 'a retired antique dealer' when he died in 1934. Having collected ceramics since 1895 he gave over seven hundred pieces to the Hull City Museum in 1915, the same year he published his catalogue[31] which included some sixty salt-glazed pieces. The auction of Cyril Earle's collection of early English pottery took place in Hanley on 27-29 May 1919, also by Charles Butters & Sons auctioneers (Fig. 139). The sale included sixty-one lots of white salt-glazed stonewares and the catalogue included one colour plate of salt-glazed wares taken directly from the Earle Collection catalogue. Several colour plates of salt-glazed stoneware were included in an advertisement placed by the auctioneers in the *Connoisseur*.

Captain Charles F.C. Luxmoore of Ashbrook Towers, Church Minshull, Middlewich, Cheshire, lent some 180 pieces from his remarkable collection of mostly white salt-glaze for exhibition to the Hanley Museum in late 1913.[32] Although his pioneering monograph on salt-glaze[33] was not published until 1924, the preface is dated February 1914, almost coincident with the Hanley exhibition. Pieces from the Luxmoore Collection were sold at Sotheby's, London, on 15 October 1959.[34]

Mr. Thomas Boynton of Norman House, Bridlington, Yorkshire, collected a wide range of English earthenware and stonewares. His concentration on pottery produced in Yorkshire led to large gifts of those wares to the Yorkshire Philosophical Society in 1916 and 1920. A catalogue of that collection was produced by Arthur Hurst in 1922.[35] The non-Yorkshire wares were sold by Charles Butters & Sons, Hanley on 23-24 March 1920 (Fig. 140). The sale included 102 lots of salt-glazed stoneware and purchasers included collectors such as Frank Freeth and Micah Salt with many lots going to dealer Cyril Andrade and a few going to Stoner and Evans. Andrade purchased a purple-ground enamelled teapot (lot 336) for the vast sum of £120 and one of the large enamelled punch pots with crabstock handle and spout (lot 354; Colour Plate 46) for £100. A figure of Spinario from the Soden-Smith collection was purchased by Frank Freeth for £21. Frank Freeth described his own collection as it was in the 1890s in F. Freeth, *Old English pottery collected and catalogued by Mr. and Mrs. F. Freeth* (London: Morgan, Thompson and Jameson, 1896).

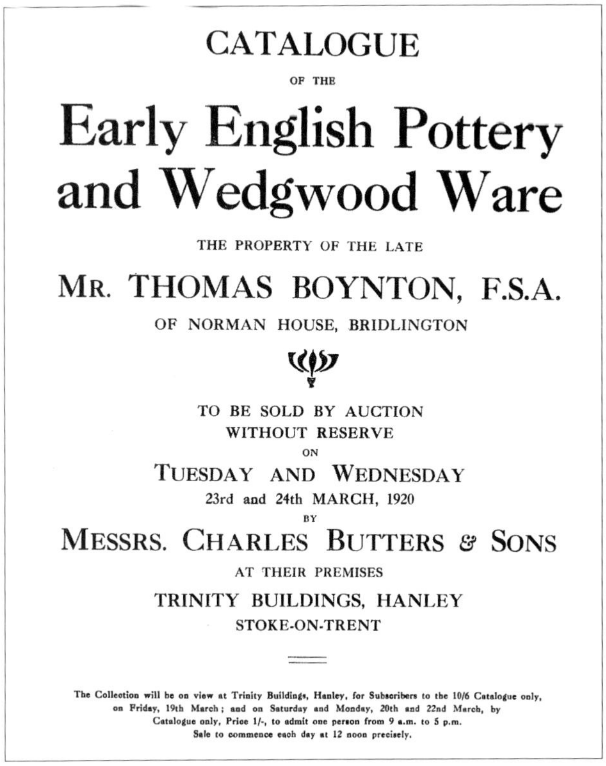
CATALOGUE
OF THE
Early English Pottery and Wedgwood Ware
THE PROPERTY OF THE LATE
MR. THOMAS BOYNTON, F.S.A.
OF NORMAN HOUSE, BRIDLINGTON
TO BE SOLD BY AUCTION
WITHOUT RESERVE
ON
TUESDAY AND WEDNESDAY
23rd and 24th MARCH, 1920
BY
MESSRS. CHARLES BUTTERS & SONS
AT THEIR PREMISES
TRINITY BUILDINGS, HANLEY
STOKE-ON-TRENT

The Collection will be on view at Trinity Buildings, Hanley, for Subscribers to the 10/6 Catalogue only, on Friday, 19th March; and on Saturday and Monday, 20th and 22nd March, by Catalogue only, Price 1/-, to admit one person from 9 a.m. to 5 p.m. Sale to commence each day at 12 noon precisely.

Fig. 140. ***Title page*** *of the catalogue of the Thomas Boynton collection of English pottery and Wedgwood Ware sold by Messrs. Charles Butters and Sons, Hanley, 23 and 24 March 1920. (Collection of Tracy and Harwood Johnson, Wallingford, Pennsylvania)*

Micah Salt, of a Buxton, Derbyshire business family, had been a keen archaeologist in the 1890s. After his death his collection was also sold by the same auctioneers at Hanley in October 1927. Wallace Elliot evidently attended the sale as the catalogue which is in the scrapbooks in the V & A had the prices in his handwriting in code. Salt-glazed items included a white cradle (lot 13), a King of Prussia teapot (lot 51), an enamel painted punch kettle (lot 53), another teapot enamel painted '*Bohea*' (lot 61), and an 8½in. (21.59cm) coffee pot (lot 68).

The Ashmolean Museum at Oxford has a little known collection of early English pottery particularly strong in white salt-glazed stoneware, the gifts of dealer Cyril Andrade and the widow of Sir Arthur Church.

Mr. F.V. de Costa Andrade, descended from a family of Portuguese Jews, was born in 1882. As mentioned, Andrade was a London antiques dealer operating from the Dalmeny Galleries, 8 Duke Street, St, James's, who specialised in European pottery and porcelain. He served for twenty years on the Westminster City Council and once made a public protest in a full suit of armour. He continued to make gifts of pottery and porcelain to the Ashmolean Museum throughout his lifetime.

Sir Arthur Herbert Church, K.C.V.O., F.R.S., who was born in 1834 and studied at Lincoln College, Oxford, was an eminent scientist. Professor of Chemistry at the Royal Agricultural College and then at the Royal Academy of Fine Arts, he discovered various minerals including churchite, a British cerium phosphate. Ceramics historians will remember Professor Church for the books he wrote on the subject. He died in 1915 and his widow, Dame Jemima, gave part of the collection to the Ashmolean, including the salt-glazed stoneware, which, according to the terms of her husband's will, would come to the museum after her death, which was in 1929.

One of the most well-known collections of early English pottery amassed by Charles J. Lomax sold at Sotheby's London on 7 April 1937, but of the 179 lots only nine were white salt-glazed stoneware.

Several other collections which included salt-glaze were given to British museums. One of the most important was the Glaisher collection, given to the Fitzwilliam Museum after the death of James Whitbread Lee Glaisher (1848-1928) on 12 January 1929. Glaisher was a Sc.D. Fellow of Trinity College with an astute eye for early English ceramics. His collection numbered more than three thousand objects, mostly pottery, acquired over a thirty year period. The salt-glazed stoneware did not feature as prominently among his collecting as delftware and lead-glazed earthenware, but a number of Fulham pieces were amongst his bequest. A catalogue of the collection was prepared by Bernard Rackham and published in 1935, a reprint of which came out in 1987.[36]

The Manchester Whitworth Institute mounted a loan exhibition of pottery 'representing the renaissance of pottery and its subsequent development in England from about 1670 to 1800' in 1912. The donors and organisers listed in the foreword to the catalogue[37] were: Mr. C.J. Lomax, Dr. E.J. Sidebotham, Mr. Frank Falkner, Mr.

Edward Sheldon, Dr. A.T. Blease, Mr. F. Dykes, and Mr. George Stoner, many of the names who lent to the Burlington Fine Arts Exhibition in 1914.

Thomas Greg (1858-1920) was another lender to the Burlington Fine Arts Exhibition and, although he lived in London, his Cheshire roots made Manchester a logical choice for the disposal of his famous collection of English pottery. Collected between 1880 and 1920 his gift of nearly one thousand pieces was the first gift of decorative arts to be given to the City of Manchester, and remains one of the most significant.[38]

One other collector who has largely faded into obscurity was J. Henry Griffith of Birmingham. Herbert Read wrote a three part article on his salt-glazed collection for the *Connoisseur* published in three consecutive months from December 1924 to February 1925. Griffith had a comprehensive collection of salt-glazed stoneware particularly strong in decorated wares and figures. One rectangular scratch-blue tea canister, illustrated in the first article (No. III), is now identified as *Bovey Tracey*. Herbert Read used Griffith's collection to develop a history of the salt-glaze industry and did a commendable job of collating the current knowledge on the subject, including the influence of the seventeenth century book[39] *The Embassy to the Grand Tartar Cham* on moulded relief panels on English salt-glaze, expounded more thoroughly by Leslie Grigsby in an article in *Antiques* magazine in 1993.[40]

Littler-Wedgwood blue-glazed items, some of which were painted in opaque white enamels, were well represented in Griffith's collection. An unusual teapot with relief swag decoration painted in enamels on a mazarine blue ground is illustrated in the first article, No. IV.

The Griffith collection was rich in salt-glazed figures of people and animals, the former mainly solid white, whilst animals often had agate bodies. Griffith had an example of a Louhan seated on a lily pad with his right hand held upward, probably the one advertised for sale by Stoner & Evans in the November 1922 *Connoisseur*. He also had a figure of Spinario, a squirrel teapot, several King of Prussia teapots and two pieces commemorating the Jacobite cause.

Regrettably Read's articles contained no biographical material on J. Henry Griffith himself so one knows very little about him outside the pieces illustrated in the *Connoisseur* articles. His collection was offered for sale by Stoner & Evans in late 1925.

Latter-day collectors included Frank P. and Harriet Call Burnap who, in 1941, gave nearly one hundred pieces of salt-glaze to the Nelson-Atkins Museum in Kansas City along with a large and important collection of early English pottery. The earliest piece of dated white salt-glazed stoneware (Fig. 10, formerly in Lord Revelstoke's collection) is now in the Burnap collection in Kansas City.[41]

The collecting of salt-glazed stoneware and early English pottery in general continues with zeal. Fine salt-glaze commands prices commensurate with English porcelains of the same period. It seems probable that connoisseurs who have collected such rare and lovely white stonewares for a century and a half will continue to favour them for ever.

CHAPTER IX

Thirteen Potters and the Pots they made

The makers of white salt-glazed stoneware did not mark their products with their names, as did later potters. We have identified some 125 manufacturers, twenty-two of them associated with surviving pots and/or excavated shards. Thirteen of these are detailed in this chapter, with illustrations:

Thomas Barker, Foley, Stoke-on-Trent	c.1770s-1786
William Bourne or Burn, Burslem	c.1750
Bovey Tracey Potteries, Devon	c.1766-pre-1775
Chester White Ware Manufactory, Cheshire	c.1757-pre-1777
John Fenton and Thomas Hill, Shelton, Stoke-on-Trent	1720-1722
William Greatbatch, Fenton, Stoke-on-Trent	1762-1782
London: John Dwight and family, Fulham, London	c.1673-1737
Humphrey Palmer, Hanley, Stoke-on-Trent	c.1750-pre-1778
Rotherham: John Platt and Samuel Walker, Rotherham, Yorkshire	1766-1770
Swansea: William Coles, Swansea, Wales	1767-1778
Aaron, Thomas and John Wedgwood, Burslem	fl.1732-1776
Thomas Whieldon, Fenton Vivian	fl.1750
Thomas Whieldon and Josiah Wedgwood Fenton Vivian	1757
York: Francis Place	fl. 1683-1693

A disproportionate six of the thirteen are 'non-Staffordshire', reflecting the relative ease of excavation and identification on single sites when compared with the multiplicity of sites in North Staffordshire.

Details of the other 112 makers are in Appendices 1 or 2. Wherever the names of the 125 salt-glaze potters are referred to in this book, they are given in italics.

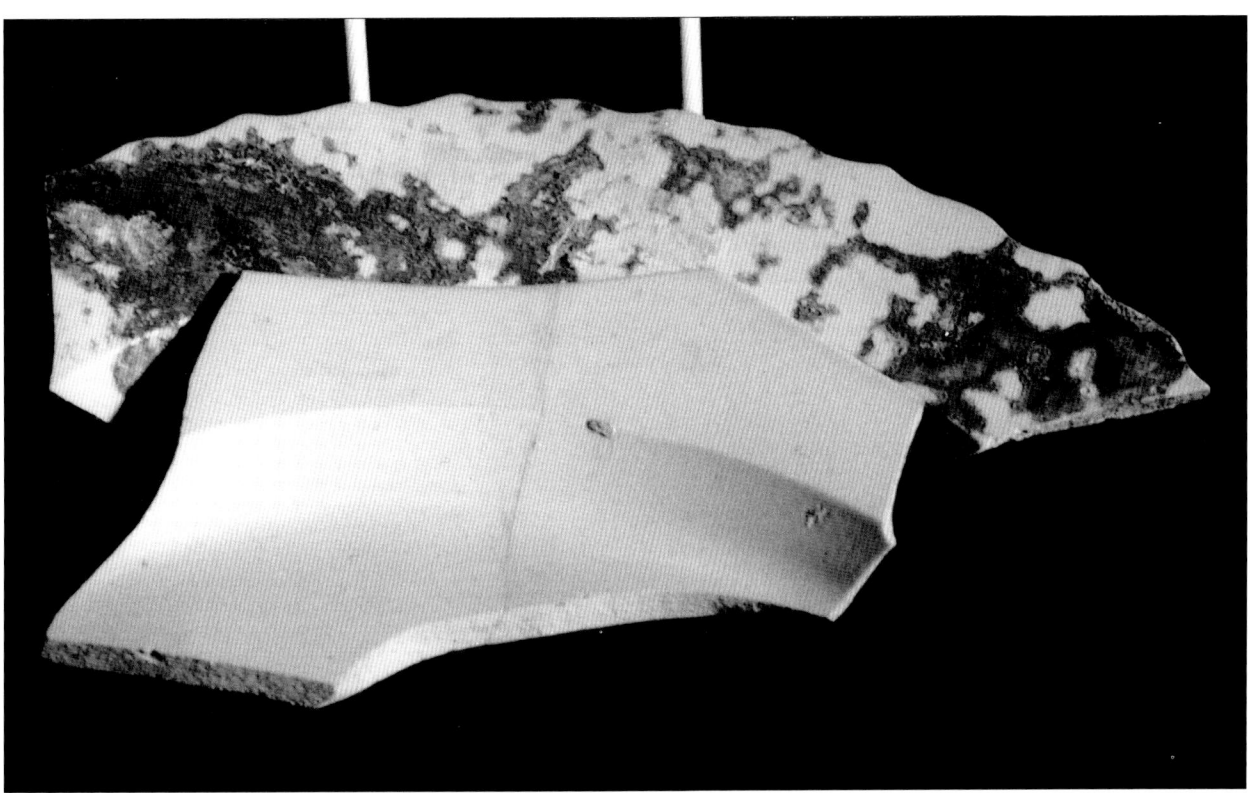

*Fig. 141. **Two plate rim fragments,** white salt-glazed stoneware, one angular rimmed, the other a waster with a scalloped rim. Excavated at the Foley site, Fenton, Staffordshire. c.1760-1780. 6⅜in. (16.19cm) maximum. (Potteries Museum and Art Gallery, Stoke-on-Trent, T3 L2)*

THOMAS BARKER
Foley, Stoke-on-Trent, c.1770s-1786

An archaeological excavation of a pottery waste dump at Foley, Fenton, in 1973-74 revealed kiln waste in the forms of red stoneware, cream-coloured ware and large quantities of white salt-glazed stoneware.[1] The 1984 report gave details of the occupants of the site, but pointed out that layers 5 to 9, containing *inter alia* white salt-glazed stoneware shards, predated the factory on the site, erected c.1780.[2]

David Barker, who wrote the 1984 report, has since published convincing evidence that Thomas Barker was the most likely manufacturer of this early ware, including the white salt-glazed shards found, inferring that Thomas Barker dumped the shards in a clay pit on vacant land opposite his own works.[3] Unless otherwise referenced, the information given here is taken from David Barker's work.

Thomas Barker was baptised 14 April 1716 at Stoke-on-Trent, and married Elizabeth Hammersley there on 6

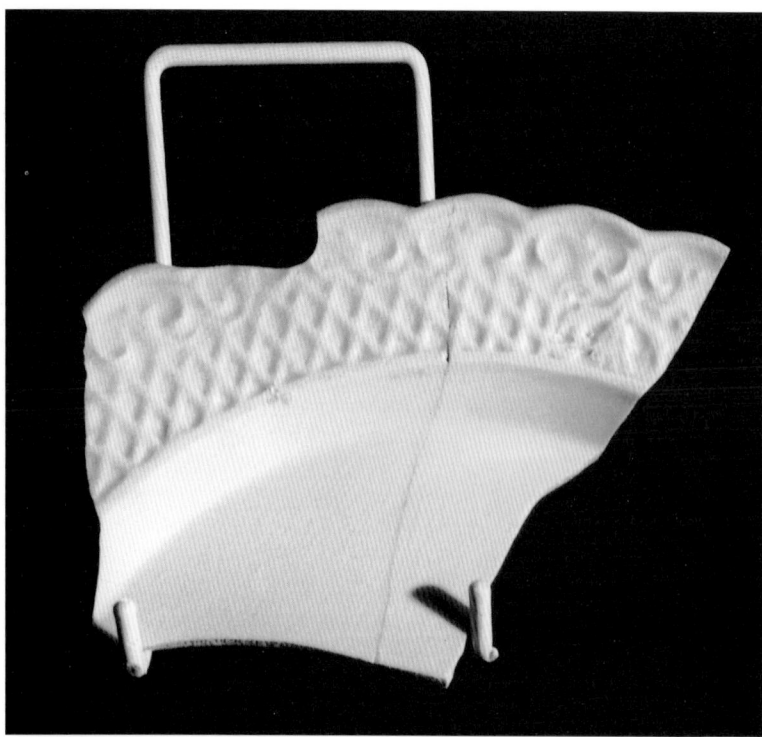

*Fig. 142. **Partially reconstructed plate rim waster**, white salt-glazed stoneware with trellis anthemion border. This unusual border was excavated at the Foley site, Fenton. c.1760-80. 5¼in. (13.34cm) long. (Potteries Museum and Art Gallery, Stoke-on-Trent)*

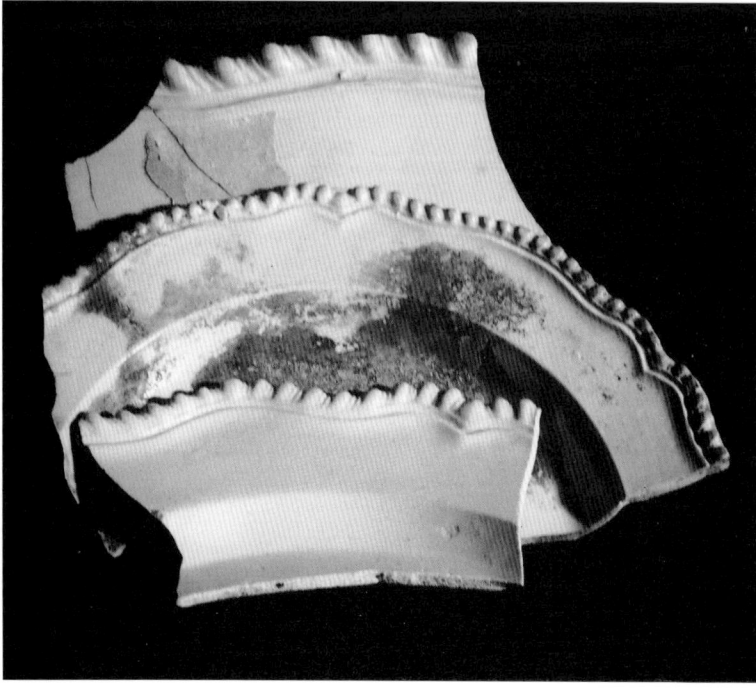

*Fig. 143. **Three plate rim fragments**, white salt-glazed stoneware with three gadroon-moulded rims. Excavated at the Foley site, Fenton, Staffordshire. c.1760-1780. 6¾in. (17.15cm) maximum. (Potteries Museum and Art Gallery, Stoke-on-Trent, T3 L2)*

September 1748. Their son Samuel was baptised at Stoke 11 March 1762.[4] Before his enterprise at Foley, Thomas Barker had been in partnership with *Robert Garner*, at Rowhouses, Fenton. Thomas Barker was buried at Stoke 28 July 1786,[5] and his will was proved at Lichfield 17 January 1787.[6] His works were likely to have been No. 115 on the 1802 map,[7] then occupied by his son, Samuel Baker (*sic*, Barker), opposite the Foley excavation site, occupied by China Millers, 409 King Street, in 2003.

White salt-glazed shards excavated on the site included plain plates without moulded borders scalloped at the rim (Fig. 141) and others moulded with unusual hatched scroll basket borders (Fig. 142), plates with bold and fine-gadrooned and beaded rims (Fig. 143) and barleycorn or seed patterns. An unusual plate with a basketweave border and a beaded edge was excavated which may be a clue to identification of some of the Foley wares (Fig.144). A barleycorn moulded sauceboat (Fig. 145) and leaf-moulded

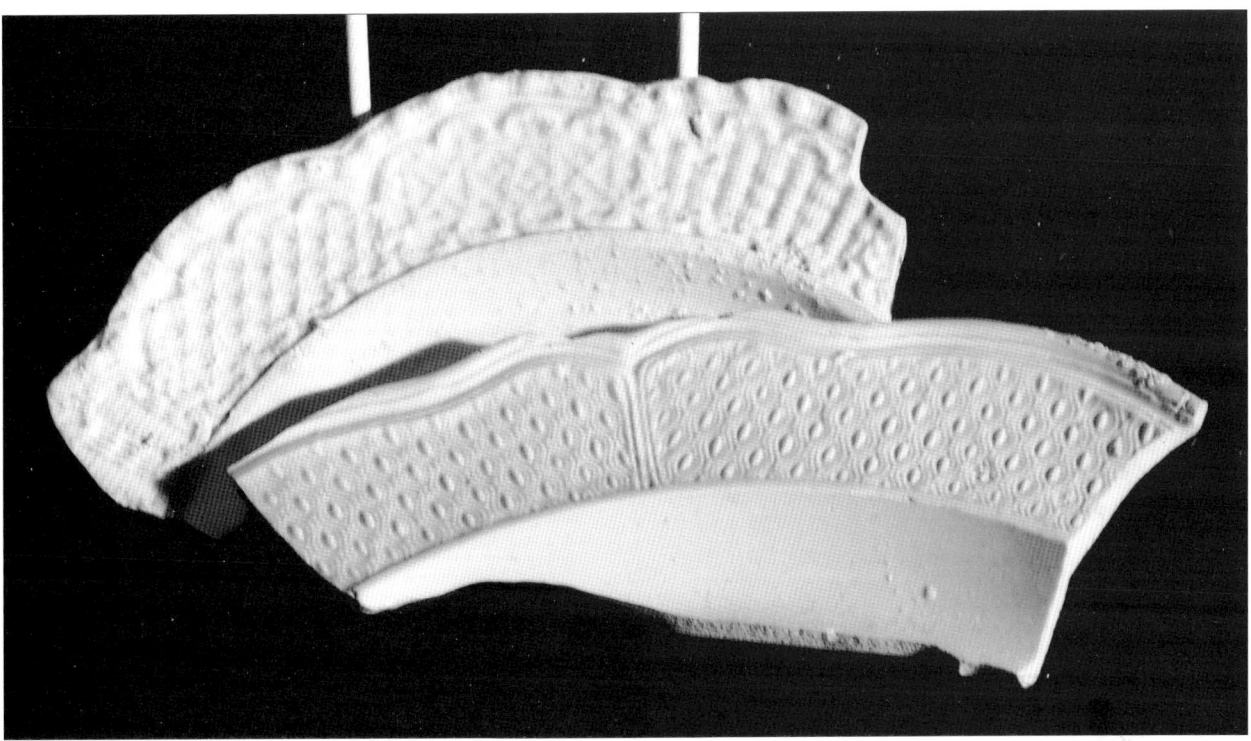

*Fig. 144. **Two plate rim fragments,** white salt-glazed stoneware moulded in the barleycorn or seed pattern and unusual basketweave border with a beaded edge. Excavated at the Foley site, Fenton, Staffordshire. c.1760-1780. 5½in. (13.97cm) maximum. (Potteries Museum and Art Gallery, Stoke-on-Trent, T3 L2)*

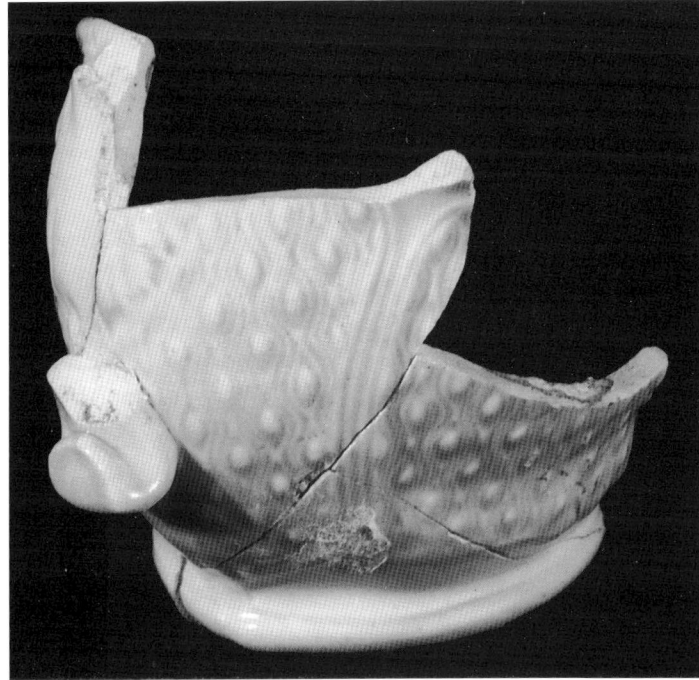

*Fig. 145. **Partially reconstructed sauceboat,** white salt-glazed stoneware moulded with the barleycorn or seed pattern with a folded handle terminal. Excavated at the Foley site, Fenton, Staffordshire. c.1760-1780. 3in. (7.62cm) high. (Potteries Museum and Art Gallery, Stoke-on-Trent, T3 L2)*

Chapter IX – Thirteen Potters and the Pots they made

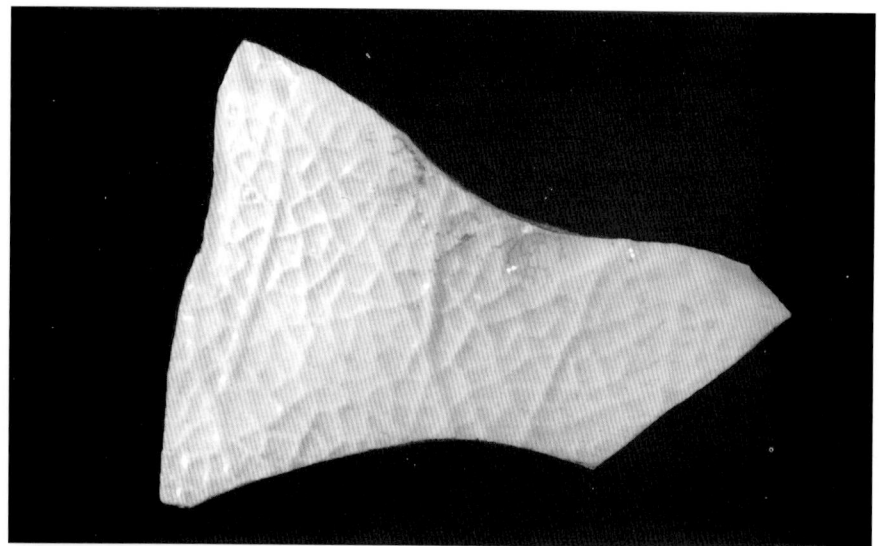

*Fig. 146. **Sauceboat waster** in white salt-glazed stoneware moulded in the form of a leaf. Excavated at the Foley site, Fenton, Staffordshire. c.1765-70. 2⅜in. (6.03cm) maximum. (Potteries Museum and Art Gallery, Stoke-on-Trent)*

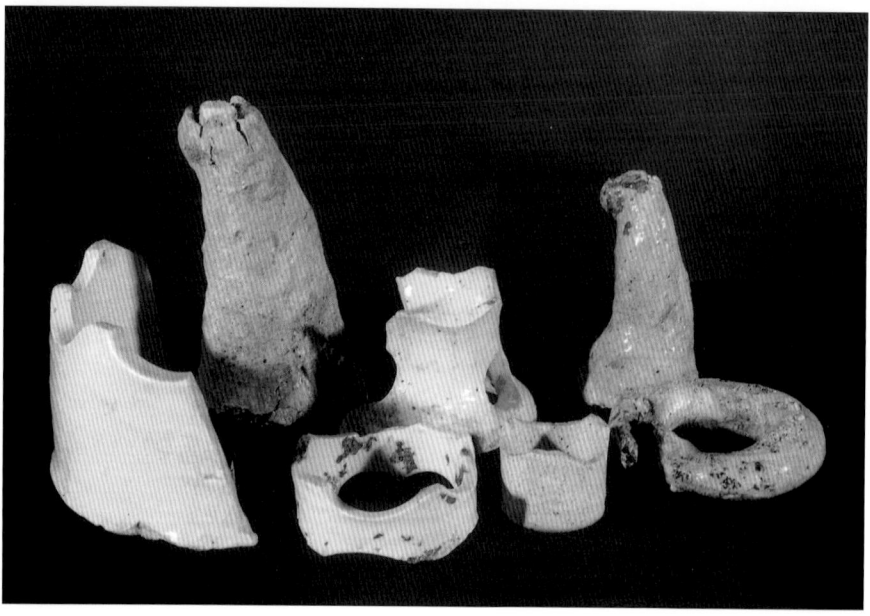

*Fig. 147. **Kiln furniture from the Foley Fenton site** including one part crown, two smaller whole crowns, two cones, a part pedestal and a ring. Staffordshire, Foley Fenton, c.1760-86. (Potteries Museum and Art Gallery, Stoke-on-Trent, T3, FKS 73)*

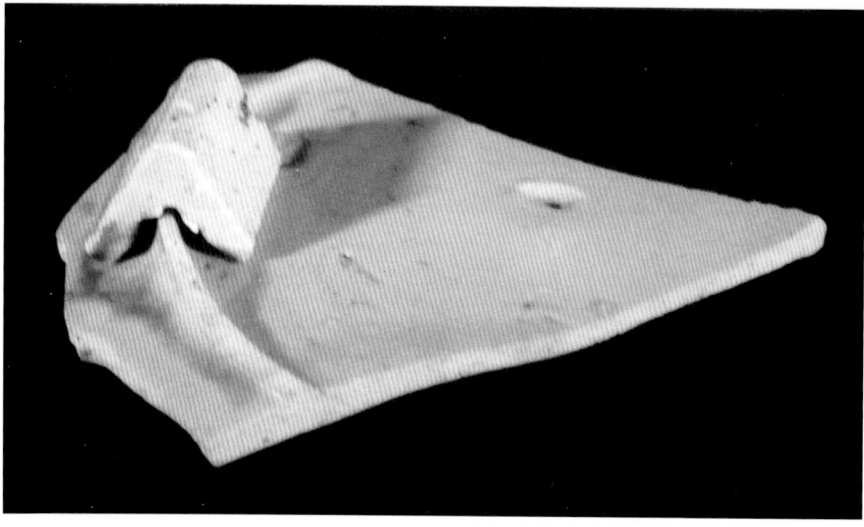

*Fig. 148. **Saucer rim (waster) with a saddle** in white salt-glazed stoneware, the upper surface is combed scratch-blue decorated. Excavated at the Foley site, Fenton, Staffordshire. c.1760-70. 2⅝in. (6.67cm) long maximum. (Potteries Museum and Art Gallery, Stoke-on-Trent, T3 L2)*

hollow-ware shards (Fig. 146) were also found. Hollow wares included pieces with reeded strap handles with fine beading at the terminal (Colour Plate 160) as well as a variety of scratch-blue teawares (Colour Plate 161). Saggars and kiln furniture included a v-shaped saddle attached to a footrim of a waster (Figs. 147, 148).[8]

Colour Plate 159. **Sauceboat,** *white salt-glazed stoneware moulded in the form of overlapping leaves seen more frequently on porcelain from Longton Hall and Chelsea than on salt-glazed stoneware. Staffordshire, possibly one of the potters operating at the Foley Fenton, c.1765. 2⅝in. (6.67cm) high. (Private collection)*

Colour Plate 160. **Three handle fragments** *in white salt-glazed stoneware with saw-tooth and ratcheted terminals. Excavated at the Foley site, Fenton, Staffordshire. c.1760. 3½in. (8.89cm) maximum. (Potteries Museum and Art Gallery, Stoke-on-Trent, T3 L2)*

Colour Plate 161. **Group of teaware fragments** *in white salt-glazed stoneware with scratch-blue decoration. maximum. Excavated at the Foley site, Fenton, Staffordshire. c.1760-70. 3in. (7.62cm). (Potteries Museum and Art Gallery, Stoke-on-Trent, T3 L2)*

WILLIAM BOURNE or BURN
12 Westport Road, Burslem, c.1750

An excavation at this site in 1974 produced evidence of a possible salt-glaze oven base: part of a floor of bricks laid in a curve, some of the bricks having glaze on their upper surface.[9] There is a possibility of further excavation on this site.

The shards located included plain white salt-glazed flat-rimmed plates (Fig. 149) and hollow wares moulded with mosaic or basketweave, gadrooned and floral borders (Figs. 150, 151). A partially reconstructed tureen with bold lion's mask and paw feet characterised by two holes on either side of the mouth was the most unusual artefact (Fig. 152). There were two waster shards with iron dipped rims and handles (Fig. 153) and portions of a teapot or patch stand (Fig. 154),

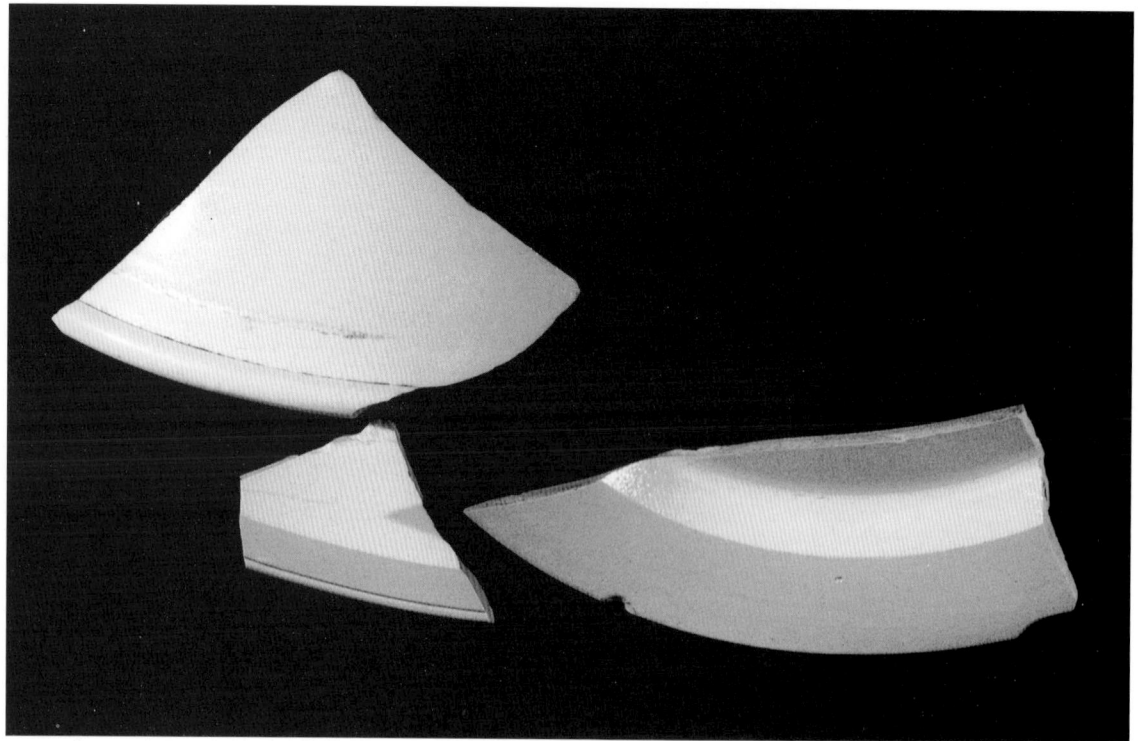

Fig. 149. **Dish rim and two plate rims** *of plain white salt-glazed stoneware excavated from the Westport Road site, Burslem. This kiln site included waster fragments from the factory of William Bourne (or Burn). Staffordshire, William Bourne (Burn), Burslem, c.1760. Dish rim, 5¼in. (13.34cm); plates, 6in. (15.24cm) and 3in. (7.62cm) respectively. (Potteries Museum and Art Gallery, Stoke-on-Trent, K2 259 1985, K2 288 1985, K2 260 1985)*

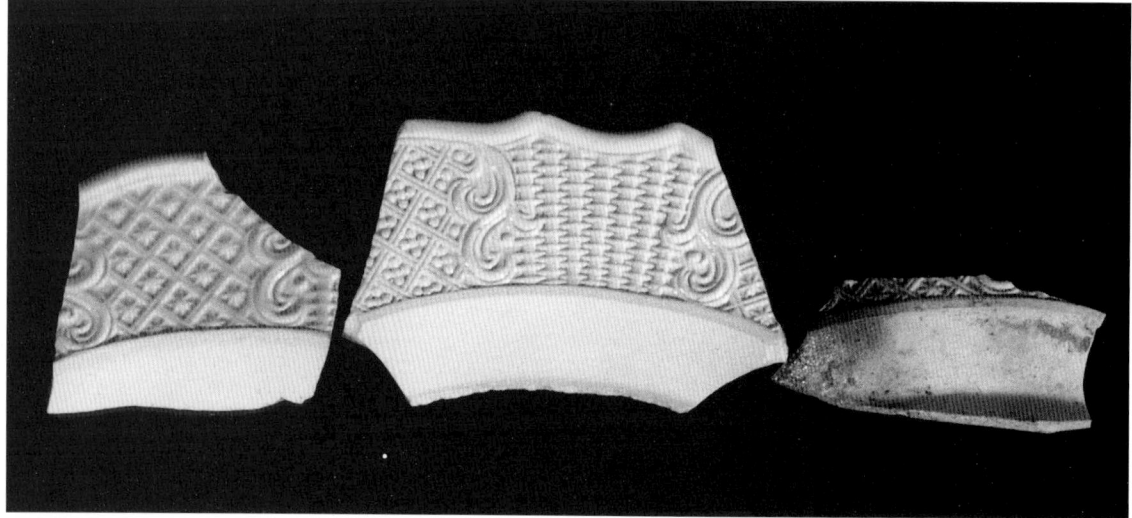

Fig. 150. **Three plate rims** *of white salt-glazed stoneware with mosaic or basketweave moulded borders excavated at the William Bourne site, Burslem. Staffordshire, William Bourne (Burn), Burslem, c.1755-65. Maximum length 3in. (7.62cm). (Potteries Museum and Art Gallery, Stoke-on-Trent, K2 264 1985 (both), K2 645 1985)*

CHAPTER IX – THIRTEEN POTTERS AND THE POTS THEY MADE

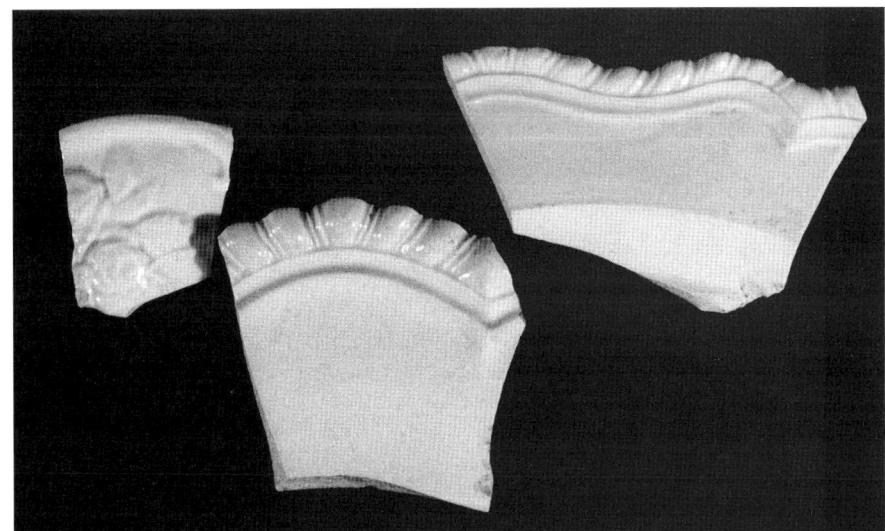

*Fig. 151. **Three rims** of white salt-glazed stoneware, one with floral moulded relief, two with gadrooned edges excavated at the William Bourne site, Burslem. Staffordshire, William Bourne (Burn), Burslem, c.1755-65. 3in. (7.62cm) maximum. (Potteries Museum and Art Gallery, Stoke-on-Trent both gadrooned edges, K2 266 1985, K2 264 1985)*

*Fig. 152. **Partially reconstructed tureen and a second foot of another tureen** in white salt-glazed stoneware, the tureen on the left moulded with the mosaic or basketweave pattern with a bold gargoyle foot, the one on the right moulded with the seed or barleycorn pattern, the same foot with a menacing grin. Excavated at the Westport Road site of William Bourne, Burslem. Staffordshire, William Bourne (Burn), Burslem, c.1755-65. 5in. (12.7cm) high, 2¾in. (6.99cm) high. (Potteries Museum and Art Gallery, Stoke-on-Trent, K2 174 1985, K2 500 1985)*

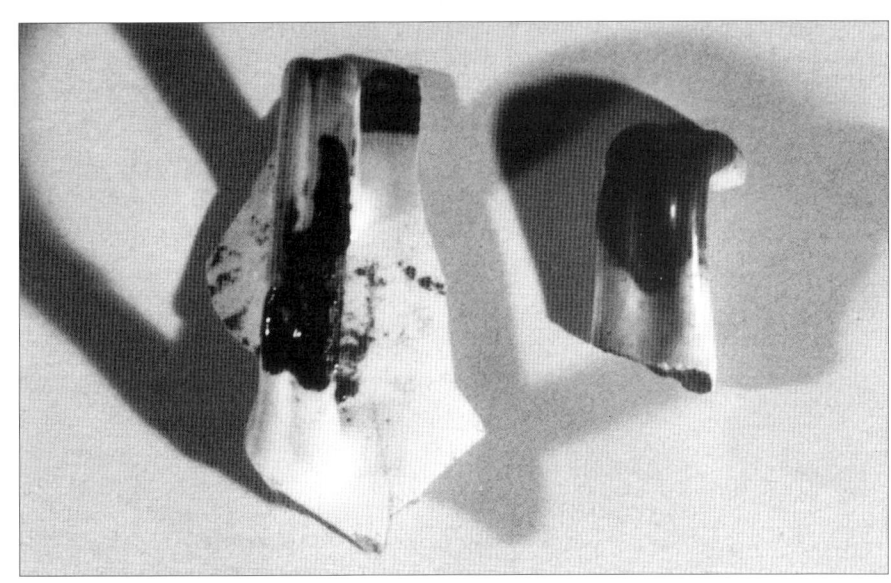

*Fig. 153. **Two waster handle shards** in white-dipped salt-glazed stoneware with iron-dipped rims and portions of the handle, excavated at the William Bourne site, Burslem. Staffordshire, William Bourne (Burn), Burslem, c.1750. Maximum 2¼in. (5.72cm). (Potteries Museum and Art Gallery, Stoke-on-Trent, L2 494 TA, L2 K2 268 1985)*

CHAPTER IX – THIRTEEN POTTERS AND THE POTS THEY MADE

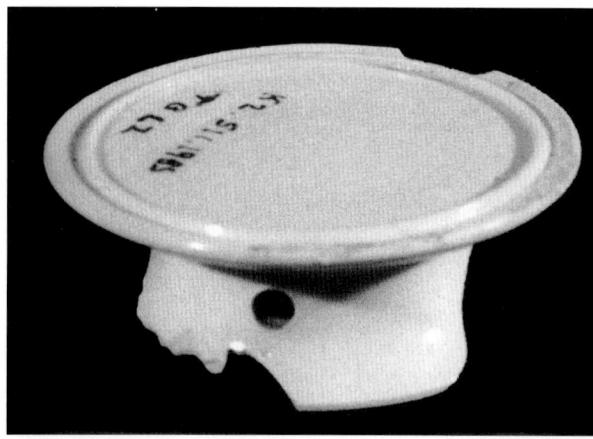

*Fig. 154. **Portion of a teapot or patch stand** in white salt-glazed stoneware with turned rim and a foot with one hole in each side, excavated at the Westport Road site of William Bourne, Burslem. Staffordshire, William Bourne (Burn), Burslem, c.1750-60. 2¼in. (5.72cm) diameter. (Potteries Museum and Art Gallery, Stoke-on-Trent, K2 511 1985)*

*Fig. 155. **Portion of a coffee cup and two cup base fragments** in white salt-glazed stoneware. One foot is a waster fragment (far right). Staffordshire, William Bourne (Burn), Burslem, c.1750-60. Cup 2⅝in. (6.67cm) high. (Potteries Museum and Art Gallery, Stoke-on-Trent, K2 499 1985, two left; K2 256 1985, waster foot)*

*Fig. 156. **Kiln furniture** excavated at the Westport Road site, Burslem, occupied by William Bourne. Some bricks in the kiln base indicated use of salt for glazing wares. The various rings, cones and saggar parts are all covered with volatilised salt. Staffordshire, William Bourne (Burn), Burslem, c.1755-65. 2⅝in. (6.67cm) maximum. (Potteries Museum and Art Gallery, Stoke-on-Trent)*

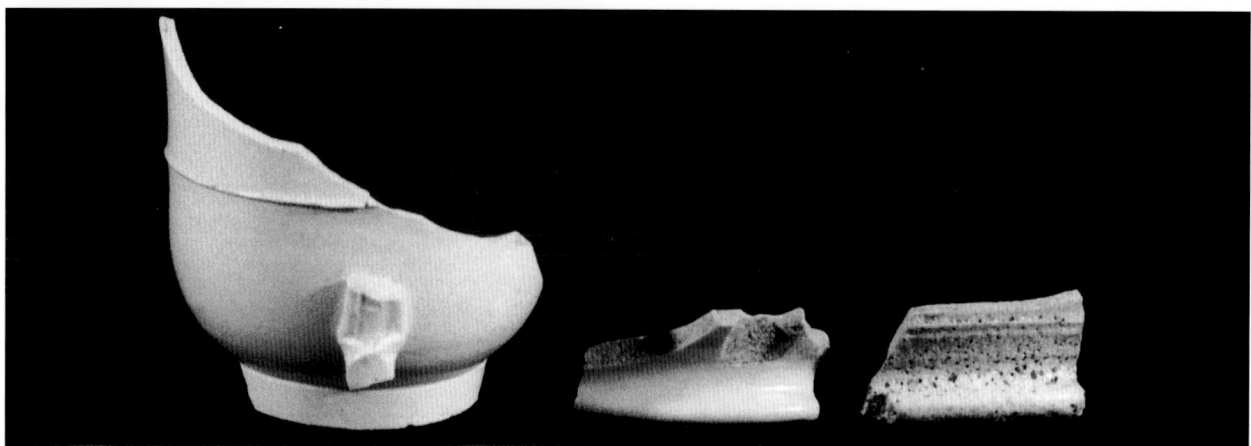

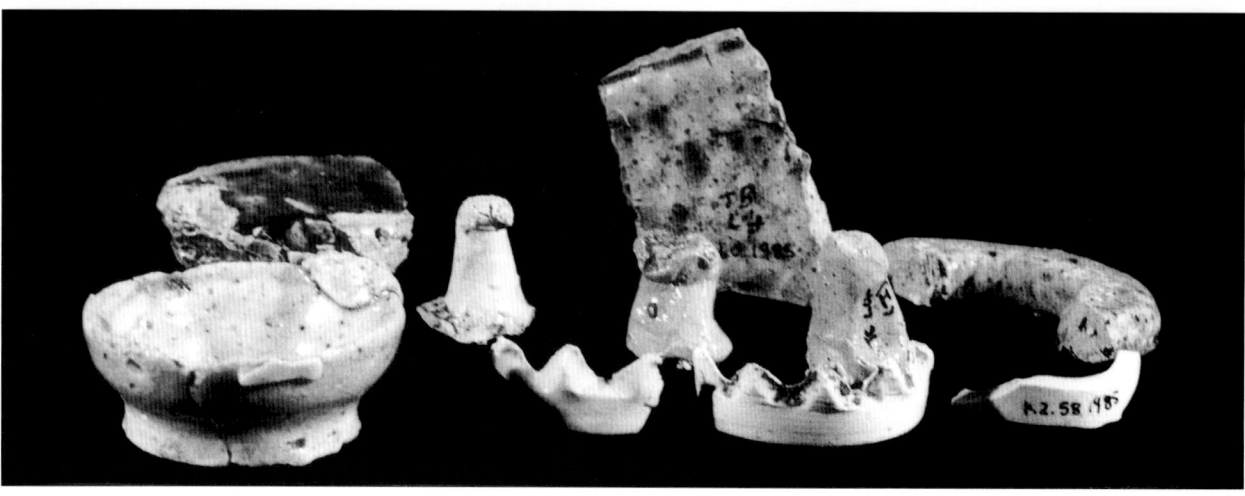

a coffee cup and two cup base fragments, one base a waster (Fig. 155), all white salt-glazed stoneware. A variety of both scratch-blue and the so-called debased scratch-blue wares for tavern mugs and chamber pots (Colour Plates 162-163) were found. Amongst the artefacts were items of kiln furniture and partial saggars, all bearing heavy coatings of volatilised salt (Fig. 156).

The 1740 and 1769 maps of Burslem offer two possible occupants for this site: No. 109, John Heath and No. 110, William Burn. Information on these maps (i.e., 'Burn's Bank rather than Bourne's Bank) suggest that that Burn's surname was most probably Bourne. 'John Heath' is too common a name in Burslem to be identified.

A William Bourne was baptised at Stoke-on-Trent on 12 October 1707, son of William and Margaret Bourne of Shelton and a William Bourne married Alice Leigh at Stoke on 2 July 1730.[10] Children of William and Alice Burn/Borne/Bourn/Bourne were baptised at *Burslem* between 1731 and 1741.[11] This information *may* relate to the possible William Bourne/Burn of the 12 Westport Road site.

Chapter IX – Thirteen Potters and the Pots they made

*Colour Plate 162. **Teaware fragments** in white salt-glazed stoneware with scratch-blue decoration excavated at the William Bourne site, Burslem. Staffordshire, William Bourne (Burn), Burslem, c.1750-65. 4⅛in. (10.48cm) maximum. (Potteries Museum and Art Gallery, Stoke-on-Trent, K2 17 1985 (saucer flowered and rouletted)*

*Colour Plate 163. **Chamber pot and mug fragments** in white salt-glazed stoneware with so-called debased scratch-blue decoration seen on utilitarian and tavern wares. Excavated at William Bourne's factory in Burslem. Staffordshire, William Bourne (Burn), Burslem, c.1755-70. Chamber rims, 3¾in. (9.53cm) maximum. (Potteries Museum and Art Gallery, Stoke-on-Trent, K2 515 1985 (both rims), K2 567 1985, K2 514 1985)*

*Colour Plate 164. **Rim fragment** of white salt-glazed stoneware moulded with small gadrooned border and decorated with grog or potter's waste (clay chips) on the rim. Staffordshire, William Bourne (Burn), Burslem, c.1755-65. 2in. (5.08cm) maximum. (Potteries Museum and Art Gallery, Stoke-on-Trent, K2 642 1985)*

Chapter IX – Thirteen Potters and the Pots They Made

BOVEY TRACEY POTTERIES
Bovey Tracey, Devon, c.1766-pre-1775

The history of the potteries at Bovey Tracey is told in papers by Norman Stretton and a monograph by Brian Adams and Anthony Thomas.[12] Only information relating to the production of white salt-glazed stoneware is given here.

The founding of a pottery at Bovey Tracey was recorded by Richard Pococke in 1750,[13] perhaps in Fore Street or Pond Garden. A rectangular kiln survived in Fore Street in Bovey Tracey town until the 1930s and was then removed to an industrial site at Heathfield,[14] where it remained in 1996. This may have been a 'London-type' salt-glazed kiln, normally used to produce brown salt-glazed stoneware. A salt-glaze saggar, and brown and white salt-glazed pots including wasters are tentatively assigned to the Fore Street site.[15]

Edmund Carthew and Company had a pottery at Bovey Heathfield in 1757[16] and William Ellis is said to have started the Indeo Pottery about 1766.[17] An excavation at Bovey Heathfield in 1992 revealed salt-glaze kiln furniture and shards, dated to 1750-70.[18] Josiah Wedgwood commented in 1775 that white salt-glazed stoneware had formerly been made at Bovey Tracey and that clay, flint and coal were available locally.[19]

Staffordshire workers were brought to Bovey Tracey in the 1750s, including one or more persons named Hammersley. Thomas Hammersley was in Bovey Tracey in 1767[20] and a John Hammersley, baptised 1763 at Horton, Staffordshire and apprenticed to *John and Richard Mare* of Hanley, salt-glaze potters, was a working potter at Bovey Tracey in 1805. Samuel Lee gave evidence at Bovey Tracey in 1789 that he was born in Burslem (baptised in 1762), apprenticed to *Isaac Warburton* and also to Taylor Stephenson (*sic*, see *Samuel Kirk and Co.*), both North Staffordshire salt-glaze potters, before coming to Bovey Tracey as a journeyman potter.[21]

White salt-glazed stoneware shards have been found at Fore Street, Indeo, Bovey Heathfield and Pond Garden sites, in the Bovey Tracey area.[22] On that evidence, teapots and other handled containers (Colour Plate 165, Fig. 157), figures (Fig. 158) and plates were made with the usual moulded borders (Colour Plate 166) as well as plain bordered plates with shaped rims (Fig. 159). Scratch-blue, typically made in teawares, was also found in abundance (Colour Plates 167, 168). One scratch-blue shard was dated *1770* (Colour Plate 170) and another (Fig. 24) had a date of *1769*.

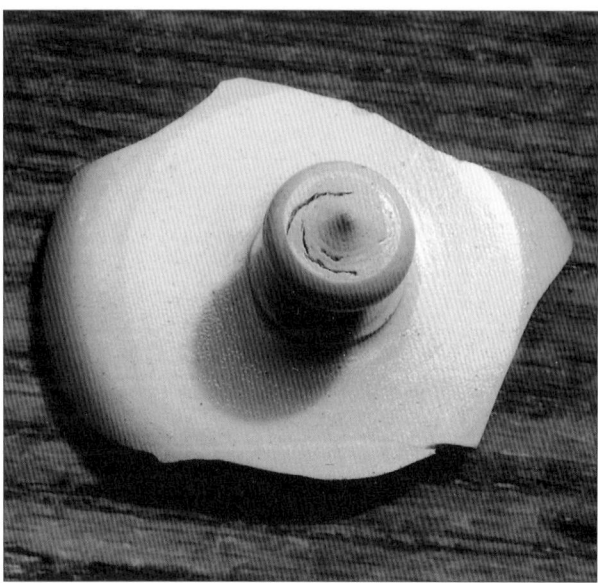

Fig. 157. **Teapot lid fragment,** *white salt-glazed stoneware excavated at the Indeo Pottery, Bovey Tracey, Devon. c.1750-60. 2⅛ x 2¾in. (5.4 x 6.99cm). (Photograph permission courtesy of Brian Adams)*

Fig. 158. **Portion of a female figure,** *white salt-glazed stoneware excavated at the Indeo Pottery, Bovey Tracey, Devon, c.1750-60. ¾ x ¾in. (1.91cm), alongside a modern reconstruction of a female holding a child. (Photograph permission courtesy of Brian Adams)*

Fig. 159. **Plate rim fragment** *of white salt-glazed stoneware moulded with dropped egg border excavated at Bovey Tracey, Devon. c.1755-65. (Photograph permission courtesy of Brian Adams)*

CHAPTER IX – THIRTEEN POTTERS AND THE POTS THEY MADE

Colour Plate 165. **Teabowl fragment,** *white engobe-slipped stoneware excavated at Bovey Tracey, Devon c.1750-60. (Photograph permission courtesy of Brian Adams)*

Colour Plate 166. **Rim fragment** *(possibly of a tureen) of white salt-glazed stoneware with gadrooned moulded relief excavated at Bovey Tracey, Devon. c.1755-65. 2¼ x 1 ¼in. (5.72 x 3.18cm). (Photograph permission courtesy of Brian Adams)*

Colour Plate 167. **Tea canister,** *white salt-glazed stoneware with heavy scratch-blue decoration inscribed* Mrs Medland October ye 8th 1770. *Bovey Tracey, Devon, c.1770. 5¼in. (13.34cm) high. (David Thorn collection)*

Colour Plate 168. **Group of scratch-blue and scratch-grey fragments** *in white salt-glazed stoneware, excavated from Bovey Tracey, Devon, c.1750-70. (Photograph permission courtesy of Brian Adams)*

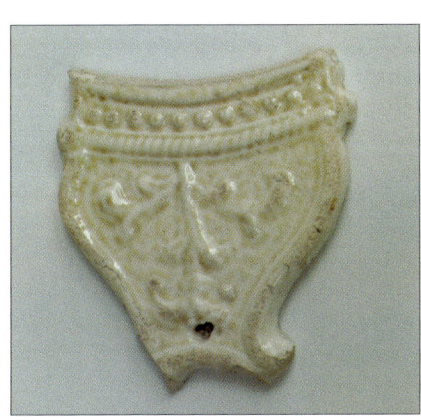

Colour Plate 169. **Porringer handle** *of moulded white salt-glazed stoneware excavated at Bovey Tracey, Devon. c.1750. 1¾in. (4.45cm) high. (Photograph permission courtesy of Brian Adams)*

Colour Plate 170. **scratch-blue fragment** *in salt-glazed stoneware dated 1770 excavated from Bovey Tracey, Devon. 1⅝ x 2⅜in. (4.13 x 6.03). (Photograph permission Courtesy of Brian Adams)*

193

*Fig. 160. **Saggar and kiln furniture** for firing white salt-glazed stoneware, Indio Pottery, Bovey Tracey, Devon. c.1750-70. Saggar 6in. (15.24cm) high. (Photograph permission courtesy of Brian Adams)*

*Fig. 161. **Group of handles** in white salt-glazed stoneware, some moulded in crabstock fashion, others pinched or of strap form with iron-dipped tip. All excavated at Bovey Tracey, Devon. c.1750-1770. 1¾in. (4.45cm) high. (Photograph permission courtesy of Brian Adams)*

CHAPTER IX – THIRTEEN POTTERS AND THE POTS THEY MADE

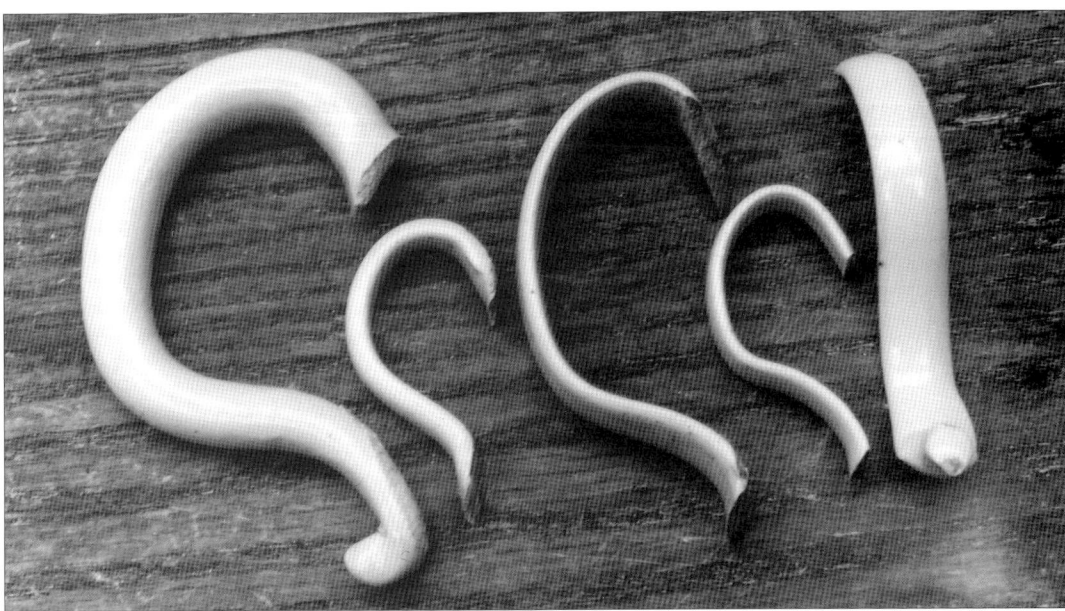

*Fig. 162. **Group of handles** in white salt-glazed stoneware mostly rolled or strap variety, excavated at Bovey Tracey, Devon. c.1750-70. 3⅛in. (7.94cm) high. (Photograph permission courtesy of Brian Adams)*

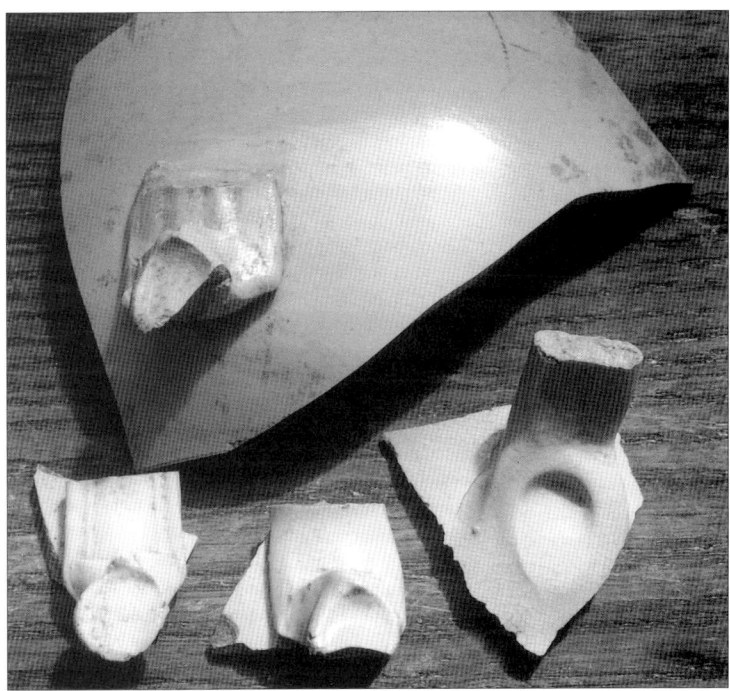

*Fig. 163. **Group of handle terminals** in white salt-glazed stoneware with thumb imprinted or pinched terminals excavated at Bovey Tracey, Devon. c.1750-60. (Photograph permission courtesy of Brian Adam)*

Sample salt-glazed shards, including wasters, of both white and white-dipped bodies (Colour Plate 165), in various common salt-glaze shapes, were (in 2003) on view at Bovey Tracey Pottery Museum. Salt-glazed kiln furniture and a fragment of a salt-glazed profile used for shaping plates have also been found (Fig. 160).[23] Excavated teapot handles run the chronological gamut from iron-dipped and crabstock (Fig. 161) to ear-shaped and pinched (Fig. 162). Strap handles were also produced and are frequently found with a thumb-imprinted terminal (Fig. 163). Porringers were also produced (Colour Plate 169).

A white salt-glazed stoneware loving cup, decorated in 'scratch-blue' and inscribed 'Joan Ellis/1766' and 'Andrew Ellis/1766' survives in America, with family provenance of being made at the Indeo Pottery.[24] A white salt-glazed stoneware tea canister, inscribed underneath 'Made by Thos. Prouse/September ye 20th/1767', is authoritatively attributed to Indeo Pottery, Bovey Tracey.[25] Other white salt-glazed tea canisters have been attributed to Bovey Tracey manufacture by their shape characteristics and inscriptions of local surnames (Colour Plate 37). A salt-glazed wall pocket or cornucopia has also been attributed to Bovey Tracey by shape.[26] Coarse redware, porcelain, tin-glazed earthenware, blackware, tortoiseshell,[27] cream-coloured and later types of pottery were also made at Bovey Tracey. Pottery production continued until 1957.[28]

CHESTER WHITE WARE MANUFACTORY
Paper Mill Lane (later Mill Street), Chester, c.1757-pre-1777

The earliest evidence of a salt-glaze pottery in Chester was an advertisement in 1757 that Randle Sorton & Co., proprietors of the Chester White Ware Manufactory, had opened a warehouse in Chester.[29] This advertisement contains the key phrase 'White Stone or Flint Ware made at their works', which confirms that white salt-glazed stoneware was being made in Chester. The detailed research by Lyn and Maurice Hillis (summarised here), which established the history of this manufacturer, was published in 1980.[30]

By 1767, 'Mr. Dicas & Co.' paid land tax for the 'Pot-House'. A lease of 1777 of 'Dwellinghouses or Cottages and Workshops' refers to a 'large oven with Funnel or pipe erected and being in the yard on the backside of the said premises … formerly made use of as a pottery for the burning or firing of Mugs'. This lease describes the location of the premises as 'in Handbridge … near to and adjoining … Paper Mill Lane [Mill Street in 1980] on the south side thereof & fronting the street on the West side thereof'.

Working potters' names found in Chester parish registers were Wm. Morrice (1758), Robt. Lloyd (1759), Robt. Shaw (1761 and 1764), all 'of Handbridge', the location of

*Fig. 164. **Saggar fragment** for salt-glazed stoneware production excavated at Mill Street, Handbridge, Chester. c.1757-pre-1777. 5½in (13.97cm) high. (Chester City Council)*

*Fig. 165. **Plate fragments; kiln support,** white salt-glazed stoneware plate excavated at Bridgegate House, Lower Bridge Street, Chester, along with a cone for supporting wares within the kiln. c.1760-75. Plate 7in. (17.78cm) diameter, cone 1½in. (3.81cm) high. (Chester City Council)*

the potworks, south of the Old Dee Bridge.

The oven remained until demolition in 1833 and building excavations in the vicinity between 1984 and 1986 produced tangible evidence of white salt-glazed stoneware manufacture: a tankard base, a jug or flask base, a plate rim with lattice/pellet, swag and basketwork pattern, a hollow ware shard (possibly of a bowl) with incised 'scratch-blue' decoration, ring supports, stilts and parts of two saggars (Fig. 164). There was also evidence of cream-ware manufacture.[31]

Parts of a white salt-glazed stoneware plate and a crude support cone were found during building excavation in the cellar of Bridgegate House, 5 Bridge Place, Lower Bridge Street, Chester (Fig. 165). The archaeologist involved suggested that the salt-glazed items found at Bridgegate House had been brought in amongst 'hard-core' for the foundations of the late Georgian house.[32] Recently, fragments of white salt-glazed stoneware wasters and saggars have been found amongst a considerable amount of other pottery in topsoil on open fields at Heronbridge, a mile or so south of the pottery site. This pottery may well have been in rubbish dumped on the fields. These salt-glazed waster and saggar fragments are likely to have originated at the Chester White Ware Manufactory.[33]

JOHN FENTON AND THOMAS HILL
Shelton Farm, Stoke-on-Trent, 1720-1722

John Fenton, owner of Shelton Farm, and his nephew Thomas Hill agreed to become partners making fine earthenware from 12 November 1720.[34] Hill had been taught by *Joshua Heath*.[35] The agreement included buying clay, salt and flint, firm evidence that they were to make white salt-glazed stoneware. They could also get local clay, which would be red-firing clay, suitable for fine redware. Fenton was to erect 'new building, workhouses and oven' at Shelton Farm, as well as using buildings already owned by him. They took over a kiln in the orchard, presumably a slip kiln. Shelton Farm site is no. 93 on the 1802 map,[36] and in 2003 was occupied by houses in Shelton Farm Road.

Within ten months, on 30 August 1721, the agreement was ended by mutual consent.[37] Hill went on to make pots elsewhere, so the raw materials and pots were divided equally. Fenton, who owned the buildings, took 'all Laths, Engines, Stampers, Mortars, Stoves, Modells, Moulds, Boards, Toolls, Utensils, Implements', hovel, ovens etc., and responsibility for employing nine men and one woman, for the next fourteen months, until 12 November 1722.

The raw materials divided included 'Clodds of Clay brought from Bridgnorth or Liverpool' and 'all unpounded fflint', and Fenton took 'punned [pounded] fflint', confirmation that ball clay and flint was used, the ingredients of white stoneware. Salt was not listed, but information elsewhere suggests that salt was purchased as required and not held in stock – see *John Baddeley* and also Appendix 1, *Thomas Wedgwood of Overhouse*.

John Fenton then took a Mr. Thomas Machin into partnership,[38] but there is no evidence that they made salt-glazed stoneware after a purchase of flint on 22 August 1722. From 1728 the Shelton Farm potwork was tenanted by *John Astbury*.[39]

Although a sequence of five kiln bases was uncovered on the site, the earliest was dated to 1730 and no evidence of a salt-glaze oven was found.[40] Salt-glaze saggars in quantity *were* found on site.

The range of vessels recovered from the site was impressive in number and in variety of shapes. Teawares, mugs and jugs prevailed. No plates were found in stratified levels.

The teawares recovered were often characterised by carved bodies, spouts and handles (Figs. 166, 177, 178, 184,

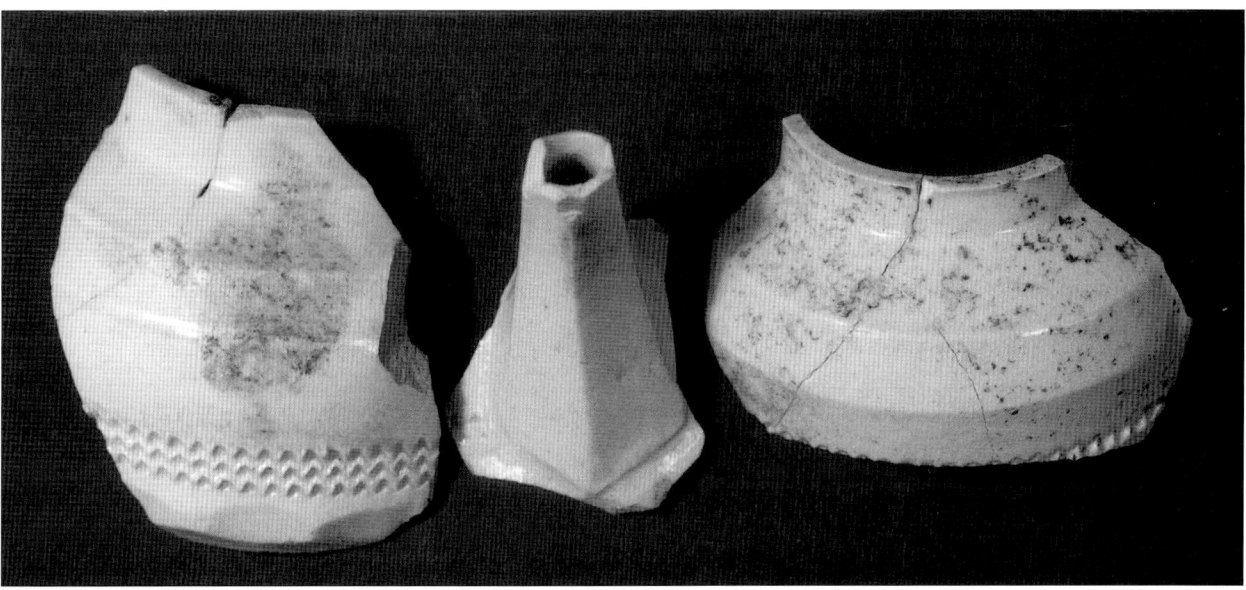

*Fig. 166. **Two teapot shoulder fragments and a spout fragment,** white salt-glazed stoneware with carved bodies and rouletted decoration all excavated at the Shelton Farm site. c.1720-22. Spout 2¼in. (5.72cm) long. (Potteries Museum and Art Gallery, Stoke-on-Trent, SFM92/G)*

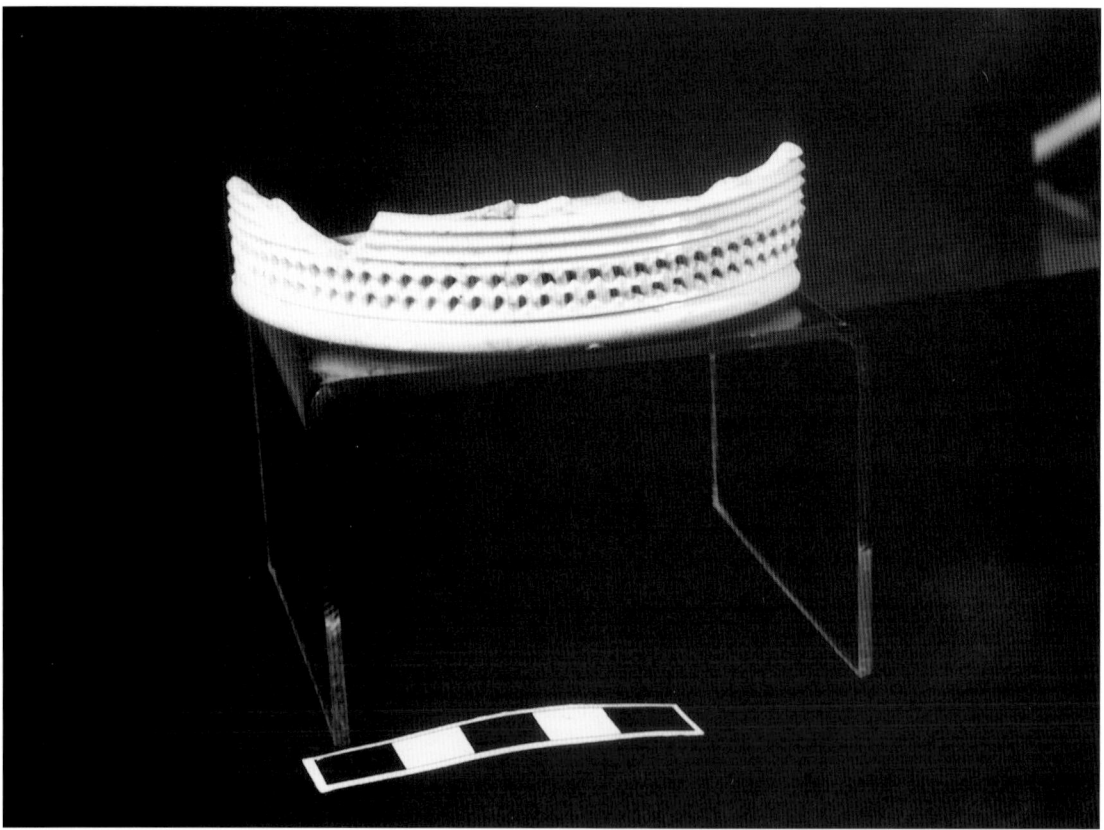

*Fig. 167. **Mug base**, white salt-glazed stoneware, rouletted and turned, excavated at the Shelton Farm site. c.1720-22. Scale in cm. (Potteries Museum and Art Gallery, Stoke-on-Trent, K7 1367)*

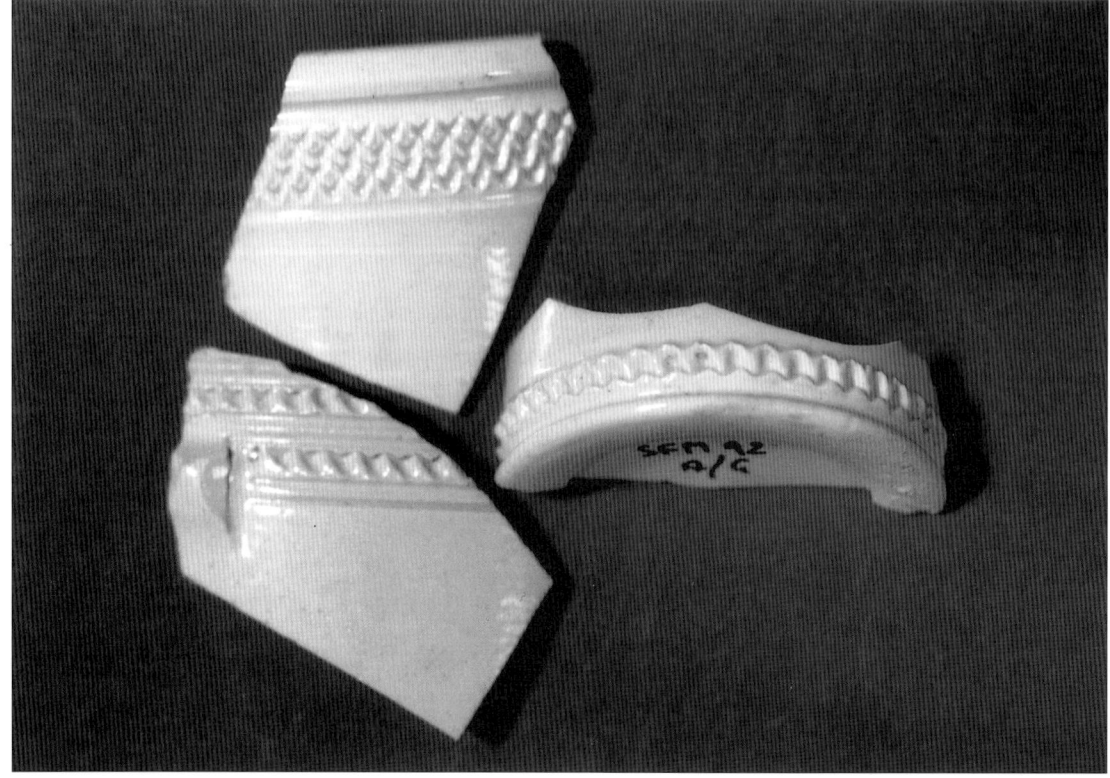

*Fig. 168. **Base and two rim fragments**, white salt-glazed stoneware with rouletted decoration excavated at the Shelton Farm site. c.1720-22. Base diameter 1⅞in. (4.76cm). (Potteries Museum and Art Gallery, Stoke-on-Trent)*

CHAPTER IX – THIRTEEN POTTERS AND THE POTS THEY MADE

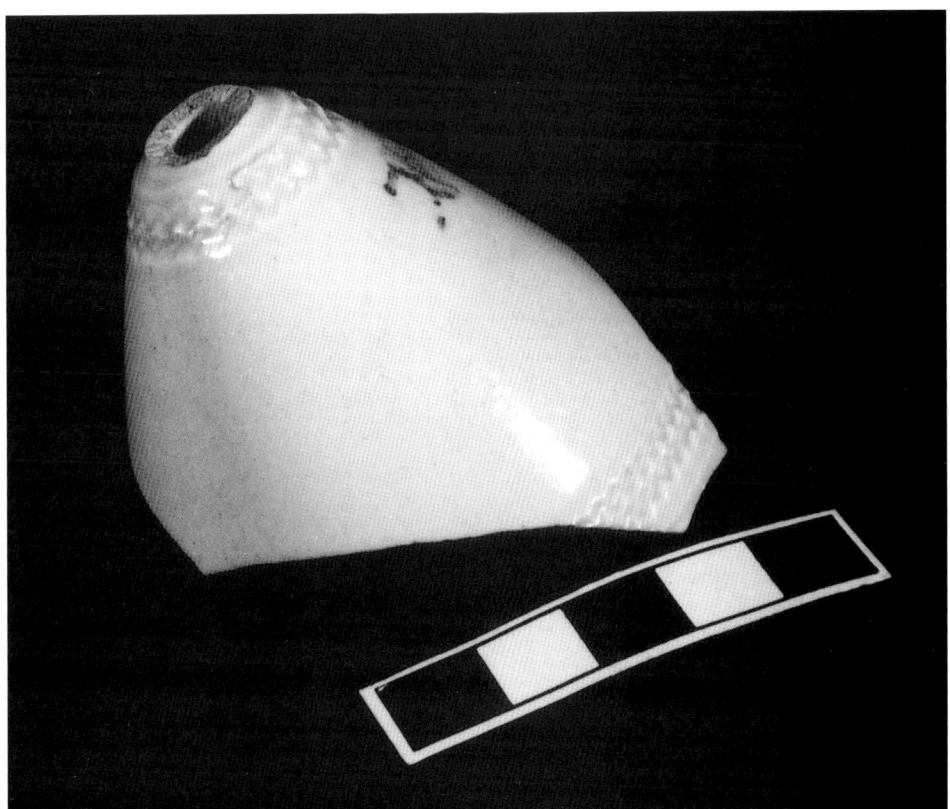

*Fig. 169. **Cone-shaped waster fragment** from a possible eggcup, white salt-glazed stoneware with rouletted decoration excavated at the Shelton Farm site. c.1720-22. Scale in cm. (Potteries Museum and Art Gallery, Stoke-on-Trent, K7 1367)*

*Fig. 170. **Teapot cover**, white salt-glazed stoneware with turned and rouletted decoration, acorn knop and square air hole, excavated at the Shelton Farm site. c.1720-22. 3in. (7.62cm) diameter. (Potteries Museum and Art Gallery, Stoke-on-Trent, SFM 92)*

185; Colour Plates 171, 173, 174). Further embellishment was sometimes achieved by rouletting around the base, shoulder or lid (Figs. 166-170). Teapot lids often had square or rectangular holes (Fig. 171), rather than the usual round ones. Cups were also made with nearly straight sides (Fig. 172) and in capuchin form (Fig. 173). The terminals on some mugs displayed a ratcheting at the base of the handle (Figs.174-175b) or a prominent parallel incision just above the kick (Fig. 179). Handles themselves are often distinctive with an ear-shaped (Fig. 177) or pinched end (Fig. 176), or the faceted top (Fig. 178). When a kick is included at the base it is often a prominent appendage (Figs. 180, 181).

Very little sprig relief decoration was found on Shelton Farm shards (Fig.184), but extant pieces with characteristic

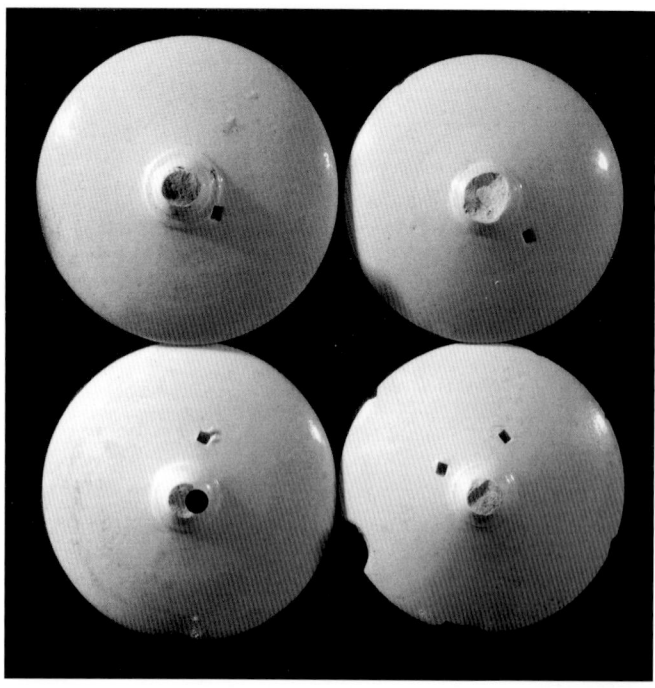

Fig. 171. **Four teapot covers,** *in white salt-glazed stoneware with square (or rectangular) air holes excavated at the Shelton Farm site. c.1720-22. 2¼in. (5.72cm) diameter. (Potteries Museum and Art Gallery, Stoke-on-Trent, SFM 92)*

Fig. 173. **Capuchin base fragment,** *white salt-glazed stoneware with waisted high foot and turned band excavated at the Shelton Farm site. c.1720-22. 1¾in. (4.45cm) diameter (across top). (Potteries Museum and Art Gallery, Stoke-on-Trent, SFM 92)*

Fig. 172. **Mug fragment,** *white salt-glazed stoneware with waisted foot and turned band at rim excavated from an unstratified portion of the Shelton Farm site. c.1720-30. Scale in cm. (Potteries Museum and Art Gallery, Stoke-on-Trent)*

CHAPTER IX – THIRTEEN POTTERS AND THE POTS THEY MADE

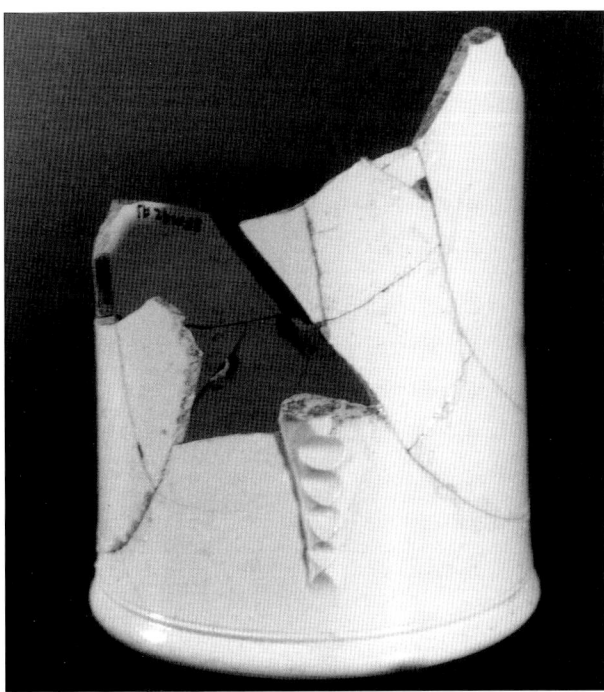

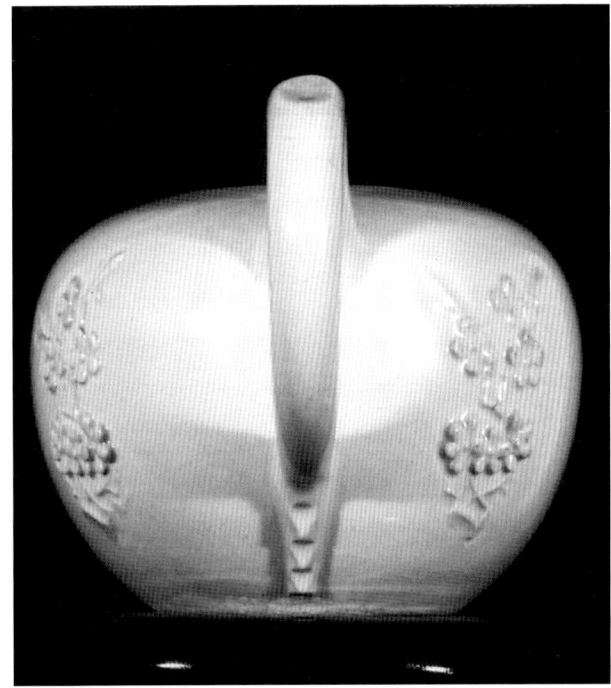

*Fig. 174. **Partially reconstructed mug base,** white salt-glazed stoneware with ratcheted handle terminal excavated at the Shelton Farm site. c.1720-22. 4⅛in. (10.48cm) base diameter. (Potteries Museum and Art Gallery, Stoke-on-Trent, SFM 92 A2)*

*Fig. 175. **Teapot,** white salt-glazed stoneware with handle illustrating the ratcheted handle terminal typical of Shelton Farm examples. This teapot also has other features associated with Shelton Farm, such as the notched handle (see fig. 178) and the early metal mould sprigging seen on redwares excavated at Shelton Farm and on some few white stonewares (see fig. 184). Probably Shelton Farm, c.1720-22. 3in. (7.62cm) high. (Private collection)*

*Fig. 175a. **Teapot** seen in fig. 175 illustrating the notched handle. Probably Shelton Farm, c.1720-22. (Private collection)*

*Fig. 175b. **Bowl fragments and cup base.** Left, white salt-glazed stoneware with turning and rouletting; right, white engobe-slipped stoneware with ratcheted handle terminal. Excavated at Shelton Farm. c.1720-22. Ratchet terminal 1⅛in. (2.86cm) maximum. (Potteries Museum and Art Gallery, Stoke-on-Trent)*

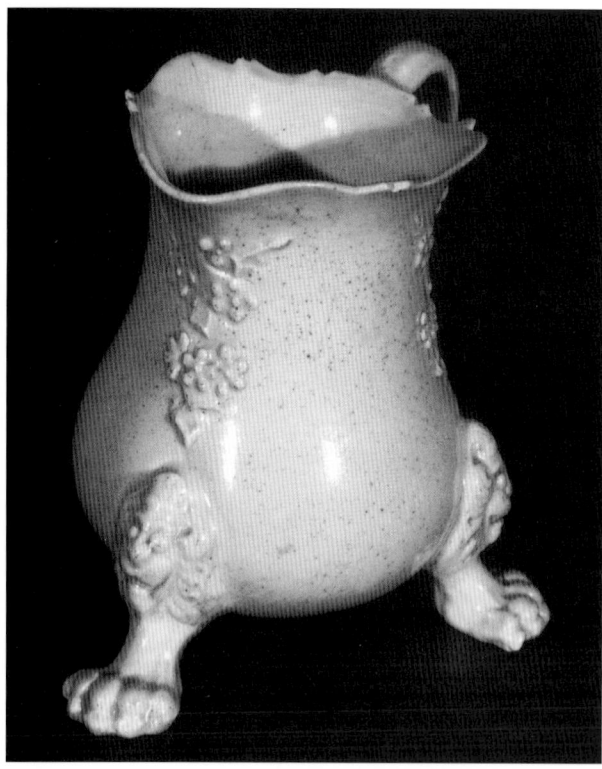

Fig. 175c. **Milk jug,** *white salt-glazed stoneware with three lion's mask feet and sprigged prunus decoration. The strap handle has the ratcheted handle at its base characteristic of wares produced at Shelton Farm. Probably Shelton Farm, c.1725-30. 3½in. (8.89cm) high. (Catzen collection)*

Fig. 175d. **Reverse of milk jug** *(fig. 175c) illustrating the ratcheted handle terminal.*

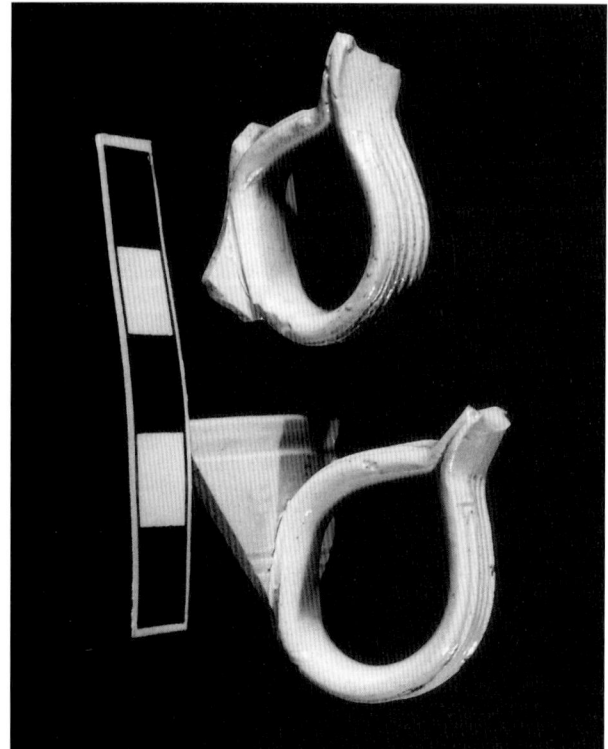

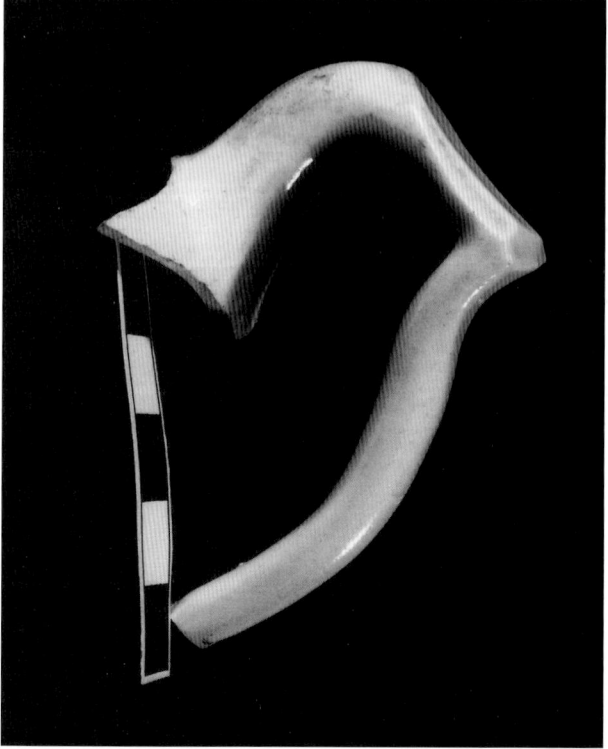

Fig. 176. **Two handle (waster) fragments** *in white salt-glazed stoneware in reeded strap form with pinched closures excavated at Shelton Farm, Stoke-on-Trent. c.1720-22. Scale in cm. (Potteries Museum and Art Gallery, Stoke-on-Trent, K7 1315)*

Fig. 177. **Handle fragment** *of white salt-glazed stoneware in a distinctive ear shape excavated at Shelton Farm, Stoke-on-Trent. c.1720-22. Scale in com. (Potteries Museum and Art Gallery, Stoke-on-Trent, K7 1340)*

CHAPTER IX – THIRTEEN POTTERS AND THE POTS THEY MADE

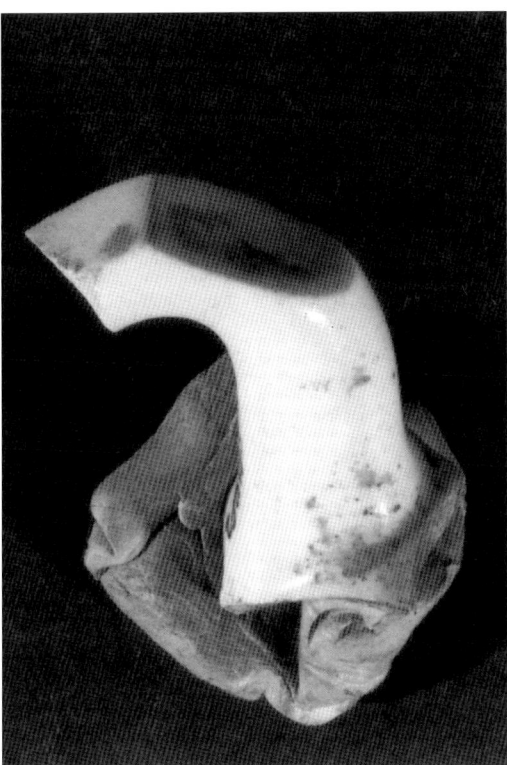

Fig. 178. **Handle fragment** *of white salt-glazed stoneware with notched form excavated at Shelton Farm, Stoke-on-Trent. c.1720-22. (Potteries Museum and Art Gallery, Stoke-on-Trent)*

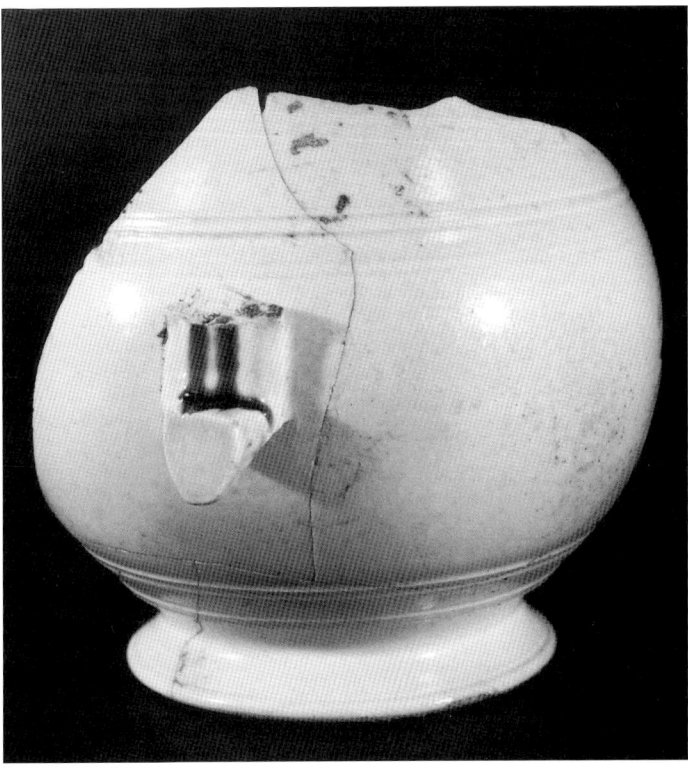

Fig. 179. **Jug base (partially reconstructed),** *white salt-glazed stoneware with turned band at foot and at the top of the bulbous base. The remaining handle has a prominent kick and distinctive parallel incised lines. The jug was excavated at Shelton Farm, Stoke-on-Trent. c.1720-22. (Potteries Museum and Art Gallery, Stoke-on-Trent)*

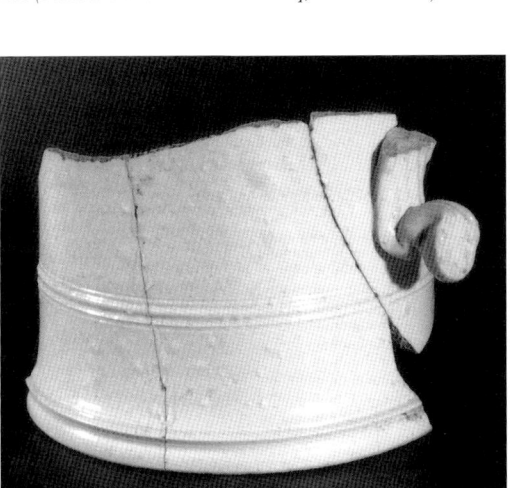

Fig. 180. **Partially reconstructed mug,** *white salt-glazed stoneware with turned base and decoration and prominent kick at the handle terminal. Excavated at the Shelton Farm site. c.1720-22. 3¼in. (8.26cm) high. (Potteries Museum and Art Gallery, Stoke-on-Trent, SFM 92 A2)*

Fig. 181. **Mug waster** *in white salt-glazed stoneware excavated at the Shelton Farm site. The mug has a reed strap handle with a prominent kick terminal. c.1720-22. Scale in cm. (Potteries Museum and Art Gallery, Stoke-on-Trent, K7 1351)*

CHAPTER IX – THIRTEEN POTTERS AND THE POTS THEY MADE

Colour Plate 171. **Teapot,** *white salt-glazed stoneware thrown and tool-cut in broad vertical facets with a rouletted band at the shoulder and pitcher-mould sprig relief designs. The ferruginous dipped embellishments are probably disguising the pulling away from the body of the white-dipped engobe slip. This teapot and a few other examples of similar teawares seem to follow closely the technology of the Dwight wares. Many features, such as the faceted body, the rouletting and the lid, spout and handle shape follow examples excavated at Shelton Farm. Probably Shelton Farm, Stoke-on-Trent, c.1720. 6in. (15.24cm) high. (Photograph courtesy of Jonathan Horne)*

Colour Plate 172. **Capuchin,** *white salt-glazed stoneware of tapered form with high foot and turned band around the lower third. The delicate strap handle has the ratcheted terminal at the base. The form is almost identical to the capuchin base fragment in fig. 175b and the terminal is similar to the ratcheting in shards in the same figure. Possibly Shelton Farm, Stoke-on-Trent, c.1720-22. (Private collection)*

CHAPTER IX – THIRTEEN POTTERS AND THE POTS THEY MADE

Colour Plate 173. **Teapot,** white salt-glazed stoneware of hexagonal form with waisted foot, faceted spout and pinched triangular-shaped handle. The panels and lid have floral sprig relief and the knop is a 'Dog of Fo'. The handle shape and spout have been excavated at Shelton Farm and the general appearance is that of the factory. Probably Shelton Farm, c.1720-30. 5in. (12.7cm) high. (Victoria and Albert Museum, C464-1949)

Colour Plate 174. **Tea canister and teapot,** white salt-glaze engobe-slip wares with panelled bodies and metal mould sprig decoration. The rims are edged in iron-dipped brown to disguise the white slip exterior which tended to pull away from the body during firing. The handle is similar to the excavated example in fig. 177 and the faceted body, spout, rouletting at the shoulder of the teapot and the sprigging are all found on shards from Shelton Farm. Probably Shelton Farm, c.1720. (Photograph courtesy of Jonathan Horne)

Colour Plate 175. **Teapot stand,** white salt-glazed stoneware with pierced foot. Staffordshire, c.1750-65. 2 x 4¾in. (5.08 x 12.07cm). (Tom Walford collection)

Shelton Farm attributes seem to indicate there was more sprig relief than the shards conveyed. Other embellishment was frequently achieved through carving or rouletting. A teapot or patch stand was one of the unusual forms excavated (Fig.183). The prominent features found on Shelton Farm shards has made identification of some extant tea and tavern wares possible; others will doubtless be forthcoming. Teabowl shards with the carved Shelton Farm walls were excavated at Deer Street, Portsmouth, New Hampshire (Fig. 187). A capuchin with the profile and the handle terminal (Colour Plates 34, 172), a teapot with a similar ratcheted handle terminal (Figs. 175, 175a) and a jug displaying the same (Figs. 175c, 175d) also has the ratcheted handle terminal. Handle distinctions are also telling as in the teapot (Colour Plate 33) and another teapot in the Victoria and Albert Museum collection which may be Shelton Farm (Colour Plates 123 and 173).

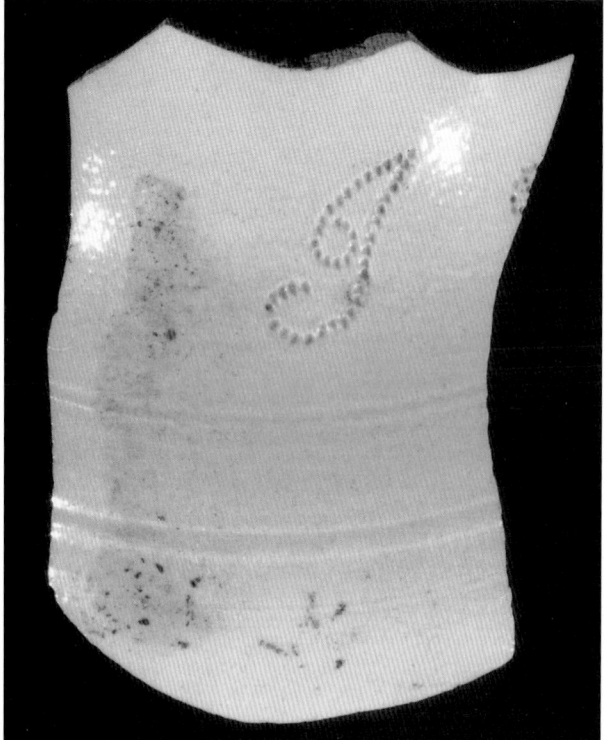

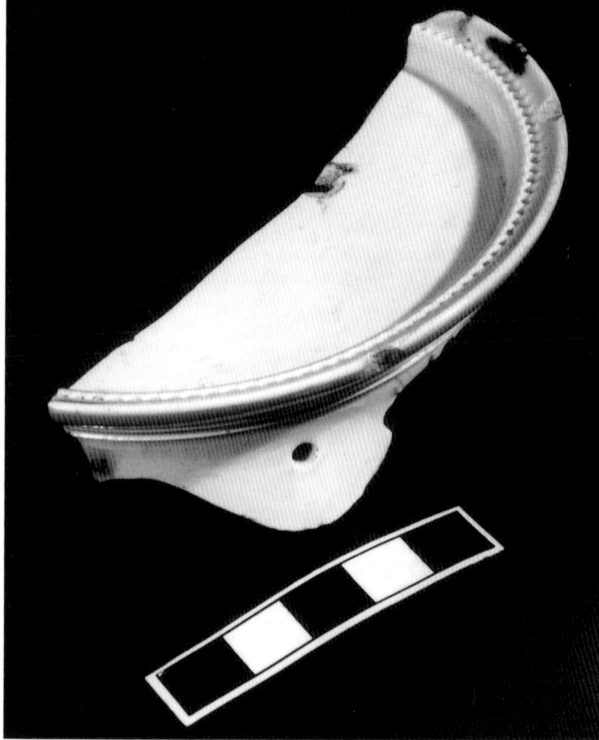

*Fig. 182. **Side from a mug** in white salt-glazed stoneware dot-incised with a J, excavated at the Shelton Farm site. c.1720-22. 3in. (7.62cm) high. (Potteries Museum and Art Gallery, Stoke-on-Trent, SFM92 A2)*

*Fig. 183. **Portion of a teapot stand** of white salt-glazed stoneware with turned and rouletted edge, the base perforated with holes, excavated from the Shelton Farm site. c.1720-22. Scale in cm. (Potteries Museum and Art Gallery, Stoke-on-Trent, K7 1349)*

*Fig. 184. **Two teapot shards** with metal stamp decoration in white salt-glazed stoneware excavated from the Shelton Farm site. c.1720-22. Scale in cm. (Potteries Museum and Art Gallery, Stoke-on-Trent, K7 1455)*

CHAPTER IX – THIRTEEN POTTERS AND THE POTS THEY MADE

*Fig. 185. **Teapot shard,** white salt-glazed stoneware with faceted sides and turned neck found on the Scornton site, home of Dr. Richard Hill, a physician and naturalist, London Town, Maryland. It is interesting to note that Hill purchased the tract of land on which the house was built in 1722, the approximate date of manufacture of the teapot. Probably Shelton Farm, Stoke-on-Trent. 1½in. (3.81cm) high. (Lost Towns Project, Anne Arundel, Maryland, 18AN46)*

*Fig. 187. **Teabowl fragment,** white salt-glazed stoneware with fluted ribs, annular turned base and waisted foot. Excavated in the fill between two houses on Deer Street, Portsmouth, New Hampshire, the teabowl is similar to ones excavated at the Shelton Farm site. Probably Shelton Farm, c.1720-22. 2⅛in. (5.4cm) wide. (Strawbery Banke Museum, Portsmouth, New Hampshire. A780)*

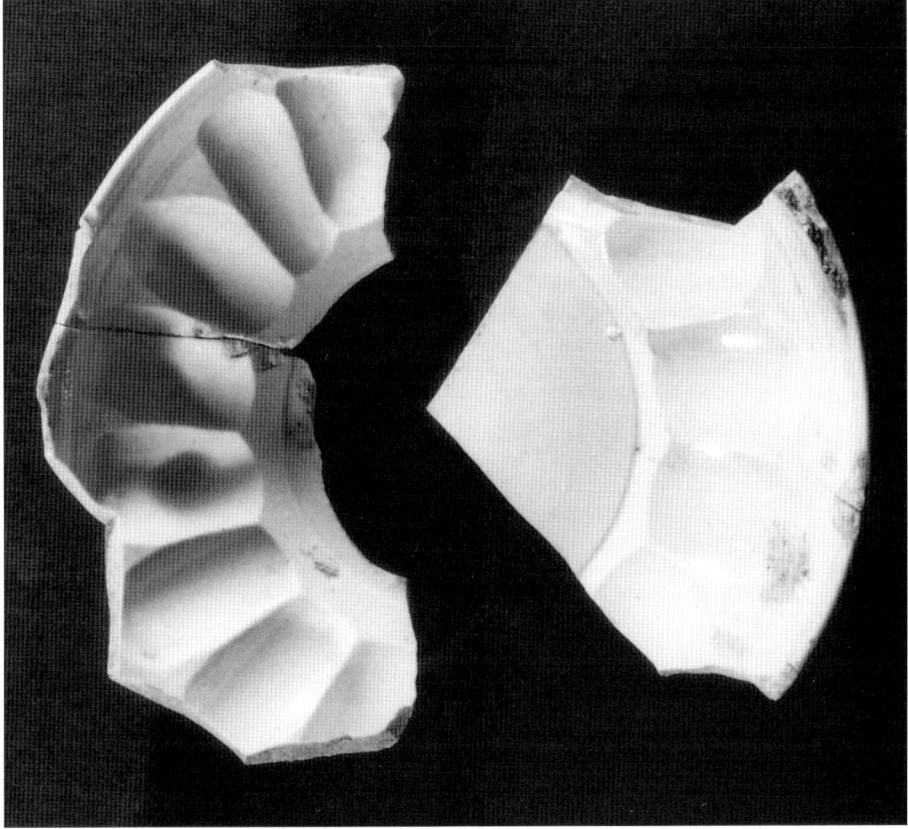

*Fig. 186. **Two fluted saucers partially reconstructed** of white salt-glazed stoneware excavated from the Shelton Farm site. These were from unstratified layers, but the modelling suggests techniques employed by Shelton Farm in other wares, such as the fine tooling or scooping out of the clay to form the prominent flutes. c.1720-22. Joined pieces 3in. (7.62cm) long. (Potteries Museum and Art Gallery, Stoke-on-Trent)*

WILLIAM GREATBATCH
Lower Lane, Fenton, 1762-1782

David Barker has written a most detailed monograph on William Greatbatch,[41] and this brief study is confined to Greatbatch's production of white salt-glazed stoneware, with information taken almost entirely from Barker's work.

Greatbatch was born c.1735 and died at Etruria, Stoke-on-Trent in April 1813.[42] He may have been employed by *Thomas Whieldon* in 1753 and he had set himself up in business as a potter by 1762.[43] Greatbatch's potworks was within the area enclosed in 2003 by Fountain Street, William Street and Manor Street, Fenton.[44] William Greatbatch remained in business there until his bankruptcy in 1782, producing all kinds of earthenware and stoneware.[45]

An intensive excavation of Greatbatch's waste dump at Glebedale Road, Fenton, from 1979 to 1981 produced evidence of Greatbatch's production of white salt-glazed stoneware, on a decreasing scale from 1762 until 1782.[46] Fragments of salt-glazed saggars and kiln furniture and shards of standard shapes of salt-glazed ware were recovered.[47]

Decoration on Greatbatch shards recovered included scratch-blue (Colour Plate 177) and enamel floral painting (Colour Plate 179). Both solid white salt-glaze and slipped white with iron rim shards were found (Colour Plate 176), and press-moulded, slip-cast and sprig relief and incised-decorated wares (Colour Plate 178) were recovered, including mugs, jugs and assorted hollow wares (Figs. 188-198).

Colour Plate 176. **Three iron-dipped rims** *of white salt-glazed stoneware. All these wasters were excavated from the Greatbatch site, Fenton. Iron-dipped rims were an early decorative technique to disguise the pulling away from the body of the white engobe slip. These shards are examples of the iron-dipped process continuing in existence for longer than would have been expected. c.1762-70. 1½ to 3in. (3.81 to 7.62cm). (Potteries Museum and Art Gallery, Stoke-on-Trent)*

Colour Plate 177. **Teabowl and saucer shards,** *white salt-glazed stoneware with scratch-blue decoration excavated at the Greatbatch site, Fenton. c.1762-70. 1¼ to 2¾in. (3.18 to 6.99cm) diameter. (Potteries Museum and Art Gallery, Stoke-on-Trent, F. 79 II)*

Colour Plate 178. **Two shards** *of white salt-glazed stoneware with incised writing ? excavated at the Greatbatch site, Fenton. c.1762-70. 1in. (2.54cm) long. (Potteries Museum and Art Gallery, Stoke-on-Trent, F. 79 I)*

Colour Plate 179. **One shard** *of white salt-glazed stoneware with enamel painting in red, yellow and green with black outlines excavated at the Greatbatch site, Fenton. c.1762-70. 2¾in. (6.99cm) maximum. (Potteries Museum and Art Gallery, Stoke-on-Trent, F. 79 II.)*

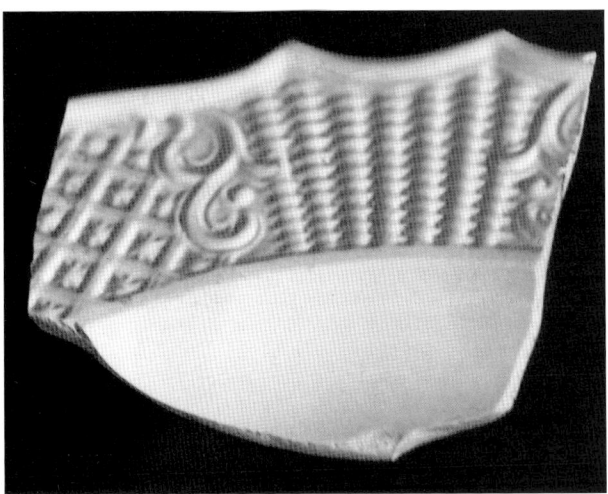

*Fig. 188. **Rim fragment from a plate** of white salt-glazed stoneware in the basketweave pattern excavated at the Greatbatch site, Fenton. c.1762-70. 3½in. (8.89cm). (Potteries Museum and Art Gallery, Stoke-on-Trent)*

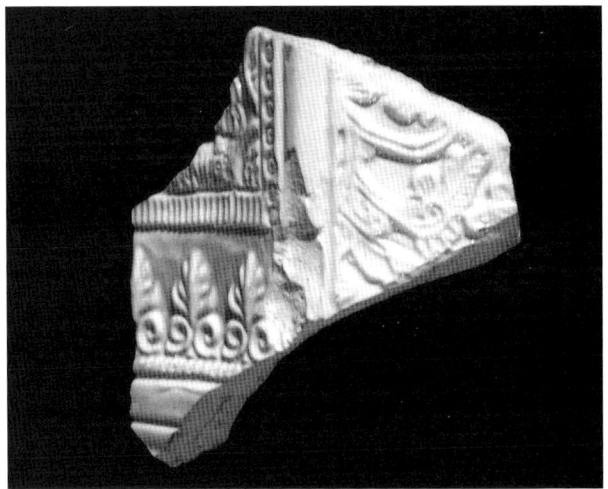

*Fig. 190. **Hexagonal teapot fragment,** white salt-glazed stoneware slip-cast. Not a waster, the fragment was excavated at the Greatbatch site, Fenton. c.1762-70. 1¾in. (4.45cm) long. (Potteries Museum and Art Gallery, Stoke-on-Trent)*

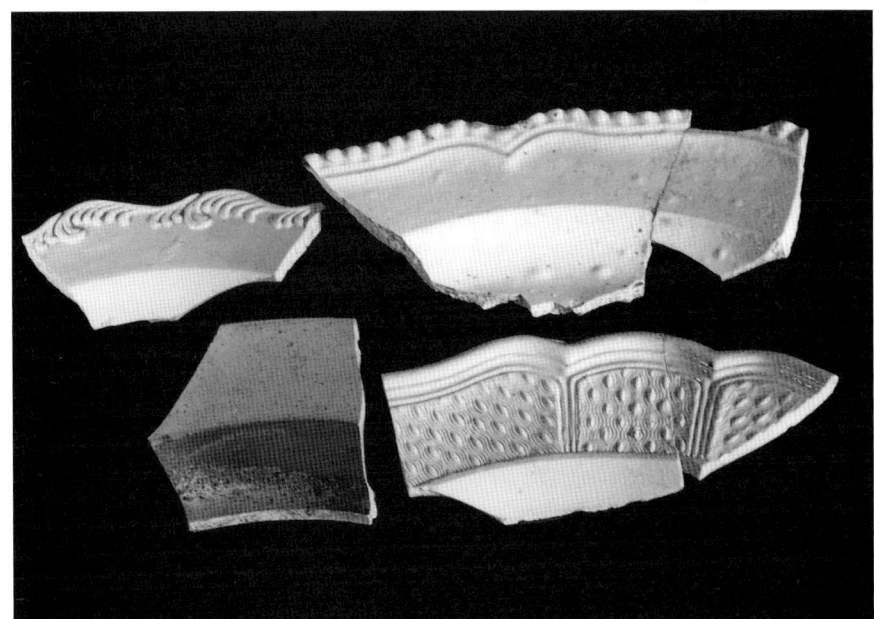

*Fig. 189. **Rim fragments from plates** of white salt-glazed stoneware in feather, gadrooned, plain and seed or barleycorn pattern excavated at the Greatbatch site, Fenton. c.1762-70. 3 to 4¾in. (7.62 to 12.07cm) widths. (Potteries Museum and Art Gallery, Stoke-on-Trent)*

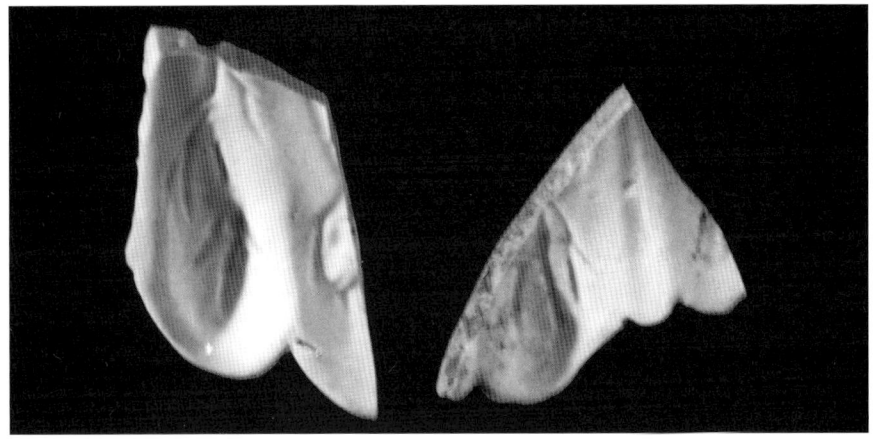

*Fig. 191. **Leaf dish shards,** white salt-glazed stoneware moulded excavated at the Greatbatch site, Fenton. c.1762-70. 1¾in. (4.45cm) maximum. (Potteries Museum and Art Gallery, Stoke-on-Trent)*

CHAPTER IX – THIRTEEN POTTERS AND THE POTS THEY MADE

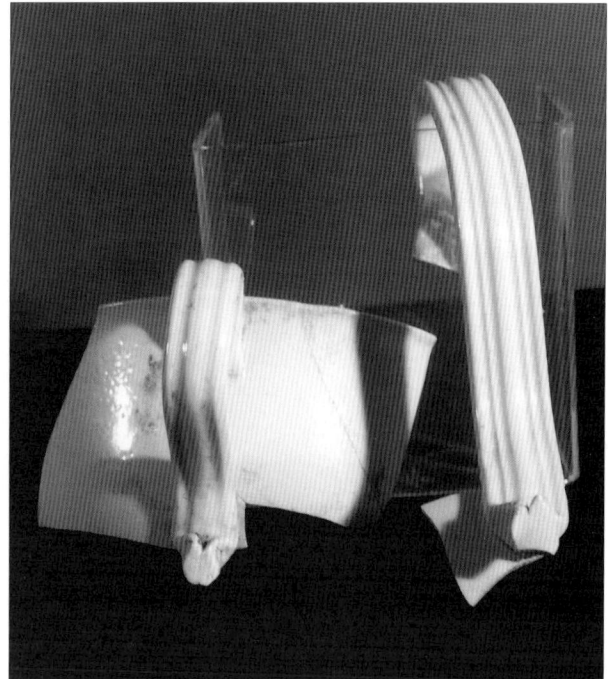

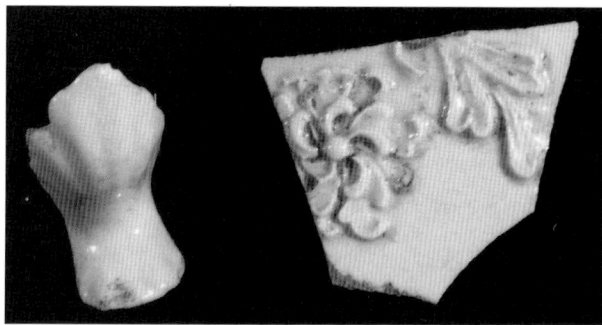

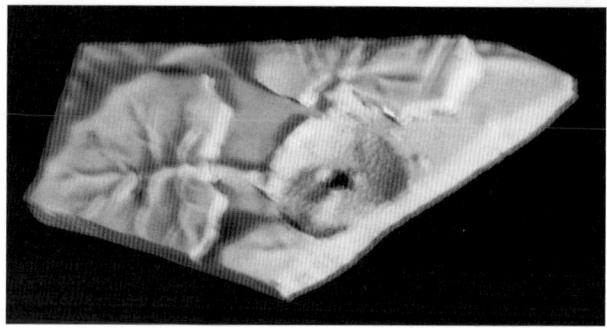

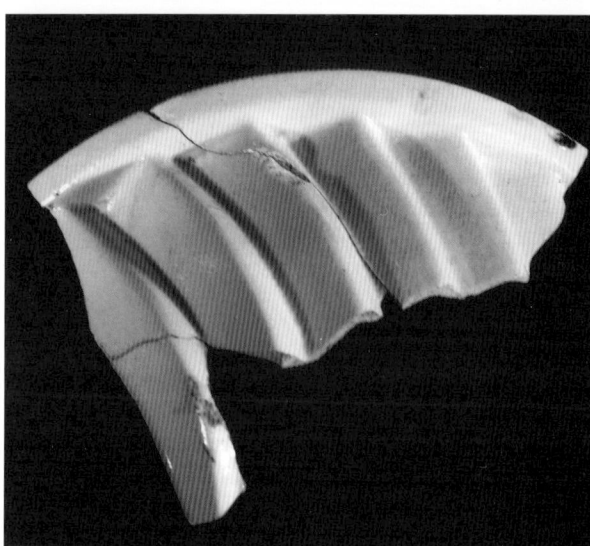

*Fig. 192. **Moulded strap handles** of white salt-glazed stoneware excavated at the Greatbatch site, Fenton. c.1762-70. Left, 2½in. (6.35cm) high, right, waster, 4½in. (11.43cm) high. (Potteries Museum and Art Gallery, Stoke-on-Trent)*

*Fig. 193. **Foot fragment and shard with leaf and applied flower** of white salt-glazed stoneware excavated at the Greatbatch site, Fenton. c.1762-70. 1¼in. (3.18cm) high. (Potteries Museum and Art Gallery, Stoke-on-Trent)*

*Fig. 194. **Lid shard with applied leaves** in white salt-glazed stoneware excavated at the Greatbatch site, Fenton. c.1762-70. 2in. (5.08cm). (Potteries Museum and Art Gallery, Stoke-on-Trent)*

*Fig. 195. **Turk's Head or bundt mould fragment** in white salt-glazed stoneware excavated at the Greatbatch site, Fenton. c.1762-70. 3¾in. (9.53cm). (Potteries Museum and Art Gallery, Stoke-on-Trent)*

*Fig. 196. **Five lid fragments** in white salt-glazed stoneware excavated at the Greatbatch site, Fenton. c.1762-70. ½ to 2in. (1.27 to 5.08cm) diameter. (Potteries Museum and Art Gallery, Stoke-on-Trent)*

CHAPTER IX – THIRTEEN POTTERS AND THE POTS THEY MADE

*Fig. 197. **Partially reconstructed jug** in white salt-glazed stoneware excavated at the Greatbatch site, Fenton. c.1762-70. 9¾in. (24.77cm) high. (Potteries Museum and Art Gallery, Stoke-on-Trent)*

*Fig. 198. **Mug waster** of white salt-glazed stoneware fused partially to saggar at base excavated at the Greatbatch site, Fenton. c.1762-70. 2½in. (6.35cm) high. (Potteries Museum and Art Gallery, Stoke-on-Trent)*

LONDON: JOHN DWIGHT, c.1673-1703
LYDIA DWIGHT, 1703-09
SAMUEL DWIGHT, 1709-1737
Fulham Pottery, London

The life of John Dwight (1630s-1703) and the history of the Fulham Pottery have been thoroughly researched.[48] Dwight studied 'civil law and physick a little but most Chymistry' at Oxford and graduated in 1661. He became a lawyer and secretary to the Bishops of Chester at Chester and later Wigan, where he experimented with ceramics. About 1672 Dwight moved to Fulham and set up a pottery there, making stoneware figures, salt-glazed stoneware and red stoneware, and experimenting with porcelain.

In April 1672 Dwight obtained a patent for fourteen years for making transparent earthenware commonly called porcelain or China and Persian ware, and stone ware vulgarly called Collogne (*sic*) Ware in England, Wales and Berwick-upon-Tweed. He obtained another fourteen year patent in 1684, this time also including Scotland and the colonies, for the same wares as before and also earthenwares called white gorges, marbled porcelain vessels, statues and figures and fine stone gorges and vessels; opaque red and dark coloured porcelain.

Between 1693 and 1697 John Dwight accused thirteen individual master potters of infringing his 1684 patent, which was for white gorges, marble porcelain vessels,

*Fig. 199. **Mug**, gorge-shaped white-slipped salt-glazed stoneware with a silver rim marked 'SS' and dated 1682. Made by John Dwight, Fulham, c.1682. 3¾in. (9.53cm) high. (Schreiber collection, Victoria and Albert Museum, Sch. II 58)*

211

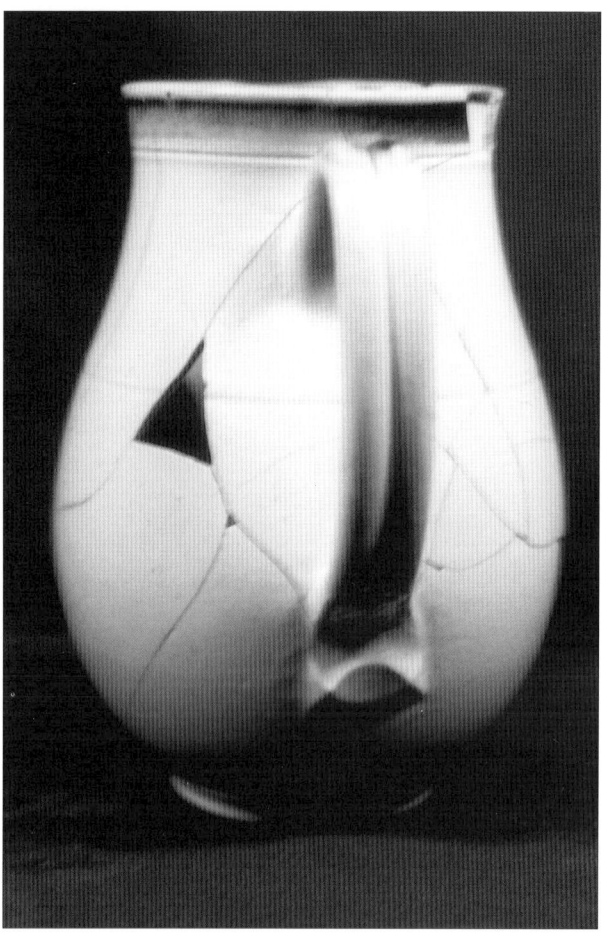

Fig. 200. A view of the typical knife-cut handle terminal on jugs and mugs of Dwight manufacture c.1700-1710. For details of this jug see Fig. 4. (Guildford Museum)

statues and figures, fine stone gorges and vessels, transparent porcelain, opacous (opaque) red and dark coloured porcelain or China and Persian wares and Cologne or Stone wares.[49] This time his accusations omitted the Cologne or Stone wares.

The ensuing litigation is helpful in defining what some of these thirteen potters were making. *John Elers and David Elers* admitted making Cologne or Stone ware and red teapots.[50] James Morley of Nottingham was found to have sold brown mugs.[51] *Cornelius Hamersley* of Staffordshire admitted that he made earthenware.[52] Of the London potters, *Mathew Garner* admitted making earthen brown cans and mugs;[53] and *Moses Johnson* admitted making China and Persian ware – and also Cologne and stone ware of which he, like the other potters, was not accused.[54] *Luke Talbot* admitted that he may have made patent wares.[55]

From the litigation, we know that *Aaron Wedgwood, Thomas Wedgwood I and Richard Wedgwood*,[56] *Moses Middleton* and *Joshua Astbury*[57] were accused of making Dwight's patent wares, but the specific types were not included in the accusations. In 1696 Thomas Wedgwood, Richard Wedgwood and other Staffordshire potters complained that Dwight was obstructing them in their trade by his patent.[58]

The nearest we come to knowing what the Wedgwoods made in the 1690s is their brother's reported statement in 1698 that Dwight was in suit with them 'for making ye ordinary glazed drinking potts in ye form (Or imitacon) of those w[hi]ch Mr. D. makes of stoneware'.[59] As the Wedgwoods and others had complained in 1696 that Dwight was obstructing them in their trade, they must have been making one or other of his patented wares. Leaving out 'Cologne or Stone wares', which were not included in the accusations, we are left with white gorges and fine stone gorges (Fig. 199) as the 'ordinary drinking glazed potts' which Wedgwoods were producing in the 1690s.

Fig. 201. **Teapot**, partially reconstructed white-slipped salt-glazed stoneware with iron-dipped upper half of the body excavated at 16 Tunsgate, Guildford. This is the only known teapot by the Dwights, Fulham, c.1700-1710. 4in. (10.16cm) high (to handle). (Guildford Museum)

Figures and busts made by Dwight (Colour Plates 2-7) are said to be salt-glazed, the bodies drab, brown, brownish white or white.[60] Fragments of two salt-glazed grey busts, and shards of white or pale grey salt-glazed gorges in imitation of Westerwald ware, some with cobalt or manganese decoration, were found on Dwight's site, dated to c.1673-75. Fine white salt-glazed stoneware shards found on site, which have been dated to the late seventeenth century, include fragments of a tankard, a teabowl, gorges and teapots, and possibly capuchins. 'Marbled' shards were found, from a tankard, capuchin, teapot cover and gorges, made from grey, white and black clays.[61] Dwight also made a great deal of ware like German brown salt-glazed stoneware.

Dwight used Dorset ball-clay and Isle of Wight sand to make his stoneware and he was aware of the use of flint.[62] Brass sprig moulds used by John Dwight are preserved.[63] Both rectangular and circular kilns were used.[64] John Dwight died in 1703, and was succeeded by his widow, Mrs. Lydia Dwight, until her death in 1709, and then by his eldest son, Samuel Dwight, until 1737.[65]

Brown salt-glazed ware continued to be made, and also white salt-glazed stoneware: tankards, gorges, tea and coffeeware in a coarse body covered with a white slip, sometimes decorated with cobalt, manganese, a brown rim, or sprigged. The quality of these wares is said to be better than the Staffordshire equivalents. This 'double-dipped' technique was stated to have been invented by Samuel Dwight,[66] possibly during his father's lifetime.

The Fulham Pottery site is at the western end of New Kings Road, London, identifiable by the preserved 1890s bottle oven. It continued to be used for pottery purposes until 1985.[67]

The pots produced by the Dwights are detailed in Chapter I and referred to throughout the book (see Figures 1, 1a, 2-6, Colour Plates 2-7, 10, 139-142). Only a sample of the identified reconstructed pieces from archaeological excavations is included here, such as the knife-cut handle kick (Fig. 200) and a teapot, the only such form to have been identified to date (Fig. 201).

HUMPHREY PALMER
Snape Marsh, Shelton, c.1750
Church Works, Town Road, Hanley, 1750-pre-1778

This study concentrates on Humphrey Palmer's probable production of white salt-glazed stoneware at two sites, Marsh Street, Shelton and Town Road, Hanley. The fullest accounts of his later career as a master potter at the Church Works, Town Road, Hanley, competitor of Wedgwood and partner of James Neale, are in Diana Edwards' *Neale Pottery and Porcelain Its Predecessors and Successors 1763-1820* (Barrie & Jenkins, 1987) and her *Black Basalt Wedgwood and Contemporary Manufacturers* (Woodbridge: Antique Collectors' Club, 1994).

Humphrey Palmer's domestic affairs appear surprising but not impossible. There appears to be only one Humphrey Palmer in the period, christened in 1725 at Chebsey, Staffs.[68] He entered into four marriages,[69] marrying Sarah Payne at Wolstanton on 1 January 1742, when he was only sixteen,[70] Ann Adams at Burslem 2 August 1750,[71] Mary Heath at Sandon, Staffs. 28 October 1751 and Hannah Ashwin at St. Martin's, Birmingham on 9 September 1777.

*Fig. 202. **Saggar for firing salt-glazed stoneware** with white salt-glazed stoneware saddle (kiln furniture) excavated at the Humphrey Palmer site, Hanley, Staffordshire. c.1750-70. 12½in. (31.75cm) diameter. (Potteries Museum and Art Gallery, Stoke-on-Trent, K3 831 1985)*

Chapter IX – Thirteen Potters and the Pots they made

Snape Marsh, Shelton

Palmer's first venture as a master potter seems to have been at Snape Marsh, Shelton, up to 1750. In 1750, *James Payne* purchased from Francis Payne (probably his father) a messuage or tenement with appurtenances in Snape Marsh, Shelton, 'part whereof is now converted into two pot ovens and hovels a stove, a smoak [sic] house and a packing house and slip kilns ... now in the holding of Humphrey Palmer'.[72] On 9 January 1752 James Payne mortgaged his house and potworks 'late in the holding of Humfry [sic] Palmer' now in Payne's possession.[73] Palmer had moved to Church Works, Hanley in 1750 – see below.

In his will of 1753 James Payne, Shelton, earth potter, mentioned his Flint ware warehouse.[74] ('Flint ware' referred to white salt-glazed stoneware at that date.) As Palmer had used Payne's potworks before him, Palmer is likely to have also produced salt-glaze, though as it was a two-oven works there might also have been production of earthenware by both Payne and Palmer.

Palmer married a Sarah Payne at Wolstanton in 1742 and, although no relationship has been found between her and James Payne, it is significant that James Payne's daughter was christened Sarah in 1740 and that Palmer was later in Payne's potworks. When Humphrey Palmer's son Thomas was buried at Hanley on 2 March 1745/46, Palmer was described as 'of Shelton'.[75] The site of Payne's potworks is likely to be on the west side of Marsh Street, perhaps near the top of Etruria Road – see *James Payne*.

Church Works, Hanley

The 1752 mortgage stated that Payne's works were *formerly* held by Palmer, so that he had already moved on. The burial of Palmer's first wife Sarah has not been traced, but he married Ann Adams on 2 August 1750. John Adams made a marriage settlement before his daughter's marriage, naming a number of fields in Hanley 'and all edifices and buildings now erecting thereon ... by one Humphrey Palmer'. If there were no children of the marriage, Palmer was to have for life the Abbey Field and Deakyn's Croft, adjoining Hanley Church, upon which 'a messuage or dwelling house and other buildings are intended to be erected by the said Humphrey Palmer'.[76] Palmer was

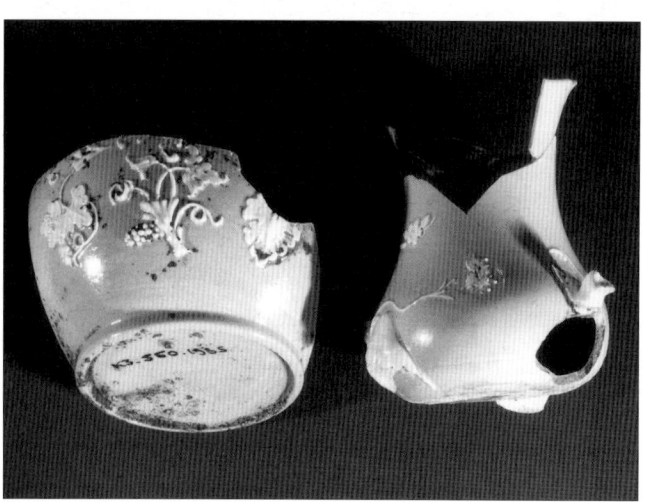

*Fig. 203. **Partially reconstructed teapot**, drab-coloured salt-glazed stoneware with white sprig relief and white crabstock handle. Excavated at the Town Road site of Humphrey Palmer's factory. c.1750-60. 3½in. (8.89cm) high at handle. (Potteries Museum and Art Gallery, Stoke-on-Trent, K3 554 1985)*

*Fig. 204. **Four lid fragments**, drab-coloured salt-glazed stoneware with white sprig relief of flowers, birds and jewel-like motifs. Excavated at Humphrey Palmer's factory, Hanley, c.1750-60. 2½in. (6.35cm) maximum diameter. (Potteries Museum and Art Gallery, Stoke-on-Trent, K3 564, 565, 556, 562, 1985)*

*Fig. 205. **Teapot and milk jug fragments**, drab-coloured salt-glazed stoneware with white sprig relief of grape leaf and vine tendrils. Excavated at Humphrey Palmer's factory, Hanley, c.1750-60. Teapot base 2⅜in. (6.03cm) diameter; milk jug 3½in. (8.89cm) high. (Potteries Museum and Art Gallery, Stoke-on-Trent, K3 550, 552 1985)*

CHAPTER IX – THIRTEEN POTTERS AND THE POTS THEY MADE

Fig. 206. **Three teapot fragments,** *drab-coloured salt-glazed stoneware with grape leaves, bunches of grapes and jewel-like ornamentation. Excavated at Humphrey Palmer's factory, Hanley, c.1750-60. 2½in. (6.35cm) long maximum. (Potteries Museum and Art Gallery, Stoke-on-Trent, K3 544, 544, 546 1985)*

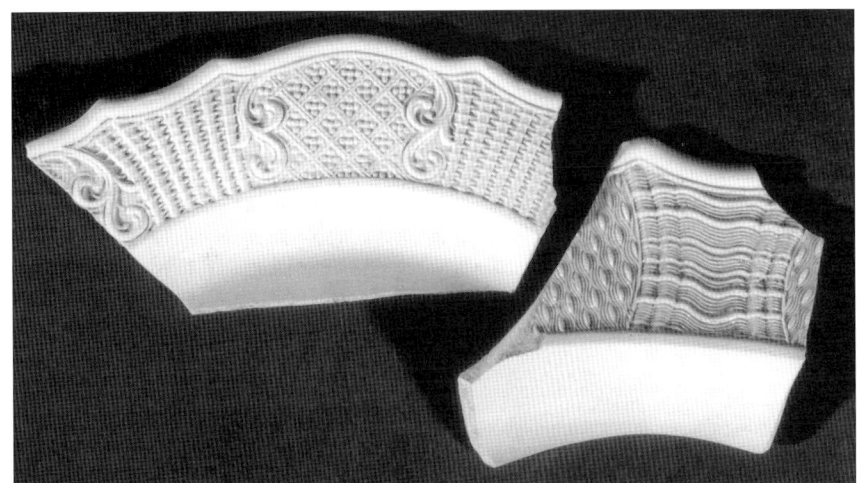

Fig. 207. **Two plate rim fragments,** *white salt-glazed stoneware moulded in the mosaic or basketweave pattern (left) and the barleycorn pattern (right). These popular patterns were manufactured by most of the potters producing salt-glaze between 1750 and 1770. Great quantities of shards with these borders were excavated from the Humphrey Palmer site, Hanley, c.1755-70. (Potteries Museum and Art Gallery, Stoke-on-Trent)*

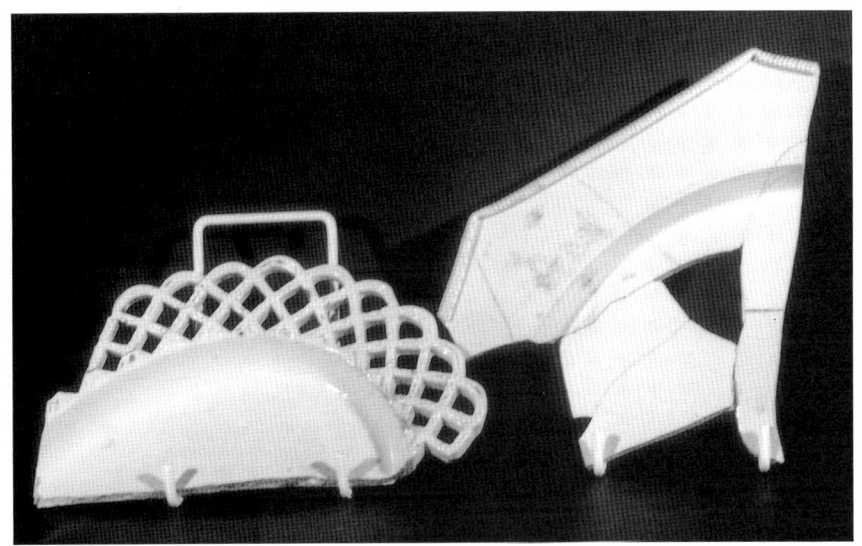

Fig. 208. **Two plates partially reconstructed,** *white salt-glazed stoneware reticulated basket stand and an octagonal plate with reeded edge. Excavated from the Humphrey Palmer site in Hanley, c.1755-70. Both 6½in. (16.51cm) long. (Potteries Museum and Art Gallery, Stoke-on-Trent, K3 241, 344 1985)*

215

Chapter IX – Thirteen Potters and the Pots they made

*Fig. 209. **Partially reconstructed soup plate (waster)** of white salt-glazed stoneware with floral moulded border. Excavated from the Humphrey Palmer site in Hanley. c.1755-70. 9⅛in. (23.18cm) diameter. (Potteries Museum and Art Gallery, Stoke-on-Trent, K3 204 1985)*

*Fig. 210. **Partially reconstructed butter dish and cover,** white salt-glazed stoneware with sprig relief grape vine decoration. Excavated from the Humphrey Palmer site in Hanley. c.1755-70. 1½ x 3⅞in. (3.81 x 9.84cm); cover 4⅛in. (10.48cm) diameter. (Potteries Museum and Art Gallery, Stoke-on-Trent, K3 238, 392 1985)*

CHAPTER IX – THIRTEEN POTTERS AND THE POTS THEY MADE

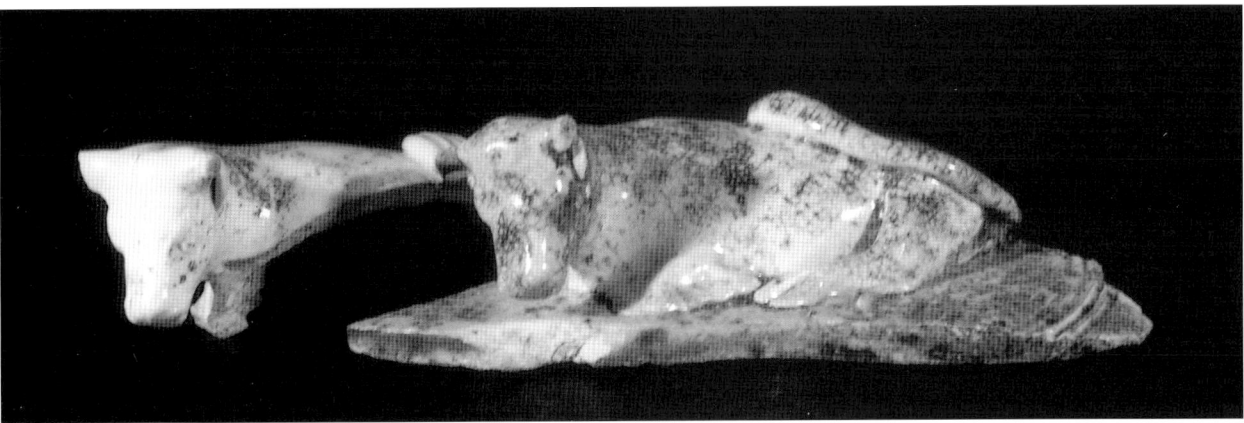

*Fig. 211. **Two waster cow knops** of moulded white salt-glazed stoneware. These cow knops are characteristically found on the covers of butter dishes. Excavated from the Humphrey Palmer site in Hanley. c.1755-70. 4in. (10.16cm) long. (Potteries Museum and Art Gallery, Stoke-on-Trent, K3 395 1985)*

*Fig. 212. **Two butter dishes, stands and covers** of press-moulded white salt-glazed stoneware with cow finials. Probably Humphrey Palmer, Hanley, c.1755-70. Left, basketweave moulded dish 4⅜in. (11.11cm) long; right, barleycorn moulded dish 5¼in. (13.34cm) long. (Potteries Museum and Art Gallery, Stoke-on-Trent, 1703, 1160)*

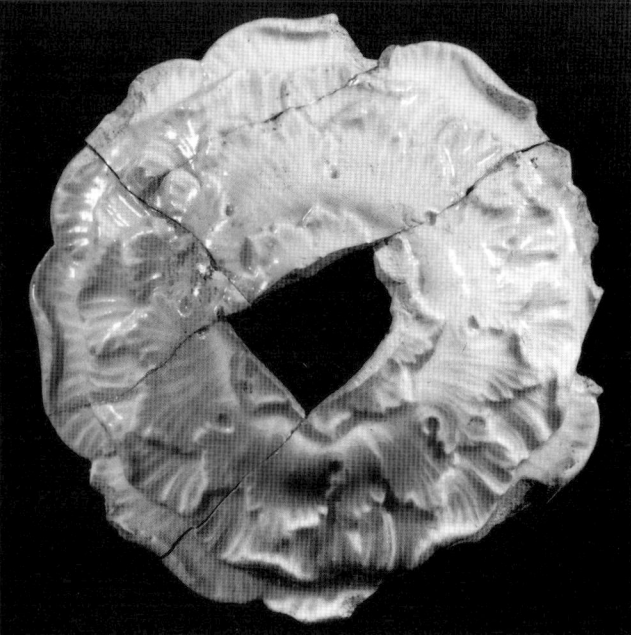

*Fig. 213. **Partially reconstructed tureen lid**, white salt-glazed stoneware press-moulded in the form of overlapping leaves. Excavated from the Humphrey Palmer site in Hanley. c.1755-65. 5½in. (13.97cm) diameter. (Potteries Museum and Art Gallery, Stoke-on-Trent, K3 217 1985)*

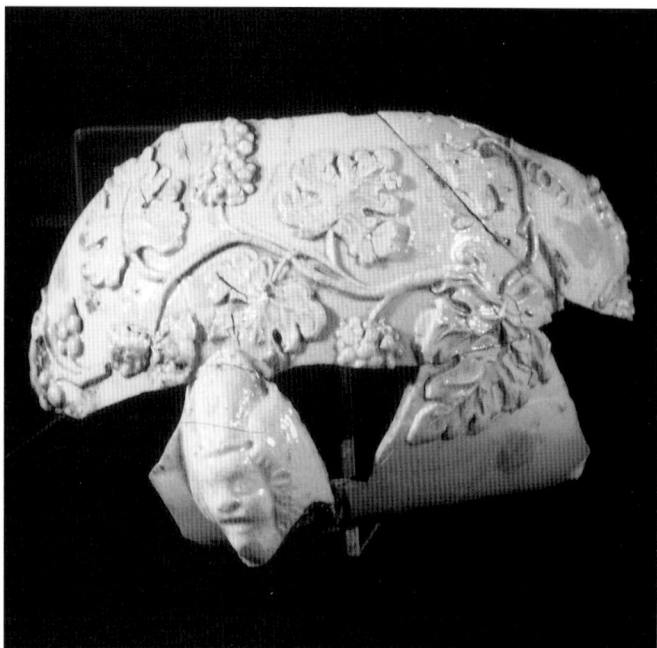

*Fig. 214. **Partially reconstructed teapot body with part foot,** white salt-glazed stoneware with heavy relief sprigging of grapes and vines. Excavated from the Humphrey Palmer site in Hanley. c.1750-65. 4in. (10.16cm) high. (Potteries Museum and Art Gallery, Stoke-on-Trent, K3 328 1985)*

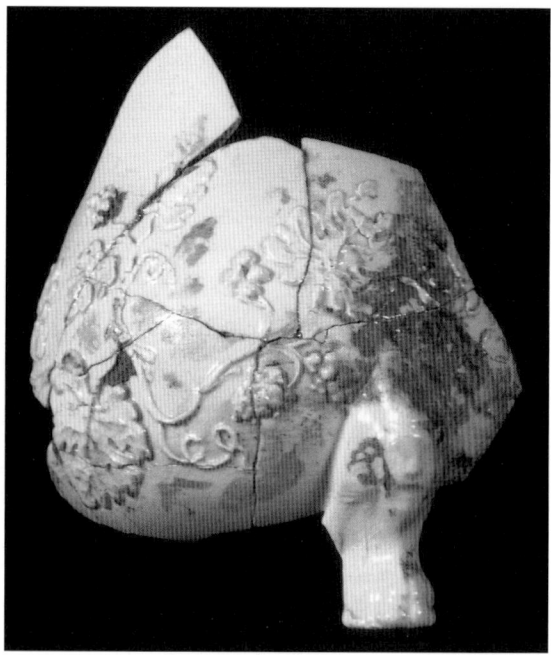

*Fig. 215. **Partially reconstructed large milk jug with foot,** white salt-glazed stoneware heavily sprigged with grape vines and a mask head moulded foot. Excavated from the Humphrey Palmer site in Hanley. c.1750-65. 4¼in. (10.8cm). (Potteries Museum and Art Gallery, Stoke-on-Trent, K3 575 1985)*

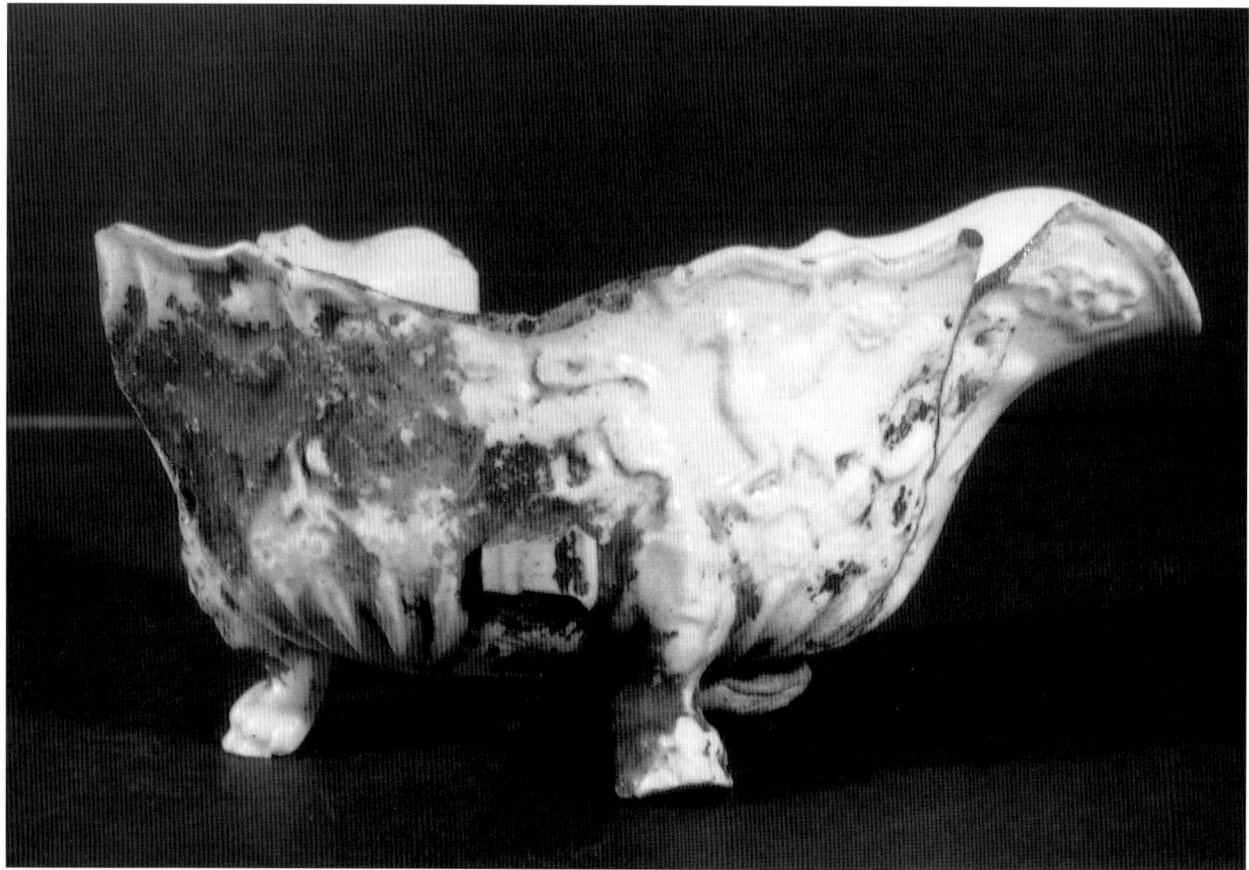

*Fig. 216. **Partially reconstructed sauceboat waster.** White salt-glazed stoneware slip-cast with birds and floral decoration. Excavated from the Humphrey Palmer site in Hanley. c.1750-65. 5¼in. (13.34cm) long. (Potteries Museum and Art Gallery, Stoke-on-Trent, K3 275 1985)*

CHAPTER IX – THIRTEEN POTTERS AND THE POTS THEY MADE

Fig. 217. **Three covers partially reconstructed,** *white salt-glazed stoneware with sprig relief decoration of grape vines, birds and flowers. Excavated from the Humphrey Palmer site in Hanley. c.1750-65. 4½in. (11.43cm) maximum. (Potteries Museum and Art Gallery, Stoke-on-Trent, K3 1017, 385, 386 1985)*

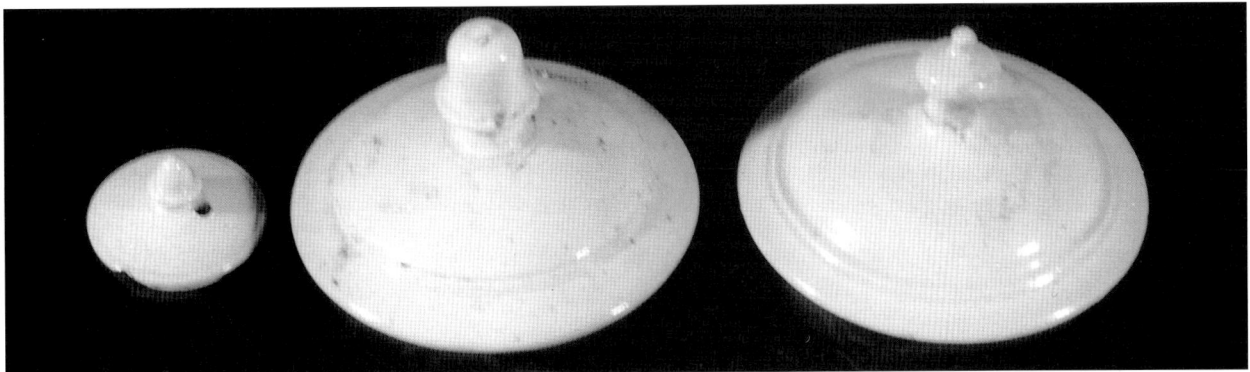

Fig. 218. **Three teapot covers,** *white salt-glazed stoneware excavated at Humphrey Palmer's factory, Hanley. c.1750-65. 2¼in. (5.72cm) maximum diameter. (Potteries Museum and Art Gallery, Stoke-on-Trent, K3 196, 196, 396 1985)*

Fig. 219. **Two finials,** *white salt-glazed stoneware moulded in the form of a wild rose. Excavated from the Humphrey Palmer site in Hanley, c.1750-65. 1¼in. (3.18cm) maximum. (Potteries Museum and Art Gallery, Stoke-on-Trent, K3 399 1985)*

219

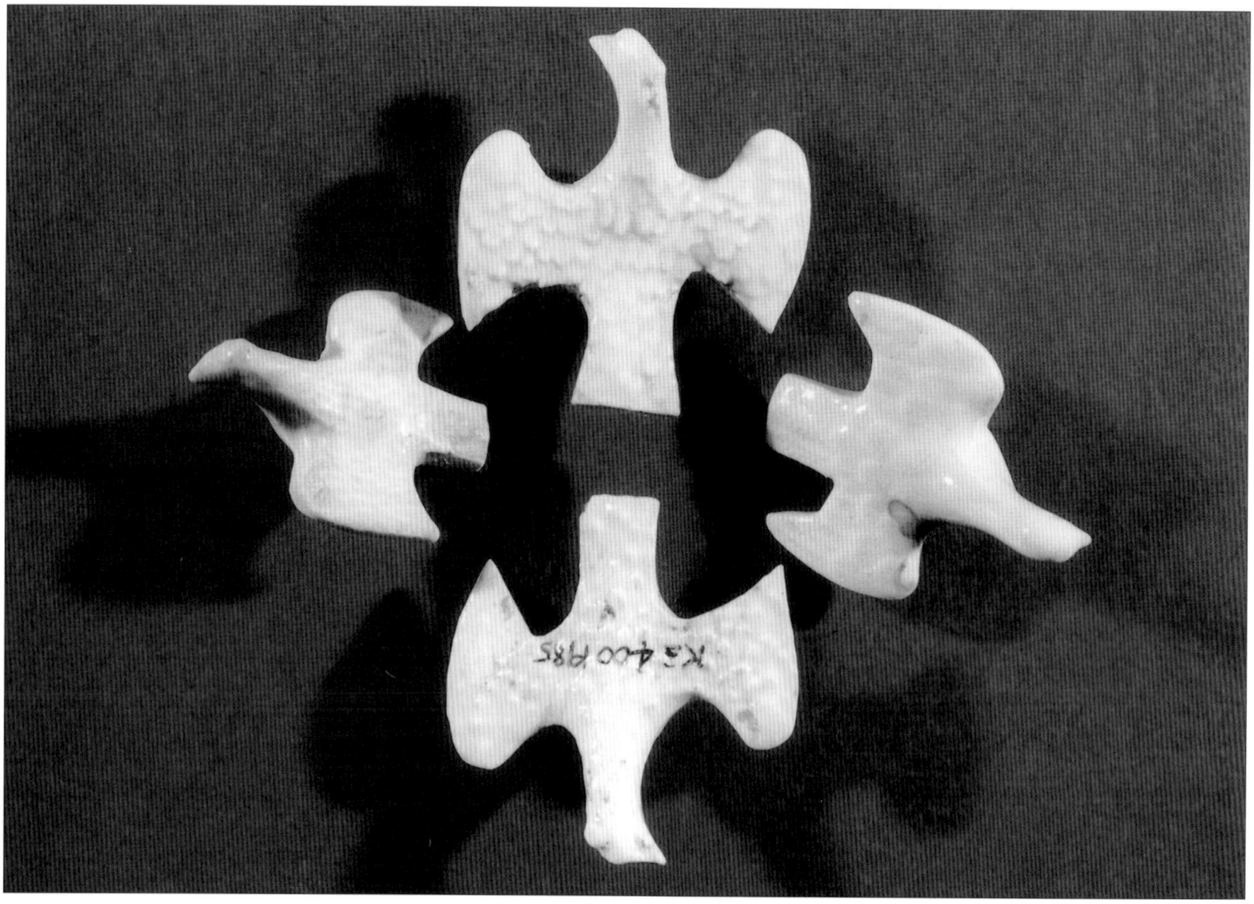

CHAPTER IX – THIRTEEN POTTERS AND THE POTS THEY MADE

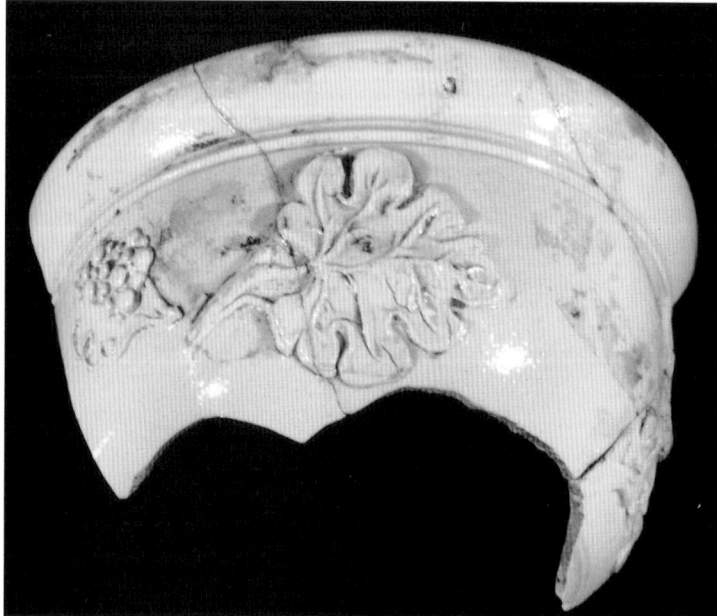

Fig. 220. **Four finials,** *white salt-glazed stoneware moulded in the form of birds found on teapot and hot milk jug lids. Excavated from the Humphrey Palmer site in Hanley. c.1750-65. 1⅝in. (4.13cm) maximum. (Potteries Museum and Art Gallery, Stoke-on-Trent, K3 400 1985)*

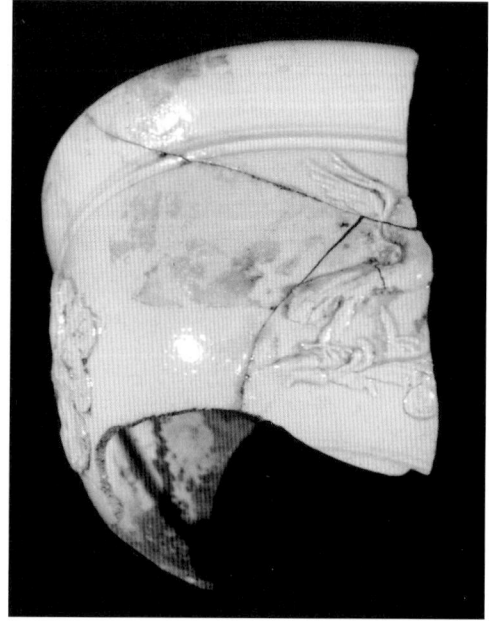

Fig. 221. **Partially reconstructed sugar bowl** *in white salt-glazed stoneware with bold sprigged relief of grape leaves and a large bird (Fig. 221a). Excavated from the Humphrey Palmer site in Hanley. c.1750-65. 3⅝in. (9.21cm) diameter. (Potteries Museum and Art Gallery, Stoke-on-Trent, K3 247 1985)*

Fig. 221a. **Partially reconstructed sugar bowl** *in Fig. 221 showing the remains of the large bird sprig relief.*

CHAPTER IX – THIRTEEN POTTERS AND THE POTS THEY MADE

Fig. 222. **Tureen and cover,** *white salt-glazed stoneware with gadrooned decoration and three mask feet. The feet on the tureen correspond to those excavated at the Humphrey Palmer factory, Town Road, Hanley (see fig. 223). Staffordshire, Humphrey Palmer's Church Works. c.1750-65. 8½in. (21.59cm) high. (Catzen collection)*

Fig. 223. **Two waster feet,** *white salt-glazed stoneware moulded with face masks and paw feet. These feet are distinctive and are found on teawares and tureens manufactured by Humphrey Palmer. Excavated at the Town Road factory site. c.1750-1765. 2½in. (6.35cm) maximum. (Potteries Museum and Art Gallery, Stoke-on-Trent, K3 19 1985)*

221

Chapter IX – Thirteen Potters and the Pots they made

*Fig. 224. **Three creamer body fragments,** white salt-glazed stoneware in the form of a pecten shell excavated from the Town Road site of Humphrey Palmer's factory. c.1750-65. 3in. (7.62cm) maximum. (Potteries Museum and Art Gallery, Stoke-on-Trent, K3 274 1985. (211)*

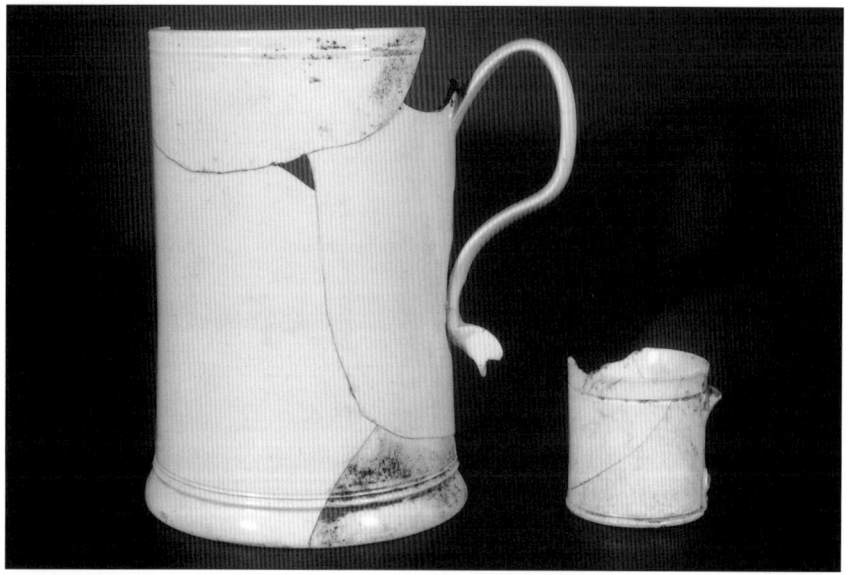

*Fig. 225. **Two partially reconstructed mugs,** white salt-glazed stoneware excavated at Town Road. Staffordshire, Humphrey Palmer, c.1750-70. 6¼; 2in. (17.15; 5.08cm) high. (Potteries Museum and Art Gallery, Stoke-on-Trent, K3 178, 180 1985)*

*Fig. 226. **Two partially reconstructed mugs,** white salt-glazed stoneware with reeded strap handles and pinch terminals. Excavated at the Town Road Palmer factory site, c.1750-1770. 3¾in. (9.53cm) high. (Potteries Museum and Art Gallery, Stoke-on-Trent, K3 182 1985)*

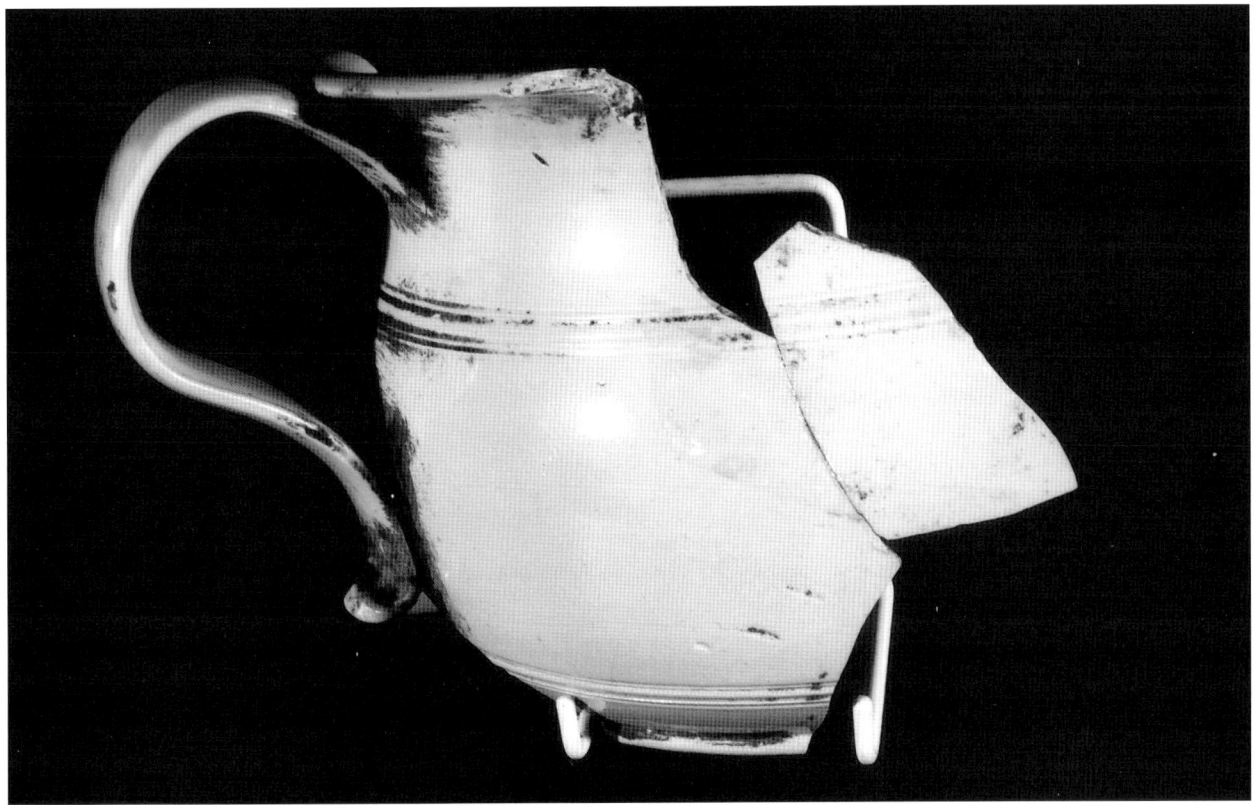

*Fig. 227. **Partially reconstructed chamber pot,** white salt-glazed stoneware with turned bands and ear-shaped handle. Excavated at the Palmer site, Hanley, c.1750-70. 5½in. (13.97cm) high. (Potteries Museum and Art Gallery, Stoke-on-Trent, K3 156.1985)*

*Fig. 228. **Group of teabowls,** white salt-glazed stoneware excavated from the Palmer site. c.1750-70. 1¾in. (4.45cm) maximum. (Potteries Museum and Art Gallery, Stoke-on-Trent, K3 233, 176 1985)*

Fig. 229. **Teabowl partially reconstructed,** translucent white salt-glazed stoneware which may have been overfired or was an experiment in porcelain production. James Neale, the successor factory to Humphrey Palmer, produced a bone china porcelain. The possibility that Palmer was also experimenting with the porcelain body seems likely. Excavated at the Palmer site, Hanley. c.1750-70. 1½ x 3in. (3.81 x 7.62cm). (Potteries Museum and Art Gallery, Stoke-on-Trent, K3 176 1985)

Fig. 230. **Porringer handle,** white salt-glazed stoneware moulded in the form of a flower. Excavated at the Palmer site, Hanley. c.1750-70. 2⅝in. (6.67cm). (Potteries Museum and Art Gallery, Stoke-on-Trent, K3 581 1985)

Fig, 231. **Three candlestick nozzles,** white salt-glazed stoneware excavated at the Palmer site, Hanley. c.1760-70. 4¼in. (10.8cm) maximum. (Potteries Museum and Art Gallery, Stoke-on-Trent, K3 576, 578 1985)

already building his 'Church Works' in mid-1750, and he continued on this site until 1778.⁷⁷

Palmer's wife Ann died and was buried at Hanley Church, allegedly on 13 May 1752, though in fact Palmer married again on 28 October 1751.⁷⁸ The Adams family historian wrote correctly that Palmer acquired the Church Works site from Ann Adams' family,⁷⁹ but the Manor Court records show much more detail about this transaction than he was aware of, and also about Palmer's later property transactions, outside the scope of this study.

An archaeological salvage excavation on the site of Palmer's works at Town Road, Hanley, revealed:

> a wide range of lead-glazed earthenware, dry-bodied stonewares and salt-glazed stonewares. The latter include white salt-glazed flat and hollow wares, scratch-blue decorated wares [Colour Plates 180-185], and the drab wares, decorated with white applied reliefs

which were 'associated with a single factory' and likely to have been produced between 1755-1760.⁸⁰ As Palmer was the first potter on the site, and building there in 1750, these excavated shards seem most likely to have been his products (Figs. 203-6; Colour Plate 186).

Moulded floral relief borders on plates (Fig. 209) were found as well as some more common 'mosaic-type' or basket, diaper and scroll borders (Fig. 207), pierced basket stands and plates with octagonal borders (Fig. 208). Many sprig relief decorated teawares were excavated (Figs. 210, 214-17, 221, 221a) as well as a variety of shapes, such as butter tubs with recumbent cow finials and a number of bird finials (Fig. 210-12, 220) for teawares. Distinctive feet with faces for teaware and tureens were excavated (Fig. 223). A tureen in a private collection has the same distinctive face mask foot (Fig. 222). Another tureen at Moffatt-Ladd House in Portsmouth, New Hampshire (Colour Plate 131) has the same feet. Palmer was also producing pecten shell teawares

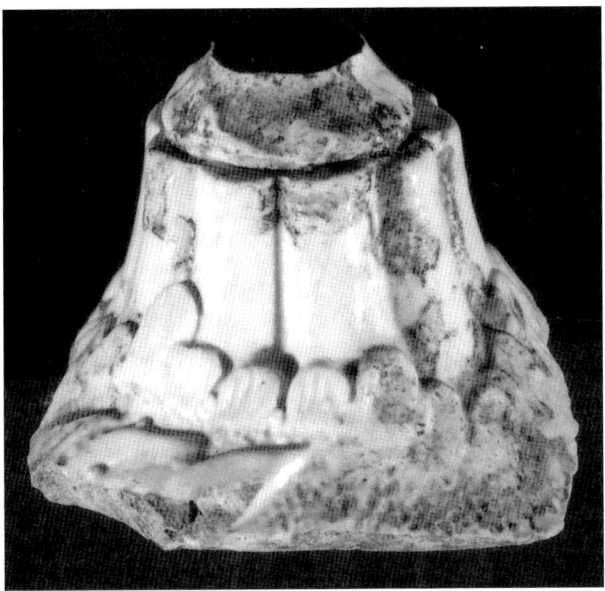

*Fig. 232. **Candlestick base**, white salt-glazed stoneware with a floral moulded base. Excavated at the Palmer site, Hanley. c.1760-70. 2in. (5.08cm) high. (Potteries Museum and Art Gallery, Stoke-on-Trent, K3 579 1985)*

*Fig. 233. **Patch or teapot stand fragment**, white salt-glazed stoneware with pierced foot and turned flange. Excavated at the Palmer site, Hanley. c.1750-70. 2¾in. (6.99cm) diameter. (Potteries Museum and Art Gallery, Stoke-on-Trent, K3 214 1985)*

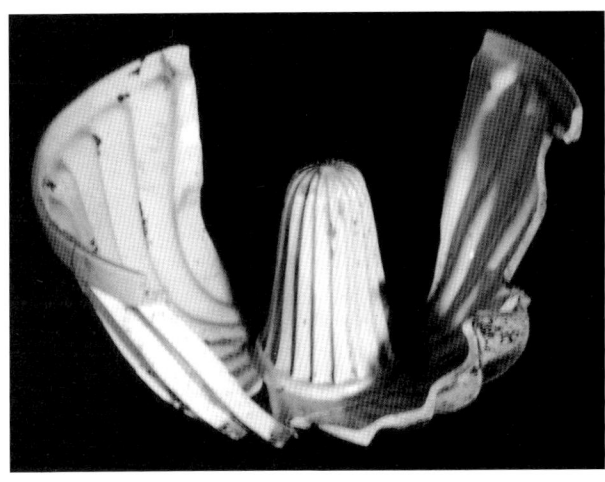

*Fig. 234. **Partially reconstructed jelly mould**, white salt-glazed stoneware slip-cast in vertical ribs. Excavated at the Palmer site, Hanley. c.1760-70. 6½in. (16.51cm) diameter. 3¼in. (8.26cm) high. (Potteries Museum and Art Gallery, Stoke-on-Trent, K3 216 1985)*

CHAPTER IX – THIRTEEN POTTERS AND THE POTS THEY MADE

Colour Plate 180. **Partially reconstructed wasters of a mug and a bowl,** *white salt-glazed stoneware with scratch-blue decoration, the mug with a large flower and the bowl with a cross-hatched geometric pattern. Staffordshire, Humphrey Palmer, Town Road, c.1750-70. Mug 3¾in. (9.53cm) high; bowl 6½in. (16.51cm) diameter. (Potteries Museum and Art Gallery, Stoke-on-Trent, K3 226 1988; K3 271 1985)*

Colour Plate 181. **Portions of two saucers,** *white salt-glazed stoneware wasters from the Humphrey Palmer site. The scratch-blue decoration utilised by Palmer employed a variety of designs. c.1750-70. 3¼; 3⅞in. (8.26; 9.84cm) diameter. (Potteries Museum and Art Gallery, Stoke-on-Trent, K3 269 1985; K3 263 1985)*

Colour Plate 182. **Teabowl and saucer waster fragments,** *white salt-glazed stoneware with unusual scratch-blue filament decoration. Humphrey Palmer, c.1750-70. teabowl 1½in. (3.81cm) high; saucer 4¼in. (10.8cm) diameter. (Potteries Museum and Art Gallery, Stoke-on-Trent, K3 249.1985)*

*Colour Plate 183. **Teabowl and saucer fragments,** white salt-glazed stoneware with unusual scratch-blue decoration. Excavated at the Humphrey Palmer site. c.1750-70. Saucer 3½in. (8.89cm) diameter. (Potteries Museum and Art Gallery, Stoke-on-Trent, K3 270, 250 1985)*

*Colour Plate 184. **Partially reconstructed bowl fragment,** white salt-glazed stoneware with scratch-blue stylised floral decoration. Excavated at the Humphrey Palmer site, c.1750-70. 4¼in. (10.8cm) high. (Potteries Museum and Art Gallery, Stoke-on-Trent, K3 1191 1985)*

*Colour Plate 185. **Two saucer wasters,** white salt-glazed stoneware with scratch-blue floral decoration. Excavated at Humphrey Palmer's Town Road site, these shards are c.1750-70. 4⅜in. (11.11cm) maximum. (Potteries Museum and Art Gallery, Stoke-on-Trent, K3 265/266 1985)*

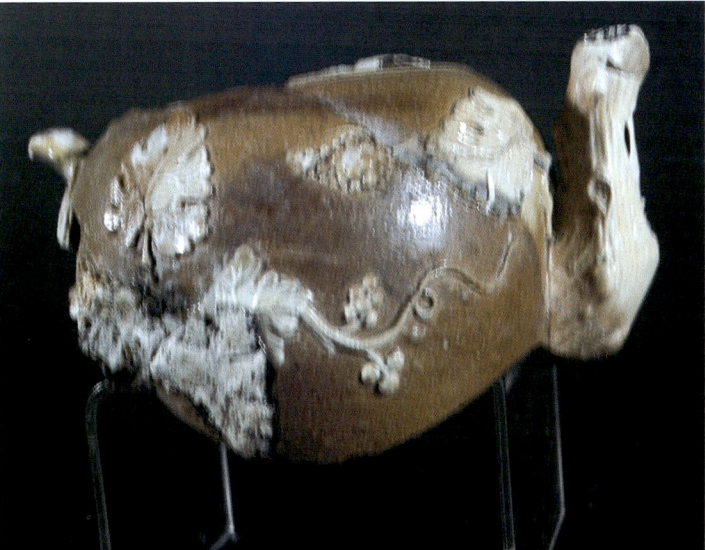

*Colour Plate 186. **Teapot waster,** over fired drab-coloured salt-glazed stoneware with white applied moulded relief grape leaf and vine tendrils, white spout and the remains of a white handle. Excavated at the Town Road site of Humphrey Palmer's factory, c.1750-60. Handle to spout 5in. (12.7cm). (Potteries Museum and Art Gallery, Stoke-on-Trent, K3 831 1985)*

*Colour Plate 187. **Two teapot fragments,** white salt-glazed stoneware with blue sprig relief decoration of the 'Girl in the tree' pattern. Excavated from the Humphrey Palmer site in Hanley. c.1750-65. 2⅝in. (6.67cm) maximum height. (Potteries Museum and Art Gallery, Stoke-on-Trent, K3 531 1985)*

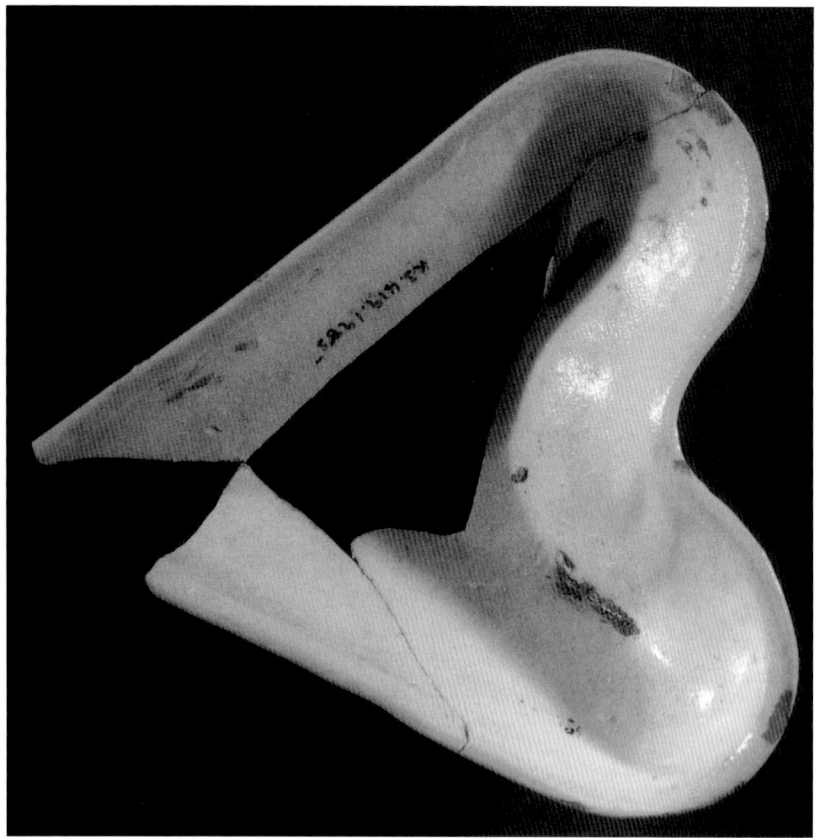

*Fig. 235. **Partially reconstructed dish,** white salt-glazed stoneware in the shape of a heart. Excavated at the Palmer site, Hanley. c.1760-70. 4in. (10.16cm) across. (Potteries Museum and Art Gallery, Stoke-on-Trent, K3 419 1985)*

*Fig. 236. **Dish,** white salt-glazed stoneware in the shape of a heart, enamel painted with playing cards and 'A TOKEN of RESPECT 1772'. Staffordshire, c.1760-70. 3⅞in. (9.84cm) long. (British Museum, 1919.5-3, 83)*

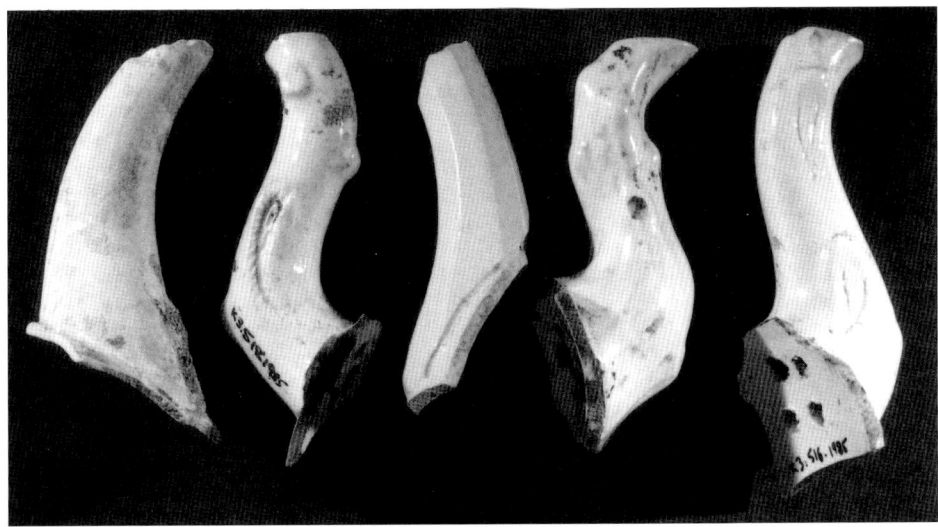

*Fig. 237. **Five teapot spouts**, white salt-glazed stoneware moulded. Left to right: plain, crabstock, carved, crabstock and modified crabstock. Excavated at the Palmer site, Hanley. c.1750-65. 3¼in. (8.26cm) maximum. (Potteries Museum and Art Gallery, Stoke-on-Trent, K3 516, 518, 522 1985)*

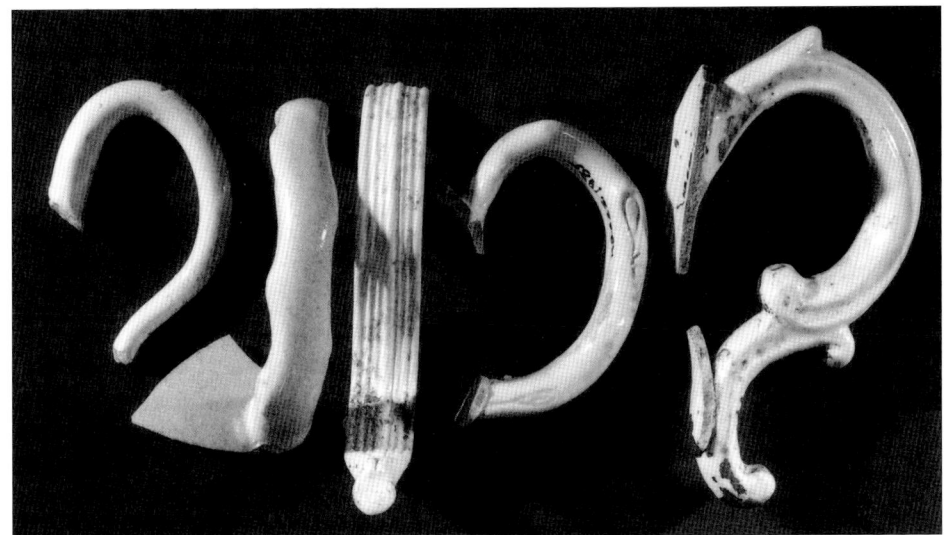

*Fig. 238. **Five teaware handles**, white salt-glazed stoneware moulded in shapes used by Humphrey Palmer on teapots and milk jugs. Excavated at the Palmer factory site, Town Road, c.1750-65. 3½in. (8.89cm) maximum. (Potteries Museum and Art Gallery, Stoke-on-Trent, K3 623, 622, 624, 626 1985)*

(Fig. 224). There was either an attempt at porcelain, or salt-glaze which was overfired, which produced translucent teabowls (Fig. 229).

Other forms include porringers (Fig. 230), candlesticks (Figs. 231-2), patch/teapot stands (Fig. 233) and heart-shaped pettys or moulds (Figs. 235-6). A large fluted bundt-type mould was recovered and partially reconstructed (Fig. 234).

Teaware spouts and handles exhibited a wide variety of shapes, from crabstock to rolled, reeded and silver shaped (Figs. 225-26). The excavation included wasters among all the shards and saggars (Fig. 202) and other kiln furniture was found in abundance. Although most wares were sprig-relief decorated or moulded with decoration, some teabowls, mugs and other ware were left undecorated (Figs. 225-29). Few enamel decorated shards seem to have been found. That Palmer was gilding his wares is indicated by a letter received from Dublin dealer George Luffingham complaining about the cost of Wedgwood's gilded wares: 'I have from Palmer in every respect preferable [gilded] work'.[81] Indeed, Palmer was producing gilded, enamelled and printed ware in creamware and enamel painting and probably gilding white salt-glazed stoneware.

There is documentary evidence that Humphrey Palmer *bought* white salt-glazed stoneware. The Sales-account book of *Thomas and John Wedgwood* shows that they sold salt-glazed ware *to* Palmer from 1759.[82] John Baddeley also sold unspecified ware worth £42 to Humphrey Palmer in 1766, paid for with 63,000 bricks and 2,900 oven bricks.[83]

The fact that Humphrey Palmer bought in white salt-glazed ware does not rule out his production of it, as he may have been supplementing his own capacity to meet particular orders. Palmer became a large-scale producer of cream-coloured and other wares and by 1759 may have been buying in salt-glazed ware to meet his customers' requirements, as did Josiah Wedgwood.

ROTHERHAM: JOHN PLATT AND SAMUEL WALKER junior
Rotherham Old Pottery, Rotherham, Yorkshire, 1766–1770

There is ample evidence of the production of white salt-glazed stoneware at Rotherham Old Pottery. 'John Platt's Journal' is a major source, but it should be borne in mind that the original journals were probably copied by him 'when he was quite an old man' and in turn that version was copied by a descendant, Mary Didham.[84]

Platt noted in his 'journal' that on 18 July 1766 he was 'Laying ye foundation for a new Case or Hovel for a White flint Work and finish it 21st August'.[85] Arthur Young visited Rotherham in 1768 and noted that 'they have a pottery, in which is made the white, cream-coloured (*Staffordshire*) and tortoiseshell earthenware'.[86]

The (undated) trade card of 'Platt & Walker At the Earthen Ware Manufactory at Rotherham in Yorkshire' tells us that they *'Make & Sell White Stone Ware, Black, Tortoise Shell, Agate, Cream Colour, &c. also Gilt & Enamel Ware'*.[87] Although a great deal of information about the Rotherham Old Pottery has survived, there is no evidence of salt-glaze manufacture after 1770.

On 11 June 1767 Platt noted 'Building a muffle or kiln for ye painted or enamel ware pottery.'[88] This would be used for firing the decoration of any of the types of ware produced and, remarkably, an enamelled white salt-glazed stoneware jug survived in family possession until 1970, inscribed 'John Platt/1767'[89] (Colour Plate 188), possibly commemorating the new facility.

An enamelled white salt-glazed punchbowl on pedestal at Colonial Williamsburg, inscribed 'I, C, / 1767',[90] has very similar numerals and might also be Platt and Walker's manufacture. John Platt recorded in his journal, between 21 June and 18 July 1766, that 'Jos Wolfe and J^{no} Cousins came here to ye Potworks'. Five years later, in 1771, he noted '23rd May. Discharged and parted with Jos. Cousins, my bookkeeper at ye Pottery'. John 'Cuzzen', baptised 10 June 1730, and Joseph 'Cousin', baptised 20 June 1735, both at Rotherham, were brothers, sons of Joseph Cuzzen/Cousin, a currier. It is conceivable that the JC/1767 (Colour Plates 189, 189a) punchbowl bears the initials of one of these brothers, most likely those of John Cousins, employed by Platt from July 1766.[91]

An enamelled salt-glaze jug in a private collection, of similar size and shape to the Platt jug, inscribed 'John / Kirkham / 1768', bears very similar lettering and numerals.[92] No connection between John Kirkham and the Rotherham Old Pottery has been found, but it is likely that the jug was made and decorated there, in the ordinary course of trade.

John Platt (1727/8-1810) was a mason-architect in South Yorkshire, whose father had come to the area c.1730 to help in the building of St. Paul's Church, Sheffield.[93] In July 1765 John Platt, William Fenney and 'Wood' agreed to start a potworks at Rotherham.[94] Fenney was the son of William Fenney senior, a glassmaker, who had come from Bolsterstone to Catcliffe, near Rotherham in 1740 to start a glassworks there.[95] Fenney left Platt in 1766 or 1767 and was paid £120 for his half-share. He was later in partnership at the *Swinton Pottery*.[96] Nothing more is known of Wood.

In December 1766 Platt took a new partner for twenty-one years, Samuel Walker junior (1742-1792),[97] a member of the Walker family who were iron and steel makers locally, with assets exceeding £31,000 in that year.[98] At the end of 1770, Platt and Walker sought an extra 'partner, on the extension of their works',[99] apparently without success. The Platt and Walker partnership lasted until 15 June 1772,

*Colour Plate 188. **Jug**, white salt-glazed stoneware with enamel decoration, inscribed for John Platt in 1767. On 11 June 1767 Platt noted that he was building a 'muffle or kiln for ye painted or enamel ware pottery' (Kiddell, ECC Transactions, Vol. 5, Part 3, 1962, 173). Yorkshire, Rotherham, John Platt, 1767. 7in. (17.78cm) high. (Victoria and Albert Museum, C67-1971)*

*Colour Plate 189. **Footed bowl,** white salt-glazed stoneware enamel decorated in similar style to the jug in Colour Plate 188 with the initials of I.C. and 1767, possibly the pottery bookkeeper of Platt and Walker, John Cousins, who worked for the pottery in 1766. Probably Rotherham (Yorkshire), John Platt, 1767. 8½in. (21.59cm) diameter. (Colonial Williamsburg Foundation, 1963-195, CG17)*

*Colour Plate 189a. **Detail of bowl** in Colour Plate 189.*

when Samuel Walker *and Son* bought out Platt for £316. Platt noted in his journal that he sold out to his great loss of money and time, though he had received £70 (presumably per annum) for himself and clerk. Capital was great already and more was needed, as they had great overseas debts not likely to be paid.[100] The partnership dissolution of the same day was of course between John Platt and Samuel Walker *the Younger*.[101]

The Walkers' intention in 1772 was to let or sell the works, which did not happen, and they owned the works until 1794.[102] Walker senior built more buildings between 1773 and 1776[103] and took William Hawley as a partner in 1776.[104] Hawley had been a master potter at Rawmarsh, nearby, since at least 1769, when he wrote to Josiah Wedgwood, asking him to find two turners as 'I think of making a little Black and Tortoise Shell Ware'.[105] Probably Walker recruited Hawley as a practical potter.

The works was at Domine Well, Rotherham, bounded by the River Don on the west.[106] Platt laid out several considerable sums in building, including laying foundations for a new case or hovel for a white flint works in July-August 1766. Eleven months later Platt built the enamel kiln and there were furnaces, ovens, warehouses, drying houses and other buildings by 1772. Heavy rain in

1767 damaged hovels and kilns (both in the plural),[107] and a map of 1774 showed that there were indeed two kilns then.[108] Two ovens would have been needed from the start, one for salt-glazing and one for lead-glazed ware.

When Samuel Walker the elder took over the works in 1772 he acquired finished and unfinished earthenware, clay wrought and unwrought, coals and flint.[109] He also took over a flint mill built on Dun Close,[110] presumably previously owned by Platt and Walker.

It is not known what time or knowledge Fenney, Wood or Walker gave to the business, but Platt himself was active, noting in his journal his times at the potworks and his travels about the Midlands, combining pottery sales and architectural work: in Lincolnshire in 1768, Yorkshire in 1768 and 1769, Staffordshire in 1769 and 1770, and in 1771 'This year much engaged in Pottery and journeys upon that business'.[111] 'John Platt' was the first signatory to the salt-glaze potters' price agreement, made 14 February 1770 (Appendix 3),[112] although his journal does not record his whereabouts on that day.

The settlement in 1772 showed that Platt was paid £70 per annum for himself and clerk. Besides Cousins and Wolfe in 1766, Platt brought in Samuel Cartledge from Burslem in 1768. At the handover in June 1772, thirteen indentured workers were transferred, including seven apprentices.[113] First on the list was Joseph Wolfe, who had been employed since 1766 and was hired for seven years in 1767, perhaps as foreman or bailiff. Arthur Young had noted in 1768 that over twenty men and forty boys were employed, the men at 9s. per week, but mostly on piece work for which they received up to 15s., and boys nine or ten years old at 2s. and 2s.6d. per week.[114]

Platt and Walker made and sold all the contemporary non-porcelain wares: 'White Stone Ware, Black, Tortoise Shell, Agate, Cream Colour, &c. also Gilt & Enamel Ware' to quote their trade card again. Like many other potters, Platt also 'bought in' ware for his customers: in 1767 he purchased two crates for £5.19s.0d. from *John Baddeley* of Shelton, paid for by 'Palmer',[115] no doubt *Humphrey Palmer*, who must have owed money to Platt.

SWANSEA: WILLIAM COLES
Cambrian Pottery, Swansea, Wales, 1767-1778

Pottery was made at Swansea from 1767 and several pieces of white salt-glazed stoneware with 'Swansea' inscriptions are known, though no wasters have been reported.

The 19 September 1764 lease of the pottery site at Swansea allowed William Coles of Cadoxton to pull down the old Copper Works in Swansea for 'carrying on a Stone Ware or Earthen Ware manufactory', and the site was referred to as 'the new Pot-house' on 3 November 1767. William Dillwyn noted in his diary for 15 July 1777 that he saw 'Stoneware and Queen's ware' being made at Swansea.[116] The site of the pottery was between High Street railway station and the River Tawe.

Four white salt-glaze stoneware items in public collections bear 'Swansea' inscriptions: a flask inscribed 'Morgan John/Swansea/March ye 28th/1768'; a jug incised 'This Jug Belongs/To the Club at the/Royel [*sic*] Oake at/The Wite [*sic*] Rock/May 5 1771'; a bowl (Colour Plates 190, 190a, Fig. 25)[117] inscribed:

Long May we live hapy[sic] may we be
Blest with Content and from all danger free
Willm Fillipes His Bowl
March 12th Swansea 1778

On the reverse:

When this you See Remember Me
And think when im Gone–
You may Look out and Seek a bout
And not find Such a one–
March 12th 1778 Swansea

and, most importantly, a tea canister inscribed 'ME/Swansea/potwork/1775'.[118]

Three major writers on Swansea pottery have considered the possibility of white salt-glazed stoneware having been made there. E.M. Nance, writing before 1942, thought that the 1768 flask and 1771 jug had a 'thin lead-glaze' and concluded that salt-glazed ware was not made at Swansea.[119] In 1967, W.J. Grant-Davidson also discussed the production of salt-glazed ware at Swansea. He thought that the 1768 flask had 'a colourless lead glaze' over the salt-glazed body and that the 1771 jug had a 'greenish-yellow lead glaze over the salt-glaze'. However, Grant-Davidson considered that the 1775 tea canister (not known to Nance) was 'undoubtedly saltglazed', and appeared to settle the matter 'in favour of the manufacture of saltglaze'.[120] With the advantage of more recent research, Jonathan Gray wrote in 2003 that 'it is clear that saltglaze was made during the early years of the factory'.[121]

The authors' opinion, based on the foregoing information, and without the opportunity to handle the pieces, is that white salt-glazed stoneware was made at Swansea from 1767 to at least 1778.

AARON WEDGWOOD, THOMAS WEDGWOOD III AND JOHN WEDGWOOD
Burslem, fl.1732-1743
THOMAS WEDGWOOD III AND JOHN WEDGWOOD
Big House Works, Burslem, 1743-1776

The survival of Thomas and John Wedgwood's sales, wages, crate and rent books, documents and white salt-glazed ware in the hands of their descendants has provided a rich source of information about Thomas and John Wedgwood, extensively discussed by A.R. Mountford, both in his degree thesis and in his classic book, *The Illustrated Guide to Staffordshire Salt-glazed Stoneware*.[122] We shall only summarise their activities here.

Pitt gave the earliest account of them,[123] that Thomas and John Wedgwood left their father, Aaron Wedgwood, a lead-ore glaze potter, about 1740 and commenced to make white salt-glazed stoneware. After initial difficulties with salt-polluted water,[124] they became very successful, and built a new large works, followed by a new house, the 'Big House', in 1750, retiring about 1763.[125] Shaw added that they made Egyptian Black before 1740, that one was an excellent thrower and the other a most skilful fireman, that they built three and later two more ovens, and made a variety of shapes of white salt-glazed ware.[126]

Documented facts are that Thomas Wedgwood III (1703-1776) and John Wedgwood (1705-1780) were the sons of Aaron Wedgwood (1666-1743), himself a master potter.[127] Aaron Wedgwood died on 21 April 1743 and his wife died the following day.[128] Subject to small legacies, he left his houses, potworks, and all his effects to his wife Mary for life and then to his sons Thomas and John Wedgwood for ever,[129] so that the brothers inherited their father's property in April 1743.

As Aaron Wedgwood was aged seventy-seven at his death, it is likely that Thomas III, aged forty, and John, aged thirty-eight, neither of them married, had been running his potworks for some years. A white salt-glazed icon depicting the Crucifixion, dated 1732 (Fig. 12), was in the hands of descendants of these Wedgwoods until 1965, when it was acquired by the Potteries Museum and Art Gallery.[130] Relying upon the date and provenance, this seems proof that Aaron, Thomas and John Wedgwood were making white salt-glazed stoneware in 1732. *William Parrott* was apprenticed to John Wedgwood of Burslem, potter, from 1736 to 1743.[131] No other John Wedgwood has been found to be a master potter in Burslem at that period, so it seems probable that it was John Wedgwood (1705-1780) to whom Parrott was apprenticed in 1736.

Thomas and John Wedgwood immediately commenced to make salt-glazed ware at their new works. A small side-handled jug (Fig. 63) amongst the salt-glazed ware handed down in the Wedgwood-Wood family has a faded ink inscription on the underside: 'The Groyel [*sic*, or Troyel] of ye first ... oven ... Nov. 24 1743'.[132] The word 'troyal' is used in a 1775 Wedgwood manuscript in a context which implies 'trial'[133] and it seems likely that this small jug is a trial from Thomas and John Wedgwood's first salt-glaze oven on their new site.

John seems to have been the dominant partner, but an account from Josiah Wedgwood to them is clearly headed 'T. & J. Wedgwood', and three statements of account in 1766, 1767 and 1769 are headed 'Thomas and John Wedgwood', clear confirmation of a partnership, the older brother Thomas always standing first.[134] Their surviving sales account book[135] starts with crates sent to customers from 1755 onward, but there is a reference to 1745 transactions on page 22 and to an 'Old Book' on pages 30 and 34, showing that this was not the first sales ledger.

Thomas and John Wedgwood's ledgers list the many shapes of salt-glazed and other ware made by them and also purchased from other potters, sold to their many customers in England, Dublin and Glasgow, and their finished and unfired ware supplied to other potters.[136] Rarities are 'blue' items, all references except one linked to *Aaron Wedgwood* as supplier. The exception is 'Gild d blue' supplied to John Griffith of Backs, Bristol, on 12 May 1759,[137] which could of course also have been bought in from Aaron Wedgwood.

Two of their price lists are included in Appendix 3.

In 1763 John Wedgwood sold to Josiah Wedgwood 'table spoons with holes, salt spoons, flower harts [*sic*, hearts], flower pickle boats, flower tryangulars [*sic*], Star Cups, Shells, Melons, and Star petty [pans]'.[138] John Wedgwood is again the sole name on an invoice of 1764 when he was providing Josiah Wedgwood with '3 dozen Artichoke cups and 3 dozen Sm[all]. Custard Cups'.[139]

In 1768 forty-two dozen plain hearts and' Starr Cups' were supplied by John Wedgwood to Josiah, the invoice bearing a personal salutation to Josiah's wife 'Love to Cousin Sally'.[140] In 1769 'double and treble Starr' [pettys] were sold to Josiah Wedgwood by John.[141] In March 1770 orders were filled for '4 dozen Fishes with Pedestal',[142] presumably footed fish moulds. Conversely, Thomas and John Wedgwood bought ware from Josiah Wedgwood between 1764 and 1766,[143] including melon tureens, square teapots, fine red teapots, printed teapots, 'King' and 'Ionic' candlesticks and gilt fruits, presumably for their customers.

Shaw wrote that 'These Brothers continued their manufactures until 1763; when they retired'.[144] The ledgers show that Shaw was wrong in detail, but, as so often happens, there may be some explanation of his statement in general. Thomas and John Wedgwood's single surviving hiring book, with information from 1758 to 1772, shows that from a maximum of thirteen employees in 1761 the numbers fell to five in 1769, including 'Left off work Nov: 11 1767 ... Began again Nov: 11 1768 & left off Nov: 11 1769'.[145] This may be construed as Wedgwoods closing down for two periods in the late 1760s, some justification for Shaw's statement. An analysis of Wedgwoods' sales account book[146] shows that they continued sales at their normal level in these two periods, but this may have been disposal of excessive stocks rather than sales of current production.

The ledgers also show the real end of Thomas and John Wedgwood's business. Between 1770 and his death in 1773, 'Cousin' *Thomas Wedgwood IV of Overhouse*, a fellow salt-glaze potter, fired eighty saggars for them, containing chamber pots, spoons, toys, gallypots, and four containing models; and they bought 40lb. of 'Clay prepared for the Wheele' from him.[147] Between October 1770 and May 1775 Thomas and John Wedgwood's ledger shows that they sold 'unfired ware' to Josiah and Thomas Wedgwood, which could be biscuit-fired, glazed and fired again to become cream-coloured ware.[148] Their invoices for these transactions, which survive in the Wedgwood Accumulation, give more details: they are for pudding cups (with and without pipes), spoons, melons, pyramids, salt moulds and shells.[149]

Their final sales were *unfired* ware to local potters, between January 1774 and December 1775, and three consignments of gallypots (ointment pots) to William Hewson at the corner of Southampton Street, Strand, London, two in 1775 and the last sale of all on 22 April 1776. These gally pots were probably those for which, in 1774 and 1775, *Josiah Wood* supplied Wedgwoods with clay to make gally pots and also fired saggars of gally pots for them.[150] It seems likely that Wedgwoods had ceased to fire ware by the end of 1773. William Hewson had been a long-standing

Chapter IX – Thirteen Potters and the Pots They Made

Colour Plate 190. **Bowl,** *white salt-glazed stoneware with scratch-blue decoration and a verse on either side:*

Long may we live hapy may we be
Blest with Content and from all danger free
Willm Fillipes His Bowl
March 12th Swansea 1778

Swansea, William Coles, 1778. Diameter 9in. (22.86cm). (Photograph courtesy of Jonathan Horne)

Colour Plate 190a. **Bowl** *(reverse side) inscribed:*

When this you See Remember Me
And think when im gone–
You may Look out and Seek about
And not find such a one–
March 12th 1778 Swansea

Swansea, William Coles, 1778. Diameter 9in. (22.86cm). (Photograph courtesy of Jonathan Horne)

Colour Plate 191. **Two shards** *of drab salt-glazed stoneware with white sprig relief decoration or berries and leaves. The interior of both has a white slip, seen often on drab stoneware milk jugs. Excavated at Thomas Whieldon's Fenton Vivian factory, c.1750-60.* 2in. (5.08cm) maximum. *(Potteries Museum and Art Gallery, Stoke-on-Trent)*

Colour Plate 192. **Two mugs,** *white engobe-slipped mugs with ferruginous dip; left the mug heavily roulette decorated with upper three-quarters iron dipped;* 6⅜in. (16.19cm) *high; right, the rim iron-dipped only,* 4in. (10.16cm) *high. Excavated at Whieldon's Fenton Vivian site, c.1750. (Potteries Museum and Art Gallery, Stoke-on-Trent, 839, K149.1978)*

*Fig. 239. **Partially reconstructed bowl** of white salt-glazed stoneware with turned band. Excavated at Thomas Whieldon's Fenton Vivian factory. c.1760. 4in. (10.16cm) high. (Potteries Museum and Art Gallery, Stoke-on-Trent, 740)*

customer from 1755 onward, sales to him diminishing year by year as presumably salt-glazed ware was replaced by cream-coloured. From 1771 to 1776, his deliveries were mostly of gallypots.[151] In 1770 there were invoices to Josiah Wedgwood for '51 pyramids'[152] and more pyramids and salt-moulds in 1775[153] from John Wedgwood, noted in his ledger as 'unfired ware'.[154]

John Wedgwood took *John Wood* as a new partner on 6 March 1776, with the intention that some rent should be paid to Thomas Wedgwood for the workhouses.[155] However, Thomas Wedgwood III died on 8 April 1776,[156] and John Wedgwood inherited all Thomas's property.[157] It seems likely that the 1776 partnership made earthenware rather than stoneware (see *John Wood*). John Wedgwood died on 20 July 1780, ending the partnership, and was succeeded as a potter by his son Thomas,[158] who was making cream-coloured ware etc. on his own account by 1784.[159]

In 1965 the Potteries Museum and Art Gallery acquired eighty-eight pieces of salt-glazed stoneware from the descendants of John Wood, great-nephew of Thomas and John Wedgwood, and himself the partner of John Wedgwood from 1776.[160] The same descendants also handed over account books and other documents relating to Thomas and John Wedgwood and it seems likely that both salt-glazed ware and papers were taken by John Wood to Brownhills when his partnership with John Wedgwood was ended by the latter's death in 1780. The pottery received in 1965 included jelly moulds (two dated 1746), sweetmeat dishes, spoons, ointment pots, boxes, a crucifix dated 1732 (Fig. 12), bowls, a teabowl and saucer, a saucer, jugs, a teapot, a caudle cup and cover, a sugar caster, a candle holder, drabware jugs, enamelled mugs, two teapot moulds and two tea canister moulds, many of them illustrated by Arnold Mountford.[161]

Thomas and John Wedgwood had two potworks. They inherited Aaron Wedgwood's 'earthenware' potworks on the west of Wedgwood Street,[162] a site now occupied by the 'Ceramica' extension of Burslem Old Town Hall and the westward widening of Wedgwood Street. Their own 'salt-glaze' works, known as the 'Big House' or 'Lower House' works, was on the east of Wedgwood Street, a site identified today by the former Post Office and surrounding buildings, north of the surviving 'Big House'.

THOMAS WHIELDON
Fenton Vivian, fl. 1750
THOMAS WHIELDON AND JOSIAH WEDGWOOD
Fenton Vivian, 1757

A comprehensive history of Thomas Whieldon was given recently by Pat Halfpenny,[163] and this account is limited to information relevant to his production of white salt-glazed stoneware.

Thomas Whieldon's parents came from Kingsley, North Staffordshire, to Stoke-on-Trent between 1705[164] and 1719, when he was baptised at Stoke.[165] He was a potter (but not necessarily a master potter) when he married Ann Shaw at Barlaston in 1744.[166] By 1747 Thomas Whieldon was tenant of a potworks at Fenton *Vivian*, and he bought this works and Fenton Hall in 1748,[167] and a nearby flint mill in 1749.[168] Whieldon is said to have continued as a potter until about 1780,[169] although recovered shards from his potworks site are regarded as 1740-70 only.[170] The site is now (2004) occupied by Tile Clearing House, 104-06 City Road, Fenton.

Thomas Whieldon owned another potworks at Fenton *Low* by 1750, tenanted by *William Meir* and then by *Edward and William Warburton*.[171] Shards found on this site in the 1920s were then ascribed to Whieldon,[172] but are now regarded as being made by Warburtons.[173]

Thomas Whieldon's memorandum book survives, and there are references to 'white' ware which probably means

CHAPTER IX – THIRTEEN POTTERS AND THE POTS THEY MADE

*Fig. 240. **Four moulded pieces** white salt-glazed stoneware, left to right: a ribbed handle, a pierced porringer handle, a rim with basketweave moulding and a face mask part foot. Excavated at Thomas Whieldon's Fenton Vivian factory. c.1750-70. 1¾in. (4.45cm) maximum. (Potteries Museum and Art Gallery, Stoke-on-Trent, 790, 823 815)*

white salt-glazed stoneware. On 27 January 1749/50, he hired John Austin for placing white (ware), and he noted a sale of '6½ p¹ mugs, white' to Mrs. Davison at an unreadable date. On 24 August 1752 he hired 'little Bet Blour to learn to flower', assumed to mean incising flowers on white salt-glazed ware, coloured in with cobalt blue.[174]

White salt-glazed stoneware shards were found at his Fenton Vivian site, together with salt-glaze oven waste, and other types of ware.[175] The range of wares found in the Fenton Vivian deposit was very impressive, but not unexpected for a Whieldon site. It included plain white (Fig. 239), dipped white (Colour Plates 192-3), Littler-Wedgwood blue (Colour Plate 194), scratch-blue (Colour Plate 195), enamelled (Colour Plates 196-7), and drab wares (Colour Plate 191). In plain white the shapes included among the usual wares moulded pieces (Fig. 240) and a very distinctive handle from a large jug or camel teapot (Fig. 241). The shapes in the dipped wares were mugs, both plain and rouletted with iron washed rims and upper portions (Colour Plate 192), and bowls or chamber pots (Colour Plate 193). The enamel-painted shards included polychrome (Colour Plate 196) and some very unusual shards of enamel blue only, very much in the Chinese *métier* (Colour Plate 197).

A biscuit creamware tile shard and a matching glazed one, found in the same excavation,[176] is of the 'Heron and Spewing Duck Fountain' design, also found on a white salt-glazed tile reliably said to have been taken from Whieldon's house.[177] This biscuit shard, albeit in creamware, and the provenance of the surviving salt-glazed example, seems adequate confirmation that Whieldon also made white salt-glazed tiles. (See Appendix 4 and Fig. 114.)

Thomas Whieldon is said to have employed Aaron Wood as a modeller and some confirmation is provided by an entry in Thomas Whieldon's notebook for 1 May 1753: 'Sett [sic, set, i.e. leased or rented] Mr Wood the house at the Mill Garden & find him fire & candle light p[er] year

[£]3.3.0 paid 25 May 1754'.[178] Wood was supposed to always work alone, so the house may have been a workshop, rather than a residence.

Thomas Whieldon had *Josiah Wedgwood* as a partner between 1754 and 1759. Writing of the 1750s, Josiah Wedgwood stated that 'White stone ware was the principal

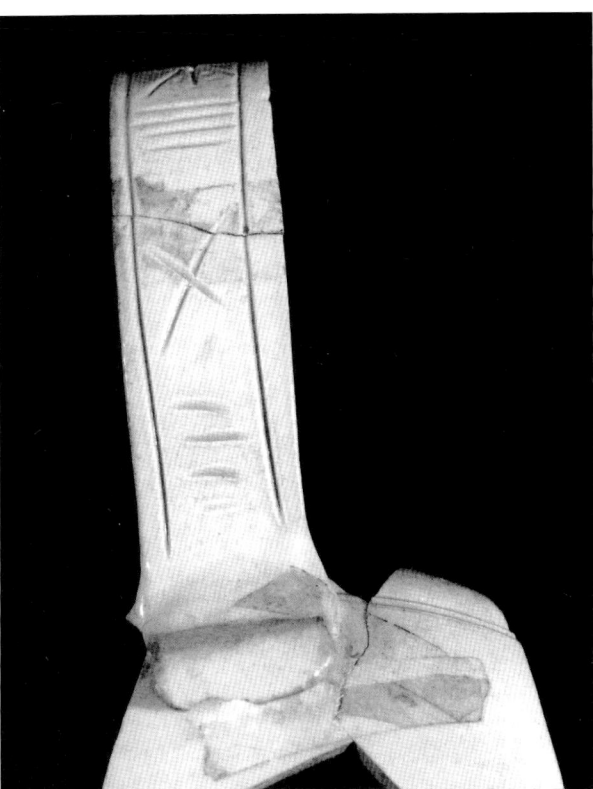

*Fig. 241. **Partially reconstructed handle** from a camel teapot? in white salt-glazed stoneware with incised decoration. Excavated at Thomas Whieldon's Fenton Vivian factory, c.1750-60. 5in. (12.7cm) high. (Potteries Museum and Art Gallery, Stoke-on-Trent, 1045)*

Chapter IX – Thirteen Potters and the Pots they made

Colour Plate 193. **Two partially reconstructed chamber pots**, *white engobe-slipped stoneware with iron-dipped rims. Excavated at Whieldon's Fenton Vivian site, c.1750. 3¼in. (8.26cm) high maximum. (Potteries Museum and Art Gallery, Stoke-on-Trent, WO750, 781)*

Colour Plate 194. **Three fragments** *of white salt-glazed stoneware with Littler-Wedgwood blue dip. The foot of a bowl is the larger shard, maximum 3in. (7.62cm), accompanied by a rim shard with a white interior and another unidentified shaped shard. Blue teapots and cups and saucers of the Littler-Wedgwood variety were being sold by Aaron Wedgwood in existing accounts from 1762 to 1764 (Wedgwood MSS 6/5030-5032). Excavated at Whieldon's Fenton Vivian site, c.1760-75. (Potteries Museum and Art Gallery, Stoke-on-Trent, 942)*

Colour Plate 195. **Three fragments** *of white salt-glazed stoneware with scratch-blue decoration. Excavated at Whieldon's Fenton Vivian site, c.1750-65. 1½in. (3.81cm) maximum. (Potteries Museum and Art Gallery, Stoke-on-Trent, 1245)*

article of our manufacture'[179] and this has been taken to mean that Whieldon and he made salt-glazed ware. It was written about thirty years later[180] and could also be understood to mean that white stoneware was the principal manufacture of North Staffordshire potters in general, in the 1750s.

However, in an account book with pages headed 'Fenton Work January 1757',[181] Josiah Wedgwood noted 'Firing White Sragers [saggars]' in every month from January to July, but not from August to December in 1657. This suggests that Whieldon and Wedgwood did make white salt-glazed ware but not after July 1757.

CHAPTER IX – THIRTEEN POTTERS AND THE POTS THEY MADE

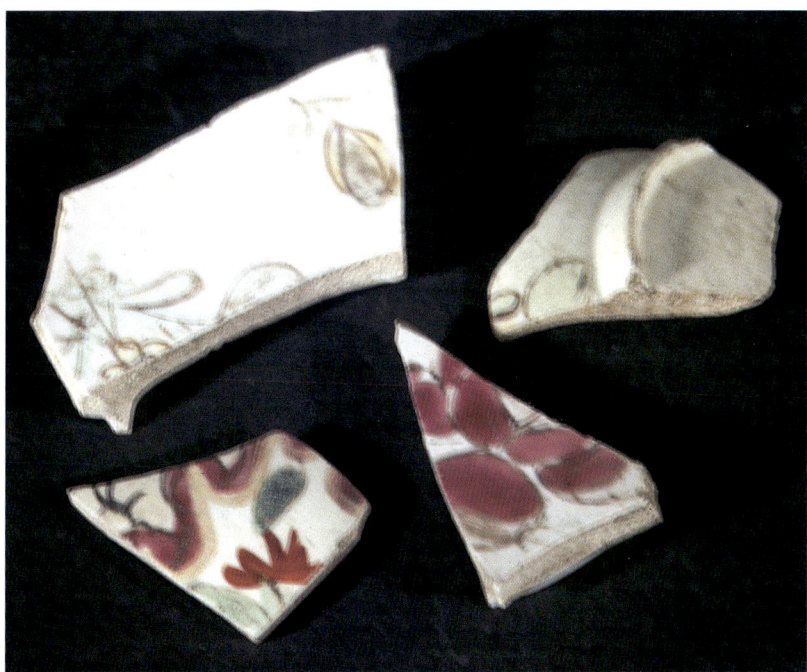

*Colour Plate 196. **Four fragments of two vessels** of white salt-glazed stoneware with enamel decoration. Excavated at Whieldon's Fenton Vivian site, c.1760-70. 2in. (5.08cm) maximum. (Potteries Museum and Art Gallery, Stoke-on-Trent, KF 2004, 2005)*

*Colour Plate 197. **Four fragments** of white salt-glazed stoneware with unusual blue enamel painting seen more commonly on delftware than salt-glaze. Excavated at Whieldon's Fenton Vivian site, c.1755-65. 1⅜in. (3.49cm) maximum. (Potteries Museum and Art Gallery, Stoke-on-Trent)*

YORK: FRANCIS PLACE
Dinsdale, County Durham and/or York, fl.1683-1693

Francis Place (1647-1728) as a potter has been subjected to thorough research.[182] He was a gentleman, artist and engraver, fifth son of Rowland Place of Dinsdale, County Durham.

The contemporary documentary evidence is that Place sold pottery to a cutler in York in 1783,[183] and that he was interested in the patents and methods of John Dwight in 1692 and 1693.[184] In 1694 Place wrote that disappointment in some other project 'and my *Pot Trade*' made him more than half-weary of projects.[185] Ralph Thoresby, the Leeds antiquary, noted in 1715 that Place had many years ago made several very delicate mugs and had given him a mug made in the Manor House at York, together with a saggar and cover.[186] An undated self-portrait of Place holding a globular mug survives (Colour Plate 1).[187]

It has been suggested that Place might have made pots in furnaces discovered at Dinsdale or at two sites in York: the stables of The King's Manor, where he lived from 1692, or the nearby King Charles I's mint on the site of St. Leonard's Hospital.[188] There is no archaeological evidence to support these conjectures.

Five finely made pots survive which are attributed to Francis Place: three salt-glazed globular mugs with ribbed necks and one salt-glazed capuchin, all in a greyish body with spiral streaks in black or brown; and one salt-glazed capuchin in a brown body.[189] The streaks, which spiral upwards from left to right, may be only surface decoration and it has been noted that similar wares, attributed to Place's contemporary John Dwight, have 'integral' spirals in the opposite, 'throwing' direction.[190]

It seems likely that Place made a small number of salt-glazed pots, some of them a greyish white.

APPENDIX 1

Thomas Wedgwoods of the Overhouse, Burslem

THOMAS WEDGWOOD IV fl. 1750s-1773
THOMAS WEDGWOOD V 1773-c.1780

The survival of documents relating to these two potters lends itself to a special study. Eldest brother of the famous Josiah Wedgwood,[1] Thomas Wedgwood IV (1717-1773) made white salt-glazed stoneware at the Overhouse Pottery, Burslem. After his death on 26 February 1773, aged fifty-six, Josiah Wedgwood was his active executor, and that is why some limited details of Thomas Wedgwood IV's business survive in the Wedgwood Archives.[2] Thomas Wedgwood's son, Thomas V, succeeded him. Josiah Wedgwood called him 'a sad Rakish boy' in February 1773, but three months later told Thomas Bentley that 'The improvement of my Nephew, & his reformation w[hi]ch is daily confirming gives me a very sensible pleasure, & I have great hopes it will be continued'.[3] When Thomas Wedgwood V died in 1786, Josiah Wedgwood also looked after his affairs. Enough information has survived to illustrate the manufacturing of white salt-glaze and its sale by both father and son.

Thomas Wedgwood (IV) 'of the Church Yard' inherited the Overhouse property from his cousin, Catherine Egerton, in 1757.[4] He already worked the pottery there, as he was described as 'of the Overhouse, potter' in his marriage settlement of 1742. Perhaps he managed the Overhouse pottery on behalf of his cousin, until he inherited it.[5]

Thomas Wedgwood IV's first wife, Isabel Beech, was sister to Mary Beech, wife of *John Harrison I*, Josiah Wedgwood's first partner. Isabel Wedgwood died in 1750.[6] When Josiah Wedgwood was apprenticed to him for five years from 1744, it was to 'Thomas Wedgwood of the Churchyard Potter',[7] so Thomas must have also run the family pottery at that time.

Josiah Wedgwood's list of Burslem potworks 1710-1715 (Fig. 26)[8] describes the 'Upper House' (Overhouse) potworks held by John Wedgwood as 'Not worked'. In Thomas Wedgwood IV's time it had six rooms and one oven. By 1784 Thomas Wedgwood V was making cream-coloured and china glazed ware[9] and after his death in 1786 Enoch Wood rented the Overhouse Works until 1796.[10] It had presumably been rebuilt by 1802 when it was rated on a value of £35,[11] probably represented by the four-oven works shown on Hargreaves' 1832 map.[12] The works was again rebuilt in 1869.[13] Much enlarged, it is still a pottery factory in 2004, occupied by Royal Stafford China, in Wedgwood Place, Burslem.

Manufacturing
An inventory made after the death of Thomas Wedgwood IV[14] showed that he had six workrooms and *one* oven in all. However, despite the modest size of his works, Thomas Wedgwood was an experienced businessman, making journeys to London and Liverpool to seek orders and collect debts. At his death his personal estate totalled over £2,500 beside his property.[15] The documents which do survive are not at all comprehensive, but are varied enough to provide 'snapshots' of how a salt-glaze potter conducted his affairs.

Raw Materials. The raw materials for making white salt-glazed stoneware are clay and flint. Materials listed in the 1773 inventory were 'Made up clay 1 tun [ton] & a half' and 'Flint 100 & 10 Pecks'.[16] 'Made up clay' would be clay mixed with flint, ready for use. The only transaction relating to clay which involved Thomas Wedgwood IV was a receipt of 3 October 1769 for £55.18s.6d. for 'Clay from Winsford to the 30th September last' bought by 'Bro[the]r Josiah Wedgwood from Thomas Wedgwood [IV]'.[17] Winsford in Cheshire, some twenty miles (32km) from Burslem, was the head of navigation on the River Weaver. The clay would be ball clay, the only white-firing clay then available in quantity, brought by sea from Dorset or Devon to the River Mersey and transferred to smaller boats to be brought up the River Weaver to Winsford, then by cart to Burslem. The same boats transported crates of ware downstream to Liverpool. It is not clear if this was a 'one-off' transaction, but there is no evidence that Thomas Wedgwood IV was a clay agent.

Thomas Wedgwood V paid freight for clay brought to Liverpool by sea: ten tons in 1776, twenty tons in 1777 and thirty tons in 1778.[18] The random survival of invoices shows that he also bought seven consignments of twenty to thirty hundredweights of clay in seven weeks in 1776.[19] In 1780, he paid cartage on two tons of clay from Longport, the nearest wharf on the recently opened Trent and Mersey Canal. Ball clay was an ingredient of the bodies of both white salt-glazed stoneware and cream-coloured earthenware.

Thomas Wedgwood IV bought £627 worth of flint from *John Baddeley* from 1764 to 1772, over 13,000 pecks in 100-peck deliveries.[20] As there were only 110 pecks in stock when Thomas Wedgwood IV died, the inference is that no stock of flint was kept, avoiding capital being tied up. His son continued to buy flint between 1774 and 1785, variously from Mr. Hales and Co. in 1774, Mr. Marsh in 1775, Mr. Antrobus, Mr. Palmer and Thomas Taylor in 1776 and Thomas Heywood in 1783 and 1785, but principally from Thomas Byerley and Co., between 1776 and 1783.[21] As was ball clay, flint was an ingredient of the bodies of both white salt-glazed stoneware and cream-coloured earthenware.

Body preparation and making ware. In 1773 the stove house, possibly containing the slip kiln,[22] also contained moulds for pressing or casting ware. '500 foot of Work Boards' was noted, perhaps a hundred boards, used for moving ware around the workshops. Elsewhere were 'Lawnes' (sieves) and slip tubs for preparing liquid body, and a beating stone for wedging the plastic body prior to throwing.

In the throwing workhouse, there was '1 w[h]eel' and 'one layth [lathe]', and in the large workhouse two 'layths' and a 'hand Layth'. Only one thrower could work at once, but there could be two or three turners, possibly the same men doing different jobs during a single day or week. A pair of screwboxes were listed next to the handling bench, for extruding handle strips.[23]

There was a 'Hot house' with '129 feet of Stone house flag[stone]s' and a '[fire] Grate' used for drying out ware prior to firing. At the time of taking the inventory there was 'Green ware 200 Doz[en]'[24] waiting to be fired.

The only patterns mentioned regularly were 'Gadroon' and 'Barley Corn', usually together, and only once 'Silver' shape. John Baylis ordered 'Pint & Qt & ½ pint mostly Silver Shape', presumably mugs or jugs in 1765.[25] There were occasional orders for 'Carv[e]d Butter Boats', which James Cotter of Liverpool wanted in 1763.[26]

The only suggestions of 'in-house' decoration were the orders for blue flowered ware and flowered plates in 1753,[27] blue flowered bowls and sugars in 1763,[28] and forty-six dozen blue and white cups and saucers in stock at Thomas Wedgwood IV's death in 1773.[29] This would be 'scratch-blue', the flower outlines incised into the unfired clay, then coloured with cobalt blue, prior to the single firing. Thomas Wedgwood V bought blue smalts in 1777 and Sapher [sic, zaffre]' in 1778 and 1779.[30] Smalt and zaffre, impure cobalt,[31] were used for 'scratch-blue' salt-glazed ware, but also for blue-painted creamware by these dates.

A debt from David Rhodes in 1767,[32] then a pottery decorator in Leeds, suggests that Rhodes bought ware from Thomas Wedgwood IV for over-glaze enamelling.

Placing and firing. The saggar house held a 'Sagger W[h]eel', the turntable used for making saggars, and 'Shoards', the round or oval plates on which the saggars were assembled. There were moulds in the 'Sagger House Chamber', perhaps the saggar 'drums' on which the saggars were shaped. The stock of saggars was valued at £4, rather than counted.

Going on to the single oven, there was 99 feet of flagstones and 'Iron Tooles' in the '[h]ovel', the shelter for the actual firing oven; and £1.1s.0d. worth of 'Bonts on the Oven' – iron bands to hold together the brickwork during firing. Incidental items around the pottery included 22,000 bricks, old bricks in the oven, lime and sand, five stools, a step-ladder, a mortar and pestle, a grinding stone and a wheel-barrow, a crane and 'Weigh Board'. The contents of a salt-glaze oven are detailed below.

Neither coal nor salt was listed in the inventory. There is no mention of coal purchased by Thomas Wedgwood IV, but his son was buying coal at weekly intervals in November 1782,[33] and this probably represents regular practice. Salt was certainly bought week by week in the early 1770s, less frequently by 1780. A page of a surviving notebook details 'Salt from Mr. Graham' purchased on the Thursday or Friday of eight successive weeks, from 20 March to 7 May, probably in 1772.[34] Eight to nine bushels were bought each week at 3s.10d. per bushel. Thomas Wedgwood V also bought salt from Mr. Graham, and another document includes a similar list of weekly purchases from 21 July to 13 October 1773.[35] Thomas Wedgwood V bought salt at 3s.9d. a bushel and 'dirty' salt at 6d. a bushel in 1776.[36] By 1780, deliveries were less frequent: nine deliveries of nine bushels each in four months,[37] indicative of lessening demand for salt-glazed ware. It is obvious that salt was bought for each oven firing and salting, and no stock kept.

Employees. There is little information about wages paid to Thomas Wedgwood IV's employees. Only three are named: Wood, Ryley and Allen. Thomas Wedgwood IV's son Thomas V, born in 1745, would also work in the pottery in some capacity, perhaps as clerk. One reference in 1764 is '27th August 1764 Paid George Wood a Fortnight Pd John Ryley a fortnight 8 Sept Pd John Ryley one week 15th Do[Sept] Paid George a Fortnight Wages & Lent him 1/3'.[38] On 8 January 1765 he noted 'Lent Dorothy Allen per dau[ghte]r Dolly a Days wages, 14th D[itt]o per son Will 2s.0d',[39] and on 5 August 1765: 'Paid George Wood his wage' and 'Paid John Ryley' wife for his wage for 3 weeks'.[40] Ryley was a tenant in 1773, when Thomas Wedgwood V paid over 'rent rece'[ive]d from Jno. Ryley 15 week £1.8.10'.[41] More of a fee than a wage is the settlement with Aaron Wood, after Thomas Wedgwood IV's death:

November 15th 1773 due five shillings to Aaron Wood from a recconing [sic, reckoning] on ye 13th February betwixt him and ye Late Mr. Wedgwood Uper [sic] house Deceas'd [received by] Thos Wedgwood [V][42]

Aaron Wood was reputed to be 'modeller to all the potters in Staffordshire'[43] and the reckoning may have been for models supplied by Aaron Wood to Thomas Wedgwood IV.

The 1773 inventory also included four horses and harness, three carts, two cows, hay, oats and wheat, and a pair of harrows, confirming that Thomas Wedgwood IV was a farmer as well as a potter.

Stock of ware and contents of a salt-glaze oven in 1773

A separate inventory[44] listed the ware of the late Mr. T. Wedgwood in 1773. It begins with 'Best White Stone Ware', followed by 'Sec[on]d White' and 'Third Ware' and finally 'Ovenfull', a total value of £172.14.10½. The oven contents are listed here, with abbreviations extended and unfamiliar terms explained, followed by the stock of ware:

[Contents of the oven in 1773]	@	£. s. d.
82 Dozen Best Sortable [various shapes, unsorted]	14d	4.15. 8
20 Dozen ditto [as above] Large Cups & Saucers	11d	18. 4
13 Dozen ditto London [size] ditto	10d.	10.10
4 Dozen ditto Inlett Teapots [recessed covers]	1/9	7. -
3 Dozen ditto Common Teapots	1/6	4. 6
97 Dozen Second Sortable	11d.	4.8.11
12 Dozen ditto Large Cups & Saucers	9d	9. -
20 Dozen ditto London ditto	8d.	13. 4
1 Dozen ditto Inlett Teapots	/3	1. 3
18 Dozen Third Sortable	9d.	13. 6
20 Dozen Plates	2/0	2. 0. 0
25 Dozen ditto	1/6	1.17. 6
6 Dozen ditto	1/3	7. 6
2 Dozen ditto	9d.	1. 6
4 Dozen Twiflers [7 or 8 inch plates]	1/4	5. 4
31 Dozen ditto	1/0	1.11. -
2 Dozen ditto	6d	1. -
360 Dozen		19. 6. 2

Assuming that the dozens were of twelve items, the oven held 4,320 pieces of ware, worth over £19. Thomas Wedgwood fired one oven per week, and these 4,230 pieces equate very neatly into one piece per minute for a twelve-hour six-day week. The 'Made up clay 1 tun & a half' was something like the amount of prepared body required for a single firing.[45]

Besides the 'Ovenfull', the 1773 inventory[46] listed all the ware in stock:

Best White Stone Ware		@	£. s. d.
322 Doz[e]n Unhandled Sortable [various shapes, unsorted]	))		
307 Dozn Handled d[itto]	)	14d	36.13. 7
67 Dozn Teap[o]ts & Coffee		18	5. 0. 6
11 Dozn Do Inlett [recessed covers]		21	19. 3
95 Dozn Cups & Sauc[e]rs Lond[o]n Size		10	3.19. 2
62 Dozn do Do Liverp[oo]l do		11	2.16.10
5½ Dozn Stoolp[a]ns [chamber-pots] 11 Inches		11	5.-½
2 Dozn Do 10 do		8	1. 4
2 Dozn Chair p[a]ns		15	2. 6
7 Dozn Cans @ 6[ ]		10	5.10
12 Dozn Chocolates & handled Cups		10	10. -
19 Dozn Turks Caps in Sizes [nesting jelly moulds]		12	19. -
1½ Dozn Slippers [slipper bed-pans?]		18	2. 3
20 Dozn Flummery [blancmange] Cups		6	10. -
8 Dozn Papboats		8	5. 4
2 Dozn Shells [sweetmeat dishes]		15	2. 6
Supposed 60 Sets Childrens Tea Toys [miniature teasets, not counted]		4	1.-.-
14 Dozn Mustard & Saffron p[o]ts		15	17. 6
32 Dozn Sauce boats in Sizes		18	2. 8. -
46 Dozn Blue & White Cups & Saucrs		14	2.13. 8
9 Groce [gross, 144] galley boxes [ointment pots]		2/6	1. 2. 6
295 Dozn Table plates [no sizes given]		18	22. 2. 6
9 Dozn Twiflers [7 or 8 inch plates]		12	9. -
27 Dozn Dishes from 18 Inches to 10	[each]	7d	9. 9. -
6 Dozn Do Small	[each]	3d	18. -
30 Dozn Nappies & Bakeing [sic] Dishes from 12 Inches to 7		2/4	3.10. -

Sec[on]d White			
489 Dozn Sortable		11	22. 8. 3
85 Dozn Cups & Saucrs		8	2.16. 8
125 Dozn 18s Plates		15	7.16. 3
32 Dozn 15 Do		12	1.12. -
38 Dozn 12 Twiflers		9	1. 8. 6
16 Dozn Bakeing Dishes & Napp[ie]s from 12 to 7 In[ches]	[each]	5	7.15. -

Third Ware			
10 Dozn Table plates		9	7. 6
20 Dozn Twiflers		7	11. 8
Sortable w[i]th Cups & Saucrs Valued at £10			10. -. -

Thomas Wedgwood IV had little ceramic ware for his domestic use. There was 'China & Glass in Beaufett [sic, Buffet] £1.1.0' and he had forty-four pewter plates, and twenty-four dishes in the kitchen.[47] His widow took with her '6 China Cups & Sawcers [sic] 2 small basons 1 spoon boat 6 small soop Plates 2 Crack[e]d bowls'.[48]

Sales
Transactions with other potters. By the 1760s, one outlet for sales was to earthenware manufacturers, who received orders for white salt-glazed stoneware along with those for their own products. Thomas Wedgwood IV made such sales to his brother Josiah in 1767-68,[49] including:

1767		£. s. d.
15th July	To 2 Stoolpans [chamber pots]	7. 0. 6
15th Oct.	To 3 Doz 2nd Qu[ar]ts [mugs?]	3. 0
1768		
30th May	To a parcel of flint ware as per bill [No price shown]	
6th June	1 Doz of plain plates	1. 6
	1 Doz of Twiflers [small plates]	1. 0
16th June	2 - 3 Quart Baking Dishes	1. 6
	2 - 3 pint D[itt]o	9
	2 Quarts Do	6
	4 Best Quart bowls	1. 0
	8 Pints Do	1. 0
16th July	3 Crates of Goods & covers, Disc[oun]t took of[f]	6. 8. 2
	Same time part of a Crate of Mugs not charg'd to the Above as Under Seconds	
	11 Doz of Quart mugs	
	6 Doz of Pints Do	
	1½ Doz of ½ pints	
	18½ Doz at 18. 6	
	Disc[oun]t 0.10	
	17. 8	17. 8
	4 Doz of 18d plates when disc[oun]t took of[f] is	5. 9
	A Large Crate & Covers	2. 4
18th Aug.	To a Water Bottle	6
31st Do	28 Doz of Table Plates at 1/6 when Disct took of is	2. 0. 0
10th Sept	1 Doz of Sauce Boats to match	2. 0
	To 6 Groce [gross, 144] of Galliboxes [ointment pots]	1. 4. 0
	To 2 Groce of Do	5. 0
	A small Crate at	1. 0
27th Do	To 41 Doz of Table Plates at 1/6 took of Disct	2.18. 6
Do	4 Doz of Do at 1/9 Disct took of is	13. 4
	To a Parcel of Flint ware	8.7½

The quantities are quite modest, suggesting that Josiah Wedgwood, then still in Burslem, was receiving small orders for salt-glazed ware along with his own staple cream-coloured ware. This same account included straw, packing, straw for thatch, hay for Josiah's horses, oats, the lay (sic, ley, pasturing) of Josiah's horses, and carriage of coals, confirmation of Thomas Wedgwood IV's farming activities.

'Discount took off' shows the practice of salt-glaze potters giving a discount to earthenware manufacturers, noted in their 1770 agreement: 'To sell to the Manufactures [sic] of Earthen wares at the Above Prices & to allow no more than seven & a half P C' Discount for Breakage & Prompt Payment'.[50] Much later, Thomas Wedgwood IV sold to 'Bror Josiah Wedgwood' 'Galliboxes [gallypots] - 2 & 3 oz', 'Flat and Soop Mosaic Table plates' and other ware on 11 March 1771.[51] His son, Thomas Wedgwood V, continued to supply salt-glazed ware to Josiah Wedgwood: besides barrels and crates of undescribed contents, '4 Doz[en] of Baskett work Plates' in 1773.[52] There would be many more transactions between the two firms, details of which have not survived.

Conversely, Thomas Wedgwood IV bought in salt-glazed ware. These were presumably items ordered by his customers which were out of stock, or else he did not make the shapes required. In 1749, *Jonah Malkin* supplied 'Mr. Thos. Wedgwood Churchyard' with 'Dipt goods' (cheaper ware): two crates of quart and pint mugs, porringers and bowls.[53] Thomas Wedgwood was already 'of the Overhouse' from 1742, so this transaction suggests that he ran two separate businesses.

In 1752, he bought a crate of square flowered (scratch-blue?) plates and dishes and scolloped flowered plates and dishes from *John Baddeley*, some invoiced with a note of London prices alongside the prices he was charged. Wedgwood also bought redware from Baddeley in 1764.[54] From *Thomas and John Wedgwood* of the Big House he bought mustard spoons, custard cups, sauceboats, star pettys and star cups, turk's caps and shells, egg spoons, melons and pudding cups between 1762 and 1771, together with hay, tiles and sixteen balls of clay, partly paid for by China Rail dishes in 1767 and stool pans in 1770. Between 1770 and 1773, Thomas Wedgwood IV repaid *Thomas and John Wedgwood* by supplying '40 lb. of Clay prepared for the Wheele', and firing eighty-four saggars for them.[55]

In 1764 Charles Kinkead of Strabane in Ireland ordered goods, noted in Thomas Wedgwood IV's order book, including 'two crates of brown mugs'.[56] Thomas Wedgwood IV probably did not make brown salt-glazed ware. He certainly bought in fifty-three dozen of 'Croutch [*sic*, crouch ware, i.e. brown salt-glazed stoneware]' at 9d. a dozen (probably mugs) and eleven dozen of jugs and bowls at 1s. a dozen from *Thomas* Cartlidge (*sic*, *Cartlich*) for Charles Kinkead in 1765.[57]

Sales to customers. Despite his single oven works, Thomas Wedgwood IV had many customers for his wares. A full list of customers, compiled from the 1767 schedule and five surviving notebooks,[58] is included in Appendix 5. Allowing for duplication of names, there were about eighty customers, mostly in London and Liverpool, but also scattered as widely as Salisbury, Hereford, Whitehaven, Newcastle upon Tyne, Durham and Coleshill near Birmingham, with one in Ireland. Other overseas consumers were presumably supplied by the Wedgwoods' customers in London or Liverpool. Only two 'trade' customers were listed in 1767: David Rhodes, debtor for £2.14s., a pottery decorator in Leeds at that date,[59] and Thomas Wedgwood IV's youngest brother, Josiah, who owed £34.

One notebook shows that Thomas Wedgwood IV made three journeys to London in 1753, 9 to 18 April, 6 to 7 August and 9 to 19 October,[60] and there is fragmentary evidence of visits to London and Liverpool in 1763, 1765, 1767, 1770 and 1771. It may be concluded that Thomas Wedgwood IV went out seeking orders and collecting debts several times a year.

Some typical orders are quoted. An order taken from Mrs. Jones, 14 April 1753, was for 'Ware Blue Flow[ere]d, Ash Colour, Image Toys, Cream Colour & tortoiseshell'.[61] A cryptic note '16 Apl 1753' shows 'for Mr. Jno Rogers Image Toys, Blue Flow[ere]d Ash coloured, new fashion'. Rogers paid Wedgwood £23.1s. on the same day.

Thomas Wedgwood IV noted 'Weight of Crates sent since Oct[obe]r 1753 on the 30th Nov[embe]r Mr Jno Rogers' a total of nine crates, for Mr. Tidmarsh four crates; and for Mr. Jno Morris three crates.[62]

Jo. Vanderkiste of 'the Boro', London, sent a mixed order to Thomas Wedgwood IV on 18 January 1763, wanting '12 pair wt [white] stone flat candlesticks', the same in leafage green, green leaves, green dessert fruit plates, and gadrooned tureens. He also wanted agate and painted yellow mugs from Josiah Wedgwood, and red china. The green ware may have been made at Thomas Wedgwood IV's Churchyard Works, like the mottled mugs mentioned below.

In 1773 Vanderkiste wanted '1 Crate of stone Galliboxes' in sizes 'by sea', and gallipots, spitting pots, chamber pots, bowls, the crate filled up with 'one Dish and 2 Dish tea potts both common and let in' by land,[63] i.e., quicker, and more expensive. 'One Dish' and '2 Dish' refer to the size of teapots, holding respectively one dish or cup and two dishes or cups of tea. 'Let in' describes teapots where the cover lies flush with the shoulder of the teapot, resting on the 'natch' or ledge.

Not all customers were in London, nor for white stoneware. Between 20 and 28 May 1765 Wedgwood noted an order for 'Mr Wm Crockett in Coleshill' for '1 Crate of Mottled mugs 14 at 9d per Doz 20 Doz of pints 7 Doz of Quarts 3 Doz of ½ pints not quite so large as the Pattern rather Taperer quite as high not quite so wide at top rather stronger below'. Coleshill near Birmingham lay on Wedgwood's route to and from London. Later in 1765 he noted that he 'Wrote a Letter to Mr Wm Fraiser Sandgate Newcastle Upon Tyne to let him know the prices of Flint ware'.[64]

John Dunbibin of Liverpool sent a long order to Josiah Wedgwood on 12 March 1764, ending 'and desire your Brother [Thomas Wedgwood IV, Overhouse] to send me 3 Crates of plates @ 18 p[*sic*]'.[65] On 4 October 1765 Thomas Wedgwood IV noted 'Mrs Dodg[s]on Pottseller in Liverp[oo]l For Mrs Forbes near the Old Dock Liverpool – 4 Crates of Best Flint Sortable with some Plates & Dishes Gadroon & Barleycorn The Mugs to be made smoothly Dutch fashion. For Mr. John Mourney Cha[mber]; Potts Jugs Cups & Sau[cers] Wash hand basons All sizes of Bowls Tankards ½ pint & p[in]ts & porringers 24s 6 8 & 12in 18in Some plates & dishes'.[66]

In 1764 Charles Kinkead, Thomas Wedgwood IV's customer in Strabane, Ireland, ordered goods 'good in the Cullor [colour] and large in the mes [measure]' and remarked that the large dishes with the fire cracks would never sell. This order is also noted in Thomas Wedgwood IV's order book, and included eleven crates and a miscellaneous list of salt-glazed wares, together with a crate of 'Goldenhill' ware, two crates of black ware, two crates of yellow porringers and 'posit [*sic*, posset]' cups and two crates of brown mugs.[67] As noted above, Thomas Wedgwood IV obtained fifty-three dozen of 'Croutch [*sic*, crouch ware, i.e. brown salt-glazed stoneware]' at 9d. a dozen (probably mugs) and eleven dozen of jugs and bowls at 1s. a dozen from Thomas Cartlidge (*Thomas Cartlich*) for Charles Kinkead in 1765.[68]

Payment for goods

Payment methods were sophisticated and varied. As shown above, Thomas Wedgwood IV went out seeking orders and collecting debts several times a year. An entry in his notebook for 9 April 1753 showed debts in London totalling £291.12s.7d. after allowing £40 for 80 crates. The debtors were only identified by crate marks: 'RD' owed £46.7s.5d. for 21 crates. A similar notebook entry for 9 October of the same year, 1753, showed debts to collect of £341, again only identified by crate mark initials.[69]

A rueful notebook entry for 16 August 1770 reads 'Memo when I settled with Mr. Samuel Ward of Brentford I allow'd him for goods just come in £22.0.0 I allowed him Dis[coun]t £1.4.0 which should have been but twelve shillings'.[70]

Jo. Vanderkiste of the Boro, London, sent a mixed order to Thomas Wedgwood IV on 18 January 1763, obliquely apologising for failure to pay by ending 'I only wait for Frost to break that I may get into the Country for to collect a little money'.[71] Vanderkiste was still explaining his delay in paying for goods in 1774. He owed £163 to Thomas Wedgwood V and pleaded that bad weather had prevented him getting out 'on circuit' to collect,[72] just as he had done in 1763.

Thomas Wedgwood IV must have had an agent in Liverpool in 1769, when John Dunbibin wrote from there to Josiah Wedgwood: 'let your brother Thos know that Mr. Tyror has lost his sight for the Pres[en]t so wou'd have him order some person else to receive [h]is money'.[73] (Robert Tyrer was a potter on Shaw's Brow in 1766.)[74]

On 20 September 1771 Thomas Wedgwood IV noted 'Then settled

with Mr. Saml. Dunbibin & due to me £51.10.0. For payment, Wedgwood could draw on Dunbibin for £20 in a month, an instalment on his debt.[75] This was a regular way of payment: as early as 4 February 1765 Wedgwood noted 'A Draft on Mr. Saml. Dunbibin & Co. For 20 0 0 payable at a month as advised 4th – Sent the above Drafts Mr. Jno. Sparrow'.[76] Wedgwood wrote to Dunbibin on the 4th to tell him that he was being drawn upon for £20 in a month's time. 'Sparrow' was a local solicitor (and later a banker) who would credit Wedgwood and arrange for the 'Draft' to be 'sold' to a London discounter, who would collect the £20 from Dunbibin on 4 March. This was the usual way of transferring credit before cheques were introduced. Mr. Dunbibin (in London) must have disputed his debt to Thomas Wedgwood IV at the end of 1770. A draft or copy letter shows that Dunbibin owed Wedgwood £101 for thirty-six crates sent via Willington (head of River Trent navigation) in a year.[77]

John Douglas of Whitehaven wrote to Josiah Wedgwood on 14 December 1763 about the problems of sending cash and unreliability of 'merchants' bills', commenting 'Your brother Thomas Bill returned of £25',[78] the implication being that Douglas had endorsed a bill (due to Douglas) for payment to be made to Thomas Wedgwood (IV), and the bill had been dishonoured.

James Omer was another London customer. Thomas Wedgwood IV noted an order from him, undated but between 12 February 1763 and 8 January 1765.[79] Perhaps in payment for this order, Wedgwood noted on 10 April 1765: 'Sent Draft to Bro[the]r John Wedgwood in London on Jas Omer for £39 0 0 payable on sight'.[80] John Wedgwood clearly acted on behalf of his brother Thomas, as he did for Josiah Wedgwood. John Wedgwood was included in Thomas' 1767 list of debtors for 1767, £5.5s., and it was Thomas Wedgwood IV who went post-haste to London when John was found drowned there on 11 June 1767.[81]

One well-known London customer not named in the 1767 list of debtors was Joseph Tidmarsh. Thomas Wedgwood IV noted an order from him on 21 September 1771,[82] and at Thomas' death, Tidmarsh owed him £59.16s.7d.[83]

Thomas Wedgwood IV's customer in Strabane, Ireland, Charles Kinkead, was on good terms with him. In 1760, Kinkead wrote from Whitchurch, Shropshire that he was on his way home from London, having spent two months in London trying to sell £900 of linen and left £825 worth unsold, but would pay Wedgwood when the linen was sold.[84]

A 1766 order from Kinkead mentioned indirect payment. Kinkead had sent 'your Bro[the]r Josiah [Wedgwood] … a bill £100 to pay him & remainder to you'.[85] In July 1767 Kinkead offered to pay his debt in November with interest 'if you think this [delay] hard';[86] and in a letter of 13 October 1768 Kinkead told Wedgwood that he would call on his way from Strabane to London and pay him.[87]

A schedule of debts owing to Thomas Wedgwood IV on 23 February 1767[88] totalled over £851 and when he died Thomas Wedgwood owed £388 and was owed £1,605.[89] It seems that most of Thomas Wedgwood IV's capital was tied up in credit to customers. His purchases were by the week: clay, coal, salt and wages were weekly outgoings. There is no record of his purchases of flint or crates, but his son bought both at weekly or fortnightly intervals.[90]

Packing and transport
Sales were only effected by packing the ware and transporting it to the customer. Most invoices for white salt-glazed ware and other pottery mention crates as the usual form of packing, but other containers were also used. An invoice of 30 March 1773, from Thomas Wedgwood to Josiah Wedgwood,[91] already quoted, names '1 Tierce & 2 Hogsheads', names for sizes of barrels. Crate-making was a specialised craft: John Walker supplied Thomas Wedgwood V with twenty-two crates and twenty-five covers in April 1775, the prices of crates varying from 1s.6d.to 2s.6d. each. Between July 1775 and June 1776 there were forty-two deliveries of a total of 192 crates, four to five crates a week.[92]

Several notebook entries draw attention to the method of carriage of ware to London customers, Wedgwood noting 'by land' or 'by sea'. Land carriage was quicker but more expensive. On 10 November 1771 Wedgwood noted '4 Crates Gadroon Plates, Dishes, Nappys [sic] By Sea Stoolpans, Basons &c. By Land' for James Atkinson of Covent Garden.[93] Another notebook entry on the same day[94] illustrates the mechanics and vicissitudes of water transport from the landlocked Potteries.

> Sent to Mrs. Mary Fullmer 3 Crates of Goods there is one Crate missing – Plates – Carriage to Willington 5/4 TWIF There was three Crates mentioned in the Bills of Lading 2 of them came to hand Ex the Sally Jno. Tinker master'.

'Willington' was the head of navigation on the River Trent. Wedgwood had sent three crates overland[95] from Burslem to Willington and paid 5s.4d. carriage. The crates were marked TW for Thomas Wedgwood and IF for Mrs. Fullmer. (A later note shows that Wedgwood dealt with Joseph Fullmer, J then being written as I.) From Willington the crates would be taken down river to Gainsborough or Hull, for trans-shipment to a sea-going vessel down the North Sea to London. Although the 'bill of lading', the receipt for the goods on board ship, showed three crates, only two arrived in London on the *Sally*, a ship captained by John Tinker. By 27 May 1772 the canal was open to Stone and Thomas Wedgwood was able to send eleven crates there to be forwarded to Hereford for Thomas Quick.[96]

Another mixed land and water route from the Potteries was by cart to Winsford in Cheshire and then by boat on the navigable Rivers Weaver and Mersey to Liverpool. Four of Wedgwood's Liverpool customers appear in the Weaver Navigation records as forwarders of 'Cratesware' from Winsford to Liverpool: John Dunbeavin (Dunbibin) and Jos. Bird in 1746,[97] and John Dalziels, John Mourney, and Dunbeavin again, in 1752.[98] On 5 July 1755 John Mourney shipped eight crates weighing ten hundredweight on the *Worrall*, master John Atherton.[99] The *Worrall* took 123 crates, eight tons in all, for sixteen different consignees. These transactions suggest that the North Staffordshire manufacturer arranged to have crates carted to Winsford 'to the order of' his Liverpool customer, and then the Liverpool merchant instructed the wharfinger at Winsford to send his crates forward to Liverpool, using the same boats which had brought up the raw clay.

Thomas Wedgwood IV's only 'overseas' customer was Charles Kinkead of Strabane in northern Ireland. Distant overseas orders for ware were presumably dealt with by Liverpool or London merchants. The formalities of exporting were explained to Thomas Wedgwood in Kinkead's request in 1764 for bills of lading and an invoice for each crate: 'there must be an invoice produced before they will admit them to an Entry upon arrival of these Goods'. The order attached was for two large crates of a great variety of salt-glazed ware, and a crate of red ware.[100]

A 1766 order from Kinkead mentioned transport. Kinkead wrote 'Below an order – get ready as fast as possible as there's som[e] ships Clear to Sail from [London]Derry for Liverpool & forward as usual'. Kinkead was well aware that ships from Londonderry to Liverpool would return from Liverpool, available to carry his order.[101]

APPENDIX 2

Salt-Glaze Potters

The dates shown in the titles of 125 pottery makers are those within which we consider that they were making white salt-glazed stoneware. We have also included details of twenty-five other potters because they have been previously said to be salt-glaze potters. For these we give our reasons why we think they were not salt-glaze makers. Samuel Spode is an obvious example. In these instances, we give no dates in their titles. When the names of the 125 salt-glaze potters are given elsewhere in this book, they are printed in italics.

The potters or places listed in this appendix are as follows:

Adams, Edward & Richard
Adams, John & John Prince
Alders, John
Alders, Thomas
Allen, John
America:
    John Bartlam
    Salem Pottery
Astbury, John
Astbury, Joshua
Astbury, Thomas
Baddeley, John, & Fletcher
Baddeley, Ralph
Baggaley, James & Brothers
Bagnall, Peter, Elizabeth
Banks, William, & John Turner
Barker, Thomas – *see* Chapter IX
Bird, Daniel
Blackwell, John
Blackwell, Joseph
Bold, James
Booth Enoch senior & George Booth
Bourne, John; Bourne, Wright & Co.
Bourne, William – *see* Chapter IX
Bovey Tracey – *see* Chapter IX
Brentford
Brindley, John
Bucknall, Joseph
Bucknall, Robert, Mary, Ralph, & Sons
Cartlich, Thomas
Chatterley, Samuel
Chester White Ware Manufactory – *see* Chapter IX
Cobb, John
Daniel, John
Daniel, Richard
Daniel, Sampson & Ralph
Daniel, Thomas I
Daniel, Thomas II
Derby:
    Cockpit Hill
    Nottingham Road
Edge, John & John Gretton
Edge, Samuel

Fenton, John & Thomas Hill – *see* Chapter IX
Ford
Garner, Robert & Co.
Glasgow: Delftfield Pottery Company
Godwin
Graham, John junior
Greatbatch, William – *see* Chapter IX
Hales, John
Hammersley, Cornelius
Harrison, John & Josiah Wedgwood
Hassells, Charles
Hassells, John
Hassells, William
Heath & Bagnall
Heath, Joshua I
Heath, Joshua II
Heath, Thomas I
Heath, Thomas II
Heath, William I
Heath, William II & Joshua Heath III
Horn, Job & - Taylor
Isleworth
Johnson, Thomas & Joseph
Keeling, Anthony
Kirk, Samuel & Co.
Leeds: Leeds Pottery
Littler, William
Liverpool: Park Lane; Dale Street
Lockett, Timothy & John
London:
    Dwight, John, Lydia, Samuel – *see* Chapter IX
    Elers, John & David
    Garner, Matthew & Luke Talbot
    Johnson, Moses
    Kishere, Joseph
    Woolwich
Lowe, John & Thomas
Malkin, Jonah
Malkin, Samuel
Mare, John, & Richard Taylor
Mare, John & Richard
Marsh, Moses
Meir, John
Meir, William
Mere, Richard
Middleton, Revd. John or Thomas
Middleton, Moses
Miles, Thomas
Mitchell, John
Mountford, Richard & John Shaw
Muchell, Richard
North-East England: Newbottle Pottery
Nottingham: James Morley
Oxford

Palmer, Humphrey – *see* Chapter IX
Parrott, William
Payne, James
Peat, John
Phillips, George & Thomas
Pool, Nicholas
Prescot
Prestonpans: William Cadell & Sons, & Co.
Rotherham: John Platt & Samuel Walker junior – *see* Chapter IX
Rothwell: John Smith & John Pullen
Shaw, Aaron
Shaw, Moses
Shaw, Ralph I
Shaw, Ralph II, Richard Bagnall & Thomas Daniel
Shaw, Thomas
Shrigley, John
Shropshire:
   Benthall
   Jackfield
Simpson, Joseph
Smith, John
Smith, Jos.
Smith, William
Spode, Samuel
Stephens, Joseph
Stevenson, Thomas
Swansea: William Coles
Swinton: William Malpass & William Fenney – *see* Chapter IX
Taylor, John
Taylor, Thomas I
Taylor, Thomas II, III, Elizabeth, & Isaiah
Taylor, William I
Taylor, William II
Twyford, William
Warburton & Stone
Warburton, Edward
Warburton, Jacob & Isaac
Warburton, John, Ann, & Son
Warburton, Joseph
Weatherby, John
Wedgwood, Aaron
Wedgwood, Aaron, Thomas III & John – *see* Chapter IX
Wedgwood, Aaron, Thomas I & Richard
Wedgwood, Burslem, Carlos
Wedgwood, John
Wedgwood, Josiah
Wedgwood, Richard
Wedgwood, Thomas I
Wedgwood, Dr. Thomas II
Wedgwood, Thomas IV, V – *see* Appendix 1
West Pans
Whieldon, Thomas, & Josiah Wedgwood – *see* Chapter IX
Whitehaven
Whitehead
Wood, John, & Ralph II, & John Wedgwood
Yates, John
York: Francis Place – *see* Chapter IX

EDWARD AND RICHARD ADAMS
fl.1767
RICHARD ADAMS
Cobridge, Staffordshire, fl.1770

Richard Adams, born 1739, died 1811, made white salt-glazed stoneware at Cobridge.[1] He signed the 1770 salt-glaze potters' price list (Appendix 3).[2] Edward and Richard Adams bought two parcels of moulds and a quantity of flint from *John Baddeley* in 1767, paid for by goods and crates.[3]

JOHN ADAMS AND JOHN PRINCE
Lane Delph, Staffordshire, n.d., 18th century

Shaw reported that 'Mr. John Adams, and Mr. John Prince were manufacturers at Lane Delph ... of Red Porcelain, and White Stone ware, and realized large fortunes'. Their turners included John Stirrup and William Hilditch,[4] both of whose families became master potters.[5]

A John Prince was christened at Stoke-on-Trent on 10 May 1731 and married Ann Swift at Trentham, Staffs., on 29 June 1760.[6]

JOHN ALDERS
Penkhull Bank, Stoke-on-Trent, c.1753-1779

Simeon Shaw wrote that 'Mr. John Aldersea [*sic*] at the manufactory in Stoke, where is now the Top Square; and his Brother Thomas [see *Thomas Alders*] of the Honey Wall, were successful in making Mottled and Cloudy, and Tortoiseshell, with lead ore and salt glazes'.[7] No firmer evidence of John Alders making salt-glazed ware has been found.

John Alders, younger brother of *Thomas Alders*, was born c.1717.[8] In 1733 he inherited a house and premises in Penkhull,[9] which had become a house and potworks by 1753.[10] John Alders died in 1779[11] and left his house and potworks at Penkhull Bank in his own occupation to his wife Elizabeth.[12] In 1782, she sold both house and potworks to George Carr, a maltster, and Carr immediately built a malthouse on the premises.[13]

The site of John Alders' works is not clear. A Duchy of Lancaster plan of encroachments in the Liberty of Penkhull, dated 1777,[14] shows No. 37, Jno. Alders' property, as two adjoining houses and garden on the west side of Hartshill Road, south of the site of the demolished Fairway House, at the entrance to derelict car parks. These were of course only 'encroachments' into Duchy land, not John Alders' leasehold potworks.

THOMAS ALDERS
Upper Cliff Bank Works, Stoke-on-Trent, c.1751-1777

As is noted for *John Alders*, Shaw wrote that 'Mr. John Aldersea [*sic*] at the manufactory in Stoke, where is now the Top Square; and his Brother Thomas of the Honey Wall, were successful in making Mottled and Cloudy, and Tortoiseshell, with lead ore and salt glazes'.[15] As with his brother John, no firmer evidence of Thomas Alders making salt-glazed ware has been found.

Thomas Alders was born c.1714,[16] eldest son of Thomas Alders of Penkhull, Stoke-on-Trent, chairmaker or yeoman, from whom he inherited a cottage in Penkhull in 1738.[17] By 1751 the cottage had become a house, warehouses, workhouses, ovens and hovels.[18] In 1777 Thomas Alders passed his house and potworks to his son-in-law, Joseph Warburton of Cobridge, potter.[19] Thomas Alders died in 1781.[20]

Joseph Warburton sold the house and potworks to John Harrison the younger of Cliff Bank, Stoke, potter (see *John Harrison and Josiah Wedgwood*), in 1788.[21] When John Harrison II's property was advertised for sale on 6 November 1802, 'Warburton's Works' was described as adjoining 'Harrison's Works'.[22] Harrison's Works have been located as along the west side of the road at the junction of Honeywall and Hartshill Road and Warburton's (formerly Thomas Alders') Works could have adjoined on either side. The 1802 map shows only one manufacturer in this location, John Harrison at Cliffgate Bank, No. 99,[23] presumably including both Warburton's and Harrison's Works.

JOHN ALLEN
Burslem?, fl.1770

John Allen signed the 1770 salt-glaze potters' price list.[24] A John Allens [sic] was buried in Burslem Churchyard 3 June 1786, and another John Allen was buried there 2 October 1791.[25] No further information has been found.

AMERICA

JOHN BARTLAM
Lane Delph, Stoke-on-Trent, England, -1763
Cain Hoy, South Carolina, America, 1765-68

Shards found at John Bartlam's Cain Hoy, South Carolina, site, under the supervision of Stanley South, suggest that he *probably* made 'Littler-Wedgwood Blue' there, and *possibly* grey or white salt-glazed ware also.[26] As Bartlam went from Lane Delph to Cain Hoy, it is reasonable to suppose that he used techniques in America with which he was already familiar in England.

Bradford Rauschenburg of the Museum of Early Southern Decorative Arts, Winston-Salem, North Carolina has thoroughly researched John Bartlam's career in England and America, and most of the following is summarised from his work.[27] Bartlam was born c.1735, and married Mary Allen of Great Fenton in 1760. In 1761-63 he was a potter at Lane Delph, buying flint from *John Baddeley*, which could have been for cream-coloured ware or stoneware.[28] The site of his works is not known.

By 1763 Bartlam was in financial difficulties and he emigrated to America, taking with him his wife, two daughters, his brother-in-law, John Allen, and others. They were shipwrecked off Madeira, but eventually reached America, except for John Allen. He turned back at Madeira and was drowned off Cornwall in a second shipwreck, in December 1763.[29]

Bartlam set up a pottery by 1765, at Cain Hoy, on the Wando River, nine miles from Charleston. He manufactured various sorts of pottery there for five years,[30] and then moved to Charleston itself in 1770, advertising that he made Queen's ware (cream-coloured ware) there. By 1772 Bartlam had moved again, to Camden, some hundred miles NNW of Charleston, where he again potted until his death c.1780. One of Bartlam's English workmen, William Ellis, went to *Salem Pottery* in 1772, where salt-glazed pottery was later made.[31]

A total of 170 'white' salt-glazed stoneware shards, and one *waster* shard of Littler-Wedgwood blue (Colour Plate 137) were found in the Cain Hoy excavation. However, no saggars, kiln furniture or any other materials associated with the production of salt-glazed stoneware were found, leading archaeologists to maintain that the shards were not made there.[32] The presence of the waster shard of Littler-Wedgwood blue salt-glazed ware remains unexplained.

SALEM POTTERY
Old Salem, Winston-Salem, North Carolina, U.S.A., fl.1782

It is a moot point whether or not Salem Pottery was still in the British Empire when salt-glazed stoneware was made there. The preliminary articles for a Peace Treaty between Britain and America were signed on 30 November 1782,[33] and Rudolph Christ asked permission to make such ware only four months earlier.

This note is based on a report by Bradford L. Rauschenberg in 1991.[34] *John Bartlam*, master potter, had been at Cain Hoy, South Carolina, since 1765. He is said to have returned to England in 1769 and recruited four more men to make pots at Charleston. William Ellis (1743-) was probably amongst them. Ellis left Bartlam and arrived at the Moravian settlement at Salem, North Carolina in December 1773, where they already had a European-style redware pottery, operated by Gottfried Aust, trained in Saxony. The Overseers decided to take advantage of Ellis' knowledge and make cream-coloured ware.

Two loads of white clay were obtained and a new kiln built, and Ellis was paid for instruction on making creamware. He had left by 5 May 1774 when it was recorded that trials of firing creamware and also stoneware had been made, using moulds rather than throwing to shape the ware.

The redware pottery continued under Aust. On 1 August 1782 one of the journeymen potters, Rudolph Christ, who had been there during Ellis' time, sought permission to start a separate pottery to make 'the Queens and salt-pottery'. Fragments of pierced salt-glazed saggars have been found on site which appear similar to those used in Britain for white salt-glazed stoneware. Plaster moulds, biscuit creamware and biscuit black 'Jackfield' ware have also been found on site, but not white salt-glazed stoneware wasters.

The inference is that Ellis had taught Christ how to make salt-glazed stoneware, creamware and Jackfield ware in 1773-74, and Christ made these types of ware at Old Salem c.1782.

JOHN ASTBURY
Shelton, Staffordshire, c.1723-43/44

John Astbury (1690-1743/44) may have made white salt-glazed stoneware at Shelton Farm, but see our entry for *Fenton and Hill*. The site is no. 93 on the 1802 map[35] and in 2003 is occupied by houses in Shelton Farm Road. When Thomas Symson applied for poor relief at Much Wenlock in 1737, he stated that he was 'born in Stoak [sic, Stoke-on-Trent parish] and worked there for one year for John Astbury fourteen years since [so 1723]'.[36] John Astbury may have made salt-glazed stoneware earlier, elsewhere in Shelton, as he is said to have been in partnership with Joshua Twyford in 1717;[37] and he was referred to as a potter in 1723 and 1724, when he bought coal from John Fenton.[38]

No family relationship with Joshua Astbury of Shelton has been found; over 1,700 Astburys have been noted in Staffordshire in three centuries.[39] John Astbury's brother *Thomas Astbury* was a potter at Lane Delph c.1725.

JOSHUA ASTBURY
Shelton, -1721

Joshua Astbury was named by *John Dwight of London* in a Bill of Complaint 4 December 1697 as one who had infringed Dwight's 1684 patent.[40] Dwight alleged that *Moses Middleton*, *Cornelius Hammersley* and Joshua Astbury of Shelton in partnership had intruded into Dwight's workhouses, learnt how to make his wares, and made copies of them for several years.

Only Hammersley replied, stating that there was no partnership, that he had used his ingenuity to improve his pots, and that he should not be punished if his wares accidentally proved to be like Dwight's. John Dwight's allegation is so widely drawn that the three Staffordshire potters might have been making any of his patented wares, and so there is no confirmation that Joshua Astbury was making salt-glazed ware at Shelton in 1697.

The alleged intrusion into Dwight's Fulham workshops may be the basis of Shaw's story of an Astbury (and a Twyford) stealing the secrets of the Elers brothers at Bradwell in the 1690s.[41] Joshua Astbury may also be the potter who was said to have discovered the use of calcined flint, discussed in Chapter IV, Raw Materials.

Joshua Astbury was baptised 14 July 1676,[42] and in a 'census' of 1701 was a boarder aged twenty-five, living with Richard Cartlich in Shelton.[43] He married Abigail Bell of Shelton[44] (b. 1679) at Caverswall on 1 July 1702.[45] She predeceased Joshua, being buried at Stoke on 18 October 1719.[46] They had six children: Ann 1704, Abigail 1707, Joshua 1711, Catharine 1714 and Dan in 1715, all baptised at Stoke,[47] and also Mary.[48]

The site of Joshua Astbury's pottery in Shelton is not known. In 1718/19 he was involved in a dispute with his neighbour John Middleton, also a potter, about smoke nuisance from Middleton's slip kiln, stove and oven[49] and this report may eventually lead to identification of his site. The arbitration award required that Middleton should rebuild his stove pipe larger than those used by Joshua Astbury at his workhouse at Shelton. The distinction between slip kiln, stove and oven suggests that the stove was a heated drying room, mentioned again below.

Joshua Astbury was buried at Stoke 10 October 1721.[50] In his will, made 5 September 1721, he called himself a yeoman (farmer) and signed with his mark, suggesting either that he could not write or that he was too ill to do so. His will was proved on 19 April 1722[51] and he left £2,000 amongst his four daughters, when they were twenty-one. He left all his freehold and copyhold messuages, lands and tenements, to his son Joshua, when he attained the age of twenty-one (in 1733).

In the accompanying inventory of Joshua Astbury's property, made 17 October 1721, he was described as a potter and the inventory shows that he was both farmer and potter, as was usual at that time. He had ten cattle, six horses, two swine, corn, hay and farm implements. Amongst his domestic items, he had thirty-nine pewter dishes and plates, a silver tankard, books, and two violins.

In his capacity as potter, Joshua Astbury had £100 worth of earthenware, burnt and unburnt (fired and unfired); two engines,[52] sifting boxes and mortars worth £9, three lathes, three vises (sic) and chocks, boards and 'Shraggers [saggars]', tubs, oven bands and two (throwing) wheels; and debts due to him of £50. His 'sifting boxes and mortars' show that he was using flint by 1721, only used at that date for making white or white-dipped salt-glazed ware. Altogether farm, domestic and pottery items were worth £435.6s.0d. His executor's accounts (see below) show that he owned a lot of land, a corn mill, rented a warehouse in London and derived payments from coal mines. Dying aged only forty-five, Joshua Astbury had become a man of substance.

Joshua Astbury's will led to a legal dispute. In 1747, one of Astbury's daughters, Mary, and her husband John Mare of Hanley, potter (see *John Baddeley* and also *John and Richard Mare*), alleged that one of Astbury's executors, John Twyford, had persuaded Joshua Astbury's son to make a will in Twyford's favour.[53] Because of this, Twyford's accounts of his executorship survive[54] and suggest that Twyford wound up Astbury's potting business by 1723.

Two days after Astbury's funeral on 10 October 1721, Twyford paid wages to twelve men, including Henry Cooper who received 12s.6d. for three weeks' wages and 'his attendance upon the stove'. There were also payments to Sarah Bryan (£1.0s.3d.) and Samuel Colclough (10s.6d.) for 'pounding fflint', the hazardous occupation of reducing calcined flintstones to dry powder, using the sifting boxes and mortars.

A week later, Twyford paid six of the twelve men for one week's work, ranging from 5s. to Richard Colclough to 7s.2d. to Wm. Walker. After that, no more wages were paid, except 'Cash for attending the Stove'. Crates (£2.0s.4d.) and salt (16s.6d.) were bought, and one of the engines was repaired for 2s. John Twyford valued the 'stock of pots' at £150, and paid 19s.0d. for carriage of three loads of ware to Birmingham on 20 January 1721/22.

Accounts paid by Twyford in winding up Astbury's affairs included one to *Aaron Shaw* for 2 tons 18 cwt. of flint, £6.16s.6d, on 26 February 1721/22, and, over a year later, £4 paid to 'John Tranter [?] for a year's rent for a warehouse at the Castle and Falcon [inn][55] London due upon Mr. Astbury's death', on 8 April 1723.

In one way, Twyford continued to deal in clay on Astbury's behalf: he received payments from a tenant, Mary Ellis, for half a pit of slip clay on 20 March 1726/27 (£1), again on 8 October 1728 (12s.6d.), and also on 18 September 1729 (10s.).

Anecdotal evidence about Joshua Astbury/Heath making white salt-glazed stoneware comes from Josiah Wedgwood's record of an 'Account of the Pottery' given by 'Steel', aged eighty-four, in 1765.[56] Steel said that 'Joshua Heath or Astbury of Shelton made white ware with the addition of flint the first in Shelton'.

THOMAS ASTBURY
Lane Delph, fl.1725

Shaw stated that 'About 1725, Mr. Thomas Astbury … commenced business at Lane Delph; first using a different kind of marl [clay] with the flint, which so varied the teint of this improved pottery, that he named it *Cream-coloured stone ware*; and this was further improved by using only the whitest native clay, and flint ground at Mothersall [Moddershall, Staffs.] mill'.[57] At this date, this could be 'off-white' salt-glazed stoneware.

Shaw also said that Thomas Astbury was a son of Mr. Astbury of Shelton, and that his works was where the Lane Delph Market-Place was in 1829. The old hovel was removed in 1823 and Charles Mason established the market in 1828.[58] The Lane Delph Market-Place is marked on an 1832 map[59] as being between (2004) King Street and Mason Street.

Joshua Astbury of Shelton had no son named Thomas; but *John Astbury* of Shelton and Thomas Astbury were both sons of John and Ann Astbury of Fenton Culvert.[60] The will of Thomas Astbury of Stoke, Husbandman (farmer), made 2 May 1750 and proved 14 August 1752, may be that of the 1725 potter.[61] It named his wife Mary and three sons: Thomas, Samuel and Joshua.

JOHN BADDELEY
Shelton, c.1749-1761
BADDELEY AND FLETCHER
Shelton, 1761-c.1763

The ceramic career of John Baddeley was researched in great detail by John Mallet, and more recently by Trevor Markin.[62] Lorna Weatherill has analysed Baddeley's surviving records.[63] This account is concerned only with his activities as a salt-glaze potter and the reader is referred to their detailed works for fuller information. John Baddeley was baptised on 26 February 1725/26 at Wolstanton Church,[64] the 'mother-church' for the north of the Potteries.

John Baddeley was in a partnership with John Mare (see *Joshua Astbury* and also *John and Richard Mare*) until about 1749.[65] In 1759 he joined a partnership to make porcelain and leased his works to Reid, Baddeley and Co: 'Buildings and places which the said John Baddiley [sic] hath usually And commonly used in making Flint Ware, Biscuit China Ware, Red & Black Ware … at Shelton'.[66] That partnership was bankrupt in 1761, but Baddeley continued trading. He formed a new partnership in 1761 with Thomas Fletcher, the Newcastle-under-Lyme mercer who had overseen his bankruptcy, and continued in business until he died in April 1771.[67]

John Baddeley, earth potter, William Ford and James Till mortgaged a potworks at Snape Marsh, Shelton in 1758. It had formerly been held by *Humphrey Palmer* and was leased to Baddeley etc. from 1 January 1752.[68] John Baddeley's works was probably that numbered 89 on the 1802 map, then unoccupied.[69] A pottery factory continued on the site, lastly Mason's Ironstone, until it was demolished in 1998.

A detailed inventory, made in 1761 when John Baddeley was bankrupt,[70] lists nothing which could be positively construed as white salt-glazed stoneware. Black, red, tortoiseshell and china ware is noted, but the only conceivable suggestion of salt-glazed ware is 'green' ware, i.e., unfired ware *of any type*.

Evidence of John Baddeley's production of white salt-glazed stoneware is as follows. In 1752, he supplied one crate of 'sq[r] flowd [square flowered?] plates' and dishes, and 'scollopt [scolloped edge] plates' and 'scollopt flowd dishes', 144 pieces altogether, to *Thomas Wedgwood IV* of Churchyard and *Overhouse, Burslem*.[71] He was sending 'stoneware' to James Lawson of Virginia in 1759.[72] Baddeley's works were described as 'commonly used for making Flint ware [the usual term for white salt-glazed stoneware] in the same year.[73] Later and conversely, John Baddeley bought nineteen crates from *Elizabeth Bagnall*, a salt-glaze potter, in 1766.[74]

A surviving account book shows that, commencing 30 June 1762, Baddeley bought fifteen deliveries of salt in 150 days from Robert Gardner, a carrier, suggesting that Baddeley fired a salt-glaze oven every ten days. The record ends on 27 November of that year, so that further payments are not known.[75] The weight of salt is not shown, but nearly all payments were for £1.10s.8d., the same weekly amount that *Thomas Wedgwood IV of Overhouse* paid in 1772 for eight bushels of salt.

John Baddeley bought 'sprigs' (presumably metal masters, to make sprig moulds) from Jos Giles, a Birmingham engraver, in 1762,[76] 'runners' (roulette wheels for beading etc.) from John Beech, clockmaker of Newcastle-under-Lyme[77] and 'blocks' (master *negative* moulds) from John Greatbatch on 21 November 1761;[78] items which could have been used equally well for cream-coloured earthenware or white salt-glazed stoneware. He bought models from 'Harrop' and 'Bullock' in 1758, and from 'W. Bullock' in 1761.[79]

At the same period, Baddeley was buying 'pin dust',[80] copper filings probably used for making green glaze, and lead,[81] showing that his production was not confined to salt-glaze. Two months before John Baddeley's death in April 1771, Wedgwood wrote that Baddeley was very ill and 'in a large and prosperous business',[82] and on 21/22 April wrote again that Baddeley made perhaps the best ware of any, and an ovenful of it per day, but had reduced the prices of his dishes (presumably cream-coloured ware]) to that of 'white stone'.[83]

A salt-glazed stoneware tureen, cover and stand, incised 'J.B' and 'J.B. 1763', in the Victoria and Albert Museum, is suggested to have been made in Baddeley's works,[84] and a stoneware basketwork 'block' incised 'J.B. 1763' is also in the Victoria and Albert Museum.[85]

John Baddeley was also a flint-grinder. His 'Mill Acct' ledger[86] shows many potters to whom he sold flint from his flint mills (see Chapter IV, Raw Materials).

RALPH BADDELEY
Shelton

The eldest son of *John Baddeley*, Ralph Baddeley has been thought to have made 'White stone ware' on the basis of Simeon Shaw's page 161. A careful reading of Shaw's pages 157-61 confirms that he was referring to *Thomas and John Wedgwood*.[87] As Ralph's father appears to have ceased making salt-glazed ware after 1763, it seems unlikely that his son would resume making eight years later, after his father's death. A 1772 account from (Ralph) Baddeley and Fletcher to Lord Hamilton at Sandon Hall, for a very large dinner and dessert service, toilet articles etc. does not state the type of ware, but the likelihood is that the major part was cream-coloured ware.[88] If any salt-glazed ware was included, it could of course have been bought in to make up the order, as his father did in 1766.

JAMES BAGGALEY AND BROTHERS
Tunstall ?, fl.1763

These potters are included on the basis of three letters to Josiah Wedgwood, who regularly accepted orders from his customers for types of ware which he did not make, including white salt-glazed stoneware. On 8 January 1763 John Dunbibin of Liverpool, potter and dealer, wrote that 'Baggaley has packed me 10 crates and will pack 10 more soon – I have paid all the three Brothers of [*sic*] for what is com'n [*sic*, coming]'.[89] In the same year, on 18 August, Thomas Wedgwood, later Josiah's partner, wrote to him from London with orders from James Taylor including '10 Crates of Baggaley's ware by sea'.[90] Dunbibin wrote again on 24 September 1763: 'order Ten Crates of Mr. James Baggaley ware' and complained that Baggaley had charged him 6d. to bring the crates to Burslem.[91]

Baggaleys' ware may or may not have been white salt-glazed stoneware. The charge for bringing to Burslem shows that their pottery was nearby but not in Burslem. A John and Sarah Baggaley had three sons, all christened at Wolstanton parish church, which included Tunstall: John, 21 February 1711, Thomas, 12 October 1718 and James, 30 July 1721,[92] who *could* have been the three brothers mentioned by Dunbibin.

PETER BAGNALL
Burslem, fl.1748-61
ELIZABETH BAGNALL
Burslem, fl.1761-64

Peter Bagnall, Burslem, potter, was buried 3 March 1761[93] and his widow was granted administration of his large estate on 27 March 1761.[94] He was probably a son of Richard Bagnall (see *Ralph Shaw II, Richard Bagnall and Thomas Daniel*) of Rushton Grange, near Cobridge.[95] His widow, Elizabeth, continued his business.[96] She was noted as a Roman Catholic in 1767, a 'potter' aged forty,[97] and was buried at Burslem 29 January 1774.[98]

Because Peter Bagnall died intestate, an unusually detailed inventory of his possessions has survived. In his house of eight rooms, the contents were valued at some £80, including an eight day clock worth £5.15s., £14.5s. in half-crown pieces, twelve pictures of the Apostles and thirty-three pewter dishes and plates. The contents of his workhouses and warehouses were worth a further £186 and he was owed £598, of which £204 were 'doubtfull debts'.[99] The largest good debt was £123 owed by Addison and Co., London dealers. L. Weatherill has estimated that Peter Bagnall's total assets, including buildings, were over £1,000.[100]

The inventory shows that Peter Bagnall had a large works for 1761: four warehouses, a packing house, sliphouse, throwing house, turning house with a room over, an 'outshore' (lean-to building) adjoining the hovel, two or more ovens, and an 'Old Stove' (perhaps a drying room).

In the sliphouse there was a slip pan and three lawns (sieves), and £3 worth of 'Slip made', 20 pecks of ground flint, £2 of clay ready for throwing and £1.12s. of clay in balls, presumably ball clay as bought in. An old oven with three bands and a very bad oven full of saggars were each valued at £3, and there was £6 worth of 'Unburnt Ware'.

Peter Bagnall had three lathes and two wheels, squeezing boxes, turning tools, plaster, 500 feet of boards, and a crank of an old wheel, which would have been for a kick- or crank-wheel rather than a great-wheel. He also had a 'Glazing Ladder', assumed to be used for throwing salt into the oven.

In the warehouses there were large stocks of pottery, best, seconds and thirds: cups and saucers, punch bowls, washing basins, sugar bowls, double coffees, oblong dishes, decanters, teapots, mustard pots, flowered saucers, carved round dishes, cream jugs, cans, salts, plates, twifflers, fruit plates, petty pans and fruit baskets; and, in different sizes, mugs, basins, chamber pots, stoolpans, carved sauceboats and dishes, valued at £88, together with unsorted ware at £4.10s. Terms such as 'flowered' and 'carved' are typical descriptions of salt-glazed ware.

Packing was provided for by baskets worth 4s.6d. and 4lb. weight of cording. For his little horse, a lame chestnut mare and two mules, he had three pack saddles, three pairs of panniers and a pair of leather bags.

Evidence that Peter Bagnall made salt-glazed ware is provided by a transaction where he bought ware from salt-glaze potter *Jonah Malkin* of Burslem in 1748: 6 crates of 'dipt' best and seconds; and paid for it in December, partly in cash and *partly by 4 crates of best and seconds dipt*. In 1749, Bagnall took 363 dozen of dipt white for £15.2s. from Malkin.¹⁰¹ On 30 August 1754 twenty-four crates were shipped from Winsford down the River Weaver to Liverpool for Peter Bagnall.¹⁰²

Peter Bagnall's widow, Elizabeth Bagnall, continued to trade. In 1764, she sold to Josiah Wedgwood both plain dishes and table plates,¹⁰³ as well as sixty-three dozen white cups and saucers of pattern No. 1 for 10d. per dozen and forty-two cups and saucers of pattern No. 2 for the same price;¹⁰⁴ and later three dozen barley-corn pattern dishes and two dozen 'Mosage [sic, Mosaic?] & Basket' dishes, each for 10d. per dozen.¹⁰⁵ In the same year, she bought twelve dozen salt-glazed teaspoons in two sizes from *Thomas and John Wedgwood*, charged 12s. 'to allow profitt',¹⁰⁶ presumably to make up an order. Elizabeth Bagnall sold nineteen crates of unspecified ware worth £38.18s.11d. to *John Baddeley* in 1766.¹⁰⁷

WILLIAM BANKS AND JOHN TURNER
c.1759-1763
WILLIAM BANKS
1763-c.1776
'Spode Works', Stoke-upon-Trent

'Mr. R.[sic] Bankes' is said by Shaw to have made white stoneware with John Turner, about 1756, on part of the Spode factory site, in Stoke. Shaw also said that Josiah Spode I was employed by Banks 'on White Stone Ware, and for Cream Colour, Scratched, and Blue Painted'.¹⁰⁸ Shaw's 1829 recording of oral history often contains elements of facts now available.

William Banks and John Turner bought a potworks at Stoke-on-Trent on 7 November 1759, described as 'newly erected' when Benjamin Lewis, yeoman (farmer) transferred it to his son, Taylor Lewis, potter, in 1751. Turner transferred his share of the works to Banks on 7 December 1763, and probably went to Lane End (Longton).¹⁰⁹ Banks sold the site on 29 February 1764 (perhaps to pay out Turner), but continued as a tenant manufacturer there, possibly until Josiah Spode bought the site on 29 February 1776.¹¹⁰ This site was part of the present-day (2004) Spode factory site.

William Banks, Stoke, potter, insured his buildings in 1763 for £500, including four hovels suggesting four ovens, a chamber to make dishes in, two Lathouses (lathe houses), a painting house and three 'Smoakhouse's,¹¹¹ a large works for that time.

A William Banks was christened 9 September 1720 at Uttoxeter, son of William and Elizabeth. He might have been the nephew of Elizabeth Banks of Uttoxeter, who married *John Philip Elers* on 7 September 1699,¹¹² but no relationship has been found.

Banks was also a dealer in pottery and his 'painting house' might have been for any kind of ware. *Thomas and John and Wedgwood* sold redware to Mr. Banks & Co. in 1758 and unspecified crates in 1759.¹¹³ John Robertson advertised the dissolution of a partnership between Messrs. Banks and Robertson at the Staffordshire Warehouse in St. Paul's Churchyard on 14 July 1759. Robertson moved to what had formerly been the Longton Hall warehouse and Banks continued at the Staffordshire Warehouse.¹¹⁴ Thirteen years later, in 1772, William Banks, dealer in china, glass and earthenware, was at No. 7 Lombard Street, London, where he insured his utensils and stock for £500.¹¹⁵

THOMAS BARKER, Foley, Stoke-on-Trent, c.1770s-1786
See Chapter IX

DANIEL BIRD
Stoke-on-Trent, c.1700
DANIEL BIRD
Stoke-on-Trent, c.1720
DANIEL BIRD
Cliff Bank, Stoke-on-Trent, fl.-1753

Bird's reputation as a white salt-glazed stoneware potter rests solely on Simeon Shaw. He wrote:

At the top of Stoke, called Cliff Bank, is the manufactory, (now [1829] occupied by Mr. Thomas Mayer, a very intelligent potter,) where Mr. Daniel Bird first ascertained the exact proportion of Flint required by the several kinds of clay, to prevent the pottery cracking in the oven; and for which he was first called the *Flint Potter*. His remains lie under a dilapidated tomb at the steeple end of the old church; and the inscription mentions that he was by accident killed at Twickenham, near London.

Again, later in his *History*:

Mr. Daniel Bird's productions at the manufactory at Cliff Bank (which Mr. T. Mayer now [1829] occupies,) were very lucrative: Agate Buttons, Knife Hafts, and Flint ware, salt glaze, by which he speedily realised a handsome fortune. He was distinguished by the appellation of the *Flint Potter*, because he is believed to have first ascertained the exact quantity of flint proper to be mixed with the clays to form the body of the Pottery.¹¹⁶

Shaw also mentioned Bird in his *Chemistry of Pottery* (1837): writing of development in pottery bodies, Shaw stated 'the *white stone-ware*, from which the transition was easy to the *flint-ware*, by Daniel Bird, of Stoke'.¹¹⁷ Shaw's statement that Daniel Bird first found the proportion of flint required calls for a Daniel Bird who was active in the 1690-1720 period, when flint began to be used in Staffordshire. A Daniel Bird who could have been active in that period was baptised at Stoke on 7 February 1670/71, son of Thomas and Anne Bird.

A second Daniel Bird,¹¹⁸ was baptised at Stoke 13 February 1697/98, son of William Bird and Elizabeth Meer, and it was probably he who married Elizabeth Rowley at Stoke 10 April 1721. He could have been actively engaged in potting by 1720, rather late for the first research into proportion of flint.

A third Daniel Bird, whose baptism is not recorded, married Mary Johnson at Norton-in-the Moors near Stoke on 15 October 1743; and their son, yet another Daniel, was christened at Stoke on 13 June 1746.¹¹⁹ B. Hillier's research showed that John Turner was apprenticed to a Daniel Bird of Penkhull, Stoke, earth potter, on 25 March 1753,¹²⁰ presumably the third one. That Daniel Bird was buried at Stoke on 10 November 1753.¹²¹ He died intestate and his widow Mary was granted administration.¹²²

Mary Bird, widow, married Hugh Booth of Stoke, potseller, at Whitmore on 14 September 1757 and Bird's works continued to be held by the Booth family.¹²³ In 1802 it was still in their hands, No. 100 on the 1802 map, occupied by Booth and Sons.¹²⁴ The site was occupied in 2003 by Caudwell Communications, east of the junction of Hartshill Road and Shelton New Road, Stoke.

The Bird family is discussed by M.R. Parkinson in *The Incomparable Art* (Manchester: City Art Gallery, 1969), 20-22, in connection with a slipware mould.

JOHN BLACKWELL
Elder Road, Cobridge, c.1784

John Blackwell of Cobridge is named as a maker of white salt-glazed stoneware because of his listing as a maker of blue and white stoneware, cream and painted ware, in a 1784 directory.¹²⁵ Two years earlier he had supplied cobalt and unidentified pottery to Josiah and Thomas Wedgwood, Etruria.¹²⁶

John Blackwell remained a pottery manufacturer at Cobridge until his death on 27 August 1804,¹²⁷ by 1796 in partnership with Andrew Blackwell.¹²⁸ John Blackwell married Teresa Warburton 12 October 1788 at Stoke.¹²⁹

John Blackwell's works, No. 59 on the 1802 map,¹³⁰ was said to be later Furnival's, east of Elder Road, site of Magnet Ltd. in 2004.

He insured his house, works and contents for £550 in 1786; in 1789 for £300, and his house and contents only in January 1804.[131]

It was noted by Shaw[132] that 'Crystals of Cobalt [were] first brought into this Country [North Staffordshire] by Mr. Mark Walklett, and Mr. John Blackwell', oral history confirmed in essence by Blackwell's sale of cobalt to Wedgwoods in 1782.

JOSEPH BLACKWELL
Cobridge, c.1784-1787

Joseph Blackwell of Cobridge was listed as a 'Manufacturer of Blue and White Stone Ware, Cream and painted Wares' in 1784,[133] and as a manufacturer of Staffordshire-ware in 1795.[134] The site of Blackwell's Cobridge works is not known, but he had a warehouse in Strand Street, Liverpool in 1790, which he insured for £400.[135]

He supplied 'White stone' to Josiah and Thomas Wedgwood in 1787: 6 oval plain dishes 14 inch at 10d.; 6 ditto 12 inch at 6d. and 6 ditto 10 inch at 3d., total value 9s., on 25 June; and a hogshead (barrel) of similar dishes, 10 inch, 11 inch, 12 inch and 14 inch round flat plates, soup plates and a plain sauce tureen and stand for £6.0s.10d. on 16 August in the same year.[136] Other accounts between Blackwell and Wedgwood do not specify stone ware: an interesting one for 13 October 1786 is for 'Firing Coach pots',[137] perhaps Blackwell firing (and salt-glazing?) shapes which Wedgwood made and he did not.

Joseph Blackwell married Mary Warburton at Newcastle-under-Lyme on 3 February 1780; and married again at Newcastle on 28 June 1788 to Mary Whitfield.[138] He died in 1795 and was buried at Burslem on 27 December.[139] Simeon Shaw wrote in 1829 that Mr. Joseph Blackwell of Cobridge was 'recently at Caltagone [Italy]',[140] but this obviously refers to another person of the same name.

JAMES BOLD
Burslem, fl.1761-63

Firm evidence of Bold's production of salt-glazed ware lies in a lengthy account of ware supplied to Josiah Wedgwood between 5 July 1761 and 25 May 1764.[141] Amongst unspecified types of ware, it included Blue Basons at 12d., Blue Sugar Basons at 8d. and 6d., '1 doz Blew Tpts [teapots] at 10d, Best' endorsed 'Not very good', all on 4 May 1764, and a dozen blue teapots omitted from a 24 April 1762 account. 'Blue' is considered to refer to 'Littler-Wedgwood Blue' salt-glazed ware. James Bold had died in 1763 and the bill was headed 'to Charlotte Bold', receipted on 24 November 1764 by James Bold's executors, see below. Earlier, James Bould (*sic*) had supplied 'Red Sprig'd ware to *Jonah Malkin* in 1749: quart jugs, pint jugs, pint mugs, half-pints, butter dishes, half-pint basins, teapots and cups, together with black teapots.[142]

Other inter-potter transactions involved the purchase of Tortoiseshell cups and saucers and melon tureens and cups and saucers from Josiah Wedgwood (no date given)[143] and three dozen 'new mustard spoons' from *Thomas and John Wedgwood* on 27 November 1762.[144] The site of Bold's works is not known.

James Bold was baptised at Burslem 18 September 1717, and married Mary Simpson there 4 January 1741.[145] They had a son, John, baptised 24 October 1742,[146] and two daughters, Ann, baptised 23 December 1744 and Mary, baptised 17 December 1749.[147] Mary Bold died and was buried 16 October 1752.[148] James married again, this time to Charlotte Spencer at Burslem 17 November 1754, 'with the consent of parents',[149] so presumably Charlotte was under-age. They had two children: James Spencer baptised 18 June 1758 and Thomas baptised 11 July 1762.[150]

James Bold died in 1763 and was buried at Burslem on 28 May, aged 46.[151] In his will James Bold described himself as an 'Earth Potter', and left everything to his executors, John Bold of Congleton, stone mason and Thomas Spencer of Burslem, potseller, for the benefit of his wife Charlotte and children, until Ann and Mary were twenty-one (in 1770).[152] Charlotte Bold provided for herself earlier than that by marrying another master potter, Taylor Stevenson (see *Samuel Kirk and Co.*), at Burslem on 12 August 1764.[153]

ENOCH BOOTH SENIOR
Tunstall, fl.c.1743-1773
ENOCH AND GEORGE BOOTH
Tunstall, 1760s

Enoch Booth senior of Tunstall, potter, (1703[154]-1773) has been researched in some detail by Patricia Halfpenny,[155] particularly as a cream-coloured ware maker from c.1743 to his death in 1773.[156] William Pitt first brought Booth's name to attention in 1817 when he wrote: 'CREAM-COLOURED WARE, was first made in the year 1750, by Enoch Booth, of Tunstall'.[157]

Enoch Booth seems to have been in partnership with his brother-in-law George Booth[158] in the 1760s. It is likely that they were also cousins, but the connection has not been found. Enoch Booth's works were the two shown as No. 17 on the 1802 map,[159] then occupied by his son-in-law Anthony and also Edward Keeling. The two areas are now (2004) occupied by Phoenix, Hose and Forster Streets, and Mountfield Street.

Evidence of Enoch Booth making white salt-glazed ware is scarce and ambiguous. There is a white salt-glazed mug in the Fitzwilliam Museum (Colour Plate 14)[160] inscribed on the front '17 Enoch Booth 42', but this may well have been made for him, rather than by him or his workers. A 'Large dish, made at Tunstall, in 1757, by Enoch Booth', which *might* have been white salt-glazed stoneware, recorded in the Museum of Practical Geology in 1855, is not now known to exist.[161]

Jonah Malkin of Burslem supplied 'Mr. Enock [*sic*] Booth' with 'Dipt' quarts, pints, 'threes', best and seconds in 1748.[162] In June 1763 John Dunbibin of Liverpool, merchant and potter, complained to Wedgwood about Enoch Booth's ware being the 'most abominable for best ever seen – he's a very bad man'. Three months later, Dunbibin asked Wedgwood for one dozen 'Inameld [*sic*] white Teapots', and told Wedgwood that 'George Booth when here offered to sell Inameled [*sic*] upon moderate terms and 12 months credit – I am not fond of the name of Booth but take him to be a deal better man than his Cousin – so get them from him'.[163]

On 17 January 1764 Dunbibin sent Josiah Wedgwood an urgent order for moulded, cloudy, 'mellon' and 'collyflower' ware, and asked him to 'get me from George Booth' teapots, basons, double coffees, ewers and cups and saucers 'Enamel'd flint'.[164] Dunbibin also asked Wedgwood to ask his brother (*Thomas Wedgwood IV of Overhouse*, salt-glaze potter) to send '3 crates of plates', which might well have been *plain* salt-glazed ware. Dunbibin's letter suggests that he wanted his plain salt-glazed ware from Thomas Wedgwood and his enamelled salt-glazed ware from Booth.

Ten days later Enoch and George Booth, Tunstall, invoiced Wedgwood for almost identical items of 'Enam'd Ware'.[165] Enoch Booth had supplied Josiah Wedgwood with ball clay, roof tiles, floor tiles and zaffre (colour) in 1762-63, and Enoch and George Booth bought cream-coloured ware from Josiah Wedgwood in 1764.[166]

There is an ambiguous statement in an order from Addison and Abernathy, Hermitage Street, Wapping, to Josiah Wedgwood in 1763 for various shapes. Abernathy noted 'The above I mean to be White Stone the same shapes as those sent [in] Green ... pray send us all the new patterns you can make ... oval sallad [*sic*] Dishes Green & White would sell well of the French pattern – Mr. Booth is making some of them of 3 Sizes, 10, 12, & 14 Inches'.[167] It is not clear whether or not these dishes were salt-glazed.

In 1767, *Thomas and John Wedgwood* of Burslem, themselves eminent salt-glazed ware potters, received from Aaron Wedgwood 'Enamell Teapots he had of Mr. E. Booth' worth 7s. Between 1767 and 1772, *Thomas and John Wedgwood* supplied Enoch Booth senior with a variety of spoons both fired and unfired; and 'custerd[s] [*sic*]' and artichoke saucers in 1772. They bought from him enamelled teapots of unspecified body, 'cream [-coloured?] cups and saucers', and roof tiles.[168]

The evidence above shows that Enoch Booth dealt in various commodities. In his will made 27 February 1773[169] he described himself as a potter, and it seems certain that he did make cream-coloured ware. It can be said with some justification that he and George Booth enamelled white salt-glazed stoneware, and possibly made it.

JOHN BOURNE
Burslem, 1770-1774
BOURNE, WRIGHT AND CO.
Burslem, 1787

John Bourn [*sic*] signed the salt-glaze potters' price list in 1770.[170] In the same year John Bourne of Burslem sold nine dozen barleycorn soup plates to Josiah Wedgwood's partner, Thomas Wedgwood at 18d. and 21d., the prices agreed for 17 inch and 18 inch dishes.[171]

Thomas and John Wedgwood of the Big House, Burslem, salt-glaze potters, sold twenty dozen *unfired* custard cups to John Bourne on 18 February 1772 and supplied their customer William Kell of Newcastle upon Tyne with '12 Doz Cups – John Bourne' value 12s.0d. on 12 May of the same year.[172] These are examples of inter-trading between salt-glaze potters.

In 1773 Bourne sold white ware to Josiah Wedgwood, and in 1774 white soup plates.[173] By 1776 Bourne was supplying Wedgwood with tortoiseshell cups and saucers, and in 1784 enamelled cream-colour cups and saucers, and quart mugs.[174] Bourne may have been making all three kinds of ware from 1770 and Wedgwood's requirements may have altered over the years. John Bourne, potter, was buried at Burslem 15 November 1785.[175]

A new firm, Bourne, Wright and Co., Burslem, supplied Messrs (Josiah) Wedgwoods with '12 Doz. White Stone Champts [chamber pots] 2d [seconds] @ 16d. 16[s].0[d].' on 20 March 1787.[176]

WILLIAM BOURNE or BURN
12 Westport Road, Burslem, c.1750
See Chapter IX

BOVEY TRACEY POTTERIES
Bovey Tracey, Devon, c.1766-pre-1775
See Chapter IX

BRENTFORD, Middlesex
c.1759

Jean Hellot (1685-1766) was a French scientist, who left notes which are now part of his *Collections d'Arts et de Sciences* in the Bibliothèque Centrale de la Ville de Caen in Normandy.[177] Amongst these papers are Hellot's notes of information given to him by 'Broillet alias Fribourg', who had been to England in 1758-59, and seen white pottery made there. At the end of these notes, quoting Broillet, Hellot wrote (translated by B. Dragesco): 'The finest white pottery of England, glazed by the vapour of salt, is called *Ware* and is made [in] *Schtaffshire*, 110 miles away from London, and at *Brenforth*, 7 miles away [from London]. Broillet also described the manufacture of salt-glazed ware, possibly near *Oxford*.

'Schtaffshire' is obviously Staffordshire and 'Brenforth' seems likely to be Brentford, Middlesex. It has been suggested[178] that Brentford refers to *Isleworth*, three miles away, where pottery production had begun c.1757, but there is as yet no evidence of salt-glaze production there. There is a reference to a Daniel Turner's Pottery at Brentford in the 1770s,[179] which might have been Broillet's 1758-59 'Brenforth' salt-glazed pottery.

JOHN BRINDLEY
Market Place?, Burslem
fl.1761-1772

John Brindley (1718-*c*.1793)[180] married Ann Rogers 8 October 1748 at Wolstanton.[181] Between 1760 and 1772 John Brindley was in partnership with his brother, James Brindley (the canal engineer), *John Shrigley* of Burslem, potter and John Simpson of Hanley, potter in land, buildings and works in Burslem, presumably the site of his potworks. Shrigley and John Brindley bought out the other two in 1772, when James Brindley died, and divided the property between them.[182] In 1802 a house and potworks in the Market Place, Burslem, was owned by a John Brindley, suggesting that this was the site of John Brindley's 1760s works.[183]

John Brindley took ten shares (£2,000) in the proposed Trent and Mersey Canal in 1766, and was a member of the Committee of Management.[184] He built potworks on the canal side at Longport in 1773,[185] possibly marking the end of his Burslem town business.

John and James Brindley were also partners in buying the Turnhurst estate in 1760, including the Golden Hill Colliery,[186] thus owning a source of coal for his pottery.

William Adams (1746-1805), later a master potter, is said to have been apprenticed to John Brindley, presumably in the 1760s.[187]

Brindley was supplying Josiah Wedgwood with wares from 1764 to at least 1768, which seem likely to have been white salt-glazed stoneware. Several documents exist for 1764 when Wedgwood bought 'Basket Work' plates, dishes and 'sosbots' from Brindley in various sizes, but he also bought in cups and saucers and mugs.[188] In April 1768 Brindley supplied Wedgwood with a substantial number of 'Inda [*sic*]' pattern 'Dishes' amounting to £14.16s.4d.[189]

John Brindley had traded with Mary Forbes of Liverpool up to 1764, when she owed him £34.11s.0d.[190] Brindley sold 'Dishes Gadroon' 13, 14 and 15 inches, and 'do. Mosake [mosaic]' 15 inches between 29 August 1761 and March 1762 to Jos. and Richard Marsh of Burslem, for £2.17s.8d. He received £1.2s.5d. at the settlement of Marshs' insolvency.[191] Brindley also sold 'Tureanes [tureens]' and other goods to *Thomas Wedgwood IV, Overhouse*, Burslem between 1766 and 1771, and the account was receipted for him in 1774.[192]

JOSEPH BUCKNALL
Cobridge, c.1760-1764

Jos. Bucknall of Cowbridge [*sic*, Cobridge] supplied Josiah Wedgwood with white tea toys, chamber pots, 'Barley Corn' plates and 'twyflers' [*sic*, twifflers, small plates], gadroon dishes, sauce boats and tureens in 1764, and offered 'Barley Corn' tureens and many other designs of sauce boats, all items typical of white salt-glazed stoneware at that date. *Per contra*, Bucknall ordered cream colour, cauliflower, melon, green sprig, purple and yellow, pine apple, fluted pearl green gilt and image toys from Wedgwood, 'a crate at least' for Bucknall's customer Mr. Wheeler.[193] Another customer was Mrs. Mary Forbes of Liverpool, who owed Jos. Bucknall £27.11s.3d. in September 1764 and had to offer security for any further supplies.[194]

Joseph Bucknall bought six dozen teaspoons from *Thomas and John Wedgwood* for 6s. in 1760, the account cleared five years later 'by carriage of goods from Manchester and Birmingham 3s, by 2s. cash and 1s. "abated"'.[195] The carriage account referred to Joseph Bucknall's carrying business, which he wanted to sell in 1760, waggon, cart and packhorses 'with the goodwill of the stage of carriage from Manchester to Birmingham and Coventry', as he intended to follow the earthenware trade only. In fact he took a partner and continued to carry.[196] A Joseph Bucknall married Ann Bagnall of Stoke at Burslem in 1758, and a Joseph Bucknall was buried at Burslem in 1764.[197] The Bucknall family (probably taking its name from the nearby village of Bucknall) were noted as potters in Cobridge in 1657,[198] and there were several branches in the 1760s – see *Ralph and Robert Bucknall*, next. They were Roman Catholics, and records of baptisms rarely survive.

ROBERT BUCKNALL
Cobridge, 1770
MARY BUCKNALL AND CO.
Cobridge, 1771
RALPH BUCKNALL
Cobridge, 1775
RALPH BUCKNALL AND SON(S)
Cobridge, 1777-c.1781

Robert Bucknall signed the 1770 price list as a salt-glaze potter,[199] and Robert Bucknall of Cobridge died 5 September 1770, aged thirty-two.[200] A bill from Mary Bucknall and Co. to Josiah Wedgwood, undated, for white lead, was receipted 13 July 1771 on behalf of Robert Bucknall's executors. Mary Bucknall, widow, Cobridge, was buried at Burslem 8 March 1777.[201] (See the note above, under *Joseph Bucknall*, for the Bucknall family of Cobridge.)

One of Josiah Wedgwood's customers, C.W. Krause of Brunswick, Germany, thanked Wedgwood for Mr. Bucknall's address at Cobridge in 1774, and said he would not fail to make use of him.[202] Although Wedgwood was willing to help his customers to buy salt-glazed ware direct, he still received orders himself, which he asked Bucknalls to fulfil.

In 1775 Ralph Bucknall, Cobridge, probably son of Robert, supplied Wedgwoods with chocolates and saucers, bowls, milkpots, sugar dishes and covers, cups and saucers and teapots, all Best Blue, cups and saucers 2nd Blue, and Barley, Indian and Basket dishes, flat plates and soup plates, together with gadroon and plain items, all descriptions of salt-glazed ware.[203] When his son, Robert, wrote to Thomas Wedgwood at Etruria in the same year, he addressed 'Useful Thomas' as 'Dear Uncle' and signed himself 'Your m[os]t affectionat Nephew', but proof of the relationship has not been found.[204] Two years later, 1777, Ralph Bucknall and Son supplied huge quantities of Shell, Gadroon and plain wares to Josiah and Thomas Wedgwood in eighteen crates, including '42 dozen plain Chocolats X handled', still apparently salt-glazed wares.[205]

A further account in 1780 still refers to Indian, basket, and Barley (salt-glaze) patterns, but also Royal pattern sugar dishes. A 1781 directory listed Ralph Bucknall and Sons as potters at Cobridge, but a 1784 directory showed solely Robert Bucknall of Cobridge as making Queen's, blue painted etc. wares.[206] Ralph Bucknall (Papist, Cobridge) was buried 28 February 1784 at Burslem,[207] and it was presumably his son, Robert, who supplied Wedgwood with Tortoise Chocolates and Stands in that year.[208] Clearly he had turned over to earthenware production.

Robert Bucknall's works was probably No. 59 on the 1802 map,[209] a site now (2004) occupied by Douglas Street and Crane Street.

THOMAS CARTLICH
Burslem

Thomas Cartlich supplied Josiah Wedgwood with two crates of sortable 'Crouch', thirty-nine and thirty-eight dozen respectively, at 9d. per dozen in April and July 1764, his account receipted by Ann Cartlich.[210] 'Crouch ware' is considered to refer to *brown* salt-glazed ware.

John Douglas of Whitehaven was a customer of Josiah Wedgwood, and commented to him in 1763 'Crouch wanted but I have sent orders to Thos Cartledge [*sic*] myself'. In January 1764 Wedgwood was asked by Douglas to obtain a wide range of 'Crouch' jugs, mugs, tots, mustard pots, porringers and bowls from Thos Cartlich. Wedgwood was to pay him as they are made 'as they are but poor and can't afford much Creditt [*sic*]' and 'I beg you will Charge them to make them Right Misers [correct measures] according to orders or if they are not They are of very Littell [*sic*] service to me'. In April 1764 Douglas asked Wedgwood again for 'one crate of small "misered" Crouch Muges [*sic*]'.[211]

Thomas Wedgwood IV of the Overhouse obtained fifty-three dozen of 'Croutch' at 9d. a dozen (probably mugs) and eleven dozen of jugs and bowls at 1s. a dozen from Thomas Cartlidge for Charles Kinkead, his customer in Strabane, Ireland, in 1765.[212] Altogether, Thomas Cartlich seems to have been a maker of brown 'Crouch' salt-glazed ware, and not white.

A '1740' map of Burslem places Thomas Cartlich's potworks at the top of Packhorse Lane, later part of Fountain Place works.[213] Ann, wife of Thomas Cartlich, was buried 12 August 1780 and Thomas Cartlich was buried 25 July 1786, both at Burslem.[214]

SAMUEL CHATTERLEY
Shelton, Staffordshire
c.1770

The Chatterley family were potters in North Staffordshire from c.1709.[215] A Samuel Chatterley sent thirty crates of unspecified ware down the River Weaver to Liverpool as early as 1742,[216] and bought flint, china, block (negative) moulds and teapots from *John Baddeley* between 1758 and 1767, credited in 1763-67 by cash, crates ware, bowls and sugar boxes, totalling £426.[217] In one of John Baddeley's ledgers the accounts are headed 'Old Sam Chatterley', suggesting that there were two of that name in business in 1765-67.[218] 'Samel Chatterly' signed the 1770 salt-glaze potters' price list,[219] the only firm evidence of him producing white salt-glazed stoneware.

Samuel Chatterley, Shelton, potter, made his will 6 January 1778, noted at Newcastle-under-Lyme Manor Court on 7 October 1778, after his death.[220]

CHESTER WHITE WARE MANUFACTORY,
Paper Mill Lane (later Mill Street), Chester, c.1757-pre-1777
See Chapter IX

JOHN COBB
Burslem?, fl.1770

John Cobb signed the 1770 salt-glaze potters' price list.[221] Cobb's signature to this agreement confirms that he was making *white* salt-glazed stoneware in 1770, although it appears he turned to brown 'crouch' ware later. He married Ann Bagshaw at Burslem on 26 January 1770 and their son John was baptised there on 25 June 1774.[222]

Strictly, nothing more is known of him, but on 14 January 1777, Josiah Wedgwood told his partner that his head clerk, Peter Swift, had 'join'd in partnership with Mr. Cobb, my late warehouseman here [Etruria], in a work of Critch [*sic*, Crouch, i.e. brown salt-glazed] ware, such as Mr. Haywood was concern'd in at Chesterfield. He is likewise to be a Landlord at Mayday next, having taken the Leopard [Inn] in Burslem, so that I must seek out for another Clerk'.

Wedgwood told Bentley on 9 February 1778 that Swift was tired of being a landlord and 'if I will continue him in my place he will quit the public business, & give up his share of the potwork he was engaged in & sit down quietly to his desk & think of nothing further'. Two months later, 18 April 1778, Wedgwood told Bentley that Swift and Cobb had been 'losing money every day, & in the utmost distress to pay their creditors, & the weekly wages'. Wedgwood lent them about £100 to clear their debts. Wedgwood made it a condition of Swift continuing with him that he quit the potwork.[223]

There is nothing more than a common surname to connect the 1770 John Cobb with Swift's 1777-78 partner, but the surname Cobb is rare in North Staffordshire so the possibility that it was the same man must be entertained.

Swift came to Wedgwood at Burslem in 1766 on Bentley's recommendation. It is likely that he was the Peter Swift born at Liverpool in 1731.[224] He left Wedgwood in 1788.[225]

JOHN DANIEL
Burslem?, fl.1770

John Daniel signed the 1770 salt-glaze potters' price list.[1] No other firm information about him has been found. The Daniel family were potters in Burslem for many years.[2] A John Daniel was baptised at Burslem 20 February 1741/42, son of Joseph and Mary,[3] and buried at Burslem 24 November 1788, aged forty-eight.[4]

RICHARD DANIEL
Burslem, -1687

Richard Daniel of Burslem, yeoman (farmer) was buried 6 January 1686/87 at Burslem. In his will, he left 'the Service Yard in Burslem and the barne and workhouses thereupon erected' to his wife Sara for life and then to Richard, son of his brother-in-law *Aaron Wedgwood*.[5] The inventory of his possessions, made 7 January 1686/87, included 'All manner of loose bords [*sic*, ware boards] which belonge to the trade of an earthen potter and all other utensills belonging to the said trade with severall ladders'. The inclusion of ladders with his pottery utensils suggests the slight possibility that they were used for salting a potter's oven, which at that date might have been for making brown 'Crouch' salt-glazed ware.

The 'Service Yard' seems to have been near the Overhouse, in Burslem. Its name may derive from the Service-tree, a fruit tree.

SAMPSON AND RALPH DANIEL
Sneyd Street, Cobridge, fl.1762-1769

Sampson Daniel and partner of 'Cowbridge' [Cobridge] supplied white salt-glazed ware to Josiah Wedgwood in 1762 and 1763: large and small Barley Corn tureens, 'Dresden or Barley Corn tureans [*sic*]', oblong dishes, fruit plate shapes and 'Longer for Bread' shapes, large and less 'Bread Basketts or fruit' and 14, 15 and 16 inch gadroon dishes.

In return they bought teapots and 'Saffron pots' from Josiah Wedgwood.[6] They also bought salt-glazed tablespoons from *Thomas and John Wedgwood* in 1762.[7] All these transactions are good examples of potters 'buying in' to complete orders for their customers. Ralph and Sampson Daniel bought flint from *John Baddeley* in 1763 and 1765, and paid by crates and goods.[8]

Sampson (1729-?1769)[9] and Ralph Daniel (1722-1765)[10] were the younger sons of Thomas Daniel of Cobridge, gentleman, and he left them £80 each when he died on 14 November 1759, aged seventy-four.[11] A sister became Mrs. *Ann Warburton*.

It may have been this Ralph Daniel who is said to have brought from a manufactury in France a plaster mould for a table plate, of which the pattern was imitated by Aaron Wood, a model maker.[12] The French mould was said to have given the Staffordshire potters the idea of making moulds with plaster.

Sampson Daniel, late of Cobridge, potter, surviving partner of Ralph Daniel, deceased, was made bankrupt on 28 April 1767, on the petition of Thomas Daniel of Cobridge, potter (perhaps Sampson's brother, *Thomas Daniel II*), to whom Sampson owed £100 or more. His assignees sold his house, potworks, buildings etc. to Joseph Stone, Cobridge, potter (see *Warburton and Stone*) and Ralph Aston, Newcastle-under-Lyme, peruke (wig) maker in 1769 for £305.[13] In 1787 the house and works were sold to William Adams for £555.[14] The house and works were situated on the south side of Sneyd Street, Cobridge, probably no. 56 on the 1802 map.[15]

THOMAS DANIEL I
Burslem

Thomas Daniel I was one of the Staffordshire potters, including *John Wedgwood, Thomas Wedgwood I and Richard Wedgwood, Richard Muchell, Richard Mere* and *Ralph Shaw I*, who petitioned the Privy Council on 11 June 1696,[16] alleging that *John Dwight* of London was obstructing them in their trade under pretence of his 1684 patent.[17] This patent gave Dwight a fourteen-year monopoly of making white gorges, marbled porcelain vessels, statues and figures, fine stone gorges and vessels, transparent porcelain, opaque red and dark coloured porcelain or china, Persian wares and Cologne or Stone Wares. Nothing further has been found about this petition, but its instigation by the Staffordshire potters shows that they were making or wished to make ware of a type which Dwight claimed to have patented. There is no certainty that Thomas Daniel was making salt-glazed ware.

Thomas Daniel I may have been the brother of *Richard Daniel* of Burslem, farmer and potter, who died in 1686/87 and left £10 to his brother Thomas, and £5 to Thomas' son, also Thomas Daniel.[18] It is suggested that Thomas Daniel I may have occupied Birch House, in Swan Square, Burslem, in 1698.[19] The name is common in Burslem and nothing more has been found to identify this Thomas Daniel, nor prove that he made white salt-glazed stoneware.

THOMAS DANIEL II
Cobridge
fl. 1764-1770

Thomas Daniel junior was one of the potters who signed the 1770 salt-glaze potters' price list.[20] He insured his dwelling-house and pottery buildings for £200 each in 1766.[21] Thomas Daniel II of Cobridge sold 'Dutch pudding Cups' to Josiah Wedgwood in 1764 and five crates of 'Soup Dishes Baskett', Barleycorn plates, and '24 doz flats & 10 doz Soupe plates 34 doz @ 1/6 Engin^d 2.11. 0' in 1768,[22] typical descriptions of salt-glazed ware.

Thomas Daniel II bought pints, quarts and 'dipt goods' from *Jonah Malkin* in 1748-49.[23] He bought flint from *John Baddeley* in 1765 and 1767, and also cream-colour teapots, paid for by 'small plates' and 'Crates'.[24]

Thomas Daniel II appears to have been born in 1715,[25] son of Thomas Daniel, and brother of *Sampson and Ralph Daniel*, and Mrs. *Ann Warburton*. He was listed as a papist aged forty-nine in 1767,[26] and he died in 1772.[27] It was probably he who made his brother Sampson Daniel bankrupt in 1769.

DERBY

There is firm evidence of the production of white salt-glazed stoneware at Derby. Two sites are discussed below, Cockpit Hill and Nottingham Road. The evidence is an archaeological find of white salt-glazed stoneware shards with a piece of salt-glazed kiln furniture, a contemporary account with a drawing of a kiln, and a contemporary artist's kiln drawing and notes.

A Swedish industrial spy, R.R. Angerstein, visited Derby in 1754.[28] In his transcribed notes he stated that there were two factories in Derby, both established c.1751: one for china or porcelain and one for flint or white-ware. The china factory employed forty people and made only figures and flowers. The white-ware factory was much larger, and, most importantly for identification, Angerstein noted there 'Prices of whiteware from Mr. 'Rolf Steen". Ralph Steane had been a partner at the Cockpit Hill potworks from 1751, so Angerstein's notes relate to that factory.

The second contemporary report is by a French artist, made between 1768 and 1771. François Joseph Bélanger drew elevations and plans of two kilns.[29] The context suggests that both kilns were at Derby, but it is by no means certain. One kiln elevation and separate kiln plan is for porcelain, so that one could assume that this kiln was at Nottingham Road.

The purpose of the other joint kiln elevation and plan is not stated, but it is endorsed with two notes. Translated, the first note gives the quantity and frequency of salting a kiln: nine times in four and a half hours, nine pounds of salt. The second note gives a stoneware body recipe: four parts of clay to one part of flint.[30] There is very little difference in the design of the two kilns, but the presence of salt-glaze references on the second kiln drawing may imply that it was used for making salt-glazed stoneware.

Bélanger's 1768-71 sectional elevation of a salt-glaze kiln is much more sophisticated than Angerstein's 1754 sketch. Both are within protective hovels, but Bélanger's kiln has cylindrical sides and a domed roof (as did Angerstein's Chelsea kiln), whilst Angerstein's dome rises from floor level. Angerstein shows three round fireboxes whilst Bélanger shows five rectangular ones. There is nothing conclusive about these variations: the kiln may well have been completely rebuilt in the intervening fourteen years, or the drawings may be of different kilns at different works.

COCKPIT HILL, 1751-c.1780

There was a potworks at Cockpit Hill, Derby from 1751 to c.1780, on the town side of a mill leat off the River Derwent. William Butts, John Heath, Thomas Rivett and Ralph Steane commenced a partnership as potters there from 11 November 1751 and it continued through various changes of partners until John and Christopher Heath were bankrupt in 1779.[31] There have been suggestions that white salt-glazed stoneware items were made at Cockpit Hill, based on similarity of shapes to cream-coloured pieces made there.[32]

Of the partners, F. Williamson suggested that John Heath, banker, provided the capital, Thomas Rivett was the landowner and William Butts was the practical man.[33] However, Butts was already in Derbyshire in 1742 and 1743, whilst the name of the junior partner, Ralph Steane, occurs (as Ralph Steen) in marriages at Burslem in 1725, 1739 and 1749.[34] It seems more likely that Butts was the promoter and it was Steane who was recruited to bring practical knowledge of the techniques of salt-glazed stoneware from Staffordshire to Derby, especially as Angerstein said that the white-ware works originated from Newcastle in Staffordshire. Steane's name was no longer mentioned in 1758, and Butts may have taken over his role.

As noted above, R.R. Angerstein visited Derby in 1754, and recorded valuable information about the two potworks he found there. His naming of 'Rolf Steen [Ralph Steane]' at the 'white-ware factory' and his description of salting the ware identifies the Cockpit Hill works as the one producing white salt-glazed stoneware in 1754.

Angerstein noted that the whiteware factory was much larger than the porcelain works (which employed forty people on figures and flowers), and had 'two large kilns of the Chelsea type'.[35] The Chelsea kiln as sketched earlier by him was cylindrical in shape, with a domed top, an entrance set higher than the fireboxes, and four visible rectangular fireboxes, presumably indicating eight in all.[36] Angerstein's sketch of the Derby kiln shows a simple dome within a hovel, with three semi-circular fireboxes with top openings, and three rectangular holes on the shoulder, for salting. The three visible fire-boxes suggest that there were six in all ranged round the kiln. If our supposition that Steane had been recruited from Burslem in 1751 to initiate white salt-glazed stoneware production at Cockpit Hill is correct, it is likely that this kiln is representative of Burslem kilns c.1750.

Angerstein described placing the ware in saggars with 'holes in the sides to permit the entry of the salt-vapours', and stated 'towards the end [of the firing] the salt is thrown into the kiln through openings in the top'. With such a first-hand account, there can be no doubt of the production of white salt-glazed stoneware at Cockpit Hill in 1754.

He went on to tell that the body was half 'dutch pipe-clay' and half calcined and ground flint,[37] the clay also calcined and ground before mixing. (Angerstein was in serious error about the proportions of clay and flint, see Chapter V.) The mixed body was dried on a rectangular brick slip-kiln to a 'consistency convenient for throwing or modelling', described in detail under 'Body preparation' in Chapter V. 'Scratch-blue' decoration was applied when required. Angerstein noted a long list of shapes produced, with prices: simple plates, plates with modelled roses,[38] serving dishes for puddings, handled teacups, half pint, one pint and two pint [mugs?], cheese plates, six-inch diameter bowls, breadbaskets, chamber pots, sugar bowls or caskets, sugar-cups, teapots 'holding more than 1 pint' and large chamber pots. The prices ranged from 1s. for a dozen of twenty-four sugar-cups to 2s.6d. per dozen (number not stated so presumably twelve) of the 'Ditto [Ordinary plates] with modelled roses'. Seconds were sold for 1s. for the dozens shown, and 5% was allowed for breakage.[39]

When the contents of the works were offered for sale in 1780, it included enamelled and blue and white china, enamelled and plain creamware and 'a great quantity of White Stone and Brown ware'.[40] It can be inferred that the 'white stone ware' was salt-glazed, but there is no information to show whether it was current production or old stock.

NOTTINGHAM ROAD, c.1770

There was another potwork in Derby, at Nottingham Road, across the River Derwent from the town, best known for porcelain manufacture.[41] Excavations adjoining the site in 1987-90 revealed white salt-glazed shards and a piece of salt-glazed kiln furniture, adhering to part of a white salt-glazed saucer.[42] This last find strongly indicates that white salt-glazed stoneware was made somewhere in Derby, and its proximity to the Nottingham Road potworks suggests that it was made there.

Between 1768 and 1771 a French artist, François Joseph Bélanger, drew elevations and plans of two kilns.[43] The context suggests that both kilns were at Derby, but it is not certain. One kiln elevation and separate kiln plan is for porcelain, so that one could assume that this kiln was at Nottingham Road.

The purpose of the other joint kiln elevation and plan is not stated, but it is endorsed with two notes. Translated, the first note gives the quantity and frequency of salting the kiln: nine times in four and a half hours, nine pounds of salt. The second note gives a stoneware body recipe: four parts of clay to one part of flint.[44] There is very little difference in the design of the two kilns, but the presence of salt-glaze references on the second kiln drawing may imply that it was used for making salt-glazed stoneware. Whilst Angerstein's notes confirm that white salt-glazed stoneware was made at Cockpit Hill in 1754, it is possible that white salt-glaze stoneware production had commenced at Nottingham Road between then and 1768, and that Bélanger's more advanced 1768-71 salt-glaze kiln was there, substantiated by the finds of white salt-glazed shards and salt-glazed kiln furniture in 1987-90.

JOHN EDGE AND JOHN GRETTON
Fenton Vivian, c.1752

John Edge and John Gretton, potters, leased 'two Workhouses then in the holding of him the said John Peate in ffenton Vivian aforesaid one whereof is called the Whiteware Workhouse His other the Dipware Workhouse' from *John Peat* on 3 October 1752.[45] 'Whiteware' and 'Dipware' describe the two types of white salt-glazed stoneware made at that time, so that Edge and Gretton may have continued to make white salt-glazed stoneware. John Peat was always described as 'of Lane Delph', which is in the township of Fenton Vivian, but the site of Peat's 1752 workhouses is not known.

Nothing more is known of John Gretton, but a John Edge was hired as a potter by *Thomas Whieldon* of Fenton Vivian on 9 February 1751, and John Edge senior had previously been hired by Whieldon.[46] A John Edge, son of John and Elizabeth Edge, was christened at Stoke-on-Trent on 16 September 1716.[47]

SAMUEL EDGE
Burslem, c.1710-1721

Josiah Wedgwood listed Samuel Edge as a maker of 'Stone Ware' in Burslem, c.1710-1715 (Fig. 26).[48] The location of his works was described as 'Next to the West', following Isaac Ball's works 'S.W. end of the Town'. The location could be construed as somewhere in the Navigation Road area.

Samuel Edge was born c.1665 and married Alice Wedgwood in 1693.[49] When he died in 1721,[50] the inventory of his possessions included '3 Mortars & pestills [pestles]' worth £2.5s.0d.[51] These could have been used for pounding lead for lead-glazed ware, but because of their value are more likely to have been large and therefore for pounding calcined flint, used for stoneware.[52] Amongst his potting equipment, he also possessed 108 boards, two wheels and lathes, four shovels and four paddles, one iron crow(bar) and three iron pokers, two pairs of tongs, three iron bonds about the ovens and sieves. No stock of ware or raw materials was itemised.

He left all his extensive property, including workhouses, pot-houses, smokehouses and potovens (all in the plural) to his wife Alice. He also left one guinea (£1.05) to the Burslem Church-wardens 'toward the Bells'. Samuel Edge's domestic items included forty-three pewter dishes and plates, and '1 Gun & Sword'.

It seems likely that Samuel Edge made white or white-dipped salt-glazed stoneware.

JOHN FENTON AND THOMAS HILL,
Shelton Farm, Stoke-on-Trent, 1720-22
See Chapter IX

- FORD
Lower Market Place, Longton

Simeon Shaw wrote in 1829 that 'Roger Wood ... in 1756, erected the manufactory (now occupied by Mr. Sampson Bridgwood ...) on the side of the Brook at the lower Market-Place, Lane End. Here a person named Ford, for some years made common stone earthenware, and brown ware.'[53] The works was probably no. 130 on the 1802 map, east of the Crown Hotel in 2004.[54]

The ware produced by Ford seems likely to have been crouch ware or brown salt-glazed stoneware, and coarse redware. Nothing more has been found about him.[55]

ROBERT GARNER AND CO.
Row Houses, Fenton, Stoke-on-Trent

Shaw wrote 'About 1750, Mr. John Barker, with his Brother, and Mr. Robert Garner, commenced the manufactory of Shining Black, and White Stone ware, salt glaze, at the Row Houses, near the Foley, Fenton; and where afterwards they made tolerable cream colour'. Elsewhere Shaw makes another reference to Robert Garner's association with the Row Houses manufactory.[56]

Although Shaw says Garner made white salt-glazed stoneware, Robert Garner and Co. actually supplied Josiah Wedgwood with brown china teapots, ewers and pineapple jars in 1762, and brown china, tortoiseshell teapots, black teapots and cream ewers in 1763-64.[57] These are entirely different types of ware and at present there is no confirmation of Shaw's statement.

Thomas Whieldon's notebook includes several mentions of Robert Garner: Whieldon hired him in 1749; rented him a house at Fenton Hall/Bank in May 1752; paid Robert Gardner's son in December 1752; and hired 'Robert Gardner sen' for 'this year' in March 1754.[58]

A Robert Garner was baptised at Stoke-on-Trent on 28 December 1701, son of Joseph and Elizabeth. He married Jane Glass at Stoke on 19 November 1732, and their son Robert was baptised on 19 November 1733, again at Stoke.[59] These two seem to be the Robert Garners, father and son, employed by *Thomas Whieldon* between 1749 and 1754. After his period at Row Houses, Garner had moved to Longton by 1777.[60]

John Barker also worked for *Thomas Whieldon*, as did Josiah Spode I. For *Thomas Barker*, apparently John Barker's brother, a potter at Foley, 1770s-1786, see Chapter IX. Shaw said that Spode's 'elder Son (the second Josiah Spode Esq.) married the eldest daughter of Mr. John Barker of the Row Houses'.[61] In fact, she was the daughter of *Thomas* Barker.[62] In his will made in 1786,[63] Thomas Barker left a dwelling house, garden etc. at Rowhouses to his son Charles Barker.

Another reference by Shaw is that 'The manufactory where Messrs. Barker pursued their avocation, is now converted into cottages and a tavern called the Dog and Partridge.[64] If Shaw meant that the Dog and Partridge was the location of the early works of the Barker brothers *and Garner*, this is the 'Row Houses' site. D. Barker has also studied the connections between John Barker and Robert Garner, and the location of the Row Houses manufactory.[65] The Dog and Partridge public house still existed in 1928 at no. 175 King Street, Fenton,[66] a location between Fenton Spiritualist Church and The Miners Arms public house in 2004.

GLASGOW

DELFTFIELD POTTERY COMPANY
Broomielaw, Glasgow, 1750s, 1760s?

The Delftfield Pottery Company was founded in 1748 to make tin-glazed earthenware.[67] It is only included in this study because on two occasions the possible manufacture of stoneware (though not salt-glazed) was mentioned.

In 1757 the Company advertised 'a new composition ... More STRONG and DURABLE ... equal in strength with the Staffordshire Stone-ware, exceeds it greatly in beauty, and comes much cheaper'.[68] This is considered to have been tin-glazed stoneware such as was also made in Liverpool.

James Watt, who had become a partner, wrote in 1768 first that they intended to carry on a stone manufactory and, later, that he had contrived a glazing for stoneware of 'a glass of lead and tin without salts'.[69] This may have been a forerunner of the Company's manufacture of cream-coloured earthenware which is said to have begun c.1770.

White salt-glazed stoneware shards, possibly wasters, have been recovered near the Delftfield site, and are now held by the People's Palace and Kelvingrove Museums in Glasgow.[70]

GODWIN

'Godwin' is said to have supplied 'Flowered & Footed', 'Mosaic' and 'Plain, Footed' porringers to *Thomas and John Wedgwood*, Burslem, but in fact this was ware supplied by Wedgwoods to their customer, John Godwin, near Newgate, Bristol, in 1770.[71]

JOHN GRAHAM Junior
Burslem, 1784

John Graham Jun., Burslem, was listed in a 1784 directory as a 'manufacturer of white stone Earthen Ware, enamelled white and cream colour'.[72] At that time, 'white' ware might have been either white salt-glazed stoneware or else the new white earthenware. John Graham junr. was buried at Burslem on 21 April 1801, and another John Graham, presumably 'senior', aged seventy-nine, on 28 February 1808.[73]

In 1776 'Mr. Graham' paid £50 to *Thomas and John Wedgwood* for 'Wm. Wedgwood's House & Workhouse Bank [potworks]',[74] presumably in Burslem. In a list of potters in 1710-15 (Fig. 26), made many years later by Josiah Wedgwood,[75] a 'Wedgwood' works is located as 'Middle of the Town ... now Grahams'. On a

'1740' map of Burslem, William Wedgwood's *house* is located in the vicinity of the (2004) New Inn, Market Place.[76] This rather speculative 'evidence' might locate John Graham junior's potworks.

Thomas Wedgwood V of Overhouse, Burslem bought salt from *Mr. Graham* in 1772 and 1773, and 'Sapher [zaffre – blue colour]' and earthenware in 1778 and ironmongery between 1777 and 1782, from *John Graham, Burslem*. A reasonable explanation would be that John Graham senior, born c.1729, was an ironmonger in Burslem and bought a potworks for his son, John Graham junior, in 1776.

WILLIAM GREATBATCH, Lower Lane, Fenton, 1762-1782
See Chapter IX

JOHN HALES
Cobridge, c.1759-64

John Hales of Cobridge sold ware to Josiah Wedgwood in 1763 and 1764, which by description appears to have been salt-glazed: white cups, gadrooned oblongs, tureens, tureen stands; barley corn oblongs, rounds, and round baskets.[77] Josiah Wedgwood ordered salt-glazed ware from makers such as Hales because he received orders for it, which he apparently could not supply himself.

An order from Jno. Will. Pollmann of London to Wedgwood on 1 October 1763 is marked up 'Basket Pattn Ordr for Mr. Hales': flat white table plates, soup plates, oval dishes in sizes, round dishes in sizes, breakfast plates, largest size tureens with feet and oval dishes, and two smaller sizes, sauceboats in sizes, oval butter tubs with plates, mustard pots and covers, tea canisters, fruit baskets and plates, and candlesticks.[78] Other items were marked for *William Taylor (II)* to supply.

John Hales billed Wedgwood £14.2s.6d. for approximately these items on 31 of the same month, in four crates.[79] Pollmann was supplying overseas customers. Remarks in an earlier letter from Pollmann to Wedgwood[80] suggest that crates with the marks used by Hales were to be sent to Paul Jackson at Newcastle-upon-Tyne for shipment to Pollmann's directions.

By 1770 Hales was also making cream-coloured ware: supplying cream-coloured teapots to *Thomas and John Wedgwood* and buying salt-glazed shapes from them, including 'unfired Ware'.[81] There are three cream-ware vases marked 'Voyez & Hales fecit' in the British Museum, which are considered to have been made about 1770.[82] In 1775 Hales entered a partnership to make pots for twenty-one years with his stepson, William Adams (1748-1831), and Thomas Hales.[83] The partnership would continue until John Hales' death in 1791, aged fifty-five.[84] Hales and Adams were concerned in a paper mill at Stone, coal mines at Norton and a warehouse in Liverpool in 1776, and a flint mill at Cheddleton in 1782.[85] 'Mr. Hales and Co.' had supplied ground flint to *Thomas Wedgwood V of Overhouse* in 1774.[86]

P.W.L. Adams stated that Hales' works at Cobridge was on the south side of Sneyd Street,[87] but our research suggests that it was at the junction of Cobridge Road and Waterloo Road, later the Globe Pottery Works and in 2004 the site of Drayton of Stoke Ltd.'s garage.[88] Hales insured his property for £300 in 1765: house £100, household goods £50, workhouse and warehouse £100, stock and earthenware £50, total £300, an average amount.[89] Hales bought flint from *John Baddeley* in 1759-60,[90] confirming that he was in business then.

CORNELIUS HAMMERSLEY
Fowlea, Wolstanton, Staffordshire

Cornelius Hammersley of Fowle Ley was named by *John Dwight* of London in a Bill of Complaint 4 December 1697 as one who had infringed Dwight's 1684 patent to make various wares. Dwight alleged that *Moses Middleton*, Cornelius Hammersley and *Joshua Astbury* in partnership had intruded into Dwight's workhouses, learnt how to make his wares, and made copies of them for several years.[91]

Only Hammersley replied, on 31 January 1697/98, stating that there was no partnership, that he had used his ingenuity to improve his pots, and that he should not be punished if his wares accidentally proved to be like Dwight's.[92] Hammersley stated that he had inherited the estate where he then lived, in which there was clay better than ordinary, and that he made the best earthenware that he could. Tantalisingly, Hammersley did not say what kind of 'earthenware' he made, but the location of his estate, Fowle Ley, is known, and it lies on the same escarpment on which the Elers brothers obtained their red-burning clay to make fine redware.[93] The probability must be that Hammersley was making fine redware, and not any kind of salt-glazed ware.

No further information has been found about potmaking on this site, but Dwight in London picked out Hammersley as one of three Staffordshire potters important enough for him to sue. It must be borne in mind that Dwight had reached agreement with the *Elers* brothers for them to continue making fine redware in late 1693, and that the Elers may have prompted Dwight to sue Hammersley, Middleton and Astbury in 1697, for copying *their* product.

The Fowlea Brook runs SSW in the main valley between Newcastle-under-Lyme and Hanley, and 'Fowl *Hay*' is located on Yates' 1775 map of Staffordshire as being west of Etruria.[94] By 22 September 1759, a house and land at Fowlea was occupied by Joseph Marsh and owned by Ralph Taylor of Hanley Green, gentleman, when Taylor left it to his nephew Job Heath.[95] Fowlea Farm still existed in 1938,[96] the site occupied by Etruria Way trading estate in 2004.

Fowlea Farm lay in Wolstanton parish, and Cornelius Hammersley was baptised at Wolstanton church on 28 January 1648/49, son of Ralph and Ursula.[97] Cornelius Hammersley had married 'Elizabeth' by 13 June 1681, when their son Cornelius was baptised at Burslem church.[98] Cornelius Hammersley was noted at Wolstanton church as overseer for Foul Lea (*sic*) in 1689-90, and his second son, John, was baptised there on 23 October 1690.[99] Cornelius Hammersley was one of many Stoke-on-Trent men who took the oath to defend and avenge King William in 1696.[100] Members of the Hammersley family appeared as pottery workers at *Bovey Tracey* in South Devon in the 1750s.[101] The name of Hammersley is quite common in North Staffordshire and no relationship with Cornelius Hammersley has been traced.

JOHN HARRISON I AND JOSIAH WEDGWOOD
c.1752-1754
JOHN HARRISON II fl.1754-1759
Cliff Bank, Stoke-on-Trent

John Harrison and Josiah Wedgwood made pottery, possibly white salt-glazed stoneware, at Cliff Bank, Stoke-on-Trent, between 1752 and 1754. The earliest accounts are in four unpublished versions of a biography of Josiah Wedgwood, which all refer to Josiah Wedgwood becoming the partner of John Harrison at Cliff Bank.[102] The one by John Leslie, written before 1800, states:

> He engaged in partnership with Mr. John Harrison, who was disposed to transfer his capital from another trade to that of pottery. The manufacture was accordingly begun at Cliffe-Bank, in 1752. But its success did not fully answer the sanguine expectations of either party; & Mr. Wedgwood finding his plans extremely cramped, determined at the end of two years, to dissolve the contract.

The next account is by Simeon Shaw,[103] writing in 1829 that Josiah Wedgwood was in partnership with Mr. Harrison at Stoke and lived there with Daniel Mayer, a mercer and draper:

> While residing there he [Josiah Wedgwood] made and supplied the tradesmen of Birmingham and Sheffield with Earthenware Hafts for Table Knives, &c. in imitation of Agate, Tortoiseshell,

Marble, and other kinds … Mr. Wedgwood here entered into partnership with Mr. Harrison, a tradesman of Newcastle, (father of the late Mr. John Harrison [II], banker, of Stoke,) and at Mr. J. Aldersea's manufactory, he made different kinds of Pottery scratched and blue, then in demand; and probably here began to employ his latent talent for speculation in different articles; for, Mr. H. being unwilling to supply further funds, a separation resulted.

The terms 'scratched' and 'blue' may be interpreted as white salt-glazed stoneware decorated with 'scratch-blue' or 'Littler-Wedgwood Blue'. Shaw's statement is the only suggestion found that Harrison and Wedgwood made salt-glazed stoneware.

John Harrison I lived from 1717 to 1798.[104] Leslie mentioned transferring from another trade, but no information has been found about Harrison's occupation before 1751. His father, also John Harrison (fl.1716-1759), was a master shoemaker in Newcastle-under-Lyme.[105] John Harrison I was married to Mary Beech in 1749, whose sister Isabel was the first wife of Josiah Wedgwood's eldest brother *Thomas Wedgwood IV of the Overhouse* from 1742 until she died in 1750.[106] Josiah Wedgwood was apprenticed to his brother Thomas from 1744 to 1749,[107] so that there would be possibilities of contact between Josiah Wedgwood and John Harrison. Accounts of Josiah Wedgwood state that his brother was unwilling to take him as a partner, and so he turned to John Harrison, who provided capital to employ Josiah Wedgwood's pottery skills.

Samuel Smiles noted a 'small green pocket-book'[108] which he considered to be a record of this partnership's orders and debts. It is in fact a record of transactions by *Thomas Wedgwood IV of the Overhouse*.[109]

John Harrison I took two cottages at Penkhull in January 1750/51 and a house there in November 1751.[110] A 1777 Duchy of Lancaster plan of encroachments in the Liberty of Penkhull[111] shows 'Mr. Harrison's Pottery' as four buildings at Cliff Bank, along the west side of the road at the junction of Honeywall and Hartshill Road, Stoke-on-Trent. The plan also shows John Harrison's house (No. 36) on the *east* side of the same road, a site now (2004) occupied by garage premises, latterly Caudwell Communications. It seems likely that Harrison converted his two 1750/51 cottages into a potworks and lived in the 1751 house opposite.

Harrison continued at Cliff Bank as a potmaker after Wedgwood's departure in 1754. He supplied *Thomas and John Wedgwood* of Burslem with plates and dishes in 1757, tortoise-shell and agate teapots in 1758, and mosaic breakfast plates and China Rail table plates in 1759. On 12 September 1759 John Harrison also supplied them with £8.4s.0d. of 'goods' for Mr. Read, which became part of a large consignment sent to William Reid of Liverpool on 26 September.[112] The only items in these transactions which might be considered as salt-glazed are the mosaic and China Rail plates.

In 1777 John Harrison, Stoke, potter, insured a house at Red Lion Square Newcastle, occupied by a grocer.[113] By 1781 only John Harrison Jnr. (II) was listed as a potter at Stoke,[114] implying that John Harrison I (aged sixty-four) ceased business between 1777 and 1781 and that his son had taken over his works.

When John Harrison I made his will on 28 June 1792, with codicils up to 1798, he described himself as now or late of Newcastle under Lyme, gentleman, and he left annuities out of his messuages, buildings, lands and tenements at Cliff Bank. Subject to legacies amounting to £1,900, he left all his real and personal estates to his eldest son, John Harrison II. He appointed 'my friend, Thomas Wedgwood of the Bighouse in Burslem' (with whom he had dealt forty years earlier) an executor. John Harrison I died on 7 September 1798.[115] John Harrison II inherited his father's potworks, 'Harrison's Works'.

The name of J. Aldersea *(John Alders)* was associated with the Harrison-Wedgwood partnership by Shaw, but our studies of *John Alders* and his brother *Thomas Alders* do not show any connection with Harrison, except as neighbouring manufacturers. The two brothers had separate works at Cliff Bank: *John Alders* from c.1753 to his death in 1779, converted into a malthouse in 1782; and *Thomas Alders* from c.1751 until he transferred his works to his son-in-law Joseph Warburton in 1777. That works, later known as 'Warburton's Works', was sold to John Harrison *II* in 1788,[116] and this may account for Shaw's statement.

When John Harrison II was bankrupt in 1802, his property thus included 'Harrison's Works' and an adjoining 'Set of Potworks … commonly known by the name of Warburton's Works', both included in an advertisement of 6 November 1802.[117] At a Manor Court held 23 October 1805, John Harrison II's assignees in bankruptcy, Baddeley, Mason and Booth, transferred a potworks, formerly *Thomas Alders*, then Joseph Warburton late *John Harrison* (i.e., Warburton's Works) to William Kenwright, timber merchant.[118] On 10 December 1807 Booth and Eardley, by then assignees of John Harrison, transferred a potworks at Cliffe Bank, commonly called Harrison's works, to Josiah Spode II.[119] These two transfers disposed of both the potworks advertised in 1802: Harrison's Works and Warburton's Works.

CHARLES HASSELLS
Shelton?, fl.1770

Charles Hassells was one of the master potters who signed the 1770 salt-glaze potters' price list.[120] A Charles Hassels (*sic*), son of John and Hannah, was baptised at Stoke church on 23 February 1743/44, and married Dorothy Wood at Whitmore church, Staffordshire, on 23 June 1771.[121] Charles Hassells was involved in numerous property transactions at Newcastle-under-Lyme Manor Court between 1775 and 1795,[122] suggesting that he lived in the Stoke-Shelton-Hanley area.

JOHN HASSELLS
Shelton, fl.1763-64

Information about John Hassells is fragmentary, and his inclusion as a salt-glaze potter relies upon a 1763 invoice in the Wedgwood papers, where John Hassells sold '4 dozen Bottles 4 Best W^t [£] 0.6.0' to Josiah Wedgwood.[123] In the same year *Thomas and John Wedgwood* sold £1.9s.6d. spoons and melons to Mr. John Hassells 'out of w[hi]ch am to allow profitt' and received 'goods' from him value £5.[124] When Mary Forbes, a Liverpool pottery dealer, was insolvent in 1764, she owed £5.2s.6d. to John Hassels [*sic*].[125] John Hassells was in Bailey's 1784 directory as a potter at Shelton.

John Hassells' name appeared in property transactions recorded at Newcastle-under-Lyme Manor Court, between 1749 and 1788.[126] He made his will on 29 August 1782 and had died before 28 March 1787, when his will was copied at the Manor Court.[127] He appears to have been the brother of *William Hassells* about whom more is known. John Hassells' daughter Abigail married *John Yates* on 19 August 1775.[128]

WILLIAM HASSELLS
Shelton?

William Hassells, pot-maker, advertised in the *Ipswich Journal* of 28 April, 5 and 12 May, and 20 and 27 October 1759 that

> he is just returned from his Pot-house in Staffordshire, and has brought a large Assortment of all sorts of Stone and Earthen-Ware of the newest Patterns, viz. White Stone, blue and white ditto, Agate, Tortoise-shell, Cream Colour and Black, both gilt, painted and enamelled' and Welsh ware, glasses etc., to be sold wholesale at Bury St. Edmunds and Colchester.[129]

A William Hassells was baptised at Stoke on 18 January 1731/32, son of Ralph and Ellen.[130] No record has been found of *John Hassells*' baptism, but it seems likely that William Hassells was his brother. *William Taylor I*, a flint potter at Hanley, whose wife was named Ellen, died in 1738 and left £40 each to his two stepsons,

William Hassells and *John Hassells*, when they attained twenty-one.[131] William Hassells' name occurs in Newcastle-under-Lyme Manor Court records between 1749 and 1765, almost always in conjunction with John.[132]

William Hassells' claim that 'he is just returned from his Pot-house in Staffordshire' may refer to a warehouse rather than a potworks. Advertisements at five-month intervals suggest that he brought a load of pottery from Staffordshire on each occasion, and so he may have similarly visited other parts of the country between these journeys to East Anglia. Although he is described as a 'pot-maker' and brought 'White Stone, blue and white ditto' to Bury St. Edmunds and Colchester, it is not certain that he made white salt-glazed stoneware himself.

HEATH AND BAGNALL
Shelton, fl.1781-1787

Heath and Bagnall of Shelton sold '8 doz. Gally Pots' to Josiah Wedgwood in 1781, the receipt signed by either 'T' or 'J' Heath. 'Gally Pots' are considered to be ointment pots, and may have been white salt-glazed stoneware. Heath and Bagnall were noted as potters at Shelton in directories from 1781 to 1784. They insured their works, utensils and stock of earthenware at Shelton for £700 in 1787 and the insurance record was endorsed that their works became the property of Edmund John Burch (*sic*, Birch) in 1797.[133] Birch's works were no. 66 on the 1802 map.[134] In 2003 the site was occupied by Wilkinsons' Store in Stafford Street, Hanley.

JOSHUA HEATH I
Shelton, fl.1714-1745

Thomas Hill of *Fenton and Hill* was apprenticed to Joshua Heath of Shelton on 1 May 1714 for six years, to learn the trade of earth potter.[135] When Hill started in partnership with his wealthy uncle John Fenton in 1719/20, they made white salt-glazed stoneware. Hill would be the practical potter, with the expertise to make salt-glazed ware, and so it seems likely that he would have learnt this from his former master, Joshua Heath.

'Joshuah Heath of Shelton fflint ware potter' was named as one of the executors of the will of *William Taylor I* of Hanley, made 8 March 1738,[136] and 'fflint ware potter' was a term only applied to salt-glaze potters at that date. On 16 February 1739/40 a Dr. Richard Wilkes visited Hanley and 'was told by Mr. Jon. Burslem and Mr. Joshuah Heal [*sic*] two head Potters' about the *Elers* brothers at Bradwell Hall, probably really referring to this Joshua Heath.[137]

When Joshua Heath died in 1745, he left his house, garden, stables and buildings (but not his 'pott ovens and Buildings used in my way of trade') to his wife (Ellen) for life. His real estate,[138] including the ovens and trade buildings, went to his son *Joshua Heath II* for ninety-nine years, then to Joshua II's first son.[139]

Although no inventory was attached to his will, Joshua Heath was clearly a prosperous potter. He owned the property named above, and also buildings in Hanley and Shelton, which he charged with life annuities of £20 to his daughter Lydia, wife of the Revd. *John Middleton*, and to his wife. He also left £300 to another son, John. (Lydia was baptised at Stoke on 23 November 1715 and John on 1 September 1721.[140])

Anecdotal evidence about Joshua Heath making white salt-glazed stoneware comes from Josiah Wedgwood's record of an 'Account of the Pottery' given by 'Steel', aged eighty-four, in 1765.[141] Steel said that 'Joshua Heath or Astbury of Shelton made white ware with the addition of flint the first in Shelton'.

JOSHUA HEATH II
Shelton, fl. 1745

Joshua Heath II was baptised at Stoke-on-Trent 21 June 1718, son of Joshua Heath I and 'Hellenae'.[142] He inherited his father's 'pott ovens' and buildings used in way of trade in 1745,[143] but died within a year. His heir was his sister, Lydia Heath, who married the Reverend *John Middleton*.[144] Joshua Heath II is assumed to have followed his father as a salt-glaze potter.

THOMAS HEATH I
Lane Delph, Stoke-on-Trent
c.1744

Thomas Heath 'White ware potter of Lane Delph' and *Jonah Malkin* were named in a bond for £50 drawn up on 13 February 1744/45.[145] 'White ware' at this period can be accepted as referring to white salt-glazed stoneware. Heath bought flint from John Baddeley of Shelton in 1761-64, paid for by cash and a crate of ware.[146] By that date, cream-coloured ware (which required flint) was also being made so there is no certainty about Heath's products then.

The early historian, Simeon Shaw, stated that 'Mr. Thomas Heath, of Lane Delph, in 1710, made a good kind of Pottery, by mixing with his other clay a species obtained from the coal mines, which by high firing became a light grey' and 'He also used the Wash of Pipe Clay'.[147] This can be understood as Heath making white-dipped salt-glazed ware, but the date is not reliable. Shaw also wrote that Heath's three daughters married potters: Neale, (Humphrey) *Palmer* and Pratt; and that the site of Heath's works was occupied by a member of the Pratt family in 1829.

The Pratt family occupied several works in the area, but Shaw's reference may be to one on the north of King Street, Fenton, bounded by Vivian Road, Wallis Street, St. Matthew Street and Fenpark Road, No. 110 on the 1802 map.[148] In 1998 archaeologists keeping a 'Watching Brief' on land opposite this site recorded over a hundred white salt-glazed stoneware shards, a few scratch-blue items and some kiln furniture.[149] It is likely that these were dumped from Heath's works.

In 1769, Ralph Deakin, Lane Delph, victualler, leased property from Stanhope and Broads including 'all those buildings [in Lane Delph] erected for making pots in and late in the tenure of Thomas Heath'.[150] The exact location is not known.

THOMAS HEATH II
Old Hall, Hanley, fl.1761-1770

Thomas and John Wedgwood sold unfired ware to Thos. Heath, Old Hall, in 1770.[151] This might have been for single salt-glaze firing, or for cream-coloured ware. Shaw wrote in 1829[152] that the Old Hall manufactory was 'long the scene of the chief manufacture of Crouch ware and White stoneware Salt glaze, in Hanley, under different persons, the latter especially of Mr. Whitehead'. Conceivably, Thomas Heath was one of the 'different persons'.

Both Thomas Heath of Old Hall and *Thomas Heath* of Lane Delph bought flint from *John Baddeley* between 1761 and 1764. Heath of Old Hall paid with bricks.[153]

WILLIAM HEATH I
Shelton, fl.1758
WILLIAM HEATH II AND JOSHUA HEATH III
Shelton, fl.1763
JOSHUA HEATH III
Shelton, fl.1764-1770

William Heath bought flint from *John Baddeley* in 1758.[154] On 23 August 1763 William and Josa (Joshua) Heath of Shelton supplied Josiah Wedgwood with a crate of quart mugs, pint mugs, chamber pots and bowls, all seconds, £1.16s.0d.[155] Between 1764 and 1767, Joshua Heath bought flint, plates and 'peper [pepper] boxes' from John Baddeley, paid for in crates and plates worth £278.[156]

From this information their products could have been either

white salt-glazed stoneware or cream-coloured earthenware, but 'Josua Heath' signed the 1770 salt-glaze potters' price list,[157] confirming that he was making white salt-glazed stoneware then.

William Heath I passed all his property to his two sons William II and Joshua in January 1760,[158] but when Ralph Taylor of Hanley, gentleman, died later that year, he left a house and pothouse *occupied by his nephew William Heath (I) to him for life and then to William's two sons, William (II) and Joshua Heath (III)*.[159] William Heath of Shelton, earth potter, presumably their father, died c.1764.[160]

The brothers William Heath II and Joshua Heath III were probably Wedgwood's 1763 suppliers. Joshua II died in 1766,[161] but Joshua III lived on into the 1780s,[162] signing the price agreement in 1770. The location of their works is not known.

The relationships of the various Heath families in the Potteries are complicated and need specific study, beyond the scope of this work.

JOB HORN AND - TAYLOR
Burslem, fl.1764-1765

The evidence for Horn and Taylor of Burslem as manufacturers of salt-glazed ware is circumstantial rather than definite. In a letter from Agnes Bennet (*sic*), a Manchester dealer, to Josiah Wedgwood, written October 19, 1764,[163] she ordered tortoiseshell teapots and cream ewers from Wedgwood, to be 'put in Horn & Taylors Crates that are coming'. The letter was addressed to 'Mr. Horn & Taylor Potters in Burslem Staffordshire' endorsed 'Please give to Mr. Wedgwood'. The inference is that Bennet had sent an order for ware to Horn and Taylor and also wanted some tortoiseshell ware from Wedgwood, because Horn and Taylor did not make it.

Horn and Taylor were buying flint from John Baddeley in 1765-66, credited by 'crates'.[164] Flint was used in both salt-glazed ware and cream-coloured (including tortoiseshell) ware, but Horn and Taylor did not supply tortoiseshell ware to Agnes Bennet, suggesting that they did make salt-glazed ware.

They also traded 'goods' with *John and Thomas Wedgwood* in 1764 and 1765,[165] but Mountford has shown that John and Thomas Wedgwood both bought and sold various types of ware, so these transactions are not conclusive.

In an undated letter from *Matthew* Horne of Lambeth to Josiah Wedgwood, he offered a recipe and asks for a little money, because 'when my Brother Job and Taylor Broke I was bound for some monney [*sic*] for him – which I must pay soon'. Wedgwood referred to Horne's letter in one of his to Bentley, dated 2 December 1775: 'I have just rec'd a letter from a Matthew Horn of Lambeth'.[166]

Matthew Horne was referring to a partnership between his brother, Job Horne and Taylor, which 'broke' (became bankrupt) and for whom he was a surety. A Mathew Horn (*sic*) was baptised at Newchapel, Staffs., 20 March 1734, son of Mathew and Martha Horn; and Job Horn was baptised at Newchapel on 13 March 1736, also son of Mathew and Martha.[167] No forename is known for Taylor, a surname which occurs frequently amongst Burslem potters.

ISLEWORTH, Middlesex

A pottery at Isleworth, Middlesex (now Borough of Hounslow, London), existed from at least 1757, occupied by Joseph Shore, his family and partners until 1831. Recovery of shards from around the site by Ray Howard and colleagues, and elsewhere, has stimulated research.[168] Shards recovered include those of tin-glazed ware, coarse and fine redware, brown, *white and white-dipped salt-glazed stoneware*, creamware and pearlware, blackware and porcelain. Mr. Howard reported that:

> only one [white salt-glaze] sherd 'could be said to be a waster, and not a very impressive one at that. No evidence of any [salt-glaze] saggars or kiln furniture has been found so it would seem to be highly unlikely that salt glaze stoneware production ever took place.[169]

The existence of these white salt-glazed shards may be explained by them being fragments of discarded domestic items, or by Shore dealing in pottery which he did not make. It has been suggested that a reference to white salt-glazed stoneware being made at '*Brenforth*, 7 miles away [from London]'[170] was really to Isleworth, but see our entry for *Brentford*.

THOMAS AND JOSEPH JOHNSON
Lane End, Staffordshire, c.1760

Simeon Shaw wrote in 1829:[171]

> Opposite to the present Lane End Church, and on the (now greatly enlarged) premises occupied by Messrs. Mayer and Newbold, during many years Messrs. Thomas and Joseph Johnson made salt glaze white stone ware, as well as crouch ware, and other kinds, from clay obtained from the Brickhouse Field, the spot now covered by houses belonging to Jacob Marsh, Esq. ... these brothers of whose manufacture a bread-basket ... exhibits proof of ability in the modeller, and excellence in the materials.

No further evidence of this partnership has been found, but a Thomas Johnson, Lane End, potter, who died c.1741, had two sons, *James* and Thomas, who were then minors,[172] possibly the origin of Shaw's Thomas and Joseph. Mayer and Newbold's Lower Market Place works was probably on the site of Longton railway station.[173]

ANTHONY KEELING
Tunstall, c.1764-66

Anthony Keeling has been the subject of research principally for his production of porcelain and black basalt.[174] His involvement with the manufacture of white salt-glazed stoneware seems reasonably certain, although the evidence of his activities as a dealer raises the possibility that he may have been a 'middleman', rather than a maker.

Born c.1738, Anthony Keeling was son and grandson of earlier Anthony Keelings.[175] His father was noted as a yeoman (farmer) of Hanley Green when he died in 1758.[176] Anthony Keeling married Ann, daughter of *Enoch Booth* senior in 1760,[177] and later took over his father-in-law's potworks at Tunstall. He was already in business with Enoch Booth, sharing a warehouse in Edinburgh in 1759, later claimed to be the first warehouse for Staffordshire ware in Scotland.[178] Amongst many types of ware, he stocked 'all kinds of Staffordshire white stone ware' in 1769. A Liverpool pottery dealer, Mrs. Forbes, owed Anthony Keeling £25.17s.6d. for unspecified goods when she was insolvent in 1764.[179]

Josiah Wedgwood bought salt-glazed ware from Anthony Keeling: fine blue teapots, coffee pots, milks, basins, sugars, tea canisters in 1764 and 1765, and mazarine blue coffee pots etc. in 1765.[180] These last were invoiced from Tunstall, where his father-in-law, Enoch Booth senior, had been making cream-coloured ware for twenty years. The following year Wedgwood continued being supplied by Anthony Keeling with an even greater variety of blue wares as well as 'baskett oblongs' which appear to have been plain white.[181] 'Fine blue' and 'mazarine blue' probably refer to 'Littler-Wedgwood Blue', white stoneware covered with an overall blue slip before being salt-glazed.

The account books of *Thomas and John Wedgwood* of Burslem show that they were dealing with a *Mr.* Keeling by 1756,[182] probably not the eighteen year old Anthony. Anthony Keeling later bought salt-glazed ware from *Thomas and John Wedgwood*: melons and shells in 1764, unfired ware, white, pudding cups and spoons between 1769 and 1775; artichoke cups, custard cups, moons and suns in 1770, custards, pudding cups, star cups and star pettys in 1772.[183] These purchases could have been to supplement his own salt-glaze production, or to supply his customers with a type of ware which he did not make. The unfired ware could have been fired and salt-glazed by Keeling, or biscuit fired, glazed and sold as cream-coloured ware. He was buying clay from Josiah and Thomas Wedgwood in 1771,[184] but this could have been for either salt-glazed stoneware or for cream-coloured ware.

By 1784 Anthony Keeling was manufacturing Queen's ware, blue painted and enamelled, and Egyptian Black at Tunstall.[185] He died at Liverpool 14 January 1815, aged seventy-six.[186]

SAMUEL KIRK AND CO.
Burslem, 1763-64

Taylor Stevenson was a master potter in Burslem between 1759 and 1779, and surviving invoices in the Wedgwood Accumulation[187] show that he traded as Samuel Kirk and Co. in 1763 and 1764. One invoice is firmly endorsed by Wedgwood 'Kirk & Coy, alias Taylor Stevenson Invo 10 May 1764'.[188] No information has been found about Samuel Kirk.

Six invoices from Kirk and Co. to Josiah Wedgwood between 26 April 1763 and 6 November 1764[189] charge Wedgwood for flower (*sic*) pans, wash basins, chamber pots, water bottles, teapots, blue and white cups, Gadroon plates and soups, plain plates, milk pots, bowls, carved table plates, Barleycorn tureens, plates, soups and oblong and long dishes, and Basketwork dishes, descriptions indicative of white salt-glazed stoneware.

Another invoice from Saml. Kirk and Co. to Josiah Wedgwood[190] commences '1764 29 August To Fireing' followed by fruit dishes and fruit baskets at 1d. each, and Barleycorn sauce boats and covers at 2d. each.

These are followed on the same invoice by a long list of 'salt-glaze' shapes, at very low prices, which might also have been for firing: twig dishes and baskets, tureens and covers, more sauce-boats and covers, teapot stands, dessert twifflers, Barleycorn dishes, stands with holes, candlesticks, spoons, more fruit baskets, butter tubs and 'sortable' (assorted) ware, ending on 10 October 1764 with large 'Birds Eye' tureens and covers. This list is closed with the word 'Clay'. Prices per item range from 1d. to 4d. each, this last the charge for Birds Eye Tureens with Covers, compared with the 1770 Price List[191] charge of 18d. to 42d. each. The low prices for all these items suggest that this invoice is entirely for firing salt-glaze shaped items for Josiah Wedgwood. *John Smith* and *William Taylor II* also fired ware for Josiah Wedgwood (q.v.) at this period.

The charges from Kirk to Wedgwood for this 'fired' ware were all on Wednesdays: 29 August, 5 September, 19 September and 10 October 1764. The regularity of Wednesdays may signify the day of the week when the oven had been emptied after the traditional weekend firing, or merely the day on which Kirk and Co. made their deliveries or did their accounts.

Stevenson is referred to in letters from Jno. Douglas of Whitehaven to Josiah Wedgwood between 1763 and 1764.[192] Douglas asked Wedgwood to get 3-pint water-bottles from Taylor Stevenson on 6 October 1763 and on 14 December 1763 Douglas wrote to Wedgwood, sending his respects to Taylor Stevenson and asking him to send 'small miserd [*sic*] Quart Mugs', cups and saucers and table plates worth £20. 'Miserd' is assumed to mean 'measured', i.e. mugs stamped with the excise mark. Later Douglas sent Stevenson £32 via Wedgwood, asked for 'Second flint sortable [assorted salt-glazed ware]' and remarked 'he promised to send me some'. Douglas told Wedgwood to pay Stevenson £20 on 30 January 1764 and in April 1764 Douglas told Wedgwood that Stevenson was sending him some goods.

Stevenson bought flint from *John Baddeley* between 1759 and 1766, partly paid for by 'crates' in 1766.[193] He bought clay from *Thomas and John Wedgwood* in 1762 and sold them table plates in 1764.[194]

On 12 August 1764 Taylor Stevenson married Charlotte Bold, widow of a salt-glaze potter, *James Bold*.[195] He died in 1779 and his widow died in 1799.[196]

LEEDS, Yorkshire

LEEDS POTTERY
Jack Lane, Leeds, Yorkshire, c.1770

Debate about the possibility of white salt-glazed stoneware being produced at Leeds was ended in 1977. The discovery of 'kiln furniture including saggers, some of which showed evidence of salt-glazing' and 'stilts… some of the hand-made examples being of white salt-glazed stone-ware' in 1977 excavations adjoining the site of the Leeds Pottery[1] gave good evidence of the production of white salt-glazed stoneware there. Fragments of salt-glazed ware found on the site included the common 'barleycorn' and 'basketwork and scrollwork' patterns,[2] which may be accepted as patterns also produced at Leeds.

Further white salt-glazed stoneware shards were found on the Leeds Pottery site in 1982: plate borders moulded with common designs, the bases of a bowl and a saucer, and also two parts of a mould for an oval tureen stand, with a feather edge (seven equally-spaced barbs), leaves, and swags suspended from rams' heads.[3]

Humble, Green and Co. built the Leeds Pottery in 1770,[4] a late date for commencing to make white salt-glazed stoneware. The works continued under various owners until 1881. See *Rothwell* for further evidence of the possible production of white salt-glazed stoneware in the Leeds area.

WILLIAM LITTLER
Brownhills, Burslem, c.1745-1750

William Littler is popularly known as an early porcelain manufacturer at Longton Hall[5] and *West Pans* and the co-inventor of 'Littler-Wedgwood Blue', white salt-glazed stoneware covered with blue slip before firing. This subject is dealt with in Chapter V, under Decoration. See Colour Plates 26, 27, 91, 92, 93, 137 and 194 for examples made by various manufacturers.

The earliest account which links Littler with the manufacture of salt-glaze pottery was published by a local historian, William Pitt in 1817:[6]

> About this time [1750-1763] an improvement was made in the salt glaze by the united efforts of William Littlor [*sic*] and Aaron Wedgwood… Aaron Wedgwood [q.v.] was a manufacturer of White Stone ware, and having married Littlor's sister, they united their experience, and made repeated attempts to improve the salt glaze. The result of their experiments was the addition of … ground zaffer … [which] produced a fine smooth glassy surface

resulting in a fine blue glaze. Littler was at Longton Hall porcelain works from c.1751 to 1760.[7] His activities from 1760 to 1764 are not known, but he was at *West Pans* near Edinburgh from c.1764 to c.1777, making porcelain and also some kind of stoneware.

William Littler was baptised at Burslem on 1 December 1724, son of William and Sarah Littelor (*sic*).[8] His father, a potter with a works at Brownhills, west of Burslem, died in 1729,[9] and William inherited his father's works in 1745, when he was twenty-one.[10] He was named as an earth potter of Brownhills in December 1745 when he mortgaged his 'tenement in Burslem … houses barns stables pothouses workhouses smoakhouses [*sic*], ovens ovenhouses' and lands.[11] Further mortgages followed until in 1748 he forfeited his property to a Thomas Fletcher, who leased it back to him until November 1750.[12] After that, Littler next appears at Longton Hall in October 1751, described two years later as 'late of Hanley Green but now of Longton Hall'.[13]

No contemporary evidence has yet been found to prove that Littler made white salt-glazed stoneware, but he had a potworks at Brownhills from 1745 to 1750, and that, together with Pitt's association of Littler with the knowledge of salt-glaze ware manufacture, makes it reasonable to assume that he did so.

The location of Littler's pottery is uncertain. The site and other property was bought by John Wedgwood of the Big House, Burslem on 22 March 1750/51.[14] John Ward, writing about Brownhills in 1843, stated: 'Of the Pottery of William Littler, which existed here a century ago … no vestiges now remain; but the site of it, and the estate adjacent, belong to Mr. [John] Wood'.[15]

Ward spelt out the ownership of Brownhills House property from 1590 down to John Wood's inheritance in 1797, which did not include Littler's pottery. He also stated that in 1826 Mrs. Wood inherited more property at Brownhills from her uncle Thomas Wedgwood (heir to John Wedgwood), and that John Wood demolished his father's factory nearby and laid out the grounds in 1830.[16] William Scarratt wrote by 1905: 'In the wall surrounding the Brownhills House are still remaining the marks of the windows and gateways of some part of the works most probably occupied by Wm. Littler'.[17] Brownhills House has been demolished, and its site was occupied by Brownhills High School in 2004. Brownhills High School is on the *east* side of Brownhills Road.

The earliest map to show 'Brown hill' was published in 1775.[18] Only two buildings are shown, both on the *west* side of the Burslem to Tunstall road. One site appears to be on present-day Canal Lane, halfway between Brownhills Road and the Trent and Mersey Canal bridge, now occupied by CD Engineering and Scientific Glass Laboratories. The other is further north, on the west side of Brownhills Road. The inference from the 1775 map evidence is that Littler's potworks occupied one or other of these two sites.

William Littler's mother was Sarah Shaw, daughter of Ralph Shaw.[19] She may have been the sister of *Ralph Shaw II*, salt-glaze potter, who patented a method of making chocolate-coloured salt-glazed ware, a process which has some similarity to the technique of 'Littler-Wedgwood Blue', an interesting connection, but not surprising in a close-knit community.

LIVERPOOL

PARK LANE, c.1756
DALE STREET, no date

The information published in support of the manufacture of white salt-glazed stoneware at Liverpool is as follows:

1 Salt-glazed stilt rings (kiln furniture) found in Chorley Court, Dale Street, Liverpool in 1914.[20]

2 An advertisement in the *Liverpool Advertiser* of 16 July 1756[21] which reads: 'John Eccles and Co., Potters, at the Park Lane Pothouse, in Liverpool, make and sell all sorts of black and white earthenware, being the first of the black and white colours ever brought to perfection in Liverpool, and offered for sale at such low prices. Likewise, all sorts of blue and white earthenware in the newest China taste, wholesale and retail, at the lowest prices.' ('black and white earthenware' as new products, might be construed as 'Jackfield' black ware and white salt-glazed stoneware, as opposed to 'blue and white … in the China taste', presumably tin-glazed earthenware.)

3 A white salt-glaze tea canister, decorated and inscribed in scratch-*black* 'Henrey/Muskit /1760 L' and 'Elizabeth/Cannon/1760/Liver' is in the Liverpool Museum (see page 10). A scratch-blue salt-glazed teapot inscribed 'Henry Muskett/1760' and 'Mary Sampson/1760' is in the Royal Cornwall Museum (1960/4/389) at Truro. ('Henry Muskett' was recorded as a Liverpool potter in 1767 and, although the tea canister and teapot could have been made elsewhere, the inscriptions suggest that they were made at Liverpool.[22])

4 The 'plumper' mug. This refers to a 'scratch-blue' white salt-glazed mug incised 'Ser William / a / Plumper', the reference being to a Liverpool parliamentary election in 1761 contested by *inter alios* Sir William Meredith. Joseph Mayer said[23] that they were made to commemorate the victory of Sir William. The mug was destroyed in the 1939-45 war. ('Plumping' is casting only one vote when the elector is entitled to vote for two candidates. It seems likely that these souvenirs were made in quantity. On the evidence that salt-glazed kiln furniture has been found in Liverpool, it seems possible that they would be made there.)

5 Stoneware pots with coatings of both salt-glaze and tin-glaze. Professor Alan Smith has put forward the theory that a group of twenty or more stoneware pots appear to have been biscuit-fired, dipped in tin-glaze and re-fired in a salt-glaze kiln, though allowing that the sequence might have been salt-glaze first followed by tin-glazing. Their decorative characteristics suggest a Liverpool origin,[24] but see Chapter V, Decoration, for possible explanations of this process, which do not necessitate *manufacture* of these salt-glaze pieces in Liverpool.

6 The name of the Flint Mug Works on Parliament Street, active before 1772,[25] suggests the manufacture of white salt-glazed stoneware, often referred to as flint ware.

This body of information suggests the manufacture of white salt-glazed stoneware in Liverpool. The locations mentioned are widely separated, so that three or more potteries may have been involved. It was certainly made at *Prescot*, eight miles away, in 1751. There were of course many *customers* in Liverpool for white salt-glazed stoneware, see Chapter VI and Appendix 5.

TIMOTHY AND JOHN LOCKETT
Hole House and Bourne's Bank, Burslem, c.1784-1787

Timothy and John Lockett were listed as 'White Stone Potters' in Burslem in a 1784 directory.[26] They sold 12 'Stool Pans Best 12 inch [chamber pots]' and '3 Doz. Best Jarrs In Sizes' to Thos. Wedgwood (partner of Josiah Wedgwood) on 11 September 1787,[27] which are assumed to have been white salt-glazed stoneware.

Timothy Lockett was baptised 2 May 1748 and John Lockett was baptised 1 October 1752, both at Burslem,[28] sons of William and Elizabeth Lockett. Their father, William Lockett, was also a Burslem master potter, but no proof has been found of him producing white salt-glazed stoneware. He was buried at Burslem on 30 October 1774.[29] In William Lockett's will, made 20 October 1774 and proved 31 March 1775,[30] he left to his son Timothy, his 'potworks … at the Holehouse Bank in Burslem',[31] which are occupied by myself and John Robinson'. To his other son, John Lockett, he left his 'potworks … in the Bournes Bank Burslem'. (A John Robinson was an enameller and printer on pottery in Burslem from c.1770.[32]) William Lockett insured a 'Potworkhouse' and a sliphouse or stove, in 1767.[33]

Timothy and John Lockett dissolved their partnership on 7 November 1800, Timothy paying their debts.[34] He died at Congleton, Cheshire on 18 December 1815, 'gentleman, many years a most respectable manufacturer at Burslem'.[35] His younger brother, John, died 12 December 1819 at Burslem, aged sixty-seven.[36] No connection has been found with the Lockett family of Longton, potters.[37]

LONDON

JOHN DWIGHT, c.1673-1703; **LYDIA DWIGHT**, 1703-09; **SAMUEL DWIGHT**, 1709-1737; Fulham Pottery, London. See Chapter IX

JOHN AND DAVID ELERS
Fulham, -1691
Bradwell, Newcastle-under-Lyme, 1691-1698

There is a theoretical possibility that the Elers brothers made *brown* salt-glazed stoneware at Bradwell Hall, as there is no doubt that they knew the techniques of making it.

John and David Elers, of Germano-Dutch extraction, were potters at Bradwell Hall, near Newcastle-under-Lyme, from 1691[38] to 1698.[39] They had already been potters in London and on 20 June 1693 *John Dwight* of London sued 'John Elers and David Elers both of Fulham' and others for making ware contrary to his patent.

Elers agreed that they had made 'Brown muggs [*sic*] w[hi]ch are comonly [*sic*] called Cologne or Stone ware [brown salt-glazed stoneware]' for about three years, i.e. from 1690, which in theory could have been either in London or in Staffordshire. By 21 November 1693 the Elers brothers had reached agreement with Dwight.[40] The nature of the agreement was not given then, but over four years later it was stated that there is 'a Company of Dutchmen who (by Licence from Mr. D[wight].) make ye fine Ware in Staffordshire' and that Mr. Dwight called that ware china.[41] The agreement at least allowed Elers to make 'china'.

As early as 1739/40, a Dr. Richard Wilkes visited Hanley and 'was told by Mr. Jon. Burslem and Mr. Joshuah Heal [*sic*, see *Joshua Heath I*] two head Potters, yt. [that] some years ago a Parcel of Dutch Men came & made Pots at Bradwel [*sic*] near Newcastle : yt.one Mr. George Astbury a Joyner employ'd by them in making Lathes, & other machines at length got a Notion of the Pottery Trade : yt. he about 30 years ago [so c.1709] began to make a sort of White Ware of calcin'd Pebbles : yt. one Mr. Dwight of Fulham had a Patent for making such Kind of Muggs'.[42] The inference here is that Astbury learnt how to make white stoneware from Elers, but see our remarks about *Joshua Astbury*.

In his Commonplace Book dated 1779, Josiah Wedgwood noted an 'Account given 15 June 1765 by … Steel aged 84' that 'White glazed ware [was] first made by Dutchmen at Bradwell about the year 1693. The people of Burslem were then very much surprised with the smoke of the salt glaze, and ran in great numbers to see what was the matter; amongst whom Steel was one'.[43] Josiah Wedgwood had already agreed that the Elers made salt-glazed stoneware. He wrote to his partner Thomas Bentley on 19 July 1777 that one of the improvements made by Mr. Elers was

> Glazing our common clays with salt which produced Pot d' Grey or Stone ware, & this after they (the two Elers's) had left the country was improv'd into white Stone Ware by using the White Pipe Clay instead of the common clay of this neighbourhood, & mixing with it Flint Stones calcin'd & reduc'd by pounding into a fine powder.[44]

This letter was of course not public in 1777, but a similar statement was published anonymously in 1789: 'They [Elers brothers] brought into this country the method of glazing stone ware, by casting salt into the kiln while it is hot'. Josiah Wedgwood was the author.[45] This statement was repeated and embellished by Aikin in 1795, Nicholson in 1808, Rees c.1814, Pitt in 1817 and Parkes in 1819 (possibly in 1806).[46]

An earlier published account of the Elers making salt-glazed ware in Staffordshire was one by Dr. R. Watson in 1784:[47]

> This very curious method of glazing earthen ware, by the vapour of common salt, was introduced into England from Holland, at least it was introduced from thence into Staffordshire, about 80 years ago, by two Dutchmen. An old man informed the person, from whom I had the account, that he remembered, when he was a boy, running with others to help to extinguish, what from the smoke, they apprehended to be a fire in the pottery where the Dutchmen were working, but that their entrance was opposed by the proprietors of the pottery, who were unwilling that the cause of the smoke, which was the common salt they were using in glazing their ware, should be generally known.

The suggestion that the Elers did not make salt-glazed stoneware came first from Enoch Wood in 1814, when he noted privately 'Report says, salt glaze was made first at Bradwell about the year 1700, I have seen the foundation of the oven near the west end of the barn about 20 years since and believe it was built to fire Red China only.' In 1836 he referred to 'pieces of Salt glazed ware which they [the Elers] pretended they made at Bradwell' which he had been told were German in origin. Wood's conclusion was that the Elers pretended to make salt-glazed ware to deceive the inhabitants of Burslem while they really were making red china teapots.[48]

It was left to Simeon Shaw in 1829 to challenge publicly the manufacture of salt-glazed stoneware by Elers at Bradwell.[49] He described the surviving remains of a circular oven at Bradwell Hall and quoted local experts (including Enoch Wood) who said that it was not suitable for salt-glazing. The Elers' successors at Bradwell Hall had been required to 'take away pull downe & destroy a certain pott house or pott oven'[50] and presumably Shaw's circular oven remains was the residue. Shaw also wrote that only red unglazed porcelain and blue pottery shards had been found nearby, and specifically contradicted Parkes' assertion that the Elers introduced salt-glazing to England.

The recent detailed monograph on Elers by Gordon Elliott mentions his discovery of seventy red stoneware shards and one German grey salt-glazed shard at Bradwell Hall, and earlier discoveries of redware shards. No salt-glazed wasters or kiln furniture have so far been discovered at Bradwell and the author devotes little space to consideration of Elers making salt-glazed ware at Bradwell.[51] Nevertheless, it remains a possibility that the Elers brothers, with their confirmed ability to do so, made at least brown salt-glazed stoneware at Bradwell.

MATTHEW GARNER and LUKE TALBOT
Gravel Lane, St. Saviours, Southwark, Surrey, c.1694-1697

On 5 May 1694, *John Dwight* of London added Matthew Garner to his 1693 suit against *John and David Elers* and others, for making ware contrary to his patent.[52] Garner denied that he had obtained Dwight's secrets and said that he made 'earthen browne Canns & Muggs', being his own invention. Dwight obtained an interim injunction against Garner to bar him from making the items complained of. Garner called witnesses to show that stone gorges like Dwight's had been made for about twenty years.

Dwight brought a new action against *Luke Talbot, Richard White* and *Moses Johnson* on 6 November 1695, alleging that they had made wares similar to Dwight's patent for several years, and evidence was given that pots like Dwight's had been bought from Garner and Talbot's warehouse in Gravel Lane, Southwark. Talbot answered that he did not believe that Dwight was the first inventor of white Gorges and fine stone Gorges, that Dwight charged more than was reasonable for them, and did not make half enough for the demand. Talbot had been apprenticed to make such pots, and made them openly.[53]

Garner and his partner Luke Talbot of Gravel Lane Pottery, were bankrupt in 1697.[54] In February 1699/1700 Garner and Talbot brought an action against Nathaniel Oade, a glass seller, wherein they claimed that they had prevailed against Dwight.[55] Garner and Talbot stated then that they and Dwight were the only persons who knew how to make 'white Gorges marbled porcelane Vessells & fine stone gorges or vessels never before made in England or elsewhere', and that they had continued to make them.

Garner went to Ireland in 1697 and made tin-glazed earthenware and fine redware at Belfast.[56] 'Old Matthew Garner' was buried in Belfast on 2 September 1725.[57] Described as 'Old', he may even have been the Mathew Garner christened at St. Botolph, Aldgate, London, son of Mathew and Sarah Garner, on 26 August 1642.[58]

MOSES JOHNSON
London, c.1681-1690
St. Olave's, Southwark, London, c.1690-1695
Bear Garden, Bankside, London, c.1695-1696

Moses Johnson is identified as a maker of salt-glazed stoneware by Dwight's accusation. On 6 November 1695, *John Dwight* of

London brought an action against *Luke Talbot* (see *Matthew Garner* and he), Richard White and Moses Johnson for making wares in imitation of Dwight's new manufactures, infringing Dwight's 12 June 1684 patent. White and Johnson answered on 27 November 1695 that they did not believe that Dwight was the first inventor of his patented wares. Moses Johnson had been apprenticed for seven years as a potter and then for the last fourteen years had been a maker of earthenware in or near London, including imitations of Collogne (*sic*) and stoneware. White stated that he was not a potter, but had sometimes furnished Johnson with money. Evidence was given on 3 February 1695/96 that pots made by Johnson, and similar to those made by Dwight, were bought from Johnson's warehouse near the Bear Garden.[59]

Johnson was born c.1662, apprenticed to Thomas Harper in 1675, and took apprentices himself between 1687 and 1691. He left St. Olave's by August 1695 and took a pothouse at Bear Garden near Bankside, making 'Stone potts or Canns'.[60] White was Johnson's financial backer.[61]

Johnson was succeeded at St. Olave's by John Robins. Robins died in 1699 and an inventory of his stock includes 84,259 pieces of tin-glazed ware and 13,656 pieces of stoneware.[62] There is no positive indication of the type of stoneware, but the list includes 'thick Gorges', 'thin Gorges' and 'Capucheens [*sic*, capuchins]'.[63]

The specification of *thin* gorges and *capuchins*, contrasted with *thick* gorges, suggests that 'Dwight-type' wares were on hand in 1699. Either Robins had continued to make 'Dwight-type' wares, along with his tin-glazed pottery, or some of Moses Johnson's admitted 'Dwight-type' ware remained in Robins' warehouse. The subject was thoroughly discussed by Haselgrove and Murray in 1992.[64]

JOSEPH KISHERE
Mortlake High Street, London, SW14 c.1810

In 1872, William Chaffers quoted 'Lysons (edit. 1811)' that 'There is a small manufactory of white stoneware belonging to Mr. Joseph Kishire [*sic*].'[65] In a collection of Kishere pottery kept in St. Mary's Church at Mortlake, there are two similar 'near white' vases, one of which is marked 'Kishere'.[66] This marked piece seems to substantiate Lysons' statement that Kishere made white stoneware and is the reason for his inclusion in this book.

Joseph Kishere built a pottery on the south side of Mortlake High Street in the late 1790s. He called himself a 'Brown Stone Manufacturer' and numerous marked examples of brown salt-glazed stoneware jugs, mugs etc. survive. He was succeeded by his son William Kishere in 1835 and production ceased when William died in 1843.[67]

WOOLWICH, London, SE 18 c.1650

Excavations at Woolwich in 1974[68] revealed the base of an oval salt-glazed stoneware kiln which had produced Frechen-type brown salt-glazed stoneware. This kiln was overlaid by the base of an earthenware kiln.

The wording of the report is slightly ambiguous, but appears to state that white stoneware wasters found were *salt-glazed*, which pointed to a third undiscovered kiln. These wasters were of a highly fired smooth almost white stoneware with a clear glaze, some with cobalt blue decoration beneath the glaze. Bowls and one shallow dish, a porringer and a tankard with applied leaves and crowns, and another tankard with applied birds were found. The location of the excavation was south of the River Thames, north of Market Street, east of Surgeon Street and west of Bell Water Gate, O.S. TJ 433793.

The porringer type has been found near Frechen in Germany, dated around 1630 and a similar tankard is in the *Steinzeug* catalogue of the Kunstgewerbmuseum (now Museum für Angewandte Kunst), Cologne. It is thought that potters from Frechen may have been employed at this site. The report dates the kiln base found to c.1660, but later research suggests 1630-50.[69]

JOHN AND THOMAS LOWE
Rotten Row (Greenhead Street), Burslem, fl.1758-1775

John Lowe and Thomas Lowe signed the 1770 salt-glaze potters' price agreement.[70] *Thomas and John Wedgwood* of the Big House, Burslem, supplied Thomas Lowe with mustard spoons and teaspoons in 1758-59 and bought from him breakfast and table plates, cups, chamber pots, soups and dishes between 1763 and 1766, and a few bowls in 1770.

In a large consignment to their customer William Kell of Newcastle upon Tyne on 12 May 1772, Wedgwoods included '5½ Doz cups - Lowes'. 'Mr. John Lowe Rotten Row' was supplied with unfired ware value £4.8s.4d. by *Thomas and John Wedgwood* on 17 May 1775. These instances of inter-trading between salt-glaze potters ended when Thomas and John Lowe were insolvent in 1775 and *Thomas and John Wedgwood* received only 12s.6d. in the pound, a loss to them of £4.17s.0d.[71]

A Thomas Lowe was living in a house on the Brick House estate, Burslem, in 1747.[72] He may have been the Thomas Lowe who married Sarah Bould at Stoke on 26 July 1738 and had a son, John Lowe, baptised 7 June 1745 at Burslem.[73]

JONAH MALKIN
Hamil, Burslem, 1747-50

Jonah Malkin has been researched in detail by A.R. Mountford, and most of the information given here is from his work.[74] Jonah Malkin married Sarah Wedgwood, sister of *Thomas and John Wedgwood* of the Big House, Burslem, at Stoke-on-Trent on 18 June 1740. His father, Thomas Malkin, yeoman (farmer) left his house, other houses, outhouses, pot ovens etc. to Jonah, his eldest son, in 1745.[75] The site was on the south-east of Hamil Road, Burslem, opposite the end of Lorne Street in 2004.[76]

The earliest evidence that Jonah Malkin was a potter is in his 'Sales Ledger' for 12 December 1747,[77] when he sold 'the first oven full of Dipt white at Eight pence pr. Dozen' to Sampson Bagnall. He hired three men and two boys in May 1748, a modest workforce. The ledger shows sales until 22 March 1750/51, a variety of dishes, best and second dipt ware, porringers, mugs and jugs in sizes. He had twenty-six customers, some of them other Staffordshire potters, two in Liverpool, but also as far afield as Gloucester, Exeter and Plymouth. Their names and locations are given in Appendix 5.

On one occasion, 23 May 1748, he sold one crate of seventeen dozen *mottled* quarts to Joseph Bird for 5s.8d., less than half the price of sixteen dozen half-pint seconds at 12s.4d. 'Mottled ware' was probably once-fired buff earthenware, splashed or sprinkled with manganese before glazing, an old-fashioned and cheaper product than even seconds quality white salt-glaze stoneware. Jonah Malkin also sold 'black pickling pots' along with 'dipt white' to Richard Throup in 1748. 'Dipt white' refers to salt-glazed ware made of a cheap body, dipped in a white slip to give the appearance of white salt-glazed stoneware.

Jonah Malkin also bought in ware, presumably for his customers. He supplied Joseph Jonson of Exeter with two crates of 'Japan[ne]d flow[e]red new collor [colour] from Aaron Wedgw[oo]d' on 10 September 1749, half-pint porringers, pint mugs, half-pints, half-pint toast mugs, possibly Littler-Wedgwood Blue, although japanning is lacquering or varnishing, in various colours.[78] They were sent with his own ware, which included 'freckled' and red sprigged and black ware from James Bould (*sic*, see *James Bold*).[79] The frequent mention of 'dipt' (dipped) ware, and odd mention of 'freckled' and 'mottled' ware suggest that Jonah Malkin made the commoner types of ware. Freckled ware may refer to brown salt-glazed stoneware.

Jonah Malkin supplied flint to Benjamin Lewis[80] in 1748, and his sales to Lewis were offset by deliveries of flint, usually twelve pecks each at one shilling a peck, on sixteen occasions between February and November 1749.[81] An unexplained purchase from James Bagnall in 1748 was six pecks of bone, together with eighteen pecks of flint, offset against sales of ware to *Peter Bagnall*.[82]

Jonah Malkin borrowed money on his property, until his accumulated debts were taken over in November 1748 by Samuel Boyer, a Newcastle-under-Lyme solicitor.[83] John Wedgwood, Thomas Malkin (Jonah's brother) and Samuel Boyer took over his assets on 28 November 1749 to pay his debts, which amounted to £1,125.14s.11d.

Malkin's house and works 'at the Hammill near Burslem'[84] were bought by his brother-in-law John Wedgwood in October 1751 for £950, used to settle Jonah's debts.[85] John Wedgwood took responsibility for Malkin and his family and Malkin is named as handling cash in *Thomas and John Wedgwood's* sales account book between 1756 and 1767.[86] In a superseded will dated 21 February 1755, John Wedgwood left the 'Hammill Estate' to his brother-in-law Jonah Malkin and his wife Sarah for life, but John Wedgwood married in 1758 and made another will on 8 April 1779.[87] It is likely that Malkin worked for *Thomas and John Wedgwood* until his death in 1773. Jonah Malkin was buried at Burslem on 15 March 1773.[88]

SAMUEL MALKIN
Burslem, fl.1741-1764

Samuel Malkin supplied 'flatware' (plates or dishes) to Josiah Wedgwood from 5 November 1762 to 28 September 1764, dates which are probably limited by the chance survival of documents rather than by the full extent of their dealings.[89] The quantities supplied were: ten crates of two dozen each on three occasions and thirty crates of two dozen each on two others. All were charged at two shillings a dozen. This flatware is assumed to be white salt-glazed stoneware.

A Samuel Malkin had crates shipped for him at Winsford, Cheshire: for instance, twenty-two crates on 28 November 1741 and thirty crates on 19 June 1742, probably to Liverpool.[90] These may have also contained salt-glazed ware. He is named in the key to the '1769' picture map of Burslem as occupying a house and potworks no. 129,[91] in the vicinity of present-day Mayer Bank, Nile Street. G.J.V. Bemrose described a dump of pottery wasters exposed at Massey Square, Burslem in 1939, which he convincingly related to an earlier Samuel Malkin (1668-1741). The dump was near Mayer Bank, and shards found included brown and white salt-glaze wasters.[92]

JOHN MARE
Longton, fl.1722
RICHARD TAYLOR AND JOHN MARE
Longton, 1722-1729

It has already been noted that *John Baddeley* was in a partnership with a John Mare until about 1749.[93] There is no evidence that this partnership produced white salt-glazed stoneware. That John Mare of 'Hanley, potter', was probably the same John Mare who was involved in litigation about the will of *Joshua Astbury* in 1747.

A John Mare of Longton, earth potter, signed a partnership agreement with Richard Taylor, Newcastle-under-Lyme, ironmonger, to make 'Earthen Ware' for seven years from 11 November 1722.[94] The agreement provided for buying 'Coles, Clay, Salt, fflint and other materials', firm evidence that they were to make white or white-dipped salt-glazed stoneware:

Agreement 19 July 1722 between Richard Taylor of Newcastle under Lyme in the County of Stafford ironmonger and John Mare of Longton in the County of Stafford earth potter … agreed to become co-partners and joint traders in the Trade or Mistery of makeing Earthen Ware immediately from and after the Eleventh day of November now next ensuing for and during the term of Seven Years. [Richard Taylor advanced £50, and John Mare was to pay annual interest on £25 and pay at the end of the seven years or sooner £25 to Taylor.] John Mare shall diligently and carefully employ himself and do his best to endeavour to the utmost of his power and skill in Buying, Selling, working and finishing of all such works Earthen Wares, Materialls, Goods and Merchandise as are incident or belonging to such mistery or trade of pottmaking … for the raising of Gains and p[re]venting of Loss. [Equal shares in buying in of] Coles, Clay, Salt, fflint and other materiells (except such as are hereinafter covenanted and agreed to be found and provided by the said John Mare) … Keep just and p[er]fect Books of account and Reckoning in Writing. [No private or separate occupation] Buying Selling working or Tradeing in the aforesaid Art or Trade of Pott-making by either to the Hurt or Injury of the said Joint Trade.

John Mare shall … permit all such Boards Implements Engines and Tools relating to the said Trade whereof he is now possessed to be employed in the Carrying on of the Joint Trade … [Richard Taylor to pay him twenty shillings for the use of them, and they were to be repaired as necessary and put in good order at the end of the partnership] … And to buy one or more horses if necessary, grass, hay or straw for them … Forty shillings for each horse.

And that Daniell Mare and Thomas Mare sons of the said John Mare shall and may … be employed as servants at one shilling and sixpence per week in the first year, and advanced six pence a week yearly through the term. [Richard Taylor not to work other than keeping accounts and selling the ware.]

John Mare will by 11 November next pay arrears of rent, lewns, levies, duties, impositions already due … upon account of the Workhouses and Buildings which the said John Mare hath and holdeth

[Signed] Rich [seal] Taylor John [seal] Mare
Sealed and deliverd in the p[re]sence of J. ffenton

This agreement is an early example of an established trader in the local market town investing his money in the developing North Staffordshire pottery industry. It shows that John Mare was already a potter at Longton in 1722, with rented workhouses, boards, implements, engines and tools, and Taylor's entry into a partnership to make white salt-glazed stoneware infers that Mare was already skilled in its manufacture.

A 'Jno. Meer' and his mother enjoyed a house (in two dwellings) in Longton Manor in 1705 and 1709; and John 'Meare' was fined twopence for absence from Longton Manor Court in 1717, but was present in 1723, 1729 and 1733.[95] John Mare had two sons: Daniel and Thomas, both of an age in 1722 to be employed at apprentice wages. A John Mare of nearby Blurton was churchwarden at Trentham in 1728 and was buried there on 13 April 1742.[96] Nothing is known of the site of Mare's potworks, but it should be noted that Longton was centred around Longton Hall in the early 18th century. The present-day Longton was then known as Mear Lane End.

JOHN AND RICHARD MARE
Hanley, fl.1770

'J & Rd Mare' signed the 1770 salt-glaze potters' price agreement.[97] Shaw reproduced the 1770 agreement and went on to state 'Messrs John and Rich. *Mayer*, were making salt glaze Pottery at this time - but only their name remains; the site of their Manufactory and Residences being now partly occupied by Hanley Market Place'.[98] It seems likely that Shaw was referring to John and Richard Mare. (The works of a later John Mare are no. 68, west of Hanley Market Place, on the 1802 map.[99])

John and Richard Mare were referred to as potters at Hanley in a statement by John Hammersley to Devonshire magistrates in October 1805. He told them that he was born at Horton, Staffordshire, and apprenticed to John and Richard Mare of Hanley for six years and then worked for Richard Mare for a year.[100] Hammersley then set up business as a potter himself.

John Mare, baptised at Stoke on 4 November 1744, and Richard Mare, baptised at Stoke on 8 May 1748, both sons of John and Mary Mare, are likely to be the 1770 partners. Their father was probably the litigious partner of *John Baddeley* (see also *Joshua Astbury*).

The brothers' later history is well documented, but there is no further evidence of salt-glaze manufacture.[101] Their partnership ended 11 November 1785 and they each continued independently. Richard Mare, Hanley, potter, had died by June 1797 when his creditors were asked to send their accounts to John Mare junior, Hanley.[102] His 1797 will mentions his wife Mary, and his children John, James and Ann, all then aged under twenty-one.[103] He left three houses in Hanley, but no potworks, probably by then in the hands of John Glass.[104]

MOSES MARSH
Burslem, fl. 1710-15

Moses Marsh was one of the occupants of 'Potworks in Burslem about the year 1710 to 15', listed by Josiah Wedgwood I, c.1776 (Fig. 26).[105] The entry reads: 'Moses Marsh Stone Ware say 6 [£ per week] [Residence] Middle of the Town'. Other potters were listed as making 'Brown Stone', 'Stone or Dipp[e]d W[hi]t', or 'Stone Ware & Freckl[e]d', so the type of stoneware made by Marsh is not clear.

There are later references to a Moses Marsh as a potter at Burslem, but nothing to confirm that he made white salt-glazed stoneware. 'Moses Marsh of Burslem potter' leased land in 1748,[106] and the will of Moses Marsh, Burslem, Earth Potter, was made 5 August 1755 and proved at Lichfield on 20 October 1757.[107] There are many papers in the Wedgwood Accumulation about the failure of this Moses Marsh's sons, Isaiah and Richard Marsh, Burslem potters, in 1764, but no confirmation that they made white salt-glazed stoneware.[108]

JOHN MEIR
Fenton Vivian, Stoke-on-Trent, -1729

John Meir of Fenton Vivian made his will on 13 May 1729 and died before 24 June of the same year, when his will was proved at Lichfield.[109] The attached inventory included 'In the workhouses, shelves ware working Tools fflint burn'd & pounded, slip, shraggers [*sic* saggars], Clay & fflint unburn'd' altogether worth £60. The presence of flint in his workhouse in 1729 is evidence that Meir was engaged in the production of white or white-dipped salt-glazed stoneware. Meir had £160 owing to him, upon bonds and otherwise. He also had two mares and a cow, husbandry (farming) ware and materials relating to a colliery, indicating that he combined potting with small-scale farming and coal-mining.

Meir left property in Fenton Culvert and Penkhull to his wife Anne, charged with £400 to be shared between his four children, John, *William Meir*, Joseph and Anne, when they became aged twenty-one. Nothing more has been found about him.

WILLIAM MEIR
Snape Marsh, Shelton, fl.1759-1770

'Wm. Mier [*sic*, Meir]' was another of the salt-glaze potters who signed the 1770 price agreement.[110] William Meir was baptised son of John and Anne Meir at Stoke on 23 February 1724,[111] probably the son of *John Meir* of Fenton Vivian, salt-glaze potter. That William Meir inherited £100 when he was twenty-one in 1745.[112] William Meir had a house at Fenton *Vivian* in 1747[113] and the notebook of *Thomas Whieldon* has the following entry: 'Mr. Wm. Meir, of Fenton *Low*, for a house and pottworks [*sic*] & 3 small closes, March 25, 1750, a year's Rent due-£14-10-0'.[114] Meir was followed at Fenton Low by *Edward Warburton* in 1751,[115] and salt-glazed shards found at Fenton Low have been attributed to *Edward Warburton*.

A William Meir married Sarah Payne at Stoke on 1 July 1759.[116] She was probably the daughter of *James Payne* and William Meir could have been operating her late father's potworks at Snape Marsh, Shelton. William Meir bought flint from *John Baddeley* from 1759 to 1768. Between 1761 and 1768, the flint was paid for in crates of unspecified goods,[117] but William *Meer* of *Shelton* owed £66.3s.6d. to Baddeley in 1761,[118] which might have been for the earlier deliveries.

RICHARD MERE
Shelton

Richard Mere was one of the Staffordshire potters, including *John Wedgwood*, *Thomas Wedgwood (I)*, *Richard Wedgwood*, *Richard Muchell*, *Thomas Daniel (I)* and *Ralph Shaw (I)* who petitioned the Privy Council on 11 June 1696,[119] alleging that *John Dwight* of London was obstructing them in their trade under pretence of his 1684 patent.[120] This patent gave Dwight a fourteen-year monopoly of making white gorges, marbled porcelain vessels, statues and figures, fine stone gorges and vessels, transparent porcelain, opaque red and dark coloured porcelain or china, Persian wares and Cologne or Stone Wares.

Nothing further has been found about this petition, but its instigation by the Staffordshire potters shows that they were making or wished to make ware of a type which Dwight claimed to have patented. There is no certainty that Richard Mere was making salt-glazed ware.

Two men called Richard *Meere* lived in Shelton in 1701, aged forty-eight and fifty.[121] A Richard *Meir* was buried at Stoke on 30 March 1708.[122] In his will he was described as 'of Shelton'.[123] There is no mention of workhouses or potters' tools. A slipware dish inscribed 'Richard Meer 1686' is known,[124] and names on such dishes are often that of the maker. A 'Ric. Meere' was one of many Stoke-on-Trent men who took the oath to defend and avenge King William in 1696.[125]

REVD. JOHN or THOMAS MIDDLETON
Shelton

The Reverend *John* Middleton (1714-1802),[126] curate of Hanley, has been noted as a salt-glaze potter on the evidence of an enamelled white salt-glazed stoneware jug held at the Potteries Museum and Art Gallery. The jug is dated 1760 and inscribed underneath 'To my worthy Friend John Walter ... From J. Middleton'.[127] This is evidence of a gift, rather than of manufacture.

'Rev. *Thomas* Middleton, the Minister of (Old) Hanley Chapel' is said by Shaw to have been the secret partner of Warner Edwards (d.1759[128]) at a potworks at the bottom of Albion Street, Shelton. Shaw also said that they made 'various kinds of Pottery *with lead ore glaze* [our emphasis]'.[129] The Revd. *John* Middleton (1714-1802) was curate of Hanley. He had a son named Thomas, born at Shelton in 1745, who was also ordained and became curate to his father.[130] This may explain the confusion over forenames.

Until firm evidence is found connecting either John or Thomas Middleton with the manufacture of *salt-glazed* pottery, it seems unsafe to consider either of them a salt-glaze potter. John Middleton was the son-in-law of a salt-glaze potter, *Joshua Heath I*.

MOSES MIDDLETON
Shelton

Moses Middleton of Shelton was named by *John Dwight* of London in a Bill of Complaint 4 December 1697 as one who had infringed Dwight's 1684 patent to make various types of ware.[131]

Dwight alleged that Moses Middleton, *Cornelius Hammersley* and *Joshua Astbury* in partnership had intruded into Dwight's workhouses, learnt how to make his wares, and made copies of them for several years.

Only Hammersley replied, stating that there was no partnership, that he had used his ingenuity to improve his pots, and that he should not be punished if his wares accidentally proved to be like Dwight's. John Dwight's allegation is so widely drawn that the three Staffordshire potters might have been making any of his patented wares, and so there is no confirmation that Moses Middleton was making salt-glazed ware at Shelton in 1697.

A Moses Middleton aged twenty-seven lived at Shelton with his father, Roger and his thirty year-old brother John Middleton in 1701.[132] Nothing more has been discovered about him, but his name was certainly known to Dwight in 1697. It is possible that this Moses Middleton, a young man, had been to London by 1697 and spied upon Dwight.

THOMAS MILES
Shelton, c.1685

Shaw wrote: 'About 1685, Mr. Thomas Miles, of Shelton, mixed with the whitish clay found in Shelton, some of the fine sand from Baddeley Hedge [*sic*, Baddeley Edge, three miles north-east of Shelton], and produced a rude kind of WHITE STONE WARE'.[133] A Thomas Miles alias Pope, aged fifty, was living in Shelton in 1701, with his wife and seven children, aged from seventeen down to one,[134] and could have been the man to whom Shaw referred.

Dr. Robert Plot, who visited Staffordshire in 1680, described a Newcastle-under-Lyme pipemaker who had 'clay, a *white* and a *blew* [*sic*] which He has from between *Shelton* and *Hanley green*, whereof the *blew* clay burns the *whitest*, but not so *full* as the *white*',[135] supporting Shaw's statement about whitish clay at Shelton.

JOHN MITCHELL
(Greenhead Street), Burslem, 1736-1763

Most of our information about John Mitchell comes from Simeon Shaw, recording oral history in 1829,[136] although William Pitt had already reproduced the 1743 agreement between Mitchell and Aaron Wood in 1817.[137] Mitchell signed that agreement with a mark, suggesting that he was illiterate. He was a voter in 1747,[138] by inference a 'man of property'. It is possible that John Mitchell was the person christened at Burslem on 3 December 1703, son of Thomas Mitchell, and married to Ann Shaw at Caverswall, Staffordshire in 1728. John and Ann Mitchell had seven children baptised at Burslem between 1734 and 1754.[139]

Simeon Shaw wrote that John Mitchell had his works on the highest land in Burslem. As the demand increased for white salt-glazed stoneware made with Devonshire clay and flint, he expanded his works and built the largest hovel (shelter for the oven) of the time. John Mitchell's house and works are marked as no. 94 on the '1740' Burslem map,[140] lying on the south side of present-day Greenhead Street, within the northern end of Central Pottery, a site which might be described as the highest land in Burslem. A small archaeological excavation near the site in 1964 revealed 'large quantities of white salt-glazed sherds'. Various fragments of white salt-glazed ware were recovered and recorded, but no wasters.[141] There is the possibility of further excavation on this site.

Shaw stated that, in order to compete with *Dr. Thomas Wedgwood (II)*, Mitchell engaged Aaron Wood in 1743 for seven years from 11 November 1743. Aaron Wood was born in 1717, and had been apprenticed to *Dr. Thomas Wedgwood (II)* in 1731 for seven years, to learn turning in the lath (*sic*), handling and trimming (but not throwing).[142] On completion of his apprenticeship, Shaw said that Wood worked for *Dr. Thomas Wedgwood (II)* for five further years, until 1743.

In that year, Wood bound himself to John Mitchell under a penal bond of £10 to 'perform all such service and business whatsoever relating to the trade of an earth-potter' and was to be paid 7s. a week during the seven years, and also 10s.6d. each 11 November.[143] Wood's 7s. a week from 1743 (£18 a year) can be compared with 'Useful' Thomas Wedgwood's £22 a year when he agreed to serve his cousin Josiah Wedgwood I for six years in 1759.[144] Both were of foreman or manager status, but Wood's indenture stipulated that he should work alone 'in the business that the said John Mitchell is to employ him', implying that Wood was to do original work for Mitchell, presumably modelling.

When Pitt quoted Aaron Wood's 1743 indenture, he commented that 5s.6d. or 6s. a week was then the full weekly wage for a journeyman potter and it appeared that '7s. a week was sufficient for a man who was a modeller and had the full management of the largest manufactory in the Pottery'. In Pitt's view, Aaron Wood managed Mitchell's potworks for at least seven years, until 1750, but this hardly agrees with Wood working alone. Wood and Mitchell had some connection much later: John Mitchell wrote from Plymouth to Josiah Wedgwood on 8 May 1764, asking Wedgwood to pay Aaron Wood £25 as a matter of 'great necessity'.[145]

Mitchell also took Aaron Wood's son William as an apprentice c.1760 to learn 'flowering' and 'handling', but he left after two years and was apprenticed to Josiah Wedgwood instead.[146] ('Flowering' was incising floral decoration into unfired ware.)

Shaw went on to state that Mr. Mitchell was for some years the greatest manufacturer of the day. He had four travellers, who merely emptied their pockets when they returned from their journeys, having already paid their expenses, and were then paid 5s. or 6s. a week. They all later set up as dealers in glass and earthenware: Dean at Bridgwater, Somerset; Dale at Exeter; Dickens at Plymouth and Bowers at Falmouth. As a further example of wages, Shaw tells that Mitchell paid his lathe treaders 4d. a week. These were usually boys aged seven, employed to work the treadle which caused the turner's lathe to rotate.[147]

Ralph Shaw sued J. Mitchell in 1736 for infringement of Shaw's patent to make a chocolate-coloured salt-glazed ware,[148] suggesting that Mitchell also made such ware. In 1763 John Mitchell supplied Josiah Wedgwood with 'Teapts Inlets 24s' at 2s.9d. a dozen and common teapots, ewers, salts, 'new fashion' jugs and milkpots. An undated note from Mitchell to Wedgwood lists ware in five crates, including milk jugs 'spridged [sprigged]' and teapots 'sprig'd and legd [legged - with feet?]'.[149]

The nature of the ware is not stated, but the 2s.9d. a dozen price of 24s inlet teapots in 1763 compares reasonably with 18s inlet teapots at 2s.6d. in the 1770 white salt-glaze potters' price list.[150] '24s' and '18s' indicate the sizes of the teapots, and 'Inlet' teapots are those where the cover lies level with the teapot surface and rests on a circular ledge or 'natch'.

The allegation of making 'Chocolate brown' salt-glazed ware in 1736, 'flowering' in 1760, teapots at salt-glaze prices in 1763, and shards found nearby, together with Shaw's statement that Mitchell made white salt-glazed stoneware make it reasonably certain that Mitchell did make it.

RICHARD MOUNTFORD AND JOHN SHAW
(Howard Place), Shelton, 1750

A 1750 partnership agreement between Richard Mountford, Newcastle-under-Lyme, grocer and John Shaw of Stoke-upon-Trent, earth potter, is transcribed in 'Richard Parrott's Book 1756'.[151] They agreed to make all sorts of earthenware, particularly 'Brown China Black White Red and Tortoise Shell Ware' for fourteen years, at the work buildings at Shelton, lately built by Mountford.

It is possible that Mountford and Shaw made white salt-glazed stoneware at Shelton. In 1750, 'White' ware would mean white salt-glazed stoneware, although the complete range of wares specified suggests that the agreement was written to include all possible types, and therefore does not confirm that white ware was actually made by the partnership. 'Richard Parrott's Book 1756' was compiled by him as a notebook of examples and cases,[152] and so this 1750 agreement has no precise date and might not have been signed.

Richard Mountford received a life interest in an estate at Shelton in 1750-51, and built a house and pottery workshops on the site. Mountford was in debt by 1758, but the property remained with the Mountford family. The Mountford site is identified as being on the north side of Howard Place, Shelton, occupied in 2004 by The Elms Restaurant.[153]

Richard Mountford married Elizabeth Fernyhough at Newcastle-under-Lyme 3 October 1746, possibly the Richard Mountford who was baptised at Trentham, Staffordshire 4 April 1719, son of Henry. They had two sons: Thomas baptised at Newcastle 3 August 1746, and Richard, baptised at Newcastle 16 March 1748.

Of Richard Mountford's sons, Thomas entered into a partnership with Josiah Spode I on 11 November 1772 at the pothouses etc., rented from Elizabeth Mountford at Shelton,[154] whilst Richard married Ann, daughter of *John Baddeley* at Newcastle on 13 February 1774.[155]

John Shaw, a very common name in 18th century England, may have been he who was baptised at Stoke-on-Trent on 15 March 1713, son of John and Elizabeth. According to the agreement, Mountford, the grocer, was to provide both buildings and money to carry on the business. Shaw, the 'earth potter', would contribute the practical skills of pot-making.

RICHARD MUCHELL
Burslem

Richard Muchell was one of the Staffordshire potters, including *John Wedgwood, Thomas Wedgwood (I), Richard Wedgwood, Thomas Daniel (I), Richard Mere,* and *Ralph Shaw (I)*, who petitioned the Privy Council on 11 June 1696,[156] alleging that *John Dwight* of London was obstructing them in their trade under pretence of his 1684 patent.[157] This patent gave Dwight a fourteen-year monopoly of making white gorges, marbled porcelain vessels, statues and figures, fine stone gorges and vessels, transparent porcelain, opaque red and dark coloured porcelain or china, Persian wares and Cologne or Stone Wares.

Nothing further has been found about this petition, but its instigation by the Staffordshire potters shows that they were making or wished to make ware of a type which Dwight claimed to have patented. There is no certainty that Richard Muchell was making salt-glazed ware.

Richard *Mutchell* or Muchell married Margaret, daughter of *Aaron Wedgwood*, at Stoke on 14 January 1684/85,[158] becoming brother-in-law of the *Thomas and Richard Wedgwood* named in the petition. Aaron and Thomas, sons of *Richard Muchell* of Burslem 'Pott-turner', were apprenticed in 1700 to James Brindley of Vauxhall, assignee of *John and David Elers*, who bought Elers' potworks at Vauxhall.[159]

NORTH-EAST ENGLAND

Newcastle-upon-Tyne, Sunderland and the surrounding areas included 18th century pottery producing locations.

Gabriel Jars, a French industrial spy, went to Tyneside in 1765. In his report, he stated 'There have been set up in the vicinity of the town of Newcastle different pottery factories making all varieties except the white which we call in France *Terre d'Angleterre'*. Jars also wrote 'All the glazes used are based on lead', and described biscuit and glost firing. He said that cream-coloured ware was used for pastry in ovens, 'but mainly one uses the white ware made in Staffordshire', and in discussing coarse ware he said that the grey clay used is not able to react with salt to produce a good glaze.[160] These references to white ware and salt-glaze suggest that Jars was familiar with white salt-glazed stoneware before he went to Newcastle-upon-Tyne, and that he found no evidence of its production there.

Writing over a hundred years later, Jewitt quoted from an account given to the British Association in 1863 by Mr. C.T. Maling, an earthenware manufacturer:

> The manufacture of white earthenware was introduced into this district by Mr. Warburton, at Carr's Hill Pottery, near Gateshead, about 1730 or 1740. Those works were very successfully carried on for seventy years.[161]

If Maling was correct, white ware in 1730-40 is likely to have been white salt-glazed stoneware, but recent research has shown that John Warburton was not born until 1732,[162] and Warburton first advertised 'earthenware' in 1769 and 1770.[163] No confirmation of Maling's dates has been found.

There were of course customers in the North-East for Staffordshire salt-glaze potters (see Appendix 5), but this does not disprove local production.

NEWBOTTLE POTTERY, near Sunderland, c.1740

Francis Buckley gave a paper in 1926 on Tyneside Potteries in the 18th century.[164] He stated 'In the Northern potteries we find the fine salt glaze or "white stone" wares succeeded by fine black' and quoted a 1765 advertisement for Newbottle Pottery, which had 'a large stock of Flint and other materials, for making both White and Brown Ware, which are now made to as great perfection as in Staffordshire'.

The possibility of white salt-glazed ware being made at Newbottle is supported by a later writer, who wrote that Newbottle 'High' Pottery was founded about 1720 for common brown ware, and that 'Flint crushing mills were established there in 1740, after which the manufacture of white ware began'.[165] If the date of 1740 is correct, it is likely that the crushed flint would be used for making white salt-glazed stoneware. (An alternative use for crushed flint in 1740 would be in glass-making, established in Newcastle-upon-Tyne by 1618.[166]) Newbottle water-mill is said to have been adapted for flint grinding for potteries in the early 18th century, and the first pottery to have been launched about 1820 by the Wilson family, owners of tile kilns and the flint mill.[167] Extensive shard deposits found in field-walking at Newbottle in 2001-02 have not provided evidence of white salt-glazed stoneware manufacture there.[168]

Carr's Hill Pottery (above) was about two miles south of Newcastle-upon-Tyne and Jars could be expected to have learnt about it if salt-glazed ware had been made there for over twenty years. Newbottle Pottery was ten miles south of Newcastle and so could perhaps have escaped Jars' notice. Although lacking clear archaeological or documentary evidence in confirmation, it seems possible that white salt-glazed stoneware could have been made at Newbottle Pottery from 1740.

NOTTINGHAM

JAMES MORLEY
Nottingham

An action by *John Dwight* of London in 1693 suggested that James Morley might have made white stoneware. Together with *John and David Elers, Aaron, Thomas and Richard Wedgwood* and *Mathew Garner*, James Morley of Nottingham was accused by John Dwight of infringing his patent to make various types of ware.[169] However, on 21 November 1693 Dwight's action against Morley was restricted to Morley's sale of brown mugs,[170] with which this work is not concerned.

The Morley family's activities as *brown* salt-glaze stoneware potters at Nottingham are well documented.[171]

OXFORD, c.1755

The possibility of manufacture of white salt-glazed stoneware at Oxford depends solely on the credibility of a Swiss arcanist, Jacques Louis Brolliet. Documents left by the French chemist, Jean Hellot, record information provided by Brolliet, who visited England twice, c.1755 and 1758-59.[172] Hellot wrote a reference for Brolliet to the director of the Sèvres porcelain works on 3 February 1759, and stated that Brolliet had been in England and was able to 'get into several factories, among others the factory making the white pottery which we cannot imitate, and which he had seen on a previous trip'.[173]

Hellot recorded Brolliet's information in greater detail in his own 'private encyclopaedia'.[174] In early 1759, Brolliet gave Hellot information about the manufacture of porcelain, and also about the making of *la poterie blanche d' angleterre*, which he had learnt on a previous journey. Brolliet described clearly the making of white salt-glazed stoneware from pipeclay and flint, placing in pierced saggars, wood-firing in round ovens and glazing with salt.[175]

Hellot noted that Brolliet said that the pipeclay used was found a mile from 'Oxfort', that the French pipeclay was better than Oxford pipeclay, and that the *oven used for salt-glaze at Oxford* (our emphasis) was round in shape. Confirmation that Brolliet had been at Oxford is provided by two advertisements in *Jackson's Oxford Journal* of 11 and 25 January 1755, offering *china* for sale, made by James [*sic*] Brolliet at Oseney-mill near Oxford.[176]

Concerning a source of pipeclay near Oxford, Dr. Plot wrote before 1677:

> And at *Shotover-hill* there is a *white clay* ... which during the late wars, in the siege of *Oxford* [ended June 1646], was wholly used for making *Tobacco-pipes* there; and is still in part put to that service, mixed with another they have from *Northampton-shire*. It is also of excellent use to *Statuaries*, for making *Moddels, Gargills* [gargoyles], or *Anticks* [fanciful ornaments in sculpture].[177]

Plot wrote later in his book that the Shotover pipeclay was no longer used, but a very good tobacco-pipeclay had been found in the parish of Horsepath, since his third chapter had been printed. (Horsepath is also four miles east of Oxford and perhaps one mile from Shotover Hill.) He also described black flints found in the Chilterns, used at Henley for glass-making.[178] Pipeclay and flint, the raw materials for making white salt-glazed stoneware, were certainly obtainable within packhorse distance of Oxford.

It should be mentioned that there is a *hamlet* to the north of Stoke-on-Trent, now New Oxford but called Oxford on a map of 1775,[179] with a potworks by 1780.[180] Brolliet was definitely in the *city* of Oxford in 1755 and it is too much of a coincidence for him to have visited the Staffordshire hamlet of the same name. No independent evidence for the manufacture of white salt-glazed stoneware near the city of Oxford has been found so far. Even if the location remains doubtful, Hellot's account of Brolliet's information about English white salt-glaze stoneware manufacture in the 1750s, however and wherever obtained, seems reliable and therefore valuable.

HUMPHREY PALMER
Snape Marsh, Shelton, c.1750; Church Works, Town Road, Hanley, 1750-
See Chapter IX

WILLIAM PARROTT
Burslem, fl.1763-1770

William Parrott was one of the salt-glaze potters who signed the 1770 price agreement.[181] He was baptised at Burslem on 11 December 1720, son of Richard and Martha Parrott.[182] His father, Richard Parrott, grocer, apprenticed him to John Wedgwood of Burslem potter (see *Aaron, Thomas and John Wedgwood*) from 11 November 1736 for seven years to learn 'that part of the Potting Trade (and the said William Parrott the Apprentice not to be debarred from the lathe in the said Term) called throwing on the wheele'.[183]

William Parrott married Ann Mollard at Burslem on 8 May 1748, and they had one daughter, Ann, baptised 20 April 1753 at Burslem.[184] He died in 1776,[185] and his widow made a marriage settlement on 4 July 1778 for her daughter Ann's marriage to William Brown of Burslem, a joiner.[186] Mrs. Parrott then occupied two houses and a potwork in Burslem, her daughter's inheritance.

One of Josiah Wedgwood's customers, John Douglas of Whitehaven, Cumbria, mentioned William Parrott in three letters to Wedgwood, all in white salt-glazed stoneware contexts. On 26 April 1763 he complained that one out of sixteen crates from 'Thos Cartlich, Parrot [*sic*], Weeldon [*sic*] and Booth' had not arrived.[187] In an undated letter Douglas told Wedgwood that he had sent £20 to William Parrott;[188] and on 14 December 1763 Douglas asked Wedgwood to remind William Parrott to send him a receipt for a bill.[189] Parrott was clearly one of the potters from whom Wedgwood ordered salt-glazed ware for his customers.

JAMES PAYNE
Snape Marsh, Shelton, before 1753

The evidence that James Payne made white salt-glazed stoneware is contained in his will made 20 April 1753. James Payne, Shelton, earth potter, left all his property in trust, but gave to his wife Hannah for life 'the House adjoining to the Flint ware warehouse'.[190] He also left £100 to each of his two daughters at age twenty-one. Earlier, in 1750, James Payne had purchased from Francis Payne (probably his father) a messuage or tenement with appurtenances in Snape Marsh, Shelton, 'part whereof is now converted into two pot ovens and hovels a stove, a smoak [*sic*] house and a packing house and slip kilns ... now in the holding of *Humphrey Palmer* [our italics]'.[191] On 9 January 1752 James Payne mortgaged his house and potworks 'late in the holding of Humfry [*sic*] Palmer' now in Payne's possession.[192]

Taken together, the description of Payne as an earth potter and the specific mention of a *flint ware* warehouse in 1753, and the description of his potworks in 1752, makes it likely that James Payne had been manufacturing white salt-glazed stoneware (often called flint ware) before 1753. As there were two ovens, there might also have been production of earthenware by both Payne and Palmer.

James Payne was christened at Stafford in 1717, son of Francis and Lydia, and married Hannah Lander there in 1738. Their two daughters were both christened at Stoke, Sarah in 1740 and Lydia in 1742.[193] Payne's potworks was likely to have been on the west side of Marsh Street, perhaps near the top of Etruria Road. A 1777 map of Shelton includes no. 102, pothouse and house, and no. 103, pothouse and garden, in that location, both held by Hannah Payne.[194] Sarah Payne, presumably James Payne's daughter, married William Meir at Stoke on 1 July 1759.[195] *William Meir* was a salt-glaze potter in Shelton and could have been operating Sarah's late father's potworks at Snape Marsh, Shelton.

JOHN PEAT
Fenton Vivian, Stoke-on-Trent, fl.1752

John Peat is known through the survival of a series of property documents, dated from 1732 to 1752.[196] He was described variously as a yeoman (farmer) and an earth potter of Lane Delph when he bought Gom's Mill, a corn mill and smithy, at Longton in 1732.[197] When he sold it in 1745,[198] it had acquired a kiln, suggesting that Peat had adapted the former corn mill to be a flint mill. Peat acquired a great deal of property in Fenton before becoming insolvent in 1747, then described as of Lane Delph, a potter. His creditors sold Fenton Hall, land, a newly erected flint mill and a potworks lately built.[199] That potworks was already held by *Thomas Whieldon*, who purchased it and Fenton Hall in 1748.[200] It is not known if Peat ever produced pottery there.

John Peat's production of white salt-glazed stoneware is proved by his lease of 'two Workhouses then in the holding of him the said John Peate in ffenton Vivian aforesaid one whereof is called the Whiteware Workhouse His other the Dipware Workhouse' to *John Edge and John Gretton*, potters, on 3 October 1752.[201] 'Whiteware' and 'Dipware' describe the two types of white salt-glazed stoneware made at that time. From this document it is deduced that John Peat owned property again after his insolvency in 1747 and made salt-glazed ware at Fenton Vivian until 1752, when he let his works to others. Fenton Vivian is a large area, which includes Lane Delph,[202] and the site of Peat's 1752 workhouses is not known.

The property documents mention that his wife was called Margaret, and show that John Peat signed with his mark 'IOP'. In 1769, Ralph Deakin, Lane Delph, victualler, leased property at Lane Delph from Stanhope and Broads, including a small dwellinghouse and buildings erected for making pots, late occupied by Margaret Peat.[203] The location is not known.

A John Peat married Margaret Hatton at St. Alkmund's, Shrewsbury on 28 September 1725,[204] but no connection with the Lane Delph John Peat is known. By inheritance, marriage or success in business he had acquired substantial properties between 1732, when he was a farmer, and 1747, when he was a potter.

GEORGE AND THOMAS PHILLIPS
Green Dock, Longton, c.1764

Simeon Shaw wrote in 1829: 'About 1760, a son of Mr. Phillips, of Lane Delph, commenced the manufacture of White Stone ware, salt glaze, at Green Dock, Longton; and he afterwards made tolerable cream colour, at the same place'.[205] Shaw went on to state that Phillips received salt from either Lawton or 'the Wyches', meaning Middlewich, Nantwich and Northwich, all salt-producing centres in Cheshire.

George Bolton Phillips and Thomas Phillips were potters at Green Dock, Longton, from c.1764. The family continued as potters there until 1802, and later made cream coloured ware, as Shaw said, but there is no further evidence of salt-glaze manufacture.[206] 'Boulton Phillips' bought flint from *John Baddeley* in 1763,[207] but this could have been for either salt-glazed or cream-coloured ware. The 'Elektra' works, on their site at the junction of Clayton Street and Edensor Road, Longton, was demolished c.1975.

NICHOLAS POOL
Stoke-on-Trent, fl.1770

Nicholas Pool signed the salt-glaze potters' price agreement on 14 February 1770.[208] He seems likely to have been Nicholas Pool, son of Joseph and Jane Pool, christened at Stoke-on-Trent on 1 January 1729/30,[209] but nothing more is known of him.

PRESCOT, Lancashire, fl.1751

Esmé Lloyd and Professor Alan Smith have summarised evidence of the production of *all types* of salt-glazed stoneware at Prescot.[210] The only contemporary description of the manufacture of *white* salt-glazed stoneware was given by Dr. Richard Pococke, who visited Prescot in June 1751.[211] He wrote:

> I went on to Prescot, a litle [sic] town most delightfully situated on a hill, its steeple, windmill, glass-houses and earthenware-houses render it a very beautiful point of view ... They have two or three houses for coarse earthenware and one for the white stone, where they also make the brown stone ware

Three years later, Reinhold Angerstein visited Prescot.[212] He described two potteries making *brown* lead-glazed drinking mugs, black bottles glazed with galena (lead) and 'magnesia [surely manganese]' and chamber pots, fired in 'capsels [capsules, saggars]', in circular coal-fired ovens. There was another pottery making 'larger earthenware pots' and a fourth making sugar moulds. He made no mention of Pococke's 'white stone', but provided useful sketches of sun-pans for drying-out clay, a round oven, a crank-wheel and a string or great wheel.

Two potworks at Marshall's Acre, Prescot were advertised for sale in 1770 'for making Nottingham Ware, and the other for making Burslem ware'.[213] 'Burslem ware' might conceivably have been a reference to white salt-glazed stoneware at that date. Jewitt wrote in 1878 that white stoneware had been made at Prescot 'to a large extent', probably reporting information told to him by Thomas Spencer, third generation master potter at The Moss Pottery.[214]

PRESTONPANS, Scotland
WILLIAM CADELL AND SONS (AND COMPANY), Prestonpans. fl.1750-1790

Prestonpans is on the south shore of the Firth of Forth, nine miles east of Edinburgh. The suffix 'pans' derives from salt-pans where sea water was evaporated to produce salt. The town's name is best known for the Battle of Prestonpans, where 'Bonny Prince Charlie' defeated an English army in 1745.

Patrick McVeigh has written at length about the Prestonpans Pottery. William Cadell, a merchant, and Samuel Garbett started the pottery in 1750, with a nephew, also William Cadell, in active charge. The Cadell family were involved in various ventures, including the Carron Ironworks and shipping.[215] In July 1762 William and John Cadels (*sic*) of Prestonpans, merchants, had insured utensils for making pottery and stock, for £100, and also William Cadel's household goods for another £100.[216]

This account is confined to evidence of the production there of white salt-glazed stoneware. A grey-white stoneware bowl incised 'Prestonpans [*sic*] / 1754', in Huntly House Museum, Edinburgh, is presumably an early product of the pottery,[217] and a series of contemporary references from 1767 to 1793 confirms the continuation of salt-glaze manufacture there.

An advertisement in the *Edinburgh Evening Courant* on 6 June and 7 December 1767 intimated that William Caddell and Sons, Prestonpans Pottery, made White Stone Ware, and also Cream Ware.[218] A similar advertisement also appeared in the *Caledonian Mercury* of 6 June 1767, where the firm was described as 'William Cadell and Sons and Company'.[219]

On 8 September 1770 John Cadell of the Stone and Glass Warehouse, Luckenbooths, Edinburgh, advertised 'all sorts of White, Cream, Black and Tortoiseshell ware of the Prestonpans Manufactory'.[220] A court case which dragged on from 1774 to 1786 showed that the stock of ware at the pottery in 1774 was 79% white (salt-glazed) ware and 21% creamware. This was qualified by a statement that stoneware did not deteriorate in stock, whilst creamware crazed and broke, i.e., stoneware might have been accumulated old stock, so that the proportion to creamware might not have represented current levels of production.[221] A shipment of '50 casks stoneware to Petersburgh [St. Petersburg]' by Wm. Cadell and Co. in July 1786 has been noted.[222]

It was stated in 1776 under 'Prestonpans and Port Seton' that two potteries employed over 100 people, making 'stone and flint kinds both white and yellow as is made in Staffordshire, as good in quality and good for the money'.[223] In 1793, an account of Prestonpans stated 'A manufacture of *stone ware* is carried on a little to the west of the church. It commenced about 40 years ago, and belongs to Messers. [*sic*] Cadell. White stone ware, and cream coloured ware (of late the last chiefly) are manufactured'.[224] An inventory of 1801-02, thought to be of the Prestonpans Pottery, does not list any stoneware, suggesting that manufacture had ceased.[225]

Dr. Roger Kemp recovered salt-glazed shards and a 'saddle' stilt in Prestonpans about 1968.[226] McVeigh suggested that the shards and stilts originated in Bankfoot, another pottery at Prestonpans. Bankfoot commenced in 1764, but an advertisement of 1767 names black, tortoiseshell and common brown earthenware as being made there, and does not mention stoneware.[227]

ROTHERHAM, Yorkshire : JOHN PLATT AND SAMUEL WALKER junior
Rotherham Old Pottery, Rotherham, 1766-70
See Chapter IX

ROTHWELL

JOHN SMITH AND JOHN PULLEN
Rothwell Potworks, Rothwell, Yorkshire, c.1768

In 1767, a pottery was founded at Rothwell, some four miles south-east of Leeds, by John Smith of Stainbrough, Yorkshire and John Pullen of Wath, Yorkshire, a mason.[1] A 1973 report on 'The Rothwell Pottery and its Wares' states that:

> there is some reason to suppose that a salt-glaze kiln was operating there as well [as at Rotherham, see Chapter IX for *John Platt and Samuel Walker junior*]. Unfortunately Platt's valuation [of Rothwell Pottery in 1772] records nothing that would confirm this but several white salt-glazed fragments have been found on the site, three of which are illustrated.[2]

The illustrated fragments are not wasters, so do not themselves prove the production of salt-glazed ware on site.

A 1770 deed listed 'three Ovens ... for the baking of Delphtware' and an April 1773 advertisement for the pottery included 'a large hovel containing 3 kilns, and capable of containing 4'. John Platt's valuation in 1772 was more specific: '2 kilns and the pot kiln in the Hovel'.[3] Platt was himself both a mason-architect and a salt-glaze potter, so he was a capable valuer for a pottery. If one kiln was specifically for 'pots', the other kilns must have been for enamelled ware. Enamelling was certainly done at Rothwell: the flint mill, also in the sale, included 'a small pan for grinding of enamel colours' and '3 spacious rooms, well lighted and fitted up, for the Enamel work'.[4] Platt described John Smith as 'the painter' in 1772.

Platt also listed 'the Green ware & Bisket [biscuit ware]'.[5] The existence of biscuit ware confirms that twice-fired earthenware was made at Rothwell, and unglazed creamware shards were found on site. The single 'pot kiln' must have been used for both biscuit and glost firing of this creamware by 1772, so could not have been used for salt-glazing. It is concluded that there is no positive evidence of the production of white salt-glazed stoneware at Rothwell and the only possibility is that production of it ceased before 1772.

It is tempting to link John Smith at Rothwell from 1767 with the *John Smith* who was at Burslem and Hanley until 1766, but no positive evidence of a connection has been found.

AARON SHAW I -1713
AARON SHAW II 1713-
AARON SHAW III 1735-1736
Burslem

'Aaron Shaw' was listed by Josiah Wedgwood I as making 'Stone or Dipp'd wit [dipped white]' ware in Burslem about 1710-15 (Fig. 26).[6] An Aaron Shaw (I) died in 1713 and was buried at Burslem on 17 November.[7] His will, made 7 September 1709,[8] shows that he was a potter, with 'workhouses, warehouses, pottovens [sic] and buildings' which he left to his wife Katharine for life and then to his son Aaron Shaw junior (II). Josiah Wedgwood's list, made sixty years later, is the only suggestion that Aaron Shaw I made white salt-glazed stoneware.

Aaron Shaw junior (II) was christened 25 November 1691 at Burslem. He had married 'Joane' by 5 November 1714 when their son, also Aaron (III) was christened at Burslem. The date of death of his mother has not been established,[9] but in the normal course of events Aaron Shaw II would have inherited his father's potworks. When his son Aaron III died, £4.2s.0d. of his 'earthenware' was in the hands of 'Aaron Shaw father'.

A 'Mr. Aaron Shaw' was buried at Burslem on 19 April 1754,[10] possibly Aaron Shaw II. When *John Shrigley* made his will in 1780,[11] he left 'My House and Potworks in Burslem with all the lands belonging formerly the estate of Aaron Shaw and lately held by William Taylor of New Chapel' to his daughter Mary Morris for life. The use of 'Mr.' in the parish register and Shrigley's reference to Aaron Shaw's estate suggests a 'man of property' but there is no certainty that this was Aaron Shaw II.

Aaron Shaw III, born in 1714, married Ann Morley at Alfreton, Derbyshire on 6 October 1735. Ann Morley, daughter of Thomas and Anne, was christened 15 July 1718 at South Wingfield, Derbyshire. Aaron Shaw III died in 1736/37[12] aged only twenty-two, intestate, and his widow, aged eighteen, was granted administration on 13 April 1737 under the guardianship of Joseph Shaw of South Wingfield Mills, Derbyshire, 'Pott maker'.[13] He and Stephen Shaw, also of South Wingfield Mills, potmaker, gave the usual bond for her, and her father, Thomas Morley, witnessed the bond. This contact between two salt-glaze pottery-making areas, thirty miles apart, is not surprising.

The inventory made after the death of Aaron Shaw III leaves no doubt that he was a salt-glaze potter. Actual ware included a hundred dozen of flint ware £5; burned flint ware £35 and green ware turned and unturned £3.15s.0d. Materials named were nine pecks of ground flint and seventeen balls of clay at 11d. per ball, mixed slip ready for drying and beaten clay. Equipment included a paddle and four lawns (sieves) for preparing the 'body', lathe and wheel, together with forty-nine boards (for carrying ware). Apart from 'flint ware', the most significant proof of salt-glaze manufacture was 'planks for scaffolding at the oven'. There was no mention of farming equipment, but he had three saddle horses.

MOSES SHAW
Burslem, c.1710-15

'Moses Shaw' was listed by Josiah Wedgwood I as making 'Stone Ware & Freckl[e]d' in 'Middle of the Town' at Burslem about 1710-15 (Fig. 26).[14] 'Stone Ware & Freckled' can be assumed to include salt-glazed ware at that date, though not necessarily white.

Nothing more is known about this Moses Shaw. The name is quite common in Burslem. Burials of 'Moses Shaw' are recorded in 1730, 1743, 1744, 1747/48 (*Mr.* Moses Shaw) and 1755.[15]

RALPH SHAW I
Burslem

Ralph Shaw (I) was one of the Staffordshire potters, including *John Wedgwood, Thomas Wedgwood (I), Richard Wedgwood, Richard Muchell, Thomas Daniel (I)* and *Richard Mere*, who petitioned the Privy Council on 11 June 1696,[16] alleging that *John Dwight* of London was obstructing them in their trade under pretence of his 1684 patent.[17] This patent gave Dwight a fourteen-year monopoly of making white gorges, marbled porcelain vessels, statues and figures, fine stone gorges and vessels, transparent porcelain, opaque red and dark coloured porcelain or china, Persian wares and Cologne or Stone Wares.

Nothing further has been found about this petition, but its instigation by the Staffordshire potters shows that they were making or wished to make ware of a type which Dwight claimed to have patented. There is no certainty that Ralph Shaw I was making salt-glazed ware.

In 1718/19, a Ralph Shaw of Burslem, earth potter, was an arbitrator in a dispute between *Joshua Astbury* and his neighbour John Middleton, also a potter, about smoke nuisance from Middleton's stove and oven in Shelton.[18] Ralph Shaw was a common name in North Staffordshire and it has not proved possible to identify the one who signed the petition. 'Ra. Shaw sen.' and 'Ra. Shaw jun.' were two of many Burslem men who took the oath to defend and avenge King William in 1696.[19]

RALPH SHAW II, RICHARD BAGNALL AND THOMAS DANIEL
Burslem, fl.1733-37

'Ralph Shawe of Burslem ... earth potter' obtained a patent on 24 April 1733 for a ware 'of a true chocolate colour, striped with white ... and glazed with salt' (Colour Plate 90).[20] This subject is dealt with in Chapter V, Decoration. In his specification of his patent, Ralph Shaw stated that he had been 'for many years a maker and dealer in earthenware'.

Although he was the sole patentee, Shaw had two partners, both in potmaking and in his patent. Richard Bagnall of Rushton Grange, Burslem, husbandman (farmer) died in 1737. In his will (at Lichfield JRO), made 10 August 1737 and proved 27 October 1737, he left to his wife Eleanor, 'interest on money due by trade as partner with Thomas Daniel and Mr. Shaw', and made her

> partner in my stead with Thomas Daniel and Mr. Shaw for the unexpired term of years of the Patent formerly granted us for making the Chocolate ware, leaving her for life (Provided she Continues unmarried) the Interest of whatever Profits may redound from the said Trade

Eleanor Bagnall died in 1747, and was buried at Burslem on 14 November 'a papist', by which time the (fourteen years[21]) patent would have expired. No evidence has been found that Richard Bagnall himself was a salt-glaze potter.

Simeon Shaw was the first to describe Ralph Shaw's patent, and also a subsequent court case when J[ohn]. Mitchell was unsuccessfully sued by Ralph Shaw in 1736 for infringement of his patent.[22] Ralph Shaw was also described as an early user of a slip kiln. Simeon Shaw stated that Ralph Shaw migrated to France, but this has not been substantiated elsewhere.

Ralph Shaw was a common name in Burslem and four of that name were buried there, in 1740, 1754, 1757 and 1759,[23] so that it is not possible to identify when the part-owner of the patent died. He may have been the uncle of *William Littler* who became known for developing what is now known as 'Littler-Wedgwood Blue' salt-glazed ware. William Littler's mother was Sarah Shaw, daughter of a Ralph Shaw.[24] She may have been the sister of Ralph Shaw, whose patented process has some similarity to the production of 'Wedgwood-Littler Blue', an interesting connection, but not surprising in a close-knit community.

THOMAS SHAW
Burslem, fl.1764-1765

The chance survival of contemporary documents mentioning Thomas Shaw gives an interesting picture of inter-potter trading in the 1760s: salt-glaze potters supplying each other and also creamware potters buying from salt-glaze potters for their customers.

Thomas Shaw, Burslem, supplied Josiah Wedgwood with salt-glazed ware in 1764: plain dishes, baking dishes, plain plates, Barleycorn sauceboats and 'Petties' (small dishes[25]) on 20 April; Barleycorn pattern oblong dishes, table plates and breakfast plates, chamberpots and quart washbasins on 2 August; 'unburn'd' saucers, London size cups and saucers on 17 August; and plain cups and saucers on 29 October.[26] The bodies of white salt-glaze and creamware were the same, so Shaw's 'unburn'd saucers' would be 'green', unfired ware, which Wedgwood could fire biscuit, glaze and fire glost, to make creamware saucers.

In September 1765, Thomas Shaw bought unspecified goods from *Thomas and John Wedgwood*, Burslem, salt-glaze potters, paid for by 15s. worth of 'goods'.[27] Shaw also supplied salt-glazed ware to *John Baddeley*. On 7 November 1765, Baddeley asked his partner, Thomas Fletcher, for £84 cash to pay Thomas Shaw for ware which Baddeley had sold to James Tidmarsh, a London dealer. Thomas Shaw bought flint and 'crates' from John Baddeley in the same year.[28]

An advertisement in the London *Daily Advertiser* for 18 January 1766 told that Thomas Shaw, earth-potter, late of Burslem, had left there ten weeks before, supposedly to go to London. If he enquired at Anderton's Coffee House in Fleet Street, he would hear of something greatly to his advantage.[29] 'Ten weeks before' takes us back to the date when John Baddeley paid £84 to Shaw!

A Thomas Shaw was baptised at Burslem on 11 July 1731, son of Ralph Shawe and Mary Thursfield, and another on 2 September 1739, son of Aaron and Elizabeth Shaw,[30] either of whom could be this Thomas Shaw. The key to a '1769' map of Burslem (made sixty years later)[31] shows Thomas Shaw's *house* at Sitch Rock, now in Westport Road.

JOHN SHRIGLEY
Market Place, Burslem, fl.1763

The positive evidence that John Shrigley was a salt-glaze potter is that he supplied white salt-glazed stoneware to Josiah Wedgwood in 1763: specifically '2 Large Barley Corn Turiens [sic] [£]0.7.0 and 2 Middle Do [£]0.6.0.'[32] Amongst other 'men of affairs' in Burslem, Josiah Wedgwood signed a promissory note to Shrigley and four other men in April 1763 to pay various amounts when the turnpike accounts were settled. To Shrigley he owed £1.5.8.[33] Wedgwood settled the turnpike account with Shrigley in August of the same year.[34]

John Shrigley married Ann Adams at Burslem on 3 October 1736 and leased Hadderidge potworks from her father.[35] It is said that about 1750 Shrigley built a house on the north side of Burslem Town Hall, with a potworks behind, and that he was one of the principal potters in Burslem.[36] Also, that in 1765 Shrigley built the largest hovel ever attempted in Burslem, which collapsed on completion.[37]

Factually, by 1747 John Shrigley was a man of property – he had a vote[38] – and in 1750 he rented Burslem corn water-mill. In 1750 he rented a house 'on land at the head of Crofthead' and in 1761 he was fined at the Manor Court for not removing a 'ruck [heap]' of clay or marle in the high way opposite his new workhouse.[39]

John Shrigley re-married in 1767,[40] and is referred to as a 'gentleman' in a document of 1769, suggesting that he had ceased to be an active master potter.[41] He died in 1780, and left a great deal of property.[42] It is likely that his house and potworks opposite Burslem Town Hall were on the site of what was Sadlers' Central Pottery (until 2000).

A 'rescue' archaeological excavation on the site in 1955 produced evidence of slipware, blackware and butter-pot production. Three salt-glazed items were also found, but these were not wasters: the base and part body of a buff stoneware tankard, part of a plain white saucer, and the base and part-body of a white dipped grey stoneware vessel.[43] These fragments were dated to pre-1730, before Shrigley's occupation of the site.

It is possible that Shrigley made salt-glazed pottery at Hadderidge works from 1736, but his 1763 sales to Wedgwood would be from his later potworks. In 1762 he bought 'goods' and in 1766-67 'parcels' and 'Colyflower [cauliflower ware]' from John Baddeley of Shelton,[44] presumably to meet his customers' orders for the newer ware.

SHROPSHIRE

There is firm evidence of the production of white salt-glazed stoneware in the Ironbridge Gorge area of Shropshire. Writers have reported the survival of salt-glazed saggars in garden walls etc.,[45] and there are two archaeological reports on the subject. The inference of these reports is that early production was in Benthall and later production at Jackfield.

Samuel Simpson wrote the only known contemporary reference in 1746: 'Broseley is a very large and populous village on the Severn … the Coalmines … Iron Stone, Pipes, white earthenware etc.'.[46] White earthenware in 1746 can be reasonably understood to mean white salt-glazed stoneware.

BENTHALL, no date

An archaeological investigation was carried out at the Old Vicarage,[47] Benthall, in 1978.[48] The owner of the site had retained 'a few complete saggars and one section of saltglazed bricks' when surface rubble was used to fill a disused mineshaft in the 1960s. During the investigation 'a quantity of early salt-glazed wasters' and 'fragments of the salt-glazed saggars' were found. An early '"white-dipped" salt glaze mug' fragment was found 'of the type found inside the saggars' and also the base of a white dipped salt-glazed mug, 'the upper part covered with a ferruginous wash'.[49] Eight complete salt-glazed saggars survived, three containing mug wasters stuck to the inside, presumably those retained by the owner. Evidence of a kiln on the site was not found, but the survival of salt-glazed brickwork and saggars and early types of salt-glazed ware strongly suggest that there was an early salt-glaze potworks at Benthall.

Roger Edmundson has published an illustration of a broken white salt-glazed mug fused to a saggar fragment 'found in a garden wall near the Pitts Yard pottery site, and therefore likely to have been made there'. Pitts Yard Pottery was one of three pottery sites at Benthall.[50]

JACKFIELD, 1760s-1770s

Investigation of a 'black ashy deposit' on the south bank of the River Severn, at Jackfield, was reported by J.P. Malam in 1981.[51] Shards and waster shards of white salt-glazed stoneware and numerous salt-glaze saggar fragments, items of kiln furniture and burnt flint were recovered. The shards (but not specifically the wasters) were of 'unsophisticated types remarkably similar to those from Staffordshire',[52] plates, bowls, jugs, tankards and possibly tea and coffeepots. 'Scratch-blue' decoration and moulded 'seed', 'dot and diaper, star and diaper and basket patterns in scroll-bordered panels' were found. Handles were 'invariably ribbed, often with a pronounced central spine' and some with 'a folded back lower terminal'. Whilst the non-waster shards could have come from domestic sources, the presence of salt-glaze saggars and wasters shows that production occurred nearby.

Printed evidence of the former manufacture of white salt-glazed ware at Jackfield was given in an advertisement of 21 August 1780, offering a potworks at Jackfield for sale 'having been used for making cream coloured and white stone wares' which had apparently only been in operation for ten years.[53]

Jewitt visited the area in early 1862 and met Mr. R. Thursfield there.[54] Following his visit, Jewitt wrote that salt-glazed ware was made at Jackfield (in Broseley parish) by Glover until about 1713 and then by John Thursfield, whose father came from Stoke-on-Trent. Thursfield's ware is described as

> a white stone-ware, very similar to the Staffordshire make, and on some examples flowers and other ornaments were incised and coloured; that is, the outlines were cut in while the clay was soft, and the flowers and other ornaments touched afterwards with colour ['scratch-blue ware']'.[55]

This description agrees with the finds in the riverside deposit at Jackfield described above.[56] Later, Jewitt added that 'In 1763 Mr. Simpson carried on the pottery at Jackfield, and made yellow ware, and a ware the body of which was pipe-clay and glazed with salt. This he sent down the Severn to the Bristol Channel for export to America – a trade which the American war of independence put an end to'.[57] This agrees with the 1780 advertisement for a Jackfield potworks, quoted above. Thomas Symson (*sic*, Simpson), a potter came from Staffordshire to work at Jackfield by 1731 and the Simpson family continued there until at least 1784.[58]

Potwork sites known in the area are Jackfield (Ordnance Survey reference SJ 686029) and John Miles' pottery at Ladywood (SJ 673033) in Broseley parish; and Haybrook (SJ 662019), Benthall (SJ 662020), Glasses' Pottery[59] (SJ 666021), 'Benthall Vicarage' site (SJ 668021) and Pitts Yard or Pitchyard (SJ 669025), by the New Inn in Benthall Parish.[60] It has not been possible to relate the archaeological finds to specific potworks sites. A salt-glaze saggar with white wasters attached (Colour Plate 86) is in the Jackfield Tile Museum. Although no provenance is known to the museum, it seems likely to be of local origin.

JOSEPH SIMPSON
(Greenhead Street), Burslem, fl.1761-1770

Joseph Simpson was one of the salt-glaze potters who signed the 1770 price agreement.[61] He dealt with *John Baddeley* between 1761 and 1765, buying from him flint, cauliflower teaware, blue smalts and unspecified ware, and selling to him crates and ware.[62] Joseph Simpson and Ann Stevenson, both of Burslem, were married at Newcastle-under-Lyme on 15 December 1745.[63] The 1769 sketch map of Burslem shows Jos. Simpson's house and potworks on present-day Greenhead Street, Burslem, on the north-west side of the junction with Scotia Road.[64]

Greenhead Garage is probably on this site in 2004. An excavation to make a pit there in April 2002 revealed 18th century brickwork, several *brown* salt-glaze saggars (one at least with brown salt-glaze tankards adhering), and shards of white salt-glazed stoneware, coloured glaze ware and redware.[65]

JOHN SMITH
Burslem, fl.1761-1764
Hanley, 1764-c.1766

John Smith of *Burslem* supplied Josiah Wedgwood with white salt-glazed stoneware from September 1762 to October 1764.[66] There were references to gadrooned and mosaic dishes, and 'Barley Corn T[able] Plates' and 'Barley Corn Oval Dishes with & without work'. The meaning of 'work' in this context is not understood by the authors.

On 27 October 1763 John Smith charged Wedgwood 2s. for 'wares fired', and in December 1763 Smith invoiced Wedgwood for five fruit baskets and fifty-six tureens and covers, and asked 'Sir Please to allow me the same for firing the above that you allow others'. The charges were included in a subsequent bill, endorsed by Wedgwood 'John Smith acc[oun]t of firing sundry articles'.[67] *Samuel Kirk and Co.* and *William Taylor II* also fired ware for Josiah Wedgwood (q.v.) at this period. Smith bought ware from Wedgwood: fine enamelled teapots and old fine wrought red teapots in May 1764.[68]

Smith moved from Burslem to Hanley in late 1764. In a letter from 'Hanley Green' on 24 December 1764 he told Wedgwood that he had sent him 'my bills of the ware that was fired at my house', another reference to firing green ware for Wedgwood. Excusing himself for a mistake in his bill, Smith wrote 'I was a little hurried at that time [10 November] about removeing [*sic*]'. 'Jno. Smith Handly Green' supplied 'goods' value £5 to *Thomas and John Wedgwood* of Burslem in 1765.[69]

John Smith of Burslem owed £48 to *John Baddeley* of Shelton in 1761,[70] and bought flint from Baddeley in 1763, 1765 and 1766, paying him with crates, plates, soup dishes, bills and cash.[71] It has been noted that a John Smith was a part-time carrier of flint for John Baddeley in 1761.[72]

'John Smith' must be one of the most common names in England. John Smith at Burslem and Hanley in Staffordshire until 1766 is neatly followed by John Smith at *Rothwell, Yorkshire* from 1767, but no positive evidence has been found to link the two men.

JOS SMITH
Burslem?, fl.1770

'Jos Smith' signed the 1770 salt-glaze potters' price agreement.[73] No more is known of Jos. Smith as a salt-glaze potter, but *Joseph Smith* married the widow of *Joseph Warburton*, a salt-glaze potter, on 14 January 1771.[74] Possibly it was he who signed on her behalf. That Joseph Smith, of Willington, Derbyshire, is stated to have been 'a general carrier on the canal, and was wealthy'.[75]

An alternative Joseph Smith was listed as a pottery manufacturer at Burslem in 1784, and at Tunstall in 1796, 1802 and 1805.[76] He was an ardent Methodist and 'owned considerable property in Tunstall'.[77]

WILLIAM SMITH
Burslem?, fl.1770

'Wm. Smith' was another signatory to the 1770 salt-glaze potters' price agreement, about whom nothing else is firmly known.[78] In 1767 William and Thomas Smith bought flint from *John Baddeley*, paying with 'Goods, Crates, Small plates',[79] possibly the same William. A William Smith was buried at Burslem on 2 June 1773.[80]

SAMUEL SPODE
Foley Pottery, Fenton

Samuel Spode has been described as 'the last salt-glaze potter in Staffordshire',[81] a statement traced back to A. Hayden, writing in 1925: 'Josiah Spode erected the Foley factory at Lane End for his second son, Samuel Spode, whose name occurs in the Staffordshire Directories as late as 1802; salt-glazed ware was made there up to the end of the 18th century'.[82] No reliable source has been found. Because of this statement, it has been thought desirable to study his activities, although it appears to the authors that Samuel Spode did not make salt-glazed ware.

The site of Samuel Spode's works is now (2004) occupied by the Wedgwood Seconds Shop on the south-west side of King Street, north-west of Foley Lane. An archaeological excavation of a pottery waste dump on the site in 1973-74 revealed kiln waste in the forms of red stoneware, cream-coloured ware and large quantities of white salt-glazed stoneware.[83] The report on the excavation pointed out that layers 5 to 9, containing white salt-glazed stoneware shards, pre-dated Spode's factory on the site, which was erected c.1780.[84]

David Barker, who wrote the report, has since published convincing evidence that *Thomas Barker* was the most likely manufacturer of this early ware, including the white salt-glazed shards found.[85] Thomas Barker may have had a factory on the site, or merely dumped wasters in a clay-pit there. Barker certainly had a potworks across the road from Spode's site and was the maternal grandfather of Samuel Spode.[86]

Samuel Spode was baptised 28 October 1757, son of Josiah and Ellen Spode. He married Sarah Garner 3 December 1783 in London, and died 26 January 1817.[87] It seems unlikely that a potter, starting business in his twenties, about 1780, would commence to make the out-dated salt-glazed ware. In the absence of further evidence, it is concluded that Samuel Spode did not do so.

JOSEPH STEPHENS
Cobridge, 1763-1775

Joseph Stephens was one of the salt-glaze potters who signed the 1770 price agreement.[88] He dealt largely with Josiah Wedgwood in 1763 and 1764, supplying him with Barleycorn plates, 'oblongs' from eleven to sixteen inches, dishes, round and oval dishes and tureens; plates, mugs, basins, Middle Gadroon tureens, gadroon oblongs and plates; scolloped plates, dishes from six to twelve inches, sortable ware, mugs, quart mugs, chocolates, bowls, saucers, coffees, sets of toys, teacups, chamberpots, cream jugs, teapots, and a single sugar pot.[89] The sets of toys were made up of 6 cups, 6 saucers, 1 cream jug, 1 teapot and 1 sugar pot, and Stephens supplied 120 sets at fourpence each on 3 November 1763, total cost £2.

The same group of documents included other transactions between Stephens and Wedgwood: Stephens bought clay from Wedgwood in 1772 and 1773, and supplied Wedgwood with 3,000 oven bricks and eight loads of marl (clay), 'Goods' and two dozen quart mugs in part payment, settled 14 December 1775.

Stephens also dealt with *Thomas and John Wedgwood* of the Big House, Burslem, who supplied him with unfired ware in 1768.[90] Isaiah and Richard Marsh, Burslem potters, owed Stephens £2.7s.0d. for a crate of seconds dishes in 1763,[91] and a Liverpool dealer, Mary Forbes, owed him £22.14s.3d. in 1764.[92] Stephens dealt with *John Baddeley* in 1765-66, trading crates and cash for flint, ware and candlesticks.[93]

Joseph Stephens 'Re-married' Abigail Stephens at Norton-le-Moors, Staffordshire, on 21 January 1765.[94] Abigail, wife of Joseph Stephens, aged twenty-seven, was included in a list of thirty-four papists at Burslem in 1767.[95]

THOMAS STEVENSON
Burslem, to 1757

Thomas Stevenson, born 1718, married 1743, was buried at Burslem on 1 November 1757.[96] His widow, Hannah, was granted administration of his property on 23 May 1758. The accompanying inventory describes him as of Burslem, an earth potter,[97] and lists his domestic and potting effects, worth altogether £53, which included:

Lath wheel and sagger wheel 5s.
Clay in Burslem about 50 Load £2.10s.
Warehouse Goods in the deceas'd's way of Trade as an earth Potter of various Sorts, valued & appraised, £15
Boards in the Workhouse £1
A scaffold for the Oven 5s.
Three bands of Iron to the oven £2
Saggers & oven £5
Pokers & Tongs Iron Rod Ladles & Shovels 3s.6d.
2 Tables 2 Stools & a Tressell [trestle] 4s.6d.
Flint & Chester Clay & unfired Ware £1.5s.
Salt Bag 1s.6d.
Lawn & Hair Sives [sieves] & paddle 2s.6d.
Glosing [glossing, i.e. glazing] Ladder 6d.
Clay in the ffield fifty Load £1.5s.

The mentions of a scaffold for the oven, used when throwing in salt, a salt bag, ladles (presumably for salting), and a specific 'glosing' ladder, for access to the scaffold, flint and Chester clay (ball clay, originally received from Devon through Chester) leave no doubt that Thomas Stevenson was a white salt-glazed stoneware potter.

SWANSEA, Wales:

WILLIAM COLES, Cambrian Pottery, 1767-1778
See Chapter IX

SWINTON, Yorkshire

WILLIAM MALPASS AND WILLIAM FENNEY
Swinton, South Yorkshire, 1769-1775

Swinton Pottery, often referred to as Rockingham, has been researched and written about almost from its closure in the 1840s,[98] most recently and comprehensively by Alwyn and Angela Cox.[99] It is only their archaeological investigations on the site and documentary research that has revealed that white salt-glazed stoneware was made at Swinton between 1768 and 1775. What follows is entirely drawn from their work, here gratefully acknowledged.

There had been a pottery on the site since at least 1753, on land owned by the Marquis of Rockingham, making coarse redware, slipware and, possibly, brown salt-glazed ware. It was taken over by William Malpass in 1765, and William Fenney became his partner in early 1768. Fenney had previously been a partner in a fineware pottery at Rotherham (see *John Platt and Samuel Walker junior*).

Invoices in the Wentworth Woodhouse Muniments show that Malpass and Fenney supplied 'white' items of pottery between 1769 and 1775 to Wentworth House, considered to be white salt-glazed stoneware. A wide variety of 'white' domestic ware was delivered, including chamber pots, stool pots, mugs, basins, jars, plates and sauceboats.

The shards recovered show that the white salt-glazed stoneware produced at Swinton was of high quality, equal to any produced in Staffordshire or elsewhere. An unusual moulded plate border is accurately described as 'Cockstail'. The only decorated items found were a part tea-bowl enamelled in black with a chinoiserie landscape, a shard with red enamel, and two pieces showing 'scratch-blue' decoration. Salt-glaze saggars and kiln furniture found were of standard forms.

Latecomers to the manufacture of white salt-glazed ware, Malpass and Fenney must have recruited experienced workers from elsewhere. Cream-coloured ware was also made in the same period, and enamelled dated pieces survive from 1771 onward, showing equal competence.

JOHN TAYLOR
The Hill Top or Hill, Burslem, fl.1770

John Taylor was one of the salt-glaze potters who signed the 1770 price agreement.[100] Nothing further has been found to identify him specifically, but he is probably the John Taylor of whom Simeon Shaw wrote in 1829: 'Ralph Leigh (83 years of age, in 1813) was employed by John Taylor, of the Hill Top, to look after his horses' and that John Fletcher 'worked for the brothers, W. and John Taylor of the Greenhead… J. and W. Taylor soon built each a dwelling house; the former at the *hill top*… and then they commenced making White Stone Ware'.[101] John Ward, writing ten years later, elaborated Shaw's statement to 'each erected respectable dwelling-houses, with Potworks adjacent'.[102]

John Taylor 'of the Hill' was buried at Burslem on 16 January 1773.[103]

THOMAS TAYLOR I
Burslem, to 1713

In his list of 1710-15 Burslem potters (Fig. 26), Josiah Wedgwood included Thomas Taylor (I), making £6 per week of 'Stoneware & Freckl[e]d', and living next to the north of Aaron Wedgwood, who was himself next to the Red Lion public house.[104] 'Stoneware' may be understood as some form of salt-glazed ware at that date. A 1750/1769 plan of Burslem shows nos. 109 and 110, a house and bottle oven for 'Mr. Taylor' in that situation,[105] perhaps a descendant. The location is now (2004) approximately the site of the Queen's Theatre.

'Thos. Taylor' was one of the Burslem men who took the oath to defend and avenge King William in 1696.[106] Thomas Taylor (I) of Burslem, potter, died in 1713 and left his household goods and chattels and moneys out on bond to his wife Mary. He left horses and cows; 'Potts in the Warehouse & Kiln Vallued at [£]05 00 00'; £100 out on bond etc., and £30 desperate debts.[107] L. Weatherill has interpreted this reference to a kiln as evidence of a drying kiln for either slip or pottery, but a simpler explanation is that an oven was meant.[108]

THOMAS TAYLOR II
ELIZABETH TAYLOR
THOMAS TAYLOR III AND ISAIAH TAYLOR
THOMAS TAYLOR III
Market Place and elsewhere, Burslem, c.1750-1774

A Taylor family had a potworks at the north end of Burslem Market Place between c.1712 and c.1776. The site, bounded by Market Place, Wedgwood Street and the new Ceramica extension, is now (2004) a car park and was earlier part of a Police Station.[109] Enoch Wood, well known as a potter, commissioned a plan of Burslem as it was in 1750, and his own copy of the key to the plan bears his corrections and comments.[110] A corresponding plan shows a bottle oven on Taylors' site, no. 67. The key includes '67 Thomas Taylor Potworks' and Enoch Wood endorsed the entry 'White Ware'. Enoch Wood himself occupied this site c.1786, so it seems reasonable to assume that his statement is reliable.

Thomas Taylor II (1714-1751[111]) left his house and potworks, wheels, lathes etc. to his wife Elizabeth and then to his son Thomas III (1738-1776[112]) when twenty-one.[113] His eldest son was living at Biddulph, North Staffordshire, in 1786 when he mortgaged the house and potworks,[114] then occupied by Enoch Wood.

Thomas Taylor II also left 'All my workhouses warehouses ovens hovells [sic] and other buildings yards… I lately bought of Thomas and Catharine Wedgwood' to his wife and then to his younger son Isaiah when twenty-one.[115] Isaiah Taylor was born in 1740,[116] so that in 1751 Elizabeth Taylor was left with two potworks to operate. Her sons became of age in 1759 and 1761 respectively, and they seem to have worked in partnership. The site of Isaiah Taylor's potworks is not known. An Isaiah Taylor died in 1767 and was buried at Burslem on 19 November.[117]

A group of twenty invoices from Thomas (III) and Isaiah Taylor to Josiah Wedgwood in 1763 and 1764 show that they were selling to him many types of white salt-glazed ware: four crates containing gadroon oblongs, cans, twifflers, quart mugs, chamber pots, Barleycorn flatware, washbasins, salad dishes and large teapots in their first surviving invoice of 3 February 1763 through to their last, on 18 December 1764, for oblongs, Barley Corn, in sizes from 10 inches to 13.[118]

A letter to Josiah Wedgwood from John Wyke of Liverpool watchmaker, on 23 August 1763, acknowledged receipt of seven crates £15.17s.7d. from Thos & *Josiah*[119] Taylor, and authorised Wedgwood to pay them £8 or £10 on account. Wedgwood had also obtained salt-glazed ware for Wyke from *William Taylor*. Wyke was selling these crates to a merchant in Portugal and proposed paying the remainder when he was paid. Three days later Taylor duly acknowledged receipt from Wedgwood of £8 on Mr. Wyke's account.[120]

Thomas Taylor III of Burslem bought flint and oval dishes from John Baddeley in 1765-66, paid for in bills and crates.[121] Thomas Taylor III alone sold chamber pots, white mugs and white dishes to Josiah Wedgwood in 1773-74.[122]

Archaeological excavations were made on the north Burslem Market Place site in 1998 and 1999 by the Field Unit of the Potteries Museum. The reports have not been published, but it is understood that no significant white salt-glazed shards were found.

WILLIAM TAYLOR I
Hanley, to 1738

'William Taylor of Handley, potter' was buried at Stoke on 18 May 1738.[123] His 1738 will, made by William Taylor of Hanley 'fflint Ware Potter', is sufficient to include him as a salt-glaze potter.[124] He left houses, buildings and land in Hanley to his wife Ellen and daughter Ellen, and £40 each to his stepsons *William Hassells* and *John Hassells*. Taylor appointed *Joshuah Heath* of Shelton 'fflint potter' and his brother-in-law Charles Whitehead as executors.

The inventory made at his death shows that he had nine (wooden) trenchers, twenty-four pewter dishes and plates, nineteen blue and white (tin-glaze?) plates, and four china plates, two basons and six coffee pots, in his house, a wide range of wares.

In his 'Best Ware House' he had a parcel of best flint ware valued at £16, a parcel of seconds £6, spout and other blocks £1, and thirty-two sprigs 21s. He also had a cow, three horses, three carts and harnesses, and he was owed £300; altogether a prosperous potter. No tools of trade were listed. A long wheel and a little wheel were listed in his kitchen, but these are more likely to have been spinning wheels than throwing wheels. The location of his potwork is not known.

William Taylor (I) was probably born in 1694, son of George and Ellinora Taylor, and married Ellen Taylor (sic) 17 December 1734 at Stoke. Their daughter, also Ellen, was christened at Stoke 17 June 1736.[125]

WILLIAM TAYLOR II
The Hill, Burslem, fl.1763-1776

The earliest evidence for William Taylor II of Burslem making white salt-glazed stoneware is in the Wedgwood Accumulation.[126] He invoiced Josiah Wedgwood, then in Burslem, on 24 October 1763 for one crate of barleycorn dishes, quart canisters, mustard pots, legged salts, candlesticks, carved boats, teapots and milks and another crate of one hundred dozen best cups, total £8.1s.2d.[127] The first crate bore a mark requested by John William Pollmann of London on 1 October 1763.[128] Pollmann's order was marked up by Wedgwood 'The Barley Corn from Wm. Taylor', for Taylor to supply. (Basket plain ware in this order was marked up for Mr. Hales, see *John Hales*.)

The second crate, with a different mark, agrees with an order to Wedgwood from Pollmann on 8 September 1763,[129] which Pollmann wanted sent before winter via Hull to Hamburg. Taylor's trade with Wedgwood was reciprocal: Taylor wanted melon, sprigged pearl, pineapple, leafage, 'Cocoa nut' and Indian figure ware in the same year.[130]

A September 1763 account from Taylor to Wedgwood covered the carriage of thirteen crates and a hogshead to the ferry (Willington Ferry, head of navigation on the River Trent), 'one pan of clay' which Taylor must have supplied to his neighbour, and charged Wedgwood for the firing of forty-eight candle-sticks, with another twenty-one on 14 February 1764.[131] *Samuel Kirk and Co.* and *John Smith* also fired ware for Josiah Wedgwood (q.v.) at this period.

As noted for *Thomas Taylor III and Isaiah Taylor*, John Wyke of Liverpool, watchmaker, placed large orders with Josiah Wedgwood for agate, tortoiseshell and white stoneware to go to Portugal in 1763.[132] Wyke was sorry that Wedgwood did not make all the ware, and asked him to recommend suppliers.[133] His letter to Josiah Wedgwood on 23 August 1763, acknowledged nineteen crates from Mr. Wm. Taylor, £57.3s.11d., and authorised Wedgwood to pay him £20 or £30 on account.[134] William Taylor acknowledged receipt of £20 from Mr. Wyke on 3 October 1763.[135]

Taylor's business was not of course confined to supplying Josiah Wedgwood. Samuel Fullmer of London sent an order for Cauliflower ware and enamelled teapots to Wedgwood on 23 June 1763, remarking 'As I am strange to you, ask your neighbour William Taylor for my character and pay', implying that Taylor already dealt with Fullmer.[136]

Much later, E. Mayer, Amsterdam, sent a 'small order for white ware' to 'Mr. William Taylor at the Hill at Burslem' on 9 January 1776, to be sent via Mr. R. Coddington at Gainsborough to Mr. William Holmes at Hull, in crates marked FRY. The order included common teapots, upright mugs, bowls, and London size and middle, 3rd, 4th and 5th size cups and saucers.[137]

In an accompanying letter Mayer referred to a previous delivery from Taylor, whose cups had been of good quality but the wrong shape, to be rounder and not so high in future. Moreover, many were cracked half an inch down the side. Saucers of the fourth size were to be 3¾ inches and the fifth size 3½ inches. Taylor could send any seconds of those sizes 'as you may probably not know how to dispose of them at Burslem'. Presumably there was little demand for these small sized saucers. Mayer told Taylor that he might become a customer to him for creamware. He could be sure of orders for white ware, as long as Taylor used him well.

Simeon Shaw wrote in 1829 that John Fletcher 'worked for the brothers, W. and John Taylor of the Greenhead ... J. and W. Taylor soon built each a dwelling house ... the latter at the top of the Jornell [Central Passage in 2003][138] and then they commenced making White Stone Ware'.[139] John Ward, writing ten years later, elaborated Shaw's statement to 'each erected respectable dwelling-houses, with Potworks adjacent'.[140]

WILLIAM TWYFORD
Shelton, Stoke-on-Trent, fl.1720s

Simeon Shaw was the first to associate 'Twyford' with potting, when he wrote in 1829 of *John and David Elers* at Bradwell Hall, that 'a person named *Twyford*, from Shelton, obtained employment under them' and two pages later 'Twyford and Astbury commenced and carried forward, manufactories of Red Porcelain, and White Pottery glazed with salt, amidst many small thatched dwellings in Shelton'. Later in the same book, Shaw wrote 'Mr. Twyford commenced business near Shelton Old Hall ... Mr. Astbury [*John Astbury*] commenced also in Shelton ... And both these persons made Red, Crouch and White Stone ware; using lead ore glaze for some vessels, and salt for those of more value'.[141] In 1837, Shaw credited *Josiah* Twyford with the introduction of pipe-clay to the pottery industry.[142] Shaw seems to be writing of a single individual named Twyford.

There was only one family named Twiford (sic) in Stoke-on-Trent parish in 1701: Joshua Twiford, married, aged fifty, his wife Sarah, aged forty, and two sons, William aged eleven and John aged seven, with three servants (one of them Daniel Botham aged twenty-five), a substantial household.[143] The ages given are not reliable. Joshua Twyford was baptised on 6 December 1640 (sic) at Stoke[144] and married Sarah Low at Dilhorne on 23 April 1687.[145] He was buried at Stoke on 8 September 1729.[146] His son William was baptised 2 May 1689 and his son John was baptised 12 May 1690 (sic).[147] As the Elers brothers were only in North Staffordshire between 1691 and 1698, the father, Joshua Twyford, seems most likely to be the person to whom Shaw was referring.

William Twyford of Shelton, potter, was buried at Stoke on 1 August 1729.[148] In his will[149] William Twyford left his property to his wife Ellen,[150] and then to his only son William at twenty-one (c.1749),[151] and, failing him, to his own brother John. William also provided that his daughter Ellen should have £300 out of the profits of his potting business when she was twenty-one (c.1746),[152] obviously anticipating that his business would continue. Confirming that William was the son of Joshua Twyford, he left to Daniel Botham (his father's servant in 1701, above) £4 or a cow 'in consideration of his good and faithful service to me and my family'.

It seems likely that William Twyford would be the Twyford of whom Shaw wrote that he made lead-glazed redware, and Crouch and salt-glazed white stone ware.

WARBURTON AND STONE
Burslem, fl.1768-1770

Warburton and Stone, Burslem, sold 'engine' flat plates and soup plates, flat Barley Corn plates and soup plates, and fruit dishes to Josiah Wedgwood in June 1768.[1] The meaning of 'engine' is not understood. It may refer to 'engine turning' or alternatively have been a phonetic spelling of 'Indian', either description referring to a surface moulding. In 1770 'Warburton & Stone' signed the salt-glaze potters' agreement.[2]

It has not been possible to identify which of the many Warburtons was Stone's partner. Joseph Stone married Ann Warburton at Burslem on 8 February 1764.[3] She was the daughter of John and Ann Warburton[4] and had four brothers: Thomas, Jacob, John and Joseph.[5] It seems likely that Stone would be in partnership with a Warburton brother-in-law. Thomas Warburton was his mother's partner (see *Ann Warburton and Son*), but any of the other three brothers could have been Joseph Stone's partner.

Joseph Stone, potter, aged thirty-eight, was noted as a Papist in Burslem in 1767.[6] He died in 1777.[7]

EDWARD WARBURTON
Fenton Low, fl.1751-63

White salt-glazed ware, saggars and kiln furniture were found at Fenton Low between 1900 and 1926, together with shards of other wares, and were originally attributed to *Thomas Whieldon*.[8] He was the owner of a potworks at this site from 1749 and his tenants were the manufacturers at Fenton Low. *William Meir* was the tenant on 25 March 1750, when a year's rent was due. Edward Warburton was the tenant from 25 March 1751 until 29 October 1761, when the record ceased.[9] Edward Warburton bought flint from *John Baddeley* in September 1763.[10] An Edward Warburton married Sarah Poulson in 1756 and died in 1767.[11]

William Meir may have made white salt-glazed stoneware in his apparent single year at Fenton Low, but it seems reasonable to attribute the shards to Edward Warburton, who was on the site for over ten years. Fenton Low potworks is identified on a map published in 1950.[12] In today's terms, it lay on the north-west side of Dewsbury Road, Fenton, Ordnance Survey grid reference SJ 893453. W. Emery identified a slip kiln and an 8ft.6in. diameter oven base at the site.[13]

The shards etc. recovered between 1900 and 1926 are held at the Potteries Museum and Art Gallery, Victoria and Albert Museum, Liverpool Museum, Norwich Castle Museum and the Wedgwood Museum.[14] They include salt-glazed saggars, kiln furniture, a salt-glazed pyrometer, profiles, basket-work, seed and gadrooned plate rims and scratch-blue decorated ware.[15]

JACOB AND ISAAC WARBURTON
Cobridge, fl.1763-1770

Jacob and Isaac Warburton of Cobridge supplied Barleycorn dishes in sizes from 10 inches up to 17 inches, and '[sauce] Boats' to Josiah Wedgwood in 1763.[16] They insured their potworks in 1765 for £300: house £100, pottery buildings £170, brewhouse £10, utensils and stock £20.[17] Jacob Warburton alone signed the 1770 salt-glaze potters' agreement.[18]

Jacob Warburton (c.1736-1775)[19] and Isaac Warburton (c.1740-1775)[20] were the two youngest sons of Joseph Warburton of Cobridge Gate (1694-1752).[21] He left his workshop tools to be sold for the benefit of his widow, Jacob and Isaac, and it is possible that they chose to continue his pottery business instead of selling.

JOHN WARBURTON, fl.1754-1760
JOHN WARBURTON AND SON, 1760-1761
ANN WARBURTON AND SON, 1761-c.1770
Cobridge Gate, Burslem

John Warburton was born 24 June 1720, son of Joseph Warburton[22] of Cobridge Gate, potter[23] and Abigail. His father died in 1752 and left him his Cobridge Gate estate.[24] John Warburton married Ann Daniel, born c.1713, daughter of Thomas Daniel of Cobridge, gentleman, and sister of *Sampson, Ralph and Thomas Daniel II*,[25] all salt-glaze potters. John and Ann Warburton had seven children, including Thomas, born c.1740.

Whilst in Staffordshire in 1754, Reinhold Angerstein, Swedish industrial spy, noted that he bought 'Tea pots from "Joh. Worverton [surely John Warburton?]" Each dozen consists of 12, 18 or 24 according to size. Tea pots, white ware 1s.6d.'.[26] This strongly suggests that John Warburton was making white salt-glazed stoneware in 1754.

John Warburton of Cobridge Gate died in 1761, and left Ann all his property for life, and afterwards to all their children.[27] A 26 December 1760 codicil to his 1 July 1760 will noted that Thomas had already had his share, implying that Thomas had become a partner in the meantime.

Amongst the signatories of the 1770 salt-glaze potters' price agreement was 'P[er] Pro of Ann Warburton & Son Thos Warburton',[28] confirming that the partnership had continued after John's death in 1761, and that the partnership made salt-glazed ware. Thomas Warburton was buried at Burslem 9 October 1789[29] and Ann Warburton was buried 12 August 1798, aged eighty-five.[30]

Mrs. Warburton was noted by Simeon Shaw as making 'the last improvements of Cream Colour' in 1751,[31] and is alleged to have enamelled creamware for Josiah Wedgwood.[32]

JOSEPH WARBURTON
Cobridge Gate, fl.1762-63

Joseph Warburton of Cobridge sold Barleycorn (a salt-glaze shape) plates and dishes to Josiah Wedgwood in 1763.[33] In 1762 he bought mustard spoons from *Thomas and John Wedgwood* and paid with thirty-two water bottles in 1763.[34]

Joseph Warburton was born in 1722, son of Joseph and Abigail Warburton,[35] and was an older brother of *Jacob and Isaac Warburton*. He bought land at Cobridge Gate in 1750 and built a potworks.[36] Joseph Warburton married Elizabeth Adams in 1752 and left his potworks to her when he died in 1769. She married again, to Joseph Smith in 1771, and when she died in 1792 her potworks was occupied by Thomas and Benjamin Godwin.[37]

'Jos. Smith' signed the 1770 salt-glaze potters' agreement,[38] possibly *Joseph Smith* signing on behalf of the then widow Elizabeth Warburton.

JOHN WEATHERBY
Burslem?, fl.1770

John Weatherby was another of the salt-glaze potters who signed the 1770 price agreement.[39] The only further reference to John Weatherby, potter, which has been found is his insurance of seven houses at Hanley in 1792,[40] although the Weatherby family is recorded in North Staffordshire from 1637 onward.[41] A John Weatherby was baptised at Burslem on 16 February 1737/38, son of John and Mary,[42] and either father or son might have been the 1770 potter.

John Weatherby, London pottery merchant from c.1744 and a glass maker, is well known as a partner in the Bow porcelain works from 1747; he died in 1762.[43] No connection with the salt-glaze potter has been found, other than the similarity of name.

AARON WEDGWOOD
Burslem, fl.1749-1770

Aaron Wedgwood has been linked with *William Littler* in the invention of 'Littler-Wedgwood Blue', white salt-glazed stoneware with an overall fine blue slip. The earliest account was published by a local historian, William Pitt, in 1817:[44]

> About this time [1750-1763] an improvement was made in the salt glaze by the united efforts of William Littlor [sic] and Aaron Wedgwood… Aaron Wedgwood was a manufacturer of White Stone ware, and having married Littlor's sister, they united their experience, and made repeated attempts to improve the salt glaze. The result of their experiments was the addition of … ground zaffer … [which] produced a fine smooth glassy surface.

The subject is dealt with in Chapter V, Decoration. See Colour Plates 26, 27, 91, 92, 93, 137 and 194 for examples made by various manufacturers.

Thomas and John Wedgwood sold 'Blue ware Aaron's' to William Hilcoat in 1760 and Aaron Wedgwood supplied them with 'Blew Cups &c.' in 1763.[45] Aaron Wedgwood supplied *Jonah Malkin* with porringers, mugs and toast mugs 'Japand flowred new collor' as early as 1749, but this was not necessarily 'Aaron's Blue', nor even salt-glazed ware.[46] Josiah Wedgwood bought 'blue teapots' from Aaron Wedgwood in 1763, and 'best fine blue cups and saucers' in 1764.[47]

Apart from these 'special' items, Aaron Wedgwood supplied *Thomas and John Wedgwood* with many types of white salt-glazed ware between 1761 and 1770, and Aaron occasionally included their goods in his crates between 1756 and 1766. He collected money for them and they lent him cash, fired for him when 'he was short of ware', and altogether they worked closely together.[48] They sent 'Cousen Aaron's Toys' and 'Aaron Wedgwood ... Wisling [whistling] Birds' to Bristol in 1770.[49]

Josiah Wedgwood too bought all kinds of salt-glazed ware from Aaron Wedgwood between 1762 and 1764[50] including petties (small dishes), flummery (jelly, blancmange) cups and 'unfired' plates and dishes. John Wyke, the Liverpool clockmaker, received patterns from Aaron Wedgwood in 1762.[51] In 1763 Mrs. Cadman of Penkridge told Josiah Wedgwood 'send me no Cats for I think Mr. Aaron Wedgwood has stocked me very well with Cats & Kittens for a good while. Desire Mr. Aaron Wedgwood will send me 24 white half price floure [*sic*, flower] horns to stand in the window'.[52]

Aaron Wedgwood was the eldest son of Aaron and Martha Wedgwood, baptised at Burslem on 9 March 1717.[53] His father died when he was five[54] and he was brought up by his grandfather, also Aaron (1666-1743).[55] The close working relationship between Aaron Wedgwood and *Thomas and John Wedgwood* is explained by him being their nephew and near neighbour. They refer to him in their account books as cousin, a loose term often used for nephew at that time.[56] Aaron Wedgwood married Sarah Little (*sic*), sister of William Littler, on 29 July 1738,[57] a possible reason for the cooperation in developing the blue slip described above.

In 1767-68, Aaron Wedgwood was in debt. He had supplied nine crates of goods to a Mr. Cottrell in the Borough, London in 1766. *Thomas Wedgwood IV of the Overhouse* tried to collect payment due to Aaron, stating that his creditors would get the cash if it costs them twice the money, 'the Poor Man has been confin'd in his own house for Debt upwards of twelve months' and 'he & his large family greatly distressed & in great want'.[58] Aaron Wedgwood died in 1782.[59]

The '1740' and '1769' maps of Burslem[60] show a house shared by Aaron Wedgwood and Little Aaron, on the east of what is now Wedgwood Street, between the rear of the Big House and the former Post Office. The maps do not show a potworks for Aaron Wedgwood, the site of which is not known.

AARON WEDGWOOD, THOMAS WEDGWOOD III AND JOHN WEDGWOOD, Burslem, fl.1732-1743;
THOMAS WEDGWOOD III AND JOHN WEDGWOOD,
Big House Works, Burslem, 1743-1776
See Chapter IX

AARON WEDGWOOD, THOMAS WEDGWOOD I AND RICHARD WEDGWOOD Burslem, fl.1693-1698

On 16 December 1693 Aaron Wedgwood and his sons Thomas Wedgwood I and Richard Wedgwood of Berslem (*sic*) were added to the 20 June 1693 suit of *John Dwight* of London against *John and David Elers*. The suit alleged that they had made ware contrary to Dwight's patent.[61] On 19 May 1694 it was reported to the court that the Wedgwoods had asked if they could 'answ[e]r in the country', but meanwhile they continued to make and sell the wares complained of. An interim injunction was awarded against the Wedgwoods until they answered the suit.[62]

From the litigation we know that Aaron, Thomas and Richard Wedgwood,[63] *Moses Middleton* and *Joshua Astbury*,[64] were accused of making Dwight's patent wares, but not which of the various types included in the accusation. In 1696 Thomas Wedgwood, Richard Wedgwood and other Staffordshire potters complained that Dwight was obstructing them in their trade by his patent.[65]

The nearest we come to knowing what the Wedgwoods made in the 1690s is their brother's reported statement in 1698 that Dwight was in suit with them 'for making ye ordinary glazed drinking potts in ye form (Or imitacon) of those wch Mr. D. makes of stoneware'.[66] As the Wedgwoods and others had complained in 1696 that Dwight was obstructing them in their trade, they must have been making or wished to make one or other of his patented wares. Leaving out 'Cologne or Stone wares' which were not included in the accusations, we are left with white gorges and fine stone gorges as the 'ordinary drinking glazed potts' which Wedgwoods were producing in the 1690s, presumably salt-glazed.

Dwight's Aaron Wedgwood (c.1624-1700) was the father of *Thomas Wedgwood I* and *Richard Wedgwood*,[67] and father-in-law of *Richard Muchell*. Another son, Aaron Wedgwood (1666-1743) went to *Whitehaven*, Cumbria[68] and told William Gilpen in 1698 that Dwight had been in suit particularly with his brother.[69] As Aaron his father was aged about sixty-nine in 1693, and left his pottery to his son Richard in 1695, Richard (1668-1718), although only twenty-five in 1693, was presumably the active head of the family business, the 'brother' to whom Aaron referred.

'Thos. Wedgwood', 'Ric. Wedgwood' and 'Aron Wedgwood', signing successively, were three of the Burslem men who took the oath to defend and avenge King William in 1696.[70] Aaron Wedgwood called himself 'the elder of Burslem, Yeoman [farmer]' when he made his will on 6 August 1695, proved 16 April 1701 after his death.[71] He left houses and land in Burslem and his 'potters workhouses warehouses pott ovens Libertees clay boards and all other materialls whatsoever belonging to the Art or Trade of Potting' to his son Richard.

See the separate entries for *Richard Wedgwood* and *Thomas Wedgwood I* for the sons' later activities as potters.

BURSLEM WEDGWOOD
Burslem, fl.1761-1762
CARLOS WEDGWOOD
Burslem, fl.1763-1765

Burslem Wedgwood was baptised on 16 August 1724, second son of *Dr. Thomas Wedgwood II*,[72] and died without issue in November 1762.[73] In his will of 2 November 1762,[74] Burslem Wedgwood of Burslem, potter, left his real estate to his younger brother Carlos, who appears to have continued his brother's business. Carlos Wedgwood was baptised 31 March 1726,[75] third son of Dr. Thomas Wedgwood II, and buried on 14 December 1771.[76]

The ledger of *Thomas and John Wedgwood* shows that they bought a punchbowl, jugs, very large chamberpots, quart chambers, cups and saucers, stoolpans, wash hand-basins, square plates, bowls, bottles, a melon tureen, dishes and water plates from Burslem Wedgwood between November 1761 and December 1765, although his younger brother Carlos was named in their 1765 transactions.[77]

Carlos Wedgwood bought flint from *John Baddeley* in 1763.[78] Several invoices exist which indicate that Carlos Wedgwood sold small amounts of what might be salt-glazed stoneware to Josiah Wedgwood in 1763, but they are nearly devoid of elucidating descriptions.[79]

Simeon Shaw wrote of Carlos Wedgwood that he was one of more than seven potters who went from Burslem to Chelsea China Works in 1747. They returned to Burslem and worked as salt-glaze potters, and 'Carlos Wedgwood at length commenced making white stone pottery, behind the present [1829] Wesleyan Methodist Chapel, which stands on the spot occupied by his house'.[80] Burslem Swan Bank Methodist Church and Sunday School stand in this position in 2004. The unusual forename of Carlos seems to come from his paternal grandmother, Jemima Carlos or Careless.[81]

JOHN WEDGWOOD
Overhouse, Burslem

On 11 June 1696 *John Wedgwood, Thomas Wedgwood (I), Richard Wedgwood, Richard Muchell, Thomas Daniel (I), Richard Mere, Ralph Shaw (I)* and other Staffordshire potters petitioned the Privy Council, alleging that *John Dwight* of London was obstructing them in their trade under pretence of his 1684 patent.[82] This patent gave Dwight a fourteen-year monopoly of making white gorges, marbled porcelain vessels, statues and figures, fine stone gorges and vessels, transparent porcelain, opaque red and dark coloured porcelain or china, Persian wares and Cologne or Stone Wares.[83]

Nothing further has been found about this petition, but its instigation by these Staffordshire potters shows that they were making or wished to make ware of a type which Dwight claimed to have patented. There is no certainty that John Wedgwood was making salt-glazed ware.

John Wedgwood of the Overhouse, Burslem (c.1654-1705),[84] the leader of this petition, was wealthy. Described in his will as a yeoman (farmer), nevertheless 'Materialls [sic] in the Workhouse belonging to the potting trade, and Clay & Ware' worth £17 were included in the inventory compiled after his death, together with London Ware (?), brass and pewter, silver plate and silver spoons and six pieces of gold, valued in total at £331.[85] In Josiah Wedgwood's 1776 list of Burslem Potters 1710-15 (Fig. 26), John Wedgwood's 'Upper House [Overhouse]' is noted as 'not work'd suppos'd'.[86] Nothing more is known of his activities as a potter.

JOSIAH WEDGWOOD
Burslem

Did Josiah Wedgwood make white salt-glazed stoneware in his own works at Burslem? We have found no positive evidence that he did. His family said he did not make it, but the 1829 local historian says he did. On this basis, we tentatively conclude that Josiah Wedgwood did not make white salt-glazed stoneware as an independent master potter from 1759 onward, whilst leaving the door wide open for further documentary or archaeological evidence to prove otherwise.

Personal experience Josiah Wedgwood knew all about making white salt-glazed stoneware. Born in 1730, son of a potter, Josiah Wedgwood grew up amongst salt-glaze manufacture in Burslem. From 1744 to 1749 he was apprenticed to his eldest brother *Thomas Wedgwood (IV of Overhouse)*, then or later a salt-glaze potter; between 1752 and 1754 he was junior partner of *John Harrison*, reputed to have made salt-glazed ware; and then from 1754 to 1759 junior partner of *Thomas Whieldon*, who did make salt-glazed ware.[87]

Documentary evidence We have found no contemporary documents which confirm that Josiah Wedgwood *made* white salt-glazed stoneware from 1759 onward, when he was an independent master potter, although there is plenty of evidence that he bought and sold it, quoted in this book.

Our research has shown that Josiah Wedgwood paid three 'salt-glaze' potters to fire ware for him:

Samuel Kirk and Co. in August 1764 for firing fruit dishes, fruit baskets and Barleycorn sauceboats and covers. These are followed on the same invoice by a long list of 'salt-glaze' shapes, at very low prices, which might also have been for firing.[88]

John Smith in December 1763 for firing 5 fruit baskets and 56 tureens and covers.[89]

William Taylor II in September 1763 for firing 48 candle-sticks, with another 21 in February 1764.[90]

See the respective potters in this Appendix for more details. The obvious deduction is that Josiah Wedgwood made these 'salt-glaze' shapes and sent them to the salt-glaze potters for them to fire and return to him, but we feel that this subject requires further investigation.

Archaeology Of his three known factory sites in Burslem – the 'Ivy House', the Brickhouse works and the 'Red Workhouses' – there has only been archaeological investigation on the Ivy House site. That unearthed an oven base which was of early 19th century date, and creamware, redware and salt-glazed shards, but no wasters to prove on-site production.[91]

Wedgwood's thoughts on salt-glazed ware Wedgwood had a low opinion of white stoneware. It is not clear when Wedgwood wrote his own thoughts on white stoneware, but they are set down in his experiment book, which contains details of experiments which Wedgwood *commenced* at Fenton in early 1759. The following version was re-written by Alexander Chisholm in 1781 or later:[92]

> White stone ware was the principal article of our manufacture. But this had been made a long time, and the prices were now reduced so low that the potters could not afford to bestow much expense upon it, or to make it so good in any respect as the ware would otherwise admit of – and with regard to Elegance of form, that was an object very little attended to.

Wedgwood went on to state that Tortoiseshell had been made for several years and that he had already made an imitation of agate, ending with the well-known phrase 'I saw the field was spacious, and the soil so good, as to promise an ample recompense to anyone who should labour diligently in its cultivation'.

Family biography Several draft biographies of Josiah Wedgwood survive, written and corrected around 1800 by his family and close associates.[93] The following paragraph occurs, whilst describing Wedgwood starting his own small business in 1759, after his illness during his partnership with Whieldon:

> The extent of this undertaking was determined by the state of his health, and the objects of it were of course such as he could superintend in that depressing situation. *He did not therefore make any of the great staple manufactures of the country* [our italics]

Instead, he made flower vases, green ware, tea services, pine-apple, melon, apple, pear, cauliflower and other shapes. This is the 'family' version, put together forty years after the event by people who had been close to Josiah himself, and might be thought to be writing down what he had told them.

Non-family biography Simeon Shaw wrote the 'non-family' version in 1829,[94] when seventy years had elapsed since 1759:

> Mr. Josiah Wedgwood returned to Burslem about 1760, and commenced business alone, at the small manufactory… Here he continued [after leaving Whieldon] the manufacture of Knife Hafts, Green Tiles, Tortoiseshell and Marble Plates, glazed

with lead ore, for his previously formed connections; and … engaged a second small manufactory … Here he manufactured the White Stone Pottery, then increasing in demand; and there yet remains of this kind, white Tiles, with *relief* figures, of a Heron fishing, and a Spewing-Duck fountain.

Shaw here affirms that Wedgwood made no salt-glazed ware at his first small works, the Ivy House; but he introduces a later second works, where Wedgwood *did* make salt-glazed ware. Shaw could have had his information from Enoch Wood, who was born in 1759, the year when Wedgwood set up his own works. Wood was too young to have first-hand information about events between 1759 and say 1769, but old enough to have been told recent history by older people, including Josiah Wedgwood himself. Incidentally, it seems likely that Wedgwood's former partner, *Thomas Whieldon*, made the Heron and Duck tiles.

For later reproductions of white salt-glaze ware, marked Wedgwood, see Chapter V, Replicas.

RICHARD WEDGWOOD
Burslem

Richard Wedgwood was included in Josiah Wedgwood's 1710-15 list of Burslem potters as one who made stoneware in the 'Middle of the Town' (Fig. 26).[95] A likely source of Wedgwood's list is his record of an 'Account of the Pottery' given by 'Steel', aged eighty-four, in 1765.[96] Steel said that 'Mr. Thomas Wedgwood [I] of the Red Lyon and Richard Wedgwood of the Overhouse, Burslem, made it [white ware with the addition of flint] first there'.

Richard Wedgwood was born in 1668, son of *Aaron Wedgwood*[97] and brother of *Thomas Wedgwood I*, all three sued by *John Dwight* in 1693[98] for infringing his 1684 patent.[99] This patent gave Dwight a fourteen year monopoly of making white gorges, marbled porcelain vessels, statues and figures, fine stone gorges and vessels, transparent porcelain, opaque red and dark coloured porcelain or china, Persian wares and Cologne or Stone Wares.

On 11 June 1696 *John Wedgwood, Thomas Wedgwood (I), Richard Wedgwood, Richard Muchell, Thomas Daniel (I), Richard Mere, Ralph Shaw (I)* and other Staffordshire potters petitioned the Privy Council, alleging that *John Dwight* of London was obstructing them in their trade under pretence of his 1684 patent.[100] Nothing further has been found about this petition, but its instigation by these Staffordshire potters shows that they were making or wished to make ware of a type which Dwight claimed to have patented.

When Richard's father Aaron Wedgwood died c.1700, he left houses and land in Burslem and his 'potters workhouses warehouses pott ovens Libertees clay boards and all other materialls whatsoever belonging to the Art or Trade of Potting' to his son Richard,[101] who presumably continued potting.

When he died in 1718 the inventory of his effects included 'all materials belonging to the potting trade and potts ready made' worth £30, together with £100 of 'Desperate Debts and money owing'.[102] Richard Wedgwood was a potter, but there is no certainty that he made white salt-glazed ware.

THOMAS WEDGWOOD I
Red Lion, Burslem

Thomas Wedgwood I, his father *Aaron Wedgwood* and his brother *Richard Wedgwood*,[103] were sued by *John Dwight* in 1693[104] for infringing his 1684 patent.[105] This patent gave Dwight a fourteen year monopoly of making white gorges, marbled porcelain vessels, statues and figures, fine stone gorges and vessels, transparent porcelain, opaque red and dark coloured porcelain or china, Persian wares and Cologne or Stone Wares.

On 11 June 1696 *John Wedgwood, Thomas Wedgwood (I), Richard Wedgwood, Richard Muchell, Thomas Daniel (I), Richard Mere, Ralph Shaw (I)* and other Staffordshire potters petitioned the Privy Council, alleging that *John Dwight* of London was obstructing them in their trade under pretence of his 1684 patent.[106] Nothing further has been found about this petition, but its instigation by these Staffordshire potters shows that they were making or wished to make ware of a type which Dwight claimed to have patented. There is no certainty that Thomas Wedgwood I was making salt-glazed ware.

Thomas Wedgwood I was baptised at Burslem on 18 September 1655 and was buried 29 December 1717.[107] Calling himself a 'yeoman [farmer]' in his will, proved 29 April 1718, Thomas Wedgwood I left considerable property, but made no specific mention of a potworks.[108] His brother *Richard Wedgwood* inherited their father's pottery and, apart from Dwight's ambiguous allegation, the only suggestion that Thomas Wedgwood I made white salt-glazed stoneware came from Josiah Wedgwood. In his record of an 'Account of the Pottery' given by 'Steel', aged eighty-four, in 1765,[109] 'Mr. Thomas Wedgwood [I] of the Red Lyon' was said to have been one of the first two potters in Burslem to have made white ware with the addition of flint. However, 'Dr. Thos. Wedgwood' was included in Josiah Wedgwood's 1710-15 list of Burslem potters (Fig. 26) as one who made 'Brown Stone' at 'Ruffleys'[110] – more ambiguity!

'DOCTOR' THOMAS WEDGWOOD II
Burslem, c.1731-1737

This Thomas Wedgwood (II) was baptised 25 June 1695, son of *Thomas Wedgwood I*, and was buried 20 February 1736/37.[111] He bought property in Burslem from John Taylor of Silkstone, Yorkshire on 24 June 1731, including cottages, farm buildings, and what the lawyer described as 'Potthouses workhouses warehouses beating houses molding houses throwing houses smoakhouses, Pott-ovens killns hovells [sic]' and land.[112] The extensive buildings detailed may be no more than legal phraseology to cover every possibility, but at least it shows that such buildings were known in 1731. When Thomas Wedgwood II died, six years later, the inventory referred to merely a single 'workhouse'.

Pitt recorded that, in the same year, Dr. Thomas Wedgwood (II) took Aaron Wood apprentice to learn turning, handling and trimming (not throwing) for seven years from 11 November.[113] Shaw repeated Pitt's information, and also said that Wood worked for Dr. Thomas Wedgwood for five further years, until 1743.[114] In fact Thomas Wedgwood II died in 1737 and his widow Catherine would inherit both business and apprenticeship bond. Her own sons *Burslem Wedgwood* and *Carlos Wedgwood* were too young to take over and it is possible that Aaron Wood managed her works for five years. Shaw also stated that Thomas Wedgwood (II) made coffee and teapots in agate, marbled and other natural bodies, some glazed with lead ore; 'and the white, all salt glaze'.[115]

Thomas Wedgwood II died intestate and an inventory of his effects, taken 19 March 1737, included 'In the workhouse 34 Long bords 12 short ones 0 16 0 2 Lathes & Chocks & handleing table [£] 5 0 0 A Throwing weel & wedging Board 0 15 0 [sic]'.[116]

THOMAS WEDGWOOD IV fl.1750s-1773
THOMAS WEDGWOOD V 1773- c.1780
Overhouse, Burslem
See Appendix 1

WEST PANS, Scotland

West Pans is a village on the south shore of the Firth of Forth, seven miles east of Edinburgh and, like *Prestonpans,* derives its name from local salt-pans, producing salt from sea water. There had been a pottery at West Pans from 1754.[117] *William Littler* came to West Pans in 1764, having made salt-glazed stoneware at Burslem from 1745 to 1750 and then porcelain at Longton Hall until 1760.

Littler commenced making porcelain at West Pans c.1764, and a surviving billhead dated 8 October 1766 states that Littler, china maker at West Pans, made all kinds of china and 'Also all kinds of Stone Ware, such as fine Gilded and Japand [sic] Black and Tortoise Shell Ware, &c.'.[118] He sought permission to build a windmill for flint in 1764, but there is no evidence of it being constructed.[119] There is no confirmation that Littler's 'Stone Ware' included white salt-glazed stoneware, so that his possible production of it at West Pans is 'not proven'.

Littler was last heard of in West Pans in 1777[120] and later potters made some kind of stoneware there,[121] but again there is no evidence that it was white salt-glazed ware.

THOMAS WHIELDON, Fenton Vivian, fl.1750;
THOMAS WHIELDON AND JOSIAH WEDGWOOD,
Fenton Vivian, 1757
See Chapter IX

WHITEHAVEN, Cumbria

Aaron Wedgwood (1666-1743)[122] was recruited from Burslem in 1697/98 to make earthenware near Whitehaven.[123] He was well aware of how to make salt-glazed stoneware because he told Sir John Lowther's agent in Whitehaven, William Gilpen, that *John Dwight* of Fulham was in suit particularly with his brother (see *Aaron, Thomas and Richard Wedgwood*) about making stoneware contrary to Dwight's patent.[124] Gilpen was anxious to start making pottery in the Whitehaven area. His own notes about pottery made at Fulham state that it was made from Dorset clay and Isle of Wight sand, was 'Leaded [covered in lead glaze] and then sett [sic] in the Furness [Furnace - kiln]' and that 'the inside of the Furness seems to be Leaded over',[125] not procedures that would have made salt-glazed ware.

Another Aaron Wedgwood (1671-1746)[126] was in Dearham, twelve miles north of Whitehaven, about 1704 and started a pottery about 1710,[127] but no evidence has been noted which suggests that he made salt-glazed stoneware there.

WHITEHEAD
Hanley

Simeon Shaw wrote that Mr. Whitehead of the Old Hall manufactory, Hanley, made white salt-glazed stoneware.[128] Several generations of the Whitehead family were potters,[129] and it is likely that one or other produced white salt-glazed stoneware, but no firm evidence has yet been found to confirm that they did so.

JOHN WOOD AND RALPH WOOD II
JOHN WOOD AND JOHN WEDGWOOD
Burslem
JOHN WOOD
Brownhills, Burslem

John Wood (1746-1797)[130] was involved in three businesses as a master potter, but the only firm evidence connecting him with white salt-glazed stoneware is that he bought it in the 1770s and sold it in the 1780s. He was the second son of Ralph Wood I, the modeller, and was in business at Burslem for the first time in 1772, with his brother Ralph Wood II. They bought salt-glazed ware and 'unfired ware' from *Thomas and John Wedgwood* in 1772-73,[131] but there is no information about what they made. They failed in April 1773.[132] Their elder brother, *Josiah Wood*, was also a master potter.

John Wedgwood of the Big House, Burslem took John Wood into partnership in 1776, Wood with a two-thirds share, and John Wood managed their works until John Wedgwood died in 1780.[133] Thomas and John Wedgwood had two works, one on each side of what is now called Wedgwood Street, and John Wood ran both of them. The only evidence of what was made in this period is that a 'Bisket [biscuit] oven' was built in 1776, something not needed for making salt-glazed ware, and 'Cream coloured flint' was bought in the same year,[134] suggesting that cream coloured ware was to be made.

By 1782 John Wood had sufficient cash or credit to buy an estate at Brownhills, a mile north-west of Burslem, and build a mansion and new works there.[135] Of all the transactions in his 1783-1787 sales ledger, there are only ten which included white salt-glazed stoneware, a total of 3,130 pieces, which included gallypots, twifflers, stool- and chamber-pots, bowls, cups and saucers.[136] There is a list of prices of 'Gallipots' from one to eight ounces inside the front cover of this ledger, both white stone ware and dearer ones, the body not described.

This modest quantity of 3,130 pieces in four years is not indicative of active salt-glaze production at the new works. The explanation may be that John Wood brought 'old stock' with him from *Thomas and John Wedgwood's* works in Burslem, that he 'bought in' salt-glazed ware to meet his customers' orders, or that he made much larger sales of salt-glazed ware which were not recorded in the surviving ledger.

John Wood was murdered in 1797.[137]

JOHN YATES
Shelton, fl.1758-1770

John Yates was one of the salt-glaze potters who signed the 1770 price agreement.[138] There is no further evidence of him being a salt-glaze potter, but he bought flint from *John Baddeley* from 1758 to 1767,[139] presumably used in making salt-glazed ware. He paid in 'crates' and cash, on one occasion being partly credited by '12 crucifixes'. A Mr. Yates bought a lathe from the premises of the late Moses Marsh, a Burslem potter, on 9 April 1758,[140] perhaps signifying the start of Yates' career as a potter.

John Yates was probably a son of William Yates of Newcastle-under-Lyme, currier, baptised there on 25 March 1732.[141] He was in financial difficulties in 1763. In February *Anthony Keeling* told Josiah Wedgwood that *Enoch Booth* had got the books out of Yates' hands and would endeavour to raise money to satisfy Wedgwood; and in April Enoch Booth said that 'Yates affairs [are] worse than he thought'.[142] Yates had recovered sufficiently by 1766 to take £1,200 of shares in the proposed Trent and Mersey Canal.[143]

By 1783 John Yates had turned his attention to blue-printed ware, engaging an engraver from Caughley, Shropshire.[144] He died about 1788.[145] John Yates' works, continued by his sons John and William, was on the east side of Broad Street, Shelton, no. 91 on the 1802 map,[146] probably the site in Victoria Square occupied by Evans Halshaw Ltd., motor dealers, in 2004.

YORK

FRANCIS PLACE, Dinsdale, County Durham and/or York, fl.1683-1693
See Chapter IX

APPENDIX 3

Price Lists

Three price lists have been found: the well-known 1770 agreement and two lists originally amongst the papers of *Thomas and John Wedgwood* of the Big House, Burslem. The 1770 list is for basic shapes such as dishes, tureens and cups and saucers. The other lists are for more exotic wares, suns, moons and stars, and also tenches (fish shapes) and gorns (small buckets). It is thought that these lists will be helpful in appreciating the wide range of wares made and comparative prices of the various shapes. Prices are also quoted in the main text, but may be more easily found here.

All three lists are accurate, but have been edited to make them readily comprehensible in the 21st century. All prices have been converted from shillings and pence to (pre-1971) pence only. It is notable that the 1770 price list does not mention patterns such as Mosaic, Basket or Gadroon, suggesting that at least by that date there was no distinction in prices between plain and more decorative items.

Reinhold Angerstein noted a selection of prices at Derby, Burslem and Hanley in 1754, some of which are quoted under *Derby* and *John Warburton*.[1]

14 February 1770 Price List[2]

This handwritten 1770 price list, written on contemporary paper,[3] is in the Enoch Wood Scrapbook in the Potteries Museum and Art Gallery, Ceramics Department. The names of the twenty-seven potters who signed this agreement are not individual signatures, and this may be one of a number of handwritten copies made at the time. Simeon Shaw wrote in 1829:[4]

> About 1770 the manufacture of White Stone Ware, Salt glaze, began to decline, and the Cream Colour with fluid glaze obtained the ascendancy. There were, however, some extensive manufactories continued employed therein, as is proved by the following (strictly *literal*) Copy of a Document

Shaw went on to quote the price list verbatim. We share Shaw's opinion that the potters who signed this document were salt-glaze potters, because of the phrase in the agreement at the end: 'To sell to the Manufactures [*sic*] of Earthen ware at the Above Prices'. As will be seen in the accounts of white salt-glaze potters (Chapter IX and Appendices 1 and 2), they were readily selling to creamware manufacturers by 1763. This agreement seems to be a belated attempt by the salt-glaze potters to prevent under-cutting. Not all salt-glaze potters were signatories: *Thomas and John Wedgwood* of the Big House and *Thomas Wedgwood of the Overhouse* are obvious absentees.

A facsimile and a typed transcript (with minor errors) of this price list were published in A.R. Mountford 'Documents relating to English Ceramics of the 18th & 19th centuries' in *Journal of Ceramic History* No. 8, 1975, 3-8. Apart from the verbatim agreement at the end, the following is an accurate but simplified version for ease of reference.

Shape		Best	Seconds	Remarks
		d.[5]	d.	
Dishes each[6]	10 inch[7]	3	2	Worser
	11 inch	4	3	second dishes
	12 inch	6	4	half price of best
	13 inch	8	6	
	14 inch	10	8	
	15 inch	12	10	
	16 inch	15	12	
	17 inch	18[8]	14	
	18 inch	21	16	
	19 inch	24	18	
	20 inch	30	24	
	21 inch	36	30	
Nappies[9] and baking dishes per dozen[10]	7 inch	18	12	
	8 inch	24	18	
	9 inch	30	24	
	10 inch	42	30	
	11 inch	54	42	
	12 inch	78	54	
Tureens each[11]	Large	42	30	
	Middle	33	24	
	Small	24	18	
Twifflers[12] per dozen[13]		16	12	Thirds 9d., none less than 7d.
Sauceboats per dozen[14]	Large size	30	24	
	Next size	24	21	
	Less size	21	18	
	Less size	18	15	
	Smallest	15	12	
Plates[15] per dozen[16]		24	21	Best seconds. Worser seconds 18d. A degree worser 15d., a degree worser 12d. None sold under 9d. and not to be picked but sold as they are put together.[17]

283

APPENDIX 3

Toys,[18] per dozen[19]
    covered   6   4
    handled   4   2½
    cups and saucers   3   2

Stool pans
    each[20] 12 inch   16   12
               11 inch   14   10
               10 inch   11   9
                9 inch   9   6
                8 inch   7   4

Butter tubs with stands,
    each[21]   9   6
                         7   4
                         5   3

Cups and saucers   per dozen[22]
    Holland size,[23] middle white   10   8   No cups and
    Holland size, small white   9   7   saucers under
    Holland size, middle blue[24]   14   10   6d.
    Holland size, small blue   12   8
    Irish size[25]   14   10
    London size[26]   12   9
    London size, blue and white[27]   16   12
    Three to piece ware[28]   16   12

Holland ware[29]   22   18

Sortable[30]
    White ware   18   14   No sortable
    Covered ware   24   18   under 8d.
    Inlet teapots[31] per dozen[32]   30   21
    Blue flowered[33]   22   18

(The rest of the agreement is given verbatim here)
'To allow no more than 5 P C[t] for Breakage and 5 P C[t] [per cent] C[redi]^t for ready Money.

'To sell to the Manufactures [sic] of Earthen ware at the Above Prices & to allow no more than seven & a half P C[t] [per cent] Beside Discount for Breakage & Prompt Payment.

'Wee [sic] whose Hands are hereunto Subscribed do Bind Ourselves our Heirs and Assigns in the sum of Fifty Pounds of good and Lawful Money of great Britain not to sell or cause to be sold under the within specify'd Prices as Witness our Hands This 14th Day of Feb[ruary] 1770

'John Platt   Josua Heath
John Lowe   John Bourn
John Taylor   Jos: Stephens
John Cobb   Wm Smith
Robt Bucknall   Jos: Simpson
John Daniel   John Weatherby
Thos Daniel Junr   J & R^d Mare
Richd Adams   Nicholas Pool
Sam^ll Chatterley   John Yates
Thos Lowe   Chas Hassells
John Allen   P[er] Pro of Ann
Wm Parrott   Warburton & Son
Jacob Warburton   Thos Warburton
Warburton & Stone   Wm Mier
Jos: Smith   _____ ,'

Thomas and John Wedgwood's undated salt-glazed ware price lists

These two lists are taken from photocopied documents in Stoke-on-Trent City Archives, catalogued as being part of the John Wedgwood Account Book Pottery Sales 1745–1780 (738-942461 outsize), held at the Potteries Museum and Art Gallery. The original documents are in fact not part of this book, and appear to have been 'loose leaf' lists, used by *Thomas and John Wedgwood* in pricing their invoices. Their interest lies in the great variety of shapes listed. In the first list, starting with '1 Doz least plain por[ingers]', two prices are shown without explanation. These may be respectively for 'Best' and Seconds' ware.

As with the 1770 list above, these lists have been edited for ease of reference, but are accurate in essentials. In many instances, the unit of price, 'each' or 'dozen', were omitted in the original lists. In these cases, the information has been obtained from John Wedgwood's Crate Book,[34] and the unit is shown in square brackets.

First list, page 1

1 Doz least plain por[ringers]	27d., 24d.
1 Doz	30d., 24d.
1 Doz.	39d., 30d.
1 Doz.	48d., 36d.
1 Doz	60d., 42d.
Flow'[ere]d & footed same	
Least Mosaick por[ringers]	21d., 15d.
1 Doz.	27d., 21d.
1 doz	33d., 24d.
1 Doz	48d., 36d.
Do. Flow[ere]d & Rib[be]d	
Least Gaddaroons	24d., 15d.
1 Doz.	27d., 21d.
1 Doz	36d., 24d.
1 doz	42d., 30d.
1 Doz	48d., 36d.
Large spoons	24d., 14d. [dozen]
Pap spoons	18d., 10d.
Tea Do.	12d., 8d.
Toy & Mustard Do.	9d., 6d.
Large Slippers	108d., 72d. [dozen]
Less	84d., 60d.
Very large Do.	120d.
Nest ovals 5 leaft [sic]	15d. [each]
Groce[35] Toy	48d.
Set plain Toys	9d.
Kettle & Coffee pot a Doz	18d.
Set flow[ere]d Toys	21d.
Kettle Coffee pots	3d.
Least Fishes	6d. [dozen]
Do.	9d.
Do.	12d.
Do.	15d.
Do.	18d.
Do.	21d.
Do. [Tench?]	24d.
Irish Size enlarged	24d.
Large Tench	30d.
Large & small spoon boat	24d. [dozen]
Plain square stand	30d. [dozen]
Pickle boat	~~18d.~~ & 24d. [dozen]

Large Canister	4d. [no unit found]
Less	3d.
Bundles Hearts 18 [dozen]	
Cut & [wundering?] Do. 18	
my least Hearts 12	
Flow[ere]d Hearts	18d. & 24d [dozen]
Flow[ere]d & Plain Try[angular]s	24d. [no unit found]

First list, page 2

Pudding	18d., 8d. [dozen]
	15d., 10d.
	18d., 12d.
	21d., 14d.
	24d., 16d.
	30d., 20d.
Do.	36d., 30d.
Do. with pipes	48d., 30d.
Do.	60d., 36d.
Do.	72d., 48d.
Do.	90d., 60d.
Do.	108d., 78d.
Do.	108d.
Least Mellons	18d., 12d. [dozen]
Do.	24d., 15d.
Do.	30d., 18d.
Do.	42d., 24d.
Do.	42d., 30d.
Do.	54d., 36d.
Do.	72d., 48d.
Do.	108d., 79d.
Do.	132d., 84d.
Least Custard Cups	15d., 8d. [dozen]
Do.	18d., 10d.
Do.	21d., 12d.
Do.	24d., 15d.
Do.	30d., 18d.
Do.	36d., 24d.
Do.	42d., 30d.
Artichoke Cups & Sau[cers]	12d., 8d. [dozen]
Pap boats	18d., 12d. [dozen]
Least shells	18d., 12d. [dozen]
Do.	24d., 16d.
Do.	30d., 20d.
Do.	42d., 30d.
Do.	54d., 36d.
Least square pettys	24d., 16d. [dozen]
Do.	30d., 20d.
Do.	42d., 30d.
Least star pettys	15d., 10d. [dozen]
Do.	30d., 18d.
Do.	21d., 14d.
Do.	24d., 16d.
Double Do.	30d., 16d. [dozen]
Do.	18d., 12d.
Do.	10d.
Star Cups	18d., 12d. [dozen]
Do.	18d., 12d. [sic]
Do.	21d., 14d.
Do.	24d., 16d.
Double Star Cups	12d., 8d. [dozen]
Do.	15d., 10d.
Treble Do.	12d., 8d. [dozen]
Do.	15d., 12d.
Do.	18d., 12d.
Least Suns	42d., 30d. [dozen]
Do.	48d., 30d.
Moons	36d., 24d. [dozen]
Least Grapes	30d., 18d. [no unit found]
Do.	36d., 24d.
Do.	42d., 30d.

First list, pages 3 and 4

These pages were used for calculations and only the shape names are given here.

Custard Cups	Chamber Pots
Broad Star Cups	Stool Pans
Flowered toys	Strainers
Kettles	Wash Basons
Coffee Pots	Bakers
Canisters	Ovals
Slippers	Toys
Pap Boats	Jellies
Shells	Square Pettys
Flowered Shells	Suns
Treble Stars	Moons
Star Pettys	Grap[e]s
Cups and Saucers	Sets Toys
Puddings	Cans
Gorges	

Second list, page 1

Large 5 set of Pyramids	60d. [dozen]
Less 4 set of Do. [ditto, same]	48d. [dozen]
Less 3 set of Do.	30d. [dozen]
Fluted Do.	48d. [dozen]
Fluted & Plain Do.	30d. [dozen]
Salt Mould	15d. [dozen]
Fruit Mould	72d. [dozen]
Pine Apple	84d. [dozen]
Double Prest Stars	18d. [dozen]
Treble Prest Stars	24d. [dozen]
Prest Pine Apples & Mellons	18d. or 12d. [dozen]
Large double Pine Apples	8d. [each]
Do. less	7d. [each]
Large single ditto	7d. [each]
Large double Fruit Mould	7d. [each]
Double & single Do.	6d. [each]
Less single	5d. [each]
Round Fruit Mould	7d. [each]
Crabs	5d. [each]
Large oval petty	4d. [each]
Less	2½d. [each]
3 Sorts less Fruit Moulds	3d. [each]
Large Star	3d. [each]
Less Star	1½d. [each]
Rib[be]d petty	3d. [each]
Large Cheese Mould	18d. [each]
Less	9d. [each]
Least	5d. [each]

Second list, page 2

Ovals		
Least ovals	1d.	)
Do.	1½d.	)
Do.	2d.	)
Do.	3d.	) 12 per Nest
Do.	4½d.	)
Do.	6d.	)
Do.	8d.	)

Beef Pots				Toy Candle		8d. [dozen]
	6½ Inch over 3	)		Tryangular [sic] Stands		15d. [no unit found]
	5½	2	)	Less Do.		12d.
	4½	1½	) 8d. Per Nest	Heart Do.		12d. [dozen]
	4	1	)	Less Do.		9d. [dozen]
	3½	½	)			
Sweet Meat Pots				Faces		
	2½		)	Least		6d. [each]
	2		) 7d per Nest	Mid[d]le		8d.
	1½		)	Large		12d.
	1		)			
New Turk caps			28d. Per Doz[en]	Corna Copia [Cornucopia] 2 Sizes		8d. [each]
Petty Pans			18d per Doz			
Scollopt			21d. Do.	New Turk Caps [dozen]		
Bellied Brim[m]ed Pettys 30s			21d. Per Doz	10 12 15 18		24d. 18 24d. 30d.
Bucket Gorns[36] & Ladles			8d. & 16d. or 24d.	Broad Turk Caps		14d. 16d.
			Per Doz	Bell Cups		24d. [dozen]

APPENDIX 4

Patterns, Tiles and Shapes

Patterns
Contemporary trade descriptions of salt-glazeware refer to moulded decoration, not painted patterns, apart from the ubiquitous 'flowered', meaning scratched decoration, infilled with blue or brown. In salt-glazed ware, *Thomas and John Wedgwood* supplied plates in Basket, Barleycorn, Feather edge and Gadroon shapes as well as 'Plain round' and 'Plain, Nickel Edge'; Mosaic, Shell and Vine porringers; Fluted and Gadroon sauceboats; and Figured, Gadroon and Indian teapots. *The Thomas Wedgwoods of Overhouse* supplied China rail dishes, Flat and Soop (*sic*, soup), Mosaic Table plates, Baskett work Plates, Gadroon and Barleycorn plates and dishes.

Barleycorn Also known as French or Seed pattern, Barleycorn was supplied by *Thomas and John Wedgwood*,[1] and by the *Thomas Wedgwoods of the Overhouse*. Sampson and Richard Daniel supplied 'Dresden or Barley Corn' tureens to Josiah Wedgwood in 1762-63, and *William Taylor II* supplied Barleycorn ware to Josiah Wedgwood in 1763-64.

Shards with moulded 'seed' pattern were found at *Jackfield in Shropshire*, apparently wasters from local production. *Warburton and Stone* sold flat Barley Corn plates, soup plates and fruit dishes to Josiah Wedgwood in June 1768. *William Taylor II* sold Barleycorn dishes to Josiah Wedgwood for his London customer John William Pollmann in 1763. *John Hales* sold barley corn oblongs, 'rounds' and round baskets to Josiah Wedgwood in 1763-64.

A 1764 order from Abernathy in London to Josiah Wedgwood is endorsed 'Mr. Abernathy has been in a mistake when he mentioned barley corn and French pattern as different for we understand them as one'.[2] Elizabeth Cadman ordered 'a green gilt barley corn plat[e]' from Josiah Wedgwood c.1764,[3] confirming that this shape was used for earthenware as well as salt-glazed stoneware. Henrietta Conradi of Dresden bought Barleycorn and twisted Basket ware as late as 1790.[4]

Basket-work Supplied by *Thomas and John Wedgwood*,[5] and by the *Thomas Wedgwoods of the Overhouse*. An order from Jno. Will. Pollmann of London to Josiah Wedgwood on 1 October 1763 is marked up 'Basket Pattn Ordr for Mr. Hales', meaning that the order would be passed on to *John Hales*, to supply a remarkable variety of Basket Pattern shapes: flat white table plates, soup plates, oval dishes in sizes, round dishes in sizes, breakfast plates, largest size tureens with feet and oval dishes, and two smaller sizes, sauceboats in sizes, oval butter tubs with plates, mustard pots and covers, tea canisters, fruit baskets and plates, candlesticks.[6] (Other items were marked for *William Taylor II* to supply.)

Henrietta Conradi of Dresden wanted Gadroon, Basket and Dresden patterns in 1775, and bought Barleycorn and twisted Basket ware as late as 1790.[7] *Samuel Kirk and Co.* of Burslem, salt-glaze potters, fired ware including twig dishes for Josiah Wedgwood in 1764.[8] These were Josiah Wedgwood's clay shapes, fired by Kirks, otherwise known as salt-glaze potters. 'Twig' might be construed as 'Basket'.

Birds Eye *Samuel Kirk and Co.* of Burslem, salt-glaze potters, fired ware including Birds Eye tureens for Josiah Wedgwood in 1764.[9] These were Josiah Wedgwood's clay shapes.

Carved Carved sauceboats were in the warehouse of *Peter Bagnall* in 1761. *Samuel Kirk and Co.* supplied Josiah Wedgwood with carved plates in 1763-64. In 1763 *William Taylor II* supplied Josiah Wedgwood with carved boats for William Pollmann, a London dealer. It is not known whether the 1760s carved ware was hand carved or made with a particular unrecognised moulding.

China Rail Supplied by the *Thomas Wedgwoods of the Overhouse*. This might be the same border moulding as an octagonal plate in the Potteries Museum, said to have been modelled by Aaron Wood.[10] Plates with similar borders were in the South Kensington Museum.[11] A shard (not a waster) of this design was excavated on *Thomas Whieldon's* Fenton Vivian site.[12]

Dresden *Sampson and Richard Daniel* supplied 'Dresden or Barley Corn' tureens to Josiah Wedgwood in 1762-63. Luxmoore owned a gilded bronze dessert dish model in this pattern.[13] He also reported a bronze shell pattern milk jug model – see Shell below. The purpose of these bronze models is not understood. They will not be originals, as they would have had to be cast from negative moulds. Henrietta Conradi of Dresden wanted Gadroon, Basket and Dresden patterns in 1775.[14]

Shards with moulded 'dot and diaper, star and diaper and basket patterns in scroll-bordered panels' were found at *Jackfield, Shropshire*, apparently wasters from local production.

Solon wrote in 1885[15] that

> The perforated porcelain plates and dishes brought over from Dresden gave rise to a new style of dessert services, perforated on the rim, and embossed all over with basket work, and various ornaments; for the modest admirer who could not afford the expense of such costly luxury as foreign china, fruit baskets and plates, cut out with equal delicacy, were manufactured in Salt-glaze ware, and being cheap, met with a ready sale. They were not copies, but distant reminiscences; and a certain pattern cut in the mould by *Aaron Wood*, and evincing an incontestable originality, is now in every collection.

Engined *Thomas Daniel II* sold 'Engind [*sic*]' plates to Josiah Wedgwood in 1764 and *Warburton and Stone* supplied him with 'Engine' flat and soup plates in 1768. A plate is known with an engine-turned border, in a private collection. 1764 is an early date for a Staffordshire modeller to have used an engine lathe to make a model, but Chelsea porcelain plates are known with rose-engine-turned borders, made in the 1750s.[16] There is the faint possibility of phonetic confusion between 'Engine' and 'Indian' – see 'Indian' below.

Feather Edge Supplied by *Thomas and John Wedgwood*.[17] A distinctive variant of feather edge, accurately described as 'Cockstail', was made at *Swinton, Yorkshire*.

Figured Supplied by *Thomas and John Wedgwood*.[18]

Fluted Supplied by *Thomas and John Wedgwood*.[19]

French See Barleycorn

Gadroon Supplied by *Thomas and John Wedgwood*[20] and by the *Thomas Wedgwoods of the Overhouse*. William Philpot of London ordered gadrooned plates 'all white' in 1764;[21] and Henrietta Conradi of Dresden wanted Gadroon pattern amongst others in 1775.[22]

Indian Figure There is the possibility of phonetic confusion between 'Indian' and 'Engine', see 'Engined' above. *William Taylor II*, Burslem salt-glaze potter, wanted Indian figure ware from Josiah Wedgwood in 1763,[23] and Thomas Gilbert, a London dealer, ordered square teapots with Indian figures from him c.1764.[24] Ordered from Josiah Wedgwood, 'Indian figure' is likely to have been cream-coloured earthenware.

Mosaic Supplied by *Thomas and John Wedgwood*[25] and by the *Thomas Wedgwoods of the Overhouse*. 'Fine Mosaik [*sic*] Stone Ware' occurs in a 1757 London auction advertisement,[26] and '"mosaic" design' has been authoritatively applied to a 'dot-and-diaper' moulded sauceboat model, in the Victoria and Albert Museum, illustrated with matching salt-glazed and Bow porcelain sauce-boats.[27] John Bowcock of Bow porcelain works noted 'mosaic do. [ditto, plates]' in 1756.[28] The 'dot-and-diaper' *painted* pattern occurs on a Meissen dish dated about 1740,[29] an early enough source both for Bow porcelain and for an English salt-glaze modeller.

Nut Thomas Abernathy ordered 'Nutt [*sic*]' pattern baskets and stands in white stone in 1763.[30]

Plain, Nickel Edge Supplied by *Thomas and John Wedgwood*.[31]

Plain round Supplied by *Thomas and John Wedgwood*.[32]

Roses When Angerstein visited *Derby* in 1754, he noted prices of salt-glazed ware, including 2s.6d. per dozen for plates 'with modelled roses', the most expensive price for plates.[33]

Scalloped Scollopt (*sic*) ware was supplied by *John Baddeley*.

Seed See Barleycorn

Shell Supplied by *Thomas and John Wedgwood*.[34] Luxmoore noted a 'Block for a milk jug in bronze, the same model as No. 17.', No. 17 being a shell pattern model in the Victoria and Albert Museum.[35] See also Dresden, above. By 1764 a Yorkshire dealer, Emanuel Boothroyd, told Josiah Wedgwood that 'shell teapots didn't sell any more'.[36]

Square Supplied by *John Baddeley*. Thomas Gilbert, London Chinaman, ordered square teapots c.1764.[37] 'Square' mustard pots, teapots, and chocolate cans are illustrated in later catalogues, with an upright cylinder shape.[38]

Vine Supplied by *Thomas and John Wedgwood*.[39] Luxmoore illustrated teapots which he terms 'Lovers Vine decoration', which will be heart-shaped in plan.[40]

Worcester Worcester pattern in salt-glaze was ordered by Abernathy, London in 1763.[41]

Tiles

Relief-moulded tiles were made in white salt-glazed stoneware. Anthony Ray has provided the most detailed study of these,[42] illustrating seven 'scenic' tiles, six of them in the Victoria and Albert Museum and said to be from *Thomas Whieldon's* house, as is the seventh, *The Peacock, the Turkey and the Goose,* held in Manchester City Art Gallery.[43]

Four of the Victoria and Albert tiles: *The Shepherd Dog and the Wolf, The Gardener and the Hog, The Butterfly and the Snail* and *The Old Hen and the Cock* (Fig. 114),[44] and Manchester Art Gallery's *The Peacock, the Turkey and the Goose* have subjects taken from Gay's Fables. The subject of the sixth tile illustrated by Ray, *Two Ducks and a Mill*, is thought to be from a Dutch source. The seventh shows *A Heron and Spewing Duck Fountain* – see below. Ray also illustrates two small tiles with shell moulding.

Luxmoore illustrated four salt-glaze tiles: *Farm buildings, poultry, and a well* (Ray's *The Old Hen and the Cock*), *The Peacock, the Turkey and the Goose*, and two additional subjects, *A bull tossing a bulldog* and *A farm with windmill*, all from Whieldon's house (Fig. 114).[45] The 'windmill' tile was in the Metropolitan Museum of Art in 1971.[46]

The *Heron and Spewing Duck Fountain* salt-glaze tile illustrated by Ray is matched by *creamware* shards, one biscuit and one glazed, found on the Whieldon Fenton Vivian site.[47] Taken together with the provenance of the surviving tiles, a biscuit shard is fair evidence of production on site, by Whieldon. A green-glazed creamware tile fragment of this design was found on the William Greatbatch site, but a single glazed shard is scarcely evidence of production by Greatbatch.[48] This tile design was recorded as early as 1829. Following a reference to Josiah Wedgwood making white stone pottery, Simeon Shaw wrote 'There yet remain of this kind, white Tiles, with *relief* figures, of a Heron fishing, and a Spewing-Duck fountain'.[49]

A white salt-glaze plaque representing the *Crucifixion*, 7in. x 7in. (17.78 x 17.78cm), incised 'Wm Simpkin' on the back, was exhibited at the 1913-14 Burlington Club exhibition.[50] A smaller but fairly similar white salt-glaze Crucifixion plaque, incised R B on the front, 6½in. (16.51cm) was sold at Sotheby's 26 February 1980, Lot 67.

Shapes
Many shape names will be found in the Price Lists in Appendix 3. 'Gallipots' and 'Saffron Pots' deserve explanation.

Gallipots 'A small earthen glazed pot, *esp.* one used by apothecaries for ointments and medicines' *(OED)*. *John Wood* sold white salt-glazed gallipots in 1783-87, probably from stock rather than current production. There is a list of prices of 'Gallipots' from one to eight ounces inside the front cover of his sales ledger, both white stone ware and dearer ones, the body not described. He sold '10 groce [gross, 144] Gallipots 1 2 3 & 4 [ounce capacity] in a nest [fitting inside each other]' at 3s. a gross to Mr. James Atkinson on 28 May 1783. John Lockett and Co.'s 19th century earthenware catalogue illustrates both 'Cupshape' and 'Upright' (cylindrical can shape) gallipots, nested and single, up to 16 ounce size.[51]

Saffron Pots Saffron pots were miniature teapots, used for saffron tea in the 18th century, a medicinal drink for a number of disorders, from jaundice to indigestion.[52] Saffron comes from the stamen of the autumn crocus. Ann Else, a customer (see Appendix 5), ordered plain *red* saffron pots 'with Cannon spouts' in 1762-64,[53] and *Thomas and John Wedgwood* made them in white and five sizes of 'ash [drab]' salt-glaze.[54]

APPENDIX 5

Customers for White Salt-Glazed Stoneware

Our information about customers for white salt-glazed stoneware is almost all drawn from the erratic survival of original documentation:

Jonah Malkin's sales ledger from 1747 consistently to 1750: 20 customers.
Thomas Wedgwood IV of Overhouse's notebooks, at intervals from 1752 to 1773: 73 customers.
Thomas and John Wedgwood's sales ledger and crate book, 1755 consistently to 1776: 215 customers.
Josiah Wedgwood's documents referring to the buying and selling of white salt-glazed stoneware surviving in the Wedgwood Accumulation, mostly 1763-64 with a few up to 1790: 35 customers.

Abbott, Thomas, Bath, bought crates from *Thomas and John Wedgwood* in 1755-62.[1]
Abernathy and Livie, Hermitage St., Wapping, London, ordered white stoneware from Josiah Wedgwood in 1764 – see Chapter VI.
Adams, Wm., Hereford, bought from *Thomas and John Wedgwood* in 1757-63.[2]
Addison and Abernathy, London, ordered white stoneware from Josiah Wedgwood in 1763 – see Chapter VI.
Ainsley, Sam., Newcastle-upon-Tyne, bought from *Thomas and John Wedgwood* in 1767-68.[3]
Amson, John, China Jarr, New Exchange Buildings, Strand, London, bought from *Thomas and John Wedgwood* in 1764-65.[4]
Arden, Mr., Macclesfield, ordered white salt-glazed stoneware from Josiah Wedgwood – see Chapter VI.

Arrowsmith, Wm., Richmond, bought from *Thomas and John Wedgwood* in 1767.[5]
Asbury, Joshua, bought from *Thomas and John Wedgwood* in 1772.[6]
Asbury, Matthew, bought from *Thomas and John Wedgwood* in 1765.[7]
Asbury, Richard, sen., Bridgnorth, bought from *Thomas and John Wedgwood* in 1762.[8]
Ashburner, Hannah, corner of Fleet Bridge, London, advertised 'fine Stone Ware' in 1754[9] – see Chapter VI.
Ashburnham, Lord, ordered salt-glazed ware in 1769 – see Chapter VI.
Atkinson, James, Covent Garden, London, bought from *Thomas Wedgwood IV of Overhouse* in 1771-72, including stoolpans and chambers.[10]
Bagnall, Peter, Burslem, potter, bought dipped white ware from *Jonah Malkin* in 1748-49, and spoons from *Thomas and John Wedgwood* in 1764.[11]
Bagnall, Sampson, bought dipped ware, mugs and jugs from *Jonah Malkin* in 1747-48.[12]
Bagot, Sir Walter, bought from *Thomas and John Wedgwood* in 1756-65.[13]
Baker, Mrs. Ann, York, bought from *Thomas and John Wedgwood* in 1765-67.[14]
Baker, Wm., York, bought from *Thomas and John Wedgwood* in 1764-69.[15]
Ball, Enoch, Holbeck, Leeds, bought from *Thomas and John Wedgwood* in 1768.[16]

Banks, Mr. & Co., Uttoxeter, bought from *Thomas and John Wedgwood* in 1759.[17]
Barrett, Mr., Congleton, bought gallipots from *Thomas and John Wedgwood* in 1771.[18]
Bayliss, Jno., Crispin Street, Spitalfields, London, owed money to *Thomas Wedgwood IV of Overhouse* in 1764, and bought again from him in 1765, including 'Silver Shape'.[19]
Bell, James, Newcastle-upon-Tyne, merchant, insured his stock including white and brown stoneware in 1771.[20]
Bennet, Agnes, Manchester, asked Josiah Wedgwood to put his ware in *Horn and Taylor's* crates for her, in 1764.[21]
Bennett, Thos., New Church St., Sheffield, bought from *Thomas and John Wedgwood* in 1759.[22]
Benson, Mrs. Agnes, St. Ann's Square, Manchester, bought from *Thomas and John Wedgwood* in 1761-1771, including fishes and double fishes.[23]
Bentley and Boardman, Liverpool, dealt in white salt-glazed stoneware in 1764, 1766 and 1769, and bought from *Thomas Wedgwood V of Overhouse* in 1778.[24] See Chapter VI.
Bernard, Mrs. Catharine, London, bought from *Thomas Wedgwood IV of Overhouse* in 1763.[25]
Birch, Feaston & Co., bought from *Thomas Wedgwood IV of Overhouse* in 1764.[26]
Bird, Joseph, Liverpool, bought half-pints and quarts from *Jonah Malkin* in 1748, and dipped ware half-pint, pint and quart mugs, bowls and porringers in 1749-50. Bird & Co. or Bird & Jones also bought from *Thomas Wedgwood IV of Overhouse* in 1763-65.[27]
Blackburn, Mr., Salt House, Liverpool, handled 'flint enamel Mustard pots'.[28] See Chapter VI.
Bland, Sam., Beverley, bought from *Thomas and John Wedgwood* in 1755, 1765 and 1768.[29]
Blumbly, Mrs., bought from *Thomas Wedgwood IV of Overhouse* in 1753, including ash teapots, white sprigged.[30]
Boare, James, Plymouth, bought pint, quart, middle quart and wine measure mugs from *Jonah Malkin* in 1749.[31]
Booth, Enoch junior, Tunstall, potter, bought pudding cups, spoons and unfired ware from *Thomas and John Wedgwood* in 1763.[32]
Booth, Enoch senior, Tunstall, potter and enameller, bought mugs and other ware from *Jonah Malkin* in 1748; and spoons and unfired ware from *Thomas and John Wedgwood* in 1767-72.[33]
Boothroyd, Emanuel, Lindley, Huddersfield, complained that white stoneware would not sell in 1764 – see Chapter VI.
Borrow, Mr., Bristol, bought small fruit plates from *Thomas and John Wedgwood* in 1755.[34]
Boucher, Mrs. Elizabeth, Shepherd Market, Mayfair, London, bought from *Thomas and John Wedgwood* in 1765.[35]
Bould, James, bought mustard spoons from *Thomas and John Wedgwood* in 1762.[36]
Boulton, Matthew, Soho, Birmingham, ordered white flint stone, silver pattern, terrines, dishes, plates, chamber pots from Josiah Wedgwood in 1787, for an old customer, ACP, to send via Hull by April for the only boat this year, in casks marked GZM.[37]
Bourne, Edward, bought spoons from *Thomas and John Wedgwood* in 1770.[38]
Bourne, John, Burslem, potter, bought custard cups and unfired ware from *Thomas and John Wedgwood* in 1772.[39]
Bourne & Co., Tunstall, bought from *Thomas and John Wedgwood* in 1767.[40]
Brewer, Henry, Bath, bought from *Thomas and John Wedgwood* in 1755.[41]
Brindley, Mr., was sent spoons, star pettys, double star pettys and cups, custard cups, and ash flower pots and stands and pint and quart jugs by *Thomas and John Wedgwood*, 'for his son to take to America in March 1772'.[42]
Broom, Thos., Handley Green, bought from *Thomas and John Wedgwood* in 1761.[43]

Brougham, Mrs., Newcastle-upon-Tyne, bought from *Thomas and John Wedgwood* in 1765-68.[44]
Brougham, John, China Shop, Key Side, Newcastle-upon-Tyne, advertised white stone dishes and plates in 1755, and bought from *Thomas and John Wedgwood* in 1760-63.[45]
Brown, James, near the Exchange, Manchester, bought from *Thomas and John Wedgwood* in 1768.[46]
Bryan, John, at the Bear, Basinghall Street, London, bought from *Thomas Wedgwood IV of Overhouse* in 1753 and 1763-65, including scolloped plain round dishes and 'Turks Caps'.[47]
Bryan, Sam, Lane End, potseller, 1765.[48] See Chapter VI.
Bucknall, Joseph, Cobridge, potter, bought spoons from *Thomas and John Wedgwood* in 1760.[49]
Bucknall, Mrs. Mary, Shrewsbury, bought spoons and other ware from *Thomas and John Wedgwood* in 1755.[50]
Bullin, Christopher, bought dipped ware pints and quarts from *Jonah Malkin* in 1748-49.[51]
Bullman, Mrs. Hannah, Low Street, Sunderland, bought from *Thomas and John Wedgwood* in 1757-58.[52]
Bulman, James, Carpenters Arms, Key Side, Sunderland, bought from *Thomas and John Wedgwood* in 1759 and 1761-62.[53]
Burn, I., Penkhull, bought dipped ware bowls, porringers and mugs from *Jonah Malkin* in 1749.[54]
Buxton, John, 35 St. Paul's Churchyard, London, advertised white stoneware in 1769 – see Chapter VI.
Cadman, Elizabeth, Penkridge, Ireland, bought white stoneware from *Aaron Wedgwood* in 1763 – see Chapter VI.
Cantle, Thos. & Co., bought from *Thomas and John Wedgwood* in 1755.[55]
Caravella, John, between Hollis St. and Cavendish St., London bought crates from *Thomas and John Wedgwood* in 1765, 1767-68 and 1771, including toy spoons in 1768 and pap boats, mustard spoons, slipper (pots) and chamber pots in 1771. (See also Fogg, Robert.)[56]
Carr, John, opposite Grasshopper, Mount St., Grosvenor Square, London in 1761, Flower Pot and Orange Tree, Grosvenor Square in 1762, bought from *Thomas and John Wedgwood* from 1755 to 1763.[57]
Carter, Wm., bought crates from *Thomas Wedgwood IV of Overhouse* in 1772.[58]
Catcott, George, Rackly Street, Bristol, bought from *Thomas and John Wedgwood* in 1760 and 1769-70, including toy candlesticks.[59]
Chadock, Mary, Bristol, bought from *Thomas and John Wedgwood* in 1757-69.[60]
Clark, Mr., Bristol (perhaps a carrier), bought from *Thomas and John Wedgwood* in 1771.[61]
Clarkson, John, Market St., St. James Market, London, bought 'let in' dishes and other ware from *Thomas and John Wedgwood* in 1762-63.[62]
Clive, George, Drayton, bought from *Thomas and John Wedgwood* in 1760.[63]
Coleman, A, Dundalk, Ireland, ordered white flint ware from Josiah Wedgwood in 1764 – see Chapter VI.
Coleman, Will, Hamburg, Germany, bought white stoneware from Josiah Wedgwood in 1763 – see Chapter VI.
Collerick, James, bought from *Thomas and John Wedgwood* in 1767.[64]
Colthurst, Edward, Spread Eagle Court, Finch Lane, London, bought from *Thomas Wedgwood IV of Overhouse* in c.1771, including wash hand basins, baking dishes and nappies.[65]
Conradi, Henrietta Charitas, Dresden, Germany, ordered a great deal of white salt-glazed stoneware from Josiah Wedgwood between 1777 and 1790 (see Chapter VI).[66]
Cook, Elizabeth, bought from *Thomas and John Wedgwood* in 1755-59.[67]

Cook, John, bought best dipped white from *Jonah Malkin* in 1750.[68]

Cook, Richard, bought dipped seconds and thirds from *Jonah Malkin* in 1749.[69]

Cook, Samuel, Gloucester, bought pint and quart mugs from *Jonah Malkin* in 1748; and dipped pint and quart mugs, including some lettered 'T. POPE', in 1749.[70]

Cooper and Hodgskin, Walsall, Continental merchants, ordered ware for Germany, including salt-glazed stoneware, from Josiah Wedgwood between 1764 and 1769.[71] See Chapter VI.

Cooper, John, German St., near St. James Church (London?), bought from *Thomas and John Wedgwood* in 1766.[72]

Cooper, John, Hallgreen, bought goods from *Jonah Malkin* in 1749.[73]

Corrock, Wm., Sign of the Jug within Bishops Gate (London?), bought from *Thomas and John Wedgwood* in 1765-69.[74]

Cosby, Wm., Bristol, bought from *Thomas and John Wedgwood* in 1763.[75]

Cotter, James & Co., Liverpool, bought from *Thomas Wedgwood IV of Overhouse* in 1763.[76]

Coward, Susanna, Sherborne, Dorset, bought from *Thomas and John Wedgwood* in 1762.[77]

Cowper, John, bought from *Thomas and John Wedgwood* in 1762-66.[78]

Crawly, Gertrude, Augustins Back, Bristol, bought from *Thomas and John Wedgwood* in 1760-61.[79]

Crewe, Chetwoode Esq., bought from *Thomas and John Wedgwood* in 1756.[80]

Crocket, Wm. Coleshill, owed money to *Thomas Wedgwood IV of Overhouse* in 1764, and ordered mottled mugs from him in 1765.[81]

Cross, John, Old Market, Bristol, bought from *Thomas and John Wedgwood* in 1765.[82]

Crouch, Wm., bought from *Thomas and John Wedgwood* in 1765-70, including Barley Corn ware.[83]

Dalziel, Jno., bought from *Thomas Wedgwood IV of Overhouse* in 1752.[84]

Daniel, Richd., Cobridge, bought flowered pickle boats from *Thomas and John Wedgwood* in 1765.[85]

Daniel, Sampson, Cobridge, potter, bought star pettys, star cups and flummery cups from *Thomas and John Wedgwood* in 1765.[86]

Daniel, Thomas II, Cobridge, potter, bought pints, quarts, dipped ware from *Jonah Malkin* in 1748-49.[87]

Daniells, Thos. Late, Widow Jane Daniells bought holed spoons from *Thomas and John Wedgwood* in 1769.[88]

Davis, Mrs., bought from *Thomas Wedgwood V of Overhouse* in 1778.[89]

Davis, Thomas, bought from *Thomas Wedgwood IV of Overhouse* in 1753.[90]

Davison, Thos., next the Golden Chair, Warwick Street, Golden Square, London, bought from *Thomas and John Wedgwood* in 1756-67.[91]

Denclor, Paul, Hambro' (Hamburg), bought from *Thomas and John Wedgwood* in 1757.[92]

Derby, Lady, ordered salt-glazed ware in 1769 – see Chapter VI.

Dethleffin, Christian, Hamburg, ordered white salt-glazed stoneware from Josiah Wedgwood in 1763 – see Chapter VI.

Deverell, Eliz., China Shop, Austens Back, Bristol, bought from *Thomas and John Wedgwood* in 1762.[93]

Dollery, Tho., Covent Garden, London, bought from *Thomas and John Wedgwood* in 1761-62.[94]

Douglas, John, Whitehaven, ordered what was probably white stoneware from Josiah Wedgwood, and bought from *Thomas Wedgwood IV of Overhouse* in 1763 – see Chapter VI.

Downs, Geo., Coventry, bought from *Thomas and John Wedgwood* in 1756-64 and 1771, including ash flower pots.[95]

Dunbibin, London, bought crates from *Thomas Wedgwood IV of Overhouse* in 1769-70, and wanted white cups and saucers from his son in 1773.[96]

Dunbibin, John, bought from Josiah Wedgwood in 1763, and *Thomas Wedgwood IV of Overhouse* in 1764[97] – see Chapter VI.

Dunbibin, Samuel, bought from *Thomas Wedgwood V of Overhouse* in 1771.[98]

Eaton, James, Liverpool, bought enamelled white salt-glazed ware from Josiah Wedgwood in 1763 – see Chapter VI.

Egerton, Phillip Esq., bought from *Thomas and John Wedgwood* in 1759.[99]

Else, Ann, Nottingham, ordered white salt-glazed stoneware from Josiah Wedgwood, and also bought ware from *Thomas and John Wedgwood* in 1762-64, including white flat mustard spoons c.1764 – see Chapter VI

Empson, Richd., Beverley, bought from *Thomas and John Wedgwood* in 1767-68.[100]

Falcon, Jeffrey, bought from *Thomas Wedgwood IV of Overhouse* in 1753.[101]

Falkner, Joseph, (Chester?) bought from *Thomas and John Wedgwood* in 1764.[102]

Farmer, Joseph, bought broad (*sic*) ware pints and quarts from *Jonah Malkin* in 1748-49.[103]

Farror, Joseph, Shrewsbury, bought from *Thomas and John Wedgwood* in 1759-70.[104]

Fleetwood, John, Leadenhall Street, London, advertised salt stone cups and saucers in 1757 – see Chapter VI.

Fogg, Robert, China Jarr, New Bond Street (London), bought from *Thomas and John Wedgwood* in 1758-69. (See also Caravella, John.)[105]

Forbes, Mary, near Old Dock, Liverpool, bought blue teaware, coffee cups and coffee pots and white salt-glazed ware in 1764, some for export, through Josiah Wedgwood. She was insolvent in the same year, and owed money to many potters, including *Thomas Wedgwood IV of Overhouse*. He still supplied her with 'best flint' in 1765.[106] See Chapter VI.

France, Sarah, Sheffield, bought from *Thomas and John Wedgwood* in 1759-60.[107]

Francis, Wm., owed money to *Thomas Wedgwood IV of Overhouse* in 1764.[108]

Franks, Richard etc., Bristol, bought from *Thomas and John Wedgwood* in 1757-64 and 1770, including flower horns.[109]

Frazier, Richd., Sandgate, Newcastle-upon-Tyne, bought from *Thomas and John Wedgwood* in 1768, and inquired prices of flint ware from *Thomas Wedgwood IV of Overhouse* in 1765.[110]

Fullmer, Mary, bought from *Thomas Wedgwood IV of Overhouse* in 1771, via Willington, Derbyshire.[111]

Furnivall, Thos., Below the Swan, Market Street, Manchester, bought from *Thomas and John Wedgwood* in 1768.[112]

Gardner, Hugh, London, sold stone mugs in 1769 – see Chapter VI.

Garrett, Thos., Bishopgate Street (London?), bought from *Thomas and John Wedgwood* in 1757 and previously.[113]

Gast, John, Salisbury, bought from *Thomas Wedgwood IV of Overhouse* in 1764.[114]

Gibb, John, On the Bridge, Newcastle-upon-Tyne, bought from *Thomas and John Wedgwood* in 1768.[115]

Gilbert, Thomas, Garlick Hill, London, ordered ware from Josiah Wedgwood – see Chapter VI.

Godwin, John, below Newgate, Bristol, bought white and crouch ware from *Thomas and John Wedgwood* in 1756-71, including 'Let in one dish [teapots]', and teapots 'w[hi]t[e]. ground Ash sprigs', kettles and toy bottles and basons.[116]

Graham, Wm., Liverpool, bought from *Thomas and John Wedgwood* in 1768.[117]

Gray, Benjamin, Shelton, bought table spoons from *Thomas and John Wedgwood* in 1772.[118]

Graygoose, Wm., Roydon, Essex, bought from *Thomas and John Wedgwood* in 1756.[119]

Green, Mr., Brockenhurst, near Lymington, bought from *Thomas and John Wedgwood* in 1759.[120]

Greenhalgh, James, Hanging Ditch, Manchester, bought from *Thomas and John Wedgwood* in 1771.[121]

Gresley, Sir Nigel, bought from *Thomas and John Wedgwood* in 1761.[122]

Griffith John, Backs, Bristol, bought ware including gilded blue from *Thomas and John Wedgwood* in 1759-67.[123]

Grindy, Isaac, bought dipped white pints, quarts, and sortable ware from *Jonah Malkin* in 1749.[124]

Guest, John, London, ordered what was possibly salt-glazed stoneware from Josiah Wedgwood in 1763 – see Chapter VI.

Hales, John, Cobridge, potter, bought from *Thomas and John Wedgwood* in 1770-74, including spoons, salt moulds, hearts, melons and pyramids, and unfired ware.[125]

Hall, Mary, bought from *Thomas and John Wedgwood* in 1757.[126]

Hall, Wm., Wine Street, Bristol, bought from *Thomas and John Wedgwood* in 1765.[127]

Hargrave, Richard, Stamford, sold white ware, probably salt-glazed stoneware, in 1720[128] – see Chapter VI.

Hargreaves, Geo., bought from *Thomas and John Wedgwood* in 1755.[129]

Harling, John, Tea Tree, New Church, Strand (London), bought from *Thomas and John Wedgwood* in 1757.[130]

Harrison, John, Stoke-upon-Trent, potter, bought from *Thomas and John Wedgwood* in 1757-60.[131]

Hartill, Richard, bought best and seconds dipped ware from *Jonah Malkin* in 1748.[132]

Harwell, John, Rackby Street, Bristol, bought from *Thomas and John Wedgwood* in 1761-62.[133]

Hassells, John, Shelton, potter, bought spoons and melons from *Thomas and John Wedgwood* in 1763.[134]

Hassells, William, sold blue and white stoneware in Bury St. Edmunds and Colchester in 1759 – see Chapter VI.

Haworth, Francis, Doncaster, bought from *Thomas and John Wedgwood* in 1761-66.[135]

Hayes, James, Fenchurch Street, London, ordered salt-glazed ware from Josiah Wedgwood in 1764 – see Chapter VI.

Haywood, near the Exchange, Manchester, bought from *Thomas and John Wedgwood* in 1768.[136]

Heath, Thos. II, Old Hall, Hanley, potter, bought unfired ware from *Thomas and John Wedgwood* in 1770.[137]

Hewitt, Wm., West Gate Bar, Wakefield, bought from *Thomas and John Wedgwood* in 1768.[138]

Hewson, William, Church Lane, St. Martin's (Southampton St. from 1765), London bought white salt-glazed ware from *Thomas and John Wedgwood* in 1755-1776, including gally pots, and ash beakers in 1771-76.[139]

Hilcoat, Wm., Newcastle-upon-Tyne, bought from *Thomas and John Wedgwood* in 1756-68.[140]

Hilliard, Dixon and Crewe, bought from *Thomas and John Wedgwood* in 1763.[141]

Hiscock, Elinor & Ann Hill, China Shop, Devizes, bought from *Thomas and John Wedgwood* in 1761-63.[142]

Hollins, Josh. & Thos., Hanley, potters, bought melons and unfired ware from *Thomas and John Wedgwood* in 1769-70.[143]

Holt, Sir Lester, bought from *Thomas and John Wedgwood* in 1764-65.[144]

Horner, Mr., ordered white salt-glazed stoneware from Josiah Wedgwood in 1764 – see Chapter VI.

Houghton, Mr., bought from *Thomas and John Wedgwood* in 1770, including toast mugs and venison pots.[145]

Humphrys, Martha, Swindon, bought from *Thomas and John Wedgwood* in 1768-69.[146]

Hunchton, John, Young Street, Kensington, bought from *Thomas and John Wedgwood* in 1758.[147]

Hunter, Wm., Corner Brook St., New Bond St., London, bought from *Thomas and John Wedgwood* in 1760-62.[148]

Hussey, Wm., Corner Rupert Street in Coventry Street, London, bought from *Thomas and John Wedgwood* in 1763-64.[149]

Irlam, Nathaniel, Little Suffolk St., Charing Cross, London, bought from *Thomas and John Wedgwood* in 1765-68.[150]

Jackson, Wm., Coventry, bought from *Thomas and John Wedgwood* in 1756-70, including mottled in 1761.[151]

Jacob, Rachel, Salisbury, bought from *Thomas and John Wedgwood* in 1769-70, including feather edge plates.[152]

James, Mary, near St. James's Churchyard, Bristol, owed money to *Thomas Wedgwood I of Overhouse* in 1764, and bought from *Thomas and John Wedgwood* in 1765-67.[153]

Jones, Mrs., bought from *Thomas Wedgwood IV of Overhouse* in 1753, including blue flowered and ash colour.[154]

Jonson, Joseph, Exeter, bought quarts and pints from *Jonah Malkin* in 1749, and quarts, pints, broad ware pints, wine pints, freckled wine pints and wine quarts in 1749. He also bought through *Jonah Malkin* 'Japand flowrd new collar [sic, japanned flowered new colour]' porringers, pint mugs and toast mugs from *Aaron Wedgwood* in 1749.[155]

Keeling, Anthony, Tunstall, potter, bought pudding cups with pipes, double and treble star cups and pettys, suns and moons, spoons and unfired ware from *Thomas and John Wedgwood* in 1769-75.[156]

Kell, Mr., Foot of the Side, Newcastle-upon-Tyne, bought from *Thomas and John Wedgwood* in 1769-72, including gadroon plates and fish plates.[157] See Chapter VI.

King, Elizabeth, bought seven crates of salt-glazed ware from *Thomas and John Wedgwood* in 1769-70, including mosaic porringers, ash teapots and whistling birds.[158]

King, Wm., Wine Street, Bristol, bought from *Thomas and John Wedgwood* in 1769-70.[159]

Kinkead, Charles, Strabane, Ireland, bought from *Thomas Wedgwood IV of Overhouse* in 1763-66 – see Chapter VI.

Kirby, John, Abingdon, bought from *Thomas and John Wedgwood* in 1763-64, including mustard and saffron (pots).[160]

Krause, J.D. and C.W., Hamburg, bought white salt-glazed stoneware through Cooper and Hodgskin, in the 1760s[161] – see Chapter VI.

Lambden and Woods, London, may have sold white stoneware in 1769 – see Chapter VI.

Lea, Mrs., Birmingham, bought from *Thomas and John Wedgwood* in 1764-1772, including toy cans and ash teapots.[162]

Leggatt, Rachel & Son, Great Newport Street, London, bought from *Thomas and John Wedgwood* in 1763-68.[163]

Lewis, Benjamin, bought pints and quarts from *Jonah Malkin* in 1748-49 and paid him with flint.[164]

Lewis, Ralph, Norwich, who also dealt in flints (see Chapter IV), asked Josiah Wedgwood for white enamelled cups and saucers in 1764.[165] At this date, these would be salt-glazed.

Lloyd, John, Wyle Cop, Shrewsbury, bought from *Thomas and John Wedgwood* in 1766.[166]

Lowe, John, Rotten Row, Burslem, potter, bought unfired ware from *Thomas and John Wedgwood* in 1774-75.[167]

Lowe, Thos., Burslem, potter, bought spoons from *Thomas and John Wedgwood* in 1758 and 1769, paid for by ware.[168]

Lundberg, Magnus, (Bristol) bought from *Thomas and John Wedgwood* in 1760-68.[169]

Lycett, Mr., bought from *Thomas Wedgwood IV of Overhouse* in 1753, including 'Image Toys'.[170]

Macdaniel, Domnick, bought best and seconds dipped ware from *Jonah Malkin* in 1749.[171]

McClure, Gilbert, bought from *Thomas Wedgwood IV of Overhouse* in 1763.[172]

Mahler, Peter, Hamburg, bought white stoneware from Josiah Wedgwood in 1765 – see Chapter VI.

Maidment, James, St. Paul's, London, bought from *Thomas and John Wedgwood* in 1760-62.[173]

Mainwaring, Mr., Nantwich, bought from *Thomas and John Wedgwood* in 1756.[174]

Marfitt, Thos., York, bought from *Thomas and John Wedgwood* in 1761-66.[175]

Marsh, Jos. and Richard, Burslem, potters, bought from *John Brindley* in 1761-62.[176]

Marshall, Daniel, Wakefield, bought from *Thomas and John Wedgwood* in 1756.[177]

Martin, John, Union Warehouse, Liverpool, bought from *Thomas and John Wedgwood* in 1756-57.[178]

Mawde, John, York, bought from *Thomas and John Wedgwood* in 1763-64.[179]

Mayer, E., Amsterdam, sent a small order for white ware to *William Taylor II* of Burslem in 1776.[180] See Chapter VI.

Mellor, Francis, Chesterfield, bought from *Thomas and John Wedgwood* in 1758-61.[181]

Miller, Robert, Shoreditch, London, ordered from Josiah Wedgwood in 1763-64, and from *Thomas Wedgwood IV of Overhouse* in 1771 – see Chapter VI.

Mitchell, John, no location, bought white stoneware from Josiah Wedgwood in 1763 – see Chapter VI.

Mitchil, Richard, paid *Jonah Malkin* for two crates of dipped ware in 1749.[182]

Morris, Mr. Jno., bought from *Thomas Wedgwood IV of Overhouse* in 1753, including ash colour.[183]

Mourney, John, Liverpool, bought dipped quarts and pints from *Jonah Malkin* in 1748-49; and from *Thomas Wedgwood IV of Overhouse* in 1753. He owed money to *Thomas Wedgwood IV of Overhouse* in 1764, and bought from him again in 1765, including decanters and toast cups.[184]

Neale, James, St. Pauls, London, bought from *Thomas and John Wedgwood* in 1765-66.[185]

Newman, Sarah, Glastonbury, bought from *Thomas and John Wedgwood* in 1760.[186]

Newton, Ra., bought 'broadware' from *Jonah Malkin* through Joseph Farmer (above) in 1749.[187]

Ogleby, Wm., Chester-le-Street, Co. Durham, bought from *Thomas and John Wedgwood* in 1767-69.[188]

Omer, James, London, bought from *Thomas Wedgwood IV of Overhouse* in 1764.[189]

Ormes and Bergin, 144 St. John's St., Smithfield, London. Their stock, including white stone Staffordshire ware, was for auction in 1776.[190]

Palmer, Humphrey, Handley Green, potter, bought from *Thomas and John Wedgwood* in 1759-74, including artichoke cups, kettles, 'nest ovals', 'clay' (unfired) spoons, 'Prest (pressed) Pine apple', pap boats.[191]

Parker, John, bought from *Thomas and John Wedgwood* in 1755-59 and earlier.[192]

Parson, Ann, Chester, ordered white stoneware from Josiah Wedgwood in 1763 – see Chapter VI.

Partridge, Johannah, near Bridewell, Bristol, bought from *Thomas and John Wedgwood* in 1765.[193]

Pattison, Mr., Congleton, bought from *Thomas and John Wedgwood* in 1755.[194]

Payne & Richards, bought from *Thomas and John Wedgwood* in 1745-57.[195]

Pearce, Edward, Ludlow, bought from *Thomas and John Wedgwood* in 1760.[196]

Pearson, John, New Bond Street, London, sold stoneware in 1763 – see Chapter VI.

Peart, Joshua, Bromsgrove, bought from *Thomas and John Wedgwood* in 1771-72, including 'natched teapots', ice pail buckets and ladles, and 'grapes'.[197]

Peck, Ann, Sunderland, bought from *Thomas and John Wedgwood* in 1757-66.[198]

Peers, Alice and John, Chester, ordered white ware from Josiah Wedgwood in 1763 – see Chapter VI.

Perrin, Robert, Lancaster and Liverpool, shipped white stoneware in 1763 – see Chapter VI.

Perrin, William, Marlborough, bought from *Thomas and John Wedgwood* in 1756-68.[199]

Perry, Mr., Handley Green, potter, bought unfired ware from *Thomas and John Wedgwood* in 1770.[200]

Petty, Jno., bought from *Thomas Wedgwood IV of Overhouse* in 1753.[201]

Phillips, John, Swallow Street, bought from *Thomas and John Wedgwood* in 1755-69.[202]

Philpot, William, London, ordered white stoneware from Josiah Wedgwood – see Chapter VI.

Philpot, Mr., in London, bought from *Thomas Wedgwood IV of Overhouse* in 1765, including buckets and ladles, egg stands and punchbowls.[203]

Philpott, James owed money to *Thomas Wedgwood IV of Overhouse* in 1764.[204]

Pollett, John, Manchester, bought from *Thomas and John Wedgwood* in 1768.[205]

Pollmann, Jno. Will., a London exporter, ordered white salt-glazed stoneware through Josiah Wedgwood in 1763, to be sent to Pollmann's customers via Hull and Hamburg, and also via Newcastle-upon-Tyne. Some of his salt-glaze orders were supplied by *John Hales* and *William Taylor II*.[206] See Chapter VI.

Pool, Saml., Gloucester, bought from *Thomas and John Wedgwood* in 1764.[207]

Price, Wm., Kington, Herefordshire, bought from *Thomas and John Wedgwood* in 1765-66.[208]

Quick, Thos., Hereford, bought from *Thomas and John Wedgwood* in 1767-69, and from *Thomas Wedgwood II of Overhouse* in 1772.[209]

Redshaw, Mr., bought from *Thomas and John Wedgwood* from 1760 to 1762.[210]

Reeves, Edwd., Ormen Key, Dublin, bought from *Thomas and John Wedgwood* in 1761.[211]

Reid, Wm., bought from *Thomas and John Wedgwood* in 1759-60.[212]

Reston, Wm., Newent, Glos., bought from *Thomas and John Wedgwood* in 1761-69.[213]

Revel, the late Mrs., Little Queen Street, London, stocked white stone ware in 1746 – see Chapter VI.

Rhodes, David owed money to *Thomas Wedgwood IV of Overhouse* in 1764. This would appear to be David Rhodes, earlier of Robinson and Rhodes, Leeds, enamellers.[214] (See also Robinson, Jasper & Co., below.)

Rickwood, John, next door to Smith's Coffee House, Piccadilly, London, supplied stoneware to Lady Findlater for Cullen House, Banff, in 1747.[215]

Rigby, James & Co., bought from *Thomas Wedgwood IV of Overhouse* in 1764.[216]

Roase, Mary, Lewes, bought from *Thomas and John Wedgwood* in 1757.[217]

Roberts, Saml., Gloucester, brushmaker, bought from *Thomas and John Wedgwood* in 1762-68.[218]

Robertson, John, Corner of Watling Street, St. Pauls Churchyard, London, bought from *Thomas and John Wedgwood* in 1759-63.[219]

Robinson, Jasper & Co., Briggate over against George in Leeds, bought from *Thomas and John Wedgwood* in 1761.[220] (See also Rhodes, David, above.)

Robison, Geo., Monkwearmouth, Sunderland (who succeeded Ann Sheraton, below), bought from *Thomas and John Wedgwood* in 1757-62.[221]

Rogers, James, Leominster, bought from *Thomas and John Wedgwood* in 1765.[222]

Rogers, Jno., bought image toys, blue flowered and ash coloured ware from *Thomas Wedgwood IV of Overhouse* in 1753.[223]

Rose, Thos., Everley (Wilts?), bought from *Thomas and John Wedgwood* in 1758.[224]

Rowland, Wm., Chester, bought from *Thomas and John Wedgwood* in 1759.[225]

Rowley, John, Black Friars, London, bought from *Thomas Wedgwood IV of Overhouse* in 1765.[226]

Rusted, Wm., Parliament Street, London, bought from *Thomas and John Wedgwood* in 1757.[227]

Ryan, Sylvester, no address, bought from *Thomas Wedgwood IV of Overhouse* in 1753 and 1764, including crouch ware.[228]

Sampson, Wm., Buchery, Hull, bought from *Thomas and John Wedgwood* in 1758-65.[229]

Sanger, John, Salisbury, bought from *Thomas and John Wedgwood* in 1756-65.[230]

Saywell, William, formerly Cornmarket, now Elephant and Castle, Gaol Bridge, Derby, stocked white flint and other ware in 1743.[231]

Schooman, Jacob, Emden, Germany, ordered white and enamelled white ware from Josiah Wedgwood between 1775 and 1777.[232]

Seward, William, Hamburg, ordered white stoneware from Josiah Wedgwood in 1764 – see Chapter VI.

Shaw, Thos., no address, bought from *Thomas and John Wedgwood* in 1765.[233]

Shepherd, Mrs. Amy, Darlington, bought from *Thomas and John Wedgwood* in 1755 and previously.[234]

Shepperd, Eliz., Devizes, bought from *Thomas and John Wedgwood* in 1765.[235]

Sheraton, Mrs. Ann, Monkwearmouth (later Geo. Robison, q.v.), bought from *Thomas and John Wedgwood* in 1756.[236]

Shergold, Ann, Blandford, Dorset, pottery dealer, had in stock white, blue and white and enamelled stoneware, when she died in 1759.[237]

Shrigley, John bought from *Thomas Wedgwood IV of Overhouse* in 1771.[238]

Simmons, Mrs., Bristol, bought spoons from *Thomas and John Wedgwood* in 1758.[239]

Simpson, Josia, Sheffield?, bought ware including mustard spoons from *Thomas and John Wedgwood* in 1757-60.[240]

Simpson, Thos., Hanley Green, potter, bought sortable ware from *Jonah Malkin* in 1749, and unfired ware from *Thomas and John Wedgwood* in 1771, including pickle boats and 'leaves both makes (styles?)'.[241]

Skellern, Jos., Westgate Street, Gloucester, bought from *Thomas and John Wedgwood* in 1765-67.[242]

Smith, Mr., bought from *Thomas Wedgwood V of Overhouse* in 1778.[243]

Smith, Sir Charles, ordered white stoneware from Josiah Wedgwood – see Chapter VI.

Smith, Jno., Clements Inn Passage, Clare Passage, London, bought fish plates from *Thomas Wedgwood IV of Overhouse* in 1753, owed money to him in 1764, and bought from him again in 1765.[244]

Smith, Jno. & Co., on ye Backs, Bristol, bought from *Thomas and John Wedgwood* in 1767.[245]

Smith, Thos., Swindon, bought from *Thomas and John Wedgwood* in 1768-69.[246]

Snape, Mrs., bought from *Thomas Wedgwood IV of Overhouse* in 1753.[247]

Sneyd, Ralph, Esq., Keele?, bought from *Thomas and John Wedgwood* in 1756.[248]

Statham, Mr., Liverpool, merchant, bought from *Thomas and John Wedgwood* in 1772, including flowered spoon boats.[249]

Steet, Michael, Middleton Tyas, Co. Durham, bought from *Thomas and John Wedgwood* in 1766 and previously.[250]

Stephens, Josh., Cobridge, potter, bought unfired ware from *Thomas and John Wedgwood* in 1765.[251]

Stephens, Thos., bought from *Thomas Wedgwood IV of Overhouse* in 1764.[252]

Stewart, C., opposite Argyle Building, Oxford Road (London?), bought from *Thomas and John Wedgwood* in 1766.[253]

Stewart, John, Bewsey Castle?, Derbyshire, bought from *Thomas and John Wedgwood* in 1758-59.[254]

Straphan, Wm., Queenhithe, London?, bought from *Thomas Wedgwood IV of Overhouse* in 1763-64 and from *Thomas and John Wedgwood* in 1755-67, and owed money to *Thomas Wedgwood IV of Overhouse* in 1764.[255]

Strutt, Joseph, London, bought from *Thomas Wedgwood IV of Overhouse* in 1764-65.[256]

Summerfield, William, Stoke-on-Trent, enameller and painter of earthenware, who insured his premises there in 1755, is likely to have been a customer for white salt-glazed stoneware at that date.[257]

Syson, Peter, Mount Street, London, bought from *Thomas and John Wedgwood* in 1764-69, and owed money to *Thomas Wedgwood IV of Overhouse* in 1764.[258]

Tabor, Samuel, Rotterdam, Holland, merchant, ordered white flint ware from Josiah Wedgwood in 1763 – see Chapter VI.

Talbot, Jeffrey, St. Olaves, Southwark, bought from *Thomas and John Wedgwood* in 1756.[259]

Talcot, Jeffrey and Wilson, Tooley Street, Tooley Stairs, London, bought from *Thomas and John Wedgwood* in 1757.[260]

Taylor, Ann, Durham, bought from *Thomas Wedgwood IV of Overhouse* in 1753 and 764.[261]

Taylor, James, bought blue flowered ware from *Thomas Wedgwood IV of Overhouse* in 1753.[262]

Taylor, John, Coventry, bought from *Thomas and John Wedgwood* in 1756.[263]

Taylor, Martha, in Carfax, Oxford, bought from *Thomas and John Wedgwood* in 1761.[264]

Taylor, Thos., Shelton, bought oval dishes from *Thomas and John Wedgwood* in 1765.[265]

Taylor, Wm. & Joseph, Water Lane, Bristol, bought from *Thomas and John Wedgwood* in 1768.[266]

Thomson, Richard, Upper Shadwell, facing the Virginia Planter, London, bought from *Thomas Wedgwood IV of Overhouse* in 1764.[267]

Thompson, John, Corner Argyle Street, Oxford Road, London?, bought from *Thomas and John Wedgwood* in 1764-65.[268]

Thompson, John, Sun, Newgate Street, London?, bought from *Thomas and John Wedgwood* in 1755-67.[269]

Throop, Richard, bought dipped white from *Jonah Malkin* in 1748.[270]

Tidmarsh, Mr., bought from *Thomas Wedgwood IV of Overhouse* in 1753, including Mosaic.[271]

Tidmarsh, Mrs., 4 Rosemary Lane, London, bought from *Thomas Wedgwood IV of Overhouse* in 1753.[272]

Tidmarsh, James, bought custard cups from *Thomas and John Wedgwood* in 1773; and bought other ware from *Thomas Wedgwood V of Overhouse* in 1778.[273]

Tidmarsh, John, bought blue flowered ware from *Thomas Wedgwood IV of Overhouse* in 1753, and other ware from *Thomas and John Wedgwood* in 1765.[274]

Tidmarsh, Josh., bought double coffees etc. from *Thomas Wedgwood IV of Overhouse* in 1771.[275]

Tuck, Robt. & Mary, Devizes, bought from *Thomas and John Wedgwood* in 1768-69.[276]

Turner, William, Stoke, bought pudding cups and spoons from *Thomas and John Wedgwood* in 1757-63.[277]

Turnham, Mrs., bought new fashioned flowered table plates from *Thomas Wedgwood IV of Overhouse* in 1753.[278]

Twentyman, Henry, Davie Street, Bartletts Square, London, bought from *Thomas and John Wedgwood* in 1765-66, and from *Thomas Wedgwood IV of Overhouse* in 1771.[279]

Twigg, Ann, Wakefield, bought from *Thomas and John Wedgwood* in 1757-58.[280]

Tylsley, Edwd., Navy Office, London, bought from *Thomas and John Wedgwood* in 1755.[281]

Vanderkirk/Vanderkiste, Joseph, London, bought from *Thomas Wedgwood IV of Overhouse* in 1753 and 1764, and from his son *Thomas II* in 1774 – see Chapter VI.

Vaughan, Miles, of Cork, owed money to *Thomas Wedgwood IV of Overhouse* in 1764, who took action against Vaughan in 1769.[282]

Veek, John, near the Monument, London, bought from *Thomas and John Wedgwood* in 1758.[283]

Vere, Charles, London, probably dealt in white stoneware in 1764 – see Chapter VI.

Wale, Edwd., Corner Devonshire Street, Red Lyon Square, Holborn, London, bought from *Thomas and John Wedgwood* in 1755-71, including chambers, spitting pots, and 'let in one dish [teapots]'.[284]

Warburton, Jacob, Cobridge, potter, bought spoons, stars and flowered hearts from *Thomas and John Wedgwood* in 1765.[285]

Warburton, John, Keyside, Newcastle-upon-Tyne, advertised white stone ware in 1774.[286] *Jonah Malkin* sold dipped ware to a John Warburton in 1749, no address given.[287]

Warburton, Joseph, Cobridge, potter, bought spoons from *Thomas and John Wedgwood* in 1762.[288]

Warburton, Thos., bought from *Thomas and John Wedgwood* in 1765.[289]

Ward, Mary, Salisbury, bought from *Thomas and John Wedgwood* in 1759.[290]

Ward, Samuel, Brentford, owed money to *Thomas Wedgwood IV of Overhouse* in 1764, and bought from him in 1770.[291]

Waring, Mary, Leominster, bought from *Thomas and John Wedgwood* in 1764-69.[292]

Washington, Godfrey, Doncaster, bought from *Thomas and John Wedgwood* in 1761.[293]

Watkinson, William, next to Mr. Doiley's near Exeter Change, Strand, whose bankrupt stock included 'fine white Stone ware' in 1727 (see Chapter VI).[294]

Watson, Eliz., Bromsgrove, bought from *Thomas and John Wedgwood* in 1756-72, including plates with 'Nickel edges plain' and 'Toy Babes' in 1770.[295]

Weatherby and Crowther ('Wedgrby & Croter') bought pints and quarts from *Jonah Malkin* in 1749.[296]

Wedgwood, Cousin Aaron, Burslem, potter, bought from *Thomas and John Wedgwood* in 1761-65.[297]

Wedgwood, Burslem, Burslem, potter, bought spoons from *Thomas and John Wedgwood* in 1761.[298]

Wedgwood, Carlos, Burslem, potter, bought Turks Caps from *Thomas and John Wedgwood* in 1765.[299]

Wedgwood, Jno. ('Bro[ther]'), owed money to *Thomas Wedgwood IV of Overhouse* in 1764.[300]

Wedgwood, Josiah, Burslem, potter, received orders from thirty-five customers for white salt-glazed stoneware (listed in this Appendix) and bought supplies from some thirty-three local makers (see Chapter IX and Appendices 1 and 2).

Wedgwood, Thomas (IV of Overhouse), Churchyard, Burslem, potter, bought dipped ware mugs, porringers and bowls from *Jonah Malkin* in 1749; and spoons, melons etc. from *Thomas and John Wedgwood* when he was at Overhouse in 1770-71.[301] He also bought what must be salt-glazed stoneware from John Baddeley in 1752.[302]

Wedgwood, Thomas and John, Big House, Burslem, potters, bought dishes, dipped gill mugs, half-pints, pints, quarts, wine pints and quarts, and porringers from *Jonah Malkin* in 1748-50.[303]

Weston, John owed money to *Thomas Wedgwood IV of Overhouse* in 1764, and bought from him in 1765, including 'Galliboxes'.[304]

White, Jonas owed money to *Thomas Wedgwood IV of Overhouse* in 1764.[305]

Whitehorn, Kerr, Tewkesbury, bought from *Thomas and John Wedgwood* in 1769.[306]

Whitemarsh, Mr., Salisbury, bought from *Thomas and John Wedgwood* in 1760.[307]

Wichell, Thos., Newbury, bought from *Thomas and John Wedgwood* in 1757-63.[308]

Wickstead, Sarah, in the Grove, Bath, bought from *Thomas and John Wedgwood* in 1755-65.[309]

Williams, J. & J., London, asked Josiah Wedgwood for the prices of white ware, pencilled, painted or printed, in 1763.[310]

Williams, John & Jos., Bottom Breadstreet Hill, London, bought from *Thomas and John Wedgwood* in 1758.[311]

Williams, Mary, near Goat Stairs, Bankside, Southwark, London, bought from *Thomas and John Wedgwood* in 1761-63, and white enamelled teapots from *Thomas Wedgwood IV of Overhouse* in 1763.[312]

Williams, Thos., Cannister & Jarr, Davis Street near Brook Street, Grosvenor Square, London, bought from *Thomas and John Wedgwood* in 1765.[313]

Wilson, Mr., Sandbach, bought from *Thomas and John Wedgwood* in 1765.[314]

Winter, John & Bletch, Bristol?, bought from *Thomas and John Wedgwood* in 1759-67.[315]

Winter, Thos., Everley, near Pewsey, Wilts., bought from *Thomas and John Wedgwood* in 1761.[316]

Wood, Henry, Bridge Street, Parliament Street, London, bought from *Thomas and John Wedgwood* in 1763-64.[317]

Wood, John and Ralph, Burslem, potters, bought unfired ware from *Thomas and John Wedgwood* in 1772.[318]

Wraxall & Flower, Bristol, bought from *Thomas and John Wedgwood* in 1755.[319]

Wright, Mrs. Ann, bought from *Thomas Wedgwood IV of Overhouse* in 1765, including oblong fish drainers.[320]

Wyke, John, Liverpool, clockmaker, bought from Josiah Wedgwood and *Aaron Wedgwood* in 1763, and *Thomas and John Wedgwood* on 23 July 1763 – see Chapter VI.

Wynn, Mr., Congleton, bought from *Thomas and John Wedgwood* in 1761.[321]

Yoxal, Mr., bought ware including square dishes and ash flower pots and stands from *Thomas and John Wedgwood* in 1772.[322]

Bibliography

Documentary Sources
Our principal documentary sources are:

Keele University: Wedgwood Accumulation
Lichfield Record Office: Wills and Administrations
Maryland State Archives: Inventories
New York Public Library: Arents Letterbook
Potteries Museum and Art Gallery: Thomas and John Wedgwood Papers
Staffordshire Record Office: D 1788, Aqualate Papers

Other documentary sources are shown in our endnotes.

Unpublished Sources
Elliot, Wallace, Scrapbooks (1902-1937) Victoria and Albert Museum.
Hampson, R.S., 'The Development of the Pottery Industry in Longton, 1700-1865', unpublished M.A. Thesis, Keele University, 1986.
Mountford, Arnold R., 'Thomas Wedgwood, John Wedgwood and Jonah Malkin Potters of Burslem', unpublished M.A. Thesis, Keele University, 1972.
Smith, H.A.S., 'English Queensware and its impact on the French pottery industry 1774-1814', unpublished Ph.D. Thesis, Keele University, 2002.

Published Sources

General
Blacker, J.F., *The ABC of English Salt-Glaze Stoneware from Dwight to Doulton* (London: Paul, 1922).
Coutts, Howard, *The Art of Ceramics, European Ceramic Design 1500-1830* (New Haven and London: Yale University Press, 2001).
Crafts, N.F.R., *British Economic Growth during the Industrial Revolution* (Oxford: Oxford University Press, 1985).
Freestone, I. and D. Gaimster, ed., *Pottery in the Making World Ceramic Traditions* (London: British Museum Press, 1997).
Gaimster, D., *German Stoneware 1200-1900 Archaeology and Cultural History* (London: British Museum Press, 1997).
Green, C., *John Dwight's Fulham Pottery Excavations 1971-79* (London: English Heritage, 1999).
Grigsby, Leslie, *The Henry H. Weldon Collection of English Pottery 1650-1800* (Sotheby's Publications, 1990).
Hildyard, R., *European Ceramics* (London: V&A Publications, 1999).
Hillier, B., *Pottery and Porcelain 1700-1914* (London: Weidenfeld and Nicolson, 1968).
Lockett, T.A. and P.A. Halfpenny, ed., *Stonewares & Stone chinas of Northern England to 1851* (Stoke-on-Trent: City Museum and Art Gallery, 1982).
Luxmoore, C.F.C., *"Saltglaze" with The Notes of a Collector* (Exeter: Pollard, 1924, rep. London: Holland Press, n.d., c.1970).
McKendrick, N., J. Brewer and J.H. Plumb, *The Birth of a Consumer Society The Commercialisation of Eighteenth-century England* (London: Europa, 1982; Bloomington: Indiana University Press, 1985).
Mountford, A.R., *The Illustrated Guide to Staffordshire Salt-Glazed Stoneware* (London: Barrie & Jenkins, 1971).
Pitt, W., *A Topographical History of Staffordshire...* (Newcastle-under-Lyme: Smith, 1817).
Plumb, J.H., *England in the Eighteenth Century* (Harmondsworth: Penguin, 1950).
Porter, R., *English Society in the Eighteenth Century* (Harmondsworth, 1982).
Richards, S., *Eighteenth-century ceramics Products for a civilised society* (Manchester: Manchester University Press, 1999).
Shaw, Simeon, *History of the Staffordshire Potteries* (Newton Abbot: David & Charles; New York: Praeger Publishers, 1970; originally published for the author in Hanley, 1829).
Snodin, M., ed., *Rococo Art and Design in Hogarth's England* (London: Trefoil Books/Victoria & Albert Museum, 1984).
Weatherill, L., *The Pottery Trade and North Staffordshire 1660-1760* (Manchester: Manchester University Press, 1971).
Weatherill, L., *The Growth of the Pottery Industry* (New York, 1986).
Weatherill, L., *Consumer Behaviour and Material Culture in Britain 1660-1760* (London: Routledge, 1988).
Williams, Peter and Halfpenny, Pat, *A Passion for Pottery, Further Selections from the Henry H. Weldon Collection* (Sotheby's Publications, 2000).
Young, H., *English Porcelain 1745-95 Its Makers, Design, Marketing and Consumption* (London: V&A Publications, 1999).

Chapter I: Early Development of White Salt-Glazed Stoneware
Ayres, John, Oliver Impey and J.V.G. Mallet, *Porcelain for Palaces* (London: Oriental Ceramic Society, 1990).
Beebe, Lucie, 'Rhenish Stoneware of the Renaissance' in *American Ceramic Circle Bulletin*, Number 2, 1980, 125-40.
Bimson, Mavis, 'John Dwight', *English Ceramic Circle Transactions* Vol. 5, Part 2, 1961, 95-109.
Edwards, Rhoda, 'London Potters circa 1570-1710' in *Journal of Ceramic History* No.6, 1974.
Fryer, Kevin and Andrea Selley et al., *Excavation of a Pit at 16 Tunsgate, Guildford, Surrey, 1991* (Guildford Museum, reprinted from *Post-Medieval Archaeology*, Vol. 31, 1997, 184).
Gaimster, D., *German Stoneware 1200-1900 Archaeology and Cultural History* (London: British Museum Press, 1997).
Green, Chris, *John Dwight's Fulham Pottery Excavations 1971-79* (London: English Heritage, 1999).
Horne, Jonathan, *John Dwight Master Potter of Fulham 1672-1703 and his contemporaries*, exhibition catalogue 1992.
Johnson, Harwood A., 'John Dwight of Fulham's Purchase of Land in Pennsylvania', *Ars Ceramica* Number 10, 1993, 21-25.
Korry, Patricia M., 'Francis Place, Seventeenth-Century English Potter and Man of the Enlightenment' in *Ars Ceramica*, Number 16, 2000, 40-41.
Oswald, Adrian, R.J.C. Hildyard and R.G. Hughes, *English Brown Stoneware 1670-1900* (London: Faber and Faber, 1982).

Tyler, Richard, *Francis Place*, catalogue of the exhibition at the City Art Gallery York, 9-28 April 1971.

Chapter II: Early Industrial Stonewares
Barker, David, *William Greatbatch a Staffordshire Potter* (London: Jonathan Horne, 1990).
Church, A.H., *English Earthenware made during the 17th and 18th Centuries, illustrated by specimens in the National Collections* rev. ed. (London: HMSO, 1904).
Earle, Cyril, *The Earle Collection of Early Staffordshire Pottery* (London: A. Brown and Sons, Limited, 1915).
Goodby, M., 'Moulds and Modellers in the Early 18th-century Staffordshire Potteries: Slip-Casting, Press-Moulding and the Wood Family' in *English Ceramic Circle Transactions* Vol. 17, Part 2, 2000, 216-28.
Hillis, Maurice, 'An Introduction to Ceramic Raw Materials, Bodies and Glazes', *Northern Ceramic Society Journal*, Vol. 18, 2001.
Hodgkin, John Eliot and Edith Hodgkin, *Examples of Early English Pottery Named, Dated and Inscribed* (Menston, Yorkshire, EP Publishers reprint 1973, originally published by the authors 1891).
Hume, Ivor Noël, 'The rise and fall of English white salt-glazed stoneware' in *The Magazine Antiques*, February, 1970.
Jewitt, Llewellynn, *The Ceramic Art of Great Britain* 2 Vol. (London: Virtue, 1878; New York: Scribner, Welford and Armstrong, 1878).
Mountford, Arnold R., *The Illustrated Guide to Staffordshire Salt-Glazed Stoneware* (London: Barrie & Jenkins, 1971).
Plot, Robert, *The Natural History of Stafford-shire* (Oxford: 1676).
Plourde G., Lapointe, C., *Les Objects domestiques en grès fin anglais de Place-Royale* (Quebec, Canada: Les Publications du Quebec, 1996).
Potteries Museum and Art Gallery, Stoke-on-Trent, MS Ceram., No. 4: Thomas and John Wedgwood and Jonah Malkin papers.
Shaw, Simeon, *History of the Staffordshire Potteries* (Newton Abbot: David & Charles, New York: Praeger Publishers, 1970; originally published for the author in Hanley, 1829).
Snodin, M., ed., *Rococo Art and Design in Hogarth's England* (London: Trefoil Books/Victoria & Albert Museum, 1984).
Syz, Miller and Rückert, *Catalogue of The Hans Syz Collection* (Washington, D.C.: Smithsonian Institution Press, 1979).
Tait, Hugh, 'Blocks for Spouts' in *The British Museum Quarterly*, Volume XXXVI, Number 3-4, Spring 1963.
Weatherill, L., *The Pottery Trade and North Staffordshire 1660-1760* (Manchester: Manchester University Press, 1971).
Wedgwood, Josiah C. *Staffordshire Pottery and Its History* (London: Sampson, Low, Marston & Co., Ltd (n.d., c.1912, 1923).
Young, Hilary *English Porcelain 1745-95* (London: V&A Publications, 1999).

Chapter III: The Demand for Salt-Glazed Stoneware
Bowles, Tom Parker, 'Eating Their Words: Modern British Food Writers' in *Books and Company* Issue 13, 2002.
Briggs, Asa, *A Social History of England* (London: Weidenfeld and Nicholson; New York: The Viking Press, 1983).
Chancellor, E. Beresford, *The XVIIIth Century in London* (London: B.T. Batsford, Ltd., 1920).
Coutts, Howard, *The Art of Ceramics, European Ceramic Design 1500-1830* (New Haven and London: Yale University Press, 2001).
Edwards, Diana *Tea and Sympathy Post-Revolutionary Ceramics in the Stamford Historical Society* (Stamford, Ct: Stamford Historical Society, 1981).
Ehrman, Edwina et al., *London Eats Out 500 Years of Capital Dining* (London: Museum of London, Philip Wilson, 1999).
Glanville, Phillipa and Hilary Young, *Elegant Eating, Four hundred years of dining in style* (London: V & A Publications, 2002).
Lipson, E., *The Growth of English Society* (London: A. and C. Black, 1959 (first ed. 1949)).
McKendrick, N., J. Brewer and J.H. Plumb *The Birth of a Consumer Society The Commercialisation of Eighteenth-century England* (London: Europa, 1982; Bloomington: Indiana University Press, 1985).
Reed, Michael, *The Making of Britain The Georgian Triumph 1700-1830* (London: Routledge & Kegan Paul, 1983).
Scheurleer, D.F. Lunsingh, *Chinese Export Porcelain Chine de Commande* (New York: Pitman Publishing Corporation, 1974).
Weatherill, L., *The Pottery Trade and North Staffordshire 1660-1760* (Manchester: Manchester University Press, 1971).

Chapter IV: Raw Materials
Anon., 'Ball Clays Their Occurrence, Extraction, and Uses in the Ceramic Industries' in *Ceramics* Vol. V, July 1953, 204-10.
Berg, T. and P., trans., *R R Angerstein's Illustrated Travel Diary 1753-1755 Industry in England and Wales from a Swedish perspective* (London: Science Museum, 2001).
Bulley, J.A., 'The beginnings of the Devonshire Ball-Clay Trade' in *Transactions of the Devonshire Association* Vol. LXXVII, 1955, 191-204.
Celoria, F., 'Techniques of White Salt-Glaze Stoneware Manufacture in North Staffordshire Around 1765' in *Science and Archaeology* no. 18, 1976, 25-28.
Chaloner, W.H., 'Salt in Cheshire, 1600-1870' in *Transactions of the Lancashire and Cheshire Antiquarian Society* Vol. 71, 1961, 58-74.
Copeland, R., *A short history of pottery raw materials and the Cheddleton Flint Mill* (Leek: Cheddleton Flint Mill Industrial Heritage Trust, 1972).
Durrance, E.M. and D.J.C. Laming, ed., *The Geology of Devon* (Exeter: University of Exeter, 1982).
Edwards, R., 'London Potters circa 1570-1710' in *Journal of Ceramic History* No. 6 1974, 1-139.
Gaimster, D., *German Stoneware 1200-1900 Archaeological and Cultural History* (London: British Museum Press, 1997).
Greenslade, M.W. and J.G. Jenkins, ed., *A History of the County of Stafford*, multi-vol. Vol. II (London: Oxford University Press, 1967).
Haselgrove, Dennis and John Murray, ed., 'John Dwight's Fulham Pottery 1672-1978 A Collection of Documentary Sources' in *Journal of Ceramic History* No. 11, 1979.
Hasted, E., *The History and Topographical Survey of the County of Kent* 4 vol. (Canterbury: privately, 1778).
Holdridge, D.A., 'Ball Clays and their Properties' in *Transactions of the British Ceramic Society* Vol. 55, 1956, 369-440.
Holdridge, D.A., 'Composition Variation in Ball Clays' in *Transactions of the British Ceramic Society* Vol. 58, 1959, 645-59.
Houldsworth, E., 'Blue Boulders A Little Known Sussex Industry' in *Sussex County Magazine* Vol. 14, 1940, 17-18.
Hudson, K., *The History of English China Clays Fifty Years of Pioneering and Growth* (Newton Abbot: David & Charles, n.d., c.1970).
Job, B., 'The Grinding of Flint and Bone' in *Journal of the Staffordshire Industrial Archaeology Society* No. 13, 1989, 20-28.
Job, B., *Watermills of the Moddershall Valley* (Newcastle-under-Lyme: privately, n.d., c.1985).
Latham, J.P.M., 'Dorset Clay to Staffordshire Pot' in *English Ceramic Circle Transactions* Vol. 10, Part 2, 1977, 109-17.
Mallet, J., 'John Baddeley of Shelton, an Early Staffordshire Maker of Pottery and Porcelain Parts I and II' in *English Ceramic Circle Transactions* Vol. 6, Part 2, 1966, 124-66; Part 3, 1967, 181-247.
Meredith, W.D., 'Water Mills in North Staffordshire' in *North Staffordshire Journal of Field Studies* Vol. 4, 1964, 1-10.
Muspratt, S., *Chemistry, Theoretical, Practical and Analytical* multi-vol. (Glasgow: Mackenzie, 1860).
Pitt, W., *A Topographical History of Staffordshire...* (Newcastle-under-Lyme: Smith, 1817).

P[lot], R., *The Natural History of Oxford-shire, Being an Essay toward the Natural History of England* (Oxford, 1677).

Plot, R., *The Natural History of Stafford-shire* (Oxford 1686, reprinted Didsbury: Morten, 1973).

Rolt, L.T.C., *The Potters' Field A History of the South Devon Ball Clay Industry* (Newton Abbot: David & Charles, 1974).

Shaw, Simeon, *History of the Staffordshire Potteries* (Newton Abbot: David & Charles, New York: Praeger Publishers, 1970; originally published for the author in Hanley, 1829).

Trump, H.J., *Teignmouth A Maritime History* 2nd ed. (Chichester: Phillimore, 1986).

Wakelin, A.P., *Pre-industrial trade on the River Severn: a computer-aided study of the Gloucester Port Books* (Wolverhampton: Wolverhampton University, 1991).

Weatherill, L., *The Pottery Trade and North Staffordshire 1660-1760* (Manchester: Manchester University Press, 1971).

Weatherill, L., 'Technical Change and Potters' Inventories 1660-1760' in *Journal of Ceramic History* No. 3, 1970, 3-12.

Willan, T.S., *The English Coasting Trade 1600-1750* (Manchester: Manchester University Press, 1938).

Willan, T.S., 'The Navigation of the River Weaver in the Eighteenth Century' in *Remains Historical and Literary connected with the Palatine Counties of Lancaster and Chester* Vol. III, Third series, 1951.

Wood, A.C., 'The History of Trade and Transport on the River Trent' in *Transactions of the Thoroton Society* Vol. LIV, 1950, 1-44.

Young, H., 'Evidence for Wood and Coal firing and the Design of Kilns in the 18th-century English Porcelain Industry' in *English Ceramic Circle Transactions* Vol. 17, Part 1, 1999, 1-14.

Chapter V: Making the Pots

Barker, D., 'Bits and Bobs – The Development of Kiln Furniture in the 18th-century Staffordshire pottery industry' in *English Ceramic Circle Transactions* Vol. 16, Part 3, 1998.

Berg, T. and P., trans., *R R Angerstein's Illustrated Travel Diary 1753-1755 Industry in England and Wales from a Swedish perspective* (London: Science Museum, 2001).

Blacker, J.F., *The A B C of English Salt-Glaze Stoneware from Dwight to Doulton* (London: Paul, 1922).

Celoria, F., 'Techniques of White Salt-Glaze Stoneware Manufacture in North Staffordshire around 1765' in *Science and Archaeology* no. 18, 1976.

Cook, Cyril, 'Old English Salt-glazed Plates with printed decorations' in *The Connoisseur*, June 1958.

Dragesco, B., *English Ceramics in French Archives The writings of Jean Hellot, the adventures of Jacques Louis Brolliet and the identification of the 'Girl-in-a-Swing' factory* (London: privately, 1993).

Elliott, G., *The Design Process in British Ceramic Manufacture 1750-1850* (Stoke-on-Trent: Staffordshire University Press, n.d., c.2002).

Freestone, I. and D. Gaimster, ed., *Pottery in the Making World Ceramic Traditions* (London: British Museum Press, 1997).

Gaimster, D., *German Stoneware 1200-1900 Archaeological and Cultural History* (London: British Museum Press, 1997).

Goodby, M., 'Moulds and Modellers in the Early 18th-century Staffordshire Potteries: Slip-Casting, Press-Moulding and the Wood Family' in *English Ceramic Circle Transactions* Vol. 1, Part 2, 2000.

Green, C., *John Dwight's Fulham Pottery Excavations 1971-79* (London: English Heritage, 1999).

Grigsby, Leslie, 'Johan Nieuhoff's Embassy: inspiration for relief decoration on English stoneware and earthenware' in *The Magazine Antiques*, January 1993.

Grigsby, Leslie, 'John Stalker and George Parker's Treatise: An inspiration for relief decoration on English stoneware and earthenware' in *The Magazine Antiques*, June 1993.

Grigsby, Leslie, 'Aesop's Fables on English Ceramics' in *The Magazine Antiques*, June 1994.

Haselgrove, Dennis and John Murray, ed., 'John Dwight's Fulham Pottery 1672-1978 A Collection of Documentary Sources' in *Journal of Ceramic History* No. 11, 1979.

Luxmoore, C.F.C., *"Saltglaze" with The Notes of a Collector* (Exeter: Pollard, 1924 repr. London: Holland Press, n.d.).

Mountford, A.R., *The Illustrated Guide to Staffordshire Salt-Glazed Stoneware* (London: Barrie & Jenkins, 1971).

Pitt, W., *A Topographical History of Staffordshire...* (Newcastle-under-Lyme: Smith, 1817).

Sharp, R.W., *Ceramics Ethics & Scandal* (Canada: RWD Books, 2002).

Shaw, Simeon, *History of the Staffordshire Potteries* (Newton Abbot: David & Charles, New York: Praeger Publishers, 1970; originally published for the author in Hanley, 1829).

Tait, Hugh, 'Blocks for Spouts' in *The British Museum Quarterly* Volume XXVI, Number 3-4, Spring 1963.

Tilley, Frank, 'Ravenet an Engraver for Battersea Transfers on Saltglaze Plates' in *The Antique Collector*, June 1963.

Weatherill, L., *The Pottery Trade and North Staffordshire 1660-1760* (Manchester: Manchester University Press, 1971).

Wyman, C., 'A Review of early Transfer Printing Techniques' in *English Ceramic Circle Transactions* Vol. 16, Part 3, 1998.

Young, Hilary, 'Eighteenth-century English decorators of Chinese porcelain' in *Apollo*, November 2002.

Chapter VI: Marketing in Britain and Europe

Adams, E., 'Ceramic Insurances in the Sun Company, 1776-1774' in *English Ceramic Circle Transactions* Vol. 10, Part 1, 1976, 1-38.

Adams, E., 'Women in the Eighteenth Century Ceramic Trade and some detailed Prices of that Time' in *Journal of the Northern Ceramic Society* Vol. 16, 1999, 1-21.

Barker, D., *William Greatbatch a Staffordshire Potter* (London: Horne, 1990).

Campbell, R., *The London Tradesman* (London, 1747, rep. Newton Abbot: David & Charles, 1969).

Chambers, J.D., *The Vale of Trent 1670-1800 A Regional Study of Economic Change* (Cambridge: Cambridge University Press, 1957).

Craig, R., 'Some Aspects of the Trade and Shipping of the River Dee in the Eighteenth Century' in *Transactions of the Historic Society of Lancashire and Cheshire for the Year 1962* Vol. 114, 1963, 99-128.

Deane, P. and W.A. Cole, *British Economic Growth 1688-1959 Trends and Structure* (Cambridge: Cambridge University Press, 1967).

Eland, G., ed., *Purefoy Letters 1735-1753*, 2 vol. (London: Sidgwick & Jackson, 1931).

Finer, A. and G. Savage, ed., *The Selected Letters of Josiah Wedgwood* (London: Cory, Adams & Mackay, 1965).

Greenslade, M.W. and J.G. Jenkins, ed., *A History of the County of Stafford* Vol. II, (London: Oxford University Press, 1967).

Haselgrove, D. and J. Murray, ed., 'John Dwight's Fulham Pottery 1672-1978 A Collection of Documentary Sources' in *Journal of Ceramic History* No. 11, 1979, 1-284.

Horn, B., 'Ceramic accounts found among the Seafield Muniments' in *English Ceramic Circle Transactions* Vol. 18, Part 1, 2002, 189-96.

Jenkins, J.G., ed., *A History of the County of Stafford* Vol. VIII (London: Oxford University Press, 1963).

Jewitt, L., *The Wedgwoods, being a Life of Josiah Wedgwood...* (London: Virtue, 1865).

Lindsay, J., *The Trent & Mersey Canal* (Newton Abbot: David & Charles, 1979).

Mallet, J., 'John Baddeley of Shelton An Early Staffordshire Maker of Pottery and Porcelain Part I' in *English Ceramic Circle Transactions* Vol. 6, Part 2, 1967, 124-66.

Plot, R., *The Natural History of Stafford-shire* (Oxford, 1686).

Shaw, Simeon, *History of the Staffordshire Potteries* (Newton Abbot: David & Charles, New York: Praeger Publishers, 1970; originally published for the author in Hanley, 1829).

Smith, A., *The Illustrated Guide to Liverpool Herculaneum Pottery 1796-1840* (London: Barrie & Jenkins, 1970).

Smith, A., 'John Wyke of Liverpool, and the Staffordshire Pottery Export Trade' in *Northern Ceramic Society Journal* Vol. 3, 1978-1979, 79-88.

Smith, S., 'William Hassells, Pot-Maker' in *Northern Ceramic Society Newsletter* No. 27, September 1977.

Thomas, A.L., 'Geographical aspects of the Development of Transport and Communications affecting the Pottery Industry of North Staffordshire during the Eighteenth Century' in *Collections for a History of Staffordshire 1934* ed. William Salt Archaeological Society (Kendal: Titus Wilson, 1935), 1-157.

Toppin, A.J., 'The China Trade and some London Chinamen' in *English Ceramic Circle Transactions* No 3, 1935, 37-56.

Towner, D., *Creamware* (London: Faber, 1978).

Valpy. N., 'Extracts from 18th century London Newspapers' in *English Ceramic Circle Transactions* Vol. 12 Part 2, 1985, 161-88.

Valpy, N., 'Extracts from 18th Century London Newspapers' in *English Ceramic Circle Transactions* Vol. 15, Part 2, 1994, 310-16.

Weatherill, L., 'The Business of Middleman in the English Pottery Trade before 1780' in *Business History* Vol. XXVII, No. 3, July 1986, 51-76.

Weatherill, L., 'The growth of the pottery industry in England, 1660-1815' in *Post Medieval Archaeology* No. 17, 1983, 15-46.

Weatherill, L., *The Pottery Trade and North Staffordshire 1660-1760* (Manchester: Manchester University Press, 1971).

White, A.J., 'A Stamford Potseller's Stock in 1720' in *Post Medieval Archaeology* No. 13, 1979, 290-92.

Young, H., *English Porcelain 1745-95 Its Makers, Design, Marketing and Consumption* (London: V & A Publications, 1999).

Chapter VII: English White Salt-Glazed Stoneware for the American Market

Brown III, Marley R., 'Ceramics from Plymouth, 1621-1800: The Documentary Record,' in *Ceramics in America*, Winterthur Conference Report 1972.

Detweiler, Susan, *George Washington's Chinaware* (New York: Harry N. Abrams, Inc, 1982).

Dow, George Francis, *The arts and crafts in New England, 1704-1775* (Topsfield, Massachusetts: The Wayside Press, 1927), 82-83.

Edwards, Diana, 'English Aristocrats in Maryland Society: the Ceramics of Charles Carroll of Carrollton, His Family and Contemporaries' in *American Ceramic Circle Journal*, Volume VII, 1989, 77-95.

Edwards, Diana, 'Hart-Shortridge House' in *Unearthing New England's Past: The Ceramic Evidence* (Lexington, Massachusetts: Museum of our National Heritage, 1984).

Edwards et al., 'Generations of Trash the Hart-Shortridge House, 1769-1860' in *American Ceramic Circle Journal* Vol. VI, 1988.

Estes, J. Worth, *Hall Jackson and the Purple Foxglove, Medical Practice & Research in Revolutionary America 1760-1820* (Hanover, New Hampshire: University of New England Press, 1979).

Goodby, M., 'Moulds and Modellers in the Early 18th-century Staffordshire Potteries: Slip-Casting, Press-Moulding and the Wood Family' in *English Ceramic Circle Transactions* Vol. 17, Part 2, 2000, 216-28.

Green, Chris, *John Dwight's Fulham Pottery* (London: English Heritage, 1999).

Hume, Ivor Noël, *Archaeology and Weatherburn's Tavern* (Williamsburg, Virginia: Colonial Williamsburg Archaeology Series No. 3, 1969).

Hume, Ivor Noël, *Pottery and Porcelain in Colonial Williamsburg's Archaeological Collections* (Williamsburg, Virginia: Colonial Williamsburg, 1969).

Hume, Ivor Noël, 'The rise and fall of English white salt-glazed stoneware (Part I)' in *The Magazine Antiques*, February, 1970.

Kelso, William M., *Archaeology at Monticello* (Charlottesville, Virginia: Thomas Jefferson Memorial Foundation, Inc, 1997).

Liggett, Barbara, *Archaeology at New Market Exhibit Catalogue* (Philadelphia: The Athenaeum of Philadelphia, 1978).

Mason, Francis Norton, *John Norton and Sons Merchants of London and Virginia* second edition (Newton Abbot: David & Charles, 1968).

New Hampshire Gazette.

New York Gazette.

Pennsylvania Evening Post.

Pennsylvania Gazette.

Schiffer, Margaret B., *Chester County Pennsylvania Inventories 1684-1850* (Exton, Pennsylvania: Schiffer Publishing, 1974).

South, Stanley, *The Search for John Bartlam at Cain Hoy: America's First Creamware Potter* (Columbia, S.C.: University of South Carolina Research Manuscript Series 219, 1993).

Starbuck, David R., 'America's First Summer Resort: John Wentworth's 18th Century Plantation in Wolfboro, New Hampshire' in *The New Hampshire Archaeologist*, Vol. 30, No. 1, 1989.

Stone, Gary Wheeler et al., 'Ceramics from the John Hicks Site, 1723-1743: The Material Culture' in *Ceramics in America* (Winterthur Conference Report 1972).

Yentsch, Ann Elizabeth, *A Chesapeake Family and Their Slaves: A Study in Historical Archaeology* (Cambridge: Cambridge University Press, 1994).

Chapter VIII: The Collectors

Archer, Michael, *Delftware* (London: The Stationery Office, 1997).

Bateman, Robert, *Catalogue of a Loan Collection of Old English Pottery Exhibited at the Manchester Whitworth Institute 1911-1912* (Manchester: H. Rawson and Co., 1912).

Blunt, R., ed., *Cheyne Book of Chelsea China and Pottery* (London, 1924; repr. Menston, Yorkshire: EP Publishing, 1973).

Caygill, Marjorie and John Cherry, ed., *A.W. Franks Nineteenth-Century Collecting and the British Museum,* (London: The British Museum, 1997).

Earle, C., *The Earle Collection of Early Staffordshire Pottery illustrating over seven hundred different pieces* (London: Brown, n.d., preface dated 1915).

Eatwell, Ann, 'The Collectors' or Fine Arts Club 1857-1884; the first society for collectors of the decorative arts' in *Journal of the Decorative Arts Society*, 1994.

Elliot, W., 'Reproduction and Fakes of English Eighteenth-Century Ceramics' in *English Ceramic Circle Transactions*, No. 7, Vol. 2, 1939.

Grigsby, Leslie, 'Johan Nieuhoff's Embassy: inspiration for relief decoration on English stoneware and earthenware in *The Magazine Antiques*, January 1993.

Guest, Montague, *Lady Charlotte Schreiber's Journals* 2 Vol. (London: John Lane, 1911).

Hampson, Rodney and Eileen, 'Brownfields, Victorian Potters' in *Northern Ceramic Society Journal* Vol. 4, 1980-81, 177-218.

Hurst, A., *A Catalogue of the Boynton Collection of Yorkshire Pottery* (York: Yorkshire Philosophical Society, 1922).

Illustrated Catalogue of Early English Earthenware (London: Burlington Fine Arts Club, 1914).

The Incomparable Art English Pottery from the Thomas Greg Collection (Manchester: City Art Gallery, 1969).

Herbert and Sylvia Jacobs Collection of 18th and early 19th Century English Pottery, sale catalogue 24 January 1994 (New York: Christie's, 1994).

'The Jahn Sale' in *The Connoisseur*, January 1912, 60.

Kirgate, Thomas, *A Description of the Villa of Horace Walpole... at Strawberry Hill...* (1774, with additions in 1786). This is located in the National Art Library, Victoria and Albert Museum, London.

Luxmoore, C.F.C., *"Saltglaze" with The Notes of a Collector* (Exeter: Pollard, 1924, reprinted London: Holland Press, n.d., c.1970).

Mayo, H.J., 'The auction of Lord Revelstoke's collection' in *The Connoisseur*, January 1935, 55-56.

Mountford, A.R., *The Illustrated Guide to Staffordshire Salt-Glazed Stoneware* (London: Barrie & Jenkins, 1971).

Ogilby, John, *The Embassy to the Grand Tartar of Cham* (1671).

Rackham, Bernard, *Catalogue of the Glaisher Collection of Pottery & Porcelain* 2 Vol. (Cambridge: Cambridge University Press, 1935, repr. Woodbridge: Antique Collectors' Club, 1987).

Rackham, Bernard and Herbert Read, *English Pottery: Its Development from Early Times to the end of the Eighteenth Century* (London: Ernest Benn, 1924).

Taggart, Ross E., *The Frank P. and Harriet C. Burnap Collection of English Pottery in the William Rockhill Nelson Gallery* (Kansas City: Nelson Gallery-Atkins Museum, 1953, 2nd ed. 1967).

Willett, Henry, *Catalogue of a Collection of Pottery and Porcelain illustrating Popular British History* (London: HMSO, 1899).

Wilson, David M., *The Forgotten Collector* (London: Thames and Hudson, 1984).

Chapter IX: Thirteen potters and the pots they made
Appendix 2: Salt-Glaze Potters

There are no general works on this subject. The reader is referred to the endnotes for publications referring to individual potters.

Appendix 4: Patterns, Tiles and Shapes

Goodby, M., 'Moulds and Modellers in the Early 18th-century Staffordshire Potteries: Slip-Casting, Press-Moulding and the Wood Family' in *English Ceramic Circle Transactions* Vol. 17, Part 2, 2000, 216-28.

Luxmoore, C.F.C., *"Saltglaze" with The Notes of a Collector* (Exeter: Pollard, 1924 repr. London: Holland Press, n.d.).

Mallet, J.V.G. 'Rococo in English Ceramics' in *Rococo Art and Design in Hogarth's England* ed. M. Snodin (London: Trefoil Books/Victoria & Albert Museum, 1984) 236-42.

Mountford, A.R., *The Illustrated Guide to Staffordshire Salt-Glazed Stoneware* (London: Barrie & Jenkins, 1971).

Ray, A., 'Staffordshire Tiles 1750-1840' in *English Ceramic Circle Transactions* Vol. 15, Part 2, 1994, 194-204, 195-97.

References

CHAPTER I

1. David Gaimster, *German Stoneware 1200-1800* (London: British Museum Press, 1997), 33.
2. David Gaimster, lecture, Keele University, 1999.
3. Andrew Watts, lecture, Keele University, 1999.
4. According to Paul Rado, *An Introduction to the Technology of Pottery* (Oxford: Pergamon Press, 1969), 127, with bodies rich in iron the temperature in the kiln to which the salt is added may be as great as 1300 degrees centigrade.
5. Lucie B. Beebe, 'Rhenish Stoneware of the Renaissance', *American Ceramic Circle Bulletin*, Number 2, 1980, 126.
6. Gaimster, op. cit., 251.
7. Rhoda Edwards, 'London Potters circa 1570-1710', *Journal of Ceramic History*, No. 6, 1974, 57.
8. Ibid., 56.
9. Ibid., 57.
10. Ibid.
11. Gaimster, op. cit., 211.
12. Ibid., 314.
13. Richard Tyler, *Francis Place*, catalogue of the exhibition at the City Art Gallery, York, 9-28 Apr. 1971, 42.
14. Patricia M. Korry, 'Francis Place, Seventeenth-Century English Potter and Man of the Enlightenment', *Ars Ceramica*, Number 16, 2000, 40-41.
15. Unglazed white stoneware from Siegburg was imported into England as early as 1482. Adrian Oswald, R.J.C. Hildyard and R.G. Hughes, *English Brown Stoneware 1670-1900* (London: Faber and Faber, 1982), 18.
16. Gaimster, op. cit., 251.
17. PRO Patent Roll c66/3133 reprinted in Edwards, op. cit., 56.
18. For an excellent pre-excavation account of John Dwight and his contributions see Mavis Bimson, 'John Dwight', *English Ceramic Circle Transactions* Vol. 5, 1961.
19. Edwards, op. cit., 56.
20. Chris Green, *John Dwight's Fulham Pottery Excavations 1971-79* (London: English Heritage, 1999), 2.
21. Edwards, op. cit., 56.
22. Green, op. cit., 2.
23. Edwards, op. cit., 56.
24. John Ayres, Oliver Impey and J.V.G. Mallet, *Porcelain for Palaces* (London: Oriental Ceramic Society, 1990), 16.
25. Green, op. cit., 3.
26. Edwards, op. cit., 57.
27. Ibid.
28. Ibid., 58.
29. Jonathan Horne, *John Dwight Master Potter of Fulham 1672-1703 and his contemporaries*, exhibition catalogue, 1992.
30. Edwards, op. cit., 58-9.
31. Harwood A. Johnson, 'John Dwight of Fulham's Purchase of Land in Pennsylvania', *Ars Ceramica* Number 10, 1993, 21-25.
32. Kevin Fryer and Andrea Selley et al, *Excavation of a Pit at 16 Tunsgate, Guildford, Surrey, 1991* (Guildford Museum, reprinted from *Post-Medieval Archaeology*, Vol. 31, 1997, 184).
33. Ibid., 59.

CHAPTER II

1. Chris Green, *John Dwight's Fulham Pottery Excavations 1971-79* (London: English Heritage, 1999), 336.
2. Ibid., 135-7.
3. Examples of these wares can be seen at the Guimet Museum, Paris.
4. Robert Plot, *The Natural History of Staffordshire* (Oxford: 1676).
5. Ibid., as quoted by Arnold Mountford in his unpublished M.A. thesis 'Thomas Wedgwood, John Wedgwood and Josiah Malkin Potters of Burslem' (University of Keele, 1972).
6. Wedgwood MS 96/17695, reproduced in Josiah C. Wedgwood, *Staffordshire Pottery and Its History* (London: Sampson, Low, Marston & Co., Ltd (ND) 1912, 1923), 49-53. The J.C. Wedgwood account says that Josiah Wedgwood produced this account in 1765 (p.48). The document clearly has a date of 1776 written in Wedgwood's hand although it is added later, or written with a darker ink. No other date exists on the document.
7. Ibid.
8. Simeon Shaw, *History of the Staffordshire Potteries* (New York: Praeger Publishers, 1970; originally published for the author in Hanley, 1829), 161.
9. Arnold Mountford, op. cit., 46.
10. Ibid.
11. Lorna Weatherill, *The Pottery Trade and North Staffordshire 1660-1760* (Manchester: Manchester University Press, 1971), 38.
12. Maurice Hillis, 'An Introduction to Ceramic Raw Materials, Bodies and Glazes', *Northern Ceramic Society Journal*, Vol. 18, 2001, 89.
13. Ivor Noël Hume, 'The rise and fall of English white salt-glazed stoneware', *The Magazine Antiques*, Feb., 1970, 17.
14. Wedgwood MS 96/17695.
15. Wedgwood MS WM 947, 24 Jun. 1731.
16. Shaw, op. cit., 150-2.
17. Miranda Goodby, 'Early 18th-century Staffordshire Moulds and Modellers,' *ECC Transactions* Vol.17, Part 2, 2000, 223.
18. Glaisher Collection #532.
19. British Museum G50.
20. Illustrated also by Arnold Mountford, *The Illustrated Guide to Staffordshire Salt-Glazed Stoneware* (London: Barrie & Jenkins, 1971), Pl. 222.
21. Major Cyril Earle, *The Earle Collection of Early Staffordshire Pottery* (London: A. Brown and Sons, Limited, 1915), Pl. 63.
22. Ibid., Pl. 60.
23. A.H. Church, *English Earthenware A Handbook to the Wares made in England during the Seventeenth and Eighteenth Centuries as illustrated by specimens in the National Collections* Part 1 (London: Committee of Council on Education, 1884), 57.
24. Wedgwood MS 96/17695.
25. A.R. Mountford, op. cit., 55. The Thomas and John Wedgwood and Jonah Malkin papers are in the Potteries Museum, Stoke-on-Trent, MS Ceram., No.4.
26. Llewellynn Jewitt, *Ceramic Art in Great Britain* Vol. II (New York: Scribner, Welford and Armstrong, 1878), 415-6.
27. The figures are derived from the Retail Price Index compiled by the Bank of England in Mar. 1999.
28. 'The Prices of Sundry Goods at London, 15 Mar. 1745/6', Winterthur MS, 74 x 118.
29. The London *Daily Advertiser*, 24 Aug. 1747, advertised a 'great variety of curious Tea-Pots…'.
30. Jewitt, op. cit., 416. The original account book is in the Potteries Museum, Stoke-on-Trent.
31. 11 Sept. 1755. This information is not contained in the Whieldon notebook in the Potteries Museum. It was obtained from the Duke of Bedford's private papers and we are grateful to Tom Walford for sharing it with us.
32. Ibid.
33. Linda Colley et al, *Rococo Art and Design in Hogarth's England* (London: Victoria and Albert Museum, 1984), 254.
34. London *Daily Advertiser*, 26-29 Nov. 1757.
35. 22 Jul. 1760 as quoted in David Barker, *William Greatbatch a Staffordshire Potter* (London: Jonathan Horne, 1990), 44-5.
36. Wedgwood MSS 55/30426, 29 Aug. 1761. *John Brindley* sold Messrs Jos & Richard Marsh '6 Dishes Gadrooned 13 Inches 0.3.6; 1 March 1762 2 [ditto] Mosake 15 [Inches] 0.2.0'; Josiah Wedgwood was buying in Gadrooned and 'Mos[ai]k' dishes from *John Smith* in Sept. 1762 (30/22966.)
37. Wedgwood MS 6/5047, 14 May 1752. The added shillings in superscript have a note appended which says 'Charged at London', presumably transportation costs.
38. Wedgwood MSS 6/ 31324, 20 Dec. 1762; 6/5028, 22 Apr., 25 May 1763.
39. Wedgwood MSS 6/5030, 21 Oct. 1762-4 Nov. 1763; 6/5032, 10 May 1764.
40. Wedgwood MSS 6/31324, 20 Dec. 1762; 6/5032, 10 May 1764.
41. Wedgwood MSS 31/30563, (n.d.) Mar. 1766; 31/30564, 17 Apr. 1766; 31/23001 (n.d.);31/23002, 20 Sept. 1768.
42. Wedgwood MS 30/22836, *Ralph Bucknall*,

Cobridge, 1775.
43. Hilary Young, *English Porcelain 1745-95* (London: V&A Publications, 1999), 82.
44. Syz, Miller and Rückert, *Catalogue of The Hans Syz Collection (*Washington, D.C.: Smithsonian Institution Press, 1979), 382.
45. Wedgwood MS 30/22888.
46. Wedgwood MS 30/22972, 8 Sept. 1763.
47. Wedgwood MSS 30/22836; 30/22842 (n.d.) 1775, 1780 *Ralph Bucknall*, Cobridge.
48. Wedgwood MS 30/22838, *Ralph Bucknall & Son*, Cobridge, 1777.
49. Wedgwood MS 11/9363, Josiah Wedgwood was buying in from *John Hales* '6 Oblongs bask't work 17 In. Best 0.10.0' 31 on Oct. 1763.
50. Wedgwood MS 31/23013, 31 Jul. 1764.
51. Wedgwood MS 6/30442, 27 Jun. 1763.
52. Wedgwood MSS 30/22971-22977, 31 Aug. 1763-10 Nov. 1764.
53. Wedgwood MSS 31/30920, 5 Oct.1763; 31/23025, 3 Feb. 1763.
54. Wedgwood MS 6/30461, 5 Dec. 1768.
55. Wedgwood MS 6/30932, 10 May 1768.
56. Wedgwood MS 10/30902, 1 Jun. 1768.
57. Wedgwood MS 52/9484, 12 Feb. 1770.
58. Wedgwood MSS 30/22921-22923, *Joseph Blackwell* 1781.

CHAPTER III
1. The population figures are approximate, based on Gregory King's well-informed estimates (published in 1696). The first census in Britain was 1801. Michael Reed, *The Making of Britain The Georgian Triumph 1700-1830* (London: Routledge & Kegan Paul, 1983), 10.
2. Asa Briggs, *A Social History of England* (New York: The Viking Press, 1983), 151.
3. Reed, op. cit., 12.
4. Ibid., 1.
5. Edwina Ehrman *et al, London Eats Out 500 Years of Capital Dining* (Museum of London: Philip Wilson Publisher, 1999), 31-33.
6. E. Beresford Chancellor, *The XVIIIth Century in London* (London: B.T. Batsford, Ltd., 1920), 120.
7. Ehrman, op. cit., 35.
8. Phillipa Glanville and Hilary Young, *Elegant Eating, Four hundred years of dining in style* (London: V & A Publications, 2002), 110.
9. Ehrman, op. cit., 46.
10. Ibid.
11. Briggs, op. cit., 151.
12. Reed, op. cit., 12.
13. Ehrman, op. cit., 110.
14. Glanville and Young, op. cit., 108.
15. Diana Edwards, *Tea and Sympathy Post-Revolutionary Ceramics in the Stamford Historical Society* (Stamford, Ct: Stamford Historical Society, 1981), 6.
16. Invoice from John Fleetwood, Leadenhall Street, London, 10 Oct. 1757. Winterthur MS 60 x 8.12.
17. Wedgwood MS 6/31150, 23 Feb. 1764.
18. Glanville and Young, op. cit., 7.
19. Inventory of the estate of Henry Troth (Talbot County, Maryland), Maryland State Archives, Maryland Inventories Vol. 14, 346.
20. Neil McKendrick, John Brewer and J.H. Plumb, *The Birth of a Consumer Society* (Bloomington: Indiana University Press, 1985), 197.
21. Tom Parker Bowles, 'Eating Their Words: Modern British Food Writers', *Books and Company* Issue 13, 2002, 60-1.
22. E. Lipson, *The Growth of English Society* (London: A. and C. Black, 1959 (First Ed. 1949), 89.
23. Creamware did not, as suggested in *Elegant Eating*, 11, supplant pewter on the dining table. Salt-glazed stoneware and delftware both intervened.
24. D.F. Lunsingh Scheurleer, *Chinese Export Porcelain Chine de Commande* (New York: Pitman Publishing Corporation, 1974), 57-8.
25. Howard Coutts, *The Art of Ceramics, European Ceramic Design 1500-1830* (New Haven and London: Yale University Press, 2001), 66.
26. Glanville and Young, op. cit., 48.
27. Ibid., 49.
28. There is no evidence that the dinner 'sets' of Chinese porcelain in the 17th century were matching services as were known in the 18th century, but groups of porcelains with different decoration which probably complemented each other.
29. Duke of Bedford papers, Woburn, 11 Sept. 1755. The authors thank Tom Walford for providing this information.
30. Duke of Bedford papers, 23 Jan. 1756.
31. Lipson, op. cit., 111.
32. Briggs, op. cit., 164-6.
33. Ibid., 169.
34. Lipson, op. cit., 103.
35. Lorna Weatherill, *The Pottery Trade and North Staffordshire 1660-1760* (Manchester University Press, 1971), 87.

CHAPTER IV
1. D. Gaimster, *German Stoneware 1200-1900 Archaeological and Cultural History* (London: British Museum Press, 1997), 167, 251.
2. D. Barker, *Slipware* (Princes Risborough: Shire Publications, 1993), 8.
3. D. Gage and M. Marsh, *Tobacco Containers & Accessories Their Place in Eighteenth Century European Social History* (London: Gage Bluett, 1988), 11-12, 17.
4. B.H. Charles, *Pottery and Porcelain A Dictionary of Terms* (Newton Abbot: David & Charles, 1974), 22.
5. Anon, 'Ball Clays Their Occurrence, Extraction, and Uses in the Ceramic Industries' in *Ceramics* Vol. V, Jul. 1953, 204-10, 206-07.
6. *Mineral Dossier No. 11 Ball Clay* comp. D.E. Highley (London: HMSO, 1975), 3; *The Geology of Devon* ed. E.M. Durrance and D.J.C. Laming (Exeter: University of Exeter, 1982), 293.
7. F. Singer and S.S. Singer, *Industrial Ceramics* (London: Chapman & Hall, 1963), 35-41.
8. B.H. Charles, op. cit., 22. 'Secondary' distinguishes sedimentary clays, found away from their primary source; ibid., 232.
9. D.A. Holdridge, 'Ball Clays and their Properties' in *Transactions of the British Ceramic Society* Vol. 55, 1956, 369-440; and 'Composition Variation in Ball Clays' in Vol. 58, 1959, 645-59. See also P.S. Keeling, 'A Geologist looks at Clay' in *The A.T. Green Book* (British Ceramic Research Association, 1959), 94-100.
10. R. Edwards, 'London Potters circa 1570-1710' in *Journal of Ceramic History* No. 6, 1974, 1-139, 56-59.
11. 'John Dwight's Fulham Pottery 1672-1978 A Collection of Documentary Sources' ed. D. Haselgrove and John Murray in *Journal of Ceramic History* No. 11, 1979, 1-284, 48.
12. R.P[lot], *The Natural History of Oxford-shire, Being an Essay toward the Natural History of England* (Oxford, 1677), 250-51.
13. L. Weatherill and R. Edwards, 'Pottery Making in London and Whitehaven in the Late Seventeenth Century' in *Post-Medieval Archaeology* Vol. 5, 1971, 160-81, 163, 164.
14. J.P.M. Latham, 'Dorset Clay to Staffordshire Pot' in *English Ceramic Circle Transactions* Vol. 10, Part 2, 1977, 109-17, 109.
15. A.R. Mountford & F. Celoria, 'Some examples of sources in the history of 17th Century Ceramics' in *Journal of Ceramic History* No. 1, 1968, 1-27, 2,3.
16. *Statutes at Large* (London, 1809), Vol. VIII, 42.
17. T.S. Willan, *The English Coasting Trade 1600-1750* (Manchester: Manchester University Press, 1938), 44, 156. Willan points out that 'although only 212 tons [of the 2,215 tons] were specified as 'tobacco-pipe clay', it seems probable that most, if not all, of the clay was for making pipes'. Dorset also produced stoneware clay, and it is possible that some of the 2,215 tons of clay sent to London in 1691 was for Dwight and other London stoneware potters to make their coarser ware. In half a year in 1749, Poole shipped 1,135 tons of pipe clay to London.
18. York was a major tobacco-pipe making centre in the second half of the 17th century, *vide* D. Barker, 'The Newcastle-under-Lyme Clay Tobacco Pipe Industry' in *BAR* British Series 146, 1985, 237-89, 239.
19. *R R Angerstein's Illustrated Travel Diary 1753-1755 Industry in England and Wales from a Swedish perspective* trans. T. and P. Berg (London: Science Museum, 2001), 200.
20. A.C. Wood, 'The History of Trade and Transport on the River Trent' in *Transactions of the Thoroton Society* Vol. LIV, 1950, 1-44, 18: 'The first boat … reached Derby in Jan. 1721'.
21. S. Muspratt, *Chemistry, Theoretical, Practical and Analytical* multi-vol. (Glasgow: Mackenzie, 1860), 826; K. Hudson *The History of English China Clays Fifty Years of Pioneering and Growth* (Newton Abbot: David & Charles, n.d., c.1970), 31.
22. R.P. [Robert Plot], *The Natural History of Oxford-shire…* (Oxford, 1677), 56, 65-66, 250.
23. R. Plot, *The Natural History of Stafford-shire* (Oxford, 1686), 121-23.
24. In 1829, S. Shaw located Plot's 'between Shelton and Hanley green' as 'Filcher's and Kirkham's marl pits' in his *History of the Staffordshire Potteries…* (privately, 1829, rep. Newton Abbot: David & Charles, 1970), 123.
25. Haselgrove and Murray, op. cit., 69-71, 95, 104, 122.
26. Ibid., 122.
27. Ibid., 69-71, 125.
28. W. Pitt, *A Topographical History of Stafford-shire…* (Newcastle-under-Lyme: Smith, 1817), 415-16.
29. Ibid., 417.
30. A. Grant, *North Devon Pottery: The Seventeenth Century* (Exeter: University of Exeter, 1983), 37-39, 95.
31. A.P. Wakelin, *Pre-industrial trade on the River Severn: a computer-aided study of the Gloucester Port Books* (Wolverhampton: Wolverhampton University, 1991), passim.
32. D. Defoe, *A Tour Through the Whole Island of Great Britain,* 2 vol. (1724-26, rep. London: Dent, 1928, rev. 1962), I, 261.
33. Shaw, op. cit., 69, 124, 125, 160.
34. Ibid., 125, 149.
35. Chester was a major tobacco-pipe making

centre in the second half of the 17th century, *vide* D. Barker, 1985, op cit., 237-89, 239.
36. L.T.C. Rolt, *The Potters' Field A History of the South Devon Ball Clay Industry* (Newton Abbot: David & Charles, 1974), 24-25.
37. S. Shaw described the carriage of ball clay by trains of five horses, each horse with two panniers, each holding two or three balls weighing sixty or seventy pounds, see Shaw, op. cit., 149.
38. T.S. Willan, 'The Navigation of the River Weaver in the Eighteenth Century' in *Remains Historical and Literary connected with the Palatine Counties of Lancaster and Chester* Vol. III Third series, 1951, Chapter I.
39. Ibid., 31.
40. L. Weatherill, *The Pottery Trade and North Staffordshire 1660-1760* (Manchester: Manchester University Press, 1971), 16.
41. H.J. Trump, *Teignmouth A Maritime History* 2nd ed. (Chichester: Phillimore, 1986), 48. 550,000 tons of pipe clay were exported from Teignmouth in 1995 (information from Teignmouth Museum).
42. J.A. Bulley, 'The beginnings of the Devonshire Ball-Clay Trade' in *Transactions of the Devonshire Association* Vol. LXXVII, 1955, 191-204, 195, 204. Three ships with pipe clay from Teignmouth/Exeter (and one from Belfast) arrived at Liverpool in one month in 1756, *vide* L. Burman, 'Excerpts from Williamson's Liverpool Advertiser and Mercantile Register - 1756' in *English Ceramic Circle Transactions* Vol. 17, Part 1, 1999, 34-46, 36-38.
43. Rolt, op. cit., 39.
44. Ibid., 39.
45. Berg, op. cit., 339.
46. R. Copeland, *A short history of pottery raw materials and the Cheddleton Flint Mill* (Leek: Cheddleton Flint Mill Industrial Heritage Trust, 1972).
47. J.R. Taylor and A.C. Bull, *Ceramics Glaze Technology* (Oxford: Pergamon, 1986), 16: 'Silica is the major glass-former'.
48. F. Singer and S.J. Singer, op. cit., 598.
49. Haselgrove and Murray, op. cit., 48.
50. Ibid., XVII, *Ai, Biv, Bvi*.
51. Ibid., 143, 144.
52. Plot, 1686, op. cit., 168; Pitt, op. cit., 417.
53. Berg, op. cit., 341.
54. F. Celoria, 'Techniques of White Salt-Glaze Stoneware Manufacture in North Staffordshire Around 1765' in *Science and Archaeology* no. 18, 1976, 25-28, 25.
55. H. Young, 'Evidence for Wood and Coal firing and the Design of Kilns in the 18th-century English Porcelain Industry' in *English Ceramic Circle Transactions* Vol. 17, Part 1, 1999, 1-14, 9-11. We are grateful to Dr. Helen Smith for the translation of the notes.
56. Josiah Wedgwood told the story to his partner Thomas Bentley on 19 Jul. 1777. (R. Hampson, 'Josiah Wedgwood I Ceramic Historian' in *Ars Ceramica* No. 5, 1988, 22-25, 23.)
57. Biographical information is from M.W. Greenslade, 'The Staffordshire Historians' in *Collections for a History of Staffordshire* Fourth Series, Volume Eleven, 1982, 84-97.
58. Wellcome Institute for the Study of Medicine, 183 Euston Road, London, NW1 2BP, reference MS 5006: Richard Wilkes (1691-1760), Diary and Observations from 1 Jan. 1739 to 7 Jul. 1754. Copied from the original by Richard Wilkes Unett, Wolverhampton, c.1790, pages 11 and 12. (The original text is not known to have survived.)
59. There was a Cock Inn at Redbourn, Hertfordshire, between at least 1636 and 1781 (Hertfordshire Archives, parish cards). Redbourn is on Watling Street, now the A5 road, between Dunstable and Luton.
60. Berg, op. cit., 200, 339.
61. *Lake and Rastall's Textbook of Geology* 5th ed., rev. R.H. Rastall (London: Arnold, 1941), 177.
62. East Sussex Record Office: SAS/HC 277, Manor of Meeching Court Book 1736-1780, 70.
63. J. Collard, *Maritime History of Rye* (1978), 77, 79; E. Houldsworth, 'Blue Boulders A Little Known Sussex Industry' in *Sussex County Magazine* Vol. 14, 1940, 17-18; 'He Collects Blue Flints' in *Sussex County Magazine* Vol. 29, 1955, 356.
64. Celoria, op. cit., 25.
65. Wedgwood MS 26/19117.
66. Wedgwood MSS 9/7220, 9/7239-40. Gravesend lay within the Port of London for Customs purposes, see E. Hasted, *The History and Topographical Survey of the County of Kent* 4 vol. (Canterbury: privately, 1778), I, 450.
67. Wedgwood MS 11/31161, 11/9338.
68. Staffordshire Record Office: D 1788, Vol. 99, 96-97.
69. E. Adams, 'Ceramic Insurances in the Sun Company, 1766-1774' in *English Ceramic Circle Transactions* Vol. 10, Part I, 1976, 17, 27.
70. J. Mallet, 'John Baddeley of Shelton, an Early Staffordshire Maker of Pottery and Porcelain, Part I' in *English Ceramic Circle Transactions* Vol. 6, Part 2 1966, 124-66, 141.
71. A. Young, *A Six Months Tour through the North of England...* 4 Vol. (London: Strahan, 1770), III, 307.
72. Quoted by G. Wills, 'Ceramic Causerie' in *Apollo* Vol. LXIX, Feb. 1959, 46.
73. Weatherill, op. cit., 255.
74. Flint preparation is outside the scope of this work. See Copeland, op. cit., for an authoritative and accessible account.
75. *Patents for Inventions Abridgments of the Specifications relating to Pottery* (London: Great Seal Patent Office, 1863), 4, A.D. 1726, 5 Nov. – No. 487.
76. *Burslem Parish Register* 3 vol. (Staffordshire Parish Registers Society, 1913), I, 168.
77. Lichfield Record Office: *Samuel Edge*, will made 20 Feb. 1720-21, proved 9 May 1721.
78. See L. Weatherill, 'Technical Change and Potters' Inventories 1660-1760' in *Journal of Ceramic History* No. 3 1970, 3-12, 5.
79. Staffordshire Record Office: D 1788, pcl. 67, bdle. 22.
80. *Patents for Inventions Abridgments of the Specifications relating to Pottery*. (London: Great Seal Patent Office, 1863) 4, A.D. 1726, 5 Nov. – No. 487; 5-6, A.D. 1732, 14 Jan. No. 536.
81. Lichfield Record Office: will of *John Meir*, proved 24 Jun. 1729.
82. W.D. Meredith, 'Water Mills in North Staffordshire' in *North Staffordshire Journal of Field Studies* Vol. 4, 1964, 1-10, 4-10. B. Job 'The Grinding of Flint and Bone' in *Journal of the Staffordshire Industrial Archaeology Society* No. 13, 1989, 20-28, lists nine Staffordshire flint and bone mills which remained substantially intact in 1985. B. Job, *Watermills of the Moddershall Valley* (Newcastle-under-Lyme: privately, n.d., c.1985) is a detailed study of these mills.
83. Stoke-on-Trent City Archives: SD 4842/11/1/68-69, Indentures 31 Jul., 4 Nov. 1732, Procters to Peat.
84. Ibid.: SD 4842/11/1/68-69, Indenture 1745, Peate and Bagnall to Hatrell.
85. *A History of the County of Stafford* ed. J.G. Jenkins, multi-vol. (London: Oxford University Press, 1963), VIII, 218.
86. Berg, op. cit., 339.
87. K.M. Evans, *James Brindley Canal Engineer* (Leek: Churnet Valley Books, 1997), 31-35.
88. B. Woodcroft, *An Alphabetical Index of Patentees of Inventions* (1858, repr. New York: Kelley, 1969), No. 730, 27 Sept. 1758.
89. C.T.G. Boucher, *James Brindley Engineer 1716-1772* (Norwich: Goose, 1968), 31.
90. Staffordshire Record Office: D 1788 pcl. 31, bdle. 12 pt.
91. Ibid.: within D 1788, Aqualate papers. J. Mallet has written at length on Baddeley's flint-milling activities in 'John Baddeley of Shelton, an Early Staffordshire Maker of Pottery and Porcelain Parts I and II' in *English Ceramic Circle Transactions* Vol. 6, Part 2, 1966, 124-66, Part 3, 1967, 181-247, see 203-06.
92. Shaw, op. cit., 199.
93. See International Genealogical Index, *Staffordshire*, 1992.
94. *Wolstanton Parish Registers* 2 parts (Staffordshire Parish Registers Society, 1914), Part 1, 233, Baptisms 1725/26 Feb. John s. of Ralph & Sarah *Baddeley*.
95. *A History of the County of Stafford* ed. J.G. Jenkins, multi-vol (London: Oxford University Press, 1963), VIII, 218.
96. Staffordshire Record Office: D 1788: pcl. 14 bdle. 2 pt.: Indenture 1 Sept. 1761.
97. Ibid.: pcl. 14 bdle. 2 pt.: Attested copy of Mr. *John Baddeley's* will, 2 Feb. 1771.
98. Ibid.: Vol. 97; Vol. 99, pp. 96-97.
99. Ibid.: pcl 1, bdle. 1, *John Baddeley's* letters, 17 Dec. 1763; Vol. 97, p.3; Vol. 99, pp. 96-97.
100. Ibid: Vol. 97, loose sheet.
101. Ibid.: Vol. 99, pp. 96-97.
102. Ibid.: pcl. 1, bdle. 1, *John Baddeley's* letters, 16 Mar. 1763; Vol. 97, p.3 and loose sheet.
103. Ibid.: pcl. 1, bdle. 1, *John Baddeley's* letters, 6 Oct. 1763.
104. Ibid.: pcl. 1, bdle. 1, *John Baddeley's* letters, 15 Jun. 1764.
105. Ibid.: pcl. 1, bdle. 1, *John Baddeley's* letters, 14 Jan. 1762.
106. Ibid.: pcl. 1, bdle. 1, *John Baddeley's* letters, Statement of charges at Liverpool.
107. Ibid.: Vol. 97, p.28.
108. Ibid.: pcl. 1, bdle. 1, *John Baddeley's* letters, 6 Oct. 1763, and many other references, to Vol. 99, pp. 96-97, 1767.
109. Ibid.: pcl. 1, bdle. 1, *John Baddeley's* letters, Receipt 22 Nov. 1762.
110. Ibid.: Vol. 95, 23 Nov. 1762.
111. Ibid.: Vol. 95.
112. Ibid.: Vol. 98.
113. Ibid.: Vol. 95.
114. Ibid.: Vol. 97, pp. 26, 28.
115. Ibid.: Vol. 95.
116. Ibid.: pcl. 14 bdle. 2 pt.: Indenture 1 Sept. 1761.
117. Ibid.: pcl. 14 bdle. 2 pt.: Attested copy of *John Baddeley's* will, 2 Feb. 1771.
118. A 'peck' is a dry measure, a fourth part of a bushel, or two gallons *(OED)*. It is also defined as 16 pints in volume.

119. Gaimster, op. cit., 33, 47, 46, 356-57.
120. Ibid., 44, 211, 310, 313.
121. Ibid., 310, 311, 314-15.
122. Haselgrove and Murray, op. cit., 138.
123. *A History of the County of Stafford* ed. M.W. Greenslade and J.G. Jenkins, multi-vol. (London: Oxford University Press, 1967), II, 247-51.
124. Defoe, op. cit., I, 261.
125. *The Travels through England of Dr. Richard Pococke…* ed. J.J. Cartwright 2 vol. (London: Camden Society, 1881), I, 8.
126. W.H. Chaloner, 'Salt in Cheshire, 1600-1870' in *Transactions of the Lancashire and Cheshire Antiquarian Society* Vol. 71, 1961, 58-74, 62.
127. W. Smith and W. Webb, *The Vale Royall of England or, The County Palatine of Chester…* (1656, rep. Congleton: Heads, 1990), II, 66.
128. Chaloner, op. cit., 65.
129. Willan, 1951, op. cit., 2-3.
130. W.B. Crump. 'Saltways from the Cheshire Wiches' in *Transactions of the Lancashire and Cheshire Antiquarian Society* Vol. 54, 1939, 84-102, 97.
131. Wedgwood MS 55/9839.
132. Staffordshire Record Office: D 1788, vol. 96.
133. F. Britton, *London Delftware* (London: Horne, 1987), 190. 'Bay salt' is salt obtained in large crystals by slow evaporation, originally salt obtained from sea water by the sun's heat *(OED)*.
134. Confirmed by Pitt, op. cit., 417: 'as many bushels of salt as there were mouths or fire-places to the oven (7 or 8)'. The equivalence of 56lbs to the bushel of salt was confirmed in the 1780s by R. Watson *Chemical Essays* 5 vol. (London: Evans, 1784) II, 43.
135. Wedgwood MSS 10/8003, 129/25597-25600.
136. When the contents of John Gilbert's earthenware pottery in Burslem was offered by auction in 1803, 'Rock Salt' was amongst the Raw Materials (Potteries Museum and Art Gallery, Ceramics Department: Enoch Wood Scrapbook, 73). John Gilbert's father, also John (1724-95), had a share in Marston rock salt pits (Chaloner, op. cit., 71-72). It is possible that the younger John Gilbert held a stock of salt in Burslem to sell for any purpose.
137. Celoria, op. cit., 27, 28. 'Sea salt is 'salt obtained by evaporation of sea water' *(OED)*.
138. L. Jewitt, *The Wedgwoods: being a Life of Josiah Wedgwood …* (London: Virtue, 1865), 162-63.
139. E. Hughes, *Studies in Administration and Finance 1558-1825 with special reference to the history of salt taxation in England* (Manchester: Manchester University Press, 1934), 297, duty of 5d. per gallon from 1732. From 1826, a (British) bushel is eight Imperial gallons dry measure *(OED)*, but it has varied in the past. Berg, op. cit., 244, 312, 318 quotes salt duty as 3s.2d. in 1754.
140. Calculated from the 'near £5,000 duty' paid on salt used for glazing in North Staffordshire c.1761, which equates to 30,000 bushels at 3s.4d. per bushel (of 56 lbs.). A note of salt duty payable in 1694 in the Account Book of Shrewbridge Salt Works Nantwich states 'rate of 12 pence p. Bushell allowing 56 lb weight to the Bushell' (Cheshire Record Office: DCH/Z/35). This equivalence of 56lbs to the bushel was confirmed in the 1780s by Watson, op. cit., II, 43.

CHAPTER V

1. *R R Angerstein's Illustrated Travel Diary 1753-1755, Industry in England and Wales from a Swedish perspective*, trans. T. and P. Berg (London: Science Museum, 2001).
2. B. Dragesco, *English Ceramics in French Archives The writings of Jean Hellot, the adventures of Jacques Louis Brolliet and the identification of the 'Girl-in-a-Swing' factory* (London, 1993), *passim*.
3. F. Celoria, 'Techniques of White Salt-Glaze Stoneware Manufacture in North Staffordshire around 1765' in *Science and Archaeology* no. 18, 1976, 25-28.
4. H. Young, 'Evidence for Wood and Coal firing and the Design of Kilns in the 18th-century English Porcelain Industry' in *English Ceramic Circle Transactions* Vol. 17, Part 1, 1999, 1-14, 9-11.
5. R. Watson, *Chemical Essays,* 5 vol. (London: Evans, 1784), Vol. II, 259-60.
6. R. Plot, *The Natural History of Stafford-shire* (Oxford: 1686, rep. Didsbury: Morten, 1973), 122-24.
7. Staffordshire Record Office: D 1788 pcl. 33, bdle. 1. Thomas Basset was vicar of Barlaston from 1688 to his death in 1717 (*Barlaston Parish Register 1573-1812* (Staffordshire Parish Registers Society, 1905), iv, 52).
8. C. Green, *John Dwight's Fulham Pottery Excavations 1971-79* (London: English Heritage, 1999).
9. Ibid., 20, Figs. 16, 17.
10. 'John Dwight's Fulham Pottery 1672-1978. A Collection of Documentary Sources' ed. D. Haselgrove and J. Murray, in *Journal of Ceramic History* No. 11, 1979, 144-45.
11. Plot, op. cit., 123.
12. S. Shaw, *History of the Staffordshire Potteries…* (Hanley; privately, 1829, rep. Newton Abbot: David & Charles 1970), 162.
13. A.E. Dodd, *Dictionary of Ceramics* 2nd. ed. (London: Newnes, 1967), 343.
14. Ibid., 5.
15. Dragesco, op. cit., 7.
16. Berg, op. cit., 200, 310.
17. Celoria, 'North Staffordshire', op. cit., 25.
18. Berg, op. cit., 200, Fig. 190.
19. Ibid., 339, Figs. 316, 317.
20. Celoria, 'North Staffordshire', op. cit., 25-26.
21. Ibid., 25.
22. Watson, op. cit., II, 259-60.
23. H. Young, 1999, op. cit., 9-11. We are grateful to Dr. Helen Smith for the translation of the notes.
24. Green, op. cit., 131. It is suggested (40, 131, 132, 135-39) that these dipped wares were the same as the 'double-glazed' wares made later, but 'double-glazing' hardly describes what is single dipping with clay.
25. Plot, op. cit., 123.
26. W. Pitt, *A Topographical History of Stafford-shire…* (Newcastle-under-Lyme: Smith, 1817), 417.
27. Wedgwood MS 96/17695.
28. Shaw, op. cit., 126-27.
29. A.R. Mountford, *The Illustrated Guide to Staffordshire Salt-Glazed Stoneware* (London: Barrie & Jenkins, 1971), 36.
30. Shaw, op. cit., 98-99.
31. Berg, op. cit., 303.
32. P.C.D. Brears, *The English Country Pottery Its History and Techniques* (Newton Abbot: David & Charles, 1971), 91.
33. G. Agricola, *De Re Metallica* (1550) trans. H.C. Hoover and L.H. Hoover (London: Mining Magazine, 1912; rep. New York: Dover, 1950), 548-50.
34. J. Hall, *A History of the Town and Parish of Nantwich…* (privately, 1883, rep. Didsbury: Morten, 1972), 32, 260-62.
35. Haselgrove and Murray, op. cit., 73-77, Bv.
36. Staffordshire Record Office: D (W) 1788, pcl. 61, bdle. 41. There is no positive evidence that John Middleton made white salt-glazed stoneware.
37. *Patents for Inventions: Abridgments of the Specifications relating to Pottery* (London: Commissioners of Patents, 1863), 82: A.D. 1853, 14 Jul. – No. 1669, Needham, William and Kite, James.
38. E.A. Sandeman, *Notes on the Manufacture of Earthenware* (London: Virtue, 1901), 38-39.
39. F. Celoria, 'North Staffordshire', op. cit., 25-26; and 'Techniques of Pottery-making at Newcastle-upon-Tyne in 1765' in *Science and Archaeology* no. 18, 1976, 20-24, 22.
40. K. Boney, 'Liverpool saltglazed wares' in *English Ceramic Circle Transactions* Vol. 4, Part 2, 1957, 51-57, 52.
41. Berg, op. cit., 206.
42. See Chapter VI. Wedgwood MSS 10/30168-30171.
43. See W.B. Honey, 'English Saltglazed Stoneware' in *English Ceramic Circle Transactions* No. 1, 1933, 12-22, 16.
44. British Museum: Add MSS 15,800.
45. Berg, op. cit., 341.
46. Angerstein does not mention casting, but that may only mean that he did not observe it, not that it was not being done in 1754.
47. Might Angerstein have originally written 'Ash', a term used by Staffordshire potters? Aware that Angerstein's notes have been both transcribed and translated, it is tempting to conveniently interpret his words!
48. Berg, op. cit., 338, 341.
49. A.R. Mountford, 'Thomas Wedgwood, John Wedgwood and Jonah Malkin Potters of Burslem', unpublished MA Thesis, Keele University, 1972, 74, Appendix IV, 17, 18, 19, 20, 30, 41, 42, 43.
50. See Mountford, 1971, op. cit., plates 19-29.
51. M. Goodby, 'the Lost Collection of Enoch Wood' in *Journal of the Northern Ceramic Society* Vol. 9, 1992, 123-51, 145 for 1835; F. Falkner, *The Wood Family of Burslem* (London: Chapman and Hall, 1912, repr. East Ardsley: EP Publishing, 1972), 73 for 1836.
52. H. De La Beche and T. Reeks, *Catalogue of Specimens illustrative of the Composition and Manufacture of British Pottery and Porcelain…* (London: Museum of Practical Geology, 1855), xiv, 123-24.
53. Plot, op. cit., 123.
54. See Mountford, 1971, op. cit., plate 48.
55. R. Campbell, *The London Tradesman…* (London: Gardner, 1747, repr. Newton Abbot: David & Charles, 1969), 184-85.
56. Berg, op. cit., 304, Fig. 283.
57. Ibid., 341, Fig. 319a II. The great wheel is one where a person turns a large vertical pulley, driving an endless cord around a smaller horizontal pulley on the throwing-wheel shaft.
58. Celoria, 'North Staffordshire', op. cit., 26.
59. A. Young, *A Six Months Tour through the North of England…* 4 vol. (London: Strahan, 1770), III, 308.
60. R. Reilly, *Wedgwood* 2 vol. (London: Macmillan, 1989), I, 437.
61. J. Aikin *A Description of the Country from*

Thirty to Forty Miles round Manchester (London: Stockdale, 1795, repr. New York: Kelley, 1968 (author erroneously shown as Aiken)), 528; Wedgwood MS WM 1858, quoted in R. Hampson, 'Josiah Wedgwood I Ceramic Historian' in *Ars Ceramica* No. 5 1988, 22-25, 25.
62. L.F. Salzman, *English Industries of the Middle Ages* new ed. (London: Pordes, 1970), 139, 172.
63. See F. Britton, *London Delftware* (London: Horne, 1987), 190-92, App. III, The Inventory of Nathaniel Oade (1726-27); 'The Pickleherring Potteries: an inventory [1699]' in *Post-Medieval Archaeology* 24, 1990, 61-92; 'Delftware Inventories' in *English Ceramic Circle Transactions* Vol. 15, Part 1, 1993, 59-64, 62-64, Appendix I, Gravel Lane Inventory [1726-27]. No lathes were listed.
64. G. Elliott, *John and David Elers and their Contemporaries* (London: Horne, 1998), 18-19.
65. Wellcome Library for the History and Understanding of Medicine: Western MS 5006, Wilkes diary.
66. Shaw, op. cit., 166.
67. I. Noël-Hume, 'The rise and fall of English white salt-glazed stoneware Part I' in *English Pottery and Porcelain an Historical Survey* ed. P. Atterbury (London: Owen, 1980), 16-23, 16.
68. Oral communication from Potteries Museum and Art Gallery archaeologist to one of the authors. A definitive archaeological report on this excavation had not been published by 2004.
69. See R. Hildyard, *European Ceramics* (London: V&A Publications, 1999), 89, Fig. 124, 139 for a later creamware plate-maker's profile.
70. A.R. Mountford and F. Celoria, 'Some examples of sources in the history of 17th Century Ceramics' in *Journal of Ceramic History* No. 1, 1968, 1-27, 8-9; A.R. Mountford, 'The Sadler Teapot Manufactury Site Burslem, Stoke-on-Trent, Staff.' in *City of Stoke-on-Trent Museum Archaeological Society Reports* No. 7, 1975, 1-20, 3, 7, 20.
71. D. Gaimster, *German Stoneware 1200-1900 Archaeological and Cultural History* (London: British Museum Press, 1997), 37ff.
72. See *Aaron, Thomas and John Wedgwood* for references to this type of mould.
73. See F. Celoria, 'Reports of the U.S. Consuls on the Staffordshire Potteries 1883-1892' in *Journal of Ceramic History* No. 7, 1974, 67, 45.
74. See Mountford, 1971, op. cit., plate 110 for a cream-jug case mould with prominent seam marks; and a salt-glazed sauceboat mould with seams visible, on display in the Ashmolean Museum, Oxford.
75. R.L. Hobson, *Catalogue of The Collection of English Pottery in the Department of British and Medieval Antiquities and Ethnography of the British Museum* (London: British Museum, 1903), 162, F13. Plate XLI.
76. Green, op. cit., App. 5, 265-70.
77. Elliott, 1998, op. cit., 21.
78. D. Towner 'David Rhodes – Enameller' in *English Ceramic Circle Transactions* Vol.4, Part 4, 1957, 3-13, 5.
79. *John Baddeley* of Shelton bought 'runners' from a local clockmaker in 1761-62.
80. Over four hundred positive fired clay sprig moulds survive at the Spode Works, Stoke-on-Trent, including one notably primitive woman on horseback, see M. Leese, 'The Turner Moulds' in *Northern Ceramic Society Journal* Vol. 5, 1984, 61-78, esp. Plate 32. Similar moulds are still in use (in 2004) at the Wedgwood Works at Barlaston.
81. Pitt, op. cit., 418.
82. Elliott, 1998, op. cit., 3, 18, including a quotation from Josiah Wedgwood I, written in 1777.
83. S.R. Broadbridge, 'Joseph Banks and West Midlands Industry (1767)' in *Staffordshire Industrial Archaeology Society Journal* Vol. 2, 1971, 1-18, 5.
84. J. Ward, *The Borough of Stoke-upon-Trent…* (London: Lewis, 1843, rep. East Ardsley: S.R., 1969), 262.
85. M. Goodby, 'Moulds and Modellers in the Early 18th-century Staffordshire Potteries; Slip-Casting, Press-Moulding and the Wood Family' in *English Ceramic Circle Transactions* Vol. 17, Part 2, 2000, 216-28, 220.
86. F. Rathbone, *A Catalogue of the Wedgwood Museum Etruria* (Stoke-on-Trent: Wedgwood, 1909), 57-60.
87. B. Rackham, *Early Staffordshire Pottery* (London: Faber, 1951), 22, 23, plate 36.
88. Hobson, op. cit., 170, 177, Plate XIX.
89. Mountford, 1971, op. cit., 32, plates 32, 33. A salt-glaze teapot of similar shape to this mould is in the Schreiber Collection at the Victoria and Albert Museum, but comparison of published photographs show that the relief decoration is not the same. Lady Schreiber also collected a thrown and turned white salt-glazed stoneware mug with white 'Portobello' sprigs. B. Rackham, *Catalogue of English Porcelain Earthenware Enamels and Glass collected by Charles Schreiber Esq. M.P. and The Lady Charlotte Elizabeth Schreiber and presented to the Museum in 1884* 3 vol. (London: Board of Education, 1930), II, 25-26, No. 99, Plate 19; 21, No. 71. A salt-glaze teapot also commemorating Portobello, but cast from a completely different mould, is in the Potteries Museum and Art Gallery, see Mountford, 1971, op. cit., 32, plate 82; and a similar one is in the British Museum, see Hobson, op. cit., 182, G 68, illustrated by C.F.C. Luxmoore. *'Saltglaze' with The Notes of a Collector* (Exeter: Pollard, 1924 repr. London: Holland Press, n.d.), Plate 6.
90. D. Barker, 'Discovering Staffordshire Ceramics' in *The International Ceramics Fair and Seminar 14, 15, 16, 17 June 1991* (London: Haughton, 1991), 12-18, 13, fig. 1.
91. Mountford, 1972, op. cit., Appendix IV, 17, 28 Nov. 1770.
92. See Mountford, 1971, op. cit., plates 19-21, 70-72.
93. From *Isabella; or, The Morning* by Sir Charles Hanbury Williams, quoted in B. Hillier, *Pottery and Porcelain 1700-1914 England, Europe and North America* (London: Weidenfeld and Nicolson, 1968), 282.
94. See *World Ceramics* ed. R.J. Charleston (London: Hamlyn, 1968), figs. 745-48, 752, 759.
95. Berg, op. cit., 341.
96. Ibid., 200, Fig. 190 d, 341, Fig. 319 I.
97. Broadbridge, op. cit., 5.
98. M. Bimson, 'The Significance of 'Ale-Measure' Marks' in *Post-Medieval Archaeology* 4, 1971, 165-66.
99. See Mountford, 1971, op. cit., 47, fig. 147. However, an (admittedly limited) 'silver' library has not produced any actual examples of salt-glaze prototypes.
100. E.N. Stretton in 'A Miscellany of Pieces' in *English Ceramic Circle Transactions* Vol. 5, Part 2, 1961, 74, plates 81, 82; L.B. Grigsby, 'Johan Nieuhoff's Embassy: An inspiration for relief decoration on English stoneware and earthenware' in *The Magazine Antiques* Jan. 1993, 172-83. An English translation was published by John Ogilby in London in 1669. A reprint in parts is understood to have been published in the 1740s, but has not been traced. This would have provided a 'contemporary' source for modellers working then.
101. A Designer, 'Designs and their Ownership' in *Pottery Gazette and Glass Trade Review,* 1 Jan. 1914, 66.
102. Green, op. cit., 138, Fig. 113, no. 266.
103. A. Young, 1999, op. cit., III, 308.
104. See G. Elliott, *The Design Process in British Ceramic Manufacture 1750-1850* (Stoke-on-Trent: Staffordshire University Press, n.d., c.2002), 110-15 for an up-to-date discussion of 18th century pressing and casting. No evidence is known of the use of deflocculants in casting slip in the 18th century, an additive which reduces the amount of water needed in the slip and thus speeds up casting and reduces the time needed to dry out the mould after use. However, such simple aids as salt or soda, well known to casters in 1901, are unlikely to have been overlooked in 1750.
105. A. Young, op. cit., III, 308.
106. Berg, op. cit., 199, 339.
107. Dragesco, op. cit., 22.
108. Celoria, 'Newcastle-upon-Tyne', op. cit., 23; 'North Staffordshire', op. cit., 26. Although Jars reports slip-casting of spouts, Elliott, 1998, op. cit., 117, has pointed out that cast parts will not satisfactorily attach to thrown or pressed pieces.
109. Elliott, 1998, op. cit.,19, 21.
110. Staffordshire Record Office: D 1788, Vol. 96, 7, 21 Nov., 5, 19 Dec. 1761, 30 Jan. 1762. See J. Mallet, 'John Baddeley of Shelton, an Early Staffordshire Maker of Pottery and Porcelain Parts I and II' in *English Ceramic Circle Transactions* Vol. 6, Part 2, 1966, 124-66, Part 3, 1967, 181-247, 210-11, 214, for a discussion of John Greatbatch. He was contemporary with William Greatbatch, see Barker, 1991, op. cit., 24, but no relationship has been found.
111. Staffordshire Record Office: D 1788, Vol. 102, 6, 1761-62.
112. Mountford, 1972, op. cit., Appendix III, 150.
113. Luxmoore, op. cit., esp. 23-38, 59-60, plates 44-78 (Luxmoore's introduction was dated Feb. 1914, ten years prior to publication); Mountford, 1971, op. cit., 29-34, 40, 42, 59, 63, plates 30-47, 89, 92, 94, 96, 97, 101, 104, 108-12, 154, 186, 210; M. Goodby, 2000, op. cit., *passim,* plates 4-9.
114. H.W. Dickinson, *Matthew Boulton* (Cambridge: University Press, 1937), 63.
115. C. Lever, *Goldsmiths and Silversmiths of England* (London: Hutchinson, 1975), 225.
116. George Stubbs, born in Liverpool in 1724, received his first artistic education there, see V. Morrison, *The Art of George Stubbs* (London: Headline, 1989), 8-9.
117. Falkner, op. cit., 33, 34.
118. See Lichfield Record Office: Inventory made 25 Sept. 1607 after the death of James Shaw, Newcastle, pewterer, listed his brass, pewter, moulds etc.
119. E. Meteyard, *A Group of Englishmen (1795 to 1815) being records of the Younger Wedgwoods and their Friends…* (London: Longman, Green, and Co., 1871), 246-49.

120. Shaw, op. cit., 189-90.
121. Mallet, op. cit., II, 181-247, 195.
122. *Stoke-upon-Trent Parish Registers* 4 vol. ed. P.W.L. Adams (Staffordshire Parish Registers Society, 1925), II, 330, 341; III, 487, 537.
123. D. Edwards, *Black Basalt Wedgwood and Contemporary Manufacturers* (Woodbridge: Antique Collectors' Club, 1994), 130-31, quoting T. Clifford 'William Bullock – a fine fellow' in *Christie's International Magazine* Jun. 1991, 14.
124. W.B. Honey, *English Pottery and Porcelain* 2nd.ed. (London: Black, 1945), 79.
125. Information from this source about Ralph Wood has been published by Potteries Museum staff: Mountford, 1971, op. cit., P.A. Halfpenny *English Earthenware Figures 1740-1840* (Woodbridge: Antique Collectors' Club, 1991), 69-70; and Goodby, 2000, op. cit., 216-28, 222-24.
126. Wedgwood MS: 27/19281.
127. Goodby, 2000, op. cit., 216-28, 223.
128. Hobson, op. cit., 180, G 56. The spittoon model is illustrated in Luxmoore, op. cit., 23, Plate 44. Falkner, op. cit., 24, refers to the spittoon as a vase, and reproduces the incised signature 'Aaron Wood'.
129. Hobson, op. cit., 188, G111.
130. A.H. Church, *Some Minor Arts as practised in England* (London; Seeley, 1894), 43. Church illustrates this style by a white salt-glazed stoneware rococo dessert basket, with scrolls, pierced diamonds and dot-and-diaper border, and chevron centre in Plate II.
131. L.M. Solon, *The Art of the Old English Potter* (London: Bemrose, 1883, rep. East Ardsley: EP, 1973) stated on p.77 that 'Some of the moulds made by *A. Wood* have been preserved, and bear his name scratched in the paste; one of them is in the South Kensington Museum'.
132. These agreements were first reproduced by Pitt, op. cit., 423-26.
133. See Falkner, op. cit., pedigree facing 118.
134. Pitt, op. cit., 426, 418.
135. Enoch Wood's copy of Pitt, op. cit., 421, photocopy held by authors.
136. Shaw, op. cit., 150-55.
137. Potteries Museum and Art Gallery, Ceramics Department: Thomas Whieldon's Memorandum Book, uncatalogued, 48 left.
138. Falkner, op. cit., 27.
139. Shaw, op. cit., 151.
140. Wedgwood MS 96/17812.
141. Most recently illustrated by Goodby, 2000, op. cit., 216-28, 226, fig. 12.
142. Falkner, op. cit., 21.
143. *Rococo Art and Design in Hogarth's England* ed. M. Snodin (London: Trefoil Books/ Victoria & Albert Museum, 1984), 241, 254-55, O.29.
144. Luxmoore, op. cit., 24, plate 45; 28, plate 26. See Mountford, 1971, op. cit., fig. 35 for the IS saucebout.
145. W. Chaffers, *Marks and Monograms on Pottery and Porcelain…* 3rd ed. (London: Bickers, 1872), 633.
146. P. Walton, *Creamware and other English Pottery at Temple Newsam House, Leeds A Catalogue of the Leeds Collection* (Bradford: Manningham Press, 1976), 12.
147. Mallet, op. cit., I, 141, II, 195.
148. Staffordshire Record Office: D1788, Vol. 96. Baddeley also paid a 'Greatbatch' for 'oven work' on 5 Jun. 1762.
149. Shaw, op. cit., 184, 213.
150. Barker, 1991, op. cit.
151. Shaw, op. cit., 190.
152. See Mountford, 1971, op. cit., Plates 217 to 243 for a representative selection.
153. Plot, op. cit., 123.
154. Ward, op. cit., 46 for 'a *smoke-house*, as it was termed, for drying the green ware more expeditiously'.
155. Green, op. cit., 29.
156. E. Adams 'The Bow Insurances and Related Matters' in *English Ceramic Circle Transactions* Vol. 9, Part I, 1973, 67-108, 75, 85, 104.
157. Berg, op. cit., 341., Fig. 319b, IIII.
158. Celoria, 'North Staffordshire', op. cit., 26.
159. Pitt, op. cit., 423.
160. *Pottery in the Making World Ceramic Traditions* ed. I. Freestone and D. Gaimster 1997), 125, 126, Fig. 5.
161. A. Toppin, '1. Rouse and Cullen, Merchants and Potters' in *English Ceramic Circle Transactions* [Vol. 1], No. 5, 1937, 38-48, 42-43, Fig. 1.
162. Green, op. cit., 21-28. Chris Green included a very helpful comparison of plans of early kilns, see 27, Fig. 23.
163. Ibid., 44, 193, Fig. 156. A somewhat similar arrangement is described by G. Lambert *Art Ceramique Traité Pratique de la fabrication Faïences Fines et Autres Poteries état actuel de la Fabrication de Angleterre* (Paris, 1865), 120-22, figs. 46-49, as being in use c.1865 at Maastricht in Holland and at Tamworth in England, part of a downdraught oven. Such an oven, formerly used for firing brown salt-glaze ware, is preserved at Ferrière-la-Petite, Nord, France.
164. N. Stretton, 'The Indio Pottery at Bovey Tracey' in *English Ceramic Circle Transactions* Vol. 8, Part 2, 1972, 124-36, 133-34; B. Adams and A. Thomas, *A Potwork in Devon The history and products of the Bovey Tracey potteries* [sic] *1750-1836* (Bovey Tracey: Sayce, 1996), 9, 10.
165. Berg, op. cit., 340, Fig. 318.
166. Ibid., 199-200, Fig. 190.
167. Celoria, 'North Staffordshire', op. cit., 27.
168. Dragesco, op. cit., 28. Translated by Dr. Helen Smith.
169. H. Young, 1999, op. cit., 9-11.
170. Potteries Museum and Art Gallery, Social History Department: Rough Notes, Salvation Army Site, Westport Road, Burslem.
171. Elliott, 2002, op. cit., 94-95.
172. Shaw, op. cit., 120-21.
173. Pitt, op. cit., 419.
174. Firebars were of course well known. In 1754, Angerstein mentioned a fire-*grate* beneath a Burslem slip-kiln and illustrated a roaring fire to dry plates at Hanley, complete with firebars (Berg, op. cit., 339, 341, Fig. 196b III) and Jars described a slip-kiln at Newcastle-upon-Tyne with an *iron grate*, in 1765 (Celoria, 'Newcastle-upon-Tyne, op. cit., 22.
175. Celoria, 'North Staffordshire', op. cit., 27.
176. Berg, op. cit., 340, Fig. 318, 199-200, Fig. 190.
177. Staffordshire Record Office: D 1788, V.96.
178. Thomas and John Wedgwood hired Thos Simpson in Oct. 1765 'to throw John Harrison's sagers [*sic*, saggars]', see Mountford, 1972, op. cit., 74, Appendix I, [15].
179. Green, op. cit., 180-83.
180. D. Barker, 'Bits and Bobs – The Development of Kiln Furniture in the 18th-century Staffordshire pottery industry' in *English Ceramic Circle Transactions* Vol. 16, Part 3, 1998, 318-41.
181. Celoria, 'North Staffordshire', op. cit., 27.
182. Ibid., 27.
183. Watson, op. cit., II, 266.
184. Berg, op. cit., 339.
185. Dragesco, op. cit., 26-28, translated by Dr. Helen Smith.
186. H.W. Maxwell, 'Excavations in North Staffordshire' in *English Ceramic Circle Transactions No. 1* 1933, 57-58, 57. For Wedgwood's 'cylinder', see *Josiah Wedgwood: 'the Arts and Sciences United'* exhibition catalogue (Barlaston: Wedgwood, 1978) 35-36, iii.
187. Berg, op. cit., 339.
188. Green, op. cit., 29.
189. See H. Young, 1999, op. cit., *passim*.
190. R.J. Waller, 'An Investigation of the Firing of an Up-draught Oven for Biscuit Earthenware' in *Technical Papers of the British Pottery Research Association* Vol. V, 1942, 63-74, 66, 67. The oven was at Mintons, a large 'modern' (1926) oven, efficiently fired, so that coal consumption for a small 18th century salt-glaze oven, less efficient and fired to a higher temperature, might be higher. *Thomas Wedgwood IV of Overhouse* may have had only 1½ tons of ware in his 1773 oven.
191. Berg, op. cit., 340.
192. Dragesco, op. cit., 26-28, translated by Dr. Helen Smith.
193. Berg, op. cit., 23, 340.
194. Ibid., 201, 339-40.
195. Celoria, 'North Staffordshire', op. cit., 27.
196. Watson, op. cit., II, 265.
197. Pitt, op. cit., 419.
198. Wedgwood MS 30/22942.
199. Berg, op. cit., 340, Fig. 318, 199-200, Fig. 190.
200. The foregoing is a careful conflation from the following sources: *R R Angerstein's Illustrated Travel Diary 1753-1755 Industry in England and Wales from a Swedish perspective* trans. T. and P. Berg (London: Science Museum, 2001), 201, Fig. 190, 339-41, Fig. 318; F. Celoria 'Techniques of White salt-Glaze Stoneware Manufacture in North Staffordshire around 1765' in *Science and Archaeology* no. 18, 1976, 25-28, 27; and our notes for the following potters: *John Baddeley* in 1762 and *Thomas Wedgwood IV of Overhouse* in 1772-73 for the purchase of salt, *Peter Bagnall* for a glazing ladder in 1761, *Aaron Shaw III* for planks for scaffolding in 1736 and *Thomas Stevenson* for scaffold, ladles, salt bag and 'glosing' ladder in 1757. J.F. Blacker, *The A B C of English Salt-Glaze Stoneware from Dwight to Doulton* (London: Paul, 1922), 224-31, gives a dramatic account of salting an oven at Doultons in 1922, essentially the same as 18th century practice.
201. Dragesco, op. cit., 26-28, translated by Dr. Helen Smith.
202. Green, op. cit., 11, 29.
203. A. Watts, 'Something Nasty in the Air: Lambeth Potters and the Archbishop of Canterbury' in *English Ceramic Circle Transactions* Vol. 17, Part 1, 1999, 15-28, 15-16; Letter to *Ceramic Review* Jan./Feb. 2003, 12.
204. Berg, op. cit., 342.
205. Pitt, op. cit., 419.
206. See our Chapter VI, Potters as Customers, and Mountford, 1972, op. cit., 104-21, Table C, for sales of unfired ware. In theory, unfired ware bought by one potter from another could for instance be dipped in 'Littler-

Wedgwood' blue by the buyer before firing.
207. F. Britton, 'The Pickleherring Potteries: an inventory' in *Post-Medieval Archaeology* 24 (1990), 61-92, 80
208. K.J. Barton, "The Laboratory or School of Arts" by G. Smith, published 1740 Extract from pages 90-96' in *Post-Medieval Archaeology* 2, 1969, 169-72, 170, 171.
209. Gaimster, op. cit., 41. H.C. Hoover and L.H. Hoover, translators of Agricola, op. cit.,112, 614, stated that Biringuccio was the first to mention zaffre in connection with the decoration of pottery, in 1540.
210. See R. Copeland, *Spode's Willow Pattern and other designs after the Chinese* (London: Studio Vista, 1980), 17-20, for a full account of cobalt and its use with pottery.
211. J. Turnbull, 'Scottish Cobalt and Nicholas Crisp' in *English Ceramic Circle Transactions* Vol. 16, Part 2, 1997 144-51.
212. Mallet, op. cit., I, 141,142 for examples.
213. Wedgwood MS 6/30577.
214. Wedgwood MSS 129/25597, 25598.
215. Plot, op. cit., 123. P. Williams, 'The Talbot Hotel Pit Group c.1690-1725: Exciting Finds from Tetbury' in *Northern Ceramic Society Newsletter* No. 127, Sept. 2002, 24-26, 24 suggests that 'magnas', an iron ore, was used rather than manganese.
216. Information from Gloucester Port Books per Dr. M. Wanklyn, Wolverhampton Polytechnic, lecture at Keele University, 24 Jan. 1990.
217. R.S. Edmundson, 'Benthall Pottery, Shropshire and its Salopian Art Pottery' in *Journal of the Northern Ceramic Society*, Vol. 19, 2002, 29-76, 30, 72, Fig. 72.
218. Shaw, op. cit., 177.
219. Berg, op. cit., 200, 341-42.
220. Potteries Museum and Art Gallery, Ceramics Department: Thomas Whieldon's Memorandum Book, uncatalogued, p.67.
221. R.E. Taggart, *The Frank P. And Harriet C. Burnap Collection of English Pottery in the William Rockhill Nelson Gallery* rev. and enl. ed. (Kansas City: Nelson Gallery-Atkins Museum, 1967), 74, no. 182.
222. J. Draper, *dated post-medieval pottery in northampton museum* [sic] (Northampton: Museums and Art Galleries, 1975), 26.
223. Mountford, 1971, op. cit., Plate 58.
224. Ibid., 49.
225. *Patents for Inventions. Abridgments of the Specifications relating to Pottery* (London: Commissioners of Patents, 1863) 6, A.D. 1733, 24 Apr. – No. 541. Mountford, 1971, op. cit., 41-42 quotes a fuller version of this patent.
226. Mountford, 1971, op. cit., Plates 74, 73. The unhandled cup has two white bands round its 'waist'.
227. *The International Ceramics Fair and Seminar London 1996* [Catalogue] (London: Haughton, 1996), 68.
228. P. Halfpenny, 'Thomas Whieldon: his Life and Work' in *English Ceramic Circle Transactions* Vol. 16, Part 2, 1997, 237-54, 242, fig. 6.
229. B. Rackham, *Catalogue of the Glaisher Collection of Pottery & Porcelain in the Fitzwilliam Museum Cambridge* 2 vol. (Cambridge: Cambridge University Press, 1935, repr. Woodbridge: Antique Collectors' Club, 1987), I, 80-81, no. 527; II, 44 D. The 1935 attribution to *Thomas Whieldon* on the basis of similar sprigs on an unfinished redware teapot should now be to *Edward Warburton*.

230. Shaw, op. cit., 147. Luxmoore, op. cit., 54-55 included Aaron Wood with J. Mitchell as defendants in the case, presumably from a misreading of L. Jewitt *Ceramic Art of Great Britain* 2 Vol. (London: Virtue, 1878), II, 241.
231. British Museum: Add MSS 15,800.
232. M. Goodby, 'William Littler: The Early Years' in *William Littler: An English Earth Potter 1724-1784* ed. M. Adams (Charlotte: Delhom Service League, 1999), 11-18, 12.
233. H. Coutts, *The Art of Ceramics European Ceramic Design 1500-1830* (New Haven: Yale University Press, 2001), 162.
234. G. Savage *Seventeenth and Eighteenth Century French Porcelain* (London: Barrie and Rockliff, 1960, repr. London: Spring, 1969), 135-36.
235. Most recently reported by A.R. Mountford, 'Porcelain comes to the Potteries: the pre-1760 period' in *Staffordshire Porcelain* ed. G. Godden (London: Granada, 1983), 10-30, 20.
236. Pitt, op. cit., 423; Shaw, op. cit., 168-69, 176.
237. *William Littler* of West Pans, Scotland advertised 'Japand Black' ware in 1766.
238. Mountford, 1972, op. cit., Appendix III, 14 (69 for Griffith's address).
239. Ibid., Appendix III, 60.
240. British Museum: Add. MSS 15,800.
241. As late as 1769 there is a reference 'To Mr. Wedgwood Principal Manufacturer of the Queen's Ware or commonly referred to as the Yellow Ware' in Wedgwood MS 143/29383.
242. Berg, op. cit., 341.
243. Anonymous advert: V&A Ceramics and Glass Department library, Lit. Mat. No. 88, information from Robin Hildyard..
244. Solon, op. cit., 70.
245. T.D. Chappell, 'An Adventure with Early English Pottery' in *Ceramics in America 2001*, 186-206, 203, Fig. 31.
246. A. Smith, 'An Enamelled Tin-glazed Mug at Temple Newsam House' in *Leeds Arts Calendar* No. 82, 1978, 14-19. See also A. Smith 'Stoneware in North West England' in *Stonewares & Stone chinas of Northern England to 1851* exhibition catalogue ed. T.A. Lockett and P.A. Halfpenny (Stoke-on-Trent: City Museum and Art Gallery, 1982), 25-28, 26 and 'Liverpool Earthenwares and Stonewares' in *Made in Liverpool: Liverpool Pottery and Porcelain 1700-1850* ed. M. Brown and T.A. Lockett (Liverpool: National Museums & Galleries on Merseyside, 1993), 22-26, 24-25.
247. Berg, op. cit., 310.
248. E.S. Price, *John Sadler a Liverpool Pottery Printer* (West Kirby: privately, 1948), 68; T.K. Boney, 'Liverpool Saltglazed wares' in *English Ceramic Circle Transactions* Vol. 4, Part 2, 1957, 51-57, 53; and C. Wyman, 'A Review of early Transfer Printing Techniques' in *English Ceramic Circle Transactions* Vol. 16, Part 3, 1998, 307-17, 310.
249. Wedgwood MS WM 1431.
250. Probably Benjamin or George Luffingham, Dublin, china dealers, who dealt with Josiah Wedgwood in Nov. 1763, although not for white salt-glazed stoneware. See Wedgwood MSS 6/30703, 30707, 30708.
251. John Sadler's notebook (Liverpool Central Library: 738 SAD 1), second page from back, contains an undated reference to 'Ball's best White Glaze'. The formula is printed in E.S. Price, *John Sadler a Liverpool Pottery Printer* (West Kirby: privately, 1948), 89.
252. Pitt, op. cit., 419-20. Shaw interpreted

Pitt's remarks to mean that tile painters came to the Potteries, see Shaw, op. cit., 179.
253. A 'battery' of four 20th century coal-fired enamel kilns is preserved and can be seen at 'House of Marbles', Bovey Tracey.
254. Berg, op. cit., 199, Fig. 189.
255. Campbell, op. cit., 187.
256. M. Rowlands, 'Industry and Social Change in Staffordshire 1660-1760. A Study of Probate and other records of Tradesmen' in *Lichfield and South Staffordshire Archaeological and Historical Society Transactions for 1967-8* Vol. IX, 1968, 37-58, 46.
257. See also B. Watney and R.J. Charleston, 'Petitions for Patents concerning Porcelain, Glass and Enamels with special reference to Birmingham, 'The Great Toyshop of Europe', in *English Ceramic Circle Transactions* Vol.6, Part 2, 1966, 57-123, 122, 120.
258. J.E. Nightingale, *Contributions towards the History of Early English Porcelain from Contemporary Sources* (Salisbury, 1881; repr. EP Publishing, East Ardsley, 1971), lxv-vi, xlv.
259. British Museum: Add. MSS 15,800.
260. Berg, op. cit., 310, 340, 342.
261. *Stoke-upon-Trent Parish Registers* 4 vol. (Staffordshire Parish Registers Society, 1925), III, 575, Burials, 22 Apr. 1759, Warner Edwards of Shelton.
262. P. Bradshaw, 'The Gilding of European Ceramics 1710-1840' in *Journal of the Northern Ceramic Society* Vol. 14, 1997, 81-86.
263. Mountford, 1972, op. cit., Appendix III, 14 (69 for Griffith's address).
264. D. Drakard, *Printed English Pottery: History and Humour in the reign of George III 1760-1820* (London: Horne, 1992); 'Early On-glaze Transfer Printing' in *English Ceramic Circle Transactions* Vol. 15, Part 3, 1995, 331-40; and Wyman, op. cit., 307-17 are recent studies on the subject.
265. Watney and Charleston, op. cit., 61-62.
266. C. Cook, 'Old English Salt-glazed Plates with printed decorations' in *The Connoisseur, Antique Dealers' Fair and Exhibition Number*, Jun. 1958, 39-42. F. Tilley, 'Ravenet an Engraver for Battersea Transfers on Saltglaze Plates' in *The Antique Collector* Jun. 1963, 121-28, 122, wrote on the same subject.
267. See also Mountford, 1971, op. cit., 60-62.
268. See for instance N. Stretton, 'Fable Subjects on English Pottery' in *English Ceramic Circle Transactions* Vol. 15, Part 2, 1994, 205-08, 205, for a salt-glazed plate printed in purple, reddish/brown and grey/black.
269. H. Young 'Eighteenth-century English decorators of Chinese porcelain' in *Apollo* Nov. 2002, 17-22. A major study of 18th century London decorators is awaited.
270. Mrs. D. McAlister. *William Duesbury's London Account Book 1751-1753* (London: English Porcelain Circle Monograph No. I, 1930), 64, 65.
271. Adams, 1973, op. cit., 75, 95.
272. A. Thomas, 'Geographical aspects of the Development of Transport and Communications affecting the Pottery Industry of North Staffordshire during the Eighteenth Century' in *Collections for a History of Staffordshire 1934* ed. William Salt Society (Kendal: Titus Wilson, 1935), 1-157, 58.
273. Wedgwood MSS 6/4907-4911, 8 May to 22 Jun. 1764.
274. E. Adams 'Ceramic Insurances in the Sun

Company, 1766-1774' in *English Ceramic Circle Transactions* Vol. 10, Part I, 1976, 1-38, 25.
275. Wedgwood MSS 11/30180, Tidmarsh; 30/30342, Rigby.
276. Shaw, op. cit., 168-69, 192.
277. Ibid., 178-79. One of the anonymous Dutchmen acquired a name, Horologius, see M. Goodby, 'The First Salt-Glaze Enameller' in *Northern Ceramic Society Newsletter* No. 84, Dec. 1991, 10-11, for the explanation of this. (The teapot marked W H was G23 in the Burlington Fine Arts Club 1913 exhibition.)
278. Shaw, op. cit., 178-79.
279. Mountford, 1971, op. cit., 56.
280. Mountford, 1972, op. cit., Appendix III, 105.
281. Ibid., Appendix III, 98.
282. P. Halfpenny, 'Pioneer Potter?' in *Antique Dealer & Collectors Guide,* Vol. 53, No. 11, Jun. 2000, 36-38.
283. Mountford, 1972, op. cit., Appendix III, 14 (69 for Griffith's address).
284. Ibid., Appendix III, 36.
285. D. Towner, 'The Leeds Pottery, Jack Lane, Hunslet' in *English Ceramic Circle Transactions* Vol. 3, Part 4, 1955, 173-84, 173. D. Towner wrote at greater length on 'Robinson and Rhodes, Enamellers at Leeds' in *English Ceramic Circle Transactions,* Vol. 9, Part 2, 1974, 134-39 and in his *Creamware* (London: Faber, 1978).
286. Wedgwood MS 1/665.
287. A.J.B. Kiddell, 'John Platt of Rotherham Potter and Mason-Architect' in *English Ceramic Circle Transactions* Vol. 5, Part 3, 1962, 172-175, Plate 1.
288. Ibid., 172-175, 173.
289. J.V.G. Mallet, 'Rotherham Saltglaze: John Platt's Jug' in *English Ceramic Circle Transactions* Vol. 9, Part 1, 1973, 111-14, 112-14, Plates 64, 65.
290. Mountford, 1971, op. cit., Plate 211; Colonial Williamsburg Foundation, accession number 1963.195, gift of Frank Tilley.
291. H.C. Goldweitz, 'An American Collection of English Pottery: A Chronology 1635-1778' in *English Ceramic Circle Transactions* Vol. 12, Part 1, 1984, 8-25, 17 and Plate 23 (b).
292. B. Rackham and H. Read, *English Pottery its development from early times to the end of the eighteenth century* (London: Benn, 1924, rep. East Ardsley: EP, 1972) 89-90; B. Rackham, *Victoria and Albert Museum Department of Ceramics Catalogue of English Porcelain Earthenware Enamels and Glass collected by Charles Schreiber Esq. M.P. and The Lady Charlotte Elizabeth Schreiber and presented to the Museum in 1884* 3 vol. (London: Board of Education, 1930), II, 17, Nos. 223-228.
293. J. Ressing-Wolfert and J. Daniel van Dam, 'Vroege Petit Feu-Decoraties in Delft' in *Vormen uit vuur* 2002/3 70-72, a reference kindly provided by John Mallet. See for instance R.W. Sharp, *Ceramics Ethics & Scandal* (Canada: RWD Books, 2002), 98, for a white salt-glaze stoneware coffee service decorated in Holland with a Jewish wedding scene, dated 1769.
294. See R. Hirsch, 'Dutch decorated English Creamware' in *English Ceramic Circle Transactions* Vol. 12, Part 3, 1986, 265-72, and J.L. Benson, 'Collections of Dutch decorated English Creamware' in *English Ceramic Circle Transactions* Vol. 14, Part 2, 1991, 215-27. J.L. Benson wrote more fully on the subject in 'Dutch decorated English creamware: fiction and fact' in *Medelingenblad Nederlandse Vereniging van Vrienden van de Ceramiek* Vol. 137/1, 1990/1 3-21, 'Dutch decorated English creamware: Chronology and style' in *Mededlingenblad Nederlandse Vereniging van Vrienden van de Ceramiek* Vol. 142, 1991/2, 15-24, and 'Dutch decorated English creamware: Religious and genre scenes and Dutch inscriptions' in *Mededlingenblad Nederlandse Vereniging van Vrienden van de Ceramiek* Vol. 147, 1992/4 10-23. He tentatively locates the Dutch decorators in Delft, and suggests that they bought first plain white salt-glazed stoneware for decoration and continued the practice on cream-coloured earthenware.
295. Honey, 1945, op. cit., 255.
296. T.T. Greg, *A Contribution to the History of English Pottery with Special Reference to the Greg Collection* (Manchester: City of Manchester Art Gallery, 1908), 79-80.
297. See for instance H.M. Buten, *Wedgwood ABC but not Middle E* (Merion, Pa: Buten Museum of Wedgwood, 1964) 45, for a 'salt-glaze' measure mug, c.1900, impressed Wedgwood.
298. G.W. Rhead, 'More about Salt-glaze' in *The Connoisseur,* Vol. XXVI, Jan.-Apr. 1910, 30-32, 32.
299. See Edwards, op. cit., Figure 34 for the identical shape in basalt.
300. Reilly, op. cit., II, 484, 543-44.
301. J. Jones *Minton: The First Two Hundred Years of Design and Production* (Shrewsbury: Swan Hill, 1993), 50 (illustration, left), 51.
302. P. Atterbury and Maureen Batkin, *The Dictionary of Minton* (Woodbridge: Antique Collectors' Club, 1990), 182.
303. P. Atterbury, E.P. Denker, M. Batkin *Twentieth Century Ceramics…* (London: Miller's, 1999), 37.
304. W. Elliot, 'Reproductions and Fakes of English Eighteenth-Century Ceramics' in *English Ceramic Circle Transactions,* No. 7, Vol. 2, 1939, 67-82, 72, 74, 77, 82, Plates XXIV a, c, d, XXVII a, b, XXIX c.
305. G.W. Rhead, *The Earthenware Collector* (London: Herbert Jenkins, 1920), 60. See also B. Bumpus, *Pâte-sur-Pâte: The Art of Ceramic Relief Decoration 1849-1992* (London: Barrie & Jenkins, 1992), especially 155, 200, and 'Henry Sanders, a Forgotten Pâte-sur-Pâte Artist' in *Ars Ceramica* No. 16, 2000, 62-68.
306. For instance, A. Crane, 'Thermoluminescence will play its part in restoring pottery market confidence' in *Antiques Trade Gazette,* 2 Apr. 1994, 4.
307. D. Battie, 'Sotheby's Black Museum of Ceramics' in *Apollo* Mar. 1990, 165-69; 'Visit Black Museum' in *Art Quarterly,* Winter 2002, 74.
308. The most focused study is L. Weatherill, *The Pottery Trade and North Staffordshire 1660-1760* (Manchester: Manchester University Press, 1971), which makes no distinction between types of ware, and does not touch on the 'out-potteries'.
309. Ward, op. cit., 43.
310. We count a 'manufacturer' as either a single master potter, a partnership or a family concern.
311. Reproduced in R. Copeland, *A short history of pottery raw materials and the Cheddleton Flint Mill* (Cheddleton: Cheddleton Flint Mill Heritage Trust, 1972), [11].
312. Wedgwood MS 7/5593.
313. Wedgwood MS 7/5606.
314. Berg, op. cit., 340, 342.
315. L. Jewitt, *The Wedgwoods: being a Life of Josiah Wedgwood…* (London: Virtue, 1865), 162-63.
316. A. Young, op. cit., III, 306.
317. Wedgwood MS 96/17695.
318. Pitt, op. cit., 419.
319. Shaw, op. cit., 166.
320. Wedgwood MS WM 947.
321. Berg, op. cit., 340, 342.
322. Celoria, 'North Staffordshire', op. cit., 25.
323. A. Young, op. cit., III, 306.
324. Wedgwood MS 96/17695.
325. Weatherill, op. cit., 51-52.
326. Mountford, 1972, op. cit., Appendix I.
327. See P. Mathias *The First Industrial Nation an economic history of Britain 1700-1914* (London: Methuen, 1969, 1978), 202-03 for a general discussion of 'family units'.
328. Shaw, op. cit., 166.
329. Copeland, op. cit., [11].
330. L. Jewitt, *The Wedgwoods: being a Life of Josiah Wedgwood…* (London: Virtue, 1865), 92-93.
331. Ibid., 116.
332. Mountford, 1972, op. cit., Appendix I, [16].
333. A. Young, op. cit., III, 308-09.
334. Campbell, op. cit., 187.

CHAPTER VI
1. H. Young, *English Porcelain 1745-95 Its Makers, Design, Marketing and Consumption* (London: V & A Publications, 1999), 154-77; L. Weatherill, 'The Business of Middleman in the English Pottery Trade before 1780' in *Business History* Vol. XXVII, No. 3, Jul. 1986, 51-76.
2. John Mallet, 'John Baddeley of Shelton An Early Staffordshire Maker of Pottery and Porcelain Part I' in *English Ceramic Circle Transactions* Vol. 6, Part 2, 1967, 124-66, 127.
3. 'John Dwight's Fulham Pottery 1672-1978 A Collection of Documentary Sources' ed. D. Haselgrove and J. Murray, in *Journal of Ceramic History* No. 11, 1979, 1-284, 55.
4. R. Plot, *The Natural History of Stafford-shire* (Oxford, 1686), 124. Plot gathered his information c.1680.
5. Haselgrove and Murray, op. cit., 85.
6. R. Campbell, *The London Tradesman* (London, 1747, rep. Newton Abbot: David & Charles, 1969), 188, 185. Page 188 was quoted by H. Blakey, 'The Earthenware Shop in 1747' in *Northern Ceramic Society Newsletter* No. 92, Sept. 1993, 33.
7. *A History of the County of Stafford* Vol. VIII ed. J.G. Jenkins (London: Oxford University Press, 1963), 25, 45.
8. Lichfield Record Office: James Shaw, will and inventory, proved 25 Sept. 1607.
9. B.A. Burndrett, 'A Portrait of Newcastle-under-Lyme Hatting and Textile Industry from the Restoration to the Twentieth Century', n.d., unpublished MS in Newcastle-under-Lyme Reference Library, RL 338 BUR o/s.
10. London *Daily Advertiser,* 8 Dec. 1746.
11. B. Horn, 'Ceramic accounts found among the Seafield Muniments' in *English Ceramic Circle Transactions* Vol. 18, Part 1, 2002, 189-96, 191.
12. Winterthur MS 60x8.12, 10 Oct. 1757.
13. Wedgwood MS 55/30895, Apr. or early May 1763. Edward and John Guest, St. John's Street, West Smithfield, London, potters and glass-sellers dissolved partnership 2 May 1766. John Guest ceased business at Aldersgate Street,

London, and his stock was auctioned 1-3 Mar. 1769. See N. Valpy, 'Extracts from 18th century London Newspapers' in *English Ceramic Circle Transactions* Vol. 12, Part 2, 1985, 161-88, 165-66.
14. Winterthur MS 60x 8.3, 17 May 1763.
15. A.R. Mountford, 'Thomas Wedgwood, John Wedgwood and Jonah Malkin Potters of Burslem', unpublished MA Thesis, Keele University, 1972, Appendix III, 6, 31, 56.
16. N. Valpy, 'Extracts from 18th Century London Newspapers' in *English Ceramic Circle Transactions* Vol. 15, Part 2, 1994, 310-16, 312.
17. A.J. Toppin, 'The China Trade and some London Chinamen' in *English Ceramic Circle Transactions* No 3, 1935, 37-56, 45, Plate XIX; E. Adams, 'Women in the Eighteenth Century Ceramic Trade and some detailed Prices of that Time' in *Journal of the Northern Ceramic Society* Vol. 16, 1999, 1-21, 4, 20.
18. Wedgwood MS 5/30546, 26 Jul. 1763.
19. Wedgwood MS 5/3398, 3 Jan. 1764.
20. Wedgwood MS 5/30547, 29 Jul. 1763.
21. Wedgwood MS 5/30556, n.d.
22. Wedgwood MS 5/3999, 16 Feb. 1764.
23. Wedgwood MSS 5/4002-7, 27 Mar., 1764; 13 Aug. 1764.
24. Wedgwood MS 30/22753, n.d., c.1764.
25. Wedgwood MS 5/3734, 16 Sept. 1764.
26. Wedgwood MS 6/5062, 2 May 1764.
27. Wedgwood MS 6/4986, 1 Mar. 1764.
28. Wedgwood MS 6/4654, 23 Nov. 1764.
29. London *Gazette and Daily Advertiser*, 1 Mar. 1769.
30. Winterthur MS 65x68.5, 13 Jul. 1769.
31. Winterthur MS 76x358, 4 Feb. 1769 (merchant and location unspecified).
32. Wedgwood MS 13/2555, 10 Jun. 1773. Staffordshire potters also named him 'Vanderkiste'.
33. See *The Selected Letters of Josiah Wedgwood* ed. A. Finer and G. Savage (London: Cory, Adams & Mackay, 1965), 211, for Josiah Wedgwood urging Bentley to make bas-reliefs appear scarce.
34. R.S. Hampson, 'The Development of the Pottery Industry in Longton, 1700-1865', unpublished M.A. Thesis, Keele University, 1986, I, 195.
35. A.R. Mountford, 1972, op. cit., Appendix III, 128.
36. S. Shaw, *History of the Staffordshire Potteries...* (Hanley: privately, 1829, rep. Newton Abbot: David & Charles, 1970), 155.
37. S. Smith, 'William Hassells, Pot-Maker' in *Northern Ceramic Society Newsletter* No. 27, Sept. 1977, 16-17.
38. A.J. White, 'A Stamford Potseller's Stock in 1720' in *Post Medieval Archaeology* No. 13, 1979, 290-92.
39. Wedgwood MS 55/30733, 11 Mar. 1763.
40. Wedgwood MS 14/30305, 20 May 1763.
41. Wedgwood MS 30/30144, 9 Jun. 1763.
42. Wedgwood MS 30/30145, 16 Jun. 1763.
43. Wedgwood MSS 30/22473, 9 Dec. 1764; and 30/22462-22477, 30/30141-30155 *passim*.
44. Wedgwood MS 6/4993, 16 Apr. 1763.
45. Wedgwood MS 1/724, 23 May 1763.
46. Wedgwood MSS 29/21450/51, 27 Jun. 1764; A.R. Mountford, 1972, op. cit., Appendix III, 94.
47. Wedgwood MS 30/22759, n.d., 1764.
48. Wedgwood MS 1/618, 29 Jul. 1764.
49. Wedgwood MS 30/22659, 14 Aug. 1764.
50. Wedgwood MS 5/3999, 16 Feb. 1764.
51. Wedgwood MS 16/4667, 30 Feb.1764.
52. Wedgwood MSS 6/4667-68, 30156-63.
53. 'Miser' is understood as 'measure' from the context of Douglas' letter (Wedgwood MS 6/4667, 30 Jan. 1764), e.g. 'wine misers', 'full misers', 'small misers'.
54. Joseph and Jonathan Brooks were *merchants* in Hanover Street, Liverpool in 1766, see *The Liverpool Directory, for the Year 1766...* (Liverpool: Gore, 1766, repr. Scouse Press, 1987), 29, 61, 67.
55. E. Adams, 'Ceramic Insurances in the Sun Company, 1776-1774' in *English Ceramic Circle Transactions* Vol. 10, Part 1, 1976, 1-38, 35.
56. Wedgwood MS 11/9837, 22 Nov. 1763, 6 Jul. 1764.
57. Wedgwood MS 11/9302, 2 May 1766.
58. Wedgwood MS 6/4937, 24 May 1764.
59. Finer and Savage, op. cit., 29.
60. L. Weatherill, 'The growth of the pottery industry in England, 1660-1815' in *Post Medieval Archaeology* No. 17, 1983, 15-46, 15, Appendix 1, Table A-1.
61. See A. Smith, 'John Wyke of Liverpool, and the Staffordshire Pottery Export Trade' in *Northern Ceramic Society Journal* Vol. 3, 1978-1979, 79-88, for a detailed study of these transactions.
62. Wedgwood MSS 10/30168-30171.
63. Wedgwood MS 10/30169, 26 Feb. 1763.
64. Wedgwood MS 10/30170, 20 May 1763.
65. A.R. Mountford, 1972, op. cit., Appendix III, 104.
66. Wedgwood MSS 25/18123, 18124.
67. Wedgwood MSS 9/7017; 7027, n.d., Jul. 1769, 26 Sept. 1769.
68. Wedgwood MSS 20/17411, 4 Jul. 1769; 30/22758, n.d.
69. Wedgwood MSS 1/578-592, 49/29596a.
70. Wedgwood MS 55/9841.
71. Wedgwood MS 5/30828, 2 May 1763.
72. Wedgwood MS 5/30730, 15 Oct. 1763.
73. Wedgwood MSS 6/30575-30585.
74. Wedgwood MS 6/30576.
75. Wedgwood MS 6/30577.
76. Wedgwood MS 6/30584.
77. Wedgwood MS 30/30919.
78. Wedgwood MS 6/30584.
79. Wedgwood MS 6/30582.
80. Wedgwood MS 6/30584.
81. Wedgwood MS 11/9363.
82. Wedgwood MS 6/30579, 23 Jul. 1763.
83. *Sketchley's Directory of Walsall* (1770), transcript in Walsall Library.
84. Wedgwood MSS 5/3989-3996, 30228-30242; 25/18201, 18205, 18207.
85. Wedgwood MS 5/3991.
86. Wedgwood MSS 5/30228-29.
87. Wedgwood MS 5/3992-3996, 30233-30242 *passim*; 25/18201, 18205, 18207.
88. Wedgwood MS 13/5077.
89. Wedgwood MS 36/30938; published by R. Haggar 'A Letter and Order from Amsterdam, 1776' in *Northern Ceramic Society Newsletter* No. 8, 6-7. Even this apparently 'non-Wedgwood' document is in the Wedgwood Accumulation!
90. Wedgwood MSS 7/30344,13 May 1763, 7/30345, 28 Jun. 1763, 7/5891, 13 Jul. 1764.
91. Wedgwood MS 6/30585, n.d.
92. Wedgwood MS 7/30368, 28 May 1765.
93. Wedgwood MS 7/5900, 17 Jan. 1764.
94. Wedgwood MS 55/30436, n.d., but endorsed 1763.
95. H.A.S. Smith, 'English Queensware and its impact on the French pottery industry 1774-1814', unpublished PhD Thesis, Keele University, 2002, *passim*.
96. D. Towner, *Creamware* (London: Faber, 1978), 184.
97. Wedgwood MSS 7/5564-5606, 79/13648-13665, WM 1459 Folder C.
98. N. Valpy, 'Extracts from 18th century London Newspapers' in *English Ceramic Circle Transactions* Vol. 12, Part 2, 1985, 161-88, 162; A. Smith, *The Illustrated Guide to Liverpool Herculaneum Pottery 1796-1840* (London: Barrie & Jenkins, 1970), 5
99. Wedgwood MSS 1/30215 17 Jun. 1763; 1/30217, 19 Jul. 1763.
100. Wedgwood MS 1/30219, 13 Sept. 1763.
101. Wedgwood MS 1/30214.
102. Wedgwood MS 1/30219.
103. Wedgwood MS 1/609.
104. Wedgwood MS 11/9273.
105. A.R. Mountford, 1972, op. cit., Appendix III, 64, 130, 156, 168; D. Edwards, *Neale Pottery and Porcelain Its Predecessors and Successors 1763-1820* (London: Barrie & Jenkins, 1987), 22-23.
106. Wedgwood MS 31/23008.
107. A.R. Mountford, 1972, op. cit., Appendix III, *passim*.
108. Ibid., 107-13, Tables B-E, with details in Appendix III.
109. Wedgwood MS 25/18137.
110. Wedgwood MS 96/17794.
111. Finer and Savage, op. cit., 106.
112. *R R Angerstein's Illustrated Travel Diary 1753-1755 Industry in England and Wales from a Swedish perspective* trans. T. and P. Berg (London: Science Museum, 2001).
113. Berg, op cit., 200-01.
114. Berg, op cit., 340.
115. A.R. Mountford, 1972, op. cit., Appendix IV, 10.
116. D. Barker, *William Greatbatch a Staffordshire Potter* (London: Horne, 1990) 47.
117. Wedgwood MS 11/9363.
118. Wedgwood MS 96/17804.
119. Barker, op. cit., 51.
120. P. Deane and W.A. Cole, *British Economic Growth 1688-1959 Trends and Structure* (Cambridge: Cambridge University Press, 1967), 103, Table 24: Middlesex 1701 582, 815.
121. Wedgwood MSS 29/21450-52.
122. J.K. Grebby, *An Elementary Manual of Business Methods* (London: Macdonald & Evans, 1942), Chapter XIV.
123. Wedgwood MSS 6/4667-68, 30156-63 *passim*.
124. Wedgwood MS 6/31181. Vanderkiste was also known to Staffordshire potters as 'Vanderkirk'.
125. Wedgwood MS 49/29596a.
126. A.R. Mountford, 1972, op. cit., 86.
127. Ibid., Appendix III, 58, IV, 30.
128. Staffordshire Record Office: D 1788, 79, 82.
129. Ibid., Vol. 96, 19 Sept., 22 Aug., 19 Dec., 10 Oct. 1761.
130. Wedgwood MS 6/30582.
131. *Purefoy Letters 1735-1753* ed. G. Eland, 2 vol. (London: Sidgwick & Jackson, 1931), I, 86.
132. Wedgwood MSS 10/30168, 30171.
133. A.R. Mountford, 1972, op. cit., Appendix III, 104.
134. Wedgwood MS 30/31358.

135. Lichfield Record Office: Administration for Robert Daniel, 10 Jun. 1707.
136. L. Weatherill, *The Pottery Trade and North Staffordshire 1660-1760* (Manchester: Manchester University Press, 1971), 67, 149, 150.
137. *A History of the County of Stafford* Vol. II, ed. M.W. Greenslade and J.G. Jenkins (London: Oxford University Press, 1967), 278-84; A.L. Thomas, 'Geographical aspects of the Development of Transport and Communications affecting the Pottery Industry of North Staffordshire during the Eighteenth Century' in *Collections for a History of Staffordshire 1934* ed. William Salt, Archaeological Society (Kendal: Titus Wilson, 1935), 1-157, *passim*.
138. A.R. Mountford, 1972, op. cit., Appendix IV.
139. Ibid., Appendix IV, 43-45.
140. Ibid., Appendix III, 160.
141. Ibid., Appendix III, 18, 61, 70.
142. L. Jewitt, *The Wedgwoods, being a Life of Josiah Wedgwood...* (London: Virtue, 1865), 171.
143. Shaw, op. cit., 149.
144. A.R. Mountford, 1972, op. cit., Appendix II (64).
145. R. Craig, 'Some Aspects of the Trade and Shipping of the River Dee in the Eighteenth Century' in *Transactions of the Historic Society of Lancashire and Cheshire for the Year 1962* Vol. 114, 1963, 99-128, 108-11.
146. Cheshire Record Office: LNW 9/1-10 for Tonnage Books, LNW 17/1-5 for Day Books. See Weatherill, 1971, op. cit., *passim* for a detailed study.
147. Weatherill, 1971, op. cit., 81.
148. Shaw, op. cit., 149.
149. See J.D. Chambers, *The Vale of Trent 1670-1800 A Regional Study of Economic Change* (Cambridge: Cambridge University Press, 1957), 10-12.
150. Wedgwood MS 30/22936.
151. J. Lindsay, *The Trent & Mersey Canal* (Newton Abbot: David & Charles, 1979), especially Chapter 2.
152. Wedgwood MS 10/30169.
153. Wedgwood MS WM 1459, Folder C, 30 Jul. 1782.
154. Wedgwood MS 79/13658.
155. Wedgwood MS 6/30582.
156. Wedgwood MS 25/18201.
157. Wedgwood MS 5/30234.
158. Wedgwood MSS 5/3992-3996, 30235-30242; 25/18201, 18205, 18207.
159. Wedgwood MS 7/30368, 28 May 1765.

CHAPTER VII
1. Miranda Goodby, 'Early 18th-century Staffordshire Moulds and Modellers," *Transactions of the English Ceramic Circle*, Vol. 17, Part 2, 2000, 223.
2. George Francis Dow, *The Arts and Crafts in New England, 1704-1775* (Topsfield, Massachusetts: The Wayside Press, 1927), 82-3. Dow's original mistake was published by many others including I. Noël-Hume, 'The rise and fall of English white salt-glazed stoneware' (Part I), *The Magazine Antiques*, Feb., 1970, 16.
3. 16 Aug. 1999.
4. Dow, *op cit*, 82-3.
5. Noël-Hume, 1970, 16.
6. *Boston Gazette* 10/17 Feb., as quoted in Dow, *op. cit.*, 83.
7. Margaret B. Schiffer, *Chester County Pennsylvania Inventories 1684-1850* (Schiffer Publishing, 1974), 22.
8. Maryland State Archives, Baltimore County Inventories, Vol. 5, 175.
9. Ibid., Vol. 5, 213.
10. Ibid., Vol. 14, 346.
11. 28 Nov. 1739. Rockingham County Probate Invty. 994, book 1738-46.
12. 27 Aug. 1740. Ibid., 1005, book 1738-46.
13. Maryland State Archives, Baltimore County Inventories, Vol. 21, 159.
14. Estate of Pierce Long, 1746. Rockingham County Probate Invty. 1244, book 1738-46.
15. Estate of Stephen Greenleaf, 1749. Rockingham County Probate Invty. 1446, Vol. 17, 483.
16. *Boston Gazette*, 25 Apr./2 May 1737.
17. *Pennsylvania Gazette*, 10 Jun. 1756.
18. Susan Detweiler, *George Washington's Chinaware* (New York: Harry N. Abrams, Inc, 1982), 202.
19. Ibid., 204.
20. Ibid., 200.
21. *Boston Gazette*, 10 Apr. 1754.
22. *Boston Evening Post*, 17 Jun. 1754.
23. *Pennsylvania Gazette*, 3 Mar. 1752.
24. Ibid., 30 Nov. 1752.
25. Ibid., 24 Mar. 1757.
26. *New York Gazette*, 10 May 1762.
27. Ibid., 29 Sept. 1763.
28. *Boston Gazette*, 28 May 1764.
29. Entry in Thomas Whieldon's notebook located at the Potteries Museum, Stoke-on-Trent, information courtesy Tom Walford.
30. Wedgwood MS 9/70001, 25 Sept. 1764.
31. Wedgwood MS 9/7002-3.
32. Wedgwood MS 9/7004, 15 Oct. 1764.
33. Wedgwood MS 9/7006, 8 Nov. 1764.
34. *Boston Gazette,* 13 Nov. 1758.
35. Ivor Noël Hume, *Archaeology and Wetherburn's Tavern* (Williamsburg, Virginia: Colonial Williamsburg Archaeology Series No. 3, 1969), 30, figure 19a.
36. Maryland State Archives, Anne Arundel County, Original Inventories, Box 65, Folder 4.
37. Maryland Historical Society MS 206, Vol. 1, No. 76 (contents of Doughoregan Manor). For further information on the Carroll family see Diana Edwards, 'English Aristocrats in Maryland Society: the Ceramics of Charles Carroll of Carrollton His Family and Contemporaries' *American Ceramic Circle Journal*, Volume VII, 1989.
38. Carroll's letterbook from 1771 to the early 19th century, referred to as the *Arents Letterbook*, is located in the New York Public Library.
39. Ibid., 8 Oct. 1771.
40. Ibid., 21 Sept. 1772.
41. Ibid., 14 Oct. 1773; 17 Jan. 1775. The 'stone' descriptions of bottles, sweetmeat pots and jugs may be brown stoneware, since 'white stoneware' is specified in other cases.
42. Ibid., 20 Mar. 1783; 10 Nov. 1785.
43. *New Hampshire Gazette*, 2 Oct. 1772.
44. Maryland State Archives, Baltimore County Inventories, Vol. 2i, 332.
45. *Pennsylvania Gazette,* 13 Apr. 1769.
46. Ibid., 12 Aug. 1772. The term 'blue and white stoneware with China Glaze' is not understood by the authors.
47. Ibid., 24 Apr. 1776. The *Pennsylvania Evening Post* offered 'blue and white and enamelled white stone' on 11 Jul. 1776.
48. Winterthur MS No. 87x101.
49. The exact location of Mifflin & Massey's establishment is uncertain. Their ledger is located in the Historical Society of Pennsylvania for 1760-63. They may have gone out of business around the time of the invoice (7 May 1763). Samuel and Charles Massey were merchants located on Water Street between Chestnut and Walnut Streets in 1765 having recently moved from a previous wharf location (*Pennsylvania Magazine*, Jan., 1968). Mifflin & Dean, of Front Street, were dealers in goods of the East Indies in 1765 (*Bulletin of the New York Public Library*, Vol. 39, Number 6, 'Journal of Benjamin Mifflin on a Tour from Philadelphia to Delaware and Maryland (1762)', 1935, 426. The first Philadelphia directory was 1785 and a William Massey was listed as a merchant located at 277 Front Street in 1796.
50. Probate Inventory estate of Ann Pierson, Salem (New Jersey), 15 Sept. 1750, Winterthur MS 55.17.6.
51. James Hongman, Newport, Vernon Papers, Winterthur MS 77 x 314.2, 1 May 1753.
52. Maryland State Archives, inventory of Parker Hall 1755, Baltimore County Inventories, Vol. 1, 337.
53. Estate of Henry Woodward, Anne Arundel County, Maryland, 1762. Probate Inventory estate of Joseph James, Woodstown, Salem (New Jersey). 1 Jun. 1767, Winterthur MS 57 x 14.4.
54. Ibid., Estate of Henry Woodward, Baltimore 1762; estate of Richard Piercy, St. Mary's County, Maryland Inventories, Vol. 87, 23, 1765.
55. Estate of William Payne, Baltimore, 1769. Maryland Inventories, Vol. 106, 143.
56. Probate Inventory estate of Gregory Purcell, merchant located at Puddle Dock, Portsmouth, New Hampshire, 20 Feb. 1777.
57. 5 May 1791, Winterthur MS 73 x 113.
58. *Pennsylvania Gazette*, 17 Sept. 1783.
59. Marley R. Brown III, 'Ceramics from Plymouth, 1621-1800: The Documentary Record,' *Ceramics in America*, Winterthur Conference Report 1972, 72.
60. 12 Sept. 1808, Winterthur MS 58 x 15.
61. Brown *op cit*, 70-72.
62. Frances Norton Mason, *John Norton and Sons Merchants of London and Virginia* (Newton Abbot: David & Charles, 1968), 124-5.
63. Schiffer *op cit*, 22.
64. In a barn fill on the Richard Hart site (Strawberry Banke Museum, A2087; Feature 12).
65. V-586-7 as illustrated in Barbara Liggett, *Archaeology at New Market Exhibit Catalogue* (Philadelphia: The Athenaeum of Philadelphia, 1978), 34.
66. Pat Halfpenny lecture, Keele University, Aug. 1999.
67. Stanley South, *The Search for John Bartlam at Cain Hoy: America's First Creamware Potter* (Columbia, S.C.: University of South Carolina Research Manuscript Series 219, 1993), 195.
68. Personal communication Lisa Hudgins, University of South Carolina Institute of Archaeology and Anthropology.
69. Chris Green, *John Dwight's Fulham Pottery* (London: English Heritage, 1999), 140.
70. Ibid., 135-7.
71. Anne Elizabeth Yentsch, *A Chesapeake Family and Their Slaves: A Study in Historical Archaeology* (Cambridge University Press, 1994).
72. Garry Wheeler Stone et al., 'Ceramics from the John Hicks Site, 1723-1743: The Material Culture,' *Ceramics in America* (Winterthur

Conference Report 1972), 103-125.
73. Ibid., 123.
74. Ivor Noël Hume, *Pottery and Porcelain in Colonial Williamsburg's Archaeological Collections* (Williamsburg, Virginia: Colonial Williamsburg, 1969), 16, figures 11, 12.
75. James Geddy Jnr. was the second occupant of the site on which these shards were found. Geddy's father, James, was a brass founder and Geddy Jnr. worked founding various metals, not just brass.
76. The printed plate with the *Dog in a Manger* scene was found in 1954 on the Ravenscroft site, a last quarter of the 18th century dwelling, which appears from the excavated artefacts to have belonged to a relatively prosperous family. Colonial Williamsburg archaeology catalogue number 139-28FA.
77. The excavations were conducted in several phases from 1979-1991. See William M. Kelso, *Archaeology at Monticello* (Charlottesville, Virginia: Thomas Jefferson Memorial Foundation, Inc, 1997.)
78. Diana Edwards, 'Hart-Shortridge House', *Unearthing New England's Past: The Ceramic Evidence* (Lexington, Massachusetts: Museum of our National Heritage, 1984), 73-84. Edwards et al., 'Generations of Trash, the Hart-Shortridge House, 1769-1860' *American Ceramic Circle Journal*, Vol. VI, 1988, 29-51.
79. J. Worth Estes, *Hall Jackson and the Purple Foxglove, Medical Practice & Research in Revolutionary America 1760-1820* (Hanover, New Hampshire: University of New England Press, 1979).
80. David R. Starbuck, 'America's First Summer Resort: John Wentworth's 18th Century Plantation in Wolfboro, New Hampshire,' *The New Hampshire Archaeologist*, Vol. 30, No. 1, 1989, 63-68.

CHAPTER VIII
1. Published in London by Hamish Hamilton, 1998; Penguin Books, 1999, 132.
2. Thomas Kirgate, *A Description of the Villa of Horace Walpole…at Strawberry Hill…*, 1774 (with additions in 1786). This is located in the National Art Library, Victoria and Albert Museum, London.
3. The sale was conducted by Mr. Thomas Kirby with his assistant, Mr. Otto Bernet, later of Parke Bernet which subsequently joined with Sotheby's forming Sotheby's Parke Bernet.
4. C. Earle, *The Earle Collection of Early Staffordshire Pottery illustrating over seven hundred different pieces* (London: Brown, n.d., preface dated 1915), Plate 60.
5. The Burlington Fine Arts Club was founded in 1856 by J.C. Robinson, first curator of the South Kensington Museum, a friend and kindred spirit of A.W. Franks. The membership in the club which stood at nearly 200 included nearly every prominent collector and connoisseur in the country as well as some leading society figures. Dealers in the antiques trade could not become members but could attend meetings. For further information see: Ann Eatwell, 'The Collectors' or Fine Arts Club 1857-1884; the first society for collectors of the decorative arts', *Journal of the Decorative Arts Society*, 1994.
6. *Illustrated Catalogue of Early English Earthenware* (Burlington Fine Arts Club, 1914).
7. Michael Archer, *Delftware* (London: The Stationery Office, 1997), 52.
8. Ibid., 51.
9. Montague Guest, *Lady Charlotte Schreiber's Journals* Vol. I (London: John Lane, 1911), xxix.
10. W. Elliot, 'Reproduction and Fakes of English Eighteenth-Century Ceramics', *ECC Transactions*, No. 7, Vol. 2, 1939, 67-82.
11. Introduction by J.V.G. Mallet, *Cheyne Book of Chelsea China and Pottery* (Menston, Yorkshire: EP Publishing, 1973 (2nd ed.)), xiii.
12. Wallace Elliot Scrapbooks (1902-1937), Vol. III, page 41. These are located at the Victoria and Albert Museum.
13. Bernard Rackham and Herbert Read's book *English Pottery: Its Development from Early Times to the end of the Eighteenth Century* (London: Ernest Benn) came out in Feb. 1924 in a deluxe printing of fifty copies for England and twenty-five for the United States with an additional three colour plates for £12.12s.; the ordinary edition was £6.6s.
14. Illustrated *ECC Transactions* op. cit., Plate XXVI.
15. H.J. Mayo, *The Connoisseur*, Jan. 1935, 55-6. The auction of Lord Revelstoke's collection was 20-23 Nov. 1934, the salt-glazed stoneware being sold on the second day.
16. Mallet, op. cit., xiii.
17. Archer, op. cit., 583. See J. and J. Cockerill 'Arthur Hurst Collector and Benefactor' in *Northern Ceramic Society Newsletter* No. 82 Jun. 1991, 17-21.
18. *A.W. Franks Nineteenth-Century Collecting and the British Museum*, Marjorie Caygill and John Cherry, eds., (London: The British Museum, 1997), 1. See also David M. Wilson, *The Forgotten Collector* (London: Thames and Hudson, 1984).
19. Robert H. Soden-Smith was a curator at the South Kensington Museum.
20. Caygill and Cherry, op. cit., Appendix I, 318.
21. Aileen Dawson, 'Franks and European Ceramics, Glass and Enamels', ibid., 214.
22. Henry Willett, *Catalogue of a Collection of Pottery and Porcelain illustrating Popular British History* (London: HMSO, 1899).
23. Ibid. Introduction to the catalogue by Henry Willett, Esq. Jun. 1899.
24. In A.R. Mountford, *The Illustrated Guide to Staffordshire Salt-Glazed Stoneware* (London: Barrie & Jenkins, 1971), Pl. 209.
25. Rodney and Eileen Hampson, 'Brownfields, Victorian Potters', *Northern Ceramic Society Journal* Vol. 4, 1980-81, 177-218.
26. *Staffordshire Sentinel*, 28 Oct. 1911.
27. A copy of the catalogue is in the Hanley Reference Library.
28. C.F.C. Luxmoore, *'Saltglaze' with The Notes of a Collector* (Exeter: Pollard, 1924, reprinted London: Holland Press, n.d., c.1970).
29. This 'profile' passed from Jahn to Luxmoore and was again sold on 14 Jun. 1988 by Christie's, London, as lot 48 in *The Price Glover Collection of Fine English Pottery*.
30. 'The Jahn Sale', *The Connoisseur*, Jan. 1912.
31. C. Earle, *The Earle Collection of Early Staffordshire Pottery illustrating over seven hundred different pieces* (London: Brown, n.d., preface dated 1915).
32. *Staffordshire Advertiser*, 29 Nov. 1912, 10; *Pottery Gazette and Glass Trade Review*, 1 Dec. 1913, 1424-25.
33. C.F.C. Luxmoore, *'Saltglaze' with The Notes of a Collector* (Exeter: Pollard, 1924, reprinted London: Holland Press, n.d., c.1970).
34. See *The Herbert and Sylvia Jacobs Collection of 18th and early 19th Century English Pottery*, sale catalogue 24 Jan. 1994 (New York: Christie's, 1994). lot 15.
35. A. Hurst, *A Catalogue of the Boynton Collection of Yorkshire Pottery* (Yorkshire Philosophical Society) 1922.
36. Bernard Rackham, *Catalogue of the Glaisher Collection of Pottery & Porcelain* 2 Vols. (reprint Woodbridge: Antique Collectors' Club, 1987).
37. Robert Bateman, *Catalogue of a Loan Collection of Old English Pottery Exhibited at the Manchester Whitworth Institute 1911-1912* (Manchester: H. Rawson and Co., 1912).
38. See *The Incomparable Art English Pottery from the Thomas Greg Collection* (Manchester: City Art Gallery, 1969).
39. Read referred to John Ogilby's 1671 book on *The Embassy to the Grand Tartar of Cham*.
40. Leslie Grigsby, 'Johan Nieuhoff's Embassy…', *Antiques*, Jan. 1993, 172-183.
41. Ross E. Taggart, *The Frank P. and Harriet C. Burnap Collection of English Pottery in the William Rockhill Nelson Gallery* (Kansas City: Nelson Gallery-Atkins Museum, 1953, 2nd ed. 1967, 182).

CHAPTER IX
1. D. Barker, '18th and 19th Century Ceramics excavated at the Foley Pottery, Fenton, Stoke-on-Trent' in *Staffordshire Archaeological Studies* No. 1, 1984, 63-86.
2. See P.F.C. Roden, 'Josiah Spode (1733-1797) his formative influences and the various Potworks associated with him' in *Journal of the Northern Ceramic Society* Vol. 14, 1997, 1-43, 37-40, for a discussion of the date of erection of the Foley Pottery.
3. D. Barker, 'A Group of Staffordshire Red Stonewares of the 18th century' in *English Ceramic Circle Transactions* Vol. I, Part 2, 1991, 177-98.
4. International Genealogical Index.
5. *Stoke-upon-Trent Parish Register* 3 vol. (Staffordshire Parish Registers Society, 1925), III, 722.
6. Roden, op. cit., 38 n.
7. D. Edwards and A.R. Hampson, English *Dry-Bodied Stoneware…* (Woodbridge: Antique Collectors' Club, 1998), 210-11.
8. Archaeological Department, Potteries Museum and Art Gallery, Stoke-on-Trent; in store.
9. Potteries Museum and Art Gallery, Social History Department: Rough Notes, Salvation Army Site, Westport Road, Burslem.
10. *Stoke-upon-Trent Parish Registers* 4 vol. (Staffordshire Parish Registers Society), II, 288, 418.
11. *Burslem Parish Register* 3 vol. (Staffordshire Parish Registers Society, 1913), I, 190, 192, 193, 197, 203, 210.
12. N. Stretton, 'The Indio Pottery at Bovey Tracey' in *English Ceramic Circle Transactions* Vol. 8, Part 2, 1972, 124-36 and 'Indio Pottery Bovey Tracey A Documentary Salt-Glaze Tea Caddy' in *The Antique Collector*, Aug. 1973, 196-99; and B. Adams and A. Thomas, *A Potwork in Devon The history and products of the Bovey Tracey potteries 1750-1836* (Bovey Tracey: Sayce, 1996).
13. *The Travels through England of Dr. Richard Pococke… during 1750, 1751, and later years* ed. J.J. Cartwright, 2 vol. (London: Camden Society, 1888), I, 131.
14. Stretton, 1972, op. cit., 133-34.

15. Adams and Thomas, op. cit., 9, 10.
16. Ibid., 11, 90.
17. Ibid.
18. Ibid., 13.
19. 'Josiah Wedgwood's Journey into Cornwall – I' ed. G. Wills, in *Proceedings of the Wedgwood Society* No. 1, 1956, 34-77, 47-49.
20. Adams and Thomas, op. cit., 8, 21.
21. A. Thomas, 'Notes on some Bovey Tracey Potters' in *Northern Ceramic Society Newsletter* No. 80, 15-19; International Genealogical Index for baptism dates.
22. Adams and Thomas, op. cit., 68-70.
23. Ibid., 87-88.
24. Ibid., 4, 16. Articles referring to Bovey Tracey Potteries also occur in *Northern Ceramic Society Newsletters* Nos. 16, 71 and *passim* to 90, 107, 111 and 113.
25. Stretton, 1972, op. cit., 131 and plate 87; 196-99.
26. A. Thomas, 'A Tea Canister, a Wall Pocket and a Teapot' in *Northern Ceramic Society Newsletter* No. 79, 31-34.
27. G. Wills, 'The Plymouth Porcelain Factory I' in *Apollo*, Dec. 1980, 377-85, 381.
28. S. Levitt, *Pountneys The Bristol Pottery at Fishponds 1905-1969* (Bristol: Redcliffe, 1990), 10.
29. The advertisement was first reported (in part) by T.K. Boney. 'Liverpool Saltglazed Wares' in *English Ceramic Circle Transactions* Vol. 4, Part 2, 1957, 51-57, 52; and later by N. Stretton, 'Potworks at Chester and Kidderminster' in *Northern Ceramic Society Newsletter* No. 11, Sept. 1974, 9.
30. L. and M. Hillis, 'The Chester White Ware Manufactory' in *Northern Ceramic Society Journal* Vol. 4, 1980-1981, 37-45.
31. C.N. Moore, 'Museum News' in *Northern Ceramic Society Newsletter* No. 57, Mar. 1985, 18-19; J. Axworthy and S. Ward, 'A note on an 18th century pottery site in Mill Street, Chester' (Chester City Council, Chester Archaeology, 1986, unpublished), 1-5.
32. Axworthy and Ward, op. cit. 2, 4; S. Ward, unpublished note on Bridgegate House, Apr. 1985 (Chester City Council, Chester Archaeology).
33. Letter from Ms. Julie Edwards, Chester Archaeology, 14 Aug. 2003.
34. Staffordshire Record Office: D 1788, pcl. 67, bdle. 22.
35. Ibid., Box F1, un-numbered bdle.
36. Edwards and Hampson, op. cit., 210-11.
37. Staffordshire Record Office: D 1788, pcl. 67, bdle. 22.
38. Ibid., Vol. 82; pcl. 67, No. 30.
39. The preceding information is taken from R. Hampson, 'Shelton Farm Potwork: the documentary evidence' (1996), awaiting publication by the Potteries Museum and Art Gallery, Stoke-on-Trent.
40. B. Klemperer, 'Stoke-on-Trent Rescue excavation of post-medieval pottery kilns' in *West Midlands Archaeology* No. 34, 1990, 68-70.
41. D. Barker, *William Greatbatch a Staffordshire Potter* (London: Horne, 1991).
42. *Staffordshire Advertiser*, 1 May 1813, Deaths.
43. Barker, 1991, op. cit., 29, 39, 42-43.
44. Ibid., 79.
45. Ibid., 58, 165.
46. Ibid., 67, 165.
47. Ibid., 143-44, 271.
48. J. Horne, 'John Dwight: The Master Potter of Fulham' in *John Dwight 'The Master Potter of Fulham' 1672-1703 and his contemporaries* (London: Horne, 1992), is a recent general account. Detailed documentary information is published in R. Edwards' 'London Potters circa 1570-1710' in *Journal of Ceramic History* No. 6, 1974, 1-139, 56-59; and more extensively in 'John Dwight's Fulham Pottery 1672-1978 A Collection of Documentary Sources' ed. D. Haselgrove and J. Murray in *Journal of Ceramic History* No. 11, 1979, 1-284, 2-149 and Supplement to *Journal of Ceramic History* Vol. [sic] 11, 1992 1-71, 2-29, 40, 47-57. The archaeological investigation of Dwight's pottery site at Fulham is published in great detail in C. Green, *John Dwight's Fulham Pottery Excavations 1971-79* (London: English Heritage, 1999), which also includes a concise summary of John Dwight's achievement at Fulham (33-36). The bibliographies of these publications include many more papers on the subject.
49. Haselgrove and Murray, 1979, op. cit., 83, 104, 122 for the accusations; 69-71 for the patent.
50. Ibid., 90-91, 93-94.
51. Ibid., 96, 108.
52. Ibid., 122-25.
53. Ibid., 99-100.
54. Ibid., 109-10.
55. Ibid., 107.
56. Ibid., 97.
57. Ibid., 122-24.
58. Ibid., 122.
59. Ibid., 144.
60. R.L. Hobson, *Catalogue of the Collection of English Pottery in the Department of British and Medieval Antiquities and Ethnography of the British Museum* (London: Trustees of the British Museum, 1903) 161-62; A.H. Church, *English Earthenware made during the 17th and 18th Centuries, illustrated by Specimens in the National Collections,* revised edition (London: Board of Education, 1904), 46.
61. Green, op. cit., contains a comprehensive account of shards recovered from the site and whole pieces in public collections, in Chapter 8, 75-108, Chapter 11, 131-46 and Appendix 7.
62. Ibid., 28-29.
63. Hobson, op. cit., 162-63, Plate XLI.
64. Green, op. cit., 21, 26.
65. Haselgrove and Murray, 1979, op. cit., 249-51.
66. Haselgrove and Murray, 1992, op. cit., 1-71, 52-53; Green, op. cit., 40, 131-32, 135-40.
67. Haselgrove and Murray, 1992, op. cit., 1-71, 44; *Ceramic Review* No. 132 Nov./Dec. 1991, 14.
68. *Chebsey Parish Register* (Staffordshire Parish Registers Society, 1964-65). 53: Baptisms 31 Mar. 1725 Humphrey s[on]. of Thomas & Elianor *(sic)* Palmer.
69. See the International Genealogical Index for all four marriages.
70. There is little doubt about Humphrey Palmer's age. He was the son of Thomas and Elianor *(sic)* Palmer, married at Lichfield 20 Feb. 1717/18; and Chebsey, Staffs. Parish Register shows that their six children were christened seriatim: Ann in 1719, Hannah in 1720, Mary in 1722, Margaret in 1723, *Humphrey* on 31 Mar. 1725 and Thomas in 1726.
71. *Burslem Parish Register* 3 vol. (Staffordshire Parish Registers Society, 1913), I, 235. Ann Adams is there described as 'Mrs.', a title accorded to older single women. Ann Adams was aged 29 at her marriage to Palmer.
72. Public Record Office: DL 507/15, Vol. 14, p.32, 15 Aug 1750, Francis Payne to James Payne. (Information from Mr. P. Roden.)
73. Public Record Office: DL 507/15, Vol. 14, p.83. (Information from Mr. P. Roden.)
74. Stoke-on-Trent City Archives: EMT 20/PAYNE/753, 20 Apr. 1753. (Information from the late Mr. K. Quinn.)
75. *Stoke-upon-Trent Parish Registers* 4 vol. (Staffordshire Parish Registers Society, 1925), III, 512.
76. Public Record Office: DL 507/15, Vol. 14, p.25, 25 Jul. 1750. (Information from Mr. P. Roden.)
77. Ibid.: DL 507/22, Vol. 21, p. 45, 23 Mar. 1778, transfer from Humphrey Palmer to James Neale. (Information from Mr. P. Roden.)
78. Hanley St. John's Churchyard, monumental inscription: Ann wife of Humphrey Palmer died 13 May 1752 aged 35. Ann Palmer's age is probably also wrong. Possibly she died in childbirth in May 1751. Palmer married again in October 1751: Staffordshire Record Office: microfiche 1048/1/2, Sandon Parish Register, 1751, Weddings, 28 Oct. married Humphrey Palmer of Hanley Green and Mary Heath of Lane Delph.
79. P.W.L. Adams, *A History of the Adams Family of North Staffordshire…* (London: St. Catharine Press, 1914), 197.
80. D. Barker and P. Halfpenny, *Unearthing Staffordshire Towards a new understanding of 18th century ceramics* (Stoke-on-Trent: City Museum & Art Gallery, 1990) 17-18, 60; D. Barker, 'Discovering Staffordshire Ceramics' in *The International Ceramics Fair and Seminar 14, 15, 16, 17 June 1991* (London: Haughton, 1991), 12-18, *passim*; D. Barker, 'Bits and Bobs – The Development of Kiln Furniture in the 18th-century Staffordshire pottery industry' in *English Ceramic Circle Transactions* Vol. 16, Part 3, 1998, 318-41, 323-24. A definitive account of the 1985 salvage excavation has not been seen. A variety of white salt-glazed stoneware and other wasters from the Town Road site is currently displayed in the Archaeology Gallery of the Potteries Museum and Art Gallery.
81. Wedgwood MS 6/30707, 3 Nov. 1763.
82. A.R. Mountford, 'Thomas Wedgwood, John Wedgwood and Jonah Malkin Potters of Burslem', unpublished MA Thesis, Keele University, 1972, Appendix III, 64, 130. See also our Chapter VI, Potters as Customers.
83. Staffordshire Record Office: D(W)1788, Vol. 99, p.99.
84. Information from Mr. John Griffin, taken from a microfilm of Platt documents in Rotherham Archives and Local Studies Library, gratefully acknowledged.
85. Ibid.
86. J.V.G. Mallet, 'Rotherham Saltglaze: John Platt's Jug' in *English Ceramic Circle Transactions* Vol. 9, Part 1, 1973, 111-14, 112.
87. A.J.B. Kiddell, 'John Platt of Rotherham Potter and Mason-Architect' in *English Ceramic Circle Transactions* Vol. 5, Part 3, 1962, 172-175, Plate 168.
88. Ibid., 173.
89. Mallet, op. cit., Plates 64, 65.
90. A.R. Mountford, *The Illustrated Guide to Staffordshire Salt-Glazed Stoneware* (London: Barrie & Jenkins, 1971), Plate 211; Colonial Williamsburg Foundation, accession number 1963.195, gift of Frank Tilley.
91. International Genealogical Index, confirmed and with additional information by

Mr. John Griffin. Stretching the bounds of possibility, could this Jno. Cousins be the 'Mr. Courzens' who had a painting shop' in 1763, referred to by William Greatbatch, and linked to John or Henry Curzon, painters at Stoke-on-Trent in 1762-63? See Barker, 1991, op. cit., 206.
92. H.C. Goldweitz, 'An American Collection of English Pottery: A Chronology 1635-1778' in *English Ceramic Circle Transactions* Vol. 12, Part 1, 1984, 8-25, 17 and Plate 23 (b).
93. R. Gunnis, *Dictionary of British Sculptors 1660-1851* rev. ed. (London: Abbey Library, n.d.), 308.
94. C. Ross, 'A New Piece from the Rotherham Old Pottery' in *Northern Ceramic Society Newsletter* No. 54, Jun. 1984, 2-8.
95. J.D. Griffin, *The Don Pottery 1801-1893* (Doncaster: Doncaster Museum Service, 2001), 18, note 7; D. Ashurst, *The History of South Yorkshire Glass* (Sheffield: Collis, n.d.), 28, 48.
96. H. Lawrence, *Yorkshire Pots and Potteries* (Newton Abbot: David & Charles, 1974), 120.
97. Kiddell, op. cit.,172-73.
98. J.A. Ely, *The Walkers of Rotherham* (Rotherham: Rotherham Library and Arts Centre, 1992), 5.
99. Mallet, op. cit., 111.
100. Kiddell, op. cit., 174.
101. N. Valpy, 'Extracts from 18th Century London Newspapers' in *English Ceramic Circle Transactions* Vol. 12, Part 2, 1985, 161-88, 169.
102. Lawrence, op. cit., 121.
103. Ross, op. cit., 5.
104. Lawrence, op. cit., 121.
105. Wedgwood MS 55/30900.
106. Lawrence, op. cit., 120.
107. Ross, op. cit., 7.
108. Lawrence, op. cit., 120.
109. Ross, op. cit., 3.
110. Lawrence, op. cit., 121.
111. Ross, op cit., 7-8.
112. A.R. Mountford, 'Documents relating to English ceramics of the 18th & 19th centuries' in *Journal of Ceramic History* No. 8, 1975, 3-41, 5, 8.
113. Ross, op. cit., *passim*.
114. Mallet, op. cit., 112.
115. Staffordshire Record Office: D 1788 Vol. 99, p.127.
116. E.M. Nance, *The Pottery & Porcelain of Swansea & Nantgarw* (London: Batsford, 1942, repr. 1985), 26, 10, 9.
117. Glynn Vivian Art Gallery, Swansea: accession no. 1987.6, diameter 23 cm. This bowl is referred to by R. Pugh *Welsh Pottery* (Bath: Towy, n.d., c.1995) 9, who considers that white salt-glazed stoneware was made at Swansea.
118. W.J. Grant-Davidson, 'Early Swansea Pottery, 1764-1810' in *English Ceramic Circle Transactions* Vol. 7, Part 1, 1968, 59-82, Plate 72 (a) for the 1768 flask and 1775 tea canister, both in the Royal Institution of South Wales, Swansea; Plate 78 (c) for the 1771 jug in Glynn Vivian Art Gallery, Swansea. J. Gray, 'The Ridgways in Swansea' in *English Ceramic Circle Transactions* Vol. 17, Part 2, 2001, 413-19 also illustrates the 1768 flask and 1771 jug.
119. Nance, op. cit., 13-14, plate I, B, C.
120. Grant-Davidson, op. cit., 60-61.
121. J. Gray, 'The Cambrian Pottery Before 1802' in *Welsh Ceramics in Context* Part I ed. J. Gray (Swansea: Royal Institution of South Wales, 2003), 19-38, 20.
122. Mountford, 1972, op. cit., Mountford, 1971, op. cit. Both documents and ware were in the Ceramics Department of the Potteries Museum and Art Gallery, Stoke-on-Trent in 2003.
123. W. Pitt, *Topographical History of Staffordshire…* (Newcastle-under-Lyme: Smith, 1817), 421.
124. John Wedgwood wrote an 'Essay on Pottery' in Aug. 1743 and he expressed concern about the quality of water used for making pots, see A. Mountford 'Thomas Briand – A Stranger' in *English Ceramic Circle Transactions* Vol. 7, Part 2, 1969, 87-99, 96.
125. Pitt, op. cit., 422-23.
126. S. Shaw. *History of the Staffordshire Potteries…* (Hanley: privately, 1829), 124-25, 149-50.
127. See Lichfield Record Office: will of Aaron Wedgwood, Burslem, Earth Potter, proved 20 Oct. 1743, 'my two sons Thomas and John Wedgwood'.
128. Burslem St. John's Churchyard, monumental inscription: Aaron Wedgwood died 21 Apr. 1743 aged 77; Mary his wife died 22 Apr. 1743 aged 76.
129. Lichfield Record Office: will of Aaron Wedgwood, Burslem, Earth Potter, proved 20 Oct. 1743.
130. Potteries Museum and Art Gallery: Pottery Accessions Register 472P 1963 – 38P 1968; and see Mountford, 1971, op. cit., 67-68, plate 222.
131. Mountford, 1975, op. cit., 5, 8.
132. Mountford, 1971, op. cit., 44, Plate 84.
133. Wedgwood MS 25/18628.
134. Wedgwood MSS 6/30443, 30447, 30448, 30451, 30452, 30457, 30464, 30466.
135. Mountford, 1972, op. cit., Appendix III.
136. Ibid., 104-21, Tables A-F. See our Appendix 5 for their customers by name, including fellow potters.
137. Ibid., Appendix III, 14 (69 for Griffith's address).
138. Wedgwood MS: 6/30442, 27 Jun. 1763.
139. Wedgwood MS 6/5013, 11 Jan. 1764.
140. Wedgwood MS 6/30461, 5 Dec. 1768.
141. Wedgwood MS 6/5014-17.
142. Wedgwood MS 6/30468, 7 Mar. 1770.
143. Wedgwood MSS 6/30445-30453.
144. Shaw, op. cit., 162.
145. Mountford, 1972, op. cit., Appendix I; 1971, op. cit., 33.
146. Ibid., illustration No. 6, opp. 72.
147. Ibid., Appendix III, 150.
148. Ibid., Appendix III, 151, 164.
149. Wedgwood MSS 6/ 30470; 6/5022-5025.
150. Mountford, 1972, op. cit., Appendix III, 158, 147, 164, 169.
151. Ibid., Appendix III, 4, 47, 102, 134, 169; Appendix IV, 24, 28, 38, 42, 54, 61.
152. Wedgwood MS 6/30470, 11Oct. 1770.
153. Wedgwood MS 6/5025, 17 May 1775.
154. Mountford, 1972, op. cit., Appendix III, 151, 164.
155. Ibid., Appendix II (68).
156. L. Jewitt, *The Wedgwoods: being a Life of Josiah Wedgwood…* (London: Virtue, 1865), 161, inscription on floor of vestry, St. John's Church, Burslem.
157. Mountford, 1972, op. cit., illustration No. 1, after p.25.
158. Ibid., 36, 37.
159. *Bailey's British Directory* 4 vol. (London: Bailey, 1784), Vol. 2, 391.
160. Potteries Museum and Art Gallery: Pottery Accessions Register 472P 1963 – 38P 1968.
161. Mountford, 1971, op. cit., 42, 54, 67-68, plates 22, 23, 44, 45, 79, 84, 87-89, 94, 96, 98-100, 103-05, 107, 108, 110, 115, 133-35, 139, 140, 201, 222. In many instances the descriptions in the captions are of course more precise than those in the Accessions Register.
162. R. Hampson, 'History of Burslem Market Place Area', unpublished, 3-5; copy in Stoke-upon-Trent City Archives: S 8109.
163. P. Halfpenny, 'Thomas Whieldon: his Life and Work' in *English Ceramic Circle Transactions* Vol. 16, Part 2, 1997, 237-54.
164. *Kingsley Parish Register* (Staffordshire Parish Registers Society, 1967-68), 127: 1705, 21 Feb. William son of Joseph & Alles [sic, Alice] Whieldon baptised.
165. *Stoke-upon-Trent Parish Registers* 4 vol. (Staffordshire Parish Registers Society), II, 347, Baptisms, 1719, 6 Sept. Thos. Whieldon son of Joseph & Alice.
166. *Barlaston Parish Register* (Staffordshire Parish Registers Society, 1905), 71, 1744, 19 Aug. Tho. Wheeldon [sic], potter, 22 and Anne . sp[inster], 22 both of Stoke parish, lic[ence] married.
167. A. Mountford, 'Thomas Whieldon's manufactory at Fenton Vivian' in *English Ceramic Circle Transactions* Vol. 8, Part 2, 1972, 164-82, 175-176, 181-82.
168. *A History of the County of Stafford* ed. J.G. Jenkins, multi-vol (London: Oxford University Press, 1963), VIII, 218.
169. Mountford, Whieldon, 1972, op. cit., 172.
170. Barker, 1991, op. cit., 82, suggesting 1740-60. The same author later suggested 1750-70, see D. Barker, 'Bits', 1998, op. cit., 318-41, 331.
171. Potteries Museum and Art Gallery, Ceramics Department: Thomas Whieldon's Memorandum Book, uncatalogued.
172. W. Emery, 'Notes on Whieldon Pottery' in *Transactions of the Ceramic Society* Vol. XXIV, Part IV, 1925, 339-47, 409; H.W. Maxwell, 'Excavations in North Staffordshire' in *English Ceramic Circle Transactions* No. 1, 1933, 57-58, 57; A.T. Morley Hewitt, 'Early Whieldon of the Fenton Low works' in *English Ceramic Circle Transactions* Vol. 3, Part 3, 1954, 142-54.
173. Halfpenny, op. cit., 251-52.
174. Potteries Museum and Art Gallery, Ceramics Department: Thomas Whieldon's Memorandum Book, uncatalogued: p. 70 for Austin, A opening for Davison, and p.67 for Blour. See ., op. cit., 177 for an explanation of 'flowering'.
175. Mountford, Whieldon, 1972, op. cit., 174-75, plate 130; Halfpenny, op. cit., 241-43.
176. D. Barker, *A New Perspective of the Staffordshire Potteries* (London: Horne, 1998), [8] fig. 18.
177. C.F.C. Luxmoore, *'Saltglaze' with The Notes of a Collector* (Exeter: Pollard, 1924, rep. London: Holland, n.d.), 65. A. Ray, 'Staffordshire Tiles 1750-1840' in *English Ceramic Circle Transactions* Vol. 15, Part 2, 1994, 194-204, 196 illustrates the *Heron and Spewing Duck Fountain* design on a white salt-glazed tile in the Victoria and Albert Museum.
178. Potteries Museum and Art Gallery, Ceramics Department: Thomas Whieldon's Memorandum Book, uncatalogued, 48 left.
179. Wedgwood MS 26/19117, Experiment Book, 1.
180. R. Reilly, Wedgwood *The New Illustrated Dictionary* (Woodbridge: Antique Collectors'

Club, 1995), 153.
181. Wedgwood MS 43/28700.
182. A.J. Toppin, 'A Ceramic Miscellany: I Francis Place' in *English Ceramic Circle Transactions* Vol. 3, Part 1, 65-68; R.E.G. Tyler, 'Francis Place's Pottery' in *English Ceramic Circle Transactions* Vol. 8, Part 2, 1972, 203-14; P.M. Korry 'Francis Place, Seventeenth-Century English Potter and Man of the Enlightenment' in *Ars Ceramica* Number 16, 2000, 40-49.
183. Tyler, op. cit., 204, 211.
184. Ibid., 205-06.
185. Ibid., 208.
186. Ibid., 211-12.
187. Ibid., 203 and Plate 155.
188. *The Victoria History of the County of York* 4 vol. ed. W. Page (London: Constable, 1907-25), II, 437.
189. Korry, op. cit., Figures 1, 5-8, held in the Mint Museum of Art, Charlotte, North Carolina, U.S.A; Victoria and Albert Museum, London; National Museums of Scotland, Edinburgh; British Museum, London and the Patrick Allan-Fraser of Hospitalfield Trust, Arbroath, Scotland.
190. Green, op. cit., 127.

APPENDIX 1

1. J.C. Wedgwood, *A History of the Wedgwood Family* (London: St. Catherine Press, 1908). 132.
2. Wedgwood MSS 96/17793-17845.
3. Wedgwood MS 25/18442, 3 Feb. 1773; 25/18465, 30 May 1773; Josiah Wedgwood to Thomas Bentley. Josiah Wedgwood's letters at this time tell much of Thomas Wedgwood's domestic difficulties, not relevant here.
4. J.C. Wedgwood, op. cit., 135.
5. Wedgwood, op. cit., 109, suggests that Thomas Wedgwood (IV) leased the Overhouse Pottery, but gives no evidence that he did so.
6. L.H. Mero, *Chronicle of Our Heritage – History of Some Harrison, Harris and Connected Families in England and America, 1550-1995* (Utica, Ky., privately, 1995), 43, 70, 125.
7. E. Meteyard, *the Life of Josiah Wedgwood...* 2 vol. (London: Hurst and Blackett, 1865), I, 222, n.1.
8. Wedgwood MS 96/17695, c.1776.
9. *Bailey's British Directory* 4 vol. (London: Bailey, 1784), Vol. 2, 391.
10. D. Edwards and R. Hampson, *English Dry-Bodied Stoneware Wedgwood and Contemporary Manufacturers 1774 to 1830* (Woodbridge: Antique Collectors' Club, 1998), 200.
11. Keele University Information Services: res Local Coll. DA 690.B9S8, Burslem Rate Book 1802.
12. Thomas Hargreaves, *Map of the Staffordshire Potteries, & Newcastle...* (Burslem: Thomas Hargreaves, 1832).
13. Inscription over entrance arch.
14. Wedgwood MS 96/17807, 1773.
15. Wedgwood MS 49/29596, 3 May 1780.
16. A 'peck' is 'A measure of capacity used for dry goods, the fourth part of a bushel, or two gallons' *(OED)*.
17. Wedgwood MS 50/29972, 3 Oct. 1769.
18. Wedgwood MSS 106/19953 for 1776, 10/8984B for 1777; 10/8984 for 1778.
19. Wedgwood MSS 49/29844-29850.
20. Staffordshire Record Office: D1788, Vol. 102, 98 for 1764; Vol. 99, 31 for 1765-67; Vol. 100, 44 for 1768-71 The first reference is to Thomas Wedgwood *Churchyard*, but this may be merely to identify which of the two or three Thomas Wedgwoods who were active at that date had bought the flint; Wedgwood MS 11/1992 for 1772.
21. Wedgwood MS 55/9840, 5-30.
22. William Lockett of Burslem, potter, father of *Timothy and John Lockett*, insured his 'Sliphouse or Stove' in 1767, see E. Adams, 'Ceramic Insurances in the Sun Company, 1766-1774' in *English Ceramic Circle Transactions* Vol. 10, Part I 1976, 1-38, 25.
23. *R R Angerstein's Illustrated Travel Diary 1753-1755 Industry in England and Wales from a Swedish perspective* trans. T. and P. Berg (London: Science Museum, 2001) illustrates these in Figures 190 (Derby), and 319a (Staffordshire).
24. 'Green' ware is unfired ware. 200 dozen would be over half an 'Ovenfull', of 360 dozen, prepared for the next firing.
25. Wedgwood MS 55/9841, between 4 Oct. and Nov. 1765.
26. Wedgwood MS 55/9837, Sept. 1763.
27. Wedgwood MS 55/9838.
28. Wedgwood MS 55/9837.
29. Wedgwood MS 96/17804.
30. Wedgwood MS 129/25597-25599.
31. A.E. Dodd, *Dictionary of Ceramics* 2nd ed. (London: Newnes, 1967), 290, 351.
32. Wedgwood MS 49/29596a, 23 Feb. 1767.
33. Wedgwood MS 55/9840, 14-27 Nov. 1782.
34. Wedgwood MS 55/9839. See F. Britton *London Delftware* (London: Horne, 1986) 190, for '8 Bushells of Bay salt' on hand in the Mugg Kiln Room of Nathaniel Oade, a London potter, in 1726.
35. Wedgwood MS 96/17806, 21 Jul.-13 Oct. 1773.
36. Wedgwood MSS 55/9840, p.2 from back.
37. Wedgwood MS127/25004.
38. Wedgwood MS 55/9841.
39. Wedgwood MS 55/9841.
40. Wedgwood MS 55/9841, 5 Aug. 1765.
41. Wedgwood MS 96/17806, 1773.
42. Wedgwood MS 96/17812.
43. R. Reilly, *Wedgwood: The New Illustrated Dictionary* (Woodbridge: Antique Collectors' Club, 1995), 492.
44. Wedgwood MS 96/17804.
45. The reduction in weight from prepared body to fired pots is about 25% (P. Rado, *An Introduction to the Technology of Pottery* 2nd edition (Oxford: Pergamon, 1988), 46). A random selection of twelve salt-glazed pots gave an average weight of 9oz. each, suggesting that 1½ tons of unfired body would produce 4,480 pots. The 'Ovenfull' was 360 dozen – 4,320 pots.
46. Wedgwood MS 96/17804.
47. Wedgwood MS 96/17811, 30 Jul. 1773.
48. Wedgwood MS 96/17808, 16 Mar. 1773.
49. Wedgwood MS 96/17794.
50. Appendix 3.
51. Wedgwood MS 55/30441.
52. Wedgwood MS 31/23056.
53. A.R. Mountford, 'Thomas Wedgwood, John Wedgwood and Jonah Malkin Potters of Burslem', unpublished MA Thesis, Keele University, 1972, Appendix II (20).
54. Wedgwood MS 6/5047-5048.
55. Mountford, 1972, op. cit., Appendix III, 93, 150.
56. Wedgwood MS 11/9837, p.11.
57. Wedgwood MS 55/9841, p.34.
58. Wedgwood MS 55/9837-9841.
59. David Rhodes' debt to Thomas Wedgwood IV suggests that Rhodes had bought plain white salt-glazed stoneware to decorate.
60. Wedgwood MS 55/9838.
61. It is assumed that, unless Thomas Wedgwood IV was manufacturing the non-salt-glazed items at his Churchyard Works, he took the orders and 'bought-in' from other makers to fulfil them.
62. Wedgwood MS 55/9838.
63. Wedgwood MS 13/2555.
64. Wedgwood MS 55/9841, between 20 and 28 May 1765, 29 Jul. 1765.
65. Wedgwood MS 1/609.
66. Wedgwood MS 55/9841, 4 Oct. 1765.
67. Wedgwood MS 11/9837, p.11.
68. Wedgwood MS 55/9841, p.34.
69. Wedgwood MS 55/9838.
70. Wedgwood MS 55/9839.
71. Wedgwood MS 6/31181.
72. Wedgwood MS 13/2557.
73. Wedgwood MS 1/30222.
74. *The Liverpool Directory For the Year 1766...* (Liverpool: Gore, 1766, rep. 1987) 48, 70.
75. Wedgwood MS 55/9839, 21 Sept. 1771.
76. Wedgwood MS 55/9841, 4 Feb. 1765.
77. Wedgwood MS 1/614.
78. Wedgwood MS 6/30159.
79. Wedgwood MS 55/9841.
80. Wedgwood MS 55/9841, 10 Apr. 1765.
81. *The Selected Letters of Josiah Wedgwood* ed. A. Finer and G. Savage (London: Cory, Adams & Mackay, 1965) 56-57; Wedgwood MS 32/24141.
82. Wedgwood MS 55/9839, 21 Sept. 1771.
83. Wedgwood MS 96/17809, 3 Apr. 1773.
84. Wedgwood MS 11/31085.
85. Wedgwood MS 11/9302.
86. Wedgwood MS 11/9303.
87. Wedgwood MS 11/30371.
88. Wedgwood MS 49/29596a.
89. Wedgwood MS 49/29596.
90. Wedgwood MS 55/9840, flint, 2 May 1775 to 29 Dec. 1785; crates from 5 Jun. 1775 to 11 Jan. 1777.
91. Wedgwood MS 31/23056.
92. Wedgwood MS 55/9840, 3-22.
93. Wedgwood MS 55/9839, 8-9.
94. Wedgwood MS 55/9839, 7.
95. The Trent and Mersey Canal had not reached the Potteries at this date. It was only opened from the River Trent near Willington to Stone, south of the Potteries, on 12 Nov. 1771. (J. Lindsay, *The Trent and Mersey Canal* (Newton Abbot: David & Charles, 1979), 41).
96. Wedgwood MS 55/9839.
97. Cheshire Record Office: LNW 17/2, Tonnage Book, 1745-1748.
98. Ibid., 17/4, Tonnage Book, 1750-1753, 355.
99. Ibid., 17/5, Tonnage Book, 1753-1755, 363.
100. Wedgwood MS 11/9301.
101. Wedgwood MS 11/9302.

APPENDIX 2 A-C

1. P.W.L. Adams, *A History of the Adams Family of North Staffordshire...* (London: St. Catherine Press, 1914), 315-17.
2. A.R. Mountford, 'Documents relating to English ceramics of the 18th & 19th centuries' in *Journal of Ceramic History* No. 8, 1975, 3-41, 5.
3. Staffordshire Record Office: D1788, Vol. 99, 124.
4. S. Shaw, *History of the Staffordshire Potteries...* (Hanley: privately, 1829), 175.

5. R. Hampson, 'Longton Potters 1700-1865' in *Journal of Ceramic History* Vol. 14, 1990, 27, 139.
6. International Genealogical Index.
7. Shaw, op. cit., 175.
8. 'The 1767 Return of Staffordshire Papists' in *Staffordshire Catholic History* No. 17, 1977, 34.
9. Information from Mr. P. Roden, quoting Public Record Office, DL30 507/9: Newcastle-under-Lyme Manor Court Minute Book Vol. 8, p.13, will of Simon Vinsome, presented 11 Apr. 1733.
10. Information from Mr. P. Roden, quoting Public Record Office, DL30 507/15: Newcastle-under-Lyme Manor Court Minute Book Vol.14, p.169.
11. *Stoke-upon-Trent Parish Register* 4 vol. (Staffordshire Parish Registers Society, 1925) III, 687: Funerals, 1779, 29 Jul. John Alders.
12. Information from Mr. P. Roden, quoting Public Record Office, DL30 507/22: Newcastle-under-Lyme Manor Court Minute Book Vol.21, pp. 2 and 3 from back.
13. Ibid., 507/23: Newcastle-under-Lyme Manor Court Minute Book Vol.22, pp. 88, 89.
14. Ibid.: Extract from 'Plan of Cottages and In-croachments on to land owned by The Duchy of Lancaster in the Liberty of Penkhull, 1777'. A copy is held by Potteries Museum and Art Gallery, Archaeological Department, Historic Buildings Survey.
15. Shaw, op. cit., 175.
16. 'The 1767 Return of Staffordshire Papists' in *Staffordshire Catholic History* No. 17 1977, 34.
17. Information from Mr. P. Roden, quoting Public Record Office, DL30 507/10: Newcastle-under-Lyme Manor Court Minute Book Vol. 10, p.4.
18. Ibid., 507/15: Newcastle-under-Lyme Manor Court Minute Book Vol. 14, p.81.
19. Ibid., 507/22: Newcastle-under-Lyme Manor Court Minute Book Vol. 21, p.33. This Joseph Warburton is not the salt-glaze potter described in this appendix.
20. *Stoke-upon-Trent Parish Register* 4 vol. (Staffordshire Parish Registers Society, 1925) III, 687.
21. Information from Mr. P. Roden, quoting Public Record Office, DL30 507/25: Newcastle-under-Lyme Manor Court Minute Book Vol.Vol. 24, p.31.
22. *Staffordshire Advertiser*, 6 Nov. 1802, p.1, col. 3.
23. D. Edwards and R. Hampson, *English Dry-Bodied Stoneware* ... (Woodbridge: Antique Collectors' Club, 1998) 210-11.
24. See Appendix 3.
25. *Burslem Parish Registers* 3 vol. (Staffordshire Parish Registers Society, 1913), III, 689, 711
26. S. South, 'The Search for John Bartlam at Cain Hoy: America's First Creamware Potter' in *Research Manuscript* Series 219, University of South Carolina, 1993, 1-162, Appendix, 163-300, 30-31, 33-34, 74-75.
27. B.L. Rauschenburg, 'John Bartlam, Who Established "new Pottworks in South Carolina" and Became the First Successful Creamware Potter in America' in *Journal of Early Southern Decorative Arts* Vol. XVII, No. 2, Nov. 1991, 1-79.
28. Staffordshire Record Office: D 1788, pcl.14, bdle., 2 pt., Book A, p.[1].
29. R. Hampson, 'John Bartlam's Companions to America' in *Journal of the Northern Ceramic Society* Vol. 15 1998, 79-82.
30. South, op. cit., Appendix, 163-300, 17-75.
31. B.L. Rauschenburg, 'Escape from Bartlam: The History of William Ellis of Hanley' in *Journal of Early Southern Decorative Arts* Vol. XVII, No. 2 Nov. 1991, 80-102.
32. South, op. cit., Appendix 2, 168, 173, 195.
33. C. Knight, *The Popular History of England* multi-vol. (London: Sangster, 1856-62),VI, 457.
34. B.L. Rauschenburg, 'Escape', op. cit., 80-102. A helpful description of Salem by P.W. Locklair can be found in *The Craftsman in Early America* ed. I.A.M.G. Quimby (Winterthur: Henry Francis du Pont Winterthur Museum, 1984, 273-98).
35. Edwards and Hampson, op. cit., 210-11.
36. M. Hawes, 'The Migration of Pottery Workers between Stoke-on-Trent and the Broseley Area in the Eighteenth Century' in *The Journal of the Wilkinson Society* No. 2, 1974, 7-9, 7.
37. *A History of the County of Stafford* ed. J.G. Jenkins (London: Oxford University Press, 1963), VIII, 164. The references in note 86 have been checked and no evidence has been found.
38. R. Hampson, 'Shelton Farm Potwork: the documentary evidence' in unpublished report on Shelton Farm Excavation in 1992, copy held by Archaeology Department, Potteries Museum and Art Gallery.
39. International Genealogical Index.
40. 'John Dwight's Fulham Pottery 1672-1978 A Collection of Documentary Sources' ed. D. Haselgrove and J. Murray, in *Journal of Ceramic History* No. 11, 1979, 69-71, 122-25.
41. S. Shaw, op. cit., 119-21. G. Elliott, *John and David Elers and their Contemporaries* (London: Horne, 1998), 37, also makes this suggestion.
42. International Genealogical Index.
43. Staffordshire Record Office: D (W) 1742/55.
44. Ibid.
45. International Genealogical Index.
46. *Stoke-upon-Trent Parish Register* 4 vol. (Staffordshire Parish Registers Society, 1925), III, 343: Funerals, 18 Oct. 1719, Abigail Astbury ux (wife).
47. International Genealogical Index: *Staffordshire* 1984.
48. See Lichfield Record Office: Joshua Astbury, will, proved 19 Apr. 1722.
49. Staffordshire Record Office: D1788, pcl. 61, bdle. 41.
50. *Stoke-upon-Trent Parish Register* 4 vol. (Staffordshire Parish Registers Society, 1925) III, 365: Funerals, 10 Oct. 1721 Josa Astbury potter.
51. Lichfield Record Office: Joshua Astbury, will, proved 19 Apr. 1722.
52. The purpose of these 'engines' is not known for certain. At that date an engine was any contrivance with moving parts: a pair of scissors was termed an engine by Pope in 1712 (*OED*). As they were associated in the inventory with sifting boxes and mortars, they may have been contrivances for oscillating the sifting boxes and mortars.
53. P.W.L. Adams, *Notes on some North Staffordshire Families* (Tunstall: privately, 1930), 22-23; Wedgwood MS 17949-22.
54. Staffordshire Record Office: D 1788, pcl. 5, bdle. 1.
55. The Castle and Falcon Inn was immediately outside the Alders-gate (*The A to Z of Georgian London* int. R. Hyde (London Topographical Society, Publication No. 126, 1982) 4Cc).
56. J.C. Wedgwood, *A History of the Wedgwood Family* (London: St. Catherine Press, 1908), 324.
57. Shaw, op. cit., 141, 130.
58. Ibid., 141, 130, 70.
59. T. Hargreaves, *a Map of the Staffordshire Potteries and Newcastle-under-Lyme* (Burslem: privately, 1832).
60. International Genealogical Index: John, son of John and Ann Astbury, baptised at Stoke Church 14 May 1690; Thomas, son of John and Ann Astbury, baptised at Stoke Church 4 May 1692; *The Stoke-upon-Trent Parish Listing, 1701* ed. D.A. Gatley et. al., off-print from *Collections for a History of Staffordshire 4th Series* Vol. 16 1994, 220, FC1.
61. Lichfield Record Office: Thomas Astbury, will proved 14 Aug. 1752.
62. J. Mallet 'John Baddeley of Shelton, an Early Staffordshire Maker of Pottery and Porcelain Parts I and II' in *English Ceramic Circle Transactions* Vol. 6, Part 2, 1966, 124-66, Part 3, 1967, 181-247; T. Markin 'Ralph Baddeley, Potter, of Shelton, Stoke on Trent' in *Journal of the Northern Ceramic Society* Vol. 16, 1999, 97-124.
63. L. Weatherill, *The Pottery Trade and North Staffordshire 1660-1760* (Manchester: Manchester University Press, 1971) *passim*; 'Capital and Credit in the Pottery Industry before 1770' in *Business History* Vol. XXIV, No. 3, Nov. 1982, 243-58, 248, 255-57.
64. *Wolstanton Parish Registers*. 2 parts (Staffordshire Parish Registers Society, 1914). Part 1, 233, Baptisms 1725/26 26 Feb. John s. of Ralph & Sarah Baddeley.
65. Mallet, 1966, op. cit., 126-27.
66. Ibid., 133, 164, 209.
67. Mallet, 1967, op. cit., 181-83, 185, 222.
68. The late Mr. K. Quinn's notes, from Stoke-on-Trent City Archives: EMT 7/758. Part of the property, a house adjoining the flint ware warehouse, was held by Hannah Payne, widow of *James Payne*. See also T. Markin 'Ralph Baddeley, Potter, of Shelton, Stoke on Trent' in *Journal of the Northern Ceramic Society* Vol. 16, 97-124, 100.
69. Mallet, 1967, op. cit., 186-89; Edwards and Hampson, op. cit., 210-11.
70. Mallet, 1967, op. cit., Appendix G, 226-42.
71. Wedgwood MS 6/5047.
72. T.A. Lockett 'English Porcelain and Colonial America' in *English Ceramic Circle Transactions* Vol. 16, Part 3, 1998, 283-97.
73. Mallet, 1966, op. cit., 133, 164, 209.
74. Staffordshire Record Office: D1788,Vol. 99.
75. Staffordshire Record Office: D1788,Vol. 96.
76. Staffordshire Record Office: D1788, Vol. 96; *Sketchley's Birmingham... Directory* (Birmingham: Sketchley, 1767) 24, Engravers: Giles, Joseph, Snow Hill.
77. Staffordshire Record Office: D1788, Vol. 96; Newcastle-under-Lyme Museum and Art Gallery: R.J. Washington 'Archaeological Survey of Clocks at Newcastle-under-Lyme Museum', unpublished dissertation submitted to the University of Keele for the Diploma in Archaeology, Jul. 1977, 24.
78. Staffordshire Record Office: D1788, Vol. 96. Baddeley made further purchases of blocks from 'Greatbatch' from 7 Nov. 1761 to 10 Jan. 1762, and also paid a 'Greatbatch' for 'oven work' on 5 Jun. 1762.
79. Mallet,1966, op. cit., 124-66, 141, 1967, op.

cit., 181-247, 195.
80. Staffordshire Record Office: D1788, Vol. 96.
81. Ibid., pcl. 1, bdle. 2.
82. Mallet, 1967, op. cit., 185.
83. *Letters of Josiah Wedgwood 1771 to 1780* ed. K.E. Farrar (privately 1903, rep. Didsbury: Morten, n.d., c.1973) 24.
84. Mallet, 1967, op cit., 212-13, plates 140.
85. W. Mankowitz & R.G. Haggar *The Concise Encyclopedia of English Pottery and Porcelain* (London: Deutsch, 1957) 12.
86. Staffordshire Record Office: D 1788, Vol. 95, Mill Account 1758.
87. S. Shaw, op. cit., 157-61.
88. B. Horn, 'Ceramic Bills – Discoveries of 1987' in *English Ceramic Circle Transactions* Vol. 14, Part 1, 1990, 84-92, 88-89.
89. Wedgwood MS 1/30211.
90. Wedgwood MS 50/31195.
91. Wedgwood MS 11/30185.
92. International Genealogical Index.
93. *Burslem Parish Register* 3 vol. (Staffordshire Parish Registers Society, 1913), III, 273.
94. Lichfield Record Office: Admon., Peter Bagnall, 27 Mar. 1761.
95. *A History of the County of Stafford* ed. J.G. Jenkins (London: OUP, 1963) VIII, 271-72. Rushton Grange was a centre for Roman Catholicism, and baptism and marriage records are scanty.
96. Wedgwood MS 72/22870.
97. 'The 1767 Return of Staffordshire Papists' in *Staffordshire Catholic History* No. 17 1977, 37.
98. *Burslem Parish Register* 3 vol. (Staffordshire Parish Registers Society, 1913) III, 652.
99. L. Weatherill has suggested total pottery assets of Peter Bagnall as £1,027, including an estimated £280 for his fourteen workrooms, in 'Capital and Credit in the Pottery Industry before 1770' in *Business History* Vol. XXIV No. 3 Nov. 1982, 246, 254.
100. L.M. Weatherill, 'The Growth of the Pottery Industry in England, 1660-1815' unpublished PhD. Thesis, London University, 1981, 275.
101. A.R. Mountford, 'Thomas Wedgwood, John Wedgwood and Jonah Malkin Potters of Burslem', unpublished MA Thesis, Keele University, 1972, Appendix II, (22), (62).
102. Cheshire Record Office: LNW 17/5, Winsford Tonnage Book, 1753-55, entry no. 229.
103. Wedgwood MS 30/22871, 17 Jul. 1764.
104. Wedgwood MS 30/22870, 11 Apr. 1764.
105. Wedgwood MS 30/22872, 17 Dec. 1764.
106. Mountford, 1972, op. cit., Appendix III, 54.
107. Staffordshire Record Office: D1788, Vol. 99, p. 91.
108. Shaw, op. cit., 172, 215.
109. See B. Hillier, *Master Potters of the Industrial Revolution The Turners of Lane End* (London: Cory, Adams & Mackay, 1965) and R. Hampson 'Longton Potters 1800-1865' in *Journal of Ceramic History* Vol. 14, 1990, 157-66.
110. P.F.C. Roden, 'Josiah Spode (1733-1797) his formative influences and the various Potworks associated with him' in *Journal of the Northern Ceramic Society* Vol. 14, 1997, 1-43, 10-16, 29.
111. E. Adams, 'The Bow Insurances and Related Matters' in *English Ceramic Circle Transactions* Vol. 9, Part I, 1973, 67-108, 75, 85, 104.
112. International Genealogical Index.
113. A.R. Mountford, 1972, op cit., Appendix III, 51.
114. G. Wills, 'Ceramic Causerie' in *Apollo*, Vol. LX, No. 354, Aug. 1954, 44, quoting the *London General Evening Post*, 14 Jul. 1759.
115. E. Adams, 'Ceramic Insurances in the Sun Company, 1766-1774' in *English Ceramic Circle Transactions* Vol. 10, Part I, 1976, 1-38, 36.
116. Shaw, op. cit., 63-64, 156-57.
117. S. Shaw, *The Chemistry of… Pottery* (London: Lewis, 1837, rep. London: Scott Greenwood, 1900), 416.
118. *The Stoke-upon-Trent Parish Listing, 1701* ed. D.A. Gatley et. al., off-print from *Collections for a History of Staffordshire* 4th Series Vol. 16 1994, 188, shows Daniel Bird aged three living with his widowed mother Elizabeth in Penkhull in June 1701.
119. International Genealogical Index. See *the Incomparable Art* int. M.R. Parkinson (Manchester: City Art Gallery, 1969) 20 for the ramifications of the Bird family.
120. B. Hillier, *Master Potters of the Industrial Revolution The Turners of Lane End* (London: Cory, Adams & Mackay, 1965) 3.
121. *Stoke-upon-Trent Parish Register* 3 vol. (Staffordshire Parish Registers Society, 1925), III, 552: Burials, 10 Nov. 1753, Dan Bird of Stoke Potter.
122. Hillier, op. cit., 4, 7.
123. See P. Roden, 'The Cliff Bank Works, Stoke' in *Northern Ceramic Society Newsletter* No. 94 Jun. 1994, 22-26, and No. 95, Sept. 1994, 15; and T. Markin, 'The Booth Family of Potters at Cliff Bank, Stoke-on-Trent' in *Journal of the Northern Ceramic Society* Vol. 15, 1998, 17-46 for more detailed information.
124. Edwards and Hampson, op. cit., 210-11.
125. *Bailey's British Directory* 4 vol. (London: Bailey, 1784) Vol. 2, 391.
126. Wedgwood MSS 11/210-12; WM 1459, Blackwell.
127. *Staffordshire Advertiser* 1 Sept. 1804.
128. *The Staffordshire Pottery Directory* (Hanley: Chester and Mort, n.d., c.1796).
129. International Genealogical Index.
130. Edwards and Hampson, op cit., 210-11.
131. H. Blakey, 'Fire Insurance and Ceramic History – including extracts from the Sun Fire Office Policy Registers: 1782-1793' in *Journal of the Northern Ceramic Society* Vol. 10 1993, 161-97, 179, 188; 'Sun Fire Insurance Policies from the Country Department Policy Registers' in *Northern Ceramic Society Journal* Vol. 3, 1978-1979, 101-48, 127.
132. Shaw, op. cit., 211.
133. *Bailey's British Directory* 4 vol. (London: Bailey, 1784) Vol. 2, 391.
134. *The Universal British Directory* (London: Patentees, 1791-98), 107. (1795 or later because of the reference to 'the late Mr. Wedgwood's house' on this page. Josiah Wedgwood died in 1795.)
135. H. Blakey 'Fire Insurance and Ceramic History – including extracts from the Sun Fire Office Policy Registers: 1782-1793' in *Journal of the Northern Ceramic Society* Vol. 10 1993, 189.
136. Wedgwood MSS 30/22922-23. C.F.C. Luxmoore noted this on p.43 of his 'Saltglaze,' with *The Notes of a Collector*.(1924; rep. London: Holland Press, n.d.).
137. Wedgwood MSS 11/6322, 30/22921.
138. *Newcastle-under-Lyme Parish Register* 3 vol. (Staffordshire Parish Registers Society, 1981), III, 60, 118.
139. *Burslem Parish Register* 3 vol. (Staffordshire Parish Registers Society, 1913), III, 733.
140. Shaw, op. cit., 92.
141. Wedgwood MS 6/5052.
142. A.R. Mountford, 1972, op. cit., Appendix II, (64).
143. Wedgwood MS 6/5051.
144. Mountford, 1972, op. cit., Appendix III, 24.
145. International Genealogical Index.
146. *Burslem Parish Register* 3 vol. (Staffordshire Parish Registers Society, 1913), I, 213.
147. International Genealogical Index.
148. *Burslem Parish Register* 3 vol. (Staffordshire Parish Registers Society, 1913), I, 244.
149. Ibid., II, 298.
150. Ibid., I, 262; II, 276. (James Spencer Bold, potter, Burslem, left a partnership with John Brown in 1805 (*Staffordshire Advertiser* 1 Jun. 1805)).
151. Ibid., II, 282. The inscription on his tombstone, noted by one of the authors in 1977, showed his age as forty-six.
152. Lichfield Record Office: will of James Bold, proved 17 May 1764.
153. *Burslem Parish Register* 3 vol. (Staffordshire Parish Registers Society, 1913), II, 306.
154. International Genealogical Index: Enoch, son of Ephraim and Mary Booth, baptised at Astbury, Cheshire, 1 Jul. 1703.
155. P. Halfpenny 'Pioneer Potter?' in *Antique Dealer & Collectors Guide* Vol. 53, No. 11, Jun. 2000, 36-38.
156. *Wolstanton Parish Register II* (Staffordshire Parish Registers Society, 1914) 404: Funerals, 26 Mar. 1773, Enoch Booth of Wolstanton.
157. W. Pitt, *A Topographical History of Staffordshire…* (Newcastle-under-Lyme: Smith, 1817), 421.
158. P.W.L. Adams, *A History of the Adams Family of North Staffordshire…* (London: St. Catherine Press, 1914), 374-75: George Booth built a potworks at Tunstall by 1745, which later became the Greengates Works.
159. Edwards and Hampson, op. cit., 210-11.
160. B. Rackham, *Catalogue of the Glaisher Collection of Pottery and Porcelain in the Fitzwilliam Museum Cambridge* 2 vol. (Cambridge University Press, 1935; rep. Woodbridge: Antique Collectors' Club, 1987), I, 79; II, 38.
161. H. De la Beche and T. Reeks, *Museum of Practical Geology. Catalogue of Specimens… of British Pottery and Porcelain…* (London: Eyre and Spottiswoode, 1855) 128; letter 1 Aug. 2000 from R.J.C. Hildyard, Victoria and Albert Museum.
162. A.R. Mountford, 1972, op. cit., Appendix II (6).
163. Wedgwood MSS 1/30214, 1/30219.
164. Wedgwood MS 1/609.
165. Wedgwood MS 11/9273.
166. Wedgwood MSS 11/9272, 9275-9280.
167. Wedgwood MS 5/30546, 26 Jul. 1763.
168. Mountford, 1972, op. cit., Appendix III, 98, 135; Appendix IV, 27, 34, 37. See also our Chapter VI, Potters as Customers, for the unfired ware.
169. Lichfield Record Office: will of Enoch Booth proved at Cheadle 6 May 1773.
170. Appendix 3.
171. Wedgwood MS 29/21312.
172. Mountford, 1972, op. cit., Appendix III, 159; Appendix IV, 38, 45. See also our Chapter VI, Potters as Customers, for the unfired ware.
173. Wedgwood MS 29/30922.

174. Wedgwood MSS 30/21313, 29/21314.
175. *Burslem Parish Register* 3 vol. (Staffordshire Parish Registers Society, 1913), III, 687.
176. Wedgwood MS 29/21316.
177. B. Dragesco, *English Ceramics in French Archives* (London: privately, 1993), *passim*.
178. Ibid., 13.
179. R. Howard, 'Isleworth Pottery, Recognition at last?' in *English Ceramic Circle Transactions* Vol. 16, Part 3, 1998, 345-68, 351.
180. W. Mankowitz & R.G. Haggar, *The Concise Encyclopedia of English Pottery and Porcelain* (London: Deutsch, 1957), 35.
181. International Genealogical Index.
182. P.W.L. Adams, op. cit., 117.
183. Keele University Information Services: res. Local Coll. DA 690.B6S8, *Burslem Rate Book 1802*, nos. 1523-24.
184. Wedgwood MS 32/31013; C.T.G. Boucher, *James Brindley Engineer 1716-1772* (Norwich: Goose, 1968), 96.
185. J. Ward *The Borough of Stoke-upon-Trent...* (London: Lewis, 1843) 156.
186. Boucher, op. cit., 57.
187. R. Nicholls, *Ten Generations of a Potting Family* (London: Lund, Humphries, n.d.), 38.
188. Wedgwood MSS 31/23010-23013, Mar.-Jul. 1764.
189. Wedgwood MS 31/23020, 21 Apr. 1768.
190. Wedgwood MS 1/592.
191. Wedgwood MSS 55/30426, 55/30413.
192. Wedgwood MS 12/2341.
193. Wedgwood MSS 30/22827-28, 22830-34.
194. Wedgwood MSS 1/590, 592.
195. A.R. Mountford, 1972, op. cit., Appendix III, 24.
196. *Manchester Mercury*, 22 Apr., 7 Oct. 1760.
197. *Burslem Parish Register* 3 vol. (Staffordshire Parish Registers Society, 1913), II, 301, 288.
198. *A History of the County of Stafford* ed. J.G. Jenkins (London: OUP, 1963) ,VIII, 271.
199. Appendix 3.
200. Burslem Churchyard, monumental inscription.
201. *Burslem Parish Register* 3 vol. (Staffordshire Parish Registers Society, 1913) III, 661.
202. Wedgwood MS 7/5085.
203. Wedgwood MSS 30/22836-37.
204. Wedgwood MS 30/22835.
205. Wedgwood MSS 30/22838-40.
206. *Bailey's Northern... Directory... for... 1781*, 268; *Bailey's British Directory* 4 vol. (London: Bailey, 1784), Vol. 2, 391.
207. *Burslem Parish Register* 3 vol. (Staffordshire Parish Registers Society, 1913) III, 681.
208. Wedgwood MSS 30/22845.
209. Edwards and Hampson, op. cit., Appendix 1; R.S. Hampson, *Churchill China Great British Potters since 1795* (Keele: Centre for Local History, 1994), 123-24.
210. Wedgwood MS 6/4934.
211. Wedgwood MSS 6/30156, 6/4667-68
212. Wedgwood MS 55/9841, p.34.
213. Stoke-on-Trent City Archives: S 810: W. Heaton *Reference to the Plan of the Town of Burslem... 1740* (Burslem, 1821) No. 119; SM5E, W. Heaton *Plan of the Town of Burslem... 1740* (Burslem n.d.), No. 119.
214. *Burslem Parish Register* 3 vol. (Staffordshire Parish Registers Society, 1913), III, 671, 689.
215. R. Gurnett, *Chatterley & Whitehead Potters of Hanley & Shelton* (Bishop's Stortford: privately, 1996), 12.
216. Cheshire Record Office: LNW17/1, Weaver Navigation Tonnage Book, 1741-, 105, 107.
217. Staffordshire Record Office: D 1788, Vol. 95; pcl. 14, bdle. 2, Book N19; Vol. 99, 42, 80,136; Vol. 102, 6, 73.
218. Ibid., Vol. 99, 80, 136.
219. Appendix 3.
220. Information from Mr. P. Roden: Public Record Office: DL30 507/22, Newcastle-under-Lyme Manor Court Minute Book, vol. 21, p.17 from back.
221. Appendix 3.
222. International Genealogical Index.
223. *Letters of Josiah Wedgwood 1771 to 1780* ed. K.E. Farrar (Privately, 1903-06; rep. Manchester: Morten, n.d, *c*.1973), 337-38, 403, 423.
224. International Genealogical Index: Peter son of Evan Swift baptised 7 Jul. 1731; Peter Swift married Mary Bonny 15 Jan. 1756; Peter son of Peter Swift baptised 20 Jan. 1760, all at St. Nicholas, Liverpool.
225. Edwards and Hampson, op. cit., 195.

APPENDIX 2 D-K
1. See Appendix 3.
2. See M. Berthoud, *H. & R. Daniel 1822-1846* (Wingham: Micawber, 1980).
3. International Genealogical Index.
4. Burslem Churchyard, monumental inscription.
5. Lichfield Record Office: will of Richard Daniel, proved 21 Apr. 1687.
6. Wedgwood MSS 30/22887-22894, 30/30927-30928.
7. A.R. Mountford, 'Thomas Wedgwood, John Wedgwood and Jonah Malkin Potters of Burslem', unpublished MA Thesis, Keele University, 1972, Appendix III, 24.
8. Staffordshire Record Office: D1788, Vol. 99, 71; Vol. 102, 14.
9. *Burslem Parish Register* 3 vol. (Staffordshire Parish Registers Society, 1913), III, 643, Burial 18 Dec. 1769, Sampson Daniel (Burslem).
10. M. Berthoud, op. cit., 17; *Burslem Parish Register* 3 vol. (Staffordshire Parish Registers Society, 1913), II, 29, Burial 17 Nov. 1765, Ralph Daniel.
11. Burslem Churchyard, monumental inscription; Lichfield Joint Record Office: Thomas Daniel, will proved 2 May 1760.
12. W. Pitt, *A Topographical History of Staffordshire...* (Newcastle-under-Lyme: Smith, 1817), 418. S. Shaw *History of the Staffordshire Potteries* (privately 1829, rep. Newton Abbot: David & Charles, 1970), 163, gives an elaborated version of Pitt's earlier account.
13. N. Valpy, 'Extracts from 18th Century London Newspapers' in *English Ceramic Circle Transactions* Vol. 12, Part 2 , 1985 161-88, 167, quoting the *St. James's Chronicle*, 5/7 May, 4/7 Jul. 1767. Stoke-on-Trent City Archives: EMT/10/769.
14. Stoke-on-Trent City Archives: EMT/11/787B.
15. P.W.L. Adams, *A History of the Adams Family of North Staffordshire...* (London: St. Catherine Press, 1914) Add. & Corr. K; *A History of the County of Stafford* ed. J.G. Jenkins (London: OUP, 1963), VIII, 271; D. Edwards and R. Hampson *English Dry-Bodied Stoneware...* (Woodbridge: Antique Collectors' Club, 1998) 210-11.
16. 'John Dwight's Fulham Pottery 1672-1978 A Collection of Documentary Sources' ed. D. Haselgrove and J. Murray in *Journal of Ceramic History* No. 11, 1979, 1-284, 122.
17. Ibid., 69-71.
18. *Burslem Parish Register* 3 vol. (Staffordshire Parish Registers Society, 1913), I, 117, Burials, 6 Jan. 1686/87, Richard Daniel; Lichfield Record Office: will of Richard Daniel, proved 21 Apr. 1687.
19. *A History of the County of Stafford* ed. J.G. Jenkins (London: OUP, 1963), VIII, 117, n.75.
20. See Appendix 3.
21. E. Adams, 'Ceramic Insurances in the Sun Company, 1766-1774' in *English Ceramic Circle Transactions* Vol. 10, Part I, 1976, 1-38, 22.
22. Wedgwood MSS 6/5007, 6/30932. See Appendix 4 for a discussion of 'Engind'.
23. A.R. Mountford, 1972, op. cit., Appendix II (32).
24. Staffordshire Record Office: D 1788, Vol. 99, 26, 113.
25. International Genealogical Index.
26. 'The 1767 Return of Staffordshire Papists' in *Staffordshire Catholic History* No. 17, 1977, 37.
27. *Burslem Parish Register* 3 vol. (Staffordshire Parish Registers Society, 1913), III, 649: Burials, 15 Nov. 1772, Thomas Daniel Jun, Cobridge.
28. *R R Angerstein's Illustrated Travel Diary 1753-1755 Industry in England and Wales from a Swedish perspective* trans. T. and P. Berg (London: Science Museum, 2001), 199-201.
29. H. Young, 'Evidence for Wood and Coal firing and the Design of Kilns in the 18th-century English Porcelain Industry' in *English Ceramic Circle Transactions* Vol. 17, Part 1, 1999, 1-14, 9-11.
30. We are grateful to Dr. Helen Smith for the translation of the notes. Gabriel Jars, who visited North Staffordshire about 1765, gave the proportions of clay to flint as six to one or five to one for white salt-glazed stoneware. (F. Celoria 'Techniques of White Salt-Glaze Stoneware Manufacture in North Staffordshire Around 1765' in *Science and Archaeology* no. 18 1976, 25-28, 25.)
31. F. Williamson, 'Derby Pot Manufactory known as Cockpit Hill Pottery' reprinted from *Derbyshire Archaeological Society's Journal New Series* Vol. IV 1930, 66.
32. G. Godden, 'Derby Pot Works, Cockpit Hill' in *English Ceramic Circle Transactions* Vol. 3, Part 4, 1955, 161-72, 169; D. Towner, 'The Cockpit Hill Pottery, Derby' in *English Ceramic Circle Transactions* Vol. 6, Part 3, 1967, 254-67, 265; *Ceramics of Derbyshire 1750-1975* ed. H.G. Bradley (London: privately, 1978), 276-79. We are indebted to Mr. Bradley (his letter 2 May 2001) for helpful suggestions about the possible production of white salt-glazed stoneware in Derby.
33. Williamson, op. cit., 20. Williamson was probably quoting Jewitt, who wrote about Butts being the practical man in 1758. See L. Jewitt, *The Ceramic Art of Great Britain...* 2 vol. (London: Virtue, 1878) II, 58.
34. International Genealogical Index: William Butts married Jane Trueman 30 Mar. 1742 at Sutton on the Hill, Derbyshire; and his son, also William Butts, was christened at All Saints Church, Derby 31 Mar. 1743. The name of Ralph Steen occurs in marriages at Burslem on 7 Jun. 1725, 19 May 1739 and 11 Feb. 1749.
35. Berg, op cit., xx, 22. Angerstein had been in England from September 1753 and only seen ceramic works at Chelsea and Worcester before reaching Derby. He had already described the Worcester kilns as being like

36. Ibid., xx, 22. Angerstein's own sketch of the Chelsea kiln is reproduced on p.xx of his diary. It is indicative of the problems caused by re-drawing that the re-drawn sketch of the same kiln on p. 22 seems to show two holes in the side of the kiln, left of the entrance, of which there is no sign in Angerstein's original drawing.
37. Gabriel Jars, who visited North Staffordshire about 1765, gave the proportions of clay to flint as six to one or five to one for white salt-glazed stoneware. (Celoria, op. cit., 25.)
38. Plates with modelled roses, salt-glazed or cream-coloured, are not illustrated in the following studies of Cockpit Hill: Godden, op. cit., 169; Towner, op. cit., 265; *Ceramics of Derbyshire 1750-1975* ed. H.G. Bradley (London: privately, 1978), 234-79. K.
39. Berg, op cit., 200-01.
40. Williamson, op. cit., 1-72.
41. See for instance J. Twitchett, *Derby Porcelain 1748-1848 – An Illustrated Guide* (Woodbridge: Antique Collectors' Club, 2002).
42. R. and R. Barka, 'A 1770 Kiln Dump of the Derby China Works' in *English Ceramic Circle Transactions* Vol. 15, Part 2, 1994, 229-39, 229-30, 239; D. Barker, 'Bits and Bobs – The Development of Kiln Furniture in the 18th-century Staffordshire pottery industry' in *English Ceramic Circle Transactions* Vol. 16, Part 3 1998, 318-41, 324; T. Walford 'Creamware and Saltglaze sherds from Nottingham Road Derby – with acknowledgments to William Greatbatch' in *English Ceramic Circle Transactions* Vol. 17, Part 1, 1999, 115-20, 115, 116.
43. Young, op. cit., 9-11.
44. We are grateful to Dr. Helen Smith for the translation of the notes. Gabriel Jars, who visited North Staffordshire about 1765, gave the proportions of clay to flint as six to one or five to one for white salt-glazed stoneware. (Celoria, op. cit., 25.)
45. A.R. Mountford, *The Illustrated Guide to Staffordshire Salt-Glazed Stoneware* (London: Barrie & Jenkins, 1971) 37, quoting a document then in the City Museum, Stoke-on-Trent.
46. L. Jewitt, *The Ceramic Art of Great Britain…* 2 vol. (London: Virtue, 1878), II, 416.
47. International Genealogical Index.
48. Wedgwood MS 96/17695.
49. International Genealogical Index: Samuel Edge was baptised at Burslem 15 Oct. 1665, son of Richard and Sarah. He married Alice Wedgwood at Wolstanton 24 Oct. 1693. See J.C. Wedgwood and J.G.E. Wedgwood, *Wedgwood Pedigrees…* (Kendal: Wilson, 1925), 108-09.
50. *Burslem Parish Register* 3 vol. (Staffordshire Parish Registers Society, 1913), I, 168.
51. Lichfield Record Office: Samuel Edge, will made 20 Feb. 1720-21, proved 9 May 1721. The use of the plural in describing Edge's buildings may be no more than legal caution.
52. See L. Weatherill, 'Technical Change and Potters' Inventories 1660-1760' in *Journal of Ceramic History* No. 3, 1970, 3-12, 5.
53. S. Shaw, op. cit., 171.
54. Edwards and Hampson, op. cit., 210-11.
55. R. Hampson, 'Longton Potters 1700-1865' in *Journal of Ceramic History* Vol. 14, 1990, 68.
56. S. Shaw, op. cit., 77, 173-74.
57. Wedgwood MSS 6/30925, 6/4954-55.
58. Potteries Museum and Art Gallery, Ceramics Department: Thomas Whieldon's Notebook, uncatalogued.
59. International Genealogical Index.
60. Hampson, op. cit., 72-74.
61. Shaw, op. cit., 216.
62. P.F.C. Roden, 'Josiah Spode (1733-1797)…. in *Journal of the Northern Ceramic Society* Vol. 14, 1997, 1-43, 37-38.
63. Lichfield Record Office: will of Thomas Barker, proved 16 May 1787; information by courtesy of Mr. Peter Roden.
64. S. Shaw, op. cit., 70.
65. D. Barker, 'A Group of Staffordshire Red Stonewares of the 18th century' in *English Ceramic Circle Transactions* Vol. 14, Part 2, 1991, 177-98, 192-93.
66. *Kelly's Directory of Staffordshire* 1928 (London: Kelly's Directories, 1928), 927.
67. The most complete account is J. Kinghorn and G. Quail, *Delftfield A Glasgow Pottery 1748-1823* (Glasgow: Glasgow Museums and Art Galleries, 1986). See also H.E. Kelly, 'Some Documents relating to the History of the Glasgow Delftfield Company' in *Scottish Pottery 15th Historical Review* 1993, 43-48.
68. Kinghorn and Quail, op. cit., 21.
69. *Partners in Science Letters of James Watt and Joseph Black* ed. E. Robinson and D. McKie (London: Constable, 1970), 8-12.
70. Information from Mr. Henry Kelly and Mr. Michael Donnelly, whose help is gratefully acknowledged.
71. A.R. Mountford, 1972, op. cit., 107, Appendix III, 53, 128, Appendix IV, 18.
72. *Bailey's British Directory* 4 Vol. (London: Bailey, 1784), Vol. 2, 390.
73. *Burslem Parish Registers* 4 vol. (Staffordshire Parish Registers Society, 1925), III, 759, 793.
74. A.R. Mountford, 1972, op. cit., 107, Appendix III, 171.
75. Wedgwood MS 96/17695.
76. Stoke-on-Trent City Archives: SM5E, W. Heaton, *Plan of the Town of Burslem… 1740* (Burslem n.d.), No. 106a.
77. Wedgwood MSS 11/9361-9368.
78. Wedgwood MS 6/30584.
79. Wedgwood MS 11/9363.
80. Wedgwood MS 6/30579, 23 Jul. 1763.
81. A.R. Mountford, 1972, op. cit., 107, 109, Appendix III, 154; Appendix IV, 9, 12, 23, 26, 31, 33, 38. See also our Chapter VI, Potters as Customers, for the unfired ware.
82. R.J Charleston, 'Jean Voyez' in *English Ceramic Circle Transactions* Vol. 5, Part 1, 1960, 8-41, 23.
83. P.W.L. Adams, op. cit., 132-33.
84. *Stoke-upon-Trent Parish Registers* 4 vol. (Staffordshire Parish Registers Society, 1925), III, 759; Monument in chancel of St. Peter ad Vincula Church, Stoke-on-Trent.
85. The late Mr. K. Quinn's notes from Stoke-on-Trent City Archives: EMT 13/776, EMT 15/782 and EMT 23/784.
86. Wedgwood MS 55/9840, p.5.
87. P.W.L. Adams, op.cit., Add. & Corr. K; amended by Supplement III, p.137.
88. Edwards and Hampson, op. cit., 125, and site no. 60 (west) on the 1802 map, 210-11.
89. E. Adams, 'The Bow Insurances and Related Matters' in *English Ceramic Circle Transactions* Vol. 9, Part 1, 1973, 67-108, 104.
90. Staffordshire Record Office: D1788, Vol. 95, Mill Acct 1758.
91. 'John Dwight's Fulham Pottery 1672-1978 A Collection of Documentary Sources' ed. D. Haselgrove and J. Murray, in *Journal of Ceramic History* No. 11, 1979, 69-71, 122-25.
92. Ibid., 69-71, 125.
93. Fowlea Farm was occupied by G.H. Downing's brick and tile works in the 20th century, based on the red clay available there, see E.J.D. Warrillow, *History of Etruria Staffordshire England 1760-1951* (Hanley: Etruscan Publications, 1952), 210-11.
94. W. Yates, *A Map of the County of Stafford* (1775).
95. Staffordshire Record Office: D239 M/1901-1917-1906, copy of will of Ralph Taylor, proved at Lichfield 3 Dec. 1760.
96. Ordnance Survey 25 inch map, *Staffordshire* X11.13 revised 1938, north of A53 Etruria Road. E.J.D. Warrillow, op. cit., 211, states that Fowlea farm was demolished by 1952. See his pages 126 and 336 for illustrations including Fowlea Farm.
97. *Wolstanton Parish Registers* 2 vol. (Staffordshire Parish Registers Society, 1914), I, 63.
98. *Burslem Parish Register* 3 vol. (Staffordshire Parish Registers Society, 1913), I, 109.
99. *Wolstanton Parish Registers* 2 vol. (Staffordshire Parish Registers Society, 1914), I, 165, 166.
100. J.C. Wedgwood *A History of the Wedgwood Family* (London: St. Catherine Press, 1908), 126, 322.
101. B. Adams and A. Thomas, *A Potwork in Devon The history and products of the Bovey Tracey potteries 1750-1836* (Bovey Tracey: Sayce, 1996), 8, 21.
102. Wedgwood MSS WM 1127. The other three versions are WM 1131.
103. Shaw, op. cit., 181-82.
104. L.H. Mero, *Chronicle of Our Heritage – History of Some Harrison, Harris and Connected Families in England and America, 1550-1995* (Utica, Ky., privately, 1995) 43.
105. Ibid., 39; 40 for 1722 and 1726; information from Mr. P. Roden, quoting Public Record Office: DL 30 507/9, Vol. 8, p.30 for 1733; DL 507/10, Vol. 9, p.36 for 1736.
106. Mero, op. cit., 43, 70, 125.
107. E. Meteyard, *The Life of Josiah Wedgwood…* 2 vol. (London: Hurst and Blackett, 1865), I, 222, n.1.
108. S. Smiles, *Josiah Wedgwood F.R.S. His Personal History* (London: Murray, 1894, 1905), 33-34.
109. Wedgwood MS 55/9838.
110. Mero, op. cit., 78, quoting Public Record Office DL 30 507/15 Vol. 14, pp.53, 55, 79.
111. Information from Mr. P. Roden: Extract from 'Plan of Cottages and Incroachments on to land owned by The Duchy of Lancaster in the Liberty of Penkhull, 1777'. A copy is held by Potteries Museum and Art Gallery, Archaeological Department, Historic Buildings Survey.
112. Mountford, 1972, op cit., 107, Appendix III, 39, 61.
113. H. Blakey, 'Sun Fire Insurance Records 1774-1782' in *Journal of the Northern Ceramic Society* Vol. 9, 1992, 165-81, 172.
114. *Bailey's Northern Directory*, 1781.
115. Mero, op. cit., 43-52.
116. Information from Mr. P. Roden, quoting Public Record Office: DL 30 507/25, Vol. 24, page 31.
117. *Staffordshire Advertiser*, 6 Nov. 1802, p.1, col. 3.

118. Information from Mr. P. Roden, quoting Public Record Office: DL 30 507/29, Vol. 30, page 352.
119. Ibid., 507/30, Vol. 31, page 333.
120. See Appendix 3.
121. International Genealogical Index.
122. Public Record Office: Index to DL30 507/4-507/26: Court Rolls of the Manor of Newcastle under Lyme... 1716-1795.
123. Wedgwood MS 6/5036, 23 Aug. 1763.
124. Mountford, 1972, op. cit., Appendix III, 96.
125. Wedgwood MS 1/592.
126. Public Record Office: Index to DL30 507/4-507/26: Court Rolls of the Manor of Newcastle under Lyme... 1716-1795.
127. Information from Mr. P. Roden.
128. *Stoke-on-Trent Parish Registers* 4 vol. (Staffordshire Parish Registers Society), IV, 883.
129. S. Smith, 'William Hassells...' in *Northern Ceramic Society Newsletter* No. 27 Sept. 1977, 16-17.
130. International Genealogical Index.
131. Lichfield Record Office: will of William Taylor, proved 1 Jun. 1738.
132. Public Record Office: Index to DL30 507/4-507/26: Court Rolls of the Manor of Newcastle under Lyme... 1716-1795.
133. Wedgwood MS WM 1459; R. Edmundson, 'Staffordshire Potters insured with the Salop Fire Office 1780-1825' in *Journal of the Northern Ceramic Society* Vol. 6, 1987, 81-93, 85.
134. Edwards and Hampson, op. cit., 121, 210-11.
135. Staffordshire Record Office: D 1788 box F1, un-numbered bdle.
136. Lichfield Record Office: will of William Taylor proved 1 Jun. 1738.
137. Wellcome Library for the History and Understanding of Medicine: Western MS 5006, Wilkes diary.
138. See Public Record Office: Index to DL30 507/4-507/26: Court Rolls of the Manor of Newcastle under Lyme... 1716-1795, for Joshua Heath's property transactions, 1716-1746.
139. Lichfield Joint Record Office: will of Joshua Heath of Shelton, earth potter, made 26 Apr. 1745, proved 31 Oct. 1745.
140. International Genealogical Index.
141. J.C. Wedgwood, op. cit., 324.
142. *Stoke-upon-Trent Parish Registers* 3 vol. (Staffordshire Parish Registers Society, 1913), II, 337.
143. Lichfield Record Office: will of Joshua Heath of Shelton, earth potter, made 26 Apr. 1745, proved 31 Oct. 1745.
144. Information from Mr. P. Roden.
145. Mountford, 1972, op. cit., 38.
146. Staffordshire Record Office: D 1788 Vol. 102, 32.
147. Shaw, op. cit., 68, 126-27.
148. D. Edwards and R. Hampson, op. cit., 165, 210-11.
149. Archaeological Watching Brief at Fenpark Road, Fenton, Stoke-on-Trent SJ 8977 4450 (Stoke-on-Trent Museum Field Archaeology Unit Report No. 62, Aug. 1998).
150. Stoke-on-Trent City Archives: SD 4842/42/32.
151. Mountford, 1972, op. cit., Appendix III, 153. See also our Chapter VI, Potters as Customers.
152. Shaw, op. cit., 44.
153. Staffordshire Record Office: D 1788 Vol. 102, 32, 75.
154. Ibid., Vol. 95.
155. Wedgwood MSS 6/4957-4958.
156. Staffordshire Record Office: D 1788 Vol. 102, 107; Vol. 99, 48, 111.
157. See Appendix 3.
158. Public Record Office: DL 507/17, Vol. 16, p.79, 9 Jan. 1760, surrender of all his copyhold property by William Heath the elder to his sons William Heath the younger and Joshua Heath. (Information from Mr. P. Roden.)
159. Staffordshire Record Office: D239 M/1901-1917-1906, will of Ralph Taylor, made 22 Sept. 1759, proved at Lichfield 3 Dec. 1760.
160. Public Record Office: DL 507/17, Vol. 16, p.392, 1 May 1765, presentment of the will of William Heath dated 18 Feb. 1764, transcribed on pages 3 to 5. (Information from Mr. Peter Roden.) William Heath died between these two dates.
161. *Stoke-upon-Trent Parish Registers* 3 vol. (Staffordshire Parish Registers Society, 1913), II, 612, burial 17 Dec. 1766, Wm. Heath.
162. Public Record Office: DL 507/23, Vol. 22, p.205, Joshua Heath mortgaged property on 9 Dec. 1783. (Information from Mr. P. Roden.)
163. Wedgwood MS 6/4946.
164. Staffordshire Record Office: D 1788, Vol. 99, p.77.
165. Mountford, 1972, op. cit., Appendix III, 109.
166. Wedgwood MSS 25/18628, 18627.
167. International Genealogical Index.
168. R. Howard, 'Isleworth Pottery, Recognition at last?' in *English Ceramic Circle Transactions* Vol. 16, Part 3 1998, 345-68, 350-51. An archaeological evaluation of the site in 1999 produced no evidence of the manufacture of white salt-glazed stoneware at Isleworth, see R. Howard, 'A Report on the Archaeological Evaluation of the Isleworth Pottery Site' in *English Ceramic Circle Transactions* Vol. 17, Part 2 2001, 467-69; and *Isleworth Pottery and Porcelain recent discoveries* Exhibition catalogue comp. R. Massey, J. Pearce and R. Howard (London: English Ceramic Circle, 2003), 95.
169. Howard, 1998, op. cit., 351
170. B. Dragesco, English *Ceramics in French Archives* (London; privately, 1993), 13.
171. S. Shaw, op. cit., 172.
172. Hampson, op. cit., 103, 104.
173. Ibid., 124.
174. G.A. Godden, *Encyclopaedia of British Porcelain Manufacturers* (London: Barrie & Jenkins, 1988) 441-56; D. Edwards, *Black Basalt: Wedgwood and Contemporary Manufacturers* (Woodbridge: Antique Collectors' Club, 1994), 182-83; P. Goodfellow, 'The Keeling Potteries in Tunstall' in *Journal of the Northern Ceramic* Society Vol. 16, 1999, 125-28; T. Markin, 'Anthony Keeling, china and earthenware manufacturer at Tunstall' in *Journal of the Northern Ceramic Society* Vol. 13, 1996, 35-52; 'Anthony Keeling and Company: part 1. The Potworks and partners, Edward Keeling and Samuel Perry' in *Journal of the Northern Ceramic Society* Vol. 17, 2000, 51-78.
175. International Genealogical Index: Anthony Keeling, son of Anthony and Anne, baptised at Stoke 6 Mar. 1708; Anthony Keeling married Mary Bedson at Wolstanton 16 Jun. 1737; Anthony Keeling, son of Anthony and Mary, baptised at Stoke 10 Jun. 1738.
176. *Stoke-upon-Trent Parish Registers* 4 vol. (Staffordshire Parish Registers Society, 1925), III, 571, burials, 22 Jul. 1758, Anthony Keeling of Han[ley]. Green, yeoman.
177. *Wolstanton Parish Registers* 2 vol. (Staffordshire Parish Registers Society, 1914), part I, 349: Marriages, 22 Aug 1760, Anthony Keeling of Stoke-on-Trent and Ann Booth of Wolstanton, lic.
178. M. Bimson, J. Ainslie and B. Watney, 'West Pans Story – The Scotland Manufactory' in *English Ceramic Circle Transactions* Vol. 6, Part 2, 1966 167-76, 173, quoting *Caledonian Mercury* 22 Apr. 1769; and information from Dr. Jill Turnbull, quoting *Edinburgh Courant* 8 Dec. 1759 and 22 Apr. 1769.
179. Wedgwood MS 1/592.
180. Wedgwood MSS 31/23001, 23002; Godden, 1988, op. cit., 442.
181. Wedgwood MSS 31/30563, Mar. 1766; 31/30560, 18 Mar. 1766; 31/30564 17 Apr. 1766; 31/23001(n.d.).
182. Mountford, 1972, op. cit., Appendix III, 33.
183. Ibid., Appendix III, 24, 147, Appendix IV 15, 24, 38, 42. See also our Chapter VI, Potters as Customers, for the unfired ware.
184. Wedgwood MS 31/23003.
185. *Bailey's British Directory* 4 Vol. (London: Bailey, 1784) Vol. 2, 390.
186. *Staffordshire Advertiser*, 21 Jan. 1815.
187. Wedgwood MS 30/22942-22948, 30/30934.
188. Wedgwood MS 30/22944.
189. Wedgwood MSS 30/22944-22948, 30/30934.
190. Wedgwood MS 30/22942.
191. See Appendix 3.
192. Wedgwood MSS 6/30156-30163, 6/4667-4668.
193. Staffordshire Record Office: D 1788, Vol. 95; pcl. 1, bdle. 2; Vol. 102, p.11; Vol. 99. P.74.
194. Mountford, 1972, op. cit., Appendix III, 72, 109, 113.
195. *Burslem Parish Registers* 3 vol. (Staffordshire Parish Registers Society, 1913), II, 306.
196. Ibid., III, 668, burials, 12 Nov. 1779, Taylor Stevenson; III, 751, burials, 27 Oct. 1799, Charlotte Stevenson.

APPENDIX 2 L-P

1. P. Walton, 'An Excavation on the Site of the Leeds Pottery' in *Leeds Arts Calendar* No. 82, 1978, 6-13, 9; also P. Walton, 'An Investigation of the Site of the Leeds Pottery' in *English Ceramic Circle Transactions* Vol. 10, Parts 4 and 5, 1980, 223-31, 226.
2. Walton, 1978, op. cit., 11; also 1980, op. cit., 227, plate 109a.
3. Unpublished information from Dr. Alwyn Cox and Mrs. Angela Cox, who state that the mould found is similar to one made of creamware and with a gadrooned edge, illustrated in P. Walton, *Creamware and other English Pottery at Temple Newsam House, Leeds A Catalogue of the Leeds Collection* (Bradford: Manningham Press, 1976), 97, No. 346.
4. See H. Lawrence, *Yorkshire Pots and Potteries* (Newton Abbot: David and Charles, 1974), 17-40 for a comprehensive summary of the history of the Leeds Pottery. A new study by J.D. Griffin is awaited.
5. B. Watney, *Longton Hall Porcelain* (London: Faber, 1957) is the classic account of the subject. See also R. Hampson, 'Longton Potters

1700-1865' in *Journal of Ceramic History* Vol. 14, 1990, 112-13.
6. W. Pitt, *A Topographical History of Staffordshire...* (Newcastle-under-Lyme: Smith, 1817), 422-23.
7. Watney, op. cit., 12-15; Hampson, op. cit., 112-13.
8. *Burslem Parish Register* 3 vol. (Staffordshire Parish Registers Society, 1913), I, 177.
9. Ibid., I, 187: Burials, 12 Sept. 1729, William Littler.
10. Potteries Museum and Art Gallery, Ceramics Department: Ellis Moxon papers, 71: 20/05/1724, copy of William Littler [senior]'s will 20 May 1724.
11. Ibid., 38: 25/12/1745, copy of deed.
12. M. Goodby, 'William Littler: The Early Years' in *William Littler: An English Earth Potter 1724-1784* ed. M. Adams (Charlotte: Delhom Service League, 1999), 11-18, 15-16.
13. Watney, op. cit., 52-53.
14. Potteries Museum and Art Gallery, Ceramics Department: Ellis Moxon papers, 38:25/12/1745, indenture 25 Dec. 1745, endorsed 6 Jul. 1751 that the original was in the hands of Thomas Wedgwood of Burslem; John Wedgwood Rent Book, 1751-80, back of book, purchase page.
15. J. Ward, *The Borough of Stoke-upon-Trent...* (London: Lewis, 1843), 155.
16. Ibid., 152-53.
17. W. Scarratt, *Old Times in the Potteries* (Stoke-on-Trent: privately, 1906, repr. East Ardsley: S.R. Publishers, 1969), 65.
18. W. Yates, *A Map of the County of Stafford* (1775).
19. Goodby, op. cit., 12.
20. A. Smith, 'Liverpool Earthenwares and Stonewares' in *Made in Liverpool: Liverpool Pottery and Porcelain 1700-1850* ed. M. Brown and T.A. Lockett (Liverpool: National Museums & Galleries on Merseyside, 1993), 22-26, 24.
21. Quoted by C.T. Gatty in 'The Liverpool Potteries', *Transactions of the Historic Society of Lancashire and Cheshire Session* 1880-81 Vol. XXXIII 1881, 123-68, 143.
22. The tea canister and teapot are thoroughly discussed by K. Boney, in 'Documentary Liverpool Saltglaze' in *Apollo* Dec. 1960, 183-86.
23. Joseph Mayer, *On the Art of Pottery with a History of its Progress in Liverpool* (Liverpool: Marples, 1873), 72-73.
24. A. Smith, 'An Enamelled Tin-glazed Mug at Temple Newsam House' in *Leeds Arts Calendar* No. 82, 1978, 14-19. See also A. Smith, 'Stoneware in North West England' in *Stonewares & Stone chinas of Northern England to 1851* exhibition catalogue ed. T.A. Lockett and P.A. Halfpenny (Stoke-on-Trent: City Museum and Art Gallery, 1982), 25-28, 26 and Smith, 1993, op. cit., 22-26, 24-25.
25. Smith, 1993, op. cit., 22-26, 25-26.
26. *Bailey's British Directory* 4 Vol. (London: Bailey, 1784), Vol. 2, 390.
27. Wedgwood MS 30/22815.
28. *Burslem Parish Register* 3 vol. (Staffordshire Parish Registers Society, 1913), I, 230, Christenings, 2 May 1748, Timothy, son of William and Elizabeth Lockett; I, 243, Christenings, 1 Oct. 1752, John son of William and Elizabeth Lockett.
29. Ibid., III, 654, Burials, 30 Oct. 1774, Wm. Lockett potter; also Burslem, St. John's Churchyard, monumental inscription: William Lockett of Burslem 27 Oct. 1774 aged 52; also Betty wife of the above mentioned, died 4 Oct. 1802 aged 80.
30. Lichfield Record Office: will of William Lockett, proved 31 Mar. 1775.
31. P.W.L. Adams in *Notes on some North Staffordshire Families* (Tunstall: Eardley, 1930) 4 stated that 'The Machins (Joseph Machin, and Machin & Co.) rented one of their factories from Mrs. Hawkesbury and another from Timothy Locket [sic]. It was called "The Hole House, Low Street".'
32. John Robinson of Liverpool and Burslem, enameller and printer, was discussed in *Northern Ceramic Society Newsletters* No. 50, 38-48, No. 51, 2-13, No. 52, 30-33 and No. 54, 19-22.
33. E. Adams, 'Ceramic Insurances in the Sun Company, 1766-1774' in *English Ceramic Circle Transactions* Vol. 10, Part I, 1976, 1-38, 25.
34. *Staffordshire Advertiser*, 15 Nov. 1800.
35. Ibid., 23 Dec. 1815. His widow died at Congleton on 11 Apr. 1819, aged 67, see *Staffordshire Advertiser*, 17 Apr. 1819.
36. Ibid., 1 Jan. 1820. His furniture, books etc. were sold by auction, see *Staffordshire Advertiser*, 5 Feb. 1820. See also Burslem, St. John's Churchyard, monumental inscription: Isabella, wife of John Lockett died 31 Dec. 1809 aged 56, also the above mentioned John Lockett, died 12 Dec. 1819, aged 76 (sic).
37. R. Hampson, 'Longton Potters 1700-1865' in *Journal of Ceramic History* Vol. 14, 1990, 167-12.
38. Newcastle-under-Lyme Museum: 42 6 2, Order Book No. 3 1669-1712, Corporation of Newcastle-under-Lyme, 75, '[18 Aug. 1691] Ordered that a present be made to my Lord Cheife [sic] Justice Holt att his Comeing to this Burrough from Lancaster Assizes of some of Mr David Elers earthen ware to the Vallew of three poundes or thereabouts'. Although Elers had earlier been a potter in London, it seems very likely that he was at Bradwell Hall by 1691.
39. Keele University: Sneyd document no. 151 is a lease of Bradwell Hall to William Beech dated 1 Sept. 1698 for occupation on 25 Mar. 1699. It states that Bradwell Hall etc. 'now are or late were in the possession of John Ellers Gent' and requires Beech to 'take away pull downe & destroy a certain pott house or pott oven'. If he had not already done so, John Elers was to leave Bradwell Hall by Lady Day, 25 Mar. 1699.
40. 'John Dwight's Fulham Pottery 1672-1978 A Collection of Documentary Sources' ed. D. Haselgrove and J. Murray in *Journal of Ceramic History* No. 11, 1979, 1-284, 83-96.
41. L. Weatherill and R. Edwards, 'Pottery Making in London and Whitehaven in the Late Seventeenth Century' in *Post Medieval Archaeology* Vol. 5, 1971 (1972), 160-81, 163.
42. Wellcome Library for the History and Understanding of Medicine: Western MS 5006, Wilkes diary.
43. J.C. Wedgwood, *A History of the Wedgwood Family* (London: St. Catherine Press, 1908), 324.
44. *Letters of Josiah Wedgwood 1771 to 1780* (privately 1903, repr. Didsbury: Morten, n.d.) 368, quoting Wedgwood MS 25/18772, 19 Jul. 1777.
45. R. Hampson, 'Josiah Wedgwood I Ceramic Historian' in *Ars Ceramica* No. 5, 1988, 22-25, 23.
46. J. Aikin, *A Description of The Country from thirty to forty miles round Manchester...* (London: Stockdale, 1795, repr. Kelley, 1968), 525-26; W. Nicholson, *A Dictionary of Practical and Theoretical Chemistry...* (London: Phillips, 1808) under 'Pottery'; *Rees's Manufacturing Industry (1819-20)* multi-vol. ed. N. Cossons (Newton Abbot: David & Charles, 1972), IV, 208 (The date suggested for this text is 1814); W. Pitt, *A Topographical History of Staffordshire...* (Newcastle[-under-Lyme]: Smith, 1817), 416; and S. Parkes *The Chemical Catechism...* ninth edition (London: Baldwin, Cradock, and Joy, 1819), 102 (first edition 1806).
47. R. Watson, *Chemical Essays* 3rd ed., 5 vol. (London: Evans, 1784), II, 266-67.
48. F. Falkner, *The Wood Family of Burslem* (London: Chapman and Hall, 1912, repr. East Ardsley: EP, 1972), 27, 72.
49. S. Shaw, *History of the Staffordshire Potteries...* (Hanley, privately, 1829), 111, 120-21, 187.
50. Keele University Archives: Sneyd document no. 151, a lease of Bradwell Hall to William Beech dated 1 Sept. 1698 for occupation on 25 Mar. 1699.
51. G. Elliott, *John and David Elers and their Contemporaries* (London: Horne, 1998). 15, 31, 32.
52. Haselgrove and Murray, 1979, op. cit., 97-120.
53. Ibid., 105, 115, 120-21.
54. R. Edwards, 'London Potters circa 1570-1710' in *Journal of Ceramic History* No. 6, 1974, 66.
55. Haselgrove and Murray, 1979, op. cit., 126.
56. P. Francis, 'The Belfast Potthouse, Carrickfergus Clay and the Spread of the Delftware Industry...' in *English Ceramic Circle Transactions* Vol. 15, Part 2, 1994, 267-82.
57. Ibid., 270.
58. International Genealogical Index.
59. Haselgrove and Murray, 1979, op. cit., 104-06, 109-10, 115.
60. Edwards, op. cit., 78-79.
61. Haselgrove and Murray, 1979, op. cit., 128.
62. F. Britton, 'Delftware Inventories' in *English Ceramic Circle Transactions* Vol. 15, Part 1, 1993, 59-64, 60-61 and Appendix II.
63. F. Britton, 'The Pickleherring Potteries: an inventory' in *Post-Medieval Archaeology* Vol. 24, 1990, 61-92, 71-73.
64. 'John Dwight's Fulham Pottery 1672-1978 A Collection of Documentary Sources' ed. D. Haselgrove and J. Murray, in *Supplement to Journal of Ceramic History* No. 11, 1992, 1-71, 21-24.
65. W. Chaffers *Marks and Monograms on Pottery and Porcelain...* (London: Bickers, 1872), 674.
66. See J. Howarth and R. Hildyard, *Joseph Kishere and the Mortlake Potteries* (Woodbridge: Antique Collectors' Club, 2004) generally, and 70, 128, plate 51 and Colour Plates C10, C11. D. Redstone, 'Kishere's Mortlake Pottery' in *English Ceramic Circle Transactions* Vol. 18, Part 1, 2002, 45-57, 49 terms the goblets 'creamy grey'.
67. Howarth and Hildyard, op. cit., 42, 46, 47.
68. S. Pryor and K. Blockley, 'A 17th-century Kiln Site at Woolwich' in *Post-Medieval Archaeology* Vol. 12, 1978, 30-85. See also A. Watts, 'Three Kilns' in *English Ceramic Circle Transactions* Vol. 18, Part 1, 2002, 33-36, 34-35.
69. D. Gaimster, *German Stoneware 1200-1900 Archaeology and Cultural History* (London: British Museum Press, 1997), 109.
70. See Appendix 3.

71. A.R. Mountford, 'Thomas Wedgwood, John Wedgwood and Jonah Malkin Potters of Burslem', unpublished MA Thesis, Keele University, 1972, Appendix III, 24, 148; Appendix IV, 43-45. See also our Chapter VI, Potters as Customers, for the unfired ware.
72. P.W.L. Adams, *A History of the Adams Family of North Staffordshire...* (London: St. Catherine Press, 1914) 118.
73. *Stoke-upon-Trent Parish Registers* 4 vol. (Staffordshire Parish Registers Society, 1925), III, 475, Marriages, 26 Jul. 1738, Thomas Lowe and Sarah Bould of Burslem; *Burslem Parish Registers* 3 vol. (Staffordshire Parish Registers Society, 1913), I, 222, Baptisms, 7 Jun. 1745, John son of Thomas and Sarah Lowe.
74. Mountford, 1972, op. cit.
75. Stoke-on-Trent City Archives: D 4842/18/1/23, copy of Thomas Malkin's will dated 16 May 1745. See *A History of the County of Stafford* Vol. VIII ed. J.G. Jenkins (London: Oxford University Press, 1963), 120, for a brief history of the Malkin family and the Hamil.
76. T. Hargreaves, *A Map of the Staffordshire Potteries and Newcastle-under-Lyme* (Burslem: privately, 1832), potworks named 'Hammil'; Ordnance Survey 1:2500 map, *Staffordshire XII.5 (W)* 1900, Brick and Pipe Works opposite end of Lorne Street; *Ordnance Survey Street Atlas Staffordshire* (Southampton: Ordnance Survey, 1995) 42, A1. The property is referred to as the 'Hammill' in 1748, see Stoke-on-Trent City Archives: D 4842/18/1/23, indentures, 4 and 5 Nov. 1748.
77. Mountford, 1972, op. cit., Appendix II (3)-(64). The fortunate survival of Jonah Malkin's sales ledger is because it was re-used by John Wedgwood.
78. *William Littler* of West Pans, Scotland advertised 'Japannd Black' ware in 1766.
79. Mountford, 1972, op. cit., Appendix II (64).
80. A Benjamin Lewis lived in Stoke-upon-Trent in 1751, see V. Wilkinson *Spode-Copeland-Spode The Works and its People 1770-1970* (Woodbridge: Antique Collectors' Club, 2002), 28.
81. Mountford, 1972, op. cit., Appendix II (39).
82. Ibid., Appendix II (22)-(23).
83. Stoke-on-Trent City Archives: D 4842/18/1/23, indentures, 4 and 5 Nov. 1748.
84. Advertised in *Aris's Birmingham Gazette,* 8, 15, 22, 29 Apr. 1751.
85. Mountford, 1972, op. cit., Vol. I, 41. See also Stoke-on-Trent City Archives: D 4842/15/1/26 and 37.
86. Mountford, 1972, op. cit., Appendix III, 21, 22, 51, 71, 74, 89, 93, 105, 106, 109, 113.
87. Ibid., Vol. I, 28, 29, 36, 44.
88. *Burslem Parish Register* 3 vol. (Staffordshire Parish Registers Society, 1913), III, 650.
89. Wedgwood MSS 6/5042-5046.
90. Cheshire Record Office: LNW 17/1, Weaver Navigation Early Tonnage Book 1741-55, entries nos. 52, 165.
91. Stoke-on-Trent City Archives: SM8, Plan o' the Town of Burslem 1769, no. 129; Keele University Information Services: HA 1139 B8 H3, Reference to the Plan of the Town of Burslem ..., no. 129.
92. G.J.V. Bemrose, 'Notes on the early history of Staffordshire Pottery' in *Transactions of the North Staffordshire Field Club 1938-39* Vol. LXXIV (1940), 65-70, 67-70. See also W. Mankowitz and R.G. Haggar, *The Concise Encyclopedia of English Pottery and Porcelain* (London: Deutsch, 1957), 139-40.
93. J. Mallet, 'John Baddeley of Shelton, an Early Staffordshire Maker of Pottery and Porcelain, Part I' in *English Ceramic Circle Transactions* Vol. 6, Part 2, 1966, 124-66, 126-27.
94. R. Hampson, 'Longton Potters 1700-1865' in *Journal of Ceramic History* Vol. 14, 1990, 118-20, quoting Staffordshire Record Office: D (W) 1788, parcel 40, bdle 2.
95. Staffordshire Record Office: D/593/J/22/2.
96. *Trentham Parish Registers* 2 vol. (Staffordshire Parish Register Society, 1906), I, 160, 240.
97. See Appendix 3. The name has been read as 'Moore', but the authors consider it to be Mare.
98. Shaw, op. cit., 209.
99. D. Edwards and R. Hampson, *English Dry-Bodied Stoneware ...* (Woodbridge: Antique Collectors' Club, 1998), 210-11.
100. A. Thomas, 'Notes on some Bovey Tracey Potters' in *Northern Ceramic Society Newsletter* No. 80, Dec. 1990, 15-19, 16. See also B. Adams and A. Thomas, *A Potwork in Devonshire...* (Bovey Tracey: Sayce, 1996), 39.
101. D. Edwards, *Black Basalt; Wedgwood and Contemporary Manufacturers* (Woodbridge: Antique Collectors' Club, 1994), 192-93.
102. *Staffordshire Advertiser,* 17 Jun. 1797.
103. Stoke-on-Trent City Archives: EMT 20/MARE/797.
104. Edwards and Hampson, op. cit., 133.
105. Wedgwood MS 96/17695. The manuscript is endorsed in another hand 'memorandums relative to the Pottery 1776'.
106. Keele University Archives: Sneyd MS 227.
107. Lichfield Record Office: Moses Marsh, will proved 20 Oct. 1757.
108. Wedgwood MSS principally 55/30405 to 30435, but see Wedgwood Accumulation indexes for further references.
109. Lichfield Record Office: will of John Meir, proved 24 Jun. 1729.
110. See Appendix 3.
111. *Stoke-upon-Trent Parish Registers* 4 vol. (Staffordshire Parish Registers Society, 1925), II, 372: William Meir son of John and Anne christened 23 Feb. 1723/24.
112. Lichfield Record Office: will of John Meir, proved 24 Jun. 1729.
113. A.R. Mountford, 'Thomas Whieldon's Manufactory at Fenton Vivian' in *English Ceramic Circle Transactions* Vol. 8, Part 2, 1972, 164-82, 176.
114. L. Jewitt, *The Ceramic Art of Great Britain...* 2 vol. (London: Virtue, 1878), II, 412.
115. A.T. Morley Hewitt, 'Early Whieldon of the Fenton Low Works' in *English Ceramic Circle Transactions* Vol. 3, Parts 2 and 3 1954, 142-56, 142-43; Mountford, 1972, op. cit., 164-67; and P. Halfpenny 'Thomas Whieldon: his life and work' in *English Ceramic Circle Transactions* Vol. 16, Part 2, 1997, 237-54, 238.
116. *Stoke-upon-Trent Parish Registers* 4 vol. (Staffordshire Parish Registers Society, 1925), IV, 832, marriages, 1 Jul. 1759, Wm. Meire, e.p. [earth people] & Sarah Payne, Sp[inster]., lic[ence], witness Wm. Heath.
117. Staffordshire Record Office: D(W)1788 V.95, 1759-60; V.102, p.4, 1761-64; V.99, p.50, 1765-68.
118. Ibid., pcl. 14, bdle. 2, Book A (i).
119. 'John Dwight's Fulham Pottery 1672-1978 A Collection of Documentary Sources' ed. D. Haselgrove and J. Murray in *Journal of Ceramic History* No. 11, 1979, 1-284, 122.
120. Ibid., 69-71.
121. *The Stoke-upon-Trent Parish Listing, 1701* ed. D.A. Gatley with L.M. Midgeley and S. Bateman, off-print from *Collections for a History of Staffordshire* 4th Series, Vol. 16, 1994, 171-253, 202, SH 11; 205, SH 37.
122. *Stoke-upon-Trent Parish Registers* 4 vol. (Staffordshire Parish Registers Society, 1925), II, 295.
123. Lichfield Record Office: will of Richard Meir of Shelton, proved 15 Apr. 1708.
124. R.G. Cooper, *English Slipware Dishes 1650-1850* (London: Tiranti, 1968), 36.
125. J.C. Wedgwood, op. cit., 126, 322.
126. T. Markin, 'Anthony Keeling and Company: Part 1. The Potworks and partners, Edward Keeling and Samuel Perry' in *Journal of the Northern Ceramic Society* Vol. 17, 2000, 51-78, 69, 78.
127. A.R. Mountford, *The Illustrated Guide to Staffordshire Salt-Glazed Stoneware* (London; Barrie & Jenkins, 1971) 56, plates 184, 185.
128. *Stoke-upon-Trent Parish Registers* 4 vol. (Staffordshire Parish Registers Society, 1925), III, 575, Burials, 22 Apr. 1759, Warner Edwards of Shelton.
129. S. Shaw, op. cit., 167.
130. *Bibliotheca Staffordiensis...* comp. R. Simms (Lichfield: Lomax, 1894), 307.
131. 'John Dwight's Fulham Pottery 1672-1978 A Collection of Documentary Sources' ed. D. Haselgrove and J. Murray, in *Journal of Ceramic History* No. 11 1979, 69-71, 122-25.
132. Gatley. op. cit., 208, SH67.
133. Shaw, op. cit., 109.
134. Gatley. op. cit., 207-08, SH60.
135. R. Plot, *The Natural History of Staffordshire* (Oxford: The Theatre, 1686, rep. Didsbury: Morten, 1973), 121. The date of Plot's visit to Staffordshire is confirmed in M.W. Greenslade, 'The Staffordshire Historians' in *North Staffordshire Journal of Field Studies* Vol. 16, 1976, 23-41, 29.
136. Shaw, op. cit., 147, 152-55, 189-90.
137. W. Pitt, *A Topographical History of Staffordshire...* (Newcastle-under-Lyme: Smith, 1817), 425-26.
138. Staffordshire Record Office: D 593, Staffordshire Poll Book, 1747, Voters for Pirehill Hundred 9-14 Jul., p.49, Burslem.
139. International Genealogical Index: William 22 Sept. 1734, Thomas 20 Sept. 1737, Joyce 12 Mar. 1739, Nancy Nov. 1741, Richard 20 May 1744, Jesse 15 Apr. 1747 and Amos 8 Oct. 1754, all baptised at Burslem.
140. Stoke-on-Trent City Archives: SM 5E (map) and S 810 (key).
141. A.R. Mountford, 'Greenhead St., Burslem (SJ 867499)' in *City of Stoke-on-Trent Museum Archaeological Society Reports* No. 2 for 1966 (1967) 21-25.
142. This 1731 agreement was first reproduced by W. Pitt, op. cit., 423-24.
143. Shaw, op. cit., 150-55.
144. Wedgwood MS 27/19281.
145. Wedgwood MS 6/4997.
146. Shaw, op. cit., 189-90.
147. Ibid., 152-55.
148. Ibid., 147.
149. Wedgwood MSS 6/4993-4998.
150. See Appendix 3.

151. Newcastle-under-Lyme Museum and Art Gallery: Richard Parrott's Book 1756, 219-26.
152. M.B. Rowlands, 'Industry and Social Change in Staffordshire 1660-1760. A study of probate and other records of Tradesmen' in *Lichfield and South Staffordshire Archaeological and Historical Society Transactions for 1967-8*, Vol. IX, 1968, 37-58, 55.
153. P.F.C. Roden, 'Josiah Spode (1733-1797) his formative influences and the various Pot-works associated with him' in *Journal of the Northern Ceramic Society* Vol. 14, 1997, 1-43, 24-28.
154. T.G. Cannon, *Old Spode* (London; Werner Laurie, n.d.) 70-82.
155. International Genealogical Index.
156. 'John Dwight's Fulham Pottery 1672-1978 A Collection of Documentary Sources' ed. D. Haselgrove and J. Murray in *Journal of Ceramic History* No. 11, 1979, 1-284, 122.
157. Ibid., 69-71.
158. International Genealogical Index: J.C. Wedgwood and J.G.E. Wedgwood, *Wedgwood Pedigrees...* (Kendal: Wilson, 1925) 160.
159. R. Edwards, 'London Potters circa 1570-1710' in *Journal of Ceramic History* No. 6, 1974, 1-141, 40, 62, 87.
160. F. Celoria, 'Techniques of Pottery Making at Newcastle-upon-Tyne in 1765' in *Science and Archaeology* no. 18, 1976, 20-24.
161. L. Jewitt, *The Ceramic Art of Great Britain...* 2 vol. (London: Virtue, 1878) II, 1.
162. J. Cockerill 'Warburtons - Potters of Tyneside' in *Journal of the Northern Ceramic Society* Vol. 18. 2002, 59-76, 72.
163. F. Buckley, 'Potteries on the Tyne, and other Northern Potteries during the eighteenth century' in *Archaeologia Aeliana* 4th series IV 1927, 68-82, 73, 78.
164. Ibid., 68-82.
165. *The Potteries of Sunderland and District* 3rd edition revised ed. J.T. Shaw (Sunderland Public Libraries, Museum and Art Gallery, 1968), 7.
166. T.C. Barker, *The Glassmakers Pilkington: the rise of an international company 1826-1976* (London: Weidenfeld and Nicholson, 1977), 5, 485, n.35.
167. G.E. Milburn, 'Newbottle: An Outline History' in *Durham Local History Society Bulletin* 23 Aug. 1979, copy in Sunderland Local Studies Library. 12-28, 20-21.
168. Letters to the authors from Mr. Andrew Fletcher.
169. 'John Dwight's Fulham Pottery 1672-1978 A Collection of Documentary Sources' ed. D. Haselgrove and J. Murray in *Journal of Ceramic History* No. 11, 1979, 1-284, 83-96.
170. Ibid., 96.
171. A. Parker, *Nottingham Pottery* (1933), 101, 103-07; A. Oswald, R.J.C. Hildyard and R.G. Hughes, *English Brown Stoneware 1670-1900* (London: Faber, 1982), 102-04.
172. B. Dragesco, *English Ceramics in French Archives The writings of Jean Hellot, the adventures of Jacques Louis Brolliet and the identification of the 'Girl-in-a-Swing' factory* (London, 1993).
173. Ibid., 8, 13.
174. Ibid., 7.
175. Ibid., 26-28. We are very grateful to Dr. Helen Smith for translating the account on these pages into English.
176. The 11 Jan. 1755 advertisement was first re-printed in N. Stebbing, J. Rhodes, M. Mellor, *The Industries of Oxfordshire: Oxfordshire Potters* (Woodstock: Oxfordshire Museums Service, 1980) 29; both 11 and 25 Jan. 1755 advertisements are reprinted in R. Massey 'Jacques Louis Brolliet and the Oxford China Manufactory' in *English Ceramic Circle Transactions* Vol. 17 part 1 1999, 121-25.
177. R.P. [Robert Plot], *The Natural History of Oxford-shire, Being an Essay toward the Natural History of England* (Oxford, 1677), 65-66. See also M. Mellor, *Pots and People that have shaped the heritage of medieval and later England* (Oxford: Ashmolean Museum, 1997), 12-13, 20-21.
178. Ibid., 150 [250]-251. Robert Graves, *Wife to Mr. Milton* (London: Cassell, 1942, rep. Penguin 1954), 266, made use of Plot's account: 'Powell [Mr. Justice Powell of Forrest Hill, in 1644] secured a profitable contract from Sir Thomas Tyrrell to dig china from the ochre pits in Shotover, which he sold in Oxford to the makers of tobacco pipes, who otherwise could obtain none of sufficient fineness'.
179. W. Yates, *A Map of the County of Stafford* (London, 1775).
180. Keele University, Information Services: Sneyd MS 2681, Tunstall Manor Court Rolls, presentment of Wedgwood hamlet, 1780, 24 Oct. 'Cornealers Machin a in Croat ment of one work house [Cornelius Machin, an encroachment of one workhouse]'.
181. See Appendix 3.
182. *Burslem Parish Register* 3 vol. (Staffordshire Parish Registers Society, 1913), I, 166, christenings, 11 Dec. 1720, William son of Richard & Martha Parrott.
183. Stoke-on-Trent City Archives: D .
184. *Burslem Parish Register* 3 vol. (Staffordshire Parish Registers Society, 1913), I, 230, marriages, 8 May 1748, William Parrott and Ann Mollard; I, 246, christenings, 20 Apr. 1753, Ann d. of William & Ann Parrott.
185. Ibid., III, 660, burials, 12 Sept. 1776, William Parrott.
186. Stoke-on-Trent City Archives: EMT 19/778; *Burslem Parish Register* 3 vol. (Staffordshire Parish Registers Society, 1913), II, 316, marriages, 12 Jul. 1778, James Brown of Burslem, joiner & Ann Parrott of Burslem, s[pinster]., lic[ence].
187. Wedgwood MS 6/30157.
188. Wedgwood MS 6/30162.
189. Wedgwood MS 6/30159.
190. Stoke-on-Trent City Archives: EMT 20/PAYNE/753, 20 Apr. 1753. Payne's will also mentioned a legacy to John Lander, confirmation of Payne's marriage to Hannah Lander. (Information from the late Mr. K. Quinn.)
191. Public Record Office: DL 507/15, Vol. 14, p.32, 15 Aug. 1750, Francis Payne to James Payne. (Information from Mr. P. Roden.)
192. Ibid., p.83. (Information from Mr. P. Roden.)
193. International Genealogical Index: James son of Francis and Lydia Payne christened at St. Mary's, Stafford 2 Dec. 1717; James Payne married Hannah Lander at St. Mary's Stafford 24 Jun. 1738; Sarah daughter of James and Hannah Payne christened at Stoke 14 Dec. 1740; Lydia daughter of James and Hannah Payne christened at Stoke 25 Oct. 1742.
194. Potteries Museum and Art Gallery, Archaeology Department, Historic Buildings Survey records: Plan of the Cottages and Incroachments in the Liberty of Shelton belonging to the Duchy of Lancaster [1777].
195. *Stoke-upon-Trent Parish Registers* 4 vol. (Staffordshire Parish Registers Society, 1925), IV, 832, marriages, 1759, Jul. 1, Wm. Meire, e.p. [earth potter] & Sarah Payne, Sp[inster]., lic[ence], witness Wm. Heath.
196. Potteries Museum and Art Gallery, Ceramics Department, Heathcote papers, un-catalogued.
197. Ibid., Indentures 31 Jul., 4 Nov. 1732, Procters to Peat.
198. Ibid., Indenture 1745, Peate and Bagnall to Hatrell.
199. A.R. Mountford, 'Thomas Whieldon's Manufactory at Fenton Vivian' in *English Ceramic Circle Transactions* Vol. 8 Part 2, 1972, 164-82, 175-81
200. Ibid., 181-82.
201. A.R. Mountford, *The Illustrated Guide to Staffordshire Salt-Glazed Stoneware* (London: Barrie & Jenkins, 1971), 37, quoting a document then in the Potteries Museum, Stoke-on-Trent.
202. *A History of the County of Stafford* Vol. VIII ed. J.G. Jenkins (London: Oxford University Press, 1963), 206, map of Fenton.
203. Stoke-on-Trent City Archives: SD 4842/42/32.
204. International Genealogical Index.
205. S. Shaw, op. cit., 175-76.
206. Fuller information on Phillips is in R. Hampson, 'Longton Potters 1700-1865' in *Journal of Ceramic History* Vol. 14, 1990, 130-31.
207. Staffordshire Record Office: D(W) 1788, vol. 95.
208. See Appendix 3.
209. *Stoke-upon-Trent Parish Registers* 4 vol. (Staffordshire Parish Registers Society, 1925), II, 405.
210. E. Lloyd, 'The Country Potteries of St. Helens and Prescot' in *Northern Ceramic Society Newsletter* No. 45 Mar. 1982, 14-26, 23-25; A. Smith, 'Stoneware in North West England' in *Stonewares & Stone Chinas of Northern England to 1851* ed. T.A. Lockett and P.A. Halfpenny (Stoke-on-Trent: City Museum and Art Gallery, 1982), 23-28, 23-25.
211. *The Travels through England of Dr. Richard Pococke...* ed. J.J. Cartwright 2 vol. (London: Camden Society, 1888), I, 208.
212. *RR Angerstein's Illustrated Travel Diary 1753-1755 Industry in England and Wales from a Swedish perspective* trans. T. and P. Berg (London: Science Museum, 2001), 303-05, Figs. 282, 283.
213. Liverpool Central Library Archives: ENT/1/204-209, quoting *Gore's General Advertiser* I, 16 Feb. 1770, and also referring to a later advertisement of 16 Mar. 1770, giving more details and naming Phithian & Co.
214. L. Jewitt, *The Ceramic Art of Great Britain...* 2 vol. (London: Virtue, 1878), II, 54.
215. P. McVeigh, *Scottish East Coast Potteries 1750-1840* (Edinburgh: John Donald, 1979), 7-45, 166-67, 170-81. Samuel Garbett was a founder of the Carron Ironworks and a partner in a sulphuric acid plant at Prestonpans, see J. Uglow, *The Lunar Men The Friends who made the Future 1730-1810* (London: Faber, 2002), 78 and *passim*.
216. E. Adams, 'The Bow Insurances and Related Matters' in *English Ceramic Circle Transactions* Vol. 9, Part 1, 1973, 67-108, 102.
217. McVeigh op. cit., 9, Figures 3 and 4.
218. F. Buckley, 'II.- Potteries on the Tyne, and other northern potteries during the

eighteenth Century' in *Archaeologia Aeliana of Miscellaneous Tracts relating to Antiquity* 4th Series, IV, 1927, 68-82, 75.
219. M. Bimson, 'West Pans Story – The Scotland Manufacture' in *English Ceramic Circle Transactions* Vol. 6, Part 2, 1966, 167-76, 172.
220. McVeigh op. cit., 11.
221. Ibid., 13-16.
222. Ibid., 187.
223. D. MacAlister, 'Inscribed Longton Hall Mugs' in *English Porcelain Circle Transactions* No. III, 1933, 75-80, 79.
224. G.D.R. Cruickshank, 'Cadell's Pottery, Prestonpans: Selling a Dummy' in *Scottish Pottery Society Archive* News No. 4, 1979, 1-3.
225. G. Quail, 'A Prestonpans Pottery Inventory of 1801-2' in *Scottish Pottery Society Archive News* No. 4, 1979, 58-63.
226. Letter from Dr. Roger Kemp to the authors, 4 Nov. 1999. The shards and stilt were lent for a 'Pots at the Grange' exhibition and in 1999 were in a store 'at Leith'.
227. McVeigh, op. cit., 9, 79-93, 166-67, Figure 97.

APPENDIX 2 R-T
1. H. Lawrence, *Yorkshire Pots and Potteries* (Newton Abbot: David & Charles, 1974), 40-46.
2. H. Lawrence and P. Walton, 'The Rothwell Pottery and Its Wares' in *Leeds Arts Calendar* No. 73, 1973, 4-13, 8.
3. Ibid., 4, 11, 12.
4. Ibid., 5, 11.
5. Ibid., 12.
6. Wedgwood MS 96/17695.
7. *Burslem Parish Register* 3 vol. (Staffordshire Parish Registers Society, 1913), I, 152.
8. Lichfield Record Office: Aaron Shaw, will (made 7 Sept. 1709) and inventory, proved at Cheadle 23 Apr. 1714 by Catharine [sic] Shaw. This will and inventory has been studied in detail by L. Weatherill, *The Pottery Trade and North Staffordshire 1660-1760* (Manchester: Manchester University Press, 1971), 17, 19, 28, 33, 34, 38, 39, 68, 70, 139, 149, 150, 151; and 'Technical change of potters' probate inventories 1660-1760' in *Journal of Ceramic History* No. 3, 1970, 3-12, 3, 5, 6, 7, 8.
9. *Burslem Parish Register* 3 vol. (Staffordshire Parish Registers Society, 1913), records (I, 156) the burial of Catherine Shaw on 6 Nov. 1715, and also (I, 191) the burial of another Catherine Shaw on 18 Aug. 1731.
10. Ibid., I, 250.
11. Lichfield Record Office: will of *John Shrigley*, proved 27 Apr. 1780.
12. *Burslem Parish Register* 3 vol. (Staffordshire Parish Registers Society, 1913), I, 199.
13. Lichfield Record Office: Aaron Shaw, administration and inventory 13 Apr. 1737.
14. Wedgwood MS 96/17695.
15. *Burslem Parish Register* 3 vol. (Staffordshire Parish Registers Society, 1913), I, 189, 207, 221, 229, 253.
16. 'John Dwight's Fulham Pottery 1672-1978 A Collection of Documentary Sources' ed. D. Haselgrove and J. Murray in *Journal of Ceramic History* No. 11, 1979, 1-284, 122.
17. Ibid., 69-71.
18. Staffordshire Record Office: D1788, pcl. 61, bdle. 41.
19. J.C. Wedgwood, *A History of the Wedgwood Family* (London: St. Catherine Press, 1908), 126, 323.
20. *Patents for Inventions. Abridgments of the Specifications relating to Pottery* (London: Commissioners of Patents, 1863) 6, A.D. 1733, 24 Apr. - No. 541. A.R. Mountford, *The Illustrated Guide to Staffordshire Salt-Glazed Stoneware* (London: Barrie & Jenkins, 1971), 41-42, quotes a fuller version of this patent.
21. N. Davenport, *The United Kingdom Patent System a Brief History* (Havant: Mason, 1979), 32.
22. S. Shaw, *History of the Staffordshire Potteries...*. (Hanley: privately, 1829), 147. C.F.C. Luxmoore, *"Saltglaze," with the Notes of a Collector* (1924, reprinted London: Holland Press, n.d.), 54-55 included Aaron Wood with J Mitchell as defendants in the case, presumably from a misreading of L. Jewitt *The Ceramic Art of Great Britain...* 2 Vol. (London: Virtue, 1878), II, 241.
23. *Burslem Parish Register* 3 vol. (Staffordshire Parish Registers Society, 1913), I, 208, 250, 260, 267.
24. M. Goodby, 'William Littler: The Early Years' in *William Littler: An English Earth Potter 1724-1784* ed. M. Adams (Charlotte: Delhom Service League, 1999), 11-18, 12.
25. See A.R. Mountford, *The Illustrated Guide to Staffordshire Salt-Glazed Stoneware* (London: Barrie & Jenkins, 1971), 44 and Plate 103.
26. Wedgwood MSS 31/23006-23009.
27. A.R. Mountford, 'Thomas Wedgwood, John Wedgwood and Jonah Malkin Potters of Burslem', unpublished MA Thesis, Keele University, 1972, Appendix III, 113.
28. Staffordshire Record Office: D 1788, pcl 1, bdle. 1 and Vol. 99, p.27.
29. N. Valpy, 'Extracts from 18th Century London Newspapers and Additional Manuscripts, British Library' in *English Ceramic Circle Transactions* Vol. 13, Part 1, 1987, 77-95, 90.
30. International Genealogical Index.
31. Stoke-on-Trent City Archives: SM8, Plan o' the Town of Burslem 1769; Keele University Information Services: HA 1139 B8 H3, Reference to the Plan of the Town of Burslem..., No. 1.
32. Wedgwood MS 30/22912 22 Jun. 1763.
33. Wedgwood MS 26/31256 30 Apr. 1763.
34. Wedgwood MS 30/22911 24 Aug. 1763.
35. P.W.L. Adams, *A History of the Adams Family of North Staffordshire...* (London: St. Catherine Press, 1914), 116-17.
36. J. Ward, *The Borough of Stoke-upon-Trent...* (London: Lewis, 1843), 235.
37. Shaw, op. cit., 152-53.
38. Staffordshire Record Office: D 593, Staffordshire Poll Book for 1747.
39. Keele University Information Services: Sneyd MS 228, 220, 2678.
40. *Stoke-upon-Trent Parish Registers* 4 vol. (Staffordshire Parish Registers Society, 1925), III, 854.
41. Adams, op. cit., 130.
42. *Burslem Parish Register* 3 vol. (Staffordshire Parish Registers Society, 1913), III, 670, burials, 18 Apr. 1780 John Shrigley senior; Lichfield Record Office: John Shrigley, Burslem, will proved 27 Apr. 1780. His will is discussed in detail by H. Blakey, 'John Shrigley of Burslem' in *Northern Ceramic Society Newsletter* No. 103, Sept. 1996, 19-23.
43. A.R. Mountford, 'The Sadler Teapot manufactory Site Burslem, Stoke-on-Trent, Staffs.' in *City of Stoke-on-Trent Museum Archaeological Society Reports* No. 7, 1975, 1-20, 3, 7.
44. Staffordshire Record Office: D 1788, vol. 102, p.55, vol. 99, p.82.
45. John Randall, writing in 1877, mentioned salt-glaze saggars, and said that they 'often form walls of the oldest cottages in Benthall and Broseley Wood', in *The Clay Industries... on the Banks of the Severn...* (Madeley, Salop: 1877, rep. Salop County Council Library n.d.), 22; E. Benthall 'Some XVIIIth Century Shropshire Potteries' in *Transactions of the Salop Archaeological Society* Vol. LV, 1954-56, 169; J.P. Malam, 'Garden walls and their clues to Jackfield's industrial past' in *Shropshire Magazine* Jul. 1983, 26.
46. Information from Mr. Roger Edmundson: S. Simpson *The Agreeable Historian or the Compleat English Traveller* (1746) quoted in *Ironbridge Quarterly, Newsletter of the Friends of the Ironbridge Gorge Museum* 1982.1.
47. The Old Vicarage is now (2003) named Benthall House. (Information from Mr. Roger Edmundson.)
48. J. Sandon, 'The Old Vicarage, Benthall, Broseley, Salop, Report of an archaeological investigation of the site, January 1978' in *The Journal of the Wilkinson Society* No. 6, 1978, 9-20.
49. See R.S. Edmundson, 'Benthall Pottery, Shropshire and its Salopian Art Pottery' in *Journal of the Northern Ceramic Society* Vol. 19, 2002, 29-76, 30, 72, Fig. 72.
50. Ibid., 29, 72, Fig. 73.
51. J.P. Malam, 'White Salt-glazed stoneware manufactured at Jackfield' in *West Midlands Archaeology* 24, 1981, 45-50. The site is at SJ 689029. Two excavations on the 'Jackfield' site were reported in *Post-Medieval Archaeology* 19, 1985, 179-80, probably including the information published by J.P. Malam in 1981.
52. Whilst it is known that pottery workers migrated from Staffordshire to Broseley between 1730 and 1739 (see M. Hawes, 'The Migration of Pottery Workers between Stoke-on-Trent and the Broseley area in the eighteenth century' in *The Journal of the Wilkinson Society* No. 2 1974, 7-9), it would be now more appropriate to say that the shards found were of *frequently found shapes*.
53. R. Edmundson, 'Potter or Salesman' in *Northern Ceramic Society Newsletters* 38, Jun. 1980, 24-29 and No. 40, Dec. 1980, 22. This advertisement, in *Aris's Birmingham Gazette* 21 Aug. 1780, was found by Gaye Blake Roberts and published by Roger Edmundson, who also identified the site of the potworks 'which became the Jackfield Pottery'.
54. W.H. Goss, *The Life and Death of Llewellynn Jewitt...* (London: Gray, 1889), 181-82.
55. L. Jewitt, 'Salopian China' in *The Art Journal* New Series Vol. I, 1862, 65-68, 66.
56. For a general survey of the pottery industries of Jackfield, see C. Clark and J. Alfrey, 4th Interim Report of *The Nuffield Archaeological Survey of the Ironbridge Gorge* 1988, 44-51.
57. L. Jewitt, *The Ceramic Art of Great Britain...* 2 vol. (London: Virtue, 1878), I, 304.
58. R.S. Edmundson, 'Shropshire Potters, and their associates, insured with the Salop Fire Office' in *Journal of the Northern Ceramic Society* Vol. 18, 2001, 39-57, 56.
59. Ibid., 47, 49, 55. William Thursfield insured Glass' Pottery in 1795 and 1805.
60. Information from Mr. Roger Edmundson.

(Ordnance Survey references added by the authors.)
61. Appendix 3.
62. Staffordshire Record Office: D 1788 Vol. 99, p.51; Vol 102, pp. 43, 65, 90.
63. *Newcastle-under Lyme Parish Registers* 3 vol.(Staffordshire Parish Registers Society, 1939), II, 189.
64. Stoke-on-Trent City Archives: SM8, Plan o'the Town of Burslem 1769; Keele University Information Services: HA 1139 B8 H3, Reference to the Plan of the Town of Burslem… Nos. 101, 102.
65. Based on information from Mr. Noel Boothroyd, Field Archaeology Unit, Potteries Museum and Art Gallery, 19 Apr. 2002.
66. Wedgwood MSS 30/22966-22990.
67. Wedgwood MSS 30/22976, 22978. These tureens were charged at 2½d. and 4d. for firing, according to size, compared with prices for tureens between 18d. and 42d. in the 1770 price agreement – see Appendix 3. Butter tubs and stands and sauceboats and covers on the same invoices, not marked 'Fired', were charged at prices comparable to the 1770 agreement.
68. Wedgwood MS 30/22982.
69. Mountford, 1972, op. cit., Appendix III, 96.
70. Staffordshire Record Office: D 1788, pcl. 14, bdle. 2 pt., Book A, p.[1].
71. Ibid., Vol. 95 for 1763, Vol. 99, p.36 for 1765-66.
72. L. Weatherill, *The Pottery Trade and North Staffordshire 1660-1760* (Manchester: Manchester University Press, 1971), 69.
73. See Appendix 3.
74. *Newcastle-under-Lyme Parish Registers* 3 vol. (Staffordshire Parish Registers Society, 1931, 1939, 1981) [III] 3.
75. P.W.L. Adams, op. cit., 286 and Table G; second supplement 1940, V; P.W.L. Adams, *Notes on some North Staffordshire Families…* (Tunstall: Eardley, 1930), 9, 63.
76. Directories, 1784-1805. See also W. Mankowitz & R.G. Haggar, *The Concise Encyclopedia of English Pottery and Porcelain* (London: Deutsch, 1957), 204.
77. J.T. Wilkinson, *Hugh Bourne 1772-1852* (London: Epworth Press, 1952), 56n, 87.
78. Appendix 3.
79. Staffordshire Record Office: D 1788, Vol. 99, 114.
80. *Burslem Parish Register* 3 vol. (Staffordshire Parish Registers Society, 1913), III, 651.
81. *A History of the County of Stafford* multi-vol., Vol. VIII, ed. J.G. Jenkins (London: Oxford University Press, 1963), 219.
82. A. Hayden, *Spode and his Successors* (London: Cassell, 1925), 8.
83. D. Barker, '18th and 19th Century Ceramics excavated at the Foley Pottery, Fenton, Stoke-on-Trent' in *Staffordshire Archaeological Studies* No. 1, 1984, 63-86.
84. See P.F.C. Roden, 'Josiah Spode (1733-1797) his formative influences and the various Potworks associated with him' in *Journal of the Northern Ceramic Society* Vol. 14, 1997, 1-43, 37-40, for a discussion of the date of erection of the Foley Pottery.
85. D. Barker, 'A Group of Staffordshire Red Stonewares of the 18th century' in *English Ceramic Circle Transactions* Vol. I, Part 2, 1991, 177-98.
86. Roden, op. cit., 37-40, 38.
87. Information from Mr. P. Roden.
88. Appendix 3.
89. Wedgwood MSS 30/22949-22965.
90. A.R. Mountford, 1972, op. cit., Appendix III, 113. See also our Chapter VI, Potters as Customers.
91. Wedgwood MS 55/30439.
92. Wedgwood MS 1/592.
93. Staffordshire Record Office: D 1788, Vol. 99, p.54.
94. The International Genealogical Index records the wife as 'Abigail Warburton' but the printed Parish register records the ceremony as '1765 Jos Stephens and Abigail Stephens being married according to the Order of the Scotch Kirk were Re-married in this Church of Norton by Banns Jan 21 (*Norton-le-Moors Parish Registers* 2 vol. (Staffordshire Parish Registers Society, 1942-43), II, 8.)
95. M.W. Greenslade, 'The 1767 Return of Staffordshire Papists' in *Staffordshire Catholic History* No. 17, 1977, 1-41, 36.
96. *Burslem Parish Registers* 3 vol. (Staffordshire Parish Registers Society, 1913), I, 161, christenings, 3 Jul. 1718, Thomas son of William and Jemima Steeveson [sic], I, 260. *Wolstanton Parish Register* 2 vol. (Staffordshire Parish Registers Society, 1914), I, 301, marriages, 6 Apr. 1743, Thos Stevenson and Hannah Taylor.
97. Lichfield Record Office: Tho. Stevenson, Burslem, administration, 23 May 1758.
98. H. De la Beche and T. Reeks, *Catalogue of Specimens illustrative of the Composition and Manufacture of British Pottery and Porcelain from the Occupation of Britain by the Romans to the Present Time* (London: Museum of Practical Geology, 1855), 165-67.
99. A. Cox and A. Cox, 'Recent Excavations at the Swinton Pottery: White Salt-Glazed Stoneware and Creamware Pre 1785' in *English Ceramic Circle Transactions* Vol. 11, Part 3, 1983, 232-54; A. and A. Cox, *Rockingham 1745-1842* (Woodbridge: Antique Collectors' Club, 2001), 22-33.
100. Appendix 3.
101. Shaw, op. cit., 148-49, 181.
102. J. Ward *The Borough of Stoke-upon-Trent…* (London: Lewis, 1843), 235.
103. *Burslem Parish Registers* 3 vol. (Staffordshire Parish Registers Society, 1913), III, 649.
104. Wedgwood MS 96/17695.
105. Keele University Information Services: HA 1139 B8 H3, 'Reference to the Plan of the Town of Burslem… In the Year 1750'. A corresponding '1769' plan is in Stoke-on-Trent City Archives, SM8.
106. J.C. Wedgwood, op. cit., 126, 323.
107. Lichfield Record Office: will of Thos Taylor, Burslem, proved 24 Sept. 1713. His will was made on 3 Apr. 1713, and he was buried 8 Apr. 1713 (*Burslem Parish Registers* 3 Vol. (Staffordshire Parish Registers Society, 1913), I, 152. 'Sperate' debts are those with some likelihood of being recovered (*OED*); 'desperate' debts are unlikely to be collectable.
108. L. Weatherill, 'Technical Change and Potters' Probate Inventories 1660-1760' in *Journal of Ceramic History* No. 3, 1970, 3-12, 5, 7.
109. Ordnance Survey reference SJ 869499. A detailed study of this area is in Stoke-on-Trent City Archives: S 8109, R. Hampson, 'History of Burslem Market Place Area'.
110. Keele University Information Services: HA 1139 B8 H3, 'Reference to the Plan of the Town of Burslem… In the Year 1750'. A corresponding '1769' plan is in Stoke-on-Trent City Archives, SM8.
111. *Burslem Parish Registers* 3 vol. (Staffordshire Parish Registers Society, 1913), I, 153, Thomas son of John and Elizabeth Taylor christened 21 Dec. 1714; I, 152, Mr. Thomas Taylor buried 3 Nov. 1751.
112. Ibid., I, 200, Thomas son of Thomas and Elizabeth Taylor christened 5 Feb. 1737/38; I, 242, Mr. Thomas Taylor buried 10 Apr. 1776.
113. Lichfield Record Office: will of Thomas Taylor of Burslem, potter, made 14 Nov. 1750, proved at Cheadle 29 Apr. 1752.
114. Stoke-on-Trent City Archives: D 4842/14/1/70.
115. Lichfield Record Office: will of Thomas Taylor of Burslem, potter, made 14 Nov. 1750, proved at Cheadle 29 Apr. 1752.
116. International Genealogical Index: Isaiah Taylor born at Burslem, 16 May 1740, of Thomas and Elizabeth.
117. *Burslem Parish Registers* 3 vol. (Staffordshire Parish Registers Society, 1913), III, 639.
118. Wedgwood MSS 31/23025-23050.
119. Wyke was shaky on forenames: he addressed Josiah Wedgwood as Joseph in his first letter. See A. Smith, 'John Wyke of Liverpool, and the Staffordshire Pottery Export Trade' in *Northern Ceramic Society Journal* Vol. 3 1978-1979, 79-88, for a detailed study of these transactions.
120. Wedgwood MSS 10/30171, 31/23036.
121. Staffordshire Record Office: D 1788 vol. 99, p.31.
122. Wedgwood MS 11/3004.
123. *Stoke-upon-Trent Parish Registers* 4 vol. (Staffordshire Parish Registers Society, 1925), III, 1738.
124. Lichfield Record Office: will of William Taylor, Stoke, proved 1 Jun. 1738, inventory dated 23 May 1738.
125. International Genealogical Index.
126. Wedgwood MSS 30/22929-941, 30/30916-919. These seventeen documents are dated between 12 Feb. 1763 and 3 Sept. 1764, and the incidence of one per month probably represents similar documents over a longer period, which have not survived.
127. Wedgwood MS 30/30919.
128. Wedgwood MS 6/30584.
129. Wedgwood MS 6/30582.
130. Wedgwood MSS 30/30916-18.
131. Wedgwood MS 20/22936.
132. See A. Smith, 'John Wyke of Liverpool, and the Staffordshire Pottery Export Trade' in *Northern Ceramic Society Journal* Vol. 3 1978-1979, 79-88, for a detailed study of these transactions.
133. Wedgwood MS 10/30170.
134. Wedgwood MS 10/30171.
135. Wedgwood MSS 10/30171, 30/22930.
136. Wedgwood MS 6/30676.
137. Wedgwood MS 36/30938; published by R. Haggar, 'A Letter and Order from Amsterdam, 1776' in *Northern Ceramic Society Newsletter* No. 8, 6-7.
138. See F. Hughes, *Mother Town* (Burslem: Burslem Community Development Trust, 2000), p.70 for a photograph entitled 'The Jawnels', showing Central Passage.
139. S. Shaw, op. cit., 148-49, 181.
140. J. Ward, *The Borough of Stoke-upon-Trent…* (London; Lewis, 1843), 235.

141. Shaw, op. cit., 119, 121-22, 125-26.
142. S. Shaw, *The Chemistry of Pottery...* (London: Lewis, 1837, repr. London; Scott Greenwood, 1900), 416, 417.
143. 'The Stoke-upon-Trent Parish Listing, 1701' ed. D.A. Gatley et al. in *Collections for a History of Staffordshire*, 4th series, vol. 16 (1994), 171-253, 210.
144. *Stoke-upon-Trent Parish Registers* 4 vol. (Staffordshire Parish Registers Society, 1925), I, 24, 6 Dec. 1640, Joshua f[ilius]. Wm. Twyford and Margarete.
145. International Genealogical Index.
146. *Stoke-upon-Trent Parish Registers* 4 vol. (Staffordshire Parish Registers Society, 1925) II, 409: Burials, 1 Aug. 1729, William Twyford.
147. Ibid., II, 176, 180.
148. Ibid., II, 408: Burials, 1 Aug. 1729, Wm. Twyford, marit (married).
149. Lichfield Record Office: will of Wm. Twyford Stoke proved 8 Oct. 1729.
150. *Croxden Parish Register* (Staffordshire Parish Registers Society, 1912), 23: William Twyford married Ellen Leese 12 Jun. 1724 at Croxden, Staffordshire.
151. *Stoke-upon-Trent Parish Registers* 4 vol. (Staffordshire Parish Registers Society, 1925), II, 298: William christened 18 Aug. 1728, of Wm. and Ellen Twyford.
152. Ibid., II, 381: Ellen christened 16 Apr. 1725, of Wm. and Ellen Twyford.

APPENDIX 2 W-Y
1. Wedgwood MS 10/30902.
2. Appendix 3.
3. *Burslem Parish Registers* 3 vol. (Staffordshire Parish Registers Society, 1913), II, 305: Marriages, 8 Feb. 1764, Joseph Stone of Burslem gent. & Ann Warburton of Burslem.
4. International Genealogical Index: Ann daughter of John and Ann Warburton, baptised 17 Jan. 1744/45 at Burslem.
5. Lichfield Record Office: will of John Warburton, Burslem, proved 29 Oct. 1761.
6. M.W. Greenslade, 'The 1767 Return of Staffordshire Papists' in *Staffordshire Catholic History* No. 17, 1977, 1-41, 36.
7. *Burslem Parish Registers* 3 vol. (Staffordshire Parish Registers Society, 1913), III, 663, Burials, 23 Nov. 23 1777, Joseph Stone.
8. Liverpool Central Library Archives: 942 ENT 30, wallet containing draft articles, 30/33-35; W. Emery, 'Note on Whieldon Pottery' in *Transactions of The [British] Ceramic Society* Vol. XXIV, Part IV 1925, 339-47, 409; H.W. Maxwell, 'Excavations in North Staffordshire' in *English Ceramic Circle Transactions* No. 1 1933, 57-58, 57; A.T. Morley Hewitt, 'Early Whieldon of the Fenton Low Works' in *English Ceramic Circle Transactions* Vol. 3, Part 3, 1954, 142-54 and P. Halfpenny, 'Thomas Whieldon: his life and work' in *English Ceramic Circle Transactions* Vol. 15, Part 2, 1997, 237-54, 250, 252.
9. Potteries Museum and Art Gallery, Ceramics Department: Thomas Whieldon's Memorandum Book, uncatalogued: p. 30 for William Meir, pp. 41-46 for Edward Warburton. Mr. Broad and William Warburton have been named as tenants of the potworks, but they were really tenants of farm land.
10. Staffordshire Record Office: D 1788, Vol. 95.
11. International Genealogical Index: Edward Poulson married Sarah Poulson 8 Jan. 1756 at Whitmore, Staffs; *Stoke-upon-Trent Parish Registers* 4 vol. (Staffordshire Parish Registers Society, 1925), III, 613, Burials, 16 May 1767, Edw. Warburton.
12. Hewitt, op. cit., Plate 59.
13. Emery, op. cit., 342, 345.
14. Maxwell, op. cit., 57; Hewitt, op. cit., 145-46; Halfpenny, op. cit., 250, 252.
15. Emery, op. cit., 339-47 *passim*; Maxwell, op. cit., 57-58, 57; Hewitt, op. cit., 145, 148-49; A.R. Mountford, *The Illustrated Guide to Staffordshire Salt-Glazed Stoneware* (London: Barrie & Jenkins, 1971), 34, plate 48; Halfpenny, op. cit., 252.
16. Wedgwood MS 10/8073.
17. E. Adams, 'The Bow Insurances and Related Matters' in *English Ceramic Circle Transactions* Vol. 9, Part I, 1973, 67-108, 75, 106.
18. Appendix 3.
19. *Burslem Parish Registers* 3 vol. (Staffordshire Parish Registers Society, 1913), III, 656, Jacob Warburton buried 4 Aug. 1775; Burslem St. John's Churchyard, monumental inscription: Jacob Warburton died 1 Aug. 1775 aged 39.
20. Burslem St. John's Churchyard, monumental inscription: Isaac Warburton died 13 Feb. 1775, aged 35; *Burslem Parish Registers* 3 vol. (Staffordshire Parish Registers Society, 1913) III, 655, Burials, 23 Feb. 1775, Isaac Warburton.
21. Lichfield Record Office: will of Jos Warburton, Burslem, proved 9 Nov. 1752.
22. International Genealogical Index.
23. No evidence has been found to confirm that *this* Joseph Warburton made white salt-glazed stoneware.
24. Burslem St. John's Churchyard, monumental inscription: Joseph Warburton, died 30 Jul. 1752; Lichfield Record Office: will of Joseph Warburton, proved 9 Nov. 1752.
25. Lichfield Record Office: will of Tho. Daniel, Burslem, proved 2 May 1760.
26. *R R Angerstein's Illustrated Travel Diary 1753-1755 Industry in England and Wales from a Swedish perspective* trans. T. and P. Berg (London: Science Museum, 2001), 340.
27. Lichfield Record Office: will of John Warburton, Burslem, 1 Jul. 1760, codicil dated 26 Dec. 1760, proved 29 Oct. 1761. Burslem St. John's Churchyard, monumental inscription: John Warburton of Cobridge Gate died 14 May 1761 aged 40.
28. Appendix 3.
29. *Burslem Parish Registers* 3 vol. (Staffordshire Parish Registers Society, 1913) III, 703.
30. Ibid., III, 745, buried 12 Aug 1798, Ann Warburton. Burslem St. John's Churchyard, monumental inscription; Ann Warburton, wife of John, died 10 Aug. 1798, aged 85.
31. S. Shaw, *History of the Staffordshire Potteries...* (Hanley: privately, 1829), 177.
32. R. Reilly, *Wedgwood The New Illustrated Dictionary* (Woodbridge: Antique Collectors' Club, 1995), 454.
33. Wedgwood MS 10/8076.
34. A.R. Mountford, 'Thomas Wedgwood, John Wedgwood and Jonah Malkin Potters of Burslem', unpublished MA Thesis, Keele University, 1972, Appendix III, 54.
35. International Genealogical Index.
36. P.W.L. Adams, *A History of the Adams Family of North Staffordshire...* (London: St. Catherine Press, 1914), 184.
37. Ibid., 284-90.
38. Appendix 3.
39. Appendix 3.
40. R. Edmundson 'Staffordshire Potters insured with the Salop Fire Office 1780-1825' in *Journal of the Northern Ceramic Society* Vol. 6, 1987, 81-93, 86.
41. *A History of the County of Stafford* multi-vol., Vol. VIII, ed. J.G. Jenkins (London: Oxford University Press, 1963), 250-51.
42. *Burslem Parish Registers* 3 vol. (Staffordshire Parish Registers Society, 1913), I, 198.
43. E. Adams and D. Redstone, *Bow Porcelain* (London; Faber, 1981), 16-17, 22, 25-27.
44. W. Pitt *A Topographical History of Staffordshire...* (Newcastle-under-Lyme: Smith, 1817), 422-23.
45. A.R. Mountford, 'Thomas Wedgwood, John Wedgwood and Jonah Malkin Potters of Burslem', unpublished MA Thesis, Keele University, 1972, Appendix III, 60, 98.
46. Ibid., Appendix II (64). Japanning is lacquering or varnishing. *William Littler* at West Pans, Scotland advertised 'Japand Black' in 1766, but japanning can be in various colours.
47. Wedgwood MSS 6/5030, 5032.
48. Mountford, 1972, op. cit., 107; Appendix III, 12-14, 27, 32, 37, 43, 50, 52, 58, 60, 63, 73, 79, 81, 84, 89, 94, 98, 108, 111, 120, 128.
49. Ibid., Appendix III, 111, 128; IV 19.
50. Wedgwood MSS 6/5028-5032, 31323-24.
51. Wedgwood MSS 10/30169.
52. Wedgwood MS 30/30144, 9 Jun. 1763.
53. *Burslem Parish Registers* 3 vol. (Staffordshire Parish Registers Society, 1913), I, 160: Baptisms, 2 Mar. 1717, Aaron, son of Aaron and Martha Wedgwood.
54. Ibid., I, 172: Burials, 1722, Aug. 26, Aaron Wedgwood.
55. J.C. Wedgwood, *A History of the Wedgwood Family* (London; St. Catherine Press, 1908), 141-42, 160, Chart XI (a).
56. T.V.H. FitzHugh, *The Dictionary of Genealogy*, 3rd ed. (London: Black, 1991), 83.
57. *Stoke-upon-Trent Parish Registers* 4 vol. (Staffordshire Parish Registers Society, 1925) III, 475.
58. Wedgwood MSS 96/17796-98.
59. *Burslem Parish Registers* 3 vol. (Staffordshire Parish Registers Society, III, 1913), 677: Burials, 8 Nov. 1782, Aaron Wedgwood senr.
60. Stoke-on-Trent City Archives: SM 5E, W. Heaton, *Plan of the Town of Burslem... 1740*, No. 74; S 810 W. Heaton, *Reference to the Plan of the Town of Burslem... 1740* (Burslem, 1821) No. 74, Aaron Wedgwood & Little Aaron Wedgwood Houses; SM8, *Plan o'the Town of Burslem 1769*, No. 113; Keele University Information Services: HA 1139 B8 H3, W. Heaton, *Reference to the Plan of the Town of Burslem... in 1750*, No. pt.113 Little Aaron Wedgwood, House &c., No. pt.113 Aaron Wedgwood House &c.
61. 'John Dwight's Fulham Pottery 1672-1978 A Collection of Documentary Sources' ed. D. Haselgrove and J. Murray in *Journal of Ceramic History* No. 11 1979, 1-284, 83-96, 97.
62. Ibid., 98.
63. Ibid., 97.
64. Ibid., 122-24.
65. Ibid., 122.
66. Ibid., 144.
67. J.C. Wedgwood, op. cit., 141-48, Chart XI (a).
68. This is not the Aaron Wedgwood (1671-1744) who was in Cumbria from about 1704,

see L. Weatherill and R. Edwards 'Pottery Making in London and Whitehaven in the Late Seventeenth Century' in *Post-Medieval Archaeology*, Vol. 5, 1971, 160-81, 170; and F. Sibson, *The History of the West Cumberland Potteries* (privately, 1991), 8.
69. Weatherill and Edwards, op. cit., 163.
70. Wedgwood, op. cit., 126, 323.
71. Lichfield Record Office: will of Aaron Wedgwood 16 Apr. 1701.
72. Wedgwood, op. cit., Chart X, 150; J.C. Wedgwood and J.G.E. Wedgwood, *Wedgwood Pedigrees* (Kendal: Wilson, 1925) 161; *Burslem Parish Registers* 3 vol. (Staffordshire Parish Registers Society, 1913), I, *Burslem Parish Registers* 3 vol. (Staffordshire Parish Registers Society, 1913), I, 177.
73. *Burslem Parish Registers* 3 vol. (Staffordshire Parish Registers Society, 1913), II, 278: Burials, 7 Nov. 1762, Burslem Wedgwood.
74. Stoke-on-Trent City Archives: SD 4842/14/3/2.
75. Wedgwood, op. cit., Chart X, 150; Wedgwood and Wedgwood, op. cit., 161; *Burslem Parish Registers* 3 vol. (Staffordshire Parish Registers Society, 1913) I, 181.
76. *Burslem Parish Registers* 3 vol. (Staffordshire Parish Registers Society, 1913) III, 646: Burials, 14 Dec. 1771, Carloss [sic] Wedgwood.
77. A.R. Mountford, 1972, op. cit., 107; Appendix III, 74.
78. Staffordshire Record Office: D (W) 1788, Vol. 95.
79. Wedgwood MSS 30/22924-6, 10 Feb., 5 Apr., 10 Apr. 1763.
80. Shaw, op. cit., 167.
81. Wedgwood, op. cit., Chart X, 146; Wedgwood and Wedgwood, op. cit., 161.
82. 'John Dwight's Fulham Pottery 1672-1978 A Collection of Documentary Sources' ed. D. Haselgrove and J. Murray in *Journal of Ceramic History* No. 11, 1979, 1-284, 122.
83. Ibid., 69-71.
84. Wedgwood, op. cit., Chart VIII, 116-20; Wedgwood and Wedgwood, op. cit., 98-99; *Burslem Parish Registers* 3 vol. (Staffordshire Parish Registers Society, 1913) I, 69: births 2 May 1654, John, son of Thomas & Margaret Wedgwood; I, 138, burials, 13 Apr. 1705, John Wedgwood; monumental inscription in St. John's Churchyard, Burslem: John Wedgwood, Gentleman, Overhouse, Burslem, buried 13 Apr. 1705 aged 51.
85. Lichfield Record Office: will of John Wedgwood, Burslem, proved Oct. 1705.
86. Wedgwood MS 96/17695.
87. For a recent and reliable biography, see R. Reilly, *Josiah Wedgwood 1730-1795* (London: Macmillan, 1992), or the same author's two-volume *Wedgwood* (London: Macmillan, 1989), 13-144.
88. Wedgwood MS 30/22942.
89. Wedgwood MSS 30/22976, 22978.
90. Wedgwood MS 20/22936.
91. 'Archaeological Excavation Market Place, Burslem, Stoke-on-Trent (The Ceramica Development)' in *Potteries Museum Field Archaeology Unit Report* No. 84, Mar. 2000, 36, 60.
92. Wedgwood MS 26/19117.
93. Wedgwood MSS 29/21439, W/M 1131.
94. S. Shaw, op. cit., 182-83.
95. Wedgwood MS 96/17695.
96. Wedgwood, op. cit., 324.
97. *Burslem Parish Registers* 3 vol. (Staffordshire Parish Registers Society, 1913), I, 89, Baptisms 21 Jun. 1668, Richard son of Aaron and Margaret Wedgwood; Wedgwood, op. cit., Chart X.
98. 'John Dwight's Fulham Pottery 1672-1978 A Collection of Documentary Sources' ed. D. Haselgrove and J. Murray in *Journal of Ceramic History* No. 11, 1979, 1-284, 83-96, 97.
99. Ibid., 69-71.
100. Ibid., 122.
101. Lichfield Record Office: will of Aaron Wedgwood, 16 Apr. 1701.
102. *Burslem Parish Registers* 3 vol. (Staffordshire Parish Registers Society, 1913), I, 162, Burials, 23 Oct. 1718, Richard Wedgwood; Lichfield Record Office: will of Richard Wedgwood, Burslem, proved 23 Apr. 1719. 'Sperate' debts are those with some likelihood of being recovered *(OED)*; 'desperate' debts are unlikely to be collectable.
103. Wedgwood, op. cit., Chart X.
104. 'John Dwight's Fulham Pottery 1672-1978 A Collection of Documentary Sources' ed. D. Haselgrove and J. Murray in *Journal of Ceramic History* No. 11, 1979, 1-284, 83-96, 97.
105. Ibid., 69-71.
106. Ibid., 122.
107. *Burslem Parish Registers* 3 vol. (Staffordshire Parish Registers Society, 1913), I, 71, Births, 13 Sept. 1655, Thomas son of Aron [sic] & Mary Wedgwood; I, 160, Burials, 29 Dec. 1717, Thomas Wedgwood (Doctr.); Wedgwood, op. cit., 146-47. The appellation 'Doctor' was used contemporaneously of members of the 'Red Lion' branch of the extended Wedgwood family, presumably to distinguish between holders of the same forename.
108. Lichfield Record Office: will of Thomas Wedgwood of Burslem, proved 29 Apr. 1718.
109. Wedgwood, op. cit., 324.
110. Wedgwood MS 96/17695.
111. *Burslem Parish Registers* 3 vol. (Staffordshire Parish Registers Society, 1913), I, 199, Burials, 20 Feb. 1736/37, Dr. Wedgwood; Wedgwood, op. cit., 149-50.
112. Wedgwood MS WM 947.
113. W. Pitt, *Topographical History of Staffordshire...* (Newcastle-under-Lyme: Smith, 1817), 423-24. For an explanation of 'Doctor', see note 107.
114. See S. Shaw, op. cit., 150.
115. Shaw, op. cit., 149-50.
116. Lichfield Record Office: Admon. Thomas Wedgwood Burslem 5 May 1737.
117. P. McVeigh, *Scottish East Coast Potteries 1750-1840* (Edinburgh: John Donald, 1979), 49.
118. G. Cruickshank, *Scottish Pottery a brief history* (Princes Risborough: Shire, 1987), 6.
119. A. Lane, 'William Littler of Longton Hall and West Pans, Scotland' in *English Ceramic Circle Transactions* Vol. 5, Part 2, 1961, 82-94, 87; G. Quail, 'William Littler and the Westpans China Works' in *Northern Ceramic Society Newsletter* No. 44, Dec. 1981 10-27, 16-17.
120. McVeigh, op. cit., 58.
121. McVeigh, op. cit., 47-67; G. Quail in *Northern Ceramic Society Newsletters* Nos. 44, 46, 47, 62, 63 and 64; H. Kelly, *Northern Ceramic Society Newsletter* No. 88; J. Turnbull, *Northern Ceramic Society Newsletter* No. 96.
122. Wedgwood, op. cit., Charts X, XI.(a), 151-52; Wedgwood and Wedgwood, op. cit., 173-74. Our entry for *Aaron, Thomas and Richard Wedgwood* establishes that it was this Aaron Wedgwood (1666-1743) who went to Cumbria in 1697/98.
123. L. Weatherill and R. Edwards, 'Pottery Making in London and Whitehaven in the Late Seventeenth Century' in *Post-Medieval Archaeology* Vol. 5, 1971, 160-81, 161-63.
124. Weatherill and Edwards, op. cit., 161-63; 'John Dwight's Fulham Pottery 1672-1978 A Collection of Documentary Sources' ed. D. Haselgrove and J. Murray, in *Journal of Ceramic History* No. 11, 1979, 1-284, 83-96, 97.
125. Weatherill and Edwards, op. cit., 165.
126. Wedgwood, op. cit., Chart XVI, 227; Wedgwood and Wedgwood, op. cit., 145.
127. F. Sibson, *The History of the West Cumberland Potteries* (privately, 1991), 8; Weatherill and Edwards, op. cit., 170.
128. Shaw, op. cit., 44, 210.
129. R. Gurnett, *Chatterley & Whitehead Potters of Hanley & Shelton* (privately, 1996); D. Edwards and R. Hampson, *English Dry-Bodied Stoneware Wedgwood and Contemporary Manufacturers 1774-1830* (Woodbridge: Antique Collectors' Club, 1998), 197.
130. F. Faulkner, *The Wood Family of Burslem* (London: Chapman and Hall, 1912, rep. 1972), Pedigree after p.118; *Burslem Parish Registers* 3 vol. (Staffordshire Parish Registers Society, 1913), I, 224, Christenings 20 Apr. 1746 John son of Ralph and Mary Wood; III, 737, Funerals 2 Feb. 1797, John Wood (Brownhills) wilfully murdered by - Oliver, Surgeon.
131. A.R. Mountford, 1972, op. cit., Appendix III; IV, 52, 56. See also our Chapter VI, Potters as Customers, for the unfired ware.
132. U. des Fontaines, 'John Wedgwood of Bignall End' in *Northern Ceramic Society Journal* Vol. 5, 1984, 115-31, 118, quoting Wedgwood MS 25/18453.
133. Mountford, 1972, op. cit., 103; Appendix II, 64 *passim* to 72.
134. Ibid., Appendix II, 64-65.
135. J. Ward, *The Borough of Stoke-upon-Trent...* (London: Lewis, 1843, rep. East Ardsley: S.R. Publishers, 1969), 152.
136. Potteries Museum and Art Gallery, Ceramics Department, uncatalogued: Sales Ledger John Wood of Brownhills 1783-1787.
137. *Staffordshire Advertiser*, 1 Apr. 1797.
138. Appendix 3.
139. Staffordshire Record Office: D 1788, pcl. 1, bdle 2, pp. 19, 26, 51; Vol. 99, pp. 29, 112; Vol. 102, pp. 3, 60 including '1763 Oct 28 [credited] By 12 Crucifixes'. See our Fig. 12 for an early (1732) example.
140. Wedgwood MS 55/30423.
141. *Newcastle-under-Lyme Parish Registers* 3 vol. (Staffordshire Parish Registers Society, 1931, 1939, 1981), II, 117.
142. G.A. Godden, *Encyclopaedia of British Porcelain Manufacturers* (London; Barrie & Jenkins, 1988), 442; Keele University Information Services: Wedgwood MS 50/31193.
143. Wedgwood MS 32/31013.
144. Shaw, op. cit., 214.
145. John Yates' will was made on 30 Oct. 1787 and presented at Newcastle under-Lyme Manor Court before 1 Oct. 1788 (information from Mr. P. Roden).
146. Edwards and Hampson, op. cit., 210-11.

APPENDIX 3

1. *R R Angerstein's Illustrated Travel Diary 1753-1755 Industry in England and Wales from a Swedish perspective* trans. T. and P. Berg (London:

Science Museum, 2001), 200-01, 340, 342.
2. Potteries Museum and Art Gallery, Ceramics Department: Enoch Wood's Scrap Book, I, 14.
3. See W.A. Churchill, *Watermarks in Paper in Holland, England, France, etc., in the XVII and XVIII Centuries and their Interconnection* (Amsterdam: Menno Hertzberger & Co., 1935, 1965), 69, 70, watermarks 81-84, 86.
4. S. Shaw, *History of the Staffordshire Potteries…* (Hanley; privately, 1829), 206-08.
5. 'd.' *(denarius)* represents a pre-1971 penny, 240 to £1 sterling.
6. See Wedgwood MS 30/30919: 13 inch Barley Corn dishes were sold in 1763 at 8d. each.
7. An inch is 2.54cm.
8. Over a year later, prices had declined. On 21-22 Apr. 1771 Josiah Wedgwood told his partner that 'Mr Baddeley has reduced the prices of the [cream colour] dishes to the prices of white stone Viz 17 inches for 16d – 16 inches @ 14d &c.' *(The Selected Letters of Josiah Wedgwood* ed. A. Finer and G. Savage (London: Cory, Adams & Mackay, 1965), 106).
9. Another name for a baking dish, see F. Celoria 'An Examination of Terminologies for Pottery Classification in Archaeology' in *Science and Archaeology* No. 22, 1980, 38.
10. See Wedgwood MS 31/23030. 10 inch baking dishes were sold in 1763 at 2½d. each; 11 inch baking dishes at 3d. each.
11. See Wedgwood MS 30/22947. A Barley Corn tureen and dish was sold for 42d. in 1764.
12. A small plate, see W. Mankowitz and R.G. Haggar, *The Concise Encyclopedia of English Pottery and Porcelain* (London: Deutsch, 1957), 227. Probably from Dutch *Twijfelaar*, a small plate or a small bed, an in-between sized object.
13. See Wedgwood MS 31/23029. Twifflers were sold in 1763 at 12d. a dozen.
14. See Wedgwood MS 30/22942. Sauceboats and covers were sold in 1764 for 2d. each.
15. As the price list suggests, there was only one price for plates, so perhaps only one size was made. Invoices (Wedgwood MSS 31/23027, 23029) from *Thomas and Isiaiah Taylor* to Josiah Wedgwood in 1763 include both 'Plain plates' and 'table plates' at 15d. a dozen.
16. See Wedgwood MS 31/23029. Plates were sold in 1763 at 15d. a dozen.
17. 'Not to be picked' meaning that the buyer is not allowed to select from the lot offered to him.
18. Whilst 'toy' was used in the 18th century to describe small ornamental articles in general, these items are probably toys for children in the modern sense.
19. See Wedgwood MS6/31324. Toy cups and toy saucers were sold in 1763 at 3d. each.
20. A stool pan was used in a commode. See Wedgwood MS 30/22938: (very large) 3 gallon stool pans were sold in 1764 at 24d. each.
21. As late as 1783, Mrs Conradi of Dresden bought salt-glaze butter tubs with stands from Josiah Wedgwood at 7d. each (Wedgwood MS 79/13653).
22. See Wedgwood MS 30/30934. Blue and white cups and saucers were sold in 1763 at 12d. a dozen.
23. From the prices given (Holland size 9d. and 10d., London size 12d., Irish size 14d.), it seems that they are different sizes of cups and saucers.
24. At 14d. presumably Littler-Wedgwood Blue ware, more expensive than Holland middle white.
25. See note 23.
26. See note 23.
27. 'Blue and white' suggests 'scratch-blue'.
28. 'Three to piece ware' is not understood but might refer to three items sold as one set. In John Wedgwood's Crate Book, 16, 'Three to peice[*sic*] pettys [dishes]' and '12 Handled Cups - 12 Cups - 24 Coffees & Sau[cers]' occur in the same unpriced list.
29. 'Holland ware' is not understood in this context.
30. 'Sortable' means compatible pieces.
31. 'Inlet teapots' are those where the cover rests on a narrow shelf (the 'natch') within the top opening. See *John Mitchell*, potter, for him selling inlet teapots to Josiah Wedgwood in 1763.
32. See Wedgwood MS 30/22945: 18s teapots were sold in 1764 at 18d. a dozen.
33. 'Blue flowered' could refer to sprigged ornamentation coloured blue, but at this date and at the price given (only 4d. more than sortable white) is more likely to refer to 'scratch-blue'.
34. A.R. Mountford, 'Thomas Wedgwood, John Wedgwood and Jonah Malkin Potters of Burslem', unpublished MA Thesis, Keele University, 1972, Appendix IV, *passim*.
35. Groce, gross, twelve dozen, 144 *(OED)*.
36. Gorn, dialect for gawn (from gallon), a small bucket with a long handle *(OED)*.

APPENDIX 4
1. A.R. Mountford, 'Thomas Wedgwood, John Wedgwood and Jonah Malkin Potters of Burslem', unpublished MA Thesis, Keele University, 1972, 104-06, Table A, Pottery Types made by John Wedgwood.
2. See Chapter VI, Wedgwood MS 5/3398, 3 Jan. 1764.
3. See Chapter VI, Wedgwood MSS 30/22473, 9 Dec. 1764, 30/22462-22477 30141-30155 *passim*.
4. See Chapter VI, Wedgwood MSS 7/5564-5606, 79/13648-13665, WM 1459 Folder C.
5. Mountford, 1972, op. cit., 104-06, Table A, Pottery Types made by John Wedgwood.
6. Wedgwood MS 6/30584.
7. See Chapter VI, Wedgwood MSS 7/5564-5606, 79/13648-13665, WM 1459 Folder C.
8. See Chapter VI, Wedgwood MS 30/22942.
9. See Chapter VI, Wedgwood MS 30/22942.
10. M. Goodby in 'Moulds and Modellers in the Early 18th-century Staffordshire Potteries: Slip-Casting, Press-Moulding and the Wood Family' in *English Ceramic Circle Transactions* Vol. 17, Part 2, 2000, 216-28, 225, Fig. 11. The text reference for Fig. 12, stating that matching shards were found on the site of Whieldon's factory, probably applies to Fig. 11.
11. J.F. Blacker, *The ABC of English Salt-Glaze Stoneware from Dwight to Doulton* (London: Paul, 1922), Plate opp. 78, lower left and lower right.
12. P. Halfpenny, 'Thomas Whieldon: his Life and Work' in *English Ceramic Circle Transactions* Vol. 16, Part 2, 1997, 237-54, 243, fig. 8, top right.
13. C.F.C. Luxmoore, *"Saltglaze" with The Notes of a Collector* (Exeter: Pollard, 1924 repr. London: Holland Press, n.d.), 42, 38, Plate 77. This bronze dish shape is now believed to be at Historic Deerfield, USA.
14. See Chapter VI, Wedgwood MSS 7/5564-5606, 79/13648-13665, WM 1459 Folder C.
15. L.M. Solon, *The Art of the Old English Potter* 2nd. Ed. Rev. (London: Bemrose, 1885), 191-92.
16. J.V.G. Mallet, 'Engine-turning on Chelsea Porcelain, with Considerations on its previous use at Meissen and Vincennes/Sèvres' in *English Ceramic Circle Transactions* Vol. 17, Part 3, 2001, 420-29.
17. Mountford, 1972, op. cit., 104-06, Table A, Pottery Types made by John Wedgwood.
18. Ibid., 104-06, Table A, Pottery Types made by John Wedgwood.
19. Ibid., 104-06, Table A, Pottery Types made by John Wedgwood.
20. Ibid., 104-06, Table A, Pottery Types made by John Wedgwood. 'Gaddaroons [*sic*]' are also named in Thomas and John Wedgwood's price lists – see our Appendix 3, Prices.
21. See Chapter VI, Wedgwood MS 6/4986, 1 Mar. 1764.
22. See Chapter VI, Wedgwood MSS 7/5564-5606, 79/13648-13665, WM 1459 Folder C.
23. Wedgwood MSS 30/30916-18.
24. See Chapter VI, Wedgwood MS 30/22753 (n.d.) c.1764.
25. Mountford, 1972, op. cit., 104-06, Table A, Pottery Types made by John Wedgwood. 'Mosaick [*sic*]' is also named in Thomas and John Wedgwood's price lists – see our Appendix 3, Prices.
26. N. Valpy, 'Extracts from 18th Century London Newspapers' in *English Ceramic Circle Transactions* Vol. 12, Part 2, 1985, 161-88, 182.
27. J.V.G. Mallet, 'Rococo in English Ceramics' in *Rococo Art and Design in Hogarth's England* ed. M. Snodin (London: Trefoil Books/Victoria & Albert Museum, 1984), 241, 254.
28. E. Adams and D. Redstone, *Bow Porcelain* (London: Faber, 1981), 210.
29. W.B. Honey, *European Ceramic Art from the end of the Middle Ages to about 1815 Illustrated Historical Survey* (London: Faber, 1949), 73, plate 144B.
30. See Chapter VI, Wedgwood MS 5/30546, 26 Jul. 1763.
31. Mountford, 1972, op. cit., 104-06, Table A, Pottery Types made by John Wedgwood.
32. Ibid., 104-06, Table A, Pottery Types made by John Wedgwood.
33. *R R Angerstein's Illustrated Travel Diary 1753-1755 Industry in England and Wales from a Swedish perspective* trans. T. and P. Berg (London: Science Museum, 2001), 200.
34. Mountford, 1972, op. cit., 104-06, Table A, Pottery Types made by John Wedgwood.
35. Luxmoore, op. cit., 25, Plate 48.
36. See Chapter VI, Wedgwood MS 30/22659, 14 Aug. 1764.
37. Wedgwood MS 30/22753 (n.d.) c.1764.
38. See for instance *James and Charles Whitehead manufacturers Hanley Staffordshire* int. R. Haggar (Bletchley: Drakard, n.d., c.1973) reproducing Whiteheads' 1798 catalogue, (6) no. 134, (7) nos. 9, 13, and associated illustrations.
39. Mountford, 1972, op. cit., 104-06, Table A, Pottery Types made by John Wedgwood.
40. Luxmoore, op. cit., 25, Plate 78.
41. See Chapter VI, Wedgwood MS 5/30546, 26 Jul. 1763.
42. A. Ray, 'Staffordshire Tiles 1750-1840' in *English Ceramic Circle Transactions* Vol. 15, Part 2, 1994, 194-204, 195-97.
43. 'A selection of recent important

acquisitions by Northern Museums' in *Northern Ceramic Society Journal*, Vol. 1, 1972-73, 69-70, 69, Plate 27.
44. *The Old Hen and the Cock* is illustrated in J. Horne, *A Collection of Early English Pottery* part VIII (London; Horne, 1988) (210).
45. Luxmoore, op. cit., Plates 88, 89.
46. See A.R. Mountford, *The Illustrated Guide to Staffordshire Salt-Glazed Stoneware* (London: Barrie & Jenkins, 1971), Fig. 120.
47. D. Barker, *A New Perspective of the Staffordshire Potteries* (London: Horne, 1998), (8) plate 18.
48. D. Barker, *William Greatbatch a Staffordshire Potter* (London: Horne, 1991), 253, plate 179.
49. S. Shaw, *A History of the Staffordshire Potteries…* (Hanley, privately, 1829), 183.
50. *Catalogue of a Collection of Early English Earthenware and other Works of Art* (London: Burlington Fine Arts Club, 1913), 113, no. 94.
51. J. McKeown, *Burleigh: The Story of a Pottery* (Shepton Beauchamp: Dennis, 2003), 15.
52. A. Tyzacke, on a silver saffron pot acquired by the Royal Cornwall Museum, Truro, in *National Art Collections Fund 2000 Review*, 115.
53. Wedgwood MS 29/21451.
54. Mountford, 1972, op. cit., 104-06, Table A, Pottery Types made by John Wedgwood.

APPENDIX 5
1. A.R. Mountford 'Thomas Wedgwood, John Wedgwood and Jonah Malkin Potters of Burslem', unpublished MA Thesis, Keele University, 1972, Appendix III, 13, 50, 73.
2. Ibid., Appendix III, 42.
3. Ibid., Appendix III, 62.
4. Ibid., Appendix III, 92.
5. Ibid., Appendix III, 137.
6. Ibid., Appendix III, 158; IV, 37.
7. Ibid., Appendix III, 118.
8. Ibid., Appendix III, 15.
9. A.J. Toppin 'The China Trade and some London Chinamen' in *English Ceramic Circle Transactions* No 3, 1935, 37-56, 45, Plate XIX; E. Adams 'Women in the Eighteenth Century Ceramic Trade and some detailed Prices of that Time' in *Journal of the Northern Ceramic Society* Vol. 16 1999, 1-21, 4, 20.
10. Wedgwood MS 55/9839.
11. Mountford, 1972, op. cit., Appendix II (22), (62); III, 54.
12. Ibid., Appendix II (8).
13. Ibid., Appendix III, 21, 83.
14. Ibid., Appendix III, 105.
15. Ibid., Appendix III, 105, 145.
16. Ibid., Appendix III, 44.
17. Ibid., Appendix III, 51.
18. Ibid., Appendix IV, 30.
19. Wedgwood MSS 49/29596a, 55/9841.
20. E. Adams, 'Ceramic Insurances in the Sun Company, 1766-1774' in *English Ceramic Circle Transactions* Vol. 10, Part 1, 1976, 1-38, 31.
21. Wedgwood MS 6/4946.
22. Mountford, 1972, op. cit., Appendix III, 44.
23. Ibid., Appendix III, 27, 88, 144; IV, 34.
24. Wedgwood MS 55/9838.
25. Wedgwood MS 55/9837.
26. Wedgwood MS 11/9837.
27. Mountford, 1972, op. cit., Appendix II (12), (56); Wedgwood MSS 55/9837, 55/9841.
28. Wedgwood MS 5/30730, 15 Oct. 1763.
29. Mountford, 1972, op. cit., Appendix III, 5, 124.
30. Wedgwood MS 55/9838.
31. Mountford, 1972, op. cit., Appendix II (46).
32. Ibid., Appendix III, 105.
33. Ibid., Appendix II (6), III, 135, IV, 27, 34, 37.
34. Ibid., Appendix III, 15.
35. Ibid., Appendix III, 114.
36. Ibid., Appendix III, 24.
37. Wedgwood MS 4/3265.
38. Mountford, 1972, op. cit., Appendix III, 149.
39. Ibid., Appendix III, 159; IV, 38.
40. Ibid., Appendix III, 134.
41. Ibid., Appendix III, 14.
42. Ibid., Appendix IV, 41.
43. Ibid., Appendix III, 64.
44. Ibid., Appendix III, 125.
45. *Newcastle Journal,* 5 Apr. 1755; Mountford, 1972, op. cit., Appendix III, 60.
46. Mountford, 1972, op. cit., Appendix III, 144.
47. Wedgwood MSS 11/9837, 55/9838, 55/-9841.
48. R.S. Hampson, 'The Development of the Pottery Industry in Longton, 1700-1865', unpublished Keele M.A. Thesis, 1986, I, 195; A.R. Mountford, 1972, op. cit., Appendix III, 128.
49. Mountford, 1972, op. cit., Appendix III, 24.
50. Ibid., Appendix III, 11.
51. Ibid., Appendix II (36), (40).
52. Ibid., Appendix III, 34.
53. Ibid., Appendix III, 34, 85.
54. Ibid., Appendix II (48).
55. Ibid., Appendix III, 12.
56. Ibid., Appendix III, 116, 117; IV, 36. For Caravella as a dealer, see B. Horn, 'John, 3rd Earl of Breadalbane as a Purchaser of Pottery and Porcelain' in *English Ceramic Circle Transactions* Vol. 13, Part 1, 1987, 51-55, 53 and Plate 45; and 'Ceramic Bills paid by Alexander, 4th Duke of Gordon' in *English Ceramic Circle Transactions* Vol. 15, part 3, 1995, 435-39, 436; H. Young, *English Porcelain 1745-95 Its Makers, Design, Marketing and Consumption* (London: V&A Publications, 1999), 160, n.46.
57. Mountford, 1972, op. cit., Appendix III, 1-2, 46.
58. Wedgwood MS 55/9839.
59. Mountford, 1972, op. cit., Appendix III, 59, 94, Appendix IV, 6, 19-20.
60. Ibid., Appendix III, 42.
61. Ibid., Appendix IV, 37.
62. Ibid., Appendix III, 90.
63. Ibid., Appendix III, 66.
64. Ibid., Appendix III, 15.
65. Wedgwood MS 55/9839.
66. Wedgwood MSS 7/5564-5606; 79/13648-13665; WM 1459, C.
67. Mountford, 1972, op. cit., Appendix III, 12.
68. Ibid., Appendix II (58).
69. Ibid., Appendix II (58).
70. Ibid., Appendix II (44), (52).
71. Wedgwood MSS 5/3989-3996, 30228-30242; 25/18201, 18205, 18207.
72. Mountford, 1972, op. cit., Appendix III, 25.
73. Ibid., Appendix II (24).
74. Ibid., Appendix III, 126.
75. Ibid., Appendix III, 58.
76. Wedgwood MS 55/9837.
77. Mountford, 1972, op. cit., Appendix III, 68.
78. Ibid., Appendix III, 90.
79. Ibid., Appendix III, 16.
80. Ibid., Appendix III, 21.
81. Wedgwood MSS 49/29596a, 55/9841.
82. Mountford, 1972, op. cit., Appendix III, 121.
83. Ibid., Appendix III, 122; IV, 11, 12.
84. Wedgwood MS 55/9838.
85. Mountford, 1972, op. cit., Appendix III, 113.
86. Ibid., Appendix III, 109.
87. Ibid., Appendix II, (32).
88. Ibid., Appendix III, 113.
89. Wedgwood MS 55/9838.
90. Ibid.
91. Mountford, 1972, op. cit., Appendix III, 26.
92. Ibid., Appendix III, 36.
93. Ibid., Appendix III, 16.
94. Ibid., Appendix III, 80.
95. Ibid., Appendix III, 24; IV 30.
96. Wedgwood MSS 1/614, 1/30657.
97. Wedgwood MSS 1/609, 55/9837.
98. Wedgwood MS 55/9839.
99. Mountford, 1972, op. cit., Appendix III, 21.
100. Ibid., Appendix III, 138.
101. Wedgwood MS 55/9838.
102. Mountford, 1972, op. cit., Appendix III, 54.
103. Ibid., Appendix II (42).
104. Ibid., Appendix III, 58, 63.
105. Ibid., Appendix III, 38, 91, 136.
106. Wedgwood MSS 1/578-592, 49/29596a, 55/9841.
107. Mountford, 1972, op. cit., Appendix III, 52, 63.
108. Wedgwood MS 49/29596a.
109. Mountford, 1972, op. cit., Appendix III, 41, 94, 111; IV, 20-21.
110. Ibid., Appendix III, 139; Wedgwood MS 55/9841.
111. Wedgwood MS 55/9839.
112. Mountford, 1972, op. cit., Appendix III, 145.
113. Ibid., Appendix III, 36.
114. Wedgwood MS 11/9837.
115. Mountford, 1972, op. cit., Appendix III, 139.
116. Ibid., Appendix III, 12, 53, 128, IV, 7, 18.
117. Ibid., Appendix III, 63.
118. Ibid., Appendix IV, 51.
119. Ibid., Appendix III, 11.
120. Ibid., Appendix III, 97.
121. Ibid., Appendix III, 144; IV, 34.
122. Ibid., Appendix III, 21.
123. Ibid., Appendix III, 14, 69.
124. Ibid., Appendix II (60).
125. Ibid., Appendix III, 154; IV, 9, 13, 28, 32, 38.
126. Ibid., Appendix III, 12.
127. Ibid., Appendix III, 68.
128. A.J. White, 'A Stamford Potseller's Stock in 1720' in *Post Medieval Archaeology* No. 13, 1979, 290-92.
129. Ibid., Appendix III, 8.
130. Ibid., Appendix III, 38.
131. Ibid., Appendix III, 39.
132. Ibid., Appendix II (28).
133. Ibid., Appendix III, 63.
134. Ibid., Appendix III, 96.
135. Ibid., Appendix III, 87.
136. Ibid., Appendix III, 143.
137. Ibid., Appendix III, 153.
138. Ibid., Appendix III, 127.
139. Ibid., Appendix III, 4, 47, 102, 131, 134, 169; IV, 24, 28, 38, 42, 54, 61.
140. Ibid., Appendix III, 33, 60, 123.
141. Ibid., Appendix III, 97.
142. Ibid., Appendix III, 81.
143. Ibid., Appendix III, 146.
144. Ibid., Appendix III, 118.
145. Ibid., Appendix IV, 16.
146. Ibid., Appendix III, 97.
147. Ibid., Appendix III, 45.
148. Ibid., Appendix III, 38, 92.
149. Ibid., Appendix III, 99.
150. Ibid., Appendix III, 114.
151. Ibid., Appendix III, 23.
152. Ibid., Appendix III, 79; IV, 10.
153. Wedgwood MS 49/29596a; Mountford,

1972, op. cit., Appendix III, 122.
154. Wedgwood MS 55/9838.
155. Mountford, 1972, op. cit., Appendix II (16), (64).
156. Ibid., Appendix III, 147; IV, 15, 24, 38, 42.
157. Ibid., Appendix III, 62, 160; IV, 8, 43-45.
158. Ibid., Appendix III, 79; IV, 4, 5, 8, 9.
159. Ibid., Appendix III, 79.
160. Ibid., Appendix III, 69.
161. Wedgwood MSS 5/3989-3996, 30228-30242, 13/5077, 25/18201, 18205, 18207.
162. Ibid., Appendix III, 88; IV, 48.
163. Ibid., Appendix III, 100, 115.
164. Ibid., Appendix II (39).
165. Wedgwood MSS 11/31034, 31160, 31161, 55/9338-9340.
166. Mountford, 1972, op. cit., Appendix III, 133.
167. Ibid., Appendix III, 148.
168. Ibid., Appendix III, 24, 148.
169. Ibid., Appendix III, 67, 110.
170. Wedgwood MS 55/9838.
171. Mountford, 1972, op. cit., Appendix II (30).
172. Wedgwood MS 55/9841.
173. Mountford, 1972, op. cit., Appendix III, 51, 76.
174. Ibid., Appendix III, 21.
175. Ibid., Appendix III, 84.
176. Wedgwood MS 55/30426, 55/30413.
177. Mountford, 1972, op. cit., Appendix III, 17.
178. Ibid., Appendix III, 27.
179. Ibid., Appendix III, 84.
180. Wedgwood MS 36/30938.
181. Mountford, 1972, op. cit., Appendix III, 52.
182. Ibid., Appendix II (54).
183. Wedgwood MS 55/9838.
184. Mountford, 1972, op. cit., Appendix II, (14)-(15); Wedgwood MSS 49/29596a, 55/-9838, 55/9841.
185. Mountford, 1972, op. cit., Appendix III, 101.
186. Ibid., Appendix III, 32.
187. Ibid., Appendix II, (42).
188. Ibid., Appendix III, 137.
189. Wedgwood MS 55/9837.
190. N. Valpy 'Extracts from 18th century London Newspapers' in *English Ceramic Circle Transactions* Vol. 12 Part 2 1985, 161-88, 170.
191. Mountford, 1972, op. cit., Appendix III, 64, 130, 156, 168, IV, 13, 14, 16, 17, 23, 25-28, 31, 32, 35-37, 39-42, 46-49, 51, 53-55, 57, 58, 60.
192. Ibid., Appendix III, 2.
193. Ibid., Appendix III, 108.
194. Ibid., Appendix III, 21.
195. Ibid., Appendix III, 22.
196. Ibid., Appendix III, 53.
197. Ibid., Appendix III, 33, 152; IV, 33, 50.
198. Ibid., Appendix III, 34, 86.
199. Ibid., Appendix III, 32.
200. Ibid., Appendix III, 152.
201. Wedgwood MS 55/9838.
202. Mountford, 1972, op. cit., Appendix III, 7, 99.
203. Wedgwood MS 55/9841.
204. Wedgwood MS 49/29596a.
205. Mountford, 1972, op. cit., Appendix III, 143.
206. Wedgwood MSS 6/30575-30585.
207. Mountford, 1972, op. cit., Appendix III, 15.
208. Ibid., Appendix III, 119.
209. Ibid., Appendix III, 108; Wedgwood MS 55/9839.
210. Mountford, 1972, op. cit., Appendix III, 66.
211. Ibid., Appendix III, 70.
212. Ibid., Appendix III, 61.
213. Ibid., Appendix III, 81.
214. Wedgwood MS 49/29596a. For Robinson and Rhodes (Rhodes & Co. from 1763), see D. Towner, *Creamware* (London: Faber, 1978), 128.
215. B. Horn, 'Ceramic accounts found among the Seafield Muniments' in *English Ceramic Circle Transactions* Vol. 18, Part 1, 2002, 189-96, 191.
216. Wedgwood MS 55/9837.
217. Mountford, 1972, op. cit., Appendix III, 37.
218. Ibid., Appendix III, 16.
219. Ibid., Appendix III, 51, 101.
220. Ibid., Appendix III, 36.
221. Ibid., Appendix III, 33, 85.
222. Ibid., Appendix III, 121.
223. Wedgwood MS 55/9838.
224. Mountford, 1972, op. cit., Appendix III, 53.
225. Ibid., Appendix III, 57.
226. Wedgwood MS 55/9841.
227. Mountford, 1972, op. cit., Appendix III, 38.
228. Wedgwood MSS 55/9837, 55/9838.
229. Mountford, 1972, op. cit., Appendix III, 44.
230. Ibid., Appendix III, 29, 95.
231. F. Williamson, *Derby Pot Manufactory known as Cockpit Hill Pottery,* rep. from *Derbyshire Archaeological Society's Journal* New series, Vol. IV 1930, from Derby Mercury, 3 Mar. 1742/43, col. 12.
232. Wedgwood MSS 7/5372-5386, 7/30369.
233. Mountford, 1972, op. cit., Appendix III, 113.
234. Ibid., Appendix III, 17.
235. Ibid., Appendix III, 119.
236. Ibid., Appendix III, 33.
237. J. Draper 'Inventory of Ann Shergold, ceramic dealer in Blandford, Dorset' in *Post-Medieval Archaeology* Vol. 16, 85-91 passim.
238. Wedgwood MS 55/9839.
239. Mountford, 1972, op. cit., Appendix III, 43.
240. Ibid., Appendix III, 39.
241. Ibid., Appendix II (50), III, 153; IV, 22.
242. Ibid., Appendix III, 43.
243. Wedgwood MS 55/9838.
244. Wedgwood MSS 55/9838, 49/29596a, 55/9841.
245. Mountford, 1972, op. cit., Appendix III, 121.
246. Ibid., Appendix III, 95.
247. Wedgwood MS 55/9839.
248. Mountford, 1972, op. cit., Appendix III, 21.
249. Ibid., Appendix IV, 39.
250. Ibid., Appendix III, 87.
251. Ibid., Appendix III, 113.
252. Wedgwood MS 11/9837.
253. Mountford, 1972, op. cit., Appendix III, 126.
254. Ibid., Appendix III, 27.
255. Wedgwood MS 55/9837; Mountford, 1972, op. cit., Appendix III, 10; Wedgwood MS 49/29596a.
256. Wedgwood MSS 55/9837, 55/9841.
257. E. Adams 'The Bow Insurances and Related Matters' in *English Ceramic Circle Transactions* Vol. 9, part 1, 1973, 67-108, 75, 95.
258. Mountford, 1972, op. cit., Appendix III, 104, 142; Wedgwood MS 49/29596a.
259. Mountford, 1972, op. cit., Appendix III, 18.
260. Ibid., Appendix III, 18.
261. Wedgwood MSS 55/9837, 55/9838.
262. Wedgwood MS 55/9838.
263. Mountford, 1972, op. cit., Appendix III, 19.
264. Ibid., Appendix III, 53.
265. Ibid., Appendix III, 127.
266. Ibid., Appendix III, 53.
267. Wedgwood MS 55/9837.
268. Mountford, 1972, op. cit., Appendix III, 107.
269. Ibid., Appendix III, 9.
270. Mountford, 1972, op. cit., Appendix II (18).
271. Wedgwood MS 55/9838.
272. Wedgwood MS 55/9838.
273. Mountford, 1972, op. cit., Appendix IV, 6; Wedgwood MS 55/9838.
274. Wedgwood MS 55/9838; Mountford, 1972, op. cit., Appendix III, 112.
275. Wedgwood MS 55/9839.
276. Mountford, 1972, op. cit., Appendix III, 119.
277. Ibid., Appendix III, 35.
278. Wedgwood MS 55/9838.
279. Mountford, 1972, op. cit., Appendix III, 117; Wedgwood MS 55/9839.
280. Mountford, 1972, op. cit., Appendix III, 35.
281. Ibid., Appendix III, 15.
282. Wedgwood MSS 49/29596a, 96/17800.
283. Mountford, 1972, op. cit., Appendix III, 45.
284. Ibid., Appendix III, 3, 77, 116, 148, 151; IV, 29.
285. Ibid., Appendix III, 54.
286. J. Cockerill, 'Warburtons of Tyneside' in *Journal of the Northern Ceramic Society* Vol. 18, 2001, 59-76, 64.
287. Mountford, 1972, op. cit., Appendix II (16).
288. Ibid., Appendix III, 54.
289. Ibid., Appendix III, 54.
290. Ibid., Appendix III, 59.
291. Wedgwood MSS 49/29596a, 55/9839.
292. Mountford, 1972, op. cit., Appendix III, 59.
293. Ibid., Appendix III, 87.
294. N. Valpy, 'Extracts from 18th Century London Newspapers' in *English Ceramic Circle Transactions* Vol. 15, Part 2, 1994, 310-16, 312.
295. Mountford, 1972, op. cit., Appendix III, 28, 111, IV, 8, 10-11.
296. Ibid., Appendix II (35).
297. Ibid., Appendix III, 73, 98.
298. Ibid., Appendix III, 74.
299. Ibid., Appendix III, 74.
300. Wedgwood MS 49/29596. John Wedgwood represented his youngest brother Josiah Wedgwood in Liverpool and London and evidently also his oldest brother *Thomas Wedgwood IV of Overhouse.*
301. Ibid., Appendix II (20), Appendix III, 150.
302. Wedgwood MS 6/5047.
303. Mountford, 1972, op. cit., Appendix II (3)-(5).
304. Wedgwood MSS 49/29596a, 55/9841.
305. Wedgwood MS 49/29596a.
306. Mountford, 1972, op. cit., Appendix III, 104.
307. Ibid., Appendix III, 68.
308. Ibid., Appendix III, 37, 68.
309. Ibid., Appendix III, 14.
310. Wedgwood MS 55/30836.
311. Mountford, 1972, op. cit., Appendix III, 55.
312. Ibid., Appendix III, 78; Wedgwood MS 11/9837.
313. Mountford, 1972, op. cit., Appendix III, 117.
314. Ibid., Appendix III, 118.
315. Ibid., Appendix III, 59.
316. Ibid., Appendix III, 32.
317. Ibid., Appendix III, 100.
318. Ibid., Appendix III, 161.
319. Ibid., Appendix III, 16.
320. Wedgwood MS 55/9841.
321. Mountford, 1972, op. cit., Appendix III, 79.
322. Ibid., Appendix IV, 43.

Index

Page numbers in bold type denote illustrations
The customers for white salt-glazed stoneware listed alphabetically in Appendix 5 are not indexed here

Abernathy, James, London dealer, 145, 252, Thomas, London dealer, 144, 252
acorn knop, Shelton Farm, **199**
Adams: Ann, 273, wife of Humphrey Palmer, 214, Edward and Richard, 247, 278, John and John Prince, 247, Richard, 284, William, 253, 255
Addison and Abernathy, London dealers, 144, 252
advertisements, newspaper, 159, 160, 161, 164, 165, 176
Aesop's Fables print, **136**
agate ware, 41, figure, **112**, man and dog, **104**, salt-glazed ware, 76
ageing clay, 71
alabaster models, 78, 81, moulds, **80**
Alders, John, 247, 259, Thomas, 247
Allen, Captain Ezra, inventory, 165, John, 248, 284, Mary, 248
America, 248, archaeology, 21, exports to, 274, marketing in, 159, salt-glazed ware in use, 176
Amsterdam, 142, 277, Parks, dealer, 142
Anbury, enameller, 125
Anderton's Coffee House, London, 273
Andrade, Cyril, dealer, 177, 181
Angerstein, Reinhold R., 71, 255, 256, 278, on prices, 28, 155, quoted, 271
Annapolis, Maryland, 161, **161**, *and see* Calvert
apprentices, 141, 270, to John Wedgwood, 233, wages, 266
apprenticeship, 281
archaeological evidence, 159
archaeological excavations, *see* excavations
Arden, Macclesfield, dealer, 148
armorial decoration, **131**
artichoke cups, 285
artists, Liverpool, 82
ash colour ware, *see* drab ware
Ashburner, Hannah, London dealer, 144
Ashbury, Thos., enameller, 125
Ashmolean Museum, 181
Astbury: accused by Dwight, 212, enameller, 125, flint legend, 67, George, 264, John, 248, 277, Joshua, 248-49, 267, 272, inventory, 249, Shelton, 260, Thomas, 249
Atkinson, James, London dealer, 245
Aust, Gottfried, 248
availability of salt-glazed ware in America, early, 159

Bélanger, François, 255, 256
Bacchanalian scenes, **63**
background, eighteenth century, 48
Bacon, Charles, decorator, **123**
Baddeley and Fletcher, 249
Baddeley Edge, 67, 268
Baddeley, John, 37, 244, 249, 250, 260, 261, 262, 266, 267, 269, 271, 273, 274, 275, 276, 278, 279, 282, exporting, 142, flint supplier, 241, inventory, 249, potter and flint miller, 69, prices, 155
Baddeley, Ralph, 250
Baggaley, James and brothers, 250
Bagnall: Eleanor, 250, 273, Heath and, 260, James, 266, Peter, 250-51, inventory, 250, Richard, 250-51, 273, Sampson, 365
bagpiper, figure, **103**
bakers, 285
ball clay, *see* clay
bands round ovens, 113, 242, 257, 275
Banks: Joseph, quoted, 78, William and John Turner, 251
barber's basin, **54**, 55
Barker, Thomas, Foley, 85, 184, 275
barleycorn pattern, 41, **44**, **46**, **47**, **57**, **61**, 88, 138, **141**, 149, 152, 153, 185, **185**, 242, 253, 254, 255, 258, 273, 274, 275, 277, 278, 286, Greatbatch excavation, **209**, Palmer's site, **215**
barrels, 152
Bartlam, John, potter, 165, 248, **167**
baskets, 156. 250
basketweave pattern, 41, 46, 138, 139, **140**, 149, 152, 153, **162**, 185, **185**, **188**, 251, 254, 258, 283, 286, Greatbatch excavation, **209**, Palmer's site, **215**, **225**
Battersea enamels, 123
Bear Garden, London, 264-65
bear jug, **113**
beating-houses, 281, -stone, Overhouse works, 242
Beche, Sir Henry De La, 178
Bedford, Duchess of, 57, Duke of, accounts, 37, **45**
beef pots, 286
Belfast, 264
bell pots, 286
Bennet, Agnes, dealer, 261
Bennett, Edward, Thornbury, inventory, 159
Benson, patents for grinding flint, 68
Benthall, 274
Bentley, Thomas and Samuel Boardman, Liverpool dealers, exporters, 148, 149, 151, 152, 154, 158, 160, 161
bests quality, 116
Bethnal Green Museum, 179
Bideford, 66, 69
Big House works, 232, 233, 236, 282, crucifixion piece, 233, end of business, 233, firing saggars and ware for, 233, ledgers, 232, 232, 233, partnership, 233, shapes, 233, trial jug, 233, unfired ware 233
bills: of exchange, 156, 245, of lading, 245
Birch, Edmund John, 260
bird and grapes sprigging, Palmer's site, **220**
bird: figures, **109**, finials, Palmer's site, **220**, 225

Bird, Daniel, 251
birds eye pattern, 286
bits, 114
Blackburn, Liverpool, exporter, 149
Blackwell: John, 251, 252, Joseph, 252
Blease, Dr. A.T., 182
bleeding bowl, **54**, 55
block moulds, 78, 81, 102, 250, spout and other, 277
blue and white stone ware, 28
blue: 28, **116**, **117**, 149, 160, 191, **164**, 191, **191**, **234**, 243, decoration, 117, solid, 117, under-glaze decoration, 116, ware, 149, wash, **96**, *and see* cobalt blue, Littler-Wedgwood blue, mazarine blue, scratch-blue ware, zaffre
blunging clay, 73, tank, 72
boar figure, **113**
Boardman, *see* Bentley and
boards, ware, 102, 241-42, 257, 266, 272, 275, 279, 281
boats, 284
bobs, 114
bodies, recipes, salt-glaze, 72, stoneware, 67
body preparation, 71
Bohemia, duty on stone ware, 152
Bold: Charlotte, 252, 262, James, 252, 262, 265
bone, 266
Bonnie Prince Charlie decoration, **134**
bonts, *see* bands
Booth: Enoch and George, 252, dated mug, 28, **30**, 252, enamellers, 125, enamelled ware supplier, 153, Enoch senior, 252, 253, 261, 282, Hugh, 251
Boothroyd, Emanuel, Lindley, dealer, 148
Boston: shops, 160, buyer, 161, ship for, 161
Botteslow mill, 69
bottle, enamelled, **62**
Bourn, John, 284
Bourne: John, 253, William, potter, Westport Road, 188, 190
Bourne, Wright and Co., 253
Bourne's Bank, Burslem, 263
Bovey Tracey: ball clay, 64, excavation, **193**, 195, **195**, 258, excavation shards, **192**, **195**, find shard, **34**, oven, **105**, potteries, 192, excavation, 192, **192**, **194**, Pottery Museum, 195, ware, **32**, **54**
Bow, model used by, **139**
Bowers, Falmouth, dealer, 268
bowl, inscribed, Rotherham, **231**
box, screw top, **106**
boy in the tree pattern, **169**, **174**
Boyer, Samuel, 266
Boynton ,Thomas, bequest, 179, collection sale, 181, **181**
Bradwell, 263-64
Brentford, 253
Brick House estate, Burslem, 265
Brickhouse works, Burslem, 280

bricks, oven, 275
Bridgegate House excavation, Chester, 197
Bridgnorth, 66, 157, clay from, 197
Brighton, Arnold House, 179
Brindley: James, 253, 269, engineer, mills, 68, patent fire-engine, 69, John, 253
Bristol, 157
British Museum, 179
Broad Street, Shelton, 282
Broillet Jacques Louis, alias Fribourg, 71, 253, 270
bronze models, 287
Brookes, Liverpool, hawker, 148
Brooks, John, engraver, 123
Broseley, 274
brown: decoration, 117, inlay, 117, manganese, 117 under-glaze decoration, 116
brown salt-glazed stoneware, 65, 73, 264, 265, 281, by Dwight, 213, Brownhills works, Burslem, 262-63, 282
Brush, John, Williamsburg, excavation, 168
Bryan, Sam, potseller, 146
bucket, 286, and ladle, **95**
Bucknall: Joseph, 253, Mary and Co., 254, Ralph, 254, Ralph and Son(s), 47, 254, Robert, 254, 284
Bullock, 83, W., 250, modeller, 102
bundt mould shard, Greatbatch excavation, **210**
bungs, 114
Burlington Fine Arts Club exhibition, 177, 179, 182
Burn, William, 188, 190
Burnap collection, 182
Burslem: Central Passage, 277, Ceramica, 236, 276, corn mill, 273, Jenkins, windmill, 69, ovens, 108, 256, potters 1710-15, **22**, **36**, potters' petition, 1762, 23, potworks 1710-15, 22, **36**, ware, 73, 149, 271, Westport Road, Bourne site excavation shards, **188-91**, and *passim*
Burton-on-Trent, 68
Bury St. Edmunds, 259, 260
business letters, 159
butter: dishes, Palmer's site, **216**, **217**, pots, 77
Butters, Charles and Sons, auctioneers, 180, **180**, 181, **181**
Butts, William, 256
Buxton, John, London dealer, 146
buying flint and salt, Shelton Farm, 197
buying-in salt-glazed ware, 46, 153, 243, 244, 255, by Palmer, 229, Big House, 233

Caddick, William, 82
Caddie, Alfred J., curator, 179
Cadell, William and Sons (and Company), 271
Cadman, Elizabeth, Penkridge, dealer, 147, 148, 279

329

Index

Cain Hoy, South Carolina, excavations, shard, 165, **167**
calcining flint, 68
Calvert: Elizabeth, 168, House, Annapolis, excavation, 165, **170**, **171**
Cambrian Pottery, Swansea, 232
Camden, S. Carolina, 248
camel shape teapot, **36**, **39**
Campman, enameller, 124
Canada, ball clay, 64
canal transport, 157, 158, 241, 245, 253
candlesticks, 55, **55**, **57**, **60**, **61**, cranes, **107**, nozzles, **224**, Palmer's site, **229**, rocky mound, **110**
canisters, 285, tea, Bovey Tracey, **193**
Canonsburg Pottery Company replicas, 136
cans, 285
capsels, 271
capuchins, 265, Francis Place's, 239, ratcheted handle, **204**, shape, **51**, Shelton Farm, 200, **200**
carriers, 156, 253, flint, 274
Carroll: Charles, order, 1771, **161**, family, inventories, 161
Carron ironworks, 271
Carr's Hill Pottery, 269
Cartagena commemorative ware, 27
carters: flint, 69, to Exeter, 157
Carthew, Edmund and Company, Bovey Tracey, 192
Cartlich, Thomas, 254, crouch ware, 244
carts, 157, 245
carved decoration: Deer Street, Portsmouth, NH, **206**, Shelton Farm, **197**, - pattern, 286, spout, Palmer's site, **229**, teapot, **204**, ware, 77, **147**, 242
case moulds, 78
casks, 156
caster, **61**
casting, 22, 81
cat figures, **112**, 279
Central Passage, Burslem, 277
centrepieces, 56
centres of manufacture, 48
Ceramica, Burslem, 276, extension, 236
Chagre commemorative ware, 27, **27**
chalk, 67
chamber pot, Palmer's site, **223**
Charleston, S. Carolina, 248
Charlie, Bonnie Prince, commemorative ware, **34**
Chatterley, Samuel, 254, 284
Cheddleton flint mill, 66, 258
Chelsea China Works, 279, kiln, 256
Chester: 67, 147, clay, 66, 275, dealers, 147, Dicas, Mr. & Co., 196, exports from, 157, goldsmiths, 82, Mill Street and Bridgegate House excavation shards, **196**, White Ware Manufactory, 196, **196**, excavations, **196**, 197, oven, 112
China Millers, 185
China rail pattern, 259, 287
chinamen, *see* dealers
Chinese porcelain 13, **16**, shell shape, 55
Chinoiserie decoration, **58**, **59**, **61**, **122**
chocks, 281
chocolate 52, colour, 118, pots, 53, 164, 179, set, **51**, ware, patent for, 273
Chorley sale, 177
Christ, Rudolph, 248
Church Works, Hanley, *see* Palmer, Humphrey
Church, Professor R.H., collector, 177, 178, 181
Churchyard works, Burslem, 241
Clarke, A.E., collector, 177, sale, 178
Clarke, Thomas B., collector, 177
clay chip decoration, **191**
clay: 64, 73, 81, 197, 275, 282, from Bridgnorth, Liverpool, 197, ageing or souring, 71, ball, 64, 66, 71, 213, 270, 279, 282, 301 n.17, calcined, 65, Chester, 66, Dutch, 64, export, 64, John Dwight's use of, 64, made-up 241, 243, North Devon, 66, South Devon, 66, Staffordshire, 65, pipe, 64, 65, 264, 270, 301, weathering, 71, white-burning, 64, 65
Cliff Bank, 251, 258, 259
clubs, 50
coach pot, **38**
coal: 69, 70, for firing, 115, mines, 115, 249, 258, in 1722, 66, Overhouse works, 242, weekly purchase, 115
coastal shipping, 157
cobalt blue, 116, 117, 251, 252, Cornwall, 117, Scotland, 117, *and see* blue
Cobb, John, 254, 284
Cobridge Gate, 278
Cockpit Hill, Derby, 255, 256
cockstail pattern, 276
coffee houses, 50
coffee pot, Dwight, **17**, shards, iron-dipped, **19**
Colchester, 259, 260, warehouse, 146
Coleman, Will, Hamburg, dealer, 152
Coles, William, Swansea, 232
Coleshill, near Birmingham, 244
collections, 177–82
collectors, 177–82
colliery, Golden Hill, 253
Collins, John, inventory, 160
Cologne, 11, ware, 64, 65
Colonial Williamsburg, *see* Williamsburg, Colonial
colonies West Indian, 61, American, 61
coloured glazes under salt-glaze, 120
commemoratives, 27, **27**, 34, moulds, 79, ware, 61, **162**, **163**, *and see* Portobello
complaints against Dwight, 212
condiment dishes, 56
Connoisseur, The, 177, 180
Conradi, Henrietta, Dresden, dealer, 138, 152, 153, 158, 286
contents, salt-glaze oven, Overhouse works, 242–43
Cook, Cyril, collection, 177
cookery books, 53
Cooper and Hodgskin, Walsall, exporters, 151, 158
cording for packing, 156, 250
cornucopias, **147**, 286, Bovey Tracey, 195
cost of flint, 68
costings, potworks, 1710–15, 23
Cottrell, Mr., 279
count, potters', 22
cow knops, Palmer's site, **217**, 225
crabs, 285

crabstock: shape, 79, handle, Bovey Tracey, **194**, spout, Palmer's site, **229**
crane candlesticks, **107**
crate: book, 157, marks, 149, 157, 245, 277
crates, 156, 245, pairs of, 156
cratesware, 157
Crawford, William, 66
cream-coloured ware, 55, 69, 72, 108, 176, 241, 252, 254, 258, 262, 271, 274, 276, 282, ascendancy of, 47, Chester, 197, Palmer making, 229, prices, 156
Cressey flint, 69
Crockett, Wm., Coleshill, customer, 244
Crouch ware, 65, 73, 244, 254, 255, 257
crown hole, 114
crucifixes, 282, 1732, 25, **26**
crucifixion, 288, tile, **139**
cup shapes, 53
custard cups, 285
customers: 142, 143, alphabetically, 288–94, England, 143, Europe, 144, Ireland, 143–44, London and Liverpool, 244 sales to, 244

Dakin, Thomas and William Chatterley, 71
Dale Street, Liverpool, 263
Dale, Exeter, dealer, 268
Dalziels, John, Liverpool dealer, 245
damage, 156
Daniel: family, 278, John, 255, 284, Richard, inventory, 255, Richard, Sampson and, 255, Robert, carrier, 156, Sampson and Richard, 255, Thomas, 273, Thomas I, 255, Thomas II, 46, 255, Thomas junior, 284
dated ware, 25, **25**, 27, earliest known, **24**
Dawson, Nancy, figure, **103**
dealers: European, 152, London, 144, 145, 147, 148, provincial, 146
Dean, Bridgwater, dealer, 268
Dearham, Cumbria, 282
debased scratch-blue decoration, 117, 160, **164**, 190, **191**
debtors, 156
debts, 281, to potters, 244, 245
decorating workshops, 121
decoration: 116, 121, 127–36, adds value, 116, armorial, **131**, moulded relief, **138**, sparse early, **59**, under-glaze, 116, *and see* carved decoration, enamelled decoration, sprig decoration
decorators, 124, 126, 154, independent, 16, outside, 123
Deer Street, Portsmouth, NH, carved decoration, **206**, excavation, 21, **42**, **140**, **141**, 172, **172**, **174**, **175**, **207**
Deerfield, Mass: Nims excavation shards, **141**, handle, 173, **175**
Defoe, Daniel, quoted, 66
Delaware excavation, 13, 165
Delftfield Pottery Company, 257
Delftware, 55
Delph plates, 146
demand for salt-glazed stoneware, 48–63, middle class, 53
Derby: 64, 125, 255, firemouths, 112, hovel, 112, kilns, 67, oven, 107, salt-glaze recipe, 72

Derby, Lady, customer, 149
Dethleffin, Christian, Flensburg, dealer, 152
Devon, ball clay, 64
diaper and scroll decoration, Palmer's site, 225
Dicas, Mr. & Co., Chester, 196
Dickens, Plymouth, dealer, 268
die-sinkers, 78
Dimsdale, Francis Place, 239
dining *à la française*, 56, customs, 56, hours, 55
dinner sets, 57
dipped white ware, 250, 255, 265, 271, 272, *and see* white-slipped ware
dipware warehouse, 256
discount, 155, 243, 244, 284
division of labour, 77
Dodgson, Mrs., Liverpool potseller, 244
Dog and Partridge, 257
Dog in the Manger print, **136**, 168
Dog of Fo figure, **111**, knop, **124**, **205**
dolphin spouts, **92**
Don Quixote prints, **137**
Dorset, ball clay, 64, 282
double dipped, *see* white-slipped
Douglas John, Whitehaven, customer, 148, 156, 245, 254, 262, 270
dove-colour ware, 76, 118
dozens, content of, 278
drab ware: **74**, **75**, 76, 79, **158**, ash colour, 76, 244, white sprigged, Palmer excavation, **214**, **215**, Whieldon's site, **235**, 237
drafts for payment, 245
drawing ovens, 116
drawing schools, 82
Dresden: pattern, 41, **45**, **61**, 152, 153, 255, 287, *and see* Conradi, Henrietta
dropped egg pattern, Bovey Tracey, **192**
drum, saggar, 114
drying moulds, 102, ware, 103
Dublin, 157
Duesbury, William, enameller, 124
Dunbibin: John, Liverpool, dealer, 152, 250, 148, 152, 153, 244, 245, 250, Saml., London dealer, 245
Dunstable, 67
Dutch: decoration, **135**, pudding cups, 255
Dutch-men, 264
duty on salt, 70, 139, on stone ware in Bohemia, 152
Dwight family, 165, ware, **170**
Dwight, John, 12–19, 64, 71, 248, 255, 258, 263, 264, 265, 267, 269, 272, 279, 280, 281, 282, accusations by, 211, 212, ball clay, sand and flint, 213, brown salt-glazed ware, 213, coffee pot, **17**, complaints against, 212, figures and bust, **14**, **15**, 16, 213, gorges, **16**, 178, gorge-shaped mug, **211**, his wares found in America, 62, iron-dipped teapot, **212**, knife-cut handle feature, **212**, lawsuits, 16, 65, London customers, 142, marbled decoration, 213, notebooks, 66, ovens, 105, 213, patents, 12, 16, 67, 211, Pennsylvania lease, **13**, 17, pipe clay, 64, porcelain, 16, 53, sand

INDEX

from Woolwich and Isle of Wight, 66, used sprig moulds, 213, white-slipped ware, 19
Dwight: Lydia, London, 19, 211, succeeded John Dwight, 213, Samuel, 20, **22**, 211, succeeded Lydia Dwight, 213
Dwights' Fulham Pottery site excavation, 213
Dykes, F., 182

ear shape handle, Shelton Farm, **202**
Earle, Major Cyril Thornwicke, collector, 177, sale, 180, sale catalogue, **180**
East India Company, 143
Eaton, James, Liverpool dealer, 148
Eccles, John and Co., 263
Edge: John and John Gretton, 256, 271, Samuel, **22**, 257
edge-runner mill, 58, 72
Edwards, Warner, 267, drawing book, 122
Elektra works, Longton, 271
Elers, John and David, 248, 258, 260, 263-64, 269, 277, 279, accused by Dwight, 212, fine redware, 65, oven, 109, secrets, 67, tea jar shape, **20**
Elliot, Wallace, collector, 177, 178, 179, 181
Elliott, Gordon, quoted, 264
Ellis, Andrew, 195, Joan, 195, Mary, 249, William, 192, 248
Else, Ann, Nottingham dealer, 148, 156
embossed ware, 76
enamel kiln, Rotherham, 230, painted shards, Whieldon's site, 239, 247, supplier, 121
enamelled decoration, 28, **50, 58, 59, 59, 61-63**, 116, by Greatbatch, 208, **208**
enamelled heart shaped dish, **228**
enamelled ware: 76, 153, 160, 165, **170**, 176, 252, 253, 276, from Enoch and George Booth, 153, Rotherham, **231, 232, 232**
enamellers: 121, 124, 125, 126, 154, 263
enamelling: 122, difficulty on salt-glaze, 121, recent, 136, Rothwell, 272, solid, 132
enamels, 121
engine pattern, 255, 277, 287
engines, 266
English Ceramic Circle, 178
English Porcelain Circle, 178
equipment for making, 71
European dealers, 152
Evelyn, John & Co., dealers, 177
evidence, archaeological, 159
excavations: see Annapolis, Bovey Tracey, Bridgegate House, Cain Hoy, Calvert House, Chester, Deer Street, Deerfield, Delaware, Dwights' Fulham Pottery, Fenton, Foley, Geddy James House, Greatbatch, Guildford, Hart Richard House, Hart-Shortridge House, Hay Anthony House, Jackson Dr. Hall, Jamestown, London Town, Monticello, Netherlands, Newcastle Delaware, Palmer's Church works, Portsmouth, NH, Shelton Farm, St. Mary's, Strawbery Banke, Warner House, Wentworth,

Westport Road, Whieldon's Fenton Vivian site, Williamsburg, Winnipesaukee
Exeter, 157
export: 61, exporters, 148-49, 151, exporting, 245, exports to America, 62, 142, 274, export to Europe, 142, Staffordshire, 1730, 143
extruding box, 79

Fables of Aesop print, **136**
faces, 286
faceted decoration, Shelton Farm, **207**
Fairway House, 247
Falkner, Frank, collector, 181
famille rose, famille verte palette, 59
farm animals pattern, **169**
farming, 139, 267, Thomas Wedgwood IV, 242
feather edge decoration, 262, 287, Greatbatch excavation, **209**
Fenney, William, Rotherham partner, 230, 275-76
Fenton: Foley site excavation, **47, 183-87**, Greatbatch excavation, 208, **208-11**, Fenton Low, excavation, 109, 236, 278, Fenton Vivian, *see* Whieldon, Thomas
Fenton, John and Thomas Hill, *see* Shelton Farm
fettling ware, 103
figured pattern, 287
figures: **14, 15, 16, 101-06, 108-13, 130, 131, 138**, 279, Bovey Tracey, **191**, by John Dwight, 213
Findlater, Lady, customer, 144
finial, crabstock, **98**, Palmer's site, **219, 220**
fire-bars, 113, -engine, 69, -irons, 257
firemouths: 107, 110, 112, 113, 256, salting, 116
firing ware: 114, 262, 274, 277, 280, at Overhouse works, 242, duration of, 115
fishes, 284
Fitzwilliam Museum, 181
flatware, 266
Fleetwood, John, china seller, **56**, 144
Fletcher, Baddeley and, 249, Thomas, 249, 262
flint: 66, 72, 213, 241, 255, 258, 265, 266, 274, 275, black, 65, burned and pounded, 267, calcined, 67, 71, carrier, 274, Chilterns, 270, cost, 68, from Baddeley, 260, from France, 67, 68, 69, grinding, 68, 250, Gravesend, 69, ground, 250, known by Dwight, 213, merchants, 68, 69, 258, 270, Newbottle, 269, Norfolk, 68, 69, pounded, 197, 249, Rotherham, 232, Rothwell, 272, seashore, 67, sources of, 67, transport, 68, unpounded, 197, Whieldon's, 236
Flint Mug works, 263
flint ware: 121, 160, 196, 249, 250, burned, 272, potter, 251, 260, 276, warehouse, 214, 270
flint white ware, first, 281
floral border moulding, Palmer's site, **216, 224, 225**, pattern, **189**
flowered, 285, shells, 285, (scratch-blue) ware, 243, ware, 242, 244
flowering, 237
flues, underfloor, 113

flummery cups, 279
fluted decoration, Shelton Farm, **207**, pattern, 287
Foley: excavation, **47, 183-87, 184, 187**, works, 275
Forbes, Mary, Liverpool dealer and exporter, 149, 244, 253, 259, 261
Ford, 257
foreign visitors, 71
Fowlea Farm, 258
fox handle, **92**
Fraiser, Wm., Newcastle-upon-Tyne, customer, 244
France: demand for white salt-glazed ware, 152, Montereau, manufacture of white salt-glazed ware, 152, plaster mould, 255, source of flint, 67, 68, 69, war with, 153
Franks, Augustus Wollaston, collector, 177-79
Frechen, 11
freckled ware, 265, 272, 276
Freeth, Frank, collector, 179, 181
French pattern, 149, 286, 287
fruit basket, **60**
fuel, 115, *and see* coal, wood
Fulham, 263, 282, Pottery, London, 211, 213
Fullmer, Mrs. Mary, London dealer, 245, Samuel, 277
fumes, salt-glazing, 116
Furnace mill, 69
Furnivals' works, 251

gadroon edge pattern, **44, 47, 141**, 152, **184**, 185, **191, 193, 209, 221**, 242, 253, 254, 258, 267, 274-76, 283, 284
Gainsborough, 152, 277
Gallagher, James, dealer, 165, **167**
gallypots, 148, 233, 260, 282, 288
Garbett, Samuel, 271
Gardner, Hugh, London dealer, 146
gargoyle feet, **189**
Garner, Matthew, accused by Dwight, 212, and Luke Talbot, 64, 264
Garner, Robert 185, and Co., 257, Sarah, 275
Geddy, James, Williamsburg, excavation, 168, **169, 171**
George II, mug, **96**
German porcelain shapes, 37
Germanic states, dealers, 152
Germany: salt-glazed ware, 64, salt-glazing, 69, stoneware, 11, 12, zaffre, 117
Gilbert, Thomas, London dealer, 145
gilding: 122, 123, **123**, 126, Humphrey Palmer's, 229, *and see* honey gilding
Giles, enameller, 124, Jos., Birmingham, engraver, 250
Gilpen, William, 66, 71, 103, 279, 282
girl in a tree pattern, Palmer's site, **227**
Glaisher, Dr. James W.L., collection, 171, 181
Glasgow, 257
Glasses' Pottery, 274
glaze combinations, 120, tin- and salt-glaze, 263
Glebedale Road, Fenton, *see* Greatbatch excavation
Gloucester, 66
Glover, 274

goat and bee shape, **93**
Goatshead mill, 69
Godwin, 257, Thomas and Benjamin, 278
gold leaf gilding, *see* gilding
Goldenhill ware, 244
goldsmiths, Chester, 82
Goldweitz, Harriet, collector, 177
Gollancz sale, 177
Gom's Mill, 68, 270
gorges, **16**, 264, 265, 285, **211**
gorns (buckets), 283, 286
Graham, Burslem salt merchant, 70, 242, 258, John junior, 257
grand plat ménage, frontispiece, **127**
grape and vine decoration, Palmer's site, **215, 216, 218, 219, 227**
grapes, 285, and bird sprigging, Palmer's site, **220**
Gravesend flint, 67, 68, 69
Greatbatch, John, 102, 250
Greatbatch, William, excavation, 208, **208-11**, handle shape, **48**, modeller, 83, 102
Green and Co., Humble, 262
Green Dock, Longton, 271
green ware, 249, 272, Overhouse works, 242
Greenhead Street, Burslem, 265, 268, 274, 277
Greenleaf, Stephen, inventory, 160
Greg, Thomas, collector, 178, 182
Grenzhausen, 11
Gretton, John, John Edge and, 256
Griffith, J. Henry, collector, 177, 182
grinding flint, 68, pans, 72
grits, 114, gritstone, 65, Staffordshire, 67
Guest, John, London dealer, 144
Guildford, 16 Tunsgate excavation, shards, 18, **18, 19, 20, 212**

Hadderidge potworks, 273
Haigh, Wigan, 64
Hales, John, 258, 277
Hamburg dealers, 152
Hamil, Burslem, 265, 266
Hammersley: Cornelius, 212, 258, Elizabeth, 184, John, 267, Thomas, Bovey Tracey, 192
Hancock, Robert, engraver, 123
Handbridge, Chester, 196
handlers' wages, 81
handles: Bovey Tracey excavation, **195**, Foley site, reeded, 187, **187**, strap, Greatbatch excavation, **210**, Palmer's site, 229, reeded, Palmer's site, **222**, shapes, Palmer's site, **229**, Shelton Farm, 200
Hanley: 155, 213-14, 229, 260, 266, 268-69, 282, Museum, 180, 181, oven, 105, Town Road excavation, *see* Palmer, Humphrey
Harland, Brian T., collector, sale, 178
Harper, Thomas, 265
Harrison: John I, 241, 259, 280, and Josiah Wedgwood, 258, John II, 247, 258, 259
Harrisons' works, 259
Harrop, modeller, 102, 250
Hart, Richard, House, Portsmouth, NH, excavation, **175**
Hart-Shortridge House, Portsmouth, NH, excavation, 172, **174**
Hassells, Charles, 259, 284, John, 259, 276, William, 259, 276
hawk, figure, **108, 109**
hawkers, 148

331

Hawley, William, partner, Rotherham, 231
Hay, Anthony, Williamsburg, excavation, 168, **169, 171**
Haybrook, 274
Hayes, James, London dealer, 146
Hayman, engravings, **137**
Haywood, Mr., 254
health hazards, 141
heart shape: teapot, **42**, dish, enamelled, **228**, dishes, Palmer's site, **228**, 229, stands, 286
hearts, 285
Heath: and Bagnall, 260, John and Christopher, 256, Joshua, 197, 276, 284, Joshua I, 260, 264, 267, Joshua II, 260, Joshua III, 260-61, Thomas I, 260, Thomas II, 260, William I, 260-61, William II and Joshua Heath III, 260-61
Hellot, Jean, 72, 253, 270
Heronbridge field shards, Chester, 197
Hewson, William, London, dealer, 233
Hicks, Captain, John, 168
Hilcoat, William, 279
Hill Top, Burslem, 276
Hill, The, Burslem, 276-77
Hill, Thomas, John Fenton and, *see* Shelton Farm
hiring, 141
Hobson, R.L., 170, 178
hogsheads (barrels), 156, 245
Höhr, 11
Hole House, Burslem, 263
holes, oven, 114
Holland size, 284, decoration in, 135
hollow-ware, 77
honey gilding, 123, 110, 112, 251, 256, 270, 276, *and see* gilding
Honeywall, 247
Horn(e), Matthew, 261, Job and Taylor, 261
horse: figures, **112,** mill, 68, 69, 72
Horsepath, 270
horses, 156, 157, 266, 276
hot house, Overhouse works, 242
hot water jug, 53
hours, dining, 55
house shape teapots, **40**
hovels: 110, 112, 114, 250, 251, 256, 270, 276, largest, 268, Rotherham, 230, 231, 232, Snape Marsh works, 214
Howard Place, Hanley, 268-69
Hull: 68, 69, 152, 277, City Museum, 180, exports via, 149
Humber, River, 68
Humble, Green and Co., 262
Hurst, Arthur, bequest, 179, collector, 177, 178

imports to America, 1752, 160
incised decoration: 117, Shelton Farm, 200, **203, 206,** Whieldon site shard, **237**
indentured workers, Rotherham, 232
indentures, 141, Aaron Wood, 87
Indian figure pattern, 254, 277, 287
industrial stoneware, 20
inlet teapots, 268, 284
inscribed bowl, 1754, 271, jug, 1760, 267, wares, Rotherham, 230
insurance policies, 140
inventories: 140, 159, 160, 161, 164, 165, 168, 249, 250, 255, 275, 277,

280, 281, Plymouth, Mass., 165, St. Mary's county, 168, Overhouse works, 243
Ipswich Journal, 259
Ireland, dealer, 148
Irish size, 284
iron tools, 242
Ironbridge Gorge, 273-74, saggar, **113**
iron-dipped: Greatbatch, **208**, mugs and jug, **18**, rims, 188, **189**, shards, Whieldon's site, **235**, **238**, teapot by John Dwight, **212**, ware, 17, **17, 22**, 24, **24**
ironmongery, 258
ironwork, 113, 114
Isle of Wight sand, 66, 67, 282
Isleworth, 253, 261
Ivy House mill, 69, works, Burslem, 280-81

Jackfield 274, ware, 248
Jackson: Dr. Hall, Portsmouth, NH, excavation, 173, **173, 175,** Paul, Newcastle-upon-Tyne, shipper, 151, 258
Jahn, Louis, collector, 177, 179, 180
Jamestown excavation, 62
japanned ware, 265, 282
Jars, Gabriel, 71, 269
Jefferson, Thomas, *see* Monticello
jellies, 285
Jenkins windmill, Burslem, 69
jigger, 77
Jinkeuson, Martha, jug, 179
Johnson: Joseph, 261, Moses, 64, 212, 264-65, Thomas and Joseph, 261
Jonson, Joseph, Exeter, dealer, 157, 265
jug: 1743 trial, **78**, by John Dwight, **212,** John Kirkham inscription, 230, John Platt inscription, 230, **230**

Kakiemon style, **58**
Keeling, Anthony, 261, 282, and Edward, 252
Kell, William, Newcastle-upon-Tyne, dealer, 157, 253, 265
Kentucky ball clay, 64
kettle coffee pots, 284
Killegrew, Captain William, 12
kiln furniture: 114, **190,** 262, 263, 271, Bovey Tracey, **194,** Chester, 196, Derby, 256, Foley excavation, **186,** Humphrey Palmer's Hanley site, **213,** 229
kilns: 276, Derby, 67, 255, enamel, 121, London type, 192, muffle, 121, Nottingham Road, 256, Rotherham, 230-32, slip, 72, 73, Shelton Farm, 197, sun, 73, *see also* ovens
King of Prussia, plate, **162,** teapot, **163**
Kinkead, Charles, Strabane, dealer, 148, 244, 245, 254
Kirk, Samuel and Co., 252, 262, 277
Kishere, Joseph, William, 265
knife haft, **99**
knife-cut handle feature, Dwight, **212**
Knox, Thomas, Bristol, dealer, 160
Krause, Conrad Wilhelm, 152, 254, J.D., Brunswick, customer, 151

ladder, 255, glazing, 115, 250, 275
ladle, **109**, 286, bucket and, **95**

lady figures, **101**
Lambden and Woods, London, dealers, 144, **145,** 146
Lane Delph, 249
Langerwehe, oven, 103
lathe houses, 251, wheel, 275
lathes: 76, 77, 249, 250, 257, 272, 281, 282, Overhouse works, 242
Law, Foulsham and Cole, dealers, 177
lawns, *see* sieves
lawsuits, 21
Lawton, salt, 69
lead-glaze over salt-glaze, 120
leaf and flower decoration, Greatbatch excavation, **209, 210**
leaf pattern, **186, 187,** Palmer's site, **217**
ledgers, Big House, 236
leech jar, **34**
Leeds Pottery, 262
Leopard Inn, Burslem, 254
letters, business, 159
Lewis: Benjamin, 265, Ralph, flint merchant, 68
Li tabio on lion figure, **111**
Limehouse porcelain, **100**
limestone, fossilised, decoration, **134, 163**
lion figure, **111**
lion's mask feet, 188, Shelton Farm, **202**
Litiz, Pennsylvania, advertisements, 164
Little, Nina Fletcher, sale, 177
Littler: and Company, 125, Sarah, 279, William, 118, 262, 263, 273, 278, 279, 281-82
Littler-Wedgwood blue ware: 37, **39**, 47, 117-18, **118,** 119-20, **119,** 165, **167,** 182, 248, 252, 254, 259, 261, 262, 265, 278-79, analysed, 118, shards, Whieldon's site, **238**
Liverpool, 66, 67, 68, 69, 157, 263, artists, 82, clay from, 197, exports through, 148 Museum, 278
Lockett, Timothy and John, 263, William, 263
Lomax, Charles J., collector, sale, 177, 181
London: 66, 263, Company of Glass-Sellers, 142, customers, 158, dealers, 144, major market, 61, size, 284
London Town, Maryland, Rumney's Tavern excavation shards, 18, **18, 19**, 20, 22, 23, **23**, 62, 67, 165, **167,** 170, 176, **207**
Londonderry, ship to, 245
Longton Hall, 125, 262
Louhans, figure, **105**
lovers, figures, **102**
Lowe, John, 284, and Thomas, 265, 284
Lower House works, Burslem, 236
Lower Lane, Fenton, William Greatbatch, 208
Lower Old Field Mill, 69
Lowther, Sir John, 64
Lowy sale, 177
Luffingham, George, 120, letter re Palmer gilding, 229
Luxmoore, Captain, Charles F.C., collector, 177, 178, 180, 181

Machin, Thomas, Shelton Farm, 197
Mahler, Peter, Hamburg, dealer, 152
makers of white salt-glazed ware,

137, 183, last in Staffs., 153, non-Staffordshire, 183, pottery, 246-82
making white salt-glazed stoneware, 71-141
Malkin: Jonah, 250, 260, 265, 279, sales ledger, 142, Samuel, 24-25, 266, Thomas, 265
Malpass, William and William Fenney, 275-76
managers' wages, 268
manganese, 116, 117
Mann Page, Fredericksburg, dealer, 165
manufacturers, salt-glaze, 137
marbled decoration by Dwight, 213
Marbury, rock salt, 69
Mare: John, 249, 266-67, Richard, 266-67, 284, Richard Taylor and John, 266
Market Place, Burslem, 276, Hanley, 266
marketing: home, 62, in America, 159-76, in Britain and Europe, 142-58
markets, expansion of, 61
marks, 20, crate, 149, 157, 245, 277
marl, 275
Marsh: Isaiah and Richard, 267, 275, Jacob, 261, Moses, 22, 267, 282
Marsh Street, Hanley, site of Snape Marsh works, 214
mask head: feet, Palmer's site, **218, 221,** 225, tureen, **221**
Mason's Ironstone works, 249
Massey Square, Burslem, 266
master moulds, **82-89**
master potters, 137
Maxwell, Colonel James, inventory, 160
Mayer and Newbold, 261
Mayer Bank, Burslem, 266
Mayer, Daniel, 258, E., 277, Elijah, 152, Thomas, 251
mazarine blue ware, 149
measure marks, 117, **164,** 81
measures, 254, 262
Meir: mill, 69, John, 267, William, 236, 267, 270, 278
Meissen ball clay, 64
melons, 285
Mere, Richard, 267
Meredith, Sir, William, 263
Mersey, River, 66, 69, 157, 245
middle class, 55, demand, 53
Middleton, Moses, 212, 267-68, Revd. John, 249, 260, 272, Revd. Thomas, 267
Middlewich salt, 69, 271
Mier, William, 284
Mifflin and Massey, Philadelphia dealers, 164, **166**
Miles, John, 274, Thomas, 268
Miller, Robert, London dealer, 145
mills: 58, 66, 68, 236, 249, 258, 270, 273, edge-runner, 58, 72, flint, Staffordshire, 69, horse, 72
Minton, 19th-20th century replicas, 136
Mitchell, John, 268, dealer, 148
Moddershall flint mills, 68, 69, 249
model, sauceboat, 102
modellers: 25, 81, 82, 83, 87, 88, 90, 102, 159, 237, 250, 268, 282, Aaron Wood, 242, Wedgwood's, 83
modelling, 102
models: 78, 79, 81, 102, 139, 287, alabaster, 81, clay, 81

INDEX

Moffatt-Ladd House, Portsmouth, NH, tureen, 225
Montereau, France, manufacture of white salt-glazed ware, 152
Monticello, Virginia, excavation shards, 168, **169**
moons, 283, 285
Morley, Ann, 272, James, 212, 269, Thomas, 272
Morrall, E.J., dealer, 177
Morris: Daniel, carrier, 156, Jno., customer, 244, Mary, 272
mortars and pestles, 67, 68
Mortlake, 265
Mortlocks, London, dealer, 177, 178
mosaic pattern, 41, **45**, **46**, **60**, **139**, **140**, **162**, **188**, 251, 253, 259, 274, 283, 284
Palmer's site, **215**, 225
mottled ware, 265
moulded relief decoration, **138**
moulders' wages, 81
moulding, 76, 77, press-, 57
moulding houses, 281
moulds, ceramic:, 25, 76, **77**, 79, 81, **82-89**, 102, **109**, 180, **210**, 213, 250, 277, alabaster, **80**, block, case, 78, drying, 102, from France, 255
moulds, culinary: **43**, 46, **77**, 78, cheese, 285, fruit, 285, Palmer's site, **225**, 229, salt, 285, sugar, 271
Mount Airy Plantation, 168
Mountford, Richard and John Shaw, 268-69
Mourney, John, Liverpool dealer, 245
Mow (Mole) Cop, 65, grit, 67
Muchell, Richard, 269, 279
muffle kiln, 126, enamel, Rotherham, 230
Museum of Practical Geology, collection, 178
museums, 178-82, 182, 278, *and see* individual museums by name
Muskit, Henrey, canister, **10**, Henry, 263
mustard pots, 55, **150**

Nantwich salt, 69, 272
nappies, 283
Neale, James, 153, 260, partner of Palmer, 213
Nelson-Atkins Museum, Kansas City, 182
neo-classical style, **60**
Netherlands, excavations, 142
New Inn Mill, 69
Newbottle Pottery, 269
Newcastle, Delaware, excavation, 168, **168**
Newcastle-under-Lyme, exports, 1730, 143
Newcastle-upon-Tyne, 149, 165, 244, 258, 269
Newhaven, boulder flint, 67
newspaper advertisements, 159, 160, 161, 164, 165, 176
nickel edge pattern, 287
Nieuhoff, John, 81
Norfolk flint, 68, 69
North Devon ball clay, 64, 66
North Staffordshire ovens, 107, 110
North-East England, 269
Northwich salt, 69, 271
Norton, John & Sons, London exporters, 165
Norwich Castle Museum, 278
notched handle, Shelton Farm, **203**

Nottingham, 269, brown ware, 73, 146, 160, 271
Nottingham Road, Derby, 255-56
nut pattern, 287

Oade, Nathaniel, London stoneware potter, 70, 264
octagonal plate shard, Palmer's site, **215**, 225
Old Age figure, **106**
Old Hall works, Hanley, 260, 282
Old Salem, N. Carolina, 248
Omer, James, London dealer, 245
on-glaze decoration, 121
Oseney-mill, 270
ovals, 284, 285
ovens: 109, 112, 113, 270, 272, 279, 281, bases, 188, 197, 280, biscuit, 282, Bovey Tracey, 105, bricks, 275, Burslem, 108, Chester, 196, contents, 115, 243, Derby, 107, Dwight, 105, 213, Elers', 264, emptying, 262, entrance, 115, Frechen-type, 265, Hanley, 105, Langerwehe, 103, North Staffordshire, 107, 110, number in 1761, 70, number of North Staffordshire, 139, Overhouse works, 241, 242, round and rectangular, used by Dwight, 213, salt-glaze, 256, salt-glaze, in 1761, 70, salting, 115, Shelton Farm, 197, Snape Marsh works, 214, *and see* kilns
Overhouse works, Burslem, 242-45, 280, 281, equipment, 242, raw materials, 241, stock of ware, 242
owl figure, **110**, jug, **110**
Oxford, 270, New, 270, salt-glazing, 116

Paca, Major Acquilla, inventory, 160
pack saddles, 156, 157
Packhorse Lane, Burslem, 254
packhorses, 156
packing of ware, 156, 245
paddle, 257, 272, 275
painting house, 251
Palmer, Humphrey, 77, 213, 250, 260, 270, buying-in salt-glazed ware, 153, 229, Church works excavation, **41**, **75**, **76**, 213-14, **213-229**, 225, gilding, 229, handle shape, **48**, marriages, 213, 214, Neale, James, partner of Palmer, 153, 213, 260, tureen, **162**, wife died, 225, works sites, 214
pan of clay, 277
panniers, 156, 157
pans, circular, grinding, 72
pap boats, 285
paper mill, 258
Park, Alexander, Amsterdam, 142
Park Lane, Liverpool, 263
Parrott: Richard, book, 268-69, William, 270, 284, apprenticed, 233
Parsons, Ann, Chester dealer, 147
partnerships, 139, agreement, 266, in Shaw's Patent, 273, Thomas Wedgwood III and John Wedgwood, Big House, 233
patch stand, **190**, Palmer's site, **225**, 229
patent: Ralph Shaw's, 273, for grinding flint, 68, Dwight's, infringements, 16, John Dwight's, 211

patterns: 286-88, names, 41, *and see* barleycorn, basketweave, birds eye, boy in the tree, carved, China rail, cockstail, Dresden, dropped egg, engine, farm animals, figured, floral, fluted, French, gadroon edge, girl in a tree, Indian figure, leaf, mosaic, nickel edge, nut, plain nickel edge, plain round, rose, royal, scalloped, seed, shell, square, trellis anthemion, vine and Worcester patterns
payment for goods, 154, 156, 244
Payne, James, 214, 267, 270
Peace of 1802, 153
Pearson, John, London dealer, 144, **144**
Peat, John, 270-71
Peers, Alice and John, Chester dealers, 147
Penkhull, 259
Penkridge dealer, 147
Pennsylvania, Dwight lease, 13, 17
Perrin, Robert, Lancaster, exporter, 149
personalisation by inscription, 117
petition against Dwight, 255, 1762, 139
Petrockstow ball clay, 64, 66
petties, petty pans, pettys, 229, 279, 285, 286
pew group, **100**, **101**
Phillips: and Greaves, 125, F.W., dealer, 177, George and Thomas, 271
Philpot, William, London dealer, 146
picked ware, 283
pickle boats, 284, leaf, **167**, or egg stand, **143**
pierced ware, Palmer's site, 225
pin dust, 250
pine apple 285
pipe clay, *see* clay
piped puddings, 285
Pitt, William, 65, quoted, 278
Pitts Yard, 274
Place, Francis, 12, 64, 239, mug, **11**
placing, 114, Overhouse works, 242
plain round pattern, 287
plain nickel edge pattern, 287
planks for scaffolding, 272
plaster mould, from France, 25
Plaster of Paris, 81
plates, early, 77, in America, 168, early, manufacture of, 159
Platt, John, 272, 284, journal, 230, 232, and Samuel Walker, decorators, 126, Rotherham, 230-32, trade card, 230
Plot, Dr. Robert, 22, 65, 71, 268, 270
Plumper mug, 263
Pococke, Dr. Richard, 192, 271
Pollmann, Jno. Will., London exporter, 149, 151, 157, 177, 258, 177, 277, 286
Pool, Nicholas, 271, 284
Poole ball clay 64
population, 48, London in 1700, 156, Potteries, 137
porcelain, 249, 262, attempt, Palmer's site, 229
porringers, 284, handles, **172**, Bovey Tracey, **193**, Palmer's site, 229
Portobello commemorative ware, **26**, 27, **27**, 79, **88**, **94**, 173, **175**, 178, 180
ports, 61-62, 148, 149, 157
Portsmouth, NH, archaeological

excavations: 21, **42**, 62, **62**, 165, 172, Deer Street excavation shards, **21**, **42**, **140**, **141**, **172**, **174**, **175**, **207**, Dr. Hall Jackson excavation shards, **26**, **173**, **175**, Hart-Shortridge House excavation shards, **174**, Richard Hart House excavation shards, **175**, Warner House excavation shards, **172**
Portsmouth, NH, inventories, 160
Portugal, 276, 277, customer, 158, exports to, 149
potsellers, 146
Potteries Museum and Art Gallery, 179, 180, 278
potters: as farmers, 139, 167, as customers, 153, London warehouses, 146, pottery makers, 183-282, sales records, 142, signing 1770 agreement, 270, workers, number, 140, works, 139, works, size, 24
Pratt, potter, 260
preparation of body, 71
Prescot, 263, 271
Prescott collection, 177
press-moulding, 81
pressers, wages, 81
Prestbury, Joseph, Baltimore County, inventory, 160
Prestonpans, 271
price agreement, 1770, 47, 139, 155, 177, 232, 243, 283-84
Price Glover sale, 177
price lists, 283-86, Thomas and John Wedgwood, 155
prices: and payment, 154-56, 164, 250, 1763, Burslem, 155, creamware, compared, 155, Derby, 155, 256, generally, 1745/6, 30, Hanley, 155
Prince, John, John Adams and, 247
printed ware, 116, 120, 123, 168
probate inventories, *see* inventories
profit on white salt-glazed stoneware, 154
provincial dealers, 146
prunus decoration, applied, **126**
Prussia, King of, **29**, **32**, 161, 181
puddings, 285
Pullen, John, John Smith and, 272
punch pots, **63**, enamelled, 132
punchbowl, I.C. inscription, 230
Purefoy, Mrs., customer, 156
purple from manganese, 117
Puttick & Simpson, auctioneers, 177
puzzle jug, **116**, **173**
pyramids, 285
pyrometers, 115

quarter holes, 114
Queen's Theatre, Burslem, 276

rabbit figure, agate, **112**
Rackham, Bernard, 178, 181
Raeren, 11, 12
Randle, Sorton & Co., Chester, 196
ratcheted handle, **204**, Shelton Farm, 200, **201**
Ravenet engravings, **137**
raw materials, 64-70, Overhouse works, 241
Read, Herbert, 182
recipes, salt-glaze stoneware body, 67, 72, 256
Red Lion works, Burslem, 276, 281
Red Workhouses, Burslem, 280

333

Index

Redbourn, Herts., 67
redware, coarse, 71
reeded handles, Foley, 187, **187**, Palmer's site, **222**, Shelton Farm, **202**
Reeks, Trenham, 178
Reid, Baddeley and Co., 249, William, 259
replicas, reproductions, 136, 137
restaurants, 55
reticulated basket stand shard, Palmer's site, **215**
Revel, Mrs., London, 144
Revelstoke, Lord Cecil, collector, 177, 178, 182
Rex, Samuel, Philadelphia, invoice, **167**
Rhodes, David, decorator, 126, 242, 244
rivers: transport, 66-69, 157, 245, 254, *and see* individual rivers by name
Rivett, Thomas, 256
roads, 157
Robins, John, 265
Robinson: and Rhodes, decorators, 126, John, enameller, 263
Rockingham, 275
rococo shape, **55**, **57**, **151**
Rogers, Jno., customer, 244
rolled rim, **174**
rollers, 117
rose pattern, 287
Rotherham: enamelled ware 232, hovel, ovens, 112, inscribed bowl, **231**, inscribed jug, **230**, partners, 230, salt-glaze works, 230-32, wages, 232, workers, 232
Rothwell, 262, 272
Rotten Row, Burslem, 265
rouletted decoration: **197-99**, Shelton Farm, 200, **201**, teapot, **204**, Whieldon's site, **235**
roulettes, 78, 117, 250
Rous and Cullen, oven, 105
Rous Lench sale, 177
Row Houses, 257
royal arms sprig, 118
royal pattern, **44**, 153, 254, seal, **94**
Royal Stafford China, Overhouse works, 241
Ruffleys, Burslem, 281
Rumney's Tavern, *see* London Town
runners, 78, 250
Rye, boulder flint, 67

Sadler, John, printing on salt-glaze, 120-121
Sadlers' Central Pottery, 273
saffron pots, 288
saggars: 114, 233, 242, 256, 262, 267, 271, 274, Bovey Tracey, **194**, Chester, **196**, conical cap, 115, Humphrey Palmer's Hanley site, **213**, Ironbridge, **113**, 270, Shelton Farm, **197**, side openings in, 115, wheel, 114, 275
Salem pottery, 248
Sales: 180, 181, Overhouse works, 243, to customers, 244, to other potters, 243
salt: bag, 70, buying, 258, Cheshire, 69, consumption of, 70, deliveries, 250, duty, 70, 139, for glazing, 69, 266, foreign, 69, Overhouse works, 242, rock, 66, 69, sea, 70, sources, 69, 271, Staffordshire, 69, supplier, Burslem, 242, transport,
69, 70, used per firing, 70, weekly purchases, 66, 115
salt container, **56**, or wine cup, **150**
salt-glaze: makers, 248-82, number, 138 potters supplying Wedgwood, 153
salt-glazing: 116, ascendancy, 30, decline, 46, early, 69, ovens, number in 1761, 70, Oxford method, 116, recipes, 72 *and see* ovens
Salt, Micah, collector, 181, 177, 179
salting ovens, 115, 116, 256, 264, frequency, 255, 256, holes, 114
sand, 268, Isle of Wight, used by Dwight, 213
Sandbach, Mary, cup, 178
Sauceboats: 56, **62**, waster, Palmer's site, **218**
scaffolding for salting, 115, 272, 275
scalloped, scolloped, scollopt pattern, 149, 160, 244, 275, 286, 287
scent burner, **151**, **154**
Schreiber, Lady Charlotte, collector, 177, 178
scolloped, scollopt, *see* scolloped
scratch-blue ware: 28, **29-35**, **54**, 117, 190, **191**, 242, 243, 256, 259, 274, 286, in America, 160, Bovey Tracey, 192, **193**, Chester, 197, Foley excavation, **187**, Greatbatch, 208, **208**, Palmer's site, **226**, **227**, Swansea, **234**, Whieldon's site, 237, **238**, *and see* debased scratch-blue decoration
scratch-brown decoration, 24, 28, **28**, **31**
scratched inscriptions, 117
screwboxes, Overhouse works, 242
sea salt, 70
seashore flint, 67
seconds quality ware: 116, 283, Overhouse works, 242, worser, 283
seed pattern: 41, **57**, **61**, **141**, 185, **185**, 286, 287, Greatbatch excavation, **209**
Seeman, Abraham, enamel supplier, 121
service *à la russe*, 57
Service yard, 255
sets, dinner, 57
settlement tanks, 71
Seven Years War, 158, 161
Severn, River, 66, 157
Seward, William, Hamburg, dealer, 152
Shand-Kydd, Mrs. F., sale, 177
shapes, 286-88, Big House, 233, 236
shaping, 76
Shaw: Aaron, 22, 23, Aaron I, 272, Aaron II, 272, Aaron III, 272, John, Richard Mountford and, 268-69, Joseph, 272, Moses, 22, 272, Ralph, 268, Ralph, and partners, 118, Ralph, unique bowl, 178, Ralph I, 272, Ralph, II, 263, Ralph II, Richard Bagnall and Thomas Daniel, 273, Stephen, 272, Thomas, 273
Shaw's patent, 117-18, bowl, 118
Sheldon, Edward, collector, 178, 182
shell pattern, **124**, 254, 287, Palmer's site, **222**, 225
shell shape, **40**, **41**, **82**, **93**, 285, Chinese porcelain, **36**, 55
Shelton Farm: 236, 248, 260, 270, 287, excavation, 62, **175**, shards,
21, **150**, 197, **197-203**, 200, **206-207**, shapes, **51**, types, **204**, **205**
shepherdess, figure, **130**
shippers, 151
shipwreck, 152, 158
shoe, white-slipped, **19**
Shore, Joseph and family, 261
Shortridge, Richard, House, Portsmouth, NH, excavation, 172, **174**
shredded clay decoration, **52**
Shrigley, John, 253, 272, 273
Shropshire, 273-74
Sidebotham, Dr. E.J., collector, 177, 181
Siegburg, 11, 12
sieves (lawns), 272, 275, Overhouse works, 242
sieving, 72
sifting boxes, 68
silica, 66
silver shape, 242
Simpkin, Wm., tile, **139**, 288
Simpson, Jos., 284, Joseph, 274, Mr., 274
Sitch Rock, Burslem, 273
sizes, saucer, 277, teapots, 268
slip: casting, 81, **151**, decoration, 72, 73, 81, 249, 256, 270, kilns, Snape Marsh works, 214, tubs, Overhouse works, 242
sliphouse, 250
slippers, 284, 285
slipware dish, 267
smallpox vaccine, 173
smalts, 117, 242
smelling flasks, **99**
Smith: John, 262, 274, 277, 280, and John Pullen, 272, Jos., 275, 284, Sir Charles, customer, 149, William, 275, 284
smoke houses: 103, 251, 257, 270, 281, Snape Marsh works, 214
Snape Marsh, Shelton: 249, 267, 270, Humphrey Palmer's works, 213-14
snuff box, **99**
Soden-Smith, R.H., collector, 177, 178, 181
sodium oxide, 116
Solon, L.M., collector, 177, 179, 180, quoted on Dresden pattern, 287, sale catalogue, **180**
sortable ware, 262, 275, 284
Sotheby's, 178
sources: for models, 81, of flint, 67, salt, 69
souring clay, 71
South Devon ball clay, 64, 66
South Kensington Museum, 178
Southampton, salt-glazing, 69
specialisation, 141
Spencer, Thomas, 271
Spinario, figure, **106**, 181
Spode: Josiah I, 251, 269, 275, Josiah II, 257, 259, Samuel, 275, works, 251
spoon boats, 284
spoons, **47**, 284
spout shapes, Palmer's site, **229**
sprig decoration: **49**, **50**, **53**, **54**, 117, **142**, **143**, **150**, **155**, **158**, **205**, moulds, 79, 304, n.80, Palmer's site, **214-16**, **218**, **219**, **227**, 229, 250, Shelton Farm site, **201**, **206**, used by Dwight, 213
sprigged ware, 160, drabware shards, Whieldon's site, **235**
square holes, Shelton Farm, **199**, 200, **200**
square pattern, 287, pettys, 285
squirrel shape teapot, **38**
St. Mary's, Maryland, excavation, 168
St. Olave's, London, 264-65
St. Petersburg, 271
Staffordshire enamellers, 121, 125, salt-glaze, 21
stamped decoration, Shelton Farm, **206**
stamps, metal, 78
stands, patch or teapot, **190**, **205**, 286, square, 284
stars, 283, 285
Steane, Ralph, 255, 256
Stephens, Jos., 284, Joseph, 275
Stevenson: Moses, carrier, 156, Taylor, 252, 262, Thomas, 275
stock of ware, Overhouse works, 242
Stoke-on-Trent, museum, 179
Stone, Joseph, 277-78
Stoner, George, 182, and Evans, dealers, 177, 181
stonewares, properties and technology, 11
stool pans, 284, 285
stove, 249, house, Overhouse works, 241
strainers, 285
straw for packing, 156
Strawberry Hill, 177
Strawbery Banke, Portsmouth, NH, excavations, 172
Stretton sale, 177
sugar pots, 53
Summerfield, William, enameller, 125
Sumner, Isaac, inventory, 160
sun kilns, 73, pans, 271
Sunderland, 269
suns, 283, 285
suppliers of colours, 121, 122
Sussex coast, source of flint, 67
Swan Bank Church, Burslem, 280
swans, figures, **108**
Swansea: Cambrian Pottery, 232, inscribed ware, 232, salt-glazed ware, **35**, scratch-blue inscribed bowl, **35**, **234**
sweet meat pots, 285
Swift, Peter, 254
Swinton, Yorkshire, 275-76

Tabor, Samuel, Rotterdam, dealer, 152
Talbot, Luke, Matthew Garner and, 264
tank, blunging, 72, settlement, 71
tantalus cups, 148
tax, excise, on Oriental ware, 160
taverns, 49, 50
Taylor: Elizabeth, 276, Isaiah, 276, Job Horn and, 261, John, 276, 281, 284, Ralph, 261, Richard and John Mare, 266, Thomas, 22, Thomas I, 276, Thomas II, 276, Thomas III and Isaiah Taylor, 46, 276, 277, William, 272, 276, William I, 259, 260, 276, II, 258, 277, 280, William III, 262
tea: 52, canister, Bovey Tracey, 195, canister, Muskit, **10**, 263, jar, Elers shape, **20**
teapot: curious, 144, inlet, 284, iron-dipped, John Dwight, **212**, stand, **190**, **205**, Palmer's site, **225**, 229, Shelton Farm, **206**

Teignmouth, 66
tenches, 283, 284
Tennessee ball clay 64
Thames, River, 68, source of flint, 67
thirds ware, 116, 283, Overhouse works, 242
thrower, wages, 81, Overhouse works, 242
throwing, 76
Thursfield, Mr. R., 274
Tidmarsh, James, dealer, 273, Joseph, London dealer, 245, Mr., customer, 244
tierces (barrels), 245
tiles, 281, 287-88, **138**, crucifixion, **139**, Whieldon's site, 237
Till, Edward, spout marked, 180
Tilley collection, 177
tin-glaze and salt-glaze, 120, 263, ware, 121
title deeds, 140
Town Road, Hanley, excavation, *see* Palmer, Humphrey
toys, 275, 279, 284, 285, candles, 286, shapes, 37
transfer printed decoration, **136**, **137**
transfer printing, 123
translucency, **115**
translucent colours, **50,** shard, Palmer's site, **224**
transport: 66-69, 70, 156, 157, 158, 241, 245, 254, flint, 68, 69, salt, 69, ware, 245
travellers, commercial, 146, 268
trellis anthemion pattern, **184**
Trent, River, 67, 68, 157
trial jug, Big House, 233
triangles, 285
triangular stands, 286
trimming ware, 103
Troth, Henry, inventory, 160
Truro, Royal Cornwall Museum, 263
tureens, 56
Turk's caps, 286, moulds, **77**
Turk's head mould shard, Greatbatch excavation, **210**
Turner, John, William Banks and, 251
turners, Overhouse works, 242
turning, 77
turnpike accounts, 273, roads, 157
turtle mould, **109**
twifflers, 276, 283
twig dishes, 286
Twyford, Joshua, 248, 277, Josiah 277, William, 277
Tyrer, Robert, Liverpool potter, 244

under-cutting, 283
under-glaze decoration, 116-21
unfired (unburnt) ware, 154, 253, 260, 261, 275, 273, 279, Big House, 233
Upper Cliff Bank works, 247
Upper House, Burslem, 280
utilitarian ware, 34, **42-44**, 116, **164**

Vanderkirke/Vanderkiste, Jo., Joseph, London dealer, 146, 156, 244
Vaughan, Elliott, inventory, 164
Vauxhall, 269
Vere, Charles, London dealer, 53, 146, **146**

Victoria and Albert Museum, 178, 179, 278
vine pattern, 287
vining, 79
Virginia, 250
visitors, foreign, 71
Voyez and Hales, 258

wages: 28, 249, apprentices', 266, comparative, 141, managers', 268, Overhouse works, 242, potters', 81, Rotherham, 232, *and see* indentures
Walker, Samuel: elder, Rotherham, 232, junior, Rotherham, partner, 230, John Platt and, 230
Walklett, Mark, 252
Wallace, Davidson and Johnson, Annapolis agents, 161, **161**
Walpole, Horace, collector, 177
war with France, 153
War, Seven Years, 158, 161
Warburton: and Stone, 46, 255, 277-78, 284, Ann, 255, Ann and Son, 278, 284, Edward, 267, 278, Edward and William, Fenton Low, 236, Isaac, 278, Jacob, 284, Jacob and Isaac, 278, John and Son, 278, John, carrier, 156, Joseph, 247, 275, 278, Mr., 269, Thomas, 284, works, 259
Ward, Mrs. London dealer, 156
warehouse: best, 277, Colchester, 146, Edinburgh, 261, 271, Gravel Lane, 264, Liverpool, 252, London, 146, 249, 251, Staffordshire, 260
Warner House, Portsmouth, NH, excavation, **172**, 173
Washington, Captain Lawrence, 27, George, purchases, 160
waster shards, 116, 218, 274
water mills 68
Waterworth, Will, invoice, **166**
Watson, Dr. R., 71
Watt, James, 257
wax models, 79
weather conditions, 158
Weatherby, John, 278, 284
weathering clay, 71
Weaver: Navigation, 157, 241, 245, River, 66, 68, 70, 157, 254
wedging board, 281
Wedgwood 19th century replicas, 46, 136
Wedgwood, Aaron, 118, 25, **26**, 262, 269, 276, 278-79, 282
Wedgwood, Aaron, Thomas Wedgwood I and Richard Wedgwood, 212, 279
Wedgwood, Aaron, Thomas Wedgwood III and John Wedgwood, Big House, 232, 233, 236, *and see* Wedgwood, Thomas III and John
Wedgwood, Alice, 257, Burslem, 279, 281, Carlos, 279, Carlos, 281, Doctor Thomas II, 24, 25, 268, 279, 281
Wedgwood, John, 280, 282, Big House, 232, death of, 236, 245, *and see* Wedgwood, Thomas III and John

Wedgwood, Josiah, 280-81, and John Harrison I, 258, biographies, 280, Bovey Tracey, 192, buying in, 46, customer, 153, documents, 142, experiment book, 280, Fenton account book, 238, list of potworks 1710-15, 22, **36**, partner to Whieldon, 236, 238
Wedgwood Museum, 278
Wedgwood, Richard, 22, 279, 281, Thomas and Catherine, 276, Thomas I, 279, 281
Wedgwood, Thomas III, 232, 259, death, 236, 259, *and see* Wedgwood, Thomas III and John
Wedgwood, Thomas III and John Wedgwood, 23, 25, **26**, 46, 232-36, 279, 282, price lists, 283-8, sales ledger and crate book, 142, *and see* Wedgwood, Aaron, Thomas Wedgwood III and John Wedgwood
Wedgwood, Thomas IV, 259, 280, 283, capital, 245, death, 241, farmer, 242, 243, London sales trips, 244, notebooks, 142, Overhouse works, Burslem, 241-45
Wedgwood, Thomas V, Overhouse works, Burslem, 241-45
Wedgwood, Useful Thomas, 268, Wedgwood, William, 257
Wedgwood-Littler blue, *see* Littler-Wedgwood blue ware
Weldon, Henry and Jimmy, collectors,177
Wentworth, Governor John, excavation, 173
West, Edward, flint merchant, 68
West Pans, 262, 281-82
Westerwald, 12, ball clay, 64, ware, 213
Westport Road, Burslem, excavation, 188, **188-91**, 190, 273
Wetherburn's Tavern, Williamsburg, *see* Williamsburg, Colonial
wheels: 275, crank and string, 271, saggar, 114, throwing, 76, 77, 242
Whieldon, Thomas: 34, 36, 57, 235-39, 247, 256, 270, 278, 280, 281, Aaron Wood, modeller for, 237, account book, 30, 238, employed Greatbatch, 208, flint mill, 236, hiring, 141, incised decoration, **237**, Josiah Wedgwood as partner, 238, memorandum or notebook, 236, 117, 160, 257, 267, site shards, **39**, 235, **235-39**, 239
white dipped ware, *see* white-slipped ware
white lead, 254
white salt-glazed stoneware, early development, 11-19, early industrial, 20-47
Whitehaven, 282, John Douglas, customer, 245
Whitehead, 260, 282, Charles, 276
white-slipped: by Dwights (doubledipped), 213, by Greatbatch, 208, mugs and jug, **18**, shards, Whieldon's site, **235**, **238**, shoe, **19**, ware, 17, **17**, 19, 21, 23, **23**, 24, **25**, 65, 72, 117, 257, 265, 267
wholesalers, 143

wild rose finial, Palmer's site, **219**
Wilden Ferry, 157
Wilkes, Dr. Richard, 67, 260, 264
Willett, Henry, collector, 177, 179
Williamsburg, Colonial: excavations, 168, 177, Anthony Hay House excavation shards, **169**, **171**, James Geddy House excavation shards, **44**, **169**, **171**, tureen, **162**, Wetherburn's Tavern excavation, **162**
Willington Ferry, 68, 157, 245, 277
Wilson, James, enameller, 125, Robert, inventory, 165
windmills, 68, at Jenkins, Burslem, 69
Winnipesaukee, Lake, excavation, 173
Winsford, 266, wharfinger, 148
Winterton, Lord, customer, **144**
Withering, Dr. William, Birmingham, 173
wood for firing, 115
Wood, Aaron: 82, 268, 282, apprenticed, 25, indentures, 141, master mould by, **89**, **139**, modeller, 83, 87, 88, 90, 159, 242, modeller for Whieldon, 237
Wood, Enoch: 88, 264, 276, 281, collector, 177, Overhouse works, 241, scrapbook, 283
Wood, John: and John Wedgwood, 282, and Ralph Wood II, 282, 286
Wood, Josiah, 282
Wood, Ralph I: 25, 82, modeller, 25, 83, 87, 159, 282, spout moulds by, 180
Wood, Ralph, II, 282
Wood: Rotherham partner, 230, wharfinger, Winsford, 148
Wood, William, 268, modeller, 83
Woodward, Henry, inventory, 161
Woolwich, 12, 138, 265, salt-glazing, 69, sand, 66
Worcester pattern, 287
Worcester printing on salt-glaze, 120
workers: 249, Bovey Tracey, 192, Chester, 196, Cockpit Hill, 256, individual, 141, Overhouse works, 242, pottery, number, 140, Prestonpans, 271, Rotherham, 232, Shelton Farm, 197
works, pottery, 139, 213-14, size, 140
workshops, decorating, 121
Wright, Bourne and Co., 253
Wright, Joseph, Derby, customer, 149
Wyke, John, Liverpool dealer, 149, 156, 158, 276

Yates, John, 282, 284, William, 282
York, Francis Place, 239
Yorkshire: decorators, 126, Museum, 179, Philosophical Society, 181
Young, Arthur, quoted, 23, 68, on Rotherham, 232

zaffre, 116, 117, 149, 242, 252, 258, Germany, 117 , *and see* blue
Zhongliquan, figure, **105**